THE MAJESTIC NATURE OF THE NORTH

THE MAJESTIC NATURE OF THE NORTH

Thomas Kelah Wharton's Journeys in Antebellum America through the Hudson River Valley and New England

Edited by
Steven A. Walton and Michael J. Armstrong

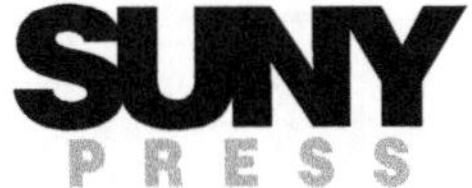

Cover images: "Portrait of Thomas Kelah Wharton from biographical note." Manuscripts and Archives Division. *The New York Public Library Digital Collections*. 1914.

"West Point from the North." Manuscripts and Archives Division. *The New York Public Library Digital Collections*. 1832.

Published by State University of New York Press, Albany

For information, contact State University of New York Press, Albany, NY
www.sunypress.edu

Library of Congress Cataloging-in-Publication Data

Names: Wharton, Thomas Kelah, 1814–1862, author. | Walton, Steven A., editor. | Armstrong, Mike (Michael J.), editor.
Title: The majestic nature of the north : Thomas Kelah Wharton's journeys in antebellum America through the Hudson River Valley and New England / edited by Steven A. Walton and Michael J. Armstrong.
Description: Albany : State University of New York Press, [2019] | Includes bibliographical references and index.
Identifiers: LCCN 2018017082 | ISBN 9781438473277 (hardcover) | ISBN 9781438473284 (pbk.) | ISBN 9781438473291 (ebook)
Subjects: LCSH: Wharton, Thomas Kelah, 1814–1862—Diaries. | Hudson River Valley (N.Y. and N.J.)—Social life and customs—19th century. | New England—Social life and customs—19th century. | Hudson River Valley (N.Y. and N.J.)—Description and travel. | New England—Description and travel. | Hudson River Valley (N.Y. and N.J.)—Biography. | New England—Biography. | Architects—United States—Biography.
Classification: LCC F127.H8 W53 2019 | DDC 917.47/304—dc23
LC record available at https://lccn.loc.gov/2018017082

Contents

List of Illustrations		vii
A Note on Transcription		xi
Preface		xiii
Acknowledgments		xvii
Abbreviations		xix
Introduction *Steven A. Walton*		1
Chapter 1	Thomas Kelah Wharton's Autobiography	31
Chapter 2	New York and the Hudson Valley, 1832–1834	37
Chapter 3	Return to the Northeast, 1853	131
Chapter 4	Biographical Register	267
Appendix	Known Works by Thomas Kelah Wharton	289
Notes		307
Index		345

Illustrations

Figure I.1	Only known likeness of Thomas Kelah Wharton, a steel-plate engraving from ca. 1860.	xx
Figure 1.1	The Diana and New York Bay from the Battery, 1830.	31
Figure 1.2	Bhurtpore Cottage, New Haven, CT.	34
Figure 1.3	The Flushing Institute (later St. Paul's College), Flushing, NY.	34
Figure 2.1	David Hosack Estate, Hyde Park, NY, 1832.	47
Figure 2.2	David Hosack Estate, Hyde Park, NY, 1832.	51
Figure 2.3	West Point from the North, 1832.	64
Figure 2.4	Works of the West Point Foundry from the head of the ravine, 1832.	67
Figure 2.5	Works of the West Point Foundry, Cold Spring, NY, 1832.	78
Figure 2.6	Crow's Nest and the Point of Constitution Island opposite West Point, 1832.	79
Figure 2.7	Village of Cold Spring and the Chapel of Our Lady, ca. 1835.	80
Figure 2.8	Residence of Gov. Kemble Esq., Cold Spring, NY, 1833.	81
Figure 2.9	Euterpe Knoll, Hyde Park, NY, 1839.	82
Figure 2.10	Crystal Cove, Hyde Park, NY, 1839.	83
Figure 2.11	Flushing Bay, Long Island with the Palisades in the distance, 1833.	85
Figure 2.12	College Point, Long Island, 1839.	87
Figure 2.13	New York from Brooklyn Heights, 1834.	102
Figure 2.14	Catskill Mountains from W. Young's, Saugerties, NY, 1840.	109
Figure 2.15	Falls of the Indian Brook opposite West Point, NY, 1834.	116

Figure 2.16 Village of Fishkill, NY from the Old Stone Bridge on Albany Road, 1834. 124

Figure 2.17 Chapel of Our Lady, Cold Spring, by Robert W. Weir, 1834. 129

Figure 3.1 View across the river looking over the Custom House, New Orleans, 1855. 132

Figure 3.2 Commerce, first high land above Cairo, 1853. 136

Figure 3.3 Peoria, Illinois River at sunset, 1853. 139

Figure 3.4 Canadian and American falls, Niagara from the Ferry Slips, 1853. 144

Figure 3.5 St. Lawrence River near Brockville, ON, 1853. 145

Figure 3.6 Rapids on the Canada side, Niagara, 1853. 153

Figure 3.7 Central gateway at Mt. Auburn Cemetery, 1853. 158

Figure 3.8 Old house, corner of Ann St. and Market Square, Boston, 1853. 160

Figure 3.9 Bridge and unfinished works at the "'Prison," Lawrence, MA, 1853. 167

Figure 3.10 Fort Warren and Boston Harbor from Hull, MA, 1853. 169

Figure 3.11 Fresh Pond near Boston, MA, 1853. 174

Figure 3.12 Old Mile Stone near Saxonville, MA, 1853. 182

Figure 3.13 Sylvan Bridge, Sudbury River, MA, 1853. 183

Figure 3.14 Chestnut tree and ferns near Saxonville, MA, 1853. 184

Figure 3.15 Cochituate Pond and Gatehouse, MA, 1853. 185

Figure 3.16 Framingham Village, MA from the Saxonville road, 1853. 192

Figure 3.17 Rapids between Goat and Moss Islands, Niagara, 1853. 194

Figure 3.18 Episcopal Church, Brookline, MA, 1853. 198

Figure 3.19 Plum Island Lights, mouth of Merrimac River, 1853. 207

Figure 3.20 Capstones on stonework at Fort Warren, Boston Harbor, 1853. 210

Figure 3.21 City of Boston from the harbor, 1853. 212

Figure 3.22 Stone quarries in Quincy, MA, 1853. 214

Figure 3.23 Boston Harbor from Quincy quarries, 1853. 215

Figure 3.24 Bluff Head, Apple Island, Governors' Island, and Deer Island, Boston Harbor, 1853. 222

Figure 3.25 "Machine for Reducing Wood to Slivers," 1854. 232

Figure 3.26 Ohio River, 1853. 247

Figure 3.27 Passing through the canal at Louisville by starlight, 1853. 249

Figure 3.28 Mississippi River near Memphis, TN, 1853. 255

Figure 3.29 Approach to Baton Rouge and state capitol of Louisiana, 1853. 259

Figure 3.30 Map of Thomas Kelah Wharton's travels, 1853. 262

Figure 4.1 Wharton and Prescott/Ladd family genealogy. 264

A Note on Transcription

Wharton's journals have been transcribed as written, with period spellings and abbreviations. Some modernization has been allowed, such as the normalization of punctuation (Wharton had a habit of using long dashes in some places where we would use either a comma or a full stop, and he rarely included the comma that should set off temporal introductory clauses), the capitalization of proper nouns and the beginning word of sentences, italicization of publication titles and ships' names, and the normalization of his erratic separation of compound words (e.g., "every where," where we would say "everywhere"). We have retained his sometimes-erratic capitalization of other nouns and his idiosyncratic spelling of place names.

Preface

The following product is the labor of many hands that have come together to make what we hope is a seamless whole. It was inspired by a little chapel overlooking the Hudson River. The chapel, Wharton's very first commission and one of his few surviving architectural designs, sits atop a granite headland at water's edge in the village of Cold Spring, NY, just above and opposite West Point (see figures 3.7 and 3.17). Built in 1833 by the proprietor of the West Point Foundry in Cold Spring, Gouverneur Kemble, for his mainly Irish, Roman Catholic workers, the chapel was restored and reopened in 1977 as a nondenominational space by the nonprofit Chapel of Our Lady Restoration, Inc. (now The Chapel Restoration, Inc.). There is an attractive account in the *New-York Mirror* of the consecration by the third Bishop of New York, John Dubois, on September 21, 1834, of this "most classical and beautiful little church," a "chaste and elegant little building," a "little temple" with a "portico . . . of the Tuscan order, of the most correct proportions," wherein it was hoped that it "might form the commencement of an era of good will among all religious denominations."[1] Although his *Journal* entry of March 19, 1833 makes clear that Wharton furnished the design details, the newspaper credits Kemble with the plan and Wharton's connection with the project is not mentioned at all in the article.[2] This may be because the illustration for the article was furnished by Robert W. Weir, the drawing instructor at West Point and the principal artist for the *New-York Mirror*, with whom—as one will see in the *Journal* entries for 1834—Wharton clashed. It is just this sort of elision of Wharton's contributions where he has fallen out of the record—of the newspaper engraving set in the 1830s and early 1840s, of the early Hudson River School of artists, and of the influential architectural circles of New York just when he might have flourished—that encouraged us to bring his autobiographical *Journal* to press.

As Mike Armstrong of Cold Spring was devoting his energies to the board of The Chapel Restoration, Steve Walton was at the same time researching the history of the West Point Foundry as an outgrowth of his then former and now renewed association with the Industrial Heritage and Archaeology program at Michigan Technological University, which conducted extensive archaeological investigations at the foundry from 2002–2008. The local Putnam County Historical Society knew of the *Journal*, and Michigan Tech researchers used some short extracts as invaluable sources for the social and visual history of the foundry. Since it was known that Wharton had designed the chapel, both researchers (who serendipitously already knew each other through an entirely unrelated academic connection to Mike's wife) lighted on the journals and discovered in them the wealth of information that cast astounding light on the antebellum world of New York and the wider Northeast.

The material for this book is all to be found in volumes one and two of the eight-volume journal now preserved in the New York Public Library with the title of *Voyage across the Atlantic in 1830 and journey from New York to our new home at Pequa* [sic], *Ohio. T.K. Wharton,* which was purchased from Wharton's widow in April 1919.[3] The first volume has an inscription in the early pages, "This book is the property of Emily J. Wharton (widow of Thomas Kelah Wharton) 'St. Luke's Home for Aged Women' 2914 Broadway, New York City."[4] Armstrong and Walton teamed up and completed a transcription of the 1830s New York section (our chapter 3; *Journal* 1, 122–310), which had been begun as a series of limited extracts of those portions related to the West Point Foundry by Vanessa M. McLean in 2006. Walton significantly amplified and extended her work, and then Armstrong completed all of the New York and Hudson Valley section. In this phase, we also discovered that the transcription of the first section of Wharton's journal covering his emigration from England to Ohio in 1830 had been published in the *Ohio Historical Society Journal* in the 1950s, and that the later volumes of the journal that recorded Wharton's life in New Orleans had been extracted in the lavishly illustrated book *Queen of the South* in 1999.[5]

As we contemplated bringing it together for publication, Armstrong, working in the archives of The Chapel Restoration, came across the typescript of both the 1830s and 1850s sections by Walter Knight Sturges from the 1980s. Sturges was an architect, most noted for the Elizabeth Ann Seaton Shrine at Battery Place in New York City. While restoring the chapel in Cold Spring from 1972 to 1977, he clearly became fascinated with Wharton as the chapel's designer, just as Armstrong had. Surviving papers in the archives mention that Sturges was working with "the University of Ohio Press" [Ohio State University Press, we assume] to publish a book called *The Life and Works of Thomas Kelah Wharton,* though it is not entirely clear why this never happened.[6] We can only assume that his 1984 typescript, with a brief twenty-four-hundred-word introduction, was to become that book. The Sturges typescript runs to more than five hundred double-spaced pages and had a few handwritten editorial revisions, but very few annotations, explanations, or references.

The story became even more complicated as we investigated the other papers that Sturges left to The Chapel Restoration when his own project failed to come to fruition. It is now clear that he had inherited the papers of Mrs. Joseph L. (Anne) Domas of Flemington, NJ, who had herself been working on a pamphlet on "Tommy" Wharton. She had been working diligently on a Wharton manuscript from about 1962–1970, apparently starting to expand it into a proposed book, but handed the papers over to Sturges because she became tied up in some other unspecified project in New Jersey. It is not entirely clear what had brought her to Wharton in the first place.

We therefore used the Sturges typescript as the basis for the 1853 summer tour section (our chapter 4; *Journal* 2, 1–294) and compared our 1830s transcription to his. Sturges had also prepared a small number of notes on both sections for his book project, inserted in pencil on his typescript, typed up in a full list, and keyed to his typescript by page number. We have in some cases retained these verbatim, indicated by a [WKS] after the text in the note, but in many cases, we merely used them as information to expand our own notes, as well as added many notes of our own. His limited biographical footnotes, for example, have all been consolidated into our much-expanded biographical register at the end of this volume.

We are pleased to bring the work of at least four people, and the assistance of at least another dozen people, working over the last fifty years, to completion. Wharton's record of New York, the Hudson River valley, Boston, and the Northeast, as well as his 1850s travels across the expanse of United States, should offer useful source material for all manner of researchers looking at social life and people in antebellum America. We hope that these sections of his journal will be of interest and use to readers and scholars of the Northeast, just as his 1850–1860s journal has brought to life antebellum and early Civil War New Orleans.

When one considers that Wharton was an unknown immigrant in 1830 and a young man coming to New York from a farm in Ohio in 1832, his success and integration into the social spheres of the lower Hudson is nothing short of amazing. No doubt it was his astounding artistic abilities that propelled him into those spheres, but it is all the more interesting that he was so heartily welcomed into the families of many of the notables he met. He must have had quite a personality to have been so quickly accepted. We hope that you, too, will come to enjoy Wharton's views of an early America and its society and nature.

Acknowledgments

Thanks to The Chapel Restoration, Inc. (formerly the Chapel of Our Lady Restoration) of Cold Spring, NY, whose interest in commemorating the skill of their architect helped bring this project to fruition. In particular, we are grateful for their preservation of the Sturges/Domas papers. Thanks also to the Industrial Heritage and Archaeology program at Michigan Technological University and their archaeological project on the West Point Foundry (2002–2008) that also learned of the journal and its illustrations.

Tracking down leads in the journal has been and continues to be great fun and endlessly fascinating. The world of Google and WorldCat has made it so much easier, though it also throws into stark relief the skill of researchers in the pre-Internet age who managed to track down much of what we know of Thomas Kelah Wharton. Still, it pays to ask people who know where to look. In this category, we need to acknowledge the assistance of The Historic New Orleans Collection for their work on Wharton, particularly the publication of large parts of his later *Journals* in *Queen of the South* (1999); the Pioneer and Historical Society of Muskingum County, Zanesville, OH for their work on the early portion of Wharton's *Journal*; Margaret D. Beasley and Matthew Reynolds at the University Archives and Special Collections of Sewanee University, Sewanee, TN for their help locating Wharton's designs for that college; Bryan Dunlap and the Constitution Island Association, Cold Spring, NY for information on the Warner brothers; Tracy Reinhardt at the Fond du Lac, WI Historical Society for help tracing Wharton's stepmother and sister-in-law's side of the family; Ruthann Tomassini at the Framingham [MA] History Center for information on Saxonville and environs; Meredith Gregg at the Jefferson County [IN] Historical Society and Janice Barnes at the Jefferson County Public Library for work on Wharton's brother, Robert John; Hubert H. McAlexander, Bobby Mitchell, and Chelius Carter with the Marshall County [MS] Historical Society, Jim Moore with the Marshall County Historical Museum, and Rev. Bruce McMillan in Holly Springs, MS for help on Wharton's in-laws, the Hullings, and St. Thomas's Hall, Holly Springs; Charlie Vasiliades at the Brighton-Allston [MA] Historical Society for checking on Aurelius Ladd's elusive estate; Mary O. Klein, archivist for the Episcopal Diocese of Maryland in Baltimore, for checking that Wharton did not apparently make much of an impression on his students who later became important Episcopal bishops, and Virginia Patterson, archivist for the Episcopal Diocese of Mississippi, for checking that he also failed to make an impression in their archives; Matthew D. Eddy at Durham University, UK for discussion on early-nineteenth-century British education, and then Otto Smart (Manchester Grammar School archivist), Chris Baylis (William Hulme's Grammar School, Manchester), Stuart Helm (Stockport Grammar School, Stockport), the staff of the Hull History Centre, and Ruth Rhynas Brown and Arthur Credland for trying to find out where Wharton went to school in the UK; and again to Ruth for helping me disentangle Dr. George Reddie's East India Company and military existence and telling me of Branwell Brontë's education; Melinda Quivik for discussions on early nineteenth-century evangelism in America; and the indefatigable Edward Margerum for lateral thinking and Internet searching that opened up a number of research avenues.

A special thanks to Lenor A.P. de Medeiros for initial compilation of the biographical register. Our wives, Liz Schevtchuk Armstrong and Alice Margerum, contributed greatly to the success of this work by astute editing, occasional research, continual discussion, and moral support.

Many fine evenings have been spent discussing Wharton with many people, including some of the great-great-great-grandchildren of the Kemble family. Sadly, Wharton's direct line ended with his son and daughter-in-law, who died issueless. We have been unable to find any lateral descendants of his line to contact about their ancestor. Curiously, though, having discovered that Wharton's stepmother is buried not far from one of our family homes in, of all places, Wisconsin, and knowing that there were nephews and nieces in both Texas and Kansas in the earlier twentieth century, we are hopeful that someone may read this book and contact us to resume the story. There is always the chance that there are still Whartons around to continue the discussions. We hope so, and hope to hear from them.

Steven A. Walton and Michael J. Armstrong
Hancock, MI and Cold Spring, NY

Abbreviations

CRA	The Chapel Restoration Archives, Cold Spring, NY
DAB	*Dictionary of American Biography*, 20 vols. (New York: Scribner's, 1928–1936)
MMA	Metropolitan Museum of Art, New York, NY
NAD	National Academy of Design, New York, NY
NONA	New Orleans Notarial Archive, New Orleans, LA
NYPL	New York Public Library, New York, NY
THNOC	The Historic New Orleans Collection, New Orleans, LA
USMA	United States Military Academy, West Point, NY
WKS	Walter Knight Sturges (see introduction pp. xiv–xv)

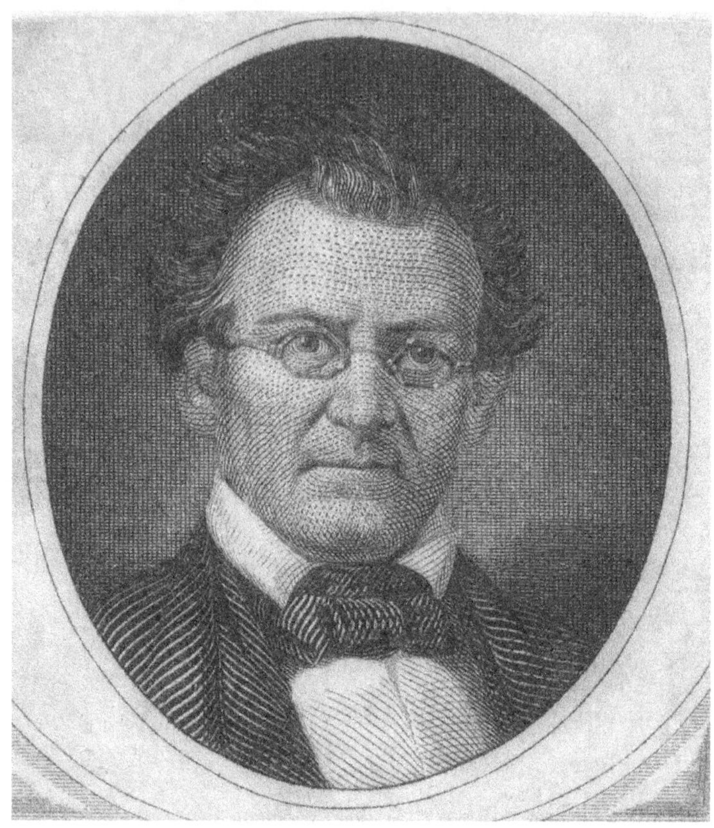

FIGURE I.1 Only known likeness of Thomas Kelah Wharton, a steel-plate engraving from ca. 1860, original source unknown. New York Public Library, Archives and Special Collections, New York.

Introduction

Steven A. Walton

Thomas Kelah Wharton transcribed his journals from his original notes into clean notebooks beginning in June 1854, when he was living in New Orleans overseeing the construction of the New Customs House for the Treasury Department. He lived at the time on Camp Street at the corner of Robin (now Euterpe Street), across from Coliseum Place Gardens in the Lower Garden District, and had just returned from a half-year's journey to Boston, "for his health." We believe that Wharton began his project as a memorial to his young son, Thomas Prescott, and went back to his original journals and started his story with his emigration from England in 1830 and first five years in America—two in Ohio and three in New York. From there he added his recent 1853 journey to Boston—unfortunately silently passing over nearly a decade—and from there his journals continued to grow over time, because we assume he did not keep a journal during those years.

The sections of the journal on his journeys in Ohio and New York are neatly transcribed, with redrawn copies of earlier illustrations from sketchbooks that do not survive. It is possible that parts of his story were re-created from memory, though enough direct quotations and names appear to indicate that there was clearly a now-lost master journal in which he kept notes. In 1833, while teaching at the Flushing Institute on Long Island, his life got busier and perhaps more mundane, and he stopped keeping detailed records except for his summer excursions on the Hudson. The death of his mother in 1834 put an end to his regular journaling, as the interlude and autobiography (see chapter 2) seem to have been added from memory to bridge the gap between when he reliably kept journals in 1830–1834 and 1853 onwards.

As an artist, educator, and architect born in England but who lived all his adult life in America, Thomas Kelah Wharton's life does not fit one simple narrative. His eye for photographic detail as an illustrator places him squarely in the ranks of talented antebellum artists, yet he never managed to directly make a career with that skill. His autobiographical text reveals a young man with strong religious interests who initially trained to be an architect. An offer of a job teaching drawing at an Episcopal boarding school pulled him away from architecture for a decade, though he returned to it when he finally settled in New Orleans. Even as a teenager, he was ever the Enlightenment gentleman, conversant in botanical taxonomy and the classics, fluent in French and German, as well as deeply influenced by the Romantics. It seems likely that his education was limited to that of English grammar school to age sixteen, and even that basic schooling is inferred from circumstantial evidence. Knowing he was the son of an immigrant merchant in Ohio does not prepare the reader to watch him mingle freely within the ranks of the Hudson River gentry by the age of eighteen. In his forties, his ability to travel the country in some considerable style characterizes the striving American bourgeoisie, and the networks of his interactions reveal a fascinating picture of social and intellectual life in antebellum America. What Wharton recorded in the Hudson River region in the 1830s and then on a trip from New Orleans to Boston in the summer of 1853 offers glimpses of America as a young nation just starting to grow out of its republican conservatism in New York and the Hudson valley, and then as a country whose democratic wealth and power were beginning to manifest themselves in Boston as it modernized out of its colonial roots.

When Wharton returned to his home in New Orleans in the fall of 1853, he concluded his observations on the family's summer trip to Boston by noting that the East teemed with "wealth, refinement, and intellectual culture," and that the Midwest and Mississippi valley had "teeming plenty and boundless resources." Still, there was "something about the genial 'South'" that he loved, despite "all its faults of climate, and . . . physical danger." Against this love, he characterized the "opulence, and magestic [*sic*] 'nature' of the more rugged and inflexible North."[1] And it was that northern nature that he sat down to document by transcribing his personal diaries into what is now volume one of an eight-volume journal. Now preserved in the New York Public Library, the journal records his travels from England to America as a teenager, initially settling in Ohio with his parents,[2] and then his adventures in trying to build a career in New York City in the early 1830s. Then, despite a gap in the journal of nearly twenty years—he seems to have stopped diarizing after the death of his mother in 1834, or at least when he sat down to recopy the diaries in the 1850s, he chose not to include that period of his life that included nearly another decade in New York, a move to Mississippi and his first marriage, and his eventual relocation to New Orleans—he chronicles his trip by steamboat, railroad, and omnibus in 1853 to visit his wife's family in Boston. The later six volumes then chronicle on a near daily basis his life in New Orleans from 1853 until his death in 1862.[3]

Written in clear, crisp penmanship and precisely illustrated, the first volume of Wharton's journal is clearly a recopying of his original diaries. In the entry for April 30, 1832, he notes that he was copying, "from the original manuscript" written in "fady ink on such paper as the Western towns then afforded, . . . which at this distance of time no body but myself could decipher." He excused himself for having chosen not to recopy some poetry he had composed: "it appears that at this point I was guilty of the enormity of 'several verses' which my maturer judgment suggests had better be omitted."[4] And although he is otherwise silent about what might have been omitted or rewritten for either clarity or propriety, this should remind us that this is not an unfiltered composition. That people could go out and buy commercially printed annual pocket diaries from their local stationer tells you that there was both a market to be met and a market to be made for this sort of behavior. The market was originally targeted at men's business lives, but soon evolved to cater to both sexes' private lives, and by just after the Civil War, diaries were a standard Christmastime gift to both parties. Many of the diaries that survive today, and certainly many of those deemed worthy of printing, demonstrate authors' consciousness of their place in an American diary tradition. Wharton was engaging in a middle-class ritual pastime,[5] and the recopying of the earlier portions of his life returned him to a more religious devotion to making nearly daily entries from the fall of 1853 until the end of his life, even including the daily temperatures at morning, noon, and evening.

All the more poignantly, we may realize that Wharton began this task of self-memorialization soon after his only child, Thomas Prescott Wharton, was born, and this work may well be his insurance letter to his son, as the Wharton men generally had weak constitutions. All three of his brothers died in their mid- to late thirties, and that, coupled with the high infant mortality of his siblings' children, may well help explain why he was so concerned with getting his memories down on paper. Wharton's health was also frail at times, which may also have given some impetus to his writing. He was more affected when he was living near the marshes of Long Island and New Orleans, and his symptoms do roughly track with ongoing bouts of weakness, chills, and fevers, suggesting a potential diagnosis of recurrent malaria, which at one point he was treated for while staying at West Point.[6] Although he was described as "tall & well proportioned," when he and his family weighed themselves for fun on the shopkeeper's scales in 1853 in Framingham, MA, we learn that he weighed only 132 pounds, suggesting a very tall, slender, and possibly frail man.[7]

Diarizing for his son turned out to be prescient, as Thomas Kelah Wharton died when his son, Thomas Prescott Wharton, was only ten years old, and even he was outlived by his mother by twenty-two years. Wharton's journal, then, offers the appropriately filtered vision that he wanted his son and the family to understand about his early life and the family's beginnings.

In the journal we learn of a man who is devout and socially skilled, yet we learn little of his direct economic status. Although he was not a man of leisure, there is never a mention of costs or cash flow. Always on the edge of the world of the artist and the literati in his younger years, we get no sense that he ran with the libertines (though his recopied diary would probably have omitted that had it been the case), and by his mature years he seems to have belonged to all the right clubs, although without explicit conceits. His words seem to avoid most notice of the fairer sex, except while he was in residence at a country estate or where he occasionally noted a female member of a larger group; later he records himself as a family man and new father, devoted to his wife and son.[8] Though apparently not a *bon vivant,* Wharton certainly attended to the notion that proper introductions mattered in a world of "fluid strangers," and he seems to have thrived in the "unexpectedness of discovering an intimate relationship in the anonymous city."[9] Although it would appear his life was full of them, servants barely register at all and laborers and mechanics make no appearance. Instead, in his earlier life, Wharton orbits as a minor satellite of the owners and engineers of the factories, of important clergymen and educators, and like so many antebellum artists, of patrons in the Hudson River valley. Later in life he takes his place among the arrived bourgeoisie who have the leisure to be tourists on the national Grand Tour. Many of the great issues of the time, such as politics and abolitionism, go virtually unmentioned, while some of the other forces then shaping America, like industrialization, get passing mention but without a clear appreciation that something profound was happening. And unlike the myriad nineteenth-century travelers to America—de Tocqueville, Dickens, Trollope, Fanny Kemble, and so on—who took it upon themselves to observe and report critically on what was developing here, Wharton seems to have taken most of the manners of his adopted country in stride. On the positive side, he is at least unlike American diarists like George Templeton Strong, a "misanthropic spokesman for the prejudices of the affluent," constantly complaining about the changes around him.[10] Ultimately, we see in Thomas Kelah Wharton's journal a man who exuded good character and talent, a man for whom social networks were key, one who grew over the course of two decades from boundlessness to impressive cosmopolitanism in mid-nineteenth-century America.[11]

The Life of Thomas Kelah Wharton

A few pages added at the beginning of the first volume of the journal records how Wharton was recalled in the early twentieth century:

> Thomas Kelah Wharton was a man of culture, refinement and polished address – a fine conversationalist – a dear lover of Nature – a Christian gentleman of the highest type. A member of the Church of England later of the American Protestant Episcopal Church. A devoted husband and father – a loyal friend – a man of rare ability & virtues – fine fair & figure tall & well proportioned. The direct heir of the Barony of Wharton dating from 1147 – An Architect by profession – planned many public & private buildings in New Orleans, La. Previous to locating in N.O. he was professor of 'The Arts of Design' and descriptive geometry in St. Paul's College (Rev[d] Dr. Muhlenberg) at College Point L.I. (about 1832). Gifted as an Artist, in early life he painted in oils (landscapes) & also made many drawings & sketches in India, Sepia & pencil & Water Colours – all of which were highly appreciated by competent judges – A large number of the pencil sketches & drawings were sold by his widow

> in 1914 to the New York Public Library 5th Ave 41st & 42nd Sts. where they are now on view. Among them, 12 'Views in Ohio,' taken when he was about 18 years old, are remarkable for delicacy of touch, finish, & fidelity to Nature.

Wharton provides a thumbnail autobiography later in his journal—which is included here as chapter 2—but more is now known of his life than he was willing to record there.

Wharton was born April 17, 1814 to Thomas Wharton Sr. and his second wife, Anne (née Barkin), in Kingston-upon-Hull, the main city on the north shore of the Humber Estuary in the East Riding of Yorkshire, England. Thomas Sr.'s first wife died young, "in the prime of life," in 1810 and as far as is known they had no children.[12] Anne was the stepdaughter of Capt. Robert Kelah of Hull, retaining her father's surname, Barkin, when her mother remarried the captain.[13] The relationship must have been a good one, as this explains how Thomas Sr. and Anne gave their first son Thomas the middle name of his maternal step-grandfather, despite it appearing nowhere else in the family tree. Thomas Sr. and Capt. Kelah had had a business relation since at least 1822, when the latter converted the 350-ton barque *Shannon*, which he had run as a whaler off Greenland in the 1810s, into a first-class passenger ship with cabins both between decks and in steerage, and retained Wharton Sr. as a ticketing agent.[14] Anne's death on September 10, 1834 made the newspapers back in Hull, clarifying the younger Wharton's own vaguely dated journal entry, where her passing "after a long protracted illness" was lamented: "Her Christian-like virtues will be long cherished by an extensive circle of friends [and] she has left a large family to deplore their sad bereavement."[15]

Wharton's younger brothers, Robert John and Charles Frederick, were christened in Cottingham, just northwest of Hull, and he and his brother Henry and sisters Marianne and Emily in Sculcoates, a northern suburb. Interestingly, Wharton was initially christened on April 19, 1814, but then there is another christening record for him at Cottingham, at age four on October 25, 1818. The family could trace its lineage back to Humphrey Wharton of Whartons, a Norman lord in the early twelfth century, and to the ancestral seat at Wharton Hall (castle) near Kirkby Stephen, Cumberland (Cumbria).[16] The line included various Lords Wharton in the sixteenth and seventeenth centuries, including some notoriously foppish ones during the Restoration, though Thomas's line diverged from a second son a generation or two after Sir Thomas Wharton (1495–1568; a follower of King Henry VIII who was best known for his victory over the Scots at the Battle of Solway Moss on November 24, 1542) was created First Baron Wharton. Thomas Kelah's immediate family had its roots in Sculcoates, and when he was born they were living on Mason Street on the northeastern edge of the city. They soon had a townhome on the developing northern edge of the city at 4 Pryme Street, a street of ship owners, clergymen, commodities merchants, and at least one lawyer and one "gentleman." This street was off the main thoroughfare of Prospect Street and less than half a mile north and west of the Humber and Old Docks (now the Princes and Queens Docks, respectively) in the harbor, convenient for Thomas Sr.'s work in the shipping and mercantile trade. At the end of the 1820s, they lived in Wyton, a rural crossing "favored for country residence by the well-to-do of Hull," about six miles northeast of Hull, apparently in charge of the toll house of the turnpike (see Wharton's *Sketchbook*, p. 65).[17]

Wharton's father immigrated to Ohio in 1829 with Wharton's younger brother, Robert John, aged eleven. Thomas Kelah left Hull in May the following year with his mother and four other siblings, arriving at New York on June 3. The *New York Spectator* noted the arrival of the barque *Diana* from Hull, and other than two named single male travelers (Wharton in his journal notes that "We had but one fellow passenger in the cabin, a Mr. Stanley from the West Riding, but were in a few days joined by a Mr. Boyd"),[18] the Mrs. Wharton and the five childern are the only other names specified: "Mrs. Wharton, Thomas K., H[enry], and C[harles] F., Emily and Mary Ann." Given that another seventy-four arrived in steerage but the Whartons were listed by name down to the youngest child, it is clear that the family was of some considerable standing at the time. Indeed, the fact that Wharton and his mother were personally taken into New York City to their lodgings by the ship's captain and that they stayed in a rooming house right in the center of the city by City Hall points to the same conclusion.

Ship owner, shipping insurance broker, and commission agent (and sometimes banker) in Exchange Alley in Hull, Thomas Wharton Sr. had made a considerable fortune in transatlantic shipping, importing everything from French burr stones to German bark and hemp to African teak and Jamaica rum, while exporting woolen goods and earthenware to places as far flung as Rio de Janeiro.[19] By 1815, he was in partnership with the Newbald family of merchants, running the brig *Gambier*, which plied the trade routes to southern Italy. In 1816 he and his partners, E. and I. Thompson, owned the three-hundred-ton copper-bottomed packet ship *Comet* under the command of Capt. John Sugden (who also incidentally captained the *Diana* that took the Wharton's to New York, suggesting the possibility that Wharton's father still had a business connection to her in 1830), which they advertised as a fast-sailing ship for New York, offering superior accommodations, "fast Between-Decks, and excellent Cabins." Seven years later Thomas Sr. held part interest in at least two other ships of about 340-ton burthen, and owned the three-hundred-ton *General Phipps* by himself, and plied the packet routes between the United Kingdom and Rio de Janeiro and Buenos Aires.[20] Unfortunately, in the autumn of 1828, Wharton and two brothers named Johnston speculated on the import of Baltic wheat from Lübeck, each paying one-third of the costs of the grain and its shipping. Wharton and at least one of the brothers signed over bills to creditors in full faith and received the cargoes and sold them, but both men went bankrupt in 1829 and the creditors were left hanging for over £3,800 (equivalent to something like £265,000 today). Ordered by the courts to surrender himself to the commissioners by April 30, 1829 to "make full discovery and disclosure of his Estate and Effects" before his creditors on the following day was too much, and he left for Ohio—although not before shipping "diverse Goods and Merchandises" to the US to be beyond the reach of his creditors. Court cases lingered into the 1830s and though creditors could claim some of their losses by 1832 and he was declared insolvent in 1833—four years after leaving for America—his bankruptcy was not finalized in England until 1841. As one lawsuit against him noted, Wharton "absconded to America" where creditors could not fully claim their debts against him, and the Wharton family began anew in Ohio.[21]

After a month-long pause in New York City, Mrs. Wharton and the children traveled via the Erie Canal and Lake Erie to Sandusky, OH, where they joined Thomas Sr. for the last leg of the trip to a farm in Piqua, OH, eighty miles due north of Cincinnati near the Indiana border. The Wharton farm, purchased in June 1829 for $2,000, consisted of 182 acres just south of present Piqua and about four or five blocks west of what is now US Route 25. It had belonged to Matthew Caldwell, who platted the town in 1807. The initial farming venture in the hinterland was not much of a success and, as Wharton put it, the entire family was "all ill-fitted for the deprivations of the backwoods," so they sold the farm in 1831 for $3,500 (making a profit) and moved to a second home in Zanesville, OH, midway between Columbus and Wheeling. There, Wharton Sr. purchased a warehousing business for $1,700 in the newly booming river town that was shortly to be connected by the National Road. The portion of Thomas Kelah's journal covering the transatlantic voyage, arrival in New York, and travel to Ohio has been previously published, so we pick up his story as he arrives in New York City in May 1832.[22]

At the age of eighteen, Wharton left the family in Ohio to New York City to take up an apprenticeship in architecture. The architect Martin E. Thompson had somehow become immediately impressed with young Wharton's drawing abilities, and had offered the young man an apprenticeship. Thompson is today best remembered for the Merchant's Exchange Building in New York (1827; burned in the Great Fire of 1835) and the Second Branch Bank of the United States (1824; its facade is now preserved at the Metropolitan Museum of Art). At the time he took on young Wharton, he was at the height of his career. How exactly Thompson knew of the young man remains something of a mystery. Wharton records in his journal that in the spring of 1832 Thompson, who had designed the Episcopal Church in Columbus, OH, "has made offers to me, thro' our friend Mr. Earl, which my Father is now considering."[23] (Mr. Earl remains an enigma, though we find out later in Wharton's journal that he lived on Beekman Street in New York City and that Wharton delivered a number of watercolors to him, perhaps as a sort of repayment for connecting him with Thompson.[24]) Thompson repeated the offer to apprentice Wharton a month later, but the Whartons were at that moment moving from Piqua to Zanesville and young Thomas claims to have left the decision to his father (and to providence). His father seems to have preferred to get young Wharton into the mercantile trades, for he proposed sending him to Philadelphia with an introduction from a Mr. Turner, and only if that did not secure him a position, then let him "go on to New York and avail [him]self of Mr. Thompson's kind offers."[25]

Despite setting up as farmers in Ohio, the Whartons enjoyed considerable financial and social capital at the time. They were clearly a family of some leisure when they arrived, as they awaited travel details from the father in Ohio, lodging at the upscale (though not palatial) boardinghouse of Thomas Slocum. They spent the month of June 1830 taking in all manner of tourist sites: "Week after week passed away like hours in the charming city, and we saw everything that was worth seeing in New York and its immediate neighbourhood."[26] This impression is further reinforced in that they were immediately befriended by a number of prominent New Yorkers and visitors to the city, notably Russell Coggeshall, a whaling magnate from Newport, Rhode Island, who also lodged at Slocum's and accompanied the family in their tourist outings. It is entirely possible that it was during their month-long respite in New York that they met Martin Thompson through Thomas Sr.'s business connections.

Thus, Wharton clearly possessed a certain social and economic cushion in his foray into the urban metropolises of Philadelphia and New York. From Wharton's later journal entries, we know that when he traveled in the 1840s and '50s, he stayed at finer hotels in cities across the country. We cannot, therefore, see him as a stereotypical farm boy coming to the city for a clerkship, with all the anxiety, class concern, and social difficulties that that entailed.[27]

When Wharton did accept Thompson's offer of employment in April 1832 and began on May 10, he had to leave the city after just a few weeks to escape a cholera epidemic.[28] In view of the fact that Wharton left Thompson's office after only a few weeks and seems not to have had a chance to produce any work for him, it is interesting to note that a friendly relationship between the two lasted through the years. Wharton often stayed with the Thompson family in the city during the years he was teaching at the Flushing Institute on Long Island, and several times Thompson offered him opportunities both to teach and to resume his work in architecture in his office.

In order to escape the cholera outbreak, in July 1832 Wharton went up the Hudson to stay on the estate of one of Thompson's clients, Dr. David Hosack, who owned what later became the Vanderbilt estate in Hyde Park. The land had been the estate of his old teacher and medical partner, Dr. Samuel Bard, and Hosack had Thompson design a mansion and other buildings on the grounds in the 1820s. Hosack was one of the leading gentlemen in New York and as Hudson gentry, his home, "the nearest thing to a salon" in the area, was filled with "books, paintings, portrait busts of his friends, and a well-stocked larder and wine cellar."[29] He welcomed all manner of notables including state and federal politicians, authors like Frances Trollope and Washington Irving, and visiting diplomats. As a strong supporter of the American Academy of Fine Arts and of young artists of talent, it is not hard to see why Hosack would be happy to have young Wharton there. At Hosack's, he met Sylvanus Thayer, superintendent of the US Military Academy at West Point, where he would continue his geometry and drawing studies and integrate himself into the lower Hudson society of the day. The "salon culture" in that stretch of the Hudson was headed by yet another man Wharton met at Hosack's that summer, Gouverneur Kemble, the proprietor of the West Point Foundry in Cold Spring. Kemble tied together artists, writers, businessmen, military officers, and all manner of men of "good taste" that bridged the Knickerbocker literary set and the Hudson River School of painting. Washington Irving and James Kirke Paulding (Kemble's brother-in-law) were also frequent guests at Kemble's with Wharton and he became known to the rising artists Thomas Cole, Asher B. Durand, William Sidney Mount, and other of the school's founders.

Wharton's career took yet another sudden turn by the fall of 1832, when he was offered and accepted a job as a teacher of art and descriptive geometry at the Flushing Institute by William Augustus Muhlenberg, a pioneer in the Episcopalian Church Schooling Movement.[30] Wharton tells us in his journal that Muhlenberg visited West Point while he was staying there with Thayer, though the connection might also have been through the Rev. Samuel Roosevelt Johnson, the pastor of St. James in Hyde Park, who Wharton met while staying with Dr. Hosack earlier that summer. On August 11, 1827, Muhlenberg had begun a grand neoclassical building that was to be called the "Flushing Institute," and the school began its first session in the spring of the following year.[31] Flushing itself was a prosperous town and wealthy agrarian enclave slightly removed from the more energetic cities of New York and Brooklyn. An English traveler in 1830 noted that Long Island's land prices made it "a situation [more] for an opulent farmer than one of limited means," describing Flushing in particular as "a neat lively village . . . [with] some excellent hotels" that had become "quite a place of resort for the butterflies of fashion."[32] Muhlenberg may well have seen this sort of location as more conducive to his vision of a conservative and upper-class Episcopal school. It may also be that this distance from Manhattan served as a slight buffer between the High Church Episcopalianism of Bishop Henry Onderdonk (whom Wharton praised as a great man in his journal on May 11, 1833 and with whom Muhlenberg was friendly) and the more formally scholastic and tepidly evangelical nature of Muhlenberg's school. In ways, it was the Flushing Institute that was "fixing the type" of church schools just as Wharton joined the school.[33]

Muhlenberg was no revivalist. He was certain that salvation came through study and introspection, somewhat at odds with the "formalist" position of the High Church that elevated liturgy and ritual as key components of faith known through the relationships of the clergy to the congregants, but even further away from the more emotive understandings of the Methodists and Baptists. At the very least, Muhlenberg was reacting against existing preparatory schools, which only gave intellectual and physical instruction; he argued that the schools needed moral instruction based in Christianity as well: "their tendency being not to 'the nurture and admonition of the Lord,' but the nurture and admonition of the world." He saw the idea of moral discipline and admonition as a "preventative," with the proper physical education "a powerful auxiliary to moral discipline"; corrective discipline, punishments, and rewards should all be based on principles and be "mild and affectionate, yet steady and uniform." As far as the intellectual education of the school went, here he did not propose anything too radical for the day:

> The ancient languages are the best ground work of liberal learning: the study of the Greek language [in English] is deemed particularly proper, because it is the depository of our faith; The art of study should be taught, the pupil being led to *think*, and acquire knowledge for himself. . . . Education should also follow the leadings of genius: Boys should be allowed to pursue those studies for which they are adapted, and not waste their time and toil in proceeds for which they are not qualified.[34]

This seemingly modern approach should not eclipse the fundamentally religious spirit of the Flushing Institute. Muhlenberg expected that the large majority of his students (and the tutors) would enter the ministry, and the school was explicitly marketed to Episcopalians *against* other colleges that were deemed a danger to their children as a result of the Second Great Awakening that made them too generally secular or shot through with excesses of the wrong strand(s) of Christianity—where "infidelity is disguising itself with the mask of rational Christianity [and] the rankest weeds of heresy are covering the soil where trees once flourished."[35] This, he thought, would create an educated class of boys who could go forth to address the social problems of the day.[36]

The institute was a success from the start and saw class after class of boys living in twelve-student sections, each under a prefect. The boys ranged in age from twelve to nineteen, and the typical graduate often went on to enter universities like Columbia, Penn, or Harvard as juniors. The school operated as a kind of extended family structure, and Muhlenberg pursued the policy of trusting the boys and placing them on their honor. A later alumnus described Muhlenberg's schools as "a family of boys, of which [Muhlenberg] was 'school-father,' the spiritual guide, friend, and father-confessor of his school-sons, not merely a schoolmaster."[37] This also seems to have been Muhlenberg's antidote to the "tent revival," itinerant free-for-alls sweeping the nation at the time, and Wharton seems to have been happy in his teaching and management of pupils. The school, however, was not the college that Muhlenberg had dreamed of.

By the mid-1830s, applications to the institute were straining resources, and at the same time, having received his degree in divinity, Muhlenberg contemplated visions of a more thoroughly equipped college.[38] To that end, he bought 175 acres of land at Strattonport just north of Flushing and, on October 15, 1836, he laid the cornerstone of what was designed to be an extensive structure that would cost about $50,000. But the building never rose above the basement story as the Panic of 1837 forced his backers to abandon him. Temporary buildings were erected for the new college, and the Flushing Institute was moved to the newly renamed College Point. There St. Paul's College opened in 1838 with a full staff of professors, including Wharton as professor of drawing. The goal of the college was again "the moral education of the students by means of a paternal and familiar discipline—and a regulation of circumstances favorable to the cultivation of sentiment and character," but the curriculum was a fusion of classical and modern subjects: seven of its twelve professors taught Latin, Greek, French, and rhetoric, but three taught mathematics, natural philosophy, and (separately) chemistry and mineralogy; courses also included Evidences of Christianity, History and Constitutional Law, and Antiquities and Geography.[39] By 1840 the college was teaching 105 students, had a seven-thousand-volume library, a property value estimated at $70,000, and an annual cost of professors' and instructors' salaries of $9,000 (a full professor of mathematics and natural philosophy was paid $1,000 per year in 1833, teaching about five hours a day). Muhlenberg tried, unsuccessfully, to get the state to allow him to confer BA degrees and the college flourished until 1844, when he moved back to New York City and two years later became rector of the Church of the Holy Communion. It eventually failed in 1848.[40]

When Muhlenberg had opened St. Paul's, it retained a general classical curriculum, but the pedagogical framework became increasingly ecclesiastical, training students at the collegiate level for missionary work in the "Western lands," and the best students for a life in the Episcopal ministry. Muhlenberg became even more set against rationalism ("a bulwark against," as he saw it, "Germanism"—Lutheranism and the rising German educational system) and against the early-nineteenth-century trend toward a more ecumenical Unitarianism in higher education, which emanated from Harvard.[41] Indeed, a number of very famous (conservative) Episcopalian churchmen and educators came up through the Flushing Institute and St. Paul's while Wharton taught there: John Barrett Kerfoot, Libertus Van Bokkelen, and James Lloyd Breck, for example, all became important Episcopal educators or bishops.

In about 1840, Wharton accepted a position at St. Thomas's Hall, a rival school back in Flushing that had been started by Rev. Francis Lister Hawks in 1839. Hawks, a North Carolinian and important theologian and church educator, had been recruited by Muhlenberg to teach rhetoric and oratory at St. Paul's in 1838 (he had also given the oration at the laying of its cornerstone in 1836 and Wharton and Hawks may have known each other in Saugerties, NY, where Hawks had his first ministry, in the early 1830s), but he lasted at St. Thomas's less than a year, choosing instead to set up his own school that charted a less strictly theological educational course. Perhaps it was Wharton's technical skills and interest in the sciences and practical building that were not in sync with the more religious nature of St. Paul's; maybe his faith had been slightly shaken by the death of his mother in 1834 or broadened the worldliness of his new stepmother, who came on the scene in 1835. His chapter and verse citations from the 1830s journal certainly give way to more curiosity about the practices of other denominations in the 1850s, though we cannot know about his faith in the later 1830s as he kept no journal at that time. He never showed any inclination toward ordination, or perhaps it was the tension felt by many in the antebellum world between the pursuit of individual success in the booming new country and the traditional social and religious ideas of society that pulled him toward Hawks's vision of education.[42]

The old Flushing Institute had become St. Ann's Hall school for girls in 1839 and Hawks built his new St. Thomas's Hall two block south. There, with fourteen instructors, the school grew to 120 students by 1841.[43] George Templeton Strong commented in his own diary that a friend had just "got back from Flushing and tells me that Hawks's school building is going up—a single Gothic quadrangle," and that the chapel was apparently "one of the most beautiful in the country."[44] By the spring of 1843, however, the finances of the school were in tatters. As Strong reported, "Hawks has exploded. St. Thomas' Hall has suspended payment." Although Hawks claimed no wrongdoing, St. Thomas's closed and Hawks left the Northeast. Wharton, clearly devoted to Hawks and the Episcopalian Church Schools Movement, followed Hawks to help found another school in Holly Springs, MS, and then eventually followed him again to New Orleans, though there they parted ways.[45]

It is clear that Wharton found his years on Long Island enjoyable and profitable. Years later he noted in his journal that,

> By the papers I see that a great "India Rubber Coat Factory" has been established on College Point Long Island, employing from 500 to 1000 hands. This was the "locus" of St. Paul's College, the darling project of Revd Dr Muhlenberg, who conducted it for seven years under very favorable auspices. Here, too, and at Flushing, but 3 miles distant, I passed some 8 years of my life in the pleasant seclusion of scholastic pursuits. What a change! The reverend Professors gone! The muses lament, The Marble porch where Wisdom went to talk with Socrates or Tully, hears no more, save the hoarse dissonance of jarring wheels.[46]

That Wharton left New York with Hawks presents an interesting counterfactual: Hawks was by this time a figure of national importance and considered to be an orator of distinction. He was also already the author of many works on religious, historical, and legal subjects well before the period of the failure at Flushing. His next venture in the South might seem hardly promising after the failure of St. Thomas's, even if Hawks was exonerated for causing the first school's failure. Wharton chose to break his ties and uproot his sisters who were studying in Astoria, leave his influential friends and family, and abandon his connections to the artistic and—in view of his lasting friendship with Martin E. Thompson—architectural world of New York. By this time, however, Wharton had spent a full decade as an educator rather than as an artist, and there are very few known works from his pen or easel from the early 1840s. Likely his inability to enter the ranks of the art world in New York, whether due to his own abilities, inclinations, or actions—or the blocking actions of others—had convinced him that his calling lay elsewhere. Hawks was clearly a brilliant man, but Wharton tells us in his autobiographical synopsis that he was possibly unstable and subject to depression due to an "impulsive nature[,] chafed and fretted by his pecuniary difficulties at Flushing." He hardly seemed like a man satisfied to remain long at the head of his college at Holly Springs, as indeed turned out to be the case.

St. Thomas's Hall for Boys in Holly Springs was founded in 1844 with Dr. Hawks as first president, and officially incorporated by the Protestant Episcopal Church in October 1845. Wharton was listed as a "proprietor" along with Hawks in the college circular.[47] Hawks had chosen the small town in northwestern Mississippi, fifty miles southeast of Memphis, both to get away from the failure of St. Thomas's in Flushing and to recoup his debts in the matter (his daughter also resided there at the time, which seems to be why he chose it). Wharton refers to the venture as a "University," leading to some confusion with the University of Holly Springs chartered in 1838 that never came to fruition, though St. Thomas's in some sense filled that goal.

Hawkes took a cautious approach, "proceeding quietly, but surely and securely, . . . in laying the foundation of an institution and a system of education, to which . . . Episcopalians may point with gratification." It would be, he had proposed, "an institution of learning, for males, of the highest order, affording all benefits of collegiate education . . . which shall extend alike to all, whether they be the sons of Episcopalians or not."[48] The school opened in locally donated buildings in January 1844 with Hawks as president and professor of English literature, John Q. Bradford teaching Latin and Greek, Lt. Claudius W. Sears (a West Point graduate and later a Confederate brigadier general) teaching mathematics, and Wharton in charge of French, German, and drawing. Tuition was $250 for the ten-month school year for boarders, $50 for day students, and included everything except books and instrumental music lessons.[49]

As soon as Hawks arrived in Mississippi, however, the state diocese offered him a bishopric—which was immediately contested at the national Episcopal convention by some who worried about his failure at St. Thomas's in New York—and he left Holly Springs that same year.[50] The school was reorganized as a military school (though it had already had "cadets" under Lieutenant Sears from the beginning), in which guise it survived until it was burned during the Civil War.[51] Having ultimately declined the Episcopal bishopric, Hawks settled in New Orleans from 1844–49 to become the fourth rector of Christ's Church and was chosen first president of the University of Louisiana (now Tulane University). By this time, his preaching reputation international, as Sir Charles Lyell, the eminent British geologist, noted in February 1846 that, "During our stay in New Orleans . . . in the principal Episcopal Church, we were fortunate in hearing Dr. Hawkes [*sic*] preach, and thought the matter and manner of his discourse deserving of his high reputation for pulpit eloquence."[52]

Wharton taught at Holly Springs for only a year before moving to New Orleans in 1845—at the same time as Hawks—with his new wife, Maria (née Huling), the daughter of a local Holly Springs judge and planter whose family also sold their plantation and bought another, fifty miles south of New Orleans.[53] It is interesting that there is no clear explanation of why Wharton only now shifted back to his initial calling in architecture when he had been an educator for a decade, or why he did not, for example, take up a position at the University of Louisiana under

Hawks. Lieutenant Sears also followed Hawks and did teach mathematics at the university from 1845 to 1859,[54] but why Wharton did not or could not avail himself of the same opportunity is unknown. Entries in his journal suggest that Wharton did stay connected with Hawks in New Orleans at first, but his autobiographical sketch merely offers that he "gradually reverted back to the occupation in which [he] commenced life, architecture."

In a way, the position he ended up in in New Orleans partly re-created what he had gone to New York for nearly twenty years before. He had already made some preliminary architectural elevations and plans for Hawks's Christ's Church, though James Gallier Sr., the contractor for the church, does not deign to name him—"the doctor [Hawks] had with him at that time a gentleman who had been the drawing master at his school, and who made a sketch design for the new church; but I had to make so many alterations in the plan, before it could be made practically fit to build from, as to make it amount to a new design"—before seeing the project to completion at least visually as Wharton had designed it.[55] His architecture career did not immediately flourish and Maria died of pulmonary consumption early that summer, so Wharton spent some of the summer and fall grieving with the Hulings at their plantation.[56] In the fall of 1848 he was appointed a clerk (i.e., draftsman and building superintendent) for the construction of the new Customs House in New Orleans. As the antebellum architectural profession began to move from craft to profession, it is clear that Wharton found a convenient niche in a full-time job as a construction superintendent for the federal government while taking private commissions for houses for well-to-do residents of New Orleans.[57]

By September 1849, Wharton became acting architect pro tem and superintendent pro tem, responsible for all building work on the Customs House project. This position lasted only two months, for in the middle of November he was upgraded to general superintendent of the building works until the spring of 1853, when ill health forced him to take a leave of absence for about eight months.[58] While the building still stands as an impressive structure at the heart of New Orleans, contemporary commentators were not always so kind about its style. Mark Twain wrote that there was no "architecture" on Canal Street:

> [T]o speak in broad, general terms, there is no architecture in New Orleans, except in the cemeteries. It seems a strange thing to say of a wealthy, far-seeing, and energetic city of a quarter of a million inhabitants, but it is true. There is a huge granite U.S. Custom-house—costly enough, genuine enough, but as a decoration it is inferior to a gasometer. It looks like a state prison.[59]

In 1851 at age thirty-seven, Wharton married his second wife, Emily Ladd Prescott, some twenty years his junior. They had a son, Thomas Prescott Wharton, the next fall, and in 1853 they took a long trip to Boston, fortuitously avoiding a serious outbreak of yellow fever in New Orleans that summer.[60] Not only does this section of the journal give a magnificent view of continental travel just as America was becoming conveniently networked through river and rail, Wharton's descriptions show Boston at its boom period, growing at nearly 20 percent a year. With Back Bay being filled in and the city changing at a rapid pace, Wharton visited a city whose population had just crested 150,000 and whose industrial boom was becoming clearer and clearer.[61] Upon his return to New Orleans that fall, he threw himself into the construction of the new Customs House and gradually became more Southern than Northern. A strong supporter of the Confederacy once the Civil War broke out, Wharton was appointed superintendent of the Customs House when his predecessor, P.G.T. Beauregard—the commander who fired the first shots on Fort Sumter—took command of Confederate units. Wharton died on May 24, 1862 at the age of forty-eight, a few weeks after the Union took New Orleans.

Antebellum Diarizing

The journals of Thomas Kelah Wharton are wonderful examples of a genre of self-reflective writing that was at once both private and yet public. For centuries authors have penned works purporting to be private but which it was entirely clear were meant for public circulation. Wharton's production is not so deliberately public as the Renaissance or Enlightenment letters that went to press before the ink was dry, nor the nineteenth-century staple of the travel journal that were kept specifically with an eye to later publication and fame. But neither is it a truly private journal under lock and key that tells all and expects to remain secret. The journal was written, at least initially, for his son, and therefore was intended at least for some private audience, but an audience beyond the author himself. It recorded Wharton's day-to-day activities, and includes some commentary on the world around him, though it tends strongly toward his personal experience rather than the affairs of the day or of the nation and offers valuable insight in terms of what he says and in what he omits.

Diaries are the private made public; they are "flesh made word,"[62] in that one becomes acquainted with a diary writer in a way that one does not when reading that same person's novel, poem, or letters. As Arthur Ponsonby, the pioneer for diary studies in the 1920s, put it, "They are better than novels, more accurate than histories, and even at times more dramatic than plays."[63] Diaries are generally thought of giving a "rare [and] intimate view" at history, or the mind of a person, or of a movement.[64] They are also at once "tantalizing," for we don't know what we will find, and there is something scandalous or wicked in reading someone else's private thoughts. Yet they do reveal things that may not be revealed in published sources, if those sources even exist. They are our surrogates for a walk though the past, filled with the banal of the weather and the writer's fits of ague as well as brushes with celebrity or royalty. But the value in them lies not necessarily in the specifics of what they reveal or record—though there is great value in that as well—but in their recording of networks of people and places and things that we might not otherwise see. Diaries can be thought of as the "ledgers of history,"[65] but they are also "kept" rather than "sent" (letters) or "shared" (stories):

> The diary, as an uncertain genre uneasily balanced between literary and historical writing, between the spontaneity of reportage and reflectiveness of the crafted text, between selfhood and events, between subjectivity and objectivity, between the private and the public, constantly disturbs attempts to summarize its characteristics within formalized boundaries."[66]

As he was recopying his journal in the company of his new bride and infant son, perhaps we should not be surprised that Wharton might omit sections in which he fell in love for the first time and began to build a life with his first wife, as well as the anguish of her death. He might have included information on his youth in Hull, but given that nowhere in his journal do we learn that the family had shifted from merchant shipping to a toll-keeper's cottage and then ran from bankruptcy in England, it makes sense that this chapter of his life, too, is elided. He was, after all, the eldest son of a prosperous shipping firm that he was no longer going to inherit, and they were now moving to, of all places, rural Ohio. The gap from 1834 to 1853 does seem to be genuine enough, but if Wharton got himself up to youthful hijinks in his days in New York, or had misadventures at or during his days off at the Flushing Institute, it is not surprising to find no mention of them in his journals. The first part of the journal from the early 1830s and from 1853 that we present in this volume, then, is an edited and occasionally editorialized reflection on his first forty years, while his later journal entries while living in New Orleans, which become more contemporary and critical of the society around him.[67]

The young Wharton arrived in New York City in the midst of its boom after the opening of the Erie Canal, just as it began to overtake Philadelphia and Boston as America's principle city. It was awash with new arrivals and quite literally bursting at its seams as it surged northward along Manhattan Island. Yet Wharton tells us a story of polite refinement of his trips up and down the Hudson, brushing elbows with some of the river's gentry, even though he would eventually fall in more with bourgeoisie artists, industrialists, and military men who occupied a refined but not aristocratic stratum. The city of prostitutes, beggars, and immigrants is entirely absent to his pen, perhaps because as a young, educated, and artistically talented English immigrant himself, he was able to immediately begin his circulations with these "better sorts." It is something short of astounding that he tells us nothing of the roiling 1830s in New York and the city that would see the overlapping worlds of Edgar Allan Poe, P.T. Barnum, and Sir John Herschel (author of the Great Moon Hoax of 1835, which seems to have entirely eluded the young artist, even though he was partly circulating in the world of the press with his *New-York Mirror* entanglement with Morris and Weir at the time).[68] Wharton's theological fervor, more ardent as a young man, may also have kept him on the straight and narrow, and once he joined the teaching staff at a theologically grounded college and found himself at a remove from the city in more genteel Flushing, it may be that he felt that he really had joined the novitiate.

There are wide areas that escaped his writing—though not, one presumes, his prodigious attention—that need to be understood to place Wharton's journal in context. Wharton has little to say about class relations or politics at all. Even world affairs don't appear in the earlier section of the journal, though by 1853 he occasionally alludes to but does not dwell on some scandals of the day, such as train accidents and murders like the 1849 Parkman-Webster murder.[69] Otherwise the huge issues of the day—from presidential elections to economic booms and busts or any discussion of slavery—make no appearance in the early years of his journals, despite the fact that we know he engaged in lively discussions on these matters with the people of some import that he met, such as at a dinner party with Gouverneur Kemble and James Kirke Paulding.[70] His later entries observe more local politics and elections, though even the onset of the Civil War elicited only a few lines of notice.[71] Though he was present in the embryonic New York artist community and nearly in the founding of groups like the National Academy of Design, he avoided editorializing on the position of the artist or the generosity or parsimony of patrons. Most of his worries are indeed quite personal. The only common thread throughout the journal is the fear of epidemics in cities. The second cholera pandemic that struck the globe from 1829–1851 killed tens of thousands and spread along transportation routes in an era that fully understood its lethality but not its waterborne mechanism or any real effective prevention. Yellow fever was similarly destructive, though through a different vector (mosquitos) and against which one could develop an acquired immunity. Though mostly contained today, we must not forget how virulent nineteenth-century epidemics were, easily carrying off 5 percent of the population in some outbreaks.[72]

Wharton makes little mention of women, other than his immediate family members and wives of acquaintances, in his 1830s entries, despite being an eligible young bachelor in the big city. One can at once perhaps catch a glimpse of his mild infatuation with refined young ladies whose paths he crossed, such as Emily Hosack, but at the same time, early-nineteenth-century masculinities being what they were, our modern eye is perhaps too prone to read Wharton's ardor for the men he meets up and down the Hudson as more than boon companionship or admiration. Given that the 1830s portion of the journal was rewritten and we know that he explicitly excised some text from his original journal, it is entirely possible that he bowdlerized events and relations during his youthful New York period. Two decades later, as a respectable married man in his trip to the Northeast, and now assured of his station and role in the world, he still only once pauses to opine how "strong women" who wore trousers made for a sight "*tout ensemble* ungraceful, inelegant to the last degree."[73]

Wharton is also curiously quiet about race throughout the first volume of the journal. Later in the 1850s he tended to be anti-abolitionist and joined the Know-Nothing Party, and he makes no reference to the ethnicity of a servant, Francis, in New Orleans who might possibly have been his slave (1860 census records do not list her in his household and Wharton is missed in the 1850 New Orleans census).[74] In fact, from the words he writes in the first volume of the journal, the only place he even encountered African Americans was on Dr. Hosack's estate in Hyde Park: he mentions in passing a "black boy" who rang the morning bell and noted with some apparent amusement the black coachman who "bent his, by the by, excellent figure, from the coach box to salute one of the Doctor's black women and begged her to 'excuse his glove.'"[75] It is likely that he was surrounded by a fair number of abolitionists in the Episcopal movement in the 1830s, and the abolition of slavery in the British empire in 1833 certainly elicited great debates in America at the time (e.g., ten days of pro-slavery rioters attacked African Americans and Englishmen in New York City), yet we hear nothing of that in his journal.[76] We know that people he associated with were abolitionists (as a US representative, Gouverneur Kemble voted for abolition in 1838, though the House motion was ultimately merely symbolic),[77] but perhaps in the 1830s Wharton's views on the matter were insufficiently developed to have made the pages of his journal, or by the time he recopied that period in the 1850s his views were changing.

By 1853, though, one would expect at least some mention. Once the Civil War broke out, Wharton took the side of the Confederacy and viewed the North as trying to destroy a way of life, and a way of life that Wharton had married into—recall his first wife's family were plantation owners and had forty-one slaves on their Holly Springs planation in 1840 and seven slaves in the 1860 federal census slave schedules—and had apparently quite contentedly adopted for more than fifteen years at that point. In 1860, a week before Secession, he noted, "News from the North indicates a gradual return to 'common sense' on the part of the canting, hypocritical, 'Black Republican' party. The anti-slavery agitation should now be set at rest *for ever*."[78] So in 1853, and again recalling that this journal was filtered for his toddler son's later eyes, perhaps Wharton trod the middle road to avoid engaging in such concerns.

Artistic Ambitions

Wharton's journals offer a glimpse at how a well-educated immigrant who was initially destined to be an artist and architect evolved into an architect and construction manager in a burgeoning country full of opportunity. His years teaching at Episcopal schools also help us understand the fluidity of the professions at the time. We ought, then, to consider the circumstances of the young and then the adult Thomas Kelah Wharton as he circulated in New York and Boston society in antebellum America. As will be seen from the included sketches in the following chapters (though these are barely half of the total in the journals), Wharton was a natural artist with a near photographic eye for detail. He began circulating in the emerging Hudson River School of artists centered around Thomas Cole, Asher B.

Durand, Frederic Church, and John Frederick Kensett, getting so far as exhibiting at the National Academy show in 1834. There, the *New-York Mirror* said he had "shown skill" in his painting of "Falls of the Indian Brook, opposite West Point" that "places him among our successful landscape painters. We understand he is a young artist from England, and we are happy to give him a welcome."[79]

Ultimately, though, he did not quite join the ranks of the noted. Perhaps his skill in oils and watercolors was underdeveloped. Perhaps it was because his pen was more suited to the world of engravings and the publication industry was still more than a decade from lavishly illustrated weeklies like *Harper's* or *Frank Leslie's*. Perhaps the allusions in the journal to conflict with Robert W. Weir, in charge of illustrations for George Pope Morris's *New-York Mirror*, hints at some larger pressures that kept him out of those ranks. Wharton had in fact gone to New York expecting to enter a master-apprentice relationship under Martin E. Thompson, but arrived just as that system was giving way to a new mode of relationships, that of education-based credentialism. The collapse of the architecture market due to the cholera scare just as Wharton arrived in New York pushed him into the latter system as he learned more technical drawing at West Point. At the same time, it wrenched him out of the world of artists and patrons, though we see him trying to keep a hand in at a personal level for a couple years. His teaching at Flushing, which would have included both artistic and technical drawing, and the fact that some of his students went on to be architects, suggests more strongly that he found a good home in the new educational system. His mix of architectural critique within aesthetics and his eye for mechanical detail appropriate for a contractor, as well as his later role as managing engineer at the New Orleans Customs House, demonstrate a breadth beyond mere artistic details and the rote of architectural orders.[80]

There can be no doubt that the well-to-do Wharton family gave their eldest son (or perhaps all their children, as we learn that Wharton's sisters were enrolled in Astoria in the 1830s) a strong classical education. Thomas not only was well versed in classical and modern poetry, he knew his Linnaean botanical classifications in Latin, and later taught German and French. Though he seems to the modern eye to have been college educated, his command of Latin and classical allusions would have been had from a strong, early-nineteenth-century grammar school. He makes no mention of boarding school or traveling to another city for lessons, although one enigmatic mention of the "intensively beautiful chimes of the churches in Manchester . . . which I used to listen to with the sensitive and delighted ears of boyhood," could possibly suggest he was also a student in that city, as does his sketching of Kirkstall Abbey in Leeds in 1929[81]. Neither does he mention any specific later schooling, so we should presumably infer that he went to the Hull Grammar School, with Rev. William Wilson as master. Alternately, by 1800 many private schools, such as Snowden's Academy in Hull, which Thomas Sr. could easily have afforded for his son, had sprung up, offering more mixed curricula for the children of the middle class that included not only classical education but natural sciences as well. At Hull, Wilson and the previous masters, Rev. John Scott and

Rev. George John Davies, had brought the Hull Grammar School forward from its strictly classical education toward a modern comprehensive one. Although the Hull Grammar School did not officially add sciences to its curriculum until the appointment of J.D. Sollitt in 1838, under Wilson the school did try to recruit a new usher to teach "the higher branches of mathematics, astronomy and fluxions included." And of course, it is also possible that his father, "an excellent, but not remarkably intellectual man,"[82] had hired private tutors for young Thomas (a distinct likelihood since advanced instruction in art was rarely offered by any grammar or private school at the time).[83] He presumably recognized the artistic talent in his son and got him a broad education, as skill in learning and with the pencil was on full display by the time he left England.

Although Wharton left teaching behind by 1850, when the New Orleans Mechanics Society, an educational college for tradesmen, was considering adding a drawing department, they sought out Wharton's opinion on the matter. His reply, printed in a New Orleans newspaper, enunciated a position that sought to give every architect, engineer, machinist, and "the operative in every other branch of industry" a good working knowledge of the "Arts of Design": "Every intelligent and well-instructed mechanic should be, to some extent," he argued, "a draughtsman."[84] He seemed to add a certain autobiographical component when he said in an aside,

> It is not expected that all mechanics should be artists, though it may be remarked, that were a proper regard paid to the subject in the education of our youth, many would eventually rise to high artistic distinction, whose abilities would otherwise be dormant.

Wharton argued that drawing was of high importance in the construction trades, *indispensable* in "ornamental construction," and many a builder, when put in charge of great works will find himself mortified by his inability to communicate a design because his artistic ability is lacking. Further, every "handicraftsman [will], without correct drawings, plans, sections, elevations, &c., continually work to disadvantage, will frequently be at a loss, and always deficient in precision and accuracy." The solution, Wharton suggested, lay in creating a professorship in the "Arts of Design" that would teach three courses on picturesque drawing, architecture, and perspective drawing. One wonders if Wharton hoped that he might be asked to fill such a chair, though it does not appear that the Mechanics Society took up the idea.

Back in New York in the 1830s, Wharton seems to have remained on the periphery of the artistic and publishing world, befriending George Pope Morris, the publisher of the *New-York Mirror*, and others. Morris's *Mirror* was "the most complete coverage of the American art scene before 1855 [whose] able editors, especially . . . Morris, not only gave this literary magazine a longevity surprising for its day, but also greatly widened its scope without reducing the contents to mere superficiality."[85] In addition, while Wharton worked for Rev. Hawks at St. Thomas's Hall, Hawks wrote frequently for and was briefly the editor of the *New York Review*. Wharton's journal of this period records his interactions with many notable artists of the day, and by 1837 he was taken seriously enough to be asked to affix his signature to a petition on copyright protections to Congress, along with twenty-nine other notables, including Morris, Samuel F. B. Morse, and Henry Longfellow.[86]

That Wharton came to circulate among the best-known artists in New York in the early 1830s was not merely a product of his excellent eye and pen, but also his initial apprenticeship to Martin E. Thomson. Thompson was an important architect, but he was also one of the three recognized architectural authorities chosen by Samuel F.B. Morse in 1826 as an architectural member of his newly formed National Academy of Design.[87] Similarly, Wharton's somewhat stilted interactions with Robert W. Weir came through West Point, with Asher B. Durand through the National Academy, and once connected with these artists, it was easy enough for him to meet William Sidney Mount, and so on.

Wharton sketched rapidly and then returned to his drawings when he wished to turn them into more formal productions. He tells us that he finished his rough pencil sketches of Niagara Falls, for example, weeks later once he was in Boston. He was quite adamant that the artist ought not invent things for their images: in searching for a place to sketch a lovely scene, he complained that,

> in no place could [the details] be assembled into a picture without falsifying the facts — either by restoring objects to what they once were, or suppressing those that now exist, in the shapes of unsightly wooden *improvements* which vitiate the picturesque every where — and I have no patience with the common vice of painters in sacrificing truth and fidelity to pictorial effect — a certain margin is always allowable to the pencil as well as the pen, especially in the play of light and shadow — atmospheric variety and other accidents, but the form and specific characteristics of all marked and leading features should be retained inviolate under any circumstances.[88]

His drawings are quite exquisite and his surviving watercolors attest to some good facility in that medium. None of his oils are known to survive, though he claims to have been making good progress on those in his visits up the Hudson in the mid-1830s. That his painting of the mountains north of West Point as seen from the ravine of the West Point Foundry that he presented to Gouverneur Kemble does not seem to have remained in Kemble's considerable collection does make one wonder what level of skill Wharton had in that medium—or it is possible that it did remain in Kemble's collection and was misattributed later.[89] Either way, it is possible that Wharton's disproportionate skill with pen over oils led him toward the world of engravings rather than paintings as the public face of his work, and this perhaps also helps explain how it is that he did not remain in the orbit of the early Hudson River School painters.

Part of his having been eclipsed as an artist is that he disseminated his works in a way that worked against his gaining any lasting public fame. Throughout his journal he notes taking finished copies of drawings and paintings to specific people, but he does not mention having tried to engage the galleries in New York. Nor was he able to regularly exhibit at places like the American Academy or the National Academy of Design. This latter is all the more curious as he was interacting with Academy members and patrons all throughout 1832–35 (and probably later) in New York and it seems odd that neither Cole nor Durand—nor Gouverneur Kemble, who was a great patron of Weir, Durand, and, later, John Gadsby Chapman—should suggest that he exhibit or propose him for membership. (Martin Thompson did plan to enroll him as a *student* at the National Academy, but the cholera evacuation quashed that plan.)[90]

One is struck throughout the journal and in his sketches that he had been fully primed in his early English education as a Romantic and fan of the picturesque movement. When we read his prose from the 1830s Atlantic crossing, we might guess he had copies of Shelley or Keats in his stateroom below. Upon leaving England: "the lofty cliffs of Flambro', shining like snow wreaths in the pure sunlight and the deep blue ocean still slumbering at their feet—myriads of sea fowl hovering around their summits and the vast Bay in their rear losing itself in the uniform brightness of the heavens"; or as he leaves New York, steaming up the Hudson for the first time: "the Shores closed in again and we were soon immersed in the deep shade of the Highlands, stupendous masses of rock shooting upward far above us into the blue heavens, and clothed with the richest foliage, ridge after ridge and one steep precipice after another."[91] He seems to have retained that sensibility throughout his life. Even as he became more of a civil engineer and architect, he would observe that "the rich olive greens of the marine Algae, clinging to the bases, all wet with the sea and specked with snow white flakes of foam, led the eye by easy gradations into the mysterious depths of colour which robed the ocean."[92]

As he began to interact with the Hudson River itself and then also got pulled into the orbit of the young Hudson River School artists, his Romantic sensibilities shine through in his words as he described the land and flora of the region. His drawings, too, consciously drip with a languid beauty that echo or even prefigure the vivid paintings of Cole or Church. It is possible that when he recopied his original sketches into the journals in the 1850s that he consciously or unconsciously upgraded the style, but even his scarce dated works, such as the 1829/36 pencil sketch of Kirkstall Abbey in Leeds, shows that he favored atmospheric effects and Romantic ruins.[93]

Wharton did not just give lip service to the Romantic idea—in the words and ideas in the journal, he seems to have hoped to bring it alive in his art: "I have for years longed to stand once more on the ocean-cliff, and watch the surges tossing and chafing at my feet, and then again those strange little eloquent fairies called 'early impressions' are ever at hand where fancy is busy." Feeling that the ocean was the true muse of emotional sensibilities, and remembering his childhood on the east Yorkshire coast, he never felt "fully satisfied with anything less redundant in all that is characteristic and engrossing in the poetry of the sea shore." He was quite content to make a bold statement that "the lover of nature will always feel that the simple ocean alone is a volume of sublimity and beauty—even apart from its varied and romantic surroundings."[94]

When Wharton went north in 1853 for his health, it is clear that he had matured both as an architect and as an architecture critic. Noting, for example, the architectural effect of the Boston Custom House, he judged that, "The Porticos are very fine and the columns exquisitely wrought in solid block, but when they are continued round the body of the building and engaged ¼ into the wall, the effect is tame and unpleasing. The Dome, too, has so much unrelieved dead work about it that it looks lumpish and oppressive." His criticism was blunt, stating that the dome had no business being there at all ("except for the fine finish it gives to the Rotunda in the interior") because a "Dome on pure Grecian Doric Temples is just as incongruous as a glossy black beaver [hat] on the head of a well-dressed woman."[95] His reproach of the architect of the Mt. Auburn Cemetery chapel is equally as scathing, calling the granite details "painfully imperfect, tho' the architect must be as much to blame as the material, from the fact that the interior, which is of strong plaster over brick, is designed with equal disregard to purity."[96]

By the 1850s, his sensibilities of the Romantic "pristine" state of nature was fully developed, as was his critical eye as an architect (reminiscent of the sort of critique by people like Andrew Jackson Downing):

> [U]pon the heights which command a noble *coup d'oeil* of the city and harbour, much marred, however, by a perfect huddle of tasteless suburban cottages, built by speculators to catch the eye of citizens who have a hankering after villas and "out of town" boxes. They cluster along the lofty terraces, and not only obscure the fine masses of the remote and middle distance, but mutilate and disfigure the bold features of the foreground which, in its primal condition, must have been very effective—large nodules and projections of pudding stone formation of a rich grey tone, filled in with smooth green turf, intersected with winding paths, and plentifully dotted over with groups of dark cedars and various species of copse wood peculiar to the soil, and the usual admixture of fine elms, oak, and hickory on the descending slopes. But all these particulars of "beautiful Nature" are fast being obliterated by a rapidly extending population.[97]

Wharton's eye for these "tasteless suburban cottages" was the negative manifestation of the same trend that gave many Bostonians a start on the suburban dream. While he criticized that view at Roxbury, he heaped praise on Aurelius Ladd's home on the banks of the Charles in Brighton, where Ladd had joined the movement for subdividing land for suburban cottages that was barely a decade old. Indeed, Wharton arrived just when and where that fundamental shift in the American landscape took place.[98]

And yet at the same time that Romanticism captivated Wharton, he remained quite devoted to Enlightenment ideas of science and nature. His constant recording of temperature and weather throughout the journal after 1854, his attention to the miles traveled in his 1853 trip, and his recording the Latin botanical names for flora he encountered upon his immigration and life in the Hudson, all speak to an educated gentleman. His writing brings to mind the young Charles Darwin, only five years

Wharton's senior, whose own HMS *Beagle* journal, written at the same moment as Wharton's New York experiences, has been described as "no dry technical treatise, [but] quite natural . . . [and including] the enthusiasms of young man filled with wonder, devoured by curiosity and absorbed in the work of investigation," leading to a journal "coloured with the spirit of adventure and invested with the charm of personality."[99] It is not surprising that Sylvanus Thayer took an immediate interest in Wharton, for not only was Thayer the head of the preeminent technical school in America at the time when the professions of engineer and architect remained intertwined and fluid, he had a strong interest in architecture himself. It should also be remembered that the curriculum at West Point was strongly influenced by French Enlightenment ideals and methods, and it was one of the few strongly scientific schools in the country at the time, some of which Wharton probably absorbed while visiting West Point.[100]

Position and Propriety

Although Thomas Wharton Sr. immigrated to what might seem like the back of beyond in 1829, he did so with what must have been considerable means and then brought his family over to capitalize on the boomtown opportunities in the Midwest. It seems that although he remained below the radar as a social notable in Ohio, the fact that his children all seem to have prospered across the country in reasonable comfort and that he remarried a well-to-do widow in New Haven (see chapter 2), shows that the family's immigration was a net success.

During his travels, Thomas Kelah Wharton took in all the sights that the rising bourgeoisie was expected to see, trading on the exclusivity and romantic sentimentalism just congealing at the time. He visits museums and botanical gardens, attends choral music (but not apparently theater) in Boston and New York, and stops to see the 1853 New York Crystal Palace exhibition on his way through the city en route home to New Orleans. When he visited Boston in 1853, it seems like he visited Mt. Auburn Cemetery and Lawrence mills because of family and business connections, respectively, but these same sites were part of the New England grand tour, taken in by European visitors "within a day or two of each other—possibly because their guides were rich Bostonians who had helped build both places."[101] Early on, he joins a mix of the Hudson River gentry and New York literati on a jaunt to the Catskill Mountain House overlooking the Hudson two-thirds the way to Albany. From his sketches, we know that some of the gaps in his journal included more travel around the greater Hudson Valley, partly for artistic views to sketch, but also to be able to get out of the city during school breaks. Yet on those breaks he also made a point to go into the city to keep contact with a certain set of cultured acquaintances and, as far as we can tell, he jumps over the Bowery to head straight for Broadway. He thus lived that concept of the combination of "art" and "nature" that was "supposed to educate, renew and uplift citizens of the world that progress was making."[102]

One author described Wharton in his more mature, New Orleans years as a typical upper-middle-class gentleman with a social circle of other Anglo-Americans, "who lived a life similar to his" along with "his loving wife and child." He was a man with a "strong sense of social responsibility, favoring the political figure whom he felt would be 'a man of family and status in the community.'" For other immigrants, though, especially the Irish, he clearly had an air of superiority: "He read eastern newspapers, took long walks stopping only long enough for 'ices,' and occasionally invited friends to his home for supper."[103] Notably, Superintendent (later Confederate General) P.G.T. Beauregard, Wharton's business and social superior, came to dinner at the Whartons' a number of times, but only once did Wharton get to go to dinner at Beauregard's. There he was "awestruck by the mansion, its furnishings, and the graciousness of Beauregard's wife," and it seems that he felt out of his league. This is all the more interesting, for as a young man at the Hosack estate in Hyde Park, NY in the summer of 1832, Wharton took it all in stride, delighted in the company of Hosack's daughters (perhaps believing he might even marry up into the family), and noted all the fine buildings, read in the library, and matched the refined taste of his hosts. He does not seem to have felt out of his league there, but perhaps time had taught him that his lot was of a middle-class professional and no more. The intervening twenty years, too, had moved Wharton and the country from a world that lionized genteel republican aristocrats on the Hudson like Hosack, to a self-made country with thriving industry and commerce,[104] and Wharton was in charge of building the massive Customs House in New Orleans that so well epitomized that prosperity. Recall that when he spent the summer in Boston, he lodged at the edge of Beacon Hill, circulated by introduction at the best clubs, and had in-laws in the developing upper-class neighborhood of the near South End (shortly eclipsed by Back Bay) and cousins-in-law with modest country estates on the Charles River.[105] We might, then, see Wharton as now a middle-class professional and an example of the rise of that class's position in American society.

Beyond his obvious artistic abilities and sensibilities addressed below, Wharton is notable for his piety, his relative affluence, and also for his constitutional infirmity. His piety is on full display in the 1830s—and recall that the journal was recopied in the 1850s, so he retained the devotion then as well—where he notes what sermons were preached and which noted reverend doctor was in town. Still, his outlook toward religion seems to have become a bit more ecumenical by the 1850s. Raised an Anglican (Church of England) in Hull, it seems natural that he gravitated to the American equivalent, the Protestant Episcopal Church, when he arrived in America. But America in the 1830s was undergoing an effervescent redefinition of religion as various iterations of the Second Great Awakening washed across the entire country by the 1820s. Although revivalism is often thought to be a rural phenomenon (and there is some truth to this), New York City in particular was roiling with new missions, evangelical poor-relief societies, and immigrant assistance leagues, all championed by new Protestant strains seeking to help and to spread the Gospel at the same time.[106] Waves of evangelical fervor saw the Episcopal Church itself partly schism between the formalists (or high church, favored by Muhlenberg) and the evangelicals, both of whom sought to give the elites of American access to evangelism without the "taint of 'enthusiasm'" of the Methodists and Baptists.[107] This heady mix offered a great variety of religious experience to the young Wharton.

He and his family remained staunch Episcopalians through and through, and Wharton quite clearly joined the more formalist strain of Episcopalianism—evangelical but not prone to revivalism—that attracted the prosperous middle class and successful business elites. His brother Robert John was an insurance cashier but also an Episcopal missionary in Madison, OH, and his other brother, Henry, remained active in the annual Episcopal conferences in Zanesville. His first wife and her well-to-do parents in Mississippi were by best estimation strong Episcopalians (his first father-in-law was also a conservative Whig at the height of that party's lifespan) who campaigned for church schools in the Memphis area and were as a group re-baptized in 1842. Even his big break in being endorsed to work with William Muhlenberg at Flushing seems to have come about by his synergy in the early 1830s with Sylvanus Thayer at West Point. That institution had been religiously evangelized between 1825 and 1830 by Charles Pettit McIlvaine, perhaps the most important of the early-nineteenth-century Episcopal reformers, who took the cadets from a cohort of nonparticipants to one of zealous, born-again officers.[108]

Episcopalianism was generally the religion of those with power and money in early-nineteenth-century America, just as his Anglicanism benefitted his family as well-to-do merchants in England (non-Anglicans were prohibited from many sectors of society).[109] Operating as an Episcopalian kept him within the orbit of many well-known businessmen and the social elites, which also benefitted his circulation in the New York circles in the early 1830s. Martin Thompson had built churches for the sect, the medical doctor and professor David Hosack and the industrialist Gouverneur Kemble were Episcopalians. Hosack is a good example of a man who shifted from Presbyterianism to Episcopalianism later in life as he circulated in elite circles, though as a non-communicant (which highlights his social, as compared to theological, engagement of such a move).[110] Wharton stayed quite tightly within the Episcopal fold throughout the 1830s and '40s, and from his journal in the 1830s one would barely even know there were other churches to be considered. He took an active interest in the theological affairs of St. Paul's at Flushing, well beyond his responsibilities as a drawing and language instructor.[111] By the 1850s, though, we see him occasionally attending other churches, sometimes out of necessity when one was full on a Sunday, but also apparently out of curiosity. He found the sermon at a Unitarian service in Boston "full of fine thoughts," and he seems to have been relatively at home at Presbyterian or even Baptist churches, even attending the Coliseum Place Baptist Church in New Orleans for a number of years in the 1850s, although he, too, chose not take communion with them.[112]

Wharton the architect was not a gentleman in the strictest sense of the word for he was not landed and he did have to "resort to the trades" for a living, but the ease with which he integrated himself into polite society and was welcomed into the households of numerous notables in New York and Boston suggests that he was more than just a good artist. Wharton eventually became a member of the board of school directors for the First District of New Orleans, continuing his educational mission in a way, and he was also an early member of the New Orleans Academy of Sciences (NOAS; founded 1854), chairman of the Library and Lyceum Committee in the city, and secretary of the board of commissioners for leveeing, draining, and reclaiming swamp lands. He remained modest, however, commenting in his journal upon his election as a fellow of NOAS,

> I must stir about and distinguish myself someway or other lest I entitle myself to such epitaph as I met with years ago in an old work on Westminster. It ran thus, "Here lies the body of Gabriel Snellow / Of Oriel College sometime Fellow, / Of him there nothing is memorial / Except that he was a Fellow of Oriel."[113]

Connectivity

One thing that may surprise a modern reader is how the individual states within the United States were at once so connected and yet so far apart. Wharton moved up and down the Hudson as we would today, yet did not go home to Ohio to attend his mother's funeral. He and his brother Robert John had to do with but an hour's hurried greeting when Thomas's Ohio River steamboat passed Madison, IN, where Robert John was living in 1853. While the opening of his journal is of great interest for the history of the early republic for some of Ohio's earliest settlers, as well as for the early phase of the Hudson River School of art and *belles lettres*, his 1853 trip is also of interest in how able he was to travel the 5,500-plus miles from New Orleans, up the Mississippi, through a young Chicago (without so much as comment) and the Great Lakes, and down to Boston in just two weeks, taking in some sights like Niagara Falls along the way. Though it is still internal rather than foreign travel, it stands as a testament to what will later become identified with the cosmopolitan in American culture as the country in the 1850s began to interconnect in ways as yet unheard of. Despite the regional differences that persevered after, and partially because of, the Civil War, Wharton gives us a glimpse of what would become an American characteristic of regional and national travel for entertainment, diversion, and for one's "health" by a wide proportion of society.

Wharton arrived in America just as it was becoming a connected country rather than a series of relatively disconnected colonies. With the opening of the Erie Canal in 1826 and the first passenger railways in 1827, the metropoles were connected with the hinterland, and then with each other. Though in his early years in New York that network was still growing, his movements throughout Ohio and the connectedness of his patrons from Philadelphia to Boston is notable. The Hudson, in particular, was the artery of the new republic's northern life:

> If passengers hurried to the landing at the sound of the horns they might see the white steamer puffing towards them, hear the distant voice of her bell, see her little boat lowered to the water, and passengers and luggage dumped into it. As with slow and dripping paddles the big packet moved majestically by, skillful boatmen in the small craft beside her sheered off, reaching the dock by the imparted impetus. Arriving passengers were hastily deposited and newcomers as hastily embarked. The thin rope connecting the long vessel in the channel with the landing boat was being paid out longer and longer. Suddenly it tightened as deck hands on the steamer began to wind it on a hand winch. Swiftly the embarkers were bumped over the water to the still moving packet. In a moment they were on board and the paddles were roaring again.[114]

In the first decades of Hudson steamboat travel (Fulton made his first successful journeys in 1807), the steamboat lines took pride in racing each other up and down the river, and if two competitors happened to draw alongside each other, they "took to spurting" and raced in "complete disregard of the safety of the passengers," until the Steamboat Inspection Act of 1853 put an end to steamboat racing. While Hudson River steamboats were a bit smaller, Great Lakes steamboats at this time were typically one hundred- to 135-foot-long side-wheelers of about one hundred to 350 tons displacement. And although Wharton was in New York a bit too early to have experienced rail travel in that area, by the time he was traveling to Mississippi and New Orleans in the 1840s, and then especially in his return to New England in 1853, we can see the East Coast and the hinterland tied together by these thin ribbons of iron. By 1848 the great essayist William Cullen Bryant observed that, "It is surprising how many persons travel, as way-passengers from place to place on the shores of these [Great] lakes. . . . They comprise, at least, half the number on board a steamboat plying between Buffalo and Chicago."[115]

In retrospect, it is striking how relatively easy it was for the Wharton family to travel from New Orleans to Boston, as well as the fact that they made the whole trip in both directions inland rather than by ocean steamer around Florida. Although in 1853 Illinois, Indiana, and Ohio had been states for half a century, or nearly so, the internal transportation connections through them had only recently been completed. In 1848, for example, it was still normal to take a lake steamer over the top of Michigan's lower peninsula to get from Chicago to Detroit, as the railroad only extended as far west as Kalamazoo. The Michigan Central advertised the overland trip as saving two days' travel time over the lake route, but that consisted of a five-hour steamboat trip across Lake Michigan to St. Joseph, a post coach that took twelve hours to cover the fifty-six miles from St. Joseph to Kalamazoo, and only there could you board the Michigan Central Railroad to cover the remaining the 146 miles to Detroit in ten hours. Travelers were lucky to do the whole trip in half again the advertised time and understandably found it "wearying."[116] A mere five years later, the Whartons made the equivalent trip of Chicago to Toledo entirely by the Southern Michigan Railroad in just over twelve hours on tracks that let their trains whiz along at more than twice the average speed the Michigan Central had promised, so probably at a running speed of triple that.

Wharton's comments about rail travel show both how frequent it was but also how dangerous it still was, or was perceived to be. On one hand, he and his fellow travelers from New Orleans seemed to race each other to the next destination by various forms of transportation, and in New England, they seem to take the train specifically because of its speed. The regional connectedness around Boston at midcentury is nothing short of astounding, as one English visitor noted:

> They who cannot afford to live in the metropolis, reside with their families at places often twenty-five miles distant, such as Ipswich, and go into their shops and counting houses every morning, paying 100 dollars (or twenty guineas), for an annual ticket on the railway, and being less than an hour at a time on the road.[117]

Still, riders were not used to traveling at dozens of miles per hour. Wharton makes mention of some of the deadly locomotive boiler explosions and accidents that remained common until after the Civil War. From the earliest days of rail travel, it was a monthly if not weekly occurrence to hear of some disaster like the fatal Hightstown rail accident in 1833, a mere two months after the Camden & Amboy Railroad replaced its horses with steam engines on the New York to Philadelphia line, where noted dignitaries including former President John Quincy Adams, steamship magnate Capt. Cornelius Vanderbilt, and the Irish actor Tyrone Power (grandfather of the silent film star by the same name) were caught in an overturned carriage when a bearing overheated and shattered an axle. Twenty-three of the twenty-four on board were injured and two died; Vanderbilt suffered a broken leg and vowed to never travel by rail again, though he eventually reneged and became the owner of the New York Central.[118] This travel also shows the rise of tourism, whether to the Catskill House on the Hudson, or to Niagara Falls, where it is somewhat exciting and depressing to learn that then, as now, one can take in a curiosities museum as well as buy moccasins. Notably the family did not stop at Niagara Falls on their way to Ohio in 1830, but it was de rigueur as the next generation headed to Boston from the Midwest in 1853. Trains and steamboats got tourists to the transit hubs, and then stages and omnibuses ran hither and yon to feed the need of local movement and for visitors' amusement, and to give people the means to reify the place in American mythography and their own place in the emerging cultural elite.[119]

Thus, the journal he kept of his life in the New York and Hudson region in the 1830s and his return to the Northeast in the 1850s neatly bookend the rise of American connectedness, at least before its momentarily being broken asunder by the War between the States. Wharton's career was one of distinction in New Orleans, yet in his earlier life we can see many avenues not taken, many connections made but not consummated. We see in these pages the development of a life that traded the dream of the riverside estate in the 1830s for the leisure of the urban subscription library in the 1850s. His journals stand as testament to a young man illustrating a young nation and its people and offer numerous insights into its culture and growth.[120]

His closing comments to his 1853 trip put it nicely in perspective, as indeed he intended:

> The wealth, refinement, and intellectual culture of the Eastern States, the teeming plenty and boundless resources of the West, have passed in review before us and successively challenged our admiration while they have ministered to our pleasure. But still there is something about the genial "South" which after all chains and rivets our love. And with all its faults of climate, and exposure to physical danger still makes one cling to it and prefer to dwell here than amid all the opulence, and magestic [*sic*] "nature" of the more rugged and inflexible North.[121]

Chapter 1

Thomas Kelah Wharton's Autobiography

[The diary ceases between 1834 and 1853, but Wharton conveniently summarized his life to date in an entry on June 3, 1854, extracted here from the *Journal*, vol. 2, pp. 378–387.]

I have been in the United States 24 years today. On the 3rd of June, 1830 at sunrise the woody hills of Neversink and Staten Island lay within a few miles of us, all glowing with lustrous sunshine. I well remember the day; it was one of intense and beautiful excitement. As we passed the Narrows and sailed up to the city of New York thro' that unrivalled Bay, every object was new to us, everything awakened a separate interest, and over all breathed an atmosphere of untainted purity, and lucid as a sapphire. It seems long, long, ago, and I recollect it now as a lovely dream. I am tempted to take a hasty review of the changes since that day.

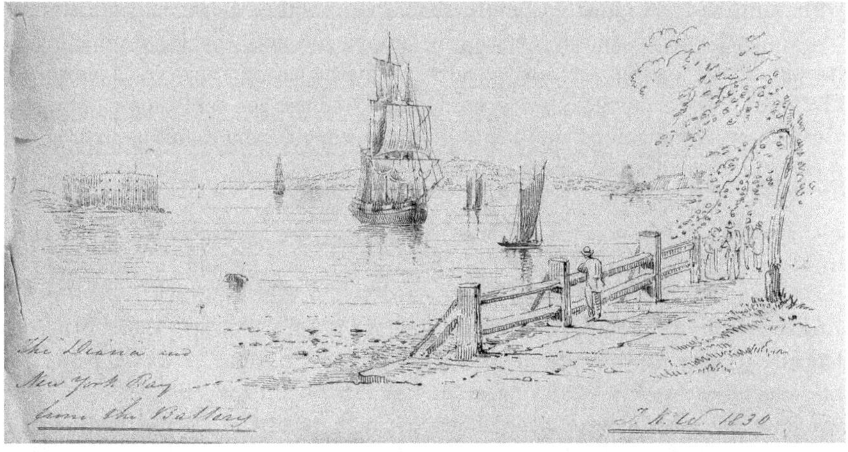

FIGURE 1.1 The Diana and New York Bay from the Battery, 1830 (*Journal*, vol. 1, p. 12). New York Public Library, Archives and Special Collections, New York.

After a delightful rest of a month in N. York at Mr. T. Slocum's in Beekman Street, we proceeded westward by the Hudson, Erie Canal and Lake, and reached our new home at Piqua, Ohio on the 17th of July. My Father had purchased an excellent farm on the Miami [river], a mile from the town. It contained about 250 acres of fine land under culture, besides woodland and two luxuriant sugar [maple] groves, a comfortable frame homestead, convenient outbuildings, and very large orchards of the choicest peaches and apples, a garden, too, in which my Father took great pride. We had no lack of society, as the neighbourhood from its fertility and healthiness had attracted many agreeable and estimable families. But the two years we spent there were by no means happy ones. My poor mother's health was very delicate and we were all ill-fitted for the deprivations of the backwoods. My Father sold the place and early in 1832 we removed to Zanesville, where he purchased a large warehouse on the Muskingum [River] and established himself in general forwarding & commission business.

In April of that year I left my dear family for the first time, and threw myself into the busy world. I went to New York and entered the office of Mr. Martin E. Thompson, Architect, and had just got fairly thro' the mysteries of the classic orders &c. when the cholera broke out in the city and I received an invitation from Dr. Hosack to take refuge for a while at his charming retreat on the Hudson at Hyde Park.

A month of uninterrupted pleasure soon slipped away, when one day amongst the frequent guests at the Doctor's sumptuous table were Col. [Sylvanus] Thayer and Mr. Governeur Kemble[1] of West Point. They both urged me to visit them before I returned to the city. Col. Thayer was at that time Superintendent of West Point and living alone, and Mr. Kemble at Coldspring opposite. When I got to the Colonel's he kindly told me that he should not think of letting me go until all danger was over in the city, so that I was soon fully domiciliated with him, and remained for more than five months, during all which time the Colonel was constantly devising means to promote my improvement and happiness. He assisted me thro' a course of mathematical study and Descriptive Geometry. He encouraged me to indulge my fondness for landscape painting by rambling with me among the scenes of enchantment around, and searching out their choicest and more latent beauties.

He introduced me to men of taste, refinement and distinction who flocked to West Point that summer, and added luster to the elegant dinner parties at the Colonel's and Mr. Kemble's amongst whom I may enumerate Mr. [James Kirke] Paulding, Washington Irving, General [Winfield] Scott, Major [Thomas Jefferson] Leslie and Mr. [Joel Roberts] Poinsett. In short it was a period of rare enjoyment and rare advantages. It has thrown a happy influence over the whole of my subsequent life, and I never can think of Col. Thayer without the liveliest emotions of pleasure and gratitude.

Among the visitors of the summer was the Revd. Dr. Muhlenberg, Principal of the Institute at Flushing, whose educational views quite won the Colonel, and prepared him to think highly of an offer I received from Dr. Muhlenberg in November to join his establishment. Accordingly, in December I left my kind friend and went to Flushing, Long Island.

During the vacation of 1833, in August and September, I crossed the mountains and revisited my family at Zanesville. My mother was in better health and we spent some happy days together. The autumn came and I parted with her for the last time. It was midnight, dark and gloomy, and I tore myself away, and the night dews fell chillingly upon me as I hurried to the stage in waiting. One year after my poor mother died. I was spending the vacation of 1834 at Flushing when the sad tidings reached me, and I immediately went up the North River to Fishkill near the mountains and spent a month by myself in that quiet and secluded village. None but those who knew her could tell how deeply I felt the loss.

I was many years at Flushing, occupying the Professorship of the Arts of Design & Descriptive Geometry at the "Institute" and studying the classics, divinity and general "belles lettres."

In the meantime, my Father was married again to Mrs. A.M. Reddie, to whom I became very much attached and we all found her a most kind and considerate step mother. Her accomplishments, too, made her society delightful. I used to spend my vacations with her at New Haven. Her place was very beautiful, surrounded by spacious gardens and ample grounds, all of which she had laid out herself with great taste, and always kept in fine order. The house, too, was her own design—Doric with canopies over the upper windows in Hindostanee fashion, conservatory on the south side with the drawing room windows opening into it, and rich clusters of grapes hanging from the glazing. What happy evenings we used to pass. My mother was a thorough musician. The piano on week days, the organ on Sundays, and my sisters were there, too, so that we had no difficulty in filling up the parts, and to my fancy our anthems were not deficient in harmony.

Bhurtpore Cottage (for so she called it to perpetuate her recollections of the East Indies), was endeared to us by a thousand pleasant incidents, but it is all changed now. Poor Henry and Charles, too, are both gone, and my Father!

In 1838 Dr. Muhlenberg purchased a fine body of land on the Sound 3 miles from Flushing, called it College Point and commenced the establishment of St. Paul's College.[2] There I spent about 2 years, when the Rev'd. Francis L. Hawks commenced the cognate Institution of St. Thomas' Hall at the Village of Flushing and I was induced to join him. It enjoyed an unprecedented reputation for a while, and the Doctor's educational abilities shone out in all their strength,

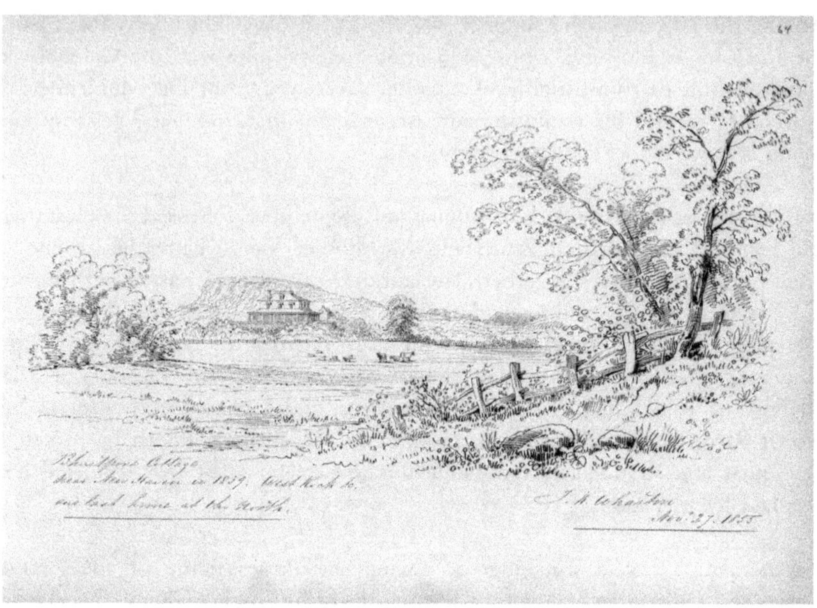

Figure 1.2 Bhurtpore Cottage, New Haven, CT (*Sketchbook*, p. 64). New York Public Library, Archives and Special Collections, New York.

but his financial talents were at fault and in April, 1843 the whole concern was in the hands of his assignees, and all my savings were absorbed in the failure. Fortunately, however, the education of my two sisters, which for some time past had devolved wholly upon me, was now just completed at the Seminary of the Rev'd. J[ohn Walker] Brown at Astoria,[3] so that the casualty was less disastrous than it would otherwise have been.

Dr. Hawks still retained the Rectorship of St. Thomas Church in New York, and after the failure at Flushing took a house for his family in Brooklyn Heights where I joined them in May, 1843. Dr. Hawks' impulsive nature was chafed and fretted by his pecuniary difficulties at Flushing, and in his despondency, he longed for the South. Accordingly, in the summer and autumn of 1843 he and I made a tour of exploration which resulted in our commencing in partnership on a University at Holly Springs, Mississippi.

On the 2nd October, 1843, we returned to Brooklyn from our Southern journey and then made arrangements for entering upon our new undertaking. I withdrew my sisters [Marianne and Emily] from Astoria and crossed the mountains with them, leaving them in the care of my brother Robert John at Cincinnati and then proceeded southward and joined Dr. Hawks & family at Holly Springs on the 1st January, 1844.

Our project went on bravely. The Doctor's peculiar talents again found a field for successful action, but unfortunately he must needs let himself be proposed for the Bishopric of Mississippi, which gave rise to new difficulties as he met with determined and successful opposition in convention on the ground of his former financial embarrassments, tho' I who knew the circumstances best have no doubt that they sprung from a want of judgment and in no respect from dishonest purpose. This new vexation made the Doctor uneasy again and he became languid in his efforts at Holly Springs.

In the summer of 1844 I went to Cincinnati to make purchases &c. for our Institution and see my sisters, and early in 1845 Dr. Hawks was induced to visit New Orleans with an offer of the rectorship of Christ's Church in that city, and an opportunity of founding a University that would make ample amends for the position we resigned in Mississippi—so he impressed me—and in May I paid a short visit to New Orleans where his family had already arrived, and he had entered upon his new charge. The prospects seemed favorable enough and I returned to wind up our affairs at Holly Springs, which I did very favorably, spent the summer there, and on the 19th Oct. was married by Dr. Hawks to the eldest daughter [Maria G.] of Judge Huling of Holly Springs.

In December, I went with my wife to New Orleans and took rooms for the winter at Mrs. Cornell's in Camp Street. In the meantime, Judge Huling sold his cotton Plantation, and purchased a sugar estate in the Parish of Plaquemines 52 miles below the city of New Orleans, to which he removed that winter.

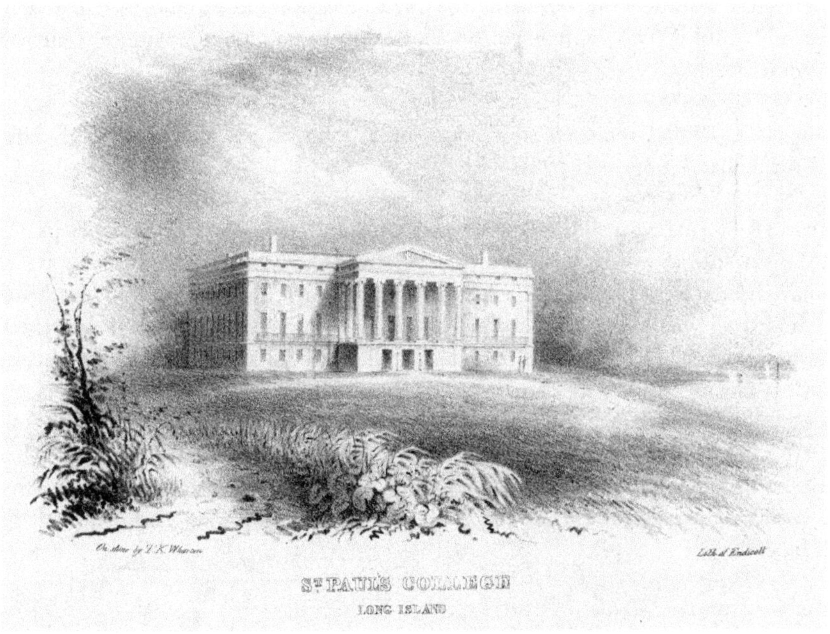

FIGURE 1.3 The Flushing Institute (later St. Paul's College), Flushing, NY. Lithograph by Endicott, after T.K. Wharton. (acc. 1946.9.207). Yale University Library, Mabel Brady Garvan Collection, New Haven, CT.

Dr. Hawks' University scheme all fell to the ground, and he confined himself in a very short time to his rectory which he resigned again with his usual facility in a couple of years and went back to New York.

In the meantime I gradually reverted back to the occupation in which I commenced life, architecture, which I was again led into from having made the designs for Christ's Church New Orleans during the last summer I spent in Holly Springs, and being engaged in making the detail drawings during the spring of 1846 with Mr. [James] Gallier, who superintended the erection of the building.[4] I made an engagement with Mr. Gallier to go into effect in the winter of '46–47, but the depressed state of architectural operations at that time prevented our carrying it out and I passed the greater part of the time during the summer and winter of '46 and the ensuing spring & summer on the Plantation pursuing closely my studies in architecture and executing some large drawings in perspective for Mr. Gallier.

In Dec. 1847 I took a house in Prytanea Street New Orleans and commenced housekeeping and in January 1848 received the appointment at the New Custom House which I have held ever since.

On the 11 April 1848 my wife [Maria Huling Wharton] fell a victim to the most fatal form of pulmonary consumption—abscess of the lungs—and I left town not long after and spent the summer on the [Hulings'] plantation.

Oct. 23 I resumed my duties at the New Custom House and pursued them steadily until I was compelled by ill health to take my northern tour last summer.

August 1, 1849 I removed to a house on Apollo Street, and October 1, 1851 to the house I now occupy.

Dec. 18 of that year I was—married to Emily [Ladd Prescott] and Sept. 23, 1852 my little boy [Thomas Prescott Wharton] was born. Last summer we all enjoyed ourselves abroad at the north. This summer we hope to enjoy ourselves at home, all well and happy around us, every comfort that we could desire, few wishes ungratified, and fewer drawbacks than fall to the lot of most persons, and in closing this hasty retrospect I cannot doubt that my experience is not dissimilar from that of almost everyone who will chose to reflect. Sorrows there have been, bitter sorrows, but the hours of happiness have far outweighed the hours of pain & grief, and even those latter might have been lightened by a better temper of mind, and a more steadfast reliance on the great anchor "Hope."

Chapter 2

New York and the Hudson Valley, 1832–1834

[Wharton provides an account of leaving Ohio to go to New York City and his life there for the next two years in his *Journal* 1: 118–310. The story of his emigration to this point was published in the *Ohio Historical Quarterly* in 1956.[1]]

May 1 [1832]
Another lovely day. The sun shines brightly upon a waste of blossoms, and the delicate little[2] yellow and blue birds flitting about everywhere.

At 10 P.M. everything was ready for departure. Mr. & Mrs. Gurney had been to say good bye, and the sad moments were hasting away, when Charles, who had been on the lookout, came to say that the Western Mail was on Main Street and would proceed in an hour's time. My Father went immediately to secure me a place. In the meantime, I received a kind parting note from Mrs. Gurney. My Father returned with the news that the Stage was full, and an Extra expected every moment also full. On the way bill of the latter were the names of our friends the "Hardcastles" of Dayton, so he went back into town to see them, leaving me to enjoy the pleasure of a reprieve. It was short lived, however, for my Father came back in a great hurry to say that Mr. Hardcastle was going no further, but would leave his wife and sister here to pursue their journey to Baltimore and I could take his vacant place. So, with a full heart I bade a long farewell, and in a very short time was on the road for the mountains. The midnight hours passed heavily, and when dawn at length came, having had no sleep and my mind confused and depressed, I gazed with careless vacancy upon the beautiful scenery of Guernsey and Belmont counties and the sweet banks of Indian Wheeling Creek. We whirled along rapidly and by noon reached the Valley of the Ohio where we crossed over by ferry to Wheeling, and I spent two hours in climbing the hills and strolling among the romantic uplands of the neighbourhood.

May 2
Having taken my place to Chambersburg [PA] at 2 o'clock I was slowly ascending Wheeling hill in a noble stage, but the roads soon became stony and

bad, and I was jolted dreadfully thro' an ever-varying succession of hills and valleys, precipices and forests, forming a small corner of Virginia, and passed into the State of Pennsylvania towards evening, after some delay occasioned by the breaking of a spring which was remedied for the time by a stout fence rail from the road side. At Washington, we changed stages and in the course of a sleepless night crossed the Monongahala (about 600 yards broad) at Williamsport [now Monongahela, PA], and the Youghiogeny (about 300 yards) just as the day was breaking over the woods and the mist floating away from the clear waters.

May 3

The 3rd and part of the 4th were spent in crossing the huge summits of the Alleghanies. The last mountain of any extent was overcome on the morning of the 4th and at noon we entered the handsome town of Chambersburg containing a population of 3,500. Slept at the Hotel, and proceeded early the next morning thro' a lovely country, the valley of the Susquehanna, and the town of Harrisburg on its banks, to the City of Lancaster where I passed the night.

May 6

The next morning's journey was thro' the best cultivated and most luxuriant agricultural country I had yet seen in the United States. The farms and farm-buildings were on a grand scale, and the frequent use of the green hawthorn hedge gave a very English look to the arable lands.

At 3 P. M. we reached Philadelphia, and I put up at the Western Hotel.[3] Being Sunday evening I attended St. Andrew's on Eighth Street, and heard the very eminent Dr. [Gregory Townsend] Bedell. The Organ and choir were enchanting. From church, I went to Mr. [Jeremiah] Warder's, 119 Race Street. He had retired early but his brother kindly invited me to breakfast with them in the morning.

May 7

Mr. Warder received me at breakfast with his accustomed warmth and after a good deal of conversation, spent the rest of the forenoon in driving round the city with me, and visiting the far-famed Waterworks at Fairmount. The great Reservoir occupies the summit of a rock 100 feet above the Schuylkill river—5 enormous, cylindrical water wheels set in motion 10 great Hydraulic Pumps which suck up the water from the Forebay of the Schuylkill and force it thro' oblique Tubes into the Reservoir above at the rate of 5,000 gallons per minute. The machinery is very simple but the power tremendous. A fine walk surrounds the reservoir, commanding the city, the beautiful banks of the Schuylkill, and the Delaware, and the buildings and contiguous grounds tasteful and ornamental. Parting with Mr. Warder I left this elegant city at noon from the Chestnut street wharf on the Steamer *Burlington*, and landed at Bordentown about 4 P.M. The broad but common-place Delaware possessed few features of much interest—shores flat and little to break their tame uniformity. The

Stages were in readiness and after leaving the highly embellished grounds of Joseph[-Napoleon] Bonaparte we proceeded at a tedious and uncomfortable pace along the sandy roads of New Jersey. Supper and beds awaited us at New Brunswick, at between 9 and 10 P.M., and at 6 the next morning I was on board the Steamer *Thistle* for New York.

May 8
The day very fine and scarce a ripple on the sluggish Raritan, which wound along between marshy banks until about noon when the well-remembered Bay opened upon us, and in an hour I again found myself among my hospitable and kind-hearted friends [the Slocums] on Beekman Street.

May 9
Called upon Mr. Jacob Harvey, firm of Abram [*sic:* Abraham] Bell & Co., Pine Street, and presented Mr. [Jeremiah] Warder's letter of introduction. He at once gave me his address and invited me to his house.

May 10
Sent off a parcel to Zanesville by a Mr. Jones.

Today I commenced with Mr. Martin E. Thompson. I am to live with his family at No. 24 Howard Street. They are very kind pleasant people, and I trust it will all result well.

Received a most welcome but desponding letter from Mamma.

May 11
I begin my architectural studies by making large drawings of the classic orders, their proportions and details.

Called at Mr. Slocum's in the evening. Their warm-heartedness towards me is as gratifying as it is unmerited.

May 12
Whole day in the office which is in the basement story of the dwelling house—drawing the orders.

May 13
Sunday. A beautiful Sabbath. I had the pleasure of again attending St. George's Chapel after a lapse of some two years. Dr. [James] Milnor preached. He has a fine, fatherly, benignant countenance, florid and healthful, with hair of snowy whiteness, his delivery solemn and impressive, and his whole manner producing a conviction of the deepest sincerity. His subject, 2 Kings 2 c.13.14. He exhorted his hearers to imitate the courageous firmness and prayerful spirit of the early prophets, in opposing the tide of iniquity, the holy fervour that burned in their breast and shone as a bright light in a darkened age. They

were men of like passions with ourselves, subject to the same weaknesses and frailty, yet they thro' faith obtained a good report. Why then may not we? Why should not their shining example animate us with holy emulation? And our desire to follow in their footsteps? They have finished their course; they have kept the faith and are now reaping immortal fruits of joy and love. Their career is before us, their influence around us. Wherefore seeing that we also are encompassed with so great a cloud of witnesses, let us lay aside-every weight and the sin which doth so easily beset us and run with patience the heavenly race and pursue with unflinching steadiness the heavenly crown.

The hymns were sung to tunes every chord of which vibrated to the recollection of former days, and the music throughout was delightful.

In the afternoon, he preached from 4 c. Philippians 6. The "Gloria in Excelsis" was exquisite. The Dr. will be absent for the ensuing fortnight.

At eight I went with Mr. Slocum to the Middle Dutch Church and heard Mr. Abilene from Mark 2 c. 17, one of a series of sermons on the depravity of man.

May 14
Still at the "Orders."

In the evening Mr. Thompson invited me to accompany his family to a rehearsal of the New York Sacred Music Soc^{y}. at the Chatham Street chapel—late theatre—large audience and parts of the performance perfectly charming, especially the chorus from the "Creation,".[4] "The heavens are telling"—but I cannot get over a repugnance to this use of sacred things.

May 16
Vegetation here is scarcely yet matured. I continue plodding on thro' the varieties in the orders from Stuart's Athens, the folio edition.[5] The time before breakfast and after tea I have at my own disposal. In the evening called at Mr. Leggett's and met Mrs. and John Van Antwerp.

May 17
Drawing the Choragac Monument of Lysicrates from Stuart.[6] In the evening I called upon Mr. Rodman in the upper part of the City and presented Mr. [Thomas] Gurney's kind note of introduction. He received me in a very friendly manner, and seemed much interested in my description of the Western country &c.

May 20
Sunday. I crossed over to Brooklyn and went to St. Ann's where I heard the Rev'd. Mr. Ilvaine [*recte*: Charles P. McIlvaine], who has the reputation of being one of the first preachers in the State. His appearance reminded me of the

Rev'd. C. [Joseph] Camidge who used to preach in Hull, and the same rich, soft, deeply toned voice. His sermon was on prayer (Romans 8.26) and so striking that I took the liberty after service to beg that he would allow me to transcribe the manuscript to send my mother which he kindly acceded to.

Dined by invitation in Beekman Street. At St. Georges in the afternoon I had the pleasure of meeting the Rev'd. Mr. Preston of Columbus, O.[7]

Took tea also at Mr. Slocum's, and went with them to the Middle Dutch Church. I find that John Van Antwerp and Mr. Crocker's grandchild are both suffering from intermittent. This would not have surprised me in the wet valley of the Sciota, but in this city, I should not have expected it.

May 21
Wrote to my friend Frederick Huntington of Hull and to my Grandmother there.

May 25
Commenced a drawing of the Tripartite Temple of Minerva Polias, Erectheus and Pandrosius.[8]

May 28
In the evening, I called upon Mr. [Jacob] Harvey. He and his lady were enjoying a bright fire in their delightful drawing room. The weather is still so cool that we require winter comforts. I had an exceedingly pleasant evening. Mr. Harvey is son in law to Dr. Hosack, who has a charming country seat at Hyde Park on the Hudson. It seems that some time ago the Doctor had expressed a wish to Mr. Thompson to have drawings of the beautiful scenery around his place by a competent pencil. Just at that time my Journal with drawings was sent to the Slocums and shown by Mr. Earl (one of the family) to Mr. Thompson, who at once mentioned me to the Doctor, and told me at our first interview that he hoped I would carry out Dr. Hosack's wish. Mr. Harvey mentioned this evening that it would be a great pleasure to Dr. Hosack to have me there on a visit, and make him some sketches, so that I shall probably go up before long. It is quite a coincidence that Mr. Warder should, on the thought of the instant, have introduced me into a family who had already heard of me thro' Mr. Thompson sometime before my return to New York.

May 30
In the evening, I went with the family to see the exhibition of the National Academy. Mr. Thompson's chief object was to introduce me to some of the leading artists, and to secure a place for me at the ensuing term as a student of the academy. He requested me to take my book of sketches[9] which were very favourably received by several artists there in the room, among whom were Mr. [Charles C.] Ingham and Mr. W[illiam Sydney] Mount. I am politely furnished with a free Ticket to the gallery for the Season.

May 31
May ends with cold rains and whistling Winds, more like the vernal equinox than the opening of summer.

June 1st, 1832
The first summer month opens with a pure sky, a mild, genial atmosphere, and a prospect of better days than in the cheerless rainy fortnight just gone by.

Spent the evening at Mr. Harvey's. Mrs. H. expects her Father, Dr. Hosack, tomorrow and wishes to have my book of drawings to shew him.

June 2
Finished the drawing of Minerva Polias.[10] In the afternoon Mr. Ingham, the painter, sent his young man to request the loan of my sketch book, but as it is at Mr. Harvey's I sent some pencil drawings in its stead.

June 3
Sunday. So chilly again and unlike June that it seemed quite a mockery for the "Ice carts" to go their accustomed rounds. Dr. Milnor gave us an admirable sermon from Acts 1c.9, dividing his discourse into three heads. 1st That the ascension of Christ was both typified and predicted, 2nd that the evidence of its having occurred is irresistible, 3rd the importance of that event in the great Plan of salvation. His closing appeal to the youth among his hearers was affecting and fervent, and to the experienced believer he spoke in terms of sincere congratulation on the happiness already attained, and counselled him to continue steadfast unto the end in the path so wisely chosen. A stranger preached in the afternoon from "Comfort ye my people."

Took tea at Mrs. Oakley's and went with Mrs. and Miss Margaret Vanantwerp to the Middle Dutch Ch., where we heard a powerful sermon on the resurrection, John 5, 28.29.

June 4
Commenced The "Propylea."

It was so cold in the evening that I had to wear my cloak down to Beekman Street. Mr. Slocum handed me a parcel from England. In spite of the late season and the bleak rains the "strawberry criers" are already going about the streets.

June 10
Sunday. Dr. Milnor assisted by the Rev'd. Mr. [James] Robinson, late of Zanesville, administered the Sacrament to a very large number of communicants. As in the "Church of England," all the non-communicants left the Church at the end of the sermon, which appears to me more beautiful and appropriate, "a little flock, as it were, shut in by grace," a people who have separated themselves

from the corruptions of the world around, and assembled to strengthen the bond of service between themselves and their Redeemer by partaking together of the distinctive ordinance of Christian faith.

June 16
My time during the week has been closely occupied. The weather has been throughout warm and summerlike.

June 17
Sunday. More terrible than the landing of the fierce Dane [i.e., Viking raids], the dreaded cholera has crossed the Atlantic and the journals of today contain fearful accounts of its first ravages in Canada. The consternation in the city is universal. Wall Street and The Exchange are crowded with eager groups waiting for the latest intelligence. The "Courrier and Enquirer" has issued an extra with every detail.[11] The event, in short, appears to engross the whole attention of the public. I have never seen so general and wide-spread an excitement.

June 19
Every preparation is now making in the city for the expected pestilence, cleansing the streets and alleys, strewing the gutters with chloride of Lime, and the druggists busily occupied in putting up specifics and prescriptions.[12] The press is multiplying precautions, advice, and statistics of the disease. Many families are already leaving the city; others preparing to do so. No cases are yet reported within the United States, but in Quebec and Montreal the mortality is appalling.

June 23
Lovely day. Spent the afternoon at Hoboken and Weehawk with my pencil.

June 26
The alarm is beginning to subside and the public mind quieting down. Dr. Milnor preached today with special reference to the Scourge from 1 Sam'l. 7c. 3,[13] no state but that of constant preparation is safe at any time, much more at so critical a juncture.

June 30
The weather during the week has been exceedingly beautiful. Cholera is spreading thro' the provinces.

Aaron Thompson and I spent the greater part of Thursday at Weehawk, where I made a sketch of "The Bay" and of "The Woods of Hoboken." Mr. and Mrs. Harvey are both attacked with intermittent, they wish me to accompany them to Hyde Park early next month, which I hope to be able to do.

Dr. Milnor, at his evening meeting yesterday preached from Gen. 32c. 10–11,[14] and towards the close made allusion again to the threatened peril. "The best preparation for cholera," he said, "is preparation of heart."

July 1, 1832
Sunday. I went to St. Thomas Church, but finding every seat occupied, I went to the Church of the Ascension in Canal Street, where I heard an eloquent sermon by The Rev'd. Martin Eastham from Phill. 2 c. 8.[15] The Right Rev'd. Bishop Onderdonk recommends that Wednesday (the 4th) be observed as a day of special religious exercises in view of the impending calamity. The exterior of the church is The Dome of The Parthenon [*recte*: Pantheon], the interior simple and elegant, the galleries supported by light columns from the Temple of Andronicius Cyrrhestes.[16] It was erected by Mr. Thompson. In the afternoon, I went to Grace Church,[17] the interior rich in Roman Ionic, elegant furniture, and a stylish fashionable audience. The organ and choir faultless and the service remarkably well read. But the sermon from Luke 14 c. 18[18] seemed to come far short of the great standard of apostolic preaching. Its diction was polished and elegant and fell upon the ear like drops of oil on a slab of marble, but there was little to warm the heart, arouse the conscience, and point the awakened sinner to the cross of Christ as the only hope of fallen man.

July 2
We had indulged some hope from the comparatively slow progress of the cholera in the Canadian provinces that this city might have remained long exempt. But no, without any intimation of its near approach it is even now among us and several cases are announced both yesterday and today—some fatal. Whether or not I shall remain in the city is uncertain but Mr. Thompson's family will have to stay, as he is closely confined to his room by severe illness. Nothing can now avail but firm reliance on the protection of the Most High, who alone can control the "pestilence that walketh in darkness, and the sickness that destroyeth at noonday."[19]

July 4
55th Anniversary of American Independence. By order of the authorities much of the uproar and parade which distinguish this day was dispensed with, and a great deal of the usual drinking in booths and low groceries prohibited so that there was far less excitement than usual. The day was very beautiful. A single company of artillery and a civic procession paraded the streets in the morning. The usual concourse of lingerers on Broadway, canton crackers [i.e., firecrackers] *ad libitum*, and fireworks in the evening. I spent the greater part of the time in the cool, shady rooms of my friends in Beekman and Fulton Streets, and the day passed quietly and pleasantly. At midnight, we were aroused by a terrible fire immediately behind us, in the Second block from Howard Street. I hurried on my clothes and went out on the roof where the scene was sublime. The flames rolled in billows and shot upwards into the lurid sky and every steeple and tower in the city was lit up with an unearthly glare. I then went round to the spot where a dense crowd was collected, and every effort went to save the furniture from the burning houses and extinguish the flames. This was soon accomplished after the destruction of three large buildings and the loss of one life by the fall of a chimney. I went back to bed again, and everything was as still and quiet as ever.

July 5
Fine airy day. Cholera on the increase. Walking down Broadway after tea I met Mrs. and John Vanantwerp and went with them to see Madame Thibault, a French lady of celebrity in miniature painting.[20] She showed us half a dozen of the finest miniatures I ever saw. They were of important European personages from life, and among them the King and Queen of Spain. Her talents are said to be thought highly of by Connoisseurs in Europe. She finishes with the utmost delicacy, and her works command the highest values.

Mrs. Vanantwerp, Margaret and John leave the city very shortly for New Rochelle in Westchester, where I am kindly invited to spend some time with them.

July 6
Beautiful weather with a refreshing breeze. The Cholera Report of today gives 37 cases, 20 deaths, in various parts of the city.

In the evening, I went to the Harveys. They have quite recovered from the ague, and Mrs. H. is busily engaged in preparing to go up the river with her Father tomorrow. The Doctor has repeated his invitation which has already been extended to me two or three times, and Mr. Harvey wishes me to accompany the party to Hyde Park tomorrow morning. On talking the matter over at The Tea table I resolved to take the "Novelty" at 7 o'clock on Monday morning next. Mr. Harvey's business requires him awhile longer in N. York. Mr. Thompson's continued illness prevents his attention to his usual employments so that I have more leisure than I may have again during the year, and in every particular this seems to be the most suitable time for a visit that I have had in view ever since my first conversation with Mr. Thompson.[21]

July 9th, 1832
New York.

The city is emptying fast, and its wonted busy streets have sunk down into a state of village-like quiet. Mr. Thompson's illness continues unabated, which detains the family in town tho' they are very anxious to leave for the Passaic, especially as the pestilence is now closer to them, the High School on Crosby Street having been converted into a Hospital. Nearly all my other friends are preparing to seek a purer air.

At half past six I shook hands with the family in Howard Street and took a hack for the [steamship] *Novelty* at the foot of Courtlandt. Her immense saloon and promenade deck were crowded—so many families anxious to escape into the country. A cold mist hung over the River, and already the 4 tall chimneys of the Steamer were pouring volumes of black smoke into the murky air. Her powerful machinery was in motion at 7 A.M., and the crowded wharves soon disappeared behind us. The Palisades and vast mountain masses beyond were involved in wreaths of vapour and the dripping moisture dimpled the still surface of the river. The curtain lifted as we passed thro' the Highlands. The rain ceased, and the clouds separated and became light and pearly. The woods and grassy slopes, green lawns and bright yellow wheat fields on either hand warmed into a richer glow with the freshening moisture of the morning.

I fell into conversation with a "Londoner"—intelligent and well-dressed but a most superb cockney, not as aspirate in his alphabet. He told me he had been staying at the "Congress'all" in New York and was now on his way to the Catskill "Mountain 'ouse." He went into raptures in describing the mountain scenery, said it far surpassed anything he had seen in Europe, and the more earnest he became the more numerous and refreshing were his "provincialisms."

At half past one P.M. I went on shore at Hyde Park Landing, found a baggage waggon to take up my trunk and cloak to Dr. Hosack's, and then followed on foot thro' the Park gate close by the Landing.[22] The Mansion itself was half a mile further on the brow of a bold eminence full 100 feet above the river. The ascent is gradual by broad winding walks, shaded by the richest foliage with gleams of the Hudson sparkling among the leaves, and beautiful lawns, with trees grouped in fine taste, a range of green houses and exquisite flower beds crown the ascent and sweep around a grand clump of forest trees leading quite up to the house which presents a noble front to the Park.

The servant who answered the bell told me that Mrs. Harvey returned to the city yesterday morning in consequence of the illness of her child, but after waiting a few minutes in the drawing room the Doctor himself received me most cordially, introduced me to his family and then pointed out the room I am to occupy during my visit, so that in a very short time I felt as much at ease as with friends of long standing. After examining the Picture-Gallery and the noble library occupying a whole story in one of the wings of the building, the Doctor took me over the grounds and pointed out their chief beauties. No expense has been spared in embellishing this splendid domain, which contains 800 acres of richly diversified surface, every feature of which has been made to contribute to the ornamental effect of the whole, and to heighten the magnificence of the River scenery which it commands. The two facades of the building, one fronting the river, the other towards the Park, shew a fine spread of enriched Italian, flanked by large well-proportioned wings. The whole designed and executed by Martin E. Thompson in his best manner. Another very tasteful edifice stands at the north end of the grounds called the "cottage," with its own separate gardens and ornamental improvements. The north and south Lodges form elegant entrances to the estate. Pavilions occupy prominent knolls. The lawns, pasterres,[23] walks and broad winding carriage drives are all kept in the highest order, and nothing can exceed the beauty of the forest groups and clumps of ornamental trees and shrubs which are disposed with the utmost skill over the whole place.[24]

We sat down to dinner at 3 and the afternoon having turned out wet and unpleasant the rest of the day was spent in examining several valuable works

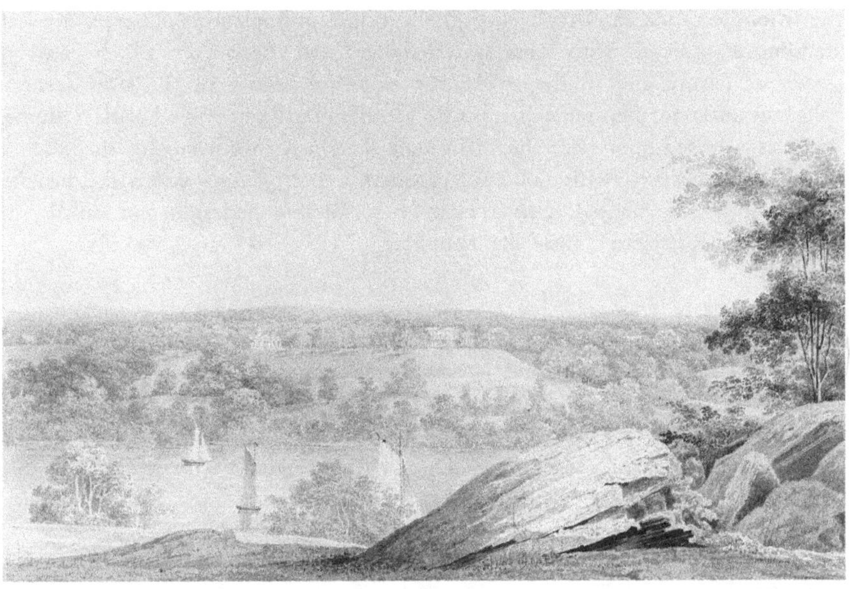

FIGURE 2.1 David Hosack Estate, Hyde Park, NY, 1832 (MMA ap1994.187.13). Metropolitan Museum of Art, New York.

&c. &c. My drawings, too, were brought out and handed round, and the Doctor said he wished me to make him several sketches to be engraved on stone to illustrate a Quarto which he is engaged upon descriptive of his place.[25] Dr. Hosack is a delightful companion, earnest and fluent, with a firm dark eye. Mrs. Hosack, formerly Mrs. Coster, is quite advanced in life and has a very pleasant winning manner. Her daughters Adeline and Laura are quite young and pretty. The Doctor's daughters Emily and Eliza are much older, rather plain, but very sprightly, intelligent and well educated, with the large black eye of their father. Mrs. Harvey is his eldest daughter, but she has gone back again. The Doctor's brother Alexander completes the family group now at home. They all seem to be exceedingly pleasant and live in a style commensurate with their superb residence.

July 10

Heavy rains, with a pleasant interval at noon which I spent in rambling over the grounds. In the afternoon, the sun broke thro' suddenly and the clouds rolled away from the distant Catskills, revealing to me for the first time their grand, shadowy outlines. Thin silvery mists still crept around their base giving additional majesty to the peaks above, the whole forming a background to the glorious scene up The Hudson from the north boundary of the estate. After sunset, the deep groves of oak and chestnut between the front lawn and the river sparkled with fire flies innumerable. These woods extend from the bottom of the ridge to the water's edge. The intervening slope is abrupt but well grassed over and is used as an enclosure for deer. The front lawn occupies the whole level plateau on the top of the ridge, and splendid old trees are left standing at intervals with seats scattered here and there from which you can survey at leisure and in the shade, the exquisite beauty of the river scenery below. A little further on a handsome Grecian Pavilion, roofed with a dome, occupies a raised spot near the main walk, and just in advance of the ridge a grassy knoll covered with tall poplars offers a pretty contrast to the heavier foliage. It is ornamented with a bust on a suitable pedestal, and called, (in imitation of Rousseau) "L'isle des Peupliers."

July 11
Wet, cold, and gloomy—Therm. in the morning 70°—bad for the fever and ague which I am sorry to find is not uncommon in this state as well as in Ohio.

Spent the day chiefly amongst the Doctor's books. It is a large and valuable collection. Played chess in the evening with Doctor Hosack, and then with Miss Emily H.

July 12
Thermometer at 8 A.M. 67°. The thick vapours have fled; a fine breeze cools the air. Distant showers and great tracts of sunshine give the spectre forms of the Catskill a grand and diversified effect. In the morning, I made a sketch of the Pavilion on a mass of rock which projects into the river, at the far north end of the estate, and of the pretty ornamental bridge over Crumelbow Creek.[26] This stream skirts the eastern portion of the park and is made to heighten its beauty. In one place its clear waters are gathered into a natural basin and spanned by the bridge in question forming with the mossy bank, and patches of grey rock a very sweet composition.

In the afternoon commenced a large view of the scene looking up the Hudson.

In the evening a cheerful fire was quite necessary.

July 12
Still showery and cool—thermometer at 67° in the Hall.

Mr. and Mrs. Coster drove up in the afternoon and happening to go to the Hall door while their carriage was in waiting I was amused at the air with which their negro coachman bent his, by the by, excellent figure, from the coach box to salute one of the Doctor's black women and begged her to "excuse his glove."

July 14
Variable weather—passing showers and noon sunshine.

The Doctor drove with me over the whole estate, and showed me his farming operations which he is conducting in one part of it.

Rest of the day drawing.

July 15
Sunday. Perfectly cloudless—whole day charming. How sweet the first breath of a Sabbath morn in such a situation as this, where every object invites to calm and joyous thought. Nature's God appears everywhere, and the beauty of his works inspires the mind with devout admiration and cheerful trust.

We receive the New York papers every morning at the breakfast table. Today they report that the cholera is still quite mild.

The Rev'd. Mr. Davis preached from "How shall we escape if we neglect so great salvation." The congregation was very much larger than I expected, especially as there is a good-sized Presbyterian church in the village. The Episcopal church is small but pretty. It stands at a short distance from the North Lodge, and the church yard is embowered with the foliage of tall locusts. It presented a lively scene this morning from the large number of handsome, stylish carriages, mixed up with the usual vehicles of a rural neighbourhood. They have a nice little organ, and good voices in the choir. "Pastoral" was sung very prettily.

The gardener furnished the dessert today with fine Citron melons, fully ripe, and the Doctor's Pinery gives proof of the superior flavour of the Pine-Apple when taken ripe from the plant. The flower beds around the conservatories are perfectly splendid. There are some things I never saw before—The Mexican Tiger flower (*Tigridia tygridifolia*)—and a fine specimen of the Indian rubber tree. Amongst the larger shrubbery the "Fringe Tree" is singularly luxuriant and ornamental.

July 16
Very pleasant morning but rainy in the afternoon. Finished tinting a drawing of the "greenhouses"[27] and commenced one of the East Front of the House.

July 17
Beautiful weather—Therm. at 6 A.M. 72°. After breakfast, I crossed the Hudson at the lower boat Ferry, and made a sketch of the river front and grounds from the high bank opposite. I then rambled far away off into the country, and climbed some rough, woody precipices which gave me fine views over Dutchess County. I returned to the Ferry, under a hot sun, at 2 o'clock. The boat was unfortunately on the other side, and there I was kept for a full hour, blowing at intervals a tin horn in the vain hope of rousing up the lazy boatman—no response but the echoes of the rocky points, until I was nearly worn out with heat, hunger, and fatigue. At length, the sound of a horn came winding across the smooth river and the boat began its tardy voyage. The ferryman told me when he got over that he had been obliged to send one of his horses to be shod[28] which was the cause of my detention, and to make amends he kindly dispensed with the usual delay, waiting for passengers, and started back at once, landing me also much above the Ferry Dock, and nearer to Dr. Hosack's.

I noticed among the shady walks today that beautiful little bird the Bohemian Waxwing (*Bombycilla garrula* or *ampilis garrulus* of Linnè). A well-drawn figure of it is given in Charles Lucien Bonaparte's elegant work on those specimens of American Ornithology not given by Wilson.[29] Both works are in the Library.

I am now looking anxiously for intelligence from Zanesville.

Cholera is still steadily increasing in New York and spreading over the neighbouring States.

July 18
Very fine weather with sheet lightening playing behind the mountains.

In the evening three dashing Phaetons drove up with a gay party of friends of the family.

July 19
Morning very fine and dewy with Thermo. 76° at 6 A.M.

A little before sunset, as Emily Hosack and another lady & myself were standing on the walk overlooking the deer park, and admiring a pair of spotted fawns which the Doctor has lately received from Long Island, a sudden and heavy rain gathered among the mountains and came rolling towards us so swiftly as to cut off our retreat to the house, so we took shelter in the Pavilion close by. But we were not detained there long. The sun broke out again in 20 minutes, and painted upon the black, turbid vapours the most perfect and brilliant rainbow I ever beheld.

The day was marked in the family by the return of young David Hosack from Tampico [Mexico] after an absence of 4 months.

July 20
Fine airy day.

Sitting with the Doctor on the Piazza after twilight I had a long conversation with him on my prospects in New York in which he kindly interests himself, and suggests plans for my advantage.

July 21
Early in the morning these beautiful grounds seemed flushed with new charms as the mist rolled away from the Catskills and the sun lighted them with clear ariel tints, like mother of pearl. The trees, lawns, and pastures borrowed additional brilliancy from the fresh dew, and the new mown grass smelt sweet and spicy in the still morning air.

I have today completed the last of five Quarto sized drawings for the Doctor, with which he is highly pleased. They are the best I can do and tinted with great care, and few things would give one greater pleasure than an approving look at them by my dear Mother.

Capt. McKennon, an intelligent Englishman from Quebec, arrived today in the steamboat. Like me he is very fond of the pencil.

I am not very well but the great kindness of all around me almost makes me forget it.

July 22

Sunday. The Rev'd. Mr. Johnson being absent there is no service at the Episcopal Church. Part of the family have gone to the Presbyterian. I remain at home as the Doctor thinks I had better take a little medicine.

The air is wonderfully pure, and the mountain peaks unusually clear and beautiful. The mountain house and its piazza is perfectly distinct thro' an excellent Telescope that stands in the Hall. It is 30 miles off and to the naked eye appears like a white spot near the summit of the most easterly mountain.

Dr. Hosack will not allow a gun to be fired in or near his pleasure grounds and it is surprising what multitudes of beautiful birds, squirrels and other graceful little creatures glance about among the walks and trees, and so fearless, too, as if conscious of protection. I spent some time in the library and was much pleased with the Life of President [Jonathan] Edwards (of Yale I think) and Witherspoon on Regeneration.[30]

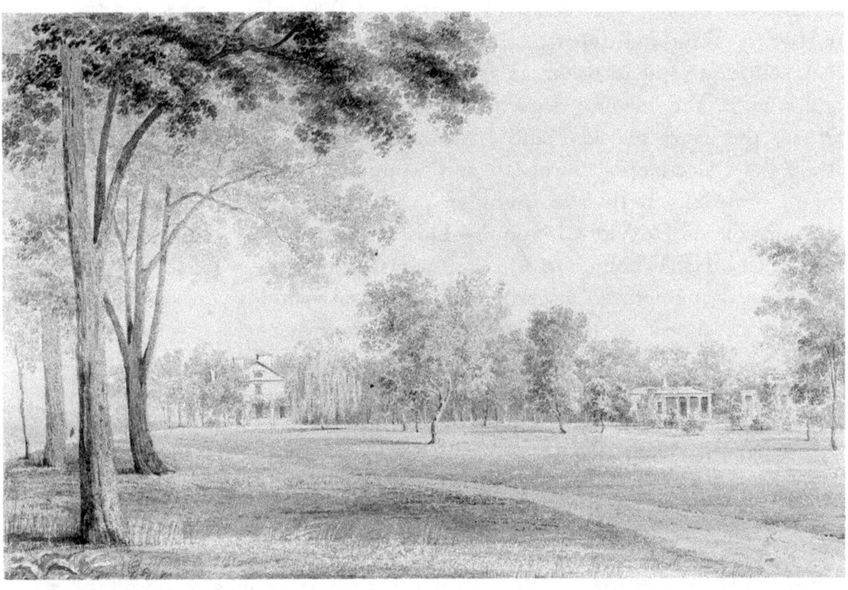

Figure 2.2 David Hosack Estate, Hyde Park, NY, 1832 (MMA ap1994.187.15). Metropolitan Museum of Art, New York.

July 23
Delightful day. Emily and Eliza Hosack and I took tea at "The Cottage" with the Allen family who live there. I am sorry to find that the dreary "fever and ague" is as prevalent here as in the rich alluvial soils of Ohio.

Scarcely a family is exempt, and the musquitoes, too, are more or less annoying. I have spent a good part of the day in drawing in my own room. How I miss the pleasant conversation with which my dear mother used to enliven me when so employed, and the animating remarks she would throw in when she noticed any thing more successful than usual in my little works, but now I am all alone.

July 24
The black boy has just rung the usual 7 o'clock bell and as I am spending the time until breakfast in the library I will try to give a little idea of it. It occupies one story of the South wing—is 38 by 23 feet and lighted by 5 handsome windows. There are two elegant black veined marble mantles with grates for anthracite coal, and the carpet, rugs, sofa, chairs &c. are in accordance with the sumptuous style of the rest of the house. Four stands contain large Portfolios of Engravings, Maps &c., and in the centre is a large mahogany reading table, with 18 capacious drawers, and covered with useful articles for study—bronze ink stands & candlesticks of elegant patterns, large atlases, and in the centre a convex Lens 7½ inches in diameter, on a neat mahogany stand, to aid in reading the finer types—in short all the decorations and conveniences are admirably adopted to the purposes of the room. It is a luxurious spot to read in—almost too much so to study in. The Books are arranged in large Mahogany cases along the walls, handsomely bound, and consist of from 4 to 5,000 volumes purchased at a cost of Twenty Thousand dollars.[31] They have been collected with great care so that they comprise some of the most valuable works in every department of literature and science. The "medical department" is of course very rich, but general "belles lettres," the "exact sciences," and "Theology" are well represented on the shelves while the collection of European and American "periodical literature" is, I am told, more complete than in any other private library in the country. Then there is a memoir of DeWitt Clinton, by Doctor Hosack,[32] of whom Clinton was a near friend, richly bound in Quarto, and reflecting great credit on the author and the artists employed in getting it up. Several volumes, too, on "Medicine" by Dr. Hosack appear on the shelves in that compartment.[33]

While employed in writing these particulars I was agreeably interrupted by a servant who came in and brought me a large letter from my mother of the 17th Inst.[34] I devoured it eagerly, and it seemed to give me new life as I have been a good deal depressed for the last day or two.

While speaking of the Library I ought to mention that the story which corresponds to it in the North wing is fitted up as a "billiard room" and a fine one it is, supplying an admirable alternative in rainy weather and good after-dinner exercise for the ladies.

As I was seated at the drawing board this morning Dr. Hosack stopped in and began to converse on a subject which has before been talked over between us—my future plans—which now seem a good deal obscured. The Doctor is clearly of the opinion that architecture in New York will disappoint me, and he thinks the prospects very slender for a good mercantile situation, but kindly suggests many ways in which I may turn my talents for drawing to advantage. He says I must on no account think of returning to the city this summer while the pestilence is there, and he and his family will leave before very long for Pennsylvania where they have been expected on a visit for some time past. He mentioned to me that a relative of his, Mrs. Coster,[35] living on an adjacent estate, had expressed a wish to receive instruction from me, and it appeared to him that I might spend some time both very agreeably and profitably in that family. It was agreed then that he should name it again to Mrs. Coster, and I went on with my drawing. However, about half an hour before dinner he came up stairs again with his pleasant smile on his countenance to say that Col. [Sylvanus] Thayer, Superintendent of the Military Academy at West Point had arrived, that he had shown him my productions, and had told him that he should feel personally interested in his showing me any attention in his power at the Point. From this favourable circumstance, he added, (and pleasure sparkled in his dark eye) he hoped good would result.

Accordingly, on the removal of the cloth after some conversation with the Colonel, who was seated next to me, I received a courteous invitation to visit him at the Point. And Mr. [Gouverneur] Kemble, a friend who accompanied him, also politely expressed to me the pleasure it would give him to have me at his house near the Point. I cannot hesitate in accepting this kindness and have little doubt that it will be to my advantage, as I am satisfied my visit to the Park has been. The chief subject over the wine, after the ladies retired, was Joseph Bonaparte's sudden and singular departure for Europe, his probable motives, whether ambitious or merely domestic. The Count de Survilliers[36] is now 62 but keenly alive as ever to the political changes of his country, and as he is one of the Doctor's circle of friends, he takes quite an interest in his movements.

July 25

Spent the time before breakfast with Col. Thayer in the Library. He is not only a very eminent man, but easy in his manner and very pleasant in conversation—very conciliating.

After a thunderstorm, the morning became very fine and it occurred to me that I might not have a better opportunity to visit the residence of a gentleman with whom I became acquainted a few evenings ago, which is prettily situated near the river about a mile south of the village. Just as I was leaving for that purpose, Col. Thayer, who was conversing with the Doctor in the Hall, followed me into the Piazza and taking my hand told me that as he intended to go back again in the morning boat he might be gone when I returned from my walk, but that he begged I would fulfill my engagement with him at West Point in a few days and make his <u>house my home as long as I could</u>. I told him I should avail myself of his kindness with pleasure and we parted. A moment after I met Mr. Kemble who repeated his invitation, and desired that if I arrived at the Point before the Col. had completed some domestic arrangements he is making that I should proceed at once to his own house on the opposite side of the river, and I shook hands with him, with this understanding.

As Mr. Allen was from home I merely stayed to make a rapid sketch of the Hudson looking south from the grounds, the Highlands in the distance and the buildings of Poughkeepsie peeping over the foliage in the middle of the view. I then hastened back and got home in time to see the two gentlemen again just before the "North America's" bell announced her approach to the landing.

After they were gone I commenced another drawing for the Doctor on the completion of which I propose taking leave of my kind and friendly entertainers at Hyde Park.

July 26

Today we have a sky without a cloud. I have now finished seven drawings for the Doctor and have just washed in the first tints of a large picture. While they are drying, I will transcribe a short allusion to this place which I find in a late Boston periodical.

From both these elegant seats (referring to the "mansion and the cottage") the eye sweeps over the noble Hudson which is nearly a mile in width—speckled at all times with the white spreading canvass or the more formidable Fulton Steamers—a richer prospect is not to be found—a more varied and fascinating view of the picturesque scarcely to be imagined. The present proprietor, Dr. David Hosack, has since the year 1794 been distinguished for assiduity and devotion to the practical duties of his profession and fulfilling the office of teacher in various of medical science in the City of New York.

Many of his works have been republished in foreign countries, and among the honors he has received from the learned Institutions of Europe, he has been elected a fellow of the Royal Society of London, and also of the Wernerian Natural History Society of Edinburg. His more recent work, the life of the late Governor DeWitt Clinton, with an account of the origin and progress of the great "Erie Canal" has been received as a splendid production, justly delineating the character of his illustrious friend, and redounding to the fame and honor of the author. Dr. Hosack sustained The Office of President of the New York Historical Society for many years, and in May 1824 was elected President of the N. York Horticultural Society. He was the Founder and Proprietor of The Elgin Botanic Garden (at Hell Gate) in 1801—the first and best in the United States—which has been purchased by the State Legislature for the purpose of completing a system of medical instruction. Altho' this eminent physician and philosopher has exchanged his professional labors during the summer months for the delightful scenes of rural and pastoral life, yet he retains a high sense of the importance of medical science and the public is still to be benefited by his literary productions.[37]

I may remark that the work on which he is now engaged will be illustrated by the drawings I have made him, while the originals, he tells me, will be enclosed in a Portfolio and placed on the drawing room centre table for the frequent inspection of his family and guests.

July 28

After breakfast, during a little talk to the Doctor, he told me he should like to compensate me for my drawings. I begged he would not say a word about it as I assured him I felt amply remunerated by the kindness shown me. This, however, he said he could not consent to, but turning the conversation for a moment he made some allusion to the larger picture I have in progress. Glad of this opportunity to escape from the subject I hastened upstairs for the piece in question, and great was my surprise when, on my return with it, he handed me a check on the Bank of New York which he had filled up in my absence, and of which he begged my acceptance, and then immediately commenced an examination of the picture, with which he and his brother (who just then stepped in) were delighted, and suggested that it would make a valuable addition to the "gallery" and that it would prove very attractive if engraved. It is 23½ inches x 16 in., and embraces all that splendid range of scenery northward from the Estate to the Catskills. They think I have been particularly successful with the sky which is nearly finished, and is by far the boldest effort I have yet attempted.

This unlooked-for addition to my resources, will, with what I have, amply supply my wants for a very long time to come, and proves how weak it is to give way to despondency and doubt in regard to provision for the future.

I observe in the library several books of travels presented to the Doctor by Sir Joseph Banks, and many others by their respective authors, including names of great celebrity in England, among the rest "Roscoe" of Liverpool, whose "Discourses"[38] are in the collection presented by himself.

The Cholera is now at Poughkeepsie, 7 miles below here. Since its first appearance in New York, above one thousand have fallen victims in that city and there is still but little abatement.

July 30

I have been busy all day with my picture, partly in the open air with the actual scene before me, and partly in my large, well lighted apartment. It is now nearly finished, and I think looks very well. I intend to present it to the Doctor. I have at length made up my mind to leave in the "Champlain" tomorrow if the weather prove favorable.

July 31
The bright sun soon purged away the mists from the Catskills and while the grass was still wet I took a farewell stroll among the splendid embellishments of the garden. Lemon trees, loaded with fine fruit, the tall India Rubber, the *althaea frutex*[39] covered with flowers, and the glossy Magnolia exhaling the sweetest perfume, a thousand other beauties, too, belonging more strictly to this latitude. I sat down in a Pavilion and having Witherspoon in my hand, as I may not ever meet with the work again, I extracted the following brief view of regeneration—

> First—that our chief end be to serve and glorify God, and that every other aim be subordinate to this. Second, that the soul rests in God as its chief happiness, and habitually prefers his favor to every other enjoyment.[40]

This appears to me a simple and comprehensive statement of the doctrine, is easily retained, and should at all times be kept in view in all our thoughts, words and actions.

The morning was chiefly spent in needful preparations. At 12 I had a little final talk with the Doctor. He gave me a letter to Col. Thayer, in which he said he had expressed himself strongly in my favour. For this and his many other attentions I thanked him suitably at the time, and secretly resolved to find some more substantial means of expressing my acknowledgements. In the meantime, the gig drove up to the door, my baggage was brought down, the parting moment came, and very soon the delightful scenes of Hyde Park lay behind me.[41]

July 31, 1832
Hyde Park, N. York

On my way to the Boat I called at the Village Post Office to leave directions about my letters. I found one from Aaron K. Thompson with the welcome intelligence that his father had recovered and would take his family at once into New Jersey until the disappearance of cholera. It was dated the 16th. Inst.

After waiting awhile at the landing the noble "Champlain" came dashing up. Her boat was instantly lowered, paddle-wheels backed, and in five minutes I was in the midst of the gay and busy crowd on board. The "North America" whirled by us near Poughkeepsie, and at 2½ P.M. we were in view of Newburg. The swelling Highlands lay in huge piles behind it and cast deep shadows over the river, which looked like a vast reservoir of melted silver, and the sky above was full of sunshine which paled down its colour to the most delicate shade of blue. Yet the air was not oppressive. A strong breeze thro' the gorge of the mountains gave it buoyancy. By and by we were within the embrace of those grand capes of granite which push boldly into the river in long perspective, and at the end of the vista on a high-level plateau appeared the buildings of the

Military Academy with their background of green mountains, and the ruins of Fort Putnam hanging high in the air above them.

I was fortunate in finding Mr. Kemble at the landing, where he was awaiting the arrival of the boat. He immediately accompanied me up the long steep ascent that leads to the Plain and in a few minutes we were at Col. Thayer's house. The Col. was at home, and welcomed me with great cordiality, pointed out a very pleasant room which he has assigned to me, and a library just opposite, then took his hat & walked over the whole establishment with me, explaining its various arrangements, and visiting the buildings appropriated to the different departments, and then, on returning to his house, he told me he expected that I should remain with him some weeks at least, and that he hoped to make them pass agreeably to me. We took supper together at Cozzen's Hotel, the Col.'s cook being away, and I retired early, and full of gratitude, not unmingled with surprise, to find so much kindness shown to a total stranger.

August 1st, 1832
Spent the day chiefly in writing.

At 4 P.M. Mr. Kemble and a small party of friends assembled, and we sat down to a sumptuous dinner. The courses one after another were delicious, the most delicate champaigne and other wines carefully iced, and lively and intelligent conversation throughout.

August 2
Today the Col. and I dined by invitation at Mr. Kemble's. At 3 o'clock we got into the barge and had a charming row around the Point of Constitution Island to Mr. Kemble's Dock at Coldspring. A shady wood path soon conducted us to his residence which is a delightful retreat, and situated not far from his great Iron works which occupy the bottom of a deep valley near the water. I enjoyed the visit extremely and the return by moonlight over the calm Hudson and beneath the shadows of those glorious mountains would have set a poet to musing for at least a month to come.

August 3
Very beautiful weather.

Having for some time past needed an aperient [laxative] I took a good dose this morning, and then, most imprudently set out on a fatiguing excursion to the summit of Crow's Nest, which is a precipitous and densely wooded mountain laying off North West from the Point. It springs from the deep water of the river in a bold, majestic sweep to the height of fourteen hundred feet, and then retires, preserving about the same elevation, far back into the country. I don't know what possessed me with such a sudden ambition to reach its top, but so it was.

I took the road leading into the country westward from the Point, and at about 1½ to 2 miles turned into a wild path leading me for a few hundred yards direct north thro' a belt of low bosky wood to the base of the mountain. Here I found the dry bed of an almost perpendicular mountain torrent, forming a monstrous furrow in the rough granite side. It was overhung with mighty forest trees, and embedded with huge detached blocks, intermixed with logs, stumps and rubbish.

"Hoc opus, hic labor."[42]

Here my toil commenced. It was a tedious, not to say perilous ascent, a vast, herculean staircase, but I surmounted it at last, and to my great disappointment still found myself hemmed in by the impervious forest, not a glimpse into the distance, and nothing to relieve the endless branches and foliage but the rich colouring of the most splendid orange Lilies I ever beheld. However, I struggled on for nearly another hour thro' the tangled underwood, and was at length rewarded by reaching a considerable plot of solid moss grown granite, without a shrub to obstruct the view, and occupying the highest point of the mountain. Up and down the Hudson the view was magnificent beyond description, and far away to the north the grand forms of the Catskill and Shonga [*sic:* Shawgunk][43] mountains almost melted into the sky. Orange and Dutchess Counties lay below, the most fertile in the State, and filled up the middle distance, and lined both sides of the noble river with scenes of enchantment such as no pen or pencil could do justice to. But even the loveliness of the scenery formed but a poor compensation for the toils I underwent in returning and the after consequences. Broiling under the fervour of an August sun I broke my way thro' a thickly matted growth of oak and other knotty underwood, sometimes losing myself altogether and nothing to guide me into the path again but conjecture and the sun above. But I persevered until I groped my way to the head of the ravine, and then soon regained the plain below. I felt very much relaxed, however, and enfeebled, so that when I sat down at 4 o'clock to the Colonel's bounteous table I took care to eat but sparingly, and finished my dinner with a cup of fine coffee. I suffered great pain until tea time but a few cups, very hot, relieved me. But as my medicine, which I took in the morning had not produced the slightest effect upon me, the Colonel, with his usual goodness, insisted that the Physician should be sent for. He came at once and before I went to bed he sent me three pills by the "orderly" which acted very favourably upon me by morning.

August 13

On the 4th (Saturday) a fever such as I had never before experienced set in, and all Sunday, Monday and Tuesday I was confined to my restless pillow, becoming weaker every hour, and sometimes suffering very much from burning heat, tho' the weather was by no means too warm. It was, indeed, unusually wet with frequent lightening. On Wednesday, the ague supervened and I had my first experience of a genuine "shake." On Thursday, I took Quinine regularly every four hours, which made the "Chill" on Friday but slight tho' the "Fever" lasted longer.

On Saturday, [took] the Quinine again and I began to convalesce rapidly. On Sunday, I escaped my chill and was able to take a walk, and breathe the pure mountain air, and enjoy the heavenly atmosphere and the splendid scenery of The Highlands. Today thro' the mercy of God I am in possession of regained health and considerable vigor, and I hope that my general constitution will be ever benefited by this tedious indisposition, as it has appeared for some time just as if it required to undergo a change. I have learnt, too, the danger of neglecting the system, and of the imprudent pursuit of unnecessary objects. To the Colonel I can never feel sufficiently grateful for his exceeding kindness. Not one cent will he permit me to pay to the Physician, but says that whatever services he has rendered me must be considered as having been rendered to his family and for which he alone is responsible. Such liberality is indeed most disinterested.

The Doctor was indefatigable in his attention to me during my illness, and the Colonel's waiter Sullivan was ever at hand to supply every little want. I had not a wish that was not immediately gratified with the minutest fidelity. If everyone had not been so very attentive to me, there is no knowing how much longer I might have suffered, as I have really been very ill.

Every breeze that sweeps over this interesting plain seems to bring new supplies of health. No one can tell how delicious is the transition from a sick chamber to the free open air of the mountains, and the weather is perfectly luxurious. The sun shines as if fresh from the hand of his Maker, and never did he shine upon a more gorgeous display of natural beauty.

As his orb sinks behind Fort Putnam the evening gun booms across the plain. The report is echoed distinctly as it strikes in succession each mountain premonitory that juts into the river. The plain is now all in motion. The cadets in their neat grey uniforms assemble for evening parade from every quarter, and groups of visitors issue from the Hotel, and come trouping towards the Colonel's house, opposite which the ranks are now drawn up and going thro' their evolutions, which are performed with exquisite precision, while the band fills the air with the richest and most inspiring harmony. They often play the "Nahant March" and the March from "Cinderella," and I have become very fond of them, but they execute everything so well that it is difficult to have any preference.[44] By and by the gay pageant is at an end and the shadows of twilight gather thick around the bases of the mountains.

Today I began to study a work on Descriptive Geometry by Professor Davies,[45] who is at the head of the Mathematical Department and author of other mathematical works.

August 14
I received today a long expected letter from my mother, but so mutilated by some accident to the mail bags that I lost a considerable part of its precious contents.

August 15
Charming weather still. Spent some time in answering my mother's letter.

At dinner, the Colonel suggested that I should pay some attention to the study of the human figure. There is an excellent gallery of casts here and the drawing department is admirably conducted under Mr. [Thomas] Gimbrede. He hinted, too, that a clergyman now here from Flushing L.I. contemplated applying for my services in drawing in his Institution.

August 16
In the afternoon, which was calm and cloudy, the Colonel and I took a long and pleasant walk together along a rude pathway which followed the bank of the river to the north—part of the way over rocks half buried in thickets, then over a smooth pebbly shore forming the outlet to a deep valley and washed by the gentle tide.

Chiefly occupied today with Geometry, the weather being unfavorable to the pencil, too cold and threatening.

August 17
Whole day gloomy and chill with considerable rain.

Chiefly Geometry within doors. At the tea table Col. Thayer proposes questions on the theorems which I have been engaged on during the day, requiring of me a sort of analysis, or general outline of the method of proof employed, but without diagrams, substituting a verbal description of the figures. This process serves to fix the chain of reasoning more firmly in my mind, and give me a clearer view of the successive steps leading to the conclusions in each demonstration.

In reply to my note the other day Cadet A.R. Johnston, son of Col. J. Johnston of Piqua, O[hio]. came and spent an hour with me this evening and talked of the far West.

August 19
Sunday. Low hung clouds entirely concealed the mountains, and dripping showers at intervals. The Liverpool Packet ship *Sheffield* arrived on Friday evening and brings the Col. his files of the *London Times* and *Bell's Weekly Messenger*. They state in general terms that cholera was on the increase in Hull and York. I have no answer yet to my letters by this ship. She passed the *Pacific* off the Floating Light,[46] by which vessel I also wrote.

At 11 the residents and visitors at the Point assembled in the Chapel. The regular chaplain being unwell, a young Methodist minister had been invited to officiate. He preached on the Solemn Theme "Prepare to Meet Thy God." The cadets were all present, and manifested great seriousness of deportment. The room is spacious and contains a good organ. There is but one service on the Sabbath.

August 20
Day throughout clear and beautiful—quite summer compared with yesterday.

Commenced a view looking up the river thro' the grand gorge of the Highlands.

In the afternoon, the Col. and I ascended the rugged mountain road which overhangs the Plain, and explored the venerable ruins of Fort Putnam. Its crumbling relics are dotted with dark cedar bushes, and the view from its lofty ramparts perfectly splendid. The soft summer air crept wooingly around it. The next time I go up I shall take my drawing materials with me.

August 21
Engaged in colouring the view commenced yesterday. In the afternoon, I walked with the Col. to a high point beyond Washington's Valley, a beautiful spot for ornamental improvement, and immediately opposite the "Cadets' Monument." We found Captain [Ethan] Hitchcock there, engaged with several gentlemen (visitors at the Point) in clearing the wood from its summit and opening the view towards the point and the waterfall opposite.

August 22
Morning dull & louring, in the afternoon a deluge of rain fell until near 4. When it ceased the Col. and I with Gen. Wood (member of Congress)[47] crossed the River to dine with Mr. Kemble, where we met Mr. James K. Paulding and lady—Mrs. [Gertrude] Paulding is a sister of Mr. Kemble. The conversation turned chiefly on the political affairs of this country and Europe and was very animated. Mr. Paulding is a gentleman of varied information and is well known as an American novel writer. His manner is quick and hasty, and his views firm and well considered. The same party will dine here tomorrow.

My water colour drawing is considerably advanced.

August 23
Very fine weather.

At 4 o'clock quite a large dinner party assembled in the dining room, including Mr. Kemble, Mr. [Thomas Jefferson] Leslie, brother to the great Painter [Charles Robert Leslie], and the Rev'd. W[illiam]. A[ugustus]. Muhlenberg, Episcopal minister at Flushing, L.I. These meetings, alternately at the Colonel's and Mr. Kemble's are the most delightful parties imaginable.

August 24
At 10 Mr. Muhlenberg called and proposed to me to take charge of the drawing department in his Institute at Flushing, containing about 60 students. I am to receive my board and the proceeds from my instruction, at the same time enjoying the general advantages of the Institution, and frequent opportunity of visiting New York with a view to my improvement in the arts of Design. He gives me six weeks or two months to deliberate on the offer and to increase

my competency for the undertaking. Soon after he left the Colonel discussed the subject with me. He thinks very favorably of it, and most generously advises that I shall remain at West Point for the next two months, pursuing my mathematical studies in connection with drawing and going thro' a course of crayon drawing on the human figure under Mr. Gimbrede, the Professor of Drawing, to whom he has already communicated his wishes, while, at the same time, I can be making sketches of the surrounding scenery which will, of course, be a profitable recreation. This, to me, is altogether a very welcome arrangement, and seems to offer more advantages than the profession of architecture.

August 25
My picture is nearly finished and seems to give Col. Thayer great pleasure. Geometry occupies part of my time, and I demonstrate the theorems regularly to the Col. at tea time, when he always adds improving remarks and interrogations.

August 26
Sunday. One of the most beautiful days we have had this summer.

Took a delightful morning walk to the ruins of Fort Putnam, and enjoyed the grand panorama all glistening with the dews of the night and the oblique glance of the early sun.

The chapel this morning was filled. The cadets ranged immediately around the pulpit, and the officers in full uniform. Every remaining seat was occupied by the numerous visitors and residents. The music was performed with great taste. Mr. Muhlenberg read our Liturgy with deep and solemn feeling and then preached a sermon which is a piece of chaste, unaffected eloquence, and affecting earnestness, I have never heard equalled in this country, and it made me long to become a member of his Institution where I should enjoy the constant benefit of his ministry. His text was Matt. 6c. 6.[48] Speaking of those worldly thoughts that will follow us even into the innermost privacy of devotion, he compared them to the birds hovering around the sacrifice of Abraham. Tho' we cannot wholly exclude them, we may resist them. Tho' we cannot hinder them from hovering around our aspirations, we may prevent their settling down upon the altar, and building their nests there, and further on "As well may you count the stars as the clusters of mercies that glow in the firmament of God's love." Mr. Muhlenberg's manner is exceedingly mild and unobtrusive and he looks like a sincere Christian.

Crossed the river in the Colonel's swift & well manned pleasure barge and dined at Mr. Kemble's.

August 27
Remarkably fine throughout. Today we had another pleasant dinner party of ten at 4 o'clock. Among the guests were Mr. Kemble, Mr. Leslie, Mr. Paulding,

and Mr. Archibald Tracy of New York, who has travelled a good deal and is a well-informed gentleman. Mr. Leslie is extremely pleasing in his manners, and the Colonel appears very fond of him. Sound sense and unaffected politeness stamp every word he utters. His lady is like her husband full of urbanity and cheerfulness, and their two little girls are interesting in every respect and remarkably well brought up. His garden is neat in the extreme and a like exactness and good order runs thro' (the Colonel tells me) both his private household and his post of duty in the Institution.

He lives in one of the Stone houses forming the front row at the Point, and directly opposite the glorious "gap" of the Highlands.

Mr. Kemble is a man of very superior mind and attainments, evidently born to command men, but very easy and affable in social intercourse.

August 28
Two young British tourists dined with us today. They have travelled over Europe and are now commencing a journey thro' this country. They seemed very intelligent and well educated.

Called on Mr. Leslie and took a pleasant stroll with him of a mile or two thro' the neighbouring woods.

August 30
A beautiful summer sky followed the mists of the morning, and the river was like a polished mirror. At 3 the Colonel, Capt. Mason, Mr. Leslie and I crossed to Coldspring and dined with Mr. Kemble. Mr. and Mrs. Paulding were there, and Miss Mary Kemble, Father [Philip] O'Reilly (a dominican) and a Mr. [John?] Travers of Ulster.[49]

August 31
Finished my River view, and presented it to the Colonel.[50]

September 1, 1832
Strong bracing wind thro' the morning and afternoon followed by a moonlight of intense purity.

From a Philadelphia paper I see the death of Mr. [Ebenezer] Buckingham by the late serious accident at Zanesville.[51]

September 2
Sunday. I was awakened by the orderly tapping at my door, with a treasure indeed, a folio sheet from Zanesville, containing not only a long letter from my mother, but something also from each of my brothers and sisters.

The services in the chapel were performed by an ignorant preacher from Vermont, which was a great disappointment. We dined with Mr. Kemble.

September 4
Commenced a course of drawing under Mr. Gimbrede.

September 5
At noon, I received a note from Mr. Kemble inviting me to return with the boat and visit with him, several points of view around Coldspring that we had before talked about, so I crossed the river and went with him to some beautiful spots. At 4 we sat down to dinner, and I returned by moonlight in the *Goode Vroue* [*The Good Wife*] a fine little sail boat of Mr. Kemble's. The wind was very high, and a strong tide set round the point of Constitution Island. The boat dashed thro' the spray in fine style and soon rounded to at the West Point Landing.

September 6
Fine mild day.

At 4 we had a pleasant dinner party. I walked home in the evening with Mr. Leslie and saw some fine engravings from his brother's pictures.

September 7
Still fine.

Commenced a view of West Point from Washington's Valley.

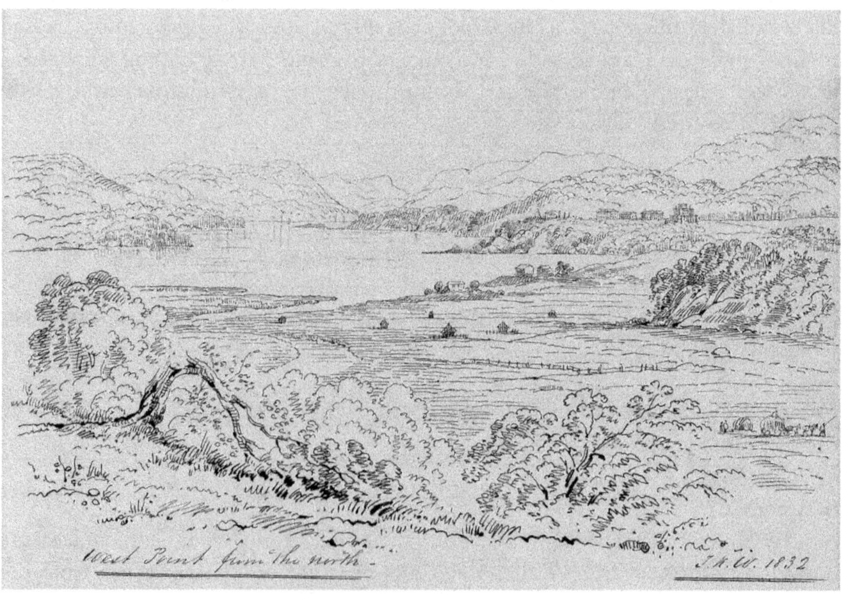

FIGURE 2.3 West Point from the North, 1832 (*Journal*, vol. 1, p. 21). New York Public Library, Archives and Special Collections, New York.

September 9
Sunday. The Rev'd. Mr. [Thomas] Warner, professor of Ethics &c. gave us a well written discourse on "Remember the Sabbath day to keep it holy."

Dined at Coldspring. Mr. and Mrs. Paulding were there, Miss Kemble, Mr. Platt, Father O'Reilly, and the two Misses Young,[52] and Miss Helen Travers, a young lady of rare beauty. We returned by moonlight and Miss Travers was in the boat with us.

September 11
The clouds of the morning gave us a succession of dreary showers in the afternoon, but before the rain the Col., Mr. Leslie and I walked to the point beyond Washington's valley. The orderly followed with my drawing board, and we criticized the outline of the piece I am now engaged on. The gentlemen pronounced all the details minutely faithful.

I am making progress with crayon drawing and mathematics.

At 4 Mr. Leslie, the Col. and I sat down to an excellent dinner to which Messrs. Kemble and Paulding were invited but were kept away by the rain. General Scott, however, and Major Mason unexpectedly made their appearance and spent the rest of the day with us.

September 12
At breakfast, I received a note from my old school fellow,[53] I. Bradley dated in New York. I wrote to him by return of post to ask him to visit me. The Col. kindly desired me to invite him to his house instead of allowing him to quarter at the Hotel.

I am left alone this evening, Col. Thayer having gone up to the [Ulster] Iron Works at Saugerties.

September 13
Beautiful day. The Col. returned by the afternoon boat.

September 18
The woods begin to change and the deep green is slowly melting into the warmer tints of autumn.

September 23
Cloudy with gloomy showers. I have finished the treatise on Common Geometry, and my view of the Point.

The Col. has already ordered the frames for this and other pictures that I have made for him of the scenery around.

September 30
Sunday. The weather during the week has been cold and variable, and the Colonel's stock of Lehigh [coal][54] came into requisition. Autumn is advancing fast. On Sunday last, Bradley arrived in the boat from New York and stayed with me until Tuesday. He seems to be well informed in English politics, for one so young.

October 1, 1832
Dreary rainy weather and so cold that we had to call in the aid of anthracite. Two handsome frames arrived for my pictures this morning but unfortunately a mistake has been made in the size, so two others are ordered to be here next Saturday.

October 2
Charming day but still cold so that one of Dr. [Eliphalet] Nott's Stoves in the Hall was by no means superfluous.

We had a very agreeable dinner party today—British [Rear-]Admiral [John Chambers] White, Mr. S. Governeur, Mr. Gov'r. Kemble, Mr. Leslie, Dr. Wheaton, Mr. Cozzens and two other gentlemen. As usual the evening passed very cheerfully. These are really very delightful banquets. Nothing can exceed the delicacy of the courses and the good taste shown in their arrangement, nor the purity and variety of the wines all sparkling from the ice, nor above all, the invariable moderation and good humour of the party which reflect honor alike on the entertainer and his guests, and it is always the same, too, at Mr. Kemble's where the "cuisine" is equally exquisite, and he has the additional advantage of female taste and management, for his sister Miss Mary Kemble lives with him and Mrs. Paulding spends a great part of the summer at his house.

October 6
Fine day after the fog cleared off.

Received a letter from Mr. Muhlenberg containing propositions to which I scarcely hesitate to accede. Col. Thayer thinks the terms sufficiently liberal when the many collateral advantages are taken into the account, and preferable to twice the compensation elsewhere. I shall suspend my decision, however, until I get a reply to a letter which I have sent off to my mother this evening.

October 14
Sunny day with a keen, bracing air.

I took tea with Mr. and Mrs. Leslie, and during the afternoon the Lieut. and I enjoyed some magnificent scenery from the heights west of Fort Putnam, looking up the River. The woods and mountains have now attained the very perfection of autumn splendour. The scarlet dogwood, the golden Hickory, the inimitable maple of the most silken brilliancy, with all the rich clusters of intermediate dyes from the still vivid green to the most sparkling and transparent yellow and carmine, present at once so dazzling a display, that the eye feasts on it with rapture, and for the moment you forget that it tells of evanescence and decay.

A while ago when this sublime scenery was clothed with the rich verdure of summer, and the eye roamed over a pleasant interchange of green forest and velvety enclosures, with what comparative indifference we dwelt upon its beauty, but now that its hour is nigh, every leaf that falls seems like the departing flight of a "golden treasure." Thus it is with our precious moments, our invaluable blessings, how little we regard them while they cluster around us, how vast seems their importance when they begin to ebb away from us, how deep our regret when they are gone forever.

October 15

The morning being delightful, Mr. Kemble came over in his barge for me, according to previous arrangement, and we proceeded together to a charming little waterfall which dashes over a fine wall of granite across the Indian Brook. The stream is one of the most secluded spots in nature, arched over by noble trees, with the sunshine glancing thro' here and there, and flecking the rich mossy face of the rocks, or lighting up the white wreaths of foam and the sparkling eddies below the cascade. It mingles with the Hudson just opposite West Point. Here Mr. Kemble handed me his "repeater" [pocket watch] that I might not miss the dinner hour and left me to pursue my sketch. I finished a careful outline by three, and then took my Drawing Board to the "Highland

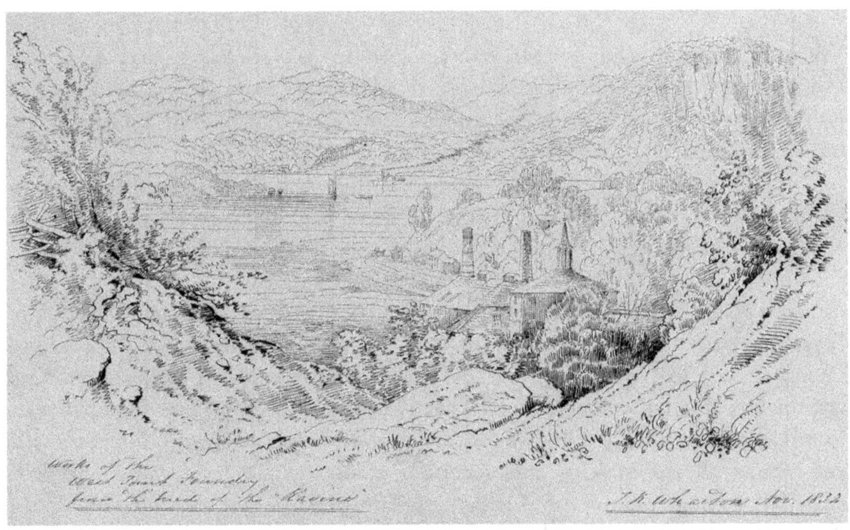

Figure 2.4 Works of the West Point Foundry from the head of the ravine, 1832 (*Journal*, vol. 1, p. 205). New York Public Library, Archives and Special Collections, New York.

School"[55] which was at no great distance, where Mr. Kemble's servant had orders to go for it, and continued my walk of about 2 miles around the beautiful heights of Phillipstown, to Mr. Kemble's to dinner. We sat down at 4 with quite a party and the exercises of the morning made me enjoy everything with threefold relish. Late in the evening while we were preparing to re-cross the river, Mr. Kemble stepped out with me onto the Piazza, and in a way that totally prevented my refusal, placed in my hands a draft on the "Foundry Association" for $50, which he urged might be of use to me in buying drawing materials, &c. Thus it is almost daily am I surprised by some new mark of the kind regard of my friends around me.

October 17
Very fine weather. At about half past two Col. Thayer and I went down to the wharf to see Mr. Kemble and his two sisters and other friends off to the city. The *North America* came by at 3, crowded with passengers. After they were all safely on board, the Colonel & I took a boat and proceeded down the river about two miles, landing near the "Sugar Loaf" mountain on the opposite side of the river. A walk of nearly a mile brought us to the top of an open ridge from which we had anticipated a fine subject for a large picture I intend painting. But our expectations were far more than realized. It was grand beyond description and greatly superior to any grouping we have either of us yet found among the Highlands. But alas! poor me, in my enthusiasm to reach an even greater elevation, in running rapidly down the intervening hollow my foot caught a little rocky projection and I came violently to the ground with my head against a stone. I was up again instantly, and after the first shock and pain had passed off, the Colonel found that I had sustained no serious injury, only a cut in the ear, and a bruise on the arm hardly worth mentioning but which, no doubt, broke the violence of the fall.

We took the boat again at Mr. Sam'l. Governeur's dock, and got back to the Point by tea time, well pleased with the result of our excursion, in having found so fine a point of view. Yet my accident somewhat marred our enjoyment but it was fortunate that it was no worse.

October 18
Very fine.

The celebrated mathematician and astronomer Professor [Ferdinand Rudolph] Hassler, and his son, dined and took tea with us. The Professor talked most fluently, but I lost much of what he said from the rapidity of his utterances, and marked foreign accent and grimace, tho' he has been no less than 20 years in this country. He is a native of Switzerland, and now over 60 years old, yet retains all the vivacity and scientific ardour which have gained for him such distinction among the "savans" of Europe. He is now engaged in the Trigonometrical survey of the coast of the United States, in which his great talents already shine conspicuous.

October 19
I have received my mother's letter of the 12th Inst., which has determined me, and I have written to Mr. Muhlenberg that I propose joining him at Flushing on the first Monday in November. This decision seems to promise well, and agree exactly with my natural taste.

October 20
After breakfast the Colonel sent his orderly to engage a boat for me, and I prepared to take a trip to the spot we selected the other day, taking my drawing board and materials with me. After a hard pull against the tide my boatsman landed me opposite "Buttermilk Falls" and I repaired to the scene of my late disaster, where I selected a suitable position, and made an outline of that splendid view, then returned to the boat at 3 and was borne rapidly up the stream by a strong south wind. It was not long before I showed the Colonel the fruits of my little voyage, and then sat down with a sharpened appetite to his ample table. This drawing is intended as a match to "[William James] Bennet's"[56] picture which is taken from the same direction as mine but much nearer the Point, so that while it embraces some of the main features, it differs totally in their combination.

I have in hand at present the large picture, one of the "Indian Falls" nearly equal in size, a view of Fort Put[nam],[57] and Dr. Hosack's large River scene (now nearly completed) all in water colours. Then I have my crayon drawing and "Descriptive Geometry."

I am, however, far from satisfied with the tardiness of my progress, and am endeavouring to acquire more fixed and prevailing habits of diligence.

It were vain to attempt a description of these Highlands at the present glowing season but I shall endeavour to introduce some of its rich tones into the picture just commenced. The silky gloss of the Maple shining here and there among the luxuriant trees that fringe either bank of the Hudson puts all other competitors to the "blush." It is like the "hectic glow" of nature, beautiful exceedingly but short lived and illusive.

October 21
Sunday. After breakfast the Colonel handed me a joint letter from my Father and mother and it is very pleasant to find that they both entirely approve of my arrangement at Flushing, so that I feel quite sanguine that it is a well-directed measure.

The subject of the Rev'd. Professor Warner's Ethical discourse this morning was "Prove all things and hold fast that which is good."[58]

Yesterday our friend Mr. Kemble sent over his "notes," and at 3 this afternoon Lieut. Leslie and I walked down together to the dock, where we were shortly joined by the rest of the party—Col. Thayer, General Winfield Scott, Capt. [Ethan] Hitchcock, Mr. Geo. P. Morris, of the *N.Y. Mirror*. The Col. introduced me to General [Winfield] Scott, and the six-oared barge being ready manned, we all took our seats astern and in a few minutes were swiftly skimming the Hudson towards Coldspring. The General is strictly speaking a fine-looking man, uncommonly tall, with a robust figure, tho' rather ordinary in its proportions, a noble head, such marked expression of earnest thought, and firm, deliberate intrepidity, combined with a dash of gentle urbaneness which seems to chase away any approach to austerity. He seems to be no ordinary character. Every look and every turn of sentiment shew penetration, sound judgment, and large and varied attainments. This is the idea I have formed of him from what I have seen today, and I believe as a military tactician and commander he is unrivalled in the American Army.

At 4 we sat down to a superb dinner, followed, as usual, on the removal of the cloth with the choicest wines, and a full flow of pleasant conversation. At a late hour coffee and wafers were handed round which, by the by, always close these elegant entertainments, with a chasse cafè, a glass of some delicious "liqueur." We then muffled ourselves in our cloaks, and the rapid barge soon landed us again at West Point. The same party are invited to dine with us tomorrow.

October 22

Lieut. Leslie and I spent the morning in the library superintending the unpacking &c. of a full-length portrait of "Monroe," admirably painted by [Thomas] Sully in his usual free and masterly style.[59]

At 4 our party assembled, Gen. Scott, Lieut. Leslie, the Rev'd. Prof. Warner, Professors [Dennis] Mahan and [Edward H.] Courtenay, a Capt. [Henry?] Smith,[60] Mr. Kemble and Mr. Morris. The dinner passed off charmingly and the General enlivened our evening by spirited and well-told anecdotes illustrative of manners on the Western frontier. His conversation is very animated, gentleman-like, and characterized by an admirable choice of language and expression.

October 25

Beautiful day with a strong breeze.

In the morning after writing to Zanesville, I set out in the boat to complete my outline from the opposite shore. When I had finished, I was passed by the Colonel and Mr. Leslie and we proceeded together to call upon Mr. S. Governeur, whose estate is just opposite West Point, and which, tho' not kept in such complete order as some others, yet in point of scenery, and natural beauty, is by far the most splendid on the river. We got back to a three o'clock dinner, of which Mr. Leslie partook with us, and a Mr. [James] Herring of N. York who is now engaged in collecting materials for an American Portrait Gallery.

October 27
The strong winds of the last few days have nearly laid the mountains bare. What foliage still remains has lost all its brilliancy. The Poplar however still rises in fresh green spires on different parts of the point, and around Mr. Sam. Governeur's residence on the opposite shore, and the large weeping willows in the Colonel's back garden are quite unscathed.

Cadet [A. R.] Johnston called upon me in the afternoon.

October 28
Sunday. A fierce northern blast swept over the plain but the Colonel's famous Lehigh fires, for which he has quite a name, made it very pleasant within doors. This place must be severely cold in winter, exposed to the entire force of the north winds which blow without but [for] the interruption thro' the gap of the Highlands. Houses are of solid granite, full of indoor comforts and abundantly supplied with anthracite, so that the people don't suffer any more than in milder situations.

Taking it the season thro' I do not think there is a place in the Union which surpasses West Point in salubrity and purity of atmosphere. In the chapel a stranger made an attempt upon that sublime text "Thou art the man," but he treated it in a lifeless and unimpressive manner.

Lieut. Leslie, Dr. Wheaton (the resident physician), Sam.[l] Governeur and Mr. Webster, one of the officers, dined with us today. Mr. Gov'r. Kemble was no doubt kept away by the inclemency of the weather. Mr. [S.] Governeur's nephew [i.e., Samuel Laurence Gouverneur] is now before the public in a long political correspondence. He is son-in-law of ex-President and by this connection has become to some extent a party in the Seminole War question, but how I don't exactly know yet.[61]

October 29
High wind, cold and clear.

My three pictures were hung today in the drawing room, and seem to give the Colonel no little pleasure which I am very glad of. Today he sent the dimensions and draught of a very handsome frame for the piece I am now engaged with, which is intended to match Mr. Bennett's picture in the same room. It makes me very happy to be able in this way to repay in some measure his great kindness to me. My long visit is now drawing to a close and I look forward to the time as to a second departure from "home."

October 30
The curves of "Crow's Nest" which a while ago were buried in the richest leafing are now bristled over with naked branches. Great patches of bare granite have thrown off the veil, and stand all exposed to the winter storm. Dark hemlocks

and cedars, however, hang in clusters among the rocks, and upon the plain the Poplar, the Lilac, and the Weeping Willow still cling to their summer suit.

Whilst engaged in my room this morning, the Col. knocked at my door and presented me with a beautiful penknife, having noticed that my own needed replacing.

I went down to the Landing at Boat time and there met Mr. Kemble and two friends whom he had just brought over to take the *Champlain* for N. York. After the usual introductions and commonplaces, one of them Mr. Henry Cary of New York gave me his address and a very pressing invitation to call and see him there. He, too, is an amateur of my favorite pursuit.

October 31
Soft dreamy Indian summer weather.

Col. Thayer and I took a long excursion in the Boat. We left at 10 and coasted along the bases of the mountains as far as Cornwall landing which is at the northern entrance of the great "Gorge" and just under "Butter Hill" [i.e., Storm King] the last mountain in that direction, and the highest of the chain, rising upwards of 1,600 feet. Nothing could be grander than the precipices which hung over us, losing their summits of stern granite in the blue mists of Indian Summer.

I made a drawing of "St. Anthony's face"[62] which is one of the wonders of the highlands. It is a bold projection of rock forming an advanced spur of "Breakneck" and in certain positions takes the form of a colossal human face in profile with a strong tuft of bushes at the chin for a beard. We were charmed with the picturesque combinations which the rocks assumed as we passed along, and in one place the Col. pointed out to me the spot where, not very long ago one "Partridge" lost his life in attempting to scale the face of the mountain in search of a vein of ore. It was on Sunday. He had already reached a high point of the almost vertical precipice, when a projecting ledge which he had clasped gave way with him and he was dashed to the bottom and killed.

We examined the stone ware Pottery, too, at Cornwall Landing, and then returned to the Point getting home at 3, soon after which we had a call from Mr. Leslie who leaves for the city tomorrow. He said he should hope to see me in the course of a few days in New York as I had told him last evening that I intended to be there on Saturday next. The Col. told him "he need expect no such thing." After he left Col. Thayer said he should not admit of my going until the 15th of next month, and that he himself should write to Mr. Muhlenberg to that effect, as he wishes me to give still more time to Descriptive Geometry &c., &c. He was so much in earnest that I could not say a word.

At 4 Mr. Kemble, Dr. Wheaton and a French gentleman sat down to dinner with us and the evening passed delightfully. The same party meets at Coldspring tomorrow.

Rime frost in the night.

November 1st, 1832
Mild Indian summer weather with a dense blue atmosphere.

Mr. Kemble's barge came over for us and at 3 the Col., Professor Dennis Mahan, and I crossed the river. At dinner, we met a Gallico-German gentleman named "Blum." It was quite late when we took our "chasse."

November 3
Very fine.

At noon, I took "Lipsy's" boat for Coldspring, and Mr. Kemble and I walked over to "Constitution Island," from which I commenced a sketch of the works of the "West Point Foundry Association" which fill up the opposite valley. They are on a great scale, and execute large government contracts, casting and boring of Cannon &c. Mr. Kemble is at their head. As he proposed taking the New York Boat he re-crossed the river with me, and spent the afternoon and took tea with us. I showed him my picture from Dr. Hosack's place with which he was highly pleased, and as much so with that now in progress for the Colonel. His off-hand frankness and liberality are beautiful traits in his character. Col. Thayer esteems him very highly, indeed, altho' they differ politically, they are just like two brothers.

November 4
Sunday. Mr. Warner gave us today an admirable sermon from Rom. 5c. 19.[63] In the afternoon I spent some time with him in his garden, and then we walked together to the Cadets' Monument above Washington's valley. His conversation is very agreeable, and he is a most amiable man, affectionate and very cheerful in his disposition. I think Mr. [Charles] McIlvaine was his predecessor as Chaplain at the Point.

November 6
Dr. Arnold, the Dentist, is on his periodical visit to the Point and the Colonel has insisted upon my having his services as my teeth have been sadly neglected.

Today he received an answer from Mr. Muhlenberg. He says, "On no account would I ask Mr. Wharton to leave you under those circumstances. I shall not, therefore, look for him at Flushing within the fortnight." It will be the 20th, then, or about that, when I leave the Point.[64]

At 4 Mr. Kemble, Dr. [Walter] Wheaton, and Mr. Cozzens sat down with us to dinner, which, as usual, from the variety of courses, took up a considerable part of the evening, and was enlivened by pleasant anecdotes &c. After the gentlemen left the Col. and I finished the day with "chess."

Often after these pleasant parties Col. Thayer walks up and down the gallery with me until bedtime and amplifies on the various topics that formed the staple of the conversation at table. His remarks are very interesting, and he always makes them contribute to my improvement.

November 7
My teeth were finished this morning, and by filling, filing and cleansing they have been greatly improved, and with proper care will last far longer than they would otherwise have done. When I asked for my account Mr. Arnold said that the Colonel had requested him to hand it to himself, and that he dared, on no account, disobey his wishes. Thus, I am again under obligation to his disinterested liberality, which I would gladly have prevented had I been permitted to do so.

November 8
After going thro' a "demonstration" in Des. Geom. at the tea table, Col. Thayer talked to me a long time on the value of mathematical study, and the importance of devoting to it a part, even if small, of each day, that thus in the progress of years my mind would become enriched with a variety of exact knowledge, which I should find of incalculable benefit, and he laid down for me many plans for my improvement, and spoke very earnestly of the many advantages I should enjoy at Flushing.

November 9
Took tea and spent a very pleasant evening with the Leslies.

November 10
We had a pleasant little party today over at Mr. Kemble's. The Colonel, Mr. Leslie, Dr. Wheaton, Mr. Cozzens, and Father O'Reilly. The moon shone charmingly as we returned in Mr. Kemble's light built barge, and his man Friday "Abrams" (one of the best oarsmen on the river) distinguished himself by the velocity with which he darted us across the beautiful river. "Abe" stutters a good deal, and is quite an original in his way, often furnishing the theme of a rich Irish joke from Father O'Reilly, who has a good deal of the "good clerk of Copmanhurst"[65] about him.

November 11
Sunday. A firm coat of ice formed in the night, yet the beautiful willows bend over the pond still dressed in living green.

Mr. Warner preached today from Matt. 25c. 46v.[66] His sermons are very fine as compositions and those of the last few Sundays have shewn more of the vitality of gospel preaching than I thought they did before.

November 12
Very fine. Dr. Wheaton and I rode down together on horseback to Fort Montgomery, some miles below the Point, which occupied the morning until 2½ P.M.

At 4 a little dinner party assembled—Mr. Leslie, Dr. Wheaton, Mr. Cozzens, Father O'Reilly and Lieut. [James H.?] Taylor.

November 16
Sky perfectly transparent, and keen, still air, ice formed to the thickness of an inch and a quarter. At 1 crossed to the Island, finished my sketch of the "Forge," made an outline of the "Mountain Pass" and at 4 joined the Col. and Mr. Kemble at the dinner table at Coldspring.

November 17
Mr. Kemble, Mr. Leslie, Professor Mahan, Lieut. Webster, and Dr. Wheaton dined with us today. Mr. Kemble pronounced my large picture of the "Highlands" a splendid piece, and Lieut. Leslie is greatly pleased with it.

November 18
Sunday. Heavy vapours clung to the mountain sides and completely concealed them. When the curtain lifted, it rose with as much regularity from the face of the river as if rolled up by art.

The usual "bugle" having by some means been omitted did not notice the lapse of time until too late for morning service.

In the afternoon, I went down to the wharf to meet Mr. Kemble, who is going to the city in the evening boat. Mr. [William] Young of Saugerties goes with him. In walking up to the Colonel's, we had some conversation on the subject of publishing in "Aquatint" my large picture. He enters into the project with warmth and his usual liberality, thinks the best plan will be to make a bargain for the copyright, and he will assist me in every way that he can, but both he and Colonel Thayer are of opinion that it had better not be attempted at all unless I can have the services of a very superior engraver, so as to preserve the full effect of the original, that it would be an injury rather than an advantage to present to the public an engraving of inferior merit.

Mr. Kemble expected that I should have been able to spend awhile with him before leaving the Highlands, but my engagement with Mr. Muhlenberg obliges me to be in New York on my way to Flushing next Wednesday.

November 20
The long looked for comet is now visible under the aspect of a bright yellowish star.[67]

This is my last day as I propose leaving in the afternoon boat tomorrow.

Boisterous weather and very cold.

In the evening, I visited for the last time Mr. Warner and the Leslies'. Mr. Leslie and I have projected an excursion to the Catskills in June next, with Mr. Kemble and whoever else we can engage to go when the time comes. Mr. L. gives a dinner party next Thursday, but as I cannot be present, they insist that I shall promise in lieu of it to eat my New Year's dinner with them, if it can be done.

On my return, I found lying on my table a handsome edition of *Davies Lights and Shadows* and a *Treatise on Optics*[68] as a present from the Col. and a letter containing a bank "check" and the kindest expression of feeling. My obligations to him are more than I can ever repay. Indeed, he seems to think that he cannot do too much for me, and it quite confuses me when I review the repeated instances of his generosity & goodness since I have been with him, and when I think how little I am entitled to them.

November 21

As soon as I heard the Colonel leaving his room I followed him into the office and acknowledged my surprise at the contents of the letter left on my Table last night, but he insisted that he only was the party obliged, and

> that he trusted he should be able at a future period to make some suitable acknowledgement. In the meantime every little advantage he could bestow he should with pleasure afford me, that whenever an opportunity occurred he should be most happy to see me and have my society, and he trusted I should be able so to arrange matters as to spend at least a portion of Mr. Muhlenberg's vacation with him, that as to my last picture (which I am inflexible in making him a present of) should it be published, he proposes subscribing for a number of copies and using his influence to obtain others. That as "Lithography" must be embraced in my plans, whatever facilities the Point does or shall offer, will be most cheerfully placed at my disposal. In short, that whatever he can do to be of service to me will only have to be made known.

At the same time, said he,

> As I always mean what I say I wish you distinctly to understand that in your visits to the Point I shall at all times be glad to have you for your company alone.

I did not know what to say as after all that the Colonel had already done for me who was so lately an entire stranger to him, it had never entered my thoughts to look for anything more, and I was quite lost in thinking over these new instances of his friendship.

At breakfast we had some conversation on the order in which my studies would be pursued to advantage, and on the benefits likely to accrue from the society and moral atmosphere of Flushing, and from the combined advantage of receiving and at the same time imparting instruction, impressing upon me the high value of moral and intellectual culture, and that rectitude of purpose and self-respect which alone can stand the shock of adversity, and bear me safely thro' the vicissitudes that may be in store for me.

West Point has become endeared to me by innumerable instances of unlooked for and unusual kindness. I leave it as if leaving a second home. It is seldom that I have become so much attached to a place, and never with greater reason, and I look forward with the hope of returning to it with the same feelings whenever an opportunity will permit me during my stay in the East.

I will here insert several sketches which will serve to elucidate some points in the scenery alluded to in the foregoing pages. They are copied from the outlines which I made with minute care at the time. I regret, however, that I preserved no outlines of the many finished pictures which I executed at the same period, as they embraced some of the very finest subjects to be found on the shores of the picturesque Hudson. The view opposite shows the "Blast Furnace" "water fall" and the entire group of buildings of Mr. Kemble's works, and the Marsh in front lying at the head of Coldspring Bay, between Constitution Island and the mainland of Putnam Co. In this drawing we look down upon the works from the head of a gravelly ravine, one side of which appears to the right of the previous view. This ravine is used to try the cannon which are cast and bored at the Foundry and its loose bed is ploughed up by the shot. The quiet, sheltered cove near Coldspring with its adjoining marsh, and the river-end of Constitution Island, occupy the middle of the picture, together with the knoll on which stand Mr. Kemble's residence and grounds but which are concealed by the groups of trees which overhang the "works." Beyond is the Hudson and above it to the right towers the lofty crest of one of the principal mountains, its granite face half buried in beautiful foliage which climbs over its very summit. What a pity that the stolidity of the early settlers should have fastened upon it such an inhuman name as the "Crow's Nest," but its noble brethren are no better off—"Bull Hill," "Breakneck," "Butter Hill," "Sugar Loaf" and "St. Anthony's nose."

The charming seclusion of "Washington's Valley" is shewn just over the end of the "Island," "Capt. Hitchcock's Point" flanking it to the right, and the "Cadets' Monument" overlooking it to the left, and a fine range of eminences covered with sunny woods lead off the eye into the remote "distance."

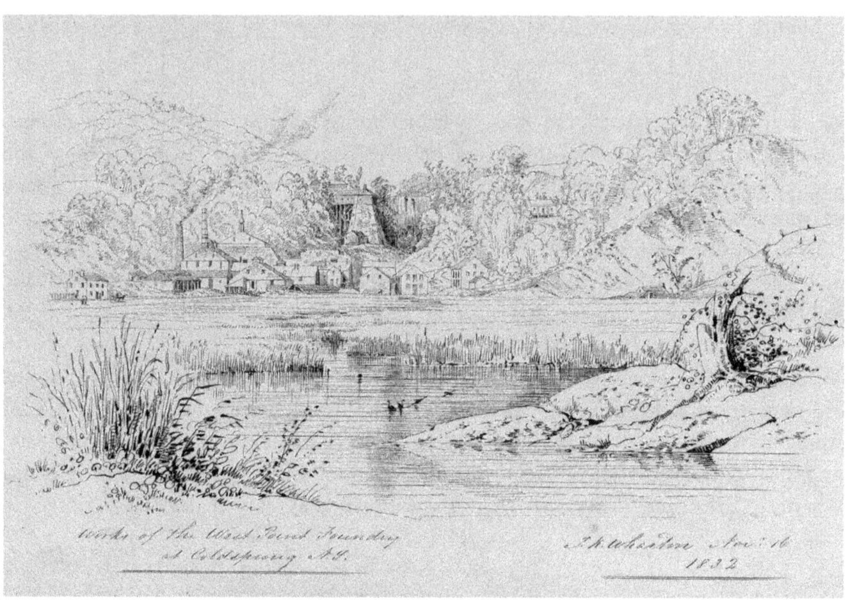

FIGURE 2.5 Works of the West Point Foundry, Cold Spring, NY, 1832 (*Journal*, vol. 1, p. 203). New York Public Library, Archives and Special Collections, New York.

"Constitution Island" is a long stony ridge for the most part covered with bosky woods, and lying just opposite West Point, midway between it and Coldspring. The remains of an old fort, or Magazine, still occupy its highest plateau, and command noble views both up and down the river, and just across the stream from the West Point Wharf, is a prominent target, near the water's edge, for the artillery practice of the "Cadets." The extremity of the Island shown in the drawing rises out of deep water in a lofty vertical wall of solid rock crowned with cedars, oak and walnut. But like all the primary formations in this region the stern face of the granite is everywhere relieved by clusters of leafage. Pines and other trees cling to rents and fissures where the only succulence seems to be the moisture which ascends from the river beneath, and the rains of heaven, and wherever a little soil has effected a lodgement, flowering shrubs and beautiful climbing plants fling their wreaths over the stony battlements. The grand swelling curves of "Crow's Nest" rise from the opposite shore and appears nowhere more majestic than from the base of this rocky Point. We used to pass round it in our frequent excursions to and from Coldspring in the barge, and always found something new to admire as the changing seasons or the changing atmosphere laid their impress upon it.

The little village of Coldspring, nestling in its pleasant cove under the shelter of the mountains, has no rival on the River for beauty of situation. It is scattered along the beach of a shallow bay in expansion of the main stream and terminates in a long wharf or steamboat landing as shown in the sketch.

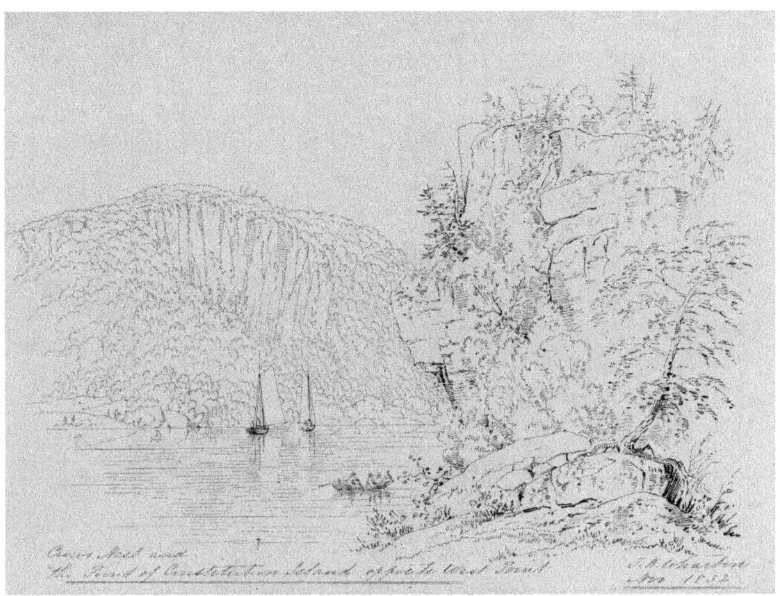

Figure 2.6 Crow's Nest and The Point of Constitution Island opposite West Point, 1832 (*Journal*, vol. 1, p. 207). New York Public Library, Archives and Special Collections, New York.

Uplands of greater or less fertility rise immediately behind it, and terraces not too sloping for cultivation, and over the whole towers the giant mass of "Bull Hill" with its jutting crags, showing bold and artistic projections amidst the umbrage of its dense woods. To the north between the bases of the mountain chain and the water's edge is a pretty fair waggon road which I remember once pursuing nearly as far as Fishkill Landing for the sake of the splendid combinations of mountain and river scenery which reward you at every step.

Southward the Bay is flanked by ledges of rock pushing out boldly into the river and fringed with pleasant woods. One of these rocky Points was selected by Mr. Kemble for his "Chapel of our Lady" and a more poetic position for a shrine could hardly be imagined. Having a vast number of Catholics employed in his works, he conceived the idea of providing them with suitable accommodations for sabbath worship, and accordingly made choice of the spot in question on which he erected a neat Tuscan chapel as shown in the sketch. He and I designed it together and indeed it is the very first architectural design I was ever engaged in.[69] At that time Father O'Reilly had charge of the Catholic congregation at Coldspring, but he was soon afterwards removed to Saugerties in Ulster Co. and thence in a few years to Patterson, New Jersey, where I lost sight of him. He was a man of thorough scholarship, thought and expressed himself with a warmth which at times bordered upon extravagance, but you could not help being interested and often startled by the originality and force of his views, and his influence over the operations in and around Coldspring was unbounded.

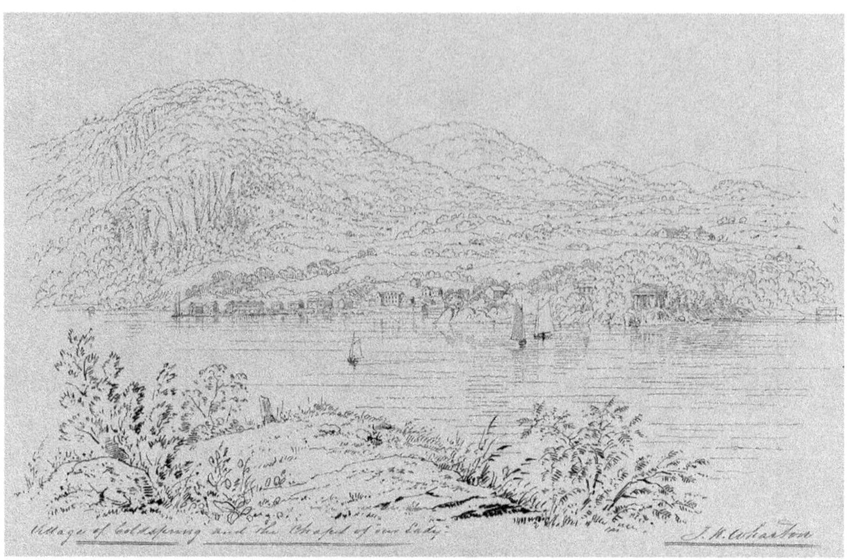

Figure 2.7 Village of Cold Spring and the Chapel of our Lady, ca. 1835 (*Journal*, vol. 1, p. 209). New York Public Library, Archives and Special Collections, New York.

The barn like structure amongst the trees on the next point of rock to the left is the old Presbyterian Church, and following the shore to the right of the "chapel" you come to Mr. Kemble's boat house, the scene to us of so many pleasant landings and embarkations.

The residence of Mr. Kemble's brother William lies concealed in the grove of trees between the chapel and the Boathouse. His family, however, used to spend but a short time in the summer here as he had an elegant mansion in town in Hudson Square.[70] Mr. Kemble's own place and the "works" would appear beyond the Boathouse to the right but they are not embraced in the view, and mention them to preserve the connection of localities among the different sketches here introduced.

The view is taken from the Point which forms the northern boundary of Washington's Valley. It is the spot where Col. Thayer and I found Capt. [Ethan] Hitchcock with a few friends clearing away the brushwood and opening the beautiful prospect on the afternoon of Augt. 21, 1832. We called it by acclamation "Hitchcock's Point."

Among the many elegant country seats on the North River, few with so unassuming an exterior contained in greater perfection those elements which go to dignify and adorn life than the residence of Mr. Kemble—everything simple and in the most refined taste, while his entertainments were sumptuous, and the most gifted spirits of the time were to [be] found at his genial table. The lawns and shrubbery around were all in character, and the view of "Crow's Nest," shewn in the pictures, was perfectly enchanting especially when the slant rays fell upon projecting rocks at eventide. Then the noble trees with garden seats under their spreading shadow, the Charming woodpath down to the boat house which we have so often threaded after an evening gathering of rare enjoyment, and the sunny Piazza with the smooth green turf in front where Washington Irving used to delight to retire with a book and lounge on the grass while the rest were grouped about within doors or on the grounds—all were beautiful exceedingly.

In the drawing room was the fine original picture of "Uncle Toby & The Widow"[71] by C.R. Leslie, R.A. and brother of our friend. A moonlight of the Bay of Naples by [R. W.] Weir[72]—one of his best—a few sunny pictures, also by Weir, a ruined Piscina in Italy,[73] and a gem by W.S. Mount—one of his "Long Island pictures," "Husking Corn"[74] is besides other works of art, all choice and of great interest.

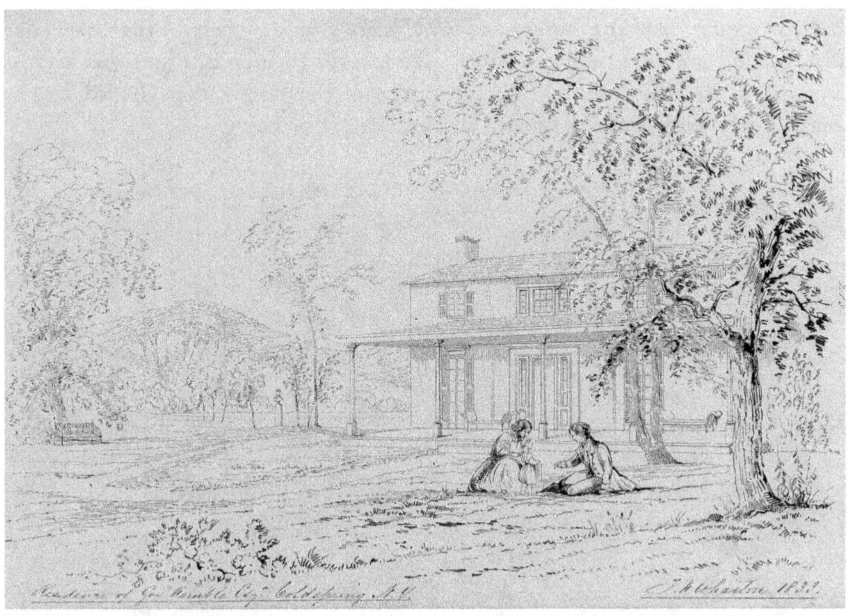

FIGURE 2.8 Residence of Gov. Kemble Esq., Cold Spring, NY, 1833 (*Journal*, vol. 1, p. 213). New York Public Library, Archives and Special Collections, New York.

This noble river view is from the curving walk along the ridge on the grounds of the late Dr. D. Hosack, leading from the principal mansion to the "cottage" at the north end of the estate. The spot chosen is just where the walk emerges from the shadow of lofty trees which border it for some distance from the houses. Here it winds over a high grassy hill with a mate just opposite crowned with a tasteful "vase" of colossal proportions, and dedicated to the goddess of "Lyric Poesy." Another walk turns off to the left and steals down the hill by the woodside, then plunges into a deep, shady dell, crosses a bridge and finally conducts you across a wide open glade to a "pavilion" occupying a broad table of granite projected out into the river and tufted with cedars and rich lichens.

Far away to the north soar the peaks of the Catskills. The highest is the "round top" seen to the right of the chain in the view, 3,590 feet above the level of the Hudson. The mountains are the engrossing feature of this superb scene, only a section of which is embraced in the view, and whether seen under the bright summer sun, or partially veiled in mist, and dashed with broad shadows, their hues are the most magical and changeful I ever looked upon. There is a weird and almost spiritual feeling about them that sometimes seems hardly to belong to earth.

"Crystal Cove" was a retired little nook at the Southern extremity of Dr. Hosack's estate. It was approached by thick shadowy woods which all at once opened upon a pebbly curve of shore flanked with points of rock which were veined with a formation of quartz crystallized into minute spiculae of peculiar brilliancy, just like the specimens which abound at Glen's Falls and Lake George, and are popularly known as Lake George diamonds. From this feature, we gave it the name, tho' the limpid purity of the waters that rippled on the beach might fairly have claimed a share in the christening.

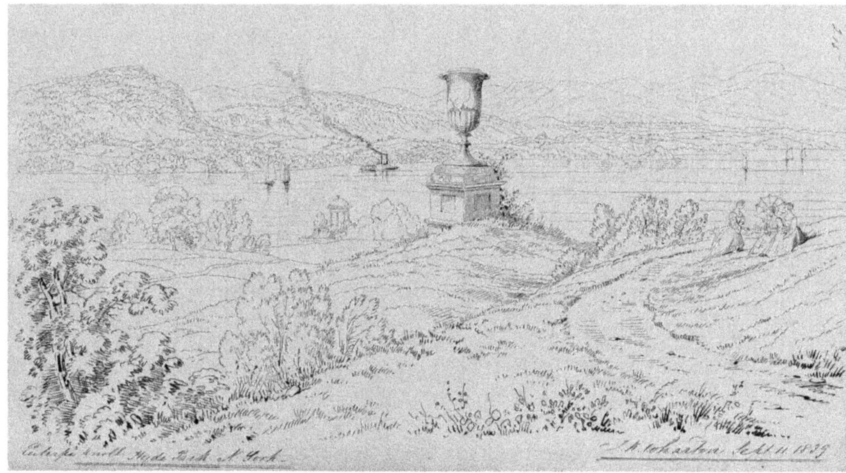

FIGURE 2.9 Euterpe Knoll. Hyde Park, NY, 1839 (*Journal*, vol. 1, p. 215). New York Public Library, Archives and Special Collections, New York.

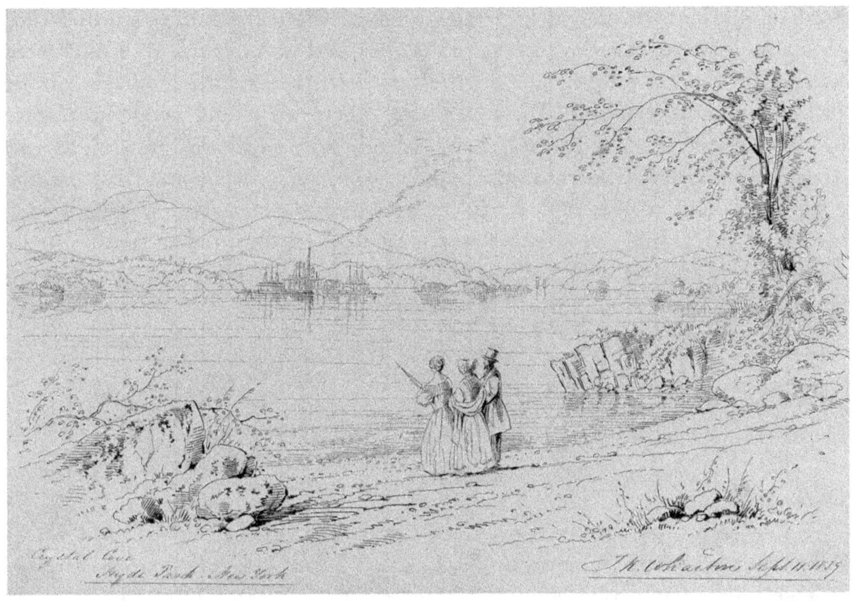

FIGURE 2.10 Crystal Cove. Hyde Park, NY, 1839 (*Journal*, vol. 1, p. 217). New York Public Library, Archives and Special Collections, New York.

Looking north you caught a glimpse of the Pavilion that bounded the upper line of the Park, then the varied shores of the River. The green island lying on its bosom—and far away in the blue, the ever-dominant Catskills from the "round top" to the extreme easterly mountain, with the mountain house shewing like a clear white spot near its crown.

In the view is introduced a "Towing Steamer" with its "freight barges" on their way to "the city." These moving masses pass so frequently that they are quite characteristic of North River Scenery, and combined with constant fleets of sloops and schooners connect the thoughts perpetually with the busy "beast of commerce" below.

The country around Flushing was rich and diversified and the shores of the Bay, with its points, and Rikers' Island, formed numerous combinations of great pastoral beauty, quiet and unobtrusive and the clear waters which flowed in from the "Sound" were dotted with sailing craft of every description—the East River being one of the avenues to the Harbour of New York.

At the head of the Bay a wide salt marsh runs far up into the island (Long Island) as is generally the case with the numerous inlets that indent this part of its shore. Flushing Creek winds thro' it and drains the high cultivated lands on either side. From one of these elevations the view is taken. The "Boat" that plyed twice a day between Flushing and the city is on her way, and the daily "stage" crossing the causeway which carries the road over the Marsh around the head of the Bay. On the high ground to the left lay the fine estate of Major Williams, beyond the Bay the grassy slopes and woodlands of Westchester, washed by the East River, and in the far distance the long level line of the Palisades on the Hudson. These were an ever present and very fine feature in the scenery of this part of Long Island, and peculiarly grateful to me. They were a visible memento, in my daily walks, of a region that had become greatly endeared to me, and as the bright sunshine brought out their strong vertical lines, I could follow the almost endless vista until my thoughts usually connected themselves with the scenes in which it is finally merged, and I could fancy myself again among the "Highlands."

Flushing, Long Island

December, 1832
One raw chilly day late in November I took the little steamboat *Linneus* (I think) and landed at Whitestone dock, where I found a light country carriage to take me and my baggage to Flushing (some 3 miles off). Mr. Muhlenberg gave me a cordial welcome to the Institute, introduced me to the professors, and in a few days' time I found myself fully established in my new home, surrounded by intelligent, well educated and gentlemanly companions, and ready to enter upon my new duties, and studies with alacrity.

There were about 60 or 70 students, and a finer set of boys it would be hard to find, or under more complete, and at the same time paternal discipline. In fact, the "Institute" composed one large family with Mr. Muhlenberg the Principal, at its head, and the several Professors and Instructors, many of them very young men educated in the Institution, were more like elder brothers and companions of the pupils than the austere taskmasters who usually fill these responsible posts. All seemed to look up to Mr. Muhlenberg with affection and reverence, and I never saw a scholastic establishment where a firm and methodical system of control was more happily blended with the strictest regard to the happiness and improvement of the inmates.

The general features of the system, both moral and educational, were taken from the famous institution of M. Fellenberg, at Berne in Switzerland, whose views our excellent Principal had fully espoused, and elaborated in his establishment with great success.

The Building was spacious, erected, if I remember rightly, at an expense of $28,000 or $30,000, consisting of a centre compartment adorned with lofty columns, and two roomy wings, the whole three stories high with full basement for dining rooms, kitchens & offices, and well distributed throughout in large dormitories, studies, recitation rooms and living apartments. The north wing was chiefly occupied by Mr. [Peter] Muhlenberg, his mother and brother (Dr. M.). It was handsomely furnished and opened upon a beautiful flower garden. The lawn in front towards the high road, contained nearly two acres of fine grassy slope, well planted, and traversed by a wide gravelled carriage drive, leading up to the "Institute," with two entrances at the ends of the enclosing fence. The grounds behind were several acres in extent, comprising a large vegetable garden, with numerous plots for the pupils to exercise their horticultural taste upon, and beyond a spacious "hippodrome" or playground, of smooth turf, with a substantial gymnasium in the centre, and encircled by a wide, well-kept walk, about the fifth of a mile round, and large trees at intervals along the boundary fences. The neighbourhood was prettily diversified with woods and pleasant fields lying on the uplands, and ponds of clear water in the hollows, so that we had no lack of pastime in the intervals of study—walking, riding, driving, skating in winter and in summer every fine evening the carriages took down large parties of us to bathe at Whitestone beach on the Sound, and after a while many of us formed ourselves into boat clubs and purchased well-built four and six oared pleasure boats which we used to keep in Flushing Creek, and on the fine summer afternoons take long excursions on the Bay and among the Islands of The East river and Sound, stopping at cool, shady cover to bathe in the lucid Salt water.

This interchange of morning study and evening exercise, had the happiest affect upon us; it effectually relieved the monotony of daily routine, while it furnished us with the purest supplies of health, and refreshed us by daily contact with the beautiful scenes of Nature. But I may as well resume the hasty notes I kept at the time, as I have been anticipating already on the last page.

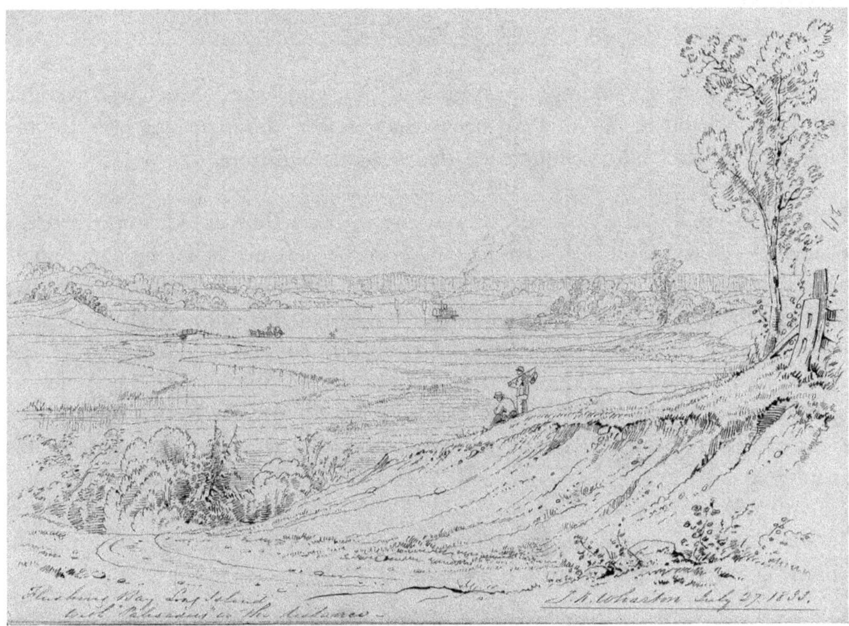

FIGURE 2.11 Flushing Bay, Long Island with the Palisades in the distance, 1833 (*Journal*, vol. 1, p. 219). New York Public Library, Archives and Special Collections, New York.

December 25, 1832
Christmas day. Mild and scarcely a cloud. At 6 the bell rang for roll-call, and at half past we all assembled in the chapel for early service. The room was brilliantly lighted and hung with a profusion of evergreens, woven into chaplets or festooned along the walls and ceiling. Bright and happy faces filled the apartment and the joyous music of the Christmas anthems pealed in rich harmony from the organ and choir. It was a beautiful and appropriate service, and closed by a warm address from the chaplain, the Rev'd. Sam'l. Seabury. There were regular services, too, both before and after dinner, and the day throughout was marked by the suspension of ordinary business and amusements. Tomorrow and the next day are holidays.

December 26
At 8 o'clock two stages and a carriage started full of boys for the city and at 9½ St. Clair W. and I followed on foot. The day was frosty and we preferred walking. It began to snow when we got about 5 miles from the city and changed to rain when we reached Brooklyn. I met Mr. J[acob] Diller, our Professor of Mathematics, and walked about the city with him, calling at Mr. [Henry] Warner's on Broome Str., but his brother (the clergyman) had just left for West Point.

At 6 P.M. I took refuge from the wet and cold at Mr. Slocum's comfortable supper table.

December 27
Rainy with clear & cold evening.

Called at Mr. J.K. Paulding's in Whitehall Str., and found Mr. Gov'r. Kemble just from Washington. We have been disappointed about an engraver for my large picture, so I have relinquished the idea of publishing.

Called and presented a note of introduction to Mr. [Thomas] Cole, the artist. I found him at the easel in his studio, and had the pleasure of seeing some noble works of his which he has just brought home from Italy. One large picture of the aqueduct in the Campagna struck me as being exceedingly fine, such a balmy evening atmosphere, and the young moon just trembling above the Appenines;[75] another picture, too, a "morning scene," I think on the Arno—it sparkled with dew drops, and the mists curled upward so freshly against the sides of the mountains. The artist himself, too, was winning and gentle in his manners.

In the evening, I joined the return party at the Walton House,[76] and we had a shivering journey of it, getting home a little after dark.

December 28
Frosty day with a brilliant sky.

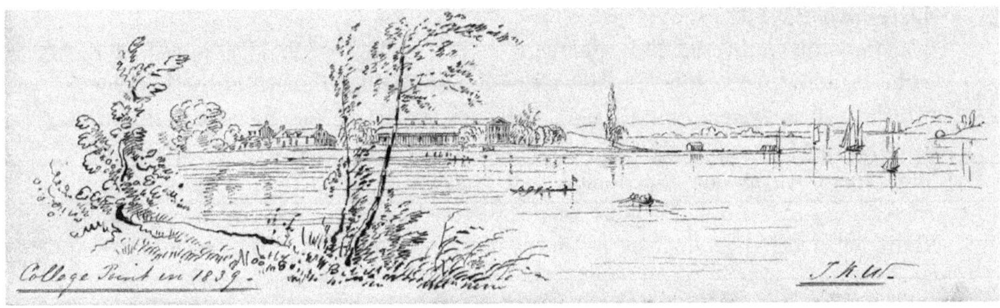

Figure 2.12 College Point, Long Island, 1839 (*Journal*, vol. 2, p. 371). New York Public Library, Archives and Special Collections, New York.

In the evening the "Eunomian Society"[77] held their 4th anniversary. Mr. Muhlenberg delivered a very neat address on their motto "Ecce Quercus."[78] Mr. Seabury followed, and Livestus [*sic*: Libertus] Van Bokkelen closed the meeting with a short and appropriate speech. The "study' was tastefully decorated for the occasion.

December 29
A little snow in the morning but very clear and calm in the afternoon.

Mr. Diller and I and several of the pupils went out to Duryee's Pond and had a few hours of excellent skating.

December 30
Sunday. Clear and sunny.

Mr. Muhlenberg preached in the morning from Luke 1: 70, and in the afternoon "We bring our years to an end as a tale that is told."[79]

I spent the calm evening hours in close reflection on the subjects suggested by the services of the day. The solemn thoughts inspired by the last Sabbath of the year, and a retrospect of the countless privileges and blessings with which its fleeting moments have been crowned, my preservation from the pestilence, and the ample provision that my Heavenly Parent has made for my happiness and welfare here, and the improvement of my moral nature to fit me for a happy eternity hereafter.

There is a thick grove of cedars with a long secluded path winding throe it, not very far from the Institute in the rear. It is so accessible and so entirely shut out from the world around that I have made choice of it to retire to whenever I wish to reflect undisturbed on any subject that occupies my mind. The quiet whisper of the breeze, the evening birds, and the distant low of the cattle all harmonized well this evening with sober thought.

December 31
Uncommonly mild and beautiful with a fine mellow sky, and a sunset of the richest gilding. 1832 bids us farewell with a smile, significative of the happiness which it has woven around us. With the dawn of the new year may the Dayspring from on high arise upon our hearts, dissolve the icy chains that bind them, warm our affections into a gracious flow, and shine upon us with increasing lustre until the "glory of the perfect day" surrounds us in that happy clime, where change shall be no more, "time no longer" but "one eternal spring encircle all."

January 1st, 1833
Flushing Institute, Long Isld. N.Y.

The studies of the "Institute" were, of course, suspended for the day. A Bible Lesson from James 4:13 to 17[80] occupied part of the morning.

At 10½ we assembled in the chapel for morning services, and Mr. Muhlenberg delivered an address from Titus 1c.4, "Grace, mercy, and peace from God the Father and the Lord Jesus Christ the Saviour." What an appropriate Sermon for the new year! Blessings then, far beyond the common good wishes uttered at this season, blessings composing the whole treasury of heaven—exhaustless, inalienable, enduring wealth—the foundation of a happy and useful life, a peaceful death, and a crown of joy thro' eternal ages.

After service all repaired to the drawing room to pay Mrs. Muhlenberg the accustomed New Year's visit, and partake of her New Year's refreshments, and at half past two we sat down to a bountiful New Year's dinner graced with noble Turkeys and other consolations peculiar to the season.

In the afternoon chess, draughts, backgammon &c. were severally put into requisition.

The weather all day delightful in the extreme, almost springlike in its mildness, and closed with a beautiful sunset, and moonlight of the intensest transparency. Towards evening Messrs. Diller, Brenneman & I took a glass of wine and cake with Mr. and Mrs. Seabury in the village and returned in time for evening prayers. The whole day passed very pleasantly and I trust not without profit.

January 2
Frosty in the night, followed by a day of extreme beauty with an air so soft as to invite the warble of the blue bird which I heard in the neighbouring woods.

Finished a coloured drawing of the Institute for Mr. Muhlenberg.

January 4
Yesterday and today have been more like April than midwinter—open windows and no fires.

Made a sketch of the "Flushing Oaks," two fine old trees rendered famous by the preaching of Thomas Fox, a Quaker of early celebrity. The old farm house opposite is also a remnant of the remote age. On the gable end is the date sixteen hundred and something.[81] Near the trees is the pleasant residence of Mr. Parsons, a fine old thrifty Quaker, and numerous families of the same sect in and around Flushing still attest to the power of "Fox's" eloquence and influence.

January 5
This climate presents strange contrasts. Last year at this time everything was bound up in ice and snow wreaths. Today the thermo. rose to 70½° in my room with the air passing freely thro' it and no fire since yesterday.

The communicants of the Institute—Messrs. [Emmanuel] Fetter, Diller, Franklin, Brenneman, Kerfort and myself met at Mr. [Samuel] Seabury's in the evening, for devotional exercises. The Sacrament will be administered tomorrow.

January 6
Sunday. Still charming spring weather.

Mr. Muhlenberg preached from "Lord thou hast heard my vows," after which the communicants to the number of 12 assembled around the altar, and as many of the students as chose to remain did so.

In the afternoon Mr. Seabury made some valuable remarks on the consistency to be maintained with the professions made at the altar, "only let your conversation be as becometh the gospel of Christ."

January 7
Quite a change from warm to cold, fine healthy and bracing.

January 8
Still colder than yesterday and threatening snow. At 4 P.M. after my drawing classes I set out on foot to New York. At the Flushing Causeway, the tide being in, had to take off shoes and stockings and make the best of an uncomfortable business, but the exercise afterwards soon restored the warmth to my collapsed feet and I got to the Williamsburg Ferry (9 miles) but little tired at 6½ o'clock. Here I had to wait half an hour for the boat, then crossed over to Grand Street Landing and reached Mr. Thompson's in Howard Street at about 8 o'clock. They appeared very glad to see me, and after tea pressed me to stay all night.

Mr. Thompson tells me that my view of the Highlands (which has been left for a while at Parker & Clover's)[82] is universally considered the best painting of that scene which has yet been made, and that Mr. Bennett was forced to confess its superiority to his own view from Phillipstown, on which account Mr. T. says Mr. Bennett would be wholly averse to engraving mine.

Mr. Thompson also says that he will use his efforts with Mr. James G. King of Weehawk[en, NJ] to call upon my pencil for the scenery around his place opposite the city, which I should like very much in the spring. Mr. T's long illness since June has prevented his resuming his regular business and he is still without an assistant, but intends taking a young Italian on trial.

They all say they are very sorry to lose me, and feel under great obligations to them for their real kindness and friendship.

In the evening, I walked down to the Atlantic near the Battery to look after a parcel I have left to be taken to Zanesville by Col. [J. T.] Fracker, and was glad to find he had done so on the 29th Ult'o.

January 9

After breakfast at Mr. Thompson's, I took my leave with a promise to make their house a home when I had occasion to visit the city.

I met Mr. Harvey on Broadway who gave me a good account of Dr. Hosack and family, and he recommended a tailor to me—Mr. Arnoux Fulton[83]—where I went and got measured for a dress coat at $22 and vest at $4.

I went on board of the Hull Packet *Dapper* & found Capt. Dickinson at the merchants', Sam'l. Hicks and Sons,[84] and was rejoiced to find that he had a small trunk for me from my grandmother. It was a great pleasure to me to shake hands with the good natured, honest hearted Captain and to observe amongst the crew the carpenter who came out with us on the *Diana* and who replaced the main-yard which was carried overboard in the gale on Pentland Firth.

I called at a locksmith's to get a key fitted to my trunk, and then hastened with it to Mr. Slocum's to examine its contents. After a greeting from Capt. Crocker and Mrs. Slocum I went upstairs with my treasure and found that it contained besides several useful articles, letters from my grandmother, Mrs. Edward Spence, R. Hustwick and the Rev'd. Thos. Dykes with a copy of "Christian Experience"[85] as a present from Robert Hustwick to Mamma, and nine Hull Papers—the intelligence all of a cheering nature from our dear friends in England, and cholera quite extinct.

Towards noon I set out again for Flushing, and again got very wet in crossing the causeway a little beyond Williamsburg, where the wide Salt Marsh was completely covered by the tide. By the time I reached Newtown I was so thoroughly tired that I had to hire a waggon, and well I did for the full spring tide was in over the long causeway around the bottom of Flushing bay, for half a mile, to the depth of 2 or 3 feet, which would have detained me on the wrong side of the deluge for some time waiting for the ebb, and I should have missed my afternoon engagement at the Institute. As it was, I got back in time, and I am now comfortably seated in the calm twilight, before a bright anthracite fire, and preparing to answer the several pleasant letters I received this morning.

January 10
Mild & cloudy with a keen air, cold stormy evening, and snow storm in the night.

January 11
Very clear, with a piercing northern blast.

January 12
Quite clear, and excessively cold. The ice is now in skating condition.

January 13
Sunday. Light clouds and very cold.

In the morning Mr. Seabury preached from Prov's. 24: 30 to the end, and in the afternoon from Eccles. 11 1v.[86]

In all our exertions, there is one encouraging truth, that should never be lost sight of—each one reclaimed to a life of virtue becomes the centre of a purifying influence, and each one acted upon by him becomes in turn another centre. The circles continually widen, and extending the idea from one generation to another, moral arithmetic would fail to compute the benefits that one humble Christian may be the means of conferring upon his race.

It is a great mistake to suppose that spiritual exercises compose the business of life—the sole occupation of the Christian—they are his food, his nourishment to sustain him in the active labours of the vineyard. The husbandman may taste of the fruit of the vine, and refresh himself under its shadow, but the spade and the pruning knife and unwearied tendance form the staple of his duties, and the burden and heat of the day will be more familiar to him than the reviving shade.

January 14
After a frosty night, we have a day of extreme beauty with a strong elastic breeze.

At 8 P.M. Messrs. [Samuel] Seabury, [Jacob W.] Diller, [John G.] Barton, [?] Babcock, [Walter E.] Franklin, [John S.] Brenneman, [John Barrett] Kerfoot and myself met in Mr. Diller's room for religious exercises and improving conversation.[87] The passage selected for consideration was Matt. 12c, 14–32v.

January 15
Still clear and frosty with signs of snow in the afternoon. At 3½ P.M. I set off for the city and walking briskly got to Williamsburg Ferry at half past 5. It snowed a little for the last few miles. Took tea at Mr. Thompson's and found

all well except himself. His health is, I fear, precarious, having been confined to the house the greater part of the time since July last, and his lungs showing symptoms of weakness. He is a truly worthy and kind hearted man, and the whole family treat me as one of themselves. I could scarcely avoid spending the night with them. Mr. William Mount, the Painter, was there. He informs me that a friend of his, a Mr. Robinson, was delighted with my North River views, and said, "if the young man persevered in his adherence to nature he would become the first water colour painter in the country." So much for poor me. I expect he said it just to encourage me. I shall think myself well off if I ever rank with even the respectable painters of the Western world.

From Mr. Thompson's I went to Mr. Henry Cary's in Hudson Square. He and Mrs. Cary received me with marks of great pleasure. In their drawing rooms, which, by the by, are splendidly furnished, I had a great treat in several original pictures of exquisite execution, by old and modern masters. One landscape by "[Jan] Both" in oil, and two watercolours of "[John] Varley" were rich indeed. Mr. and Mrs. Cary pressed me to pass the night with them, but I have promised to do so the next time I come to New York. Mr. C. wishes me to spend some days with him, that he may introduce me to several friends at whose houses I shall find valuable pictures, and begs me to visit him without ceremony whenever I can do so. Mr. Cary is a man of fine taste and very superior conversation, and Mrs. Cary's manners are very engaging and refined. They live in the best style.

Bidding them good night I went down Broadway thro' a beating rain, the weather having wholly changed, and was glad to exchange it for Mr. Harvey's delightful drawing room. Mr. and Mrs. Harvey, Emily and Eliza Hosack were there. I chatted with them for half an hour, and took some wine and blanc-mange. Gave Mr. H. a letter from the Liverpool Packet. He says that he wrote to Mr. Jeremiah Warder the other day and mentioned me very kindly, and that he wishes to introduce me to Mr. [John] McVickar of Columbia College, who has seen my drawings and desires to know me.

From Mr. Harvey's I went on to Mr. T. Slocum's and found all well and as kind as ever, and slept soundly in the room I have always occupied of late.

January 16

Before breakfast I went down to the *Sir Edward Hamilton* and got another parcel of letters and papers from Hull. The *Dapper* unhappily for me, is chartered for Constantinople.

After breakfast, I paid Mr. Cole a visit and enjoyed his conversation and delightful landscapes, and after calling at Mr. Paulding's, and Mrs. Oakley's, I transacted some matters of business, went back to Beekman Street and bidding the Slocums good bye, walked on toward the Ferry.

The day most beautiful, strong wind, and sky fleeced over with light clouds. I may mention that the cholera is again in the city but excites no alarm.

At Williamsburg, the roads being very muddy and my limbs quite stiff, I hired a wagon as far as Newtown, and walked briskly the remaining 3 miles, arriving at Flushing at about 2 P.M. in high spirits after the pleasant variety of my little trip, and with plenty of occupation for the evening amongst my English letters and Papers.

January 17
High wind in the night, followed by a clear frosty day, the wind having lulled. In the afternoon, I called at Mr. Seabury's and after fortifying ourselves against the keen air with a glass of wine we walked out together until after sunset. He hoped I would join a literary association about to be formed among the Instructors and invited me to attend a meeting to be held tomorrow evening for organization, which I shall do with pleasure. He also proposes to me a ride along the North Shore of Long Island when the leaves begin to burst.

January 18
Very fine moderate weather. Ice carts with the usual summer supply are passing into the village from the neighbouring Ponds. Flushing contains, I should think, between one and two thousand people.

January 19
Frosty, still and very clear until evening when it became cloudy and threatened snow.

January 20
Sunday. Moist and spring like with warm vapours stealing thro' the air, as if Thomson's "Steaming Power" were visibly set afloat.[88]

Mr. Muhlenberg preached an excellent discourse on "Death" and in the afternoon read a tract contrasting the last moments of the infidel "Hume"[89] with those of the eminent Dr. Finley of Princeton, N.J. The sermon of the morning led me to read with satisfaction Wilkes' Essay on "true and false repose in death."[90]

January 21
Warm and foggy, telling of springtide rather than winter.

January 22
Quite as warm as yesterday with clear sky, fires again unnecessary and very little frost on the ground.

January 23
Mild and misty. The exhalations from the neighbouring salt marshes are anything but pleasant during this warm unseasonable weather.

Last evening Mr. Seabury delivered his inaugural on taking the chair as President of the "Eumathean Society"[91] which we have just formed for our mutual improvement in polite literature.

January 26
The weather has changed, a little Snow fell yesterday, and today we have a fine bracing air and the sleighs "out" for the first time this year.

January 27
Sunday. Fine sunny atmosphere.

Mr. Seabury in the morning preached from the leading parts of the 6th Romans. In the afternoon Mr. Muhlenberg read Dwight's sermon on "Independence of mind."[92]

January 28
Pure sky with a fine keen breeze. The winter is slipping away delightfully, to the poor in New York especially, its mildness is a great blessing.

January 29
Cloudy with a little frost.

At 8 I set off in the Stage for New York, and on arrival went to Mr. Cary's in Hudson Sq. and spent a most agreeable day, staying all night.

January 30
After breakfast, Mr. Cary ordered his carriage and took me down Broadway to get my watch which I had left to be regulated, and then drove me thro' the city as far as Grand Street Ferry where I bade him adieu with a promise to repeat my visit before very long. My walk to Flushing was fatiguing as I had to hasten to be in time for my classes. Perfect Indian summer weather—chill and cloudy, however, in the afternoon, and rain at night.

January 31
Before noon the rain changed to snow and sleet. A piercing wintry wind congealed the wet, and genuine winter again reigned supreme.

February 1st, 1833
Bright and keen, with a full inch of snow on the ground, and the merry sleigh bells jingling in all directions. The roads around are admirably calculated for the sport. They are wide, smooth and undulating.

February 2
Exceedingly beautiful with a fine keen air. In the afternoon Mr. Brenneman and I enjoyed an hour or two of fine skating.

February 3
Sunday. Very beautiful day, with a most transparent sky.

In the morning Mr. Muhlenberg preached from "If any man will do his will he shall know of the doctrine whether it be of God." In the afternoon Mr. Lewis on the "Laborers in the vineyard."

February 10

Sunday. The week for the most part has been cold, clear and frosty, with one or two days of severe, dry winter weather, but since Friday night much milder. The daily routine at the Institute as usual.

Today the "south wind blows softly"[93] and the air is full of Indian summer smokiness and the blue birds warbling.

Mr. Seabury gave us today an interesting narrative of the Life and Conversion of St. Augustine, Bishop of Hippo. It is compiled by himself from existing authorities and is a deeply affecting as well as an elegant and classical production, setting in the strongest light the efficacy of a mother's prayers. "*Si mater non orasset Augustinus non praedicasset.*" ["If the mother had not prayed, Augustine would not have preached."] Mr. Seabury tells me he intends to prepare it for publication.[94]

February 16

Since the 10th the weather has been very variable, the mild, however, predominating, but today we have a deep mid-winter snow, with the sleighs glancing about everywhere, and everything sharing the buoyancy and bounding freshness of the atmosphere. The banks of snow by the roadsides have been driven by the wind into crested drifts of dazzling whiteness, light like the foam on the top of a wave, and almost blinding in the clear sunshine.

I have sent off a parcel to England by the *Sir Edward Hamilton*. Finished an oil painting of the Highlands which I intend presenting to Mr. Governeur Kemble, and a water colour of "St. Anthony's" as a present to Mr. Cary.

February 17

Sunday. Charming day, the snow melting fast.

Mr. Muhlenberg gave us an admirable sermon on the parable of the rich man and Lazarus, and in the afternoon read us an eloquent passage from "Dick's Astronomer,"[95] which I read last year at Columbus, Ohio.

February 20

Ash Wednesday. Today and for the last two days the weather has been quite like spring again and the snow all gone.

Being the first day of Lent we had a short chapel service in the morning when Mr. Muhlenberg explained the nature and design of the observance and concluded with the Solemn Litany hymn (The 56). Mr. Diller selected my favorite "Benevento," and as he touched the chords of the organ a thousand memories of home came fresh upon me, memories which the thrilling harmony of that air never fails to call up, and the delicacy of Mr. Diller's execution threw a new charm around it.

February 21
Frost in the night, today clear and bracing.

I commenced today with my class in Descriptive Geometry, consisting of Messrs. L. Van Bokkelin and John B. Kerfoot, James West and Henry Sergeant, all young men of great promise.

February 22
Washington's Birth day. Brilliant sky—keen north wind.

In the evening the "Study" was decorated with appropriate emblematic transparencies, and we had a pleasant celebration, Messrs. Barton and Brenneman delivering admirable addresses.

A capital supper followed at which Mrs. Muhlenberg gave us her company.

Earlier in the day, however, we had a very different and solemn duty to perform, the funeral of Mr. Seabury's brother who has been wasting away for some time past, it is supposed from unceasing application to study. The members of the Institute formed a long procession, the societies wearing crape with their badges. We walked to the Village Episcopal church, where Mr. Muhlenberg performed the burial service and then the whole assembly moved to the edge of the grave in the church yard, where the earth closed upon the lifeless remains, "in the sure and certain hope of a resurrection· until life eternal," for he was a true christian. This is the first time I have heard the burial service since the death of my Grandfather in 1826, who was interred in the grave yard at Sculcoates near Hull. The Service was performed in the "Sacristy" and tho' a very little boy [age 12], it made an indelible impression upon me.

February 28
The last few days have been frosty but not very cold.

In a conversation today, Mr. Muhlenberg suggested to me that it would be well for me to make Mathematics my principal study. He is pleased with my plan of teaching Descriptive Geometry with the aid of models.

March 1, 1833
Snow again covers the whole country, and the breeze piles it up in drifts and ridges.

My Geometry class finished the "first principles" today, and seem to conceive of everything, [and] think very readily. One, however, requires a good deal of extra explanation. He is far behind the others in quickness and accuracy of thought.

March 2
Very clear, but the wind blew almost a hurricane and severely cold. It shook my room and sailed the snow heaps like waves, scattering them thro' the air. At night it was so cold that altho' I had abundant covering and a glowing anthracite fire, I suffered extremely and the water froze solid in my pitchers.

March 3
Sunday. The wind has abated but it is still very cold.

We were glad to see Mr. Seabury back again in the chapel today. He preached a very serious and practical sermon upon that verse in the 51 Psalm—"Against Thee, Thee only have I sinned."[96]

March 9
After a week of keen winter a thaw has decidedly set in, and today is warm and sunny. The melting snow makes out door exercise impossible and as I have no classes today I have spent it among my books and drawings very pleasantly. I have just begun Hume's England,[97] which I am reading with great interest. I have got as far as Edward The Martyr's assassination, about 980 A.D.

March 10
Sunday. Frosty night followed by a warm day.

Mr. Muhlenberg preached a most affecting sermon on the "restoration of the widow's son" (Luke 7. 12) and the beautiful Litany hymn was again sung to the plaintive harmony of "Benevento," which sends a thrill thro' me every time I hear it. The choir is composed of the best voices among the students and instructors, and the music very impressive.

Mr. Seabury in the afternoon from Psalm 19. 11.[98]

March 11
Dull and vapory without frost.

I have been troubled for a short time past with a pain in my right side when I draw a full breath which I do not like.

March 18
During the week, there has been a gradual change to warm weather again, and the spring songsters are flocking together from every quarter.

I have received a valuable parcel from Zanesville by Mr. Sullivan, and a long expected letter from England.

March 19
Tepid air, and clear sky.

I have the following presents ready for my next visit to New York—For Mr. Kemble an elevation of the "Catholic Chapel" at Coldspring, and an oil picture of the mountains seen from the ravine at the entrance of his "Forge Valley," for Mr. Earl a water colour view of New York Bay, and for Mr. Cary St. Anthony's mountain from Fort Montgomery, also in water colours.

March 22
Spring seems to be approaching and vegetation already exhibiting signs of life. The neighbouring salt flats are vocal with innumerable frogs.

At 4 P.M. I set out on foot for the city where I have not been for nearly two months' past. At 7 I crossed at Grand Street Ferry and went direct to Doremus, Snydam and Nixon's in Pearl Street[99] to inquire for Mr. Sullivan. I learned that he was at the Franklin, and went there at once to leave a parcel for him to take to Zanesville, and sent up a message to him that I should call again in the evening. I then went to Mr. Slocum's. They had wondered a great deal at my long absence, and seemed very glad indeed to see me in such excellent health. After a little chat, I went back to the Franklin and had a pleasant interview with Mr. Sullivan who will soon see my family at Zanesville. He gave me the names of his shippers in New York, and consignees in Baltimore and directed me how to send parcels &c. thro' them to the West. I then paid a short visit to Mr. and Mrs. Harvey, and slept very soundly at Mr. Slocum's after the fatigue of the afternoon.

March 23
Very warm and beautiful throughout.

After breakfast, I called at Mr. Paulding's and sat awhile with Mrs. Paulding and Miss Mary Kemble. Mr. Kemble is expected on Tuesday form Washington. I then went to Parker and Clover's and left my oil-attempt to be framed and sent to Mr. Paulding's for Mr. Kemble. Mr. Clover intimated to me that they would be glad to have a sketch or two of mine and would like to arrange with me to supply frames in compensation for them. I saw there two fine Landscapes in oil by young [James?] Ward, and a charming Ohio River picture by [Thomas] "Cole" which I like better than any of his works I have yet seen. His two early pictures which first brought him into notice are in the collection of Dr. Hosack. They are scenes among the Catskills and painted with great force and freedom.[100]

I called in Hudson Square and found Mrs. Cary in the Drawing room without visitors, so after a little conversation, she hastened on her walking dress and went with me to Mr. Robert Weir's studio in Franklin Street. Mr. Weir's numerous orders have induced him to relinquish a little engagement with the *New York Mirror* to furnish 4 landscapes per annum at $25 each for engraving, and on seeing my Ohio sketches, shown him by Mrs. Cary he had proposed that I should succeed him. After a short conversation, it was arranged that he should see the Editor in the course of the week and let me know the result on Saturday next. He had three fine pictures on the easel which we looked at awhile and then returned to Hudson Square.

I accepted Mrs. Cary's invitation to dinner at 3, and having presented her with the view of "St. Anthony's Mountain" I returned to Beekman Street and left the "New York Bay" for Mr. Earl, then took the "Coldspring Chapel" and a note for Mr. Kemble to Mr. Paulding's, stopped at Snydam & Reed's 5 Coenties Slip, about a box to be forwarded as directed by Mr. Sullivan (the box contained cuttings) and on my way back to Hudson Square I called and sat awhile with Margaret Van Antwerp, and at Mr. Thompson's, then joined my friends at the dinner table.

Towards evening I bid them adieu promising to dine in Hudson Square again on Saturday next, then rode to Newtown and walked the rest of the way to Flushing. Supper was over when I got there but Mrs. Ash, the housekeeper, soon had Tea ready for me, which was very acceptable altho' I did not feel any the worse for so much exercise under such an inspiring atmosphere.

March 25
Beautiful weather still.

At tea Mr. Muhlenberg informed me, much to my regret, of the resignation of Col. Thayer. Mrs. Paulding told me some weeks ago that the Colonel had been a good deal irritated by the interference of the President [Jackson] with some of his decisions, conduct which even when I was at the Point he had cause to complain of, but I was in hopes the "Executive" would have discontinued the annoyance.[101]

His loss to West Point will be irreparable. He has raised it to its present high position, and I don't know where they will find a successor able to carry out fully his admirable system.

March 29
The weather today and for the last few days has been delightful, invigorating beyond measure and not too cold.

At 4½ P.M. I left Flushing, on foot, and got to the Ferry about 7, well powdered with dust. The strong East river tide swept the boat across to Grand Street in five minutes, and I went immediately to Mr. Thompson's where I agreed to spend the night. Whilst we were waiting for tea Mr. Thompson told me of a situation that he thought would be very advantageous to me if I felt at liberty to relinquish my engagement at Flushing. He appears ever on the alert for my advantage. He says that his reason for not urging me to return to his office when I was on the North River was that business in New York had been reduced to such a state of confusion by the epidemic that he had little prospect of giving me full occupation, and thought it better to leave me free to accept any offer that might promise well. He now regrets it extremely for the city has rarely been known to be in so prosperous a condition, and the amount of building is very great. His continued illness has prevented his attention to the drawing department, and he has not yet been able to find a competent assistant. The young Italian stayed with him but a short time and he derived little advantage from his services. After tea, I called at Mr. William Kemble's on Hudson Square. Mr. Governeur K. passed thro' to Coldspring a day or two ago.

March 30

After breakfast, I went to Mr. Weir's who advised me to take my "Ohio views" and shew them to Mr. [James David] Smillie, who is the Steel engraver for the *Mirror*, so I went to Mr. Cary's, where I had left the books, and met with their usual kind reception. They pressed me to pass the day and Sunday with them, but I was not able even to stay dinner as I had intended. I promised, however, to accept their politeness very soon. They appear very anxious to promote my welfare in every possible way.

After looking over two large volumes of detached drawings in pencil and water colour of extreme beauty, I bade them good morning and hastened to the engraver's. We had a conversation of full two hours. He was delighted with my specimens, and says that their high finish is the very thing to engrave from on Steel, and finds great fault with Mr. Weir's works for his purpose as they are all in oils and very difficult to transfer to the plate so as to preserve the spirit of the original. His eulogisms on mine, however, I pass over. He recommends me to undertake immediately a view of New York from Brooklyn Heights of the required size and when finished make my arrangement with Mr. Geo. Morris whom he represents as very liberal in everything connected with his Journal,[102] and he is anxious that his landscape illustrations should be of the best character.

My 12 Ohio views could be executed on steel in the best style for $3,000, and would yield about $4 per copy.[103]

I next went to Parker and Clover's about the frame I ordered last Saturday. They wish my account to run until it shall amount to the price of a small picture which they would prefer to the money. I am strongly advised to paint something for the National Academy of Design.[104]

I called at Dr. Hosack's and had the pleasure of seeing him and Emily. He was delighted with a pencil drawing of "The Pavilion" which I handed him as a present to Mrs. Hosack. He shewed me the view of the "distant Catskill" which I had painted for him, framed and hung up on the walls of a noble apartment. He invited me to stay and dine with them but I was obliged to decline. He repeated the assurance of his readiness at all times to forward my interests, and requested me to call and dine with them whenever I felt at leisure to do so.

I went on to Mr. Thompson's, took dinner and then hurried to Grand Street Ferry, toiled on thro' the dust until I fell in with the Stage from the city, which soon carried me the rest of the way and I got home just as the sun was setting, much pleased with the gratifying kindness I meet with everywhere, and the prospects before me.

March 31
Sunday. Lovely weather, grass springing fast.

This is the first day of the Passion week and the chapel services were marked with a solemnity suited to the interesting and momentous events which it commemorates.

April 1st, 1833
Very warm with a soft summer breeze.

At morning prayers Mr. M. announced that there would be an evening meeting for religious exercises every day this week at which only voluntary attendance would be required. When the time came very few members of the Institute were absent, and the remarks of Mr. Muhlenberg on John 13 c.1–17 were very beautiful. Meetings so interesting and so appropriate to the season cannot fail to be profitable to us all.

April 5
Good Friday. The week has been and continues humid and spring like.

Today the studies are suspended, and full services both morning and afternoon. The chapel hung with black. In the morning Mr. Seabury preached from "God is love," and the Litany Hymn to "Benevento" was sung as usual with exquisite beauty.

April 6
Lovely spring day. The green turf is quite cheering, and the weeping willow is already gemmed over with the young leaf buds.

Immediately after breakfast I took my portfolio and went in the Stage as far as Williamsburg Toll gate, then walked on by the Brooklyn road as I intended making my sketch of the city from the "Heights" but just before I got into Brooklyn I was seized with such a faintness, pains in the joints and chilly tremor that I could scarcely proceed and by the time I reached the Heights I was quite unfit to do anything with my pencil so I spread my handkerchief on a dry piece of grass under the cedar trees and rested for nearly an hour, which enabled me to crawl along slowly to the nearest Hotel which was on Fulton Street a quarter of a mile off. Here I took a glass of Madeira and water and sat another hour, then returned to the Heights, determined to have my sketch, altho' still suffering from the headache and languor that had so unaccountably attacked me.

I made an outline of all the principal buildings and the general plan of the picture, then set out again on my return to Flushing. Fortunately, I found an

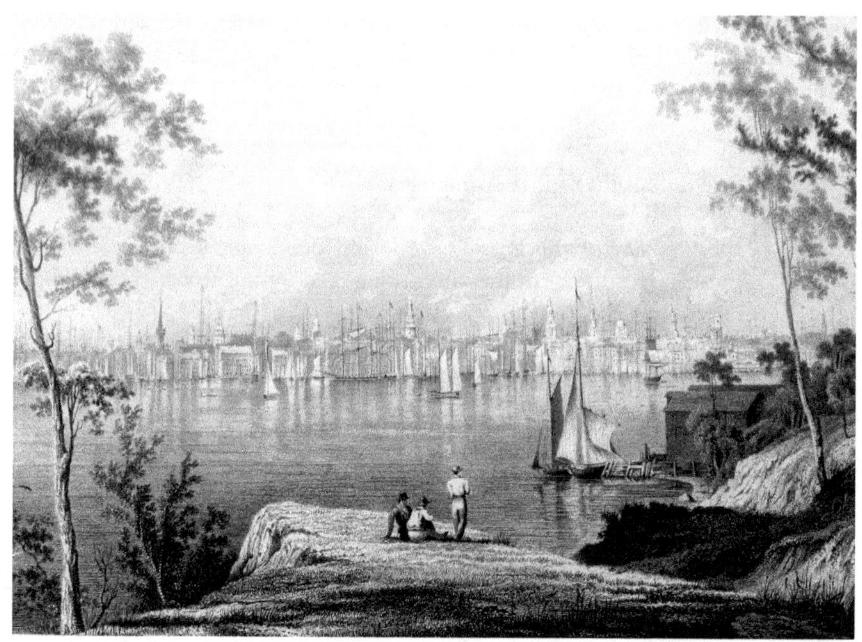

Figure 2.13 New York from Brooklyn Heights, 1834. Engraving by A.W. Graham for the *New-York Mirror*, printed by Robert Miller. Author's collection.

opportunity to ride four miles of the distance or I should not have reached there. As it was I got home with great difficulty and pain at 5 o'clock, and went to my room quite overcome with fatigue. An hour's sleep relieved me a good deal, and a cup or two of hot tea and hot foot bath afterwards, so that I rose the next morning a good deal better.

April 7

Easter Sunday. The chapel today presented a great contrast to its appearance on good Friday. White linen drapery took the place of the black crape, above the reading desk "RESURREXIT" appeared in large Roman characters and three vases of Hyacinths, and other flowers of the season, diffused an agreeable perfume thro' the room.

The Rev'd. Mr. Boyd of Philadelphia preached extempore from Matt. 28.6., "He is not here," and the Sacrament was administered to 11 communicants, the two clergymen, Mr. Muhlenberg, Mrs. Little and Mrs. Ash, five of the instructors and young Kerfoot of the Junior class. In the afternoon Mr. Boyd again preached extempore from Matt. 28, 19–20.[105] Both appeared to me admirable discourses.

Whole day cool and cloudy.

April 8
Before daylight I was awakened by a severe paroxyem of ague which, indeed, I fully expected after the attack of Saturday. The chill and headache were of long duration, followed by burning fever and intense pain round the eyes. When the man came to attend to my fire I sent for Diller who with the kindness natural to him attended to everything I needed and sent for Dr. [Asa?] Spalding. His medicines acted powerfully—calomel, salts & senna and antimony (as I had become intensely bilious) and by evening I felt light & easy, tho' too weak to stir out of bed, and a delightful letter from home by the evening mail did much to restore me.

April 9
Soon after I awoke I had Messrs. Franklin, Diller, Babcock and [Emmanuel] Fetter in my room to make enquiry after me. When they left, I dressed myself and looked out. The sky was quite transparent, and the green herbage, swept by a strong breeze, looked very cheerful, but I felt very faint having taken nothing since Sunday evening but a little thin gruel and half a square inch of toast.

"Thomas," however, soon appeared with a well loaded tray, and the Dr. came at the same time, and gave me hopes of escaping a return of the paroxysm. He gave me some tonic pills, which I took thro' the day, and remained quiet by a comfortable fire writing &c. Mr. Muhlenberg came over and sat awhile with me. My room is in the farm house of Mrs. Farrington, whose land adjoins The Institute Grounds, and is shaded by a noble walnut and plenty of fruit trees &c. Mrs. F. is very kind to me and sends me delicious currant jelly &c. Indeed, I have every attention.

April 11
Very beautiful with a strong East wind.

I am able to go out today, wrapped up in my cloak, and Dr. Spalding thinks he will have no occasion to repeat his visit, but I am a good deal reduced having had to take so much medicine. My apartment no longer looks like a sick chamber but has resumed its wanted appearance of pleasant retirement.

April 12
Moist springtide weather with a little thunder.

I had a call today from Prof. D. Mahan of West Point who says that the Colonel intends to leave the Point about the end of June, and proposes paying us a visit about the 1st of May which I rejoice to hear.

April 14
Sunday. Beautifully clear bracing weather both yesterday and today.

I feel now fully restored, and have great reason to pray that I do not become unmindful of the mercies of God because they are common.

I have received four delightful letters from friends in Hull by the Mail last evening. Mr. Muhlenberg preached from "He that believeth not is condemned already" and in the afternoon read part of Dr. Chalmer's introduction to "Baxter's Call."[106] I joined the family at dinner today for the first time since last Sunday.

April 15
Fine bracing air.

I have resumed my classes and usual employments today, and feel greatly improved, but still continue to take the Doctor's prescription of "bark" and Teneriffe, and breakfast at 8 instead of the usual Institute hour 6½.

April 17
The 19th anniversary of my birth day.

Mild and moist, highly favourable to the progress of spring which has already covered the peach and other fruit trees with fragrant blossoms.

A year ago today, returning from a long walk on the banks of the Muskingum [River] it was first proposed that I should try the East, and my success has been beyond my most flattering expectations. Still my absence from home has served but to endear it the more to me and I am now looking forward with longing hopes to the beginning of August, when I intend to cross the mountains and spend some time with my dear family. My father's business is now very favorably established in Zanesville, and everything seems to promise well. The favours of an ever-watchful Providence seem to multiply upon us on every hand.

April 20
The dawn being fresh and dewy I set out at 6 on foot for Brooklyn, breakfasted on the road, and a little after 9 reached the Heights and went to work to finish my sketch; then crossed the Fulton Ferry, called at Mr. Harvey's office, Mr. Slocum's, and the Pearl Street House to enquire after some gentleman from the West, and from there went to the old academy in Barclay Str., to see Du Bufe's famous pictures of "Adam and Eve."[107] The "Temptation" is a charming picture, the atmosphere full of golden light, and the "Eve" a perfect ideal of female loveliness. The sleeping Lion behind the figures, and the well-drawn limbs of Adam are very masterly but his Spanish looking head is the defective point in the picture. The representative and father of the whole race should exhibit the highest attainable reach of perfection, devoid of <u>nationality</u>. The "Expulsion" pleased me less but there are parts of it strikingly fine. In viewing these pictures no "thought infirm" need "alter the cheek" and that must indeed be an impure mind which could dwell upon such chaste and exquisite charms with any other emotion than that of innocent delight.

From the "Academy" I went to Mr. Smillie's and shewed him my sketch. He thinks it will be the very thing and advises me to finish it in black and white as being best to engrave from, and lends me 11 fine engravings to refer to for hints in sky &c. I returned home on the Stage, and am now at 10 P.M. sufficiently tired to enjoy a sound night's sleep.

April 21
Sunday. Balmy air, and all nature at rest under the happy sky.

Mr. Seabury preached from 2. Cor. 5–17, and described in powerful language the completeness of that change which is necessary to bring man back to that purity which he has lost.

In the afternoon from "Receive with meekness the engrafted word which is able to save your souls."

Dr. Muhlenberg played the organ today—he does so every now and then. His execution is delightful; indeed, his musical talents are of a very superior order. He seems much younger than his brother Mr. Muhlenberg.

April 25
The spring advances with rapid strides and my daily walks in the neighbourhood give me increasing pleasure. The woods and fields around are perfectly beautiful.

Today alas! I have symptoms of the intermittent again—chilly tremor, headache, pains in the joints, and excessive yawning. I am obliged to have recourse to "Salts" again.

April 26
The weather is perfectly lovely, but I am by no means free from agueish feelings. I fear the disease has taken a stronger hold upon me than I imagined.

April 30
The last few days have been almost lost to me as have been kept a close prisoner by the ague, and suffered extremely. Mr. Muhlenberg has kindly had a room provided for me in the Institute that my attendance may be more regular and everything is done to alleviate my condition.

May 6th, 1833
I have been getting weaker and weaker from the combined effect of disease and medicine, but am now beginning to recover strength again, and the intermittent seems to be overcome so that I am returning to my usual avocations and hope soon to be quite well again.

The warm season appears fairly established, and there is a luxurious softness in the air which contrasts strangely with the biting winds of winter. The *Cornus Florida* [flowering dogwood] sprinkles the woods with its white blossoms, like a firmament of stars, and multitudes of mocking birds, orioles and Tanagers hang about the blooming orchards.

May 11

The morning was ushered in by low hung clouds and dripping showers, however having finished my view for the *Mirror* I fortified myself by a hearty breakfast, and, wrapped in my cloak, went down to the Steamboat at 7 for New York. I read "Young"[108] on the way and got to the Slip at Fulton Street in about two hours. I found Mr. Smillie at his office in the "Exchange" and he assured me that he should take a real pride and interest in committing my picture to "steel."

The next thing was to see Mr. Geo. P. Morris, the Editor and Mr. Smillie went with me to his office to submit it for his approval. On the way, we called in at the exhibition of the National Academy, but O! What a falling off was there. Still there were Cole's fine Italian landscapes, and amongst the portraits there is a full length of Bishop Benj. Onderdonk by young W. Mount[109] which will greatly add to his already well merited reputation. His great forte seems to be in painting home scenes in the country, and especially on Long Island, which he executes with the spirit and fidelity of a "master."

Mr. Morris was highly gratified with the view of New York, and told me that he wished it to be immediately engraved, but that as the landscape department had been confided entirely to Mr. Weir, it would be necessary first to obtain his assent. This, however, from what had passed between Mr. Weir and myself, I regarded as a mere matter of form. Mr. Morris then handed me a large and very handsome volume which had been presented to his lady, and was already enriched by contributions from several eminent pencils, and requested to have something of mine. Mr. Morris expects that when filled the embellishments and *belles lettres* productions will be of sufficient interest & merit to lay before the public.

Mr. Smillie and I went together to Mr. Weir's. We found Messrs. [Thomas] Cole and [S.F.B.] Morse with him in his studio, but they soon left, and during the conversation that followed I was greatly surprised at Mr. Weir's total want of candour and consistency. His language was very different from that at our previous interview, and it appears that he has changed his mind about relinquishing the landscape department of the *Mirror*. He gave us to understand that the present engraving might be proceeded with, but as to the future supply (which appeared fully settled when I called with Mrs. Cary) he would not say anything satisfactory, and we left him without arriving at anything decisive. Mr. Smillie, it appears, has had more occasions than me to be disgusted with Mr. Weir's behaviour, and this morning's visit has greatly increased his bad opinion. In fact, Mr. Weir presumes so much upon his name and reputation that he seems to think he can do just as he pleases, and of course neither Mr. Morris nor Mr. Smillie wish to do anything that may give him any <u>just</u> ground to find fault. Mr. Morris, however, on hearing the result of our interview, ordered the engraving to be commenced at once, which I am glad of as Mr. Smillie's graver is the most delicate and spirited in the country, except perhaps Durand's. As to any future arrangements I shall leave them to be settled between Mr. Morris and Mr. Weir. I have already seen enough of the latter gentleman to desire but little business–intercourse with him. Tho' I respect his talents very highly, and may enjoy his society as a painter of sterling merit. I dined at Mr. Thompson's and at 5 took the Steamboat for Flushing.

May 18
A week of variable weather, daily employments in the Institute as usual.

Took the Steamboat to New York this morning. Called at Mr. Weir's to ascertain in express terms his intentions respecting the *Mirror*. I found him today very agreeable and unreserved, and he now repeated the proposition made when I first saw him. This seemed to gratify Mr. Morris highly when I saw him, and the engraver even more so.

I dined with Dr. Hosack who is just about taking his family up to Hyde Park for the summer.

After tea at Mr. Thompson's he walked with me to the Mechanic's Library.[110] He wishes to introduce me to the Directors and mature a plan for the drawing department which he desires that I should take charge of and reside with him again.

May 19
Sunday. I remained all night in the city, and went to St. George's in the morning, and in the afternoon to Ascension Church, where I heard a fine sermon from the Rev'd. Manton Eastburn on the passage "For The preaching of the cross is to them that perish foolishness &c."[111]

After service, I called at Mr. Cary's and apologized for not making my visit to him this time but hope to do so next week. Mr. Cary walked round with me to Mr. [Horatio] Wilkes' in Laight Street on the north side of the [Hudson/ St. James] Square. He introduced me to the family and we stayed some time, looked at some fine water colours by "[Hugh William] Williams" of Edinburg, an exquisite "Cole" and two "Sir Peter Lely's," undoubtedly genuine. They were obtained from Sir Joshua Reynolds by one of the family. Miss Wilkes handed me a scrap book filled with the admirable original sketches of American character by [Auguste] Hervieu, who accompanied Mrs. Trollope in her tour.[112] They are in water colour and in capital keeping. Here, as at Mr. Cary's, the rooms are filled with objects of taste. They live in the greatest elegance and affluence, and their house is frequented by the most polished circles in the city.

I took tea at Mrs. Van Antwerp's at their new and pleasant dwelling, corner of Mulberry and Grand Strts., and slept, as on the night before at Mr. Thompson's. I had felt very unwell, however, all day.

May 20
Today I bid adieu to my city friends and returned home. I took the omnibus to Yorkville by the Third Avenue. There I crossed the Ferry at Hallet's Cove, walked to Newtown, and then by a country waggon the rest of the way as the road across Flushing Marsh was entirely submerged.

May 26
Sunday. Another week lost by ague.

Dr. Spalding's Calomel and Quinine have removed the chills, but I am reduced to a state of extreme weakness, and am determined to adopt Mr. Muhlenberg's proposal of trying a change of air and relaxation among the mountains of the North River. I intend leaving here for New York on my way to West Point on Tuesday morning if strong enough for the journey.

May 27
Fully occupied in making preparations to start.

May 28
So rainy today that I am compelled to postpone leaving until tomorrow at 7 A.M.

July 9th, 1833
After quite a long interval I now resume my notice of passing incidents which has been suspended by illness and the pressure of other things. The last month of the session is fast wearing away. My daily occupations are all in regular train again, and my attacks of ague and recent journey have entailed upon me more work than usual. I give the present month to my drawing classes in lieu of time lost by illness during the quarter ending May 31, and James West requires a part of my time daily in Descriptive Geometry. The weather is warm and delightful with reviving breezes, and the country dressed in its richest summer suit.

In regard to the future I know of no situation in the East that would be so congenial to me as Flushing, is one where I could spend my time with greater profit, and in all probability I shall resume my apartment here after the vacation (at least if the plan meets the approbation of my family to whom it is submitted) and undertake the drawing department of the Institute on my own account, depending upon the number of pupils and my own success in "art" for the payment of expenses and profit. My room and attendance, board, washing, fuel & lights will not exceed $200 for the 9 months embraced in the "drawing session," (the regular scholastic session being 10 months from October 1st of each year). Then I have so many advantages here which cannot be reckoned by money values.

With respect to the *New-York Mirror* Mr. Morris has requested me to furnish him at once four drawings. One of these I have today completed in my best style, in black and white. It is a view of Clermont,[113] the seat of R. L. Livingston near Red Hook, from a sketch which I made during my recent trip to the Hudson. I shall receive $20 or $25 for it. I have also finished since my return on the 29th Ult. a view of Mr. Kemble's at Coldspring, also in black and white, which I intend for him. My indisposition seems altogether to have left me, and both physically and mentally I am in excellent working order, but I am severely annoyed by the musquitoes from the Flushing Marshes. We had none of these plagues in Ohio, and I am not yet used to them.

I am looking eagerly for an answer to my last "home letter" to determine my plans for the vacation which commences on the 1st of August, and am also expecting letters from England. Rarely have I spent a month of such varied enjoyment as the June just passed on the North River, and never have I had greater occasion to congratulate myself on the receptions, and universal goodwill I met with everywhere. I had a delightful fortnight at Mr. Governeur Kemble's, surrounded by the charming scenery of The Highlands, and enjoying the agreeable and profitable companionship of Mr. Kemble and his amiable sisters, and the numerous visitors at his hospitable and elegant home. Then another fortnight at Mr. William Young's at Saugerties, almost within the shadow of the noble "Catskills." Here, altho' before a stranger, experienced the kindest attentions especially during an unfortunate attack of ague, which seized me after a boat excursion with John [Travers or possibly Simmons?] and the young ladies up to the "Falls of Esopus Creek." We were exposed to a hot June sun all the way.

The neighbourhood of Saugerties, and the Livingston Manor on the opposite side of the River—Mr. Robt. L. Livingston's at Clermont and Mr. Robt. Tillotson's at Red Hook—supplied me with a variety of beautiful subjects for

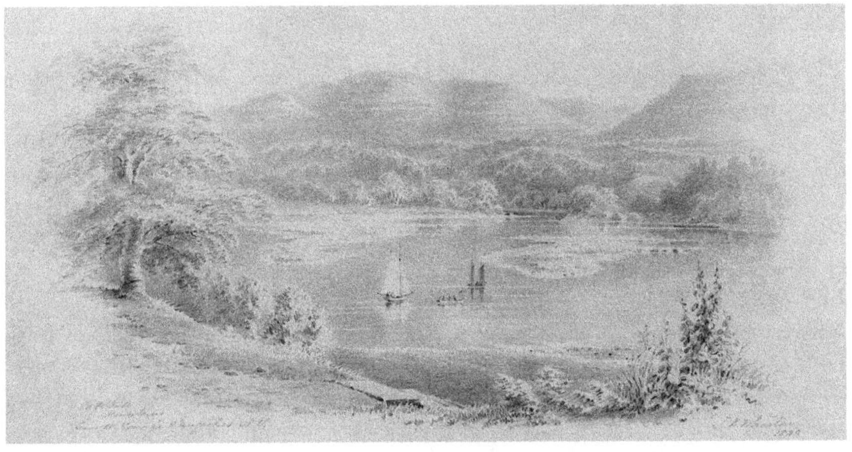

FIGURE 2.14 Catskill Mountains from W. Young's, Saugerties, NY, 1840 (NYPL drawing 22). New York Public Library, Divisions of Prints and Drawings, New York.

my pencil. Indeed, I know of but few regions richer in materials for the painter. At Mr. R. Tillotson's I spent two days with great pleasure. Mrs. Tillotson is one of the most charming women I have met with in the United States, and they have quite a large family. The view from their mansion looking across the Lawn down the Hudson is very fine. Two large Islands, clothed with wood, break the uniformity of the stream, and distant ranges of hills give a beautiful outline against the sky.

The different manufacturing works on the Creek at Saugerties are highly interesting. The rolling Mill, owned by the West Point Foundry Association, and under the management of Mr. W. Young, stands foremost.[114] Then there is a white lead factory, Henry Barclay's Paper Mill, a chair Factory, axe Factory &c., &c., the last not yet finished. The water power which supplies all this variety of heavy machinery is derived from the "Esopus Creek" which is gathered into a picturesque Lake [Barclay Pond] just above the works, and then falls over a wide pile of rocks 60 feet high into the creek below which speedily threads its way into the North river. The supply is unfailing and is admitted to the machinery by a canal cut in the solid Trap rock,[115] 20 feet wide and about one fourth of a mile in length.

In the Rolling Mill, the water wheel which turns the rollers is 24 feet diameter, & 18 broad, that working the ponderous trip-hammer 30 feet diameter 10 broad. Cylindrical race in flume conveying the water from the canal to the wheels, 5 feet diameter. Trip hammer weighs 4½ tons, and the Anvil Block which is 9½ tons was cast at the West Point Foundry, and is the heaviest casting ever made in this country. The Camerling[116] raising the Hammer is 8½ tons, having 5 teeth. The Hammer averages 90 strokes per minute, but when required will give as high as 120. The motion is communicated from the water wheel by a cog wheel on its shaft 14 feet diameter, to a pinion wheel on the shaft of the Camerling 4½ feet diameter, the rotation of which latter (The Camerling) works the hammer.

The Paper Manufacture is an extremely beautiful, simple, and speedy operation. The Mill packs no less than 1500 Reams per week.

On the 27th June, I took my last look at the Catskills, passed the night with Mr. Kemble and arrived in New York the following evening. Took up my quarters at Mr. Thompson's and reached home the next day, June 29th.

July 13, 1833

Between 6 and 7 I set off for New York on foot, the morning mild & fresh with a thin veil of clouds. Myriads of musquitoes in crossing the Marsh. Thousands of fine raspberries and wild blackberries along the road side to cool the blood, but the latter part of the walk was very hot and oppressive, and when I got to town I had to go about so much in the midday sun that I was kept in a profuse perspiration the whole time. I am convinced that the heat of a New York summer, and the habits of living would never suit me, and it will be far better to remain in the country at Flushing.

At 10 I crossed the East River, called at Mrs. Van Antwerp's, Mr. Cary's and Mr. Thompson's, then went to the lower part of the city.

Mr. Morris was absent from the city on the North River. Mr. Smillie, I find, has not yet finished his plate of the "Departure of the Israelites" which he must do before he begins mine.

At Mr. Slocum's I found all as usual.

Having taken a lunch at the Exchange in Wall Street, went to Mr. James K. Paulding's to give him the "view" for Mr. Kemble. Mr. P. was so much pleased with it that he suggested to have it introduced into the *Mirror* with a descriptive article from his own pen, and kindly offers to use his influence with Mr. Morris in my favor.

I named the difficulty of selecting suitable subjects, but he thinks he can easily settle that for me and that any of my outlines of North River scenery might be taken with the certainty that they would be superior to anything that has yet appeared in that periodical. This Mr. Paulding said without reserve. He gave me a pressing invitation to dine with him, but I was obliged today to decline. I left the view of "Clermont" with him to be handed to Mr. Morris. I returned to Flushing by the afternoon "Boat" and slept soundly after the fatigues of the day.

July 15
I have been confined to my bed this afternoon by another attack of ague. In the evening I received an answer to my last letter home. It has determined me as to the vacation. I shall proceed with as little delay as possible after the 1st Augt. to Zanesville and spend the whole vacation and part of October with my dear family, and then return to Flushing for another session. This arrangement will prevent my paying promised visits to Mr. Kemble, Mr. Governeur, Mr. Young and Mr. Tillotson, and of seeing Leslie, the Painter, who is expected at West Point from England in October, but I propose taking the Baltimore route in going, and the northern route by the New York Canal and North River in returning and pay a short visit to each of the gentlemen who have invited me on my way down.

July 19
The weather has been charming for the last few days with fine breezes.

The hour for my ague has passed without a symptom, and I indulge a hope that it has taken a final leave. My mind is so full of the promised pleasures of home that I can scarcely think of anything else, yet I rejoice that it is settled for me to return again to Flushing.

July 21

Sunday. Mr. Muhlenberg in preaching from Prov's. 4, 14.15, took occasion to express the strongest disapproval of stage performances as at present conducted. He used the following language,

> One presumptive argument against the Theatre, which would lead us to condemn it before examining it for ourselves, is this—good and reflecting men in every age have recorded their opinions against it. Thus, even among the ancient heathen we find their sages condemning the Theatre. Plato says, "Plays raise the passions and pervert the use of them and are dangerous to morality."[117]

Again

> The diversions of the Stage are prejudicial to temper and sobriety. They swell anger and desire, feelings are cherished, which ought to be dreaded, virtue loses ground, reason grows weak, vice makes an insensible approach, and steals upon us in the disguise of pleasure. Rollin tells us that the wise Solon expressed his dislike to an exhibition of this kind by striking his staff upon the ground. According to Livy professed players were degraded from their tribes and were not allowed to serve in the army. The story of [Decimus] Laberius shews us how the Romans regarded the profession of an actor; compelled by Ceasar at an advanced period of life to appear on the stage to recite some of his own works, he declared his character as a Roman citizen sullied and disgraced. "After having lived" said he, "sixty years with honor, I left my house this morning a Roman knight but shall return to it this evening an infamous stage player. Alas, I have lived a day too long." Cato strenuously opposed the establishment of a regular Theatre, asserting that it would be to Rome a more dangerous Carthage than that which they had just destroyed. Other testimony from the same quarter might be easily added, but what has been addressed is enough to shew that it does not require the existence of the superior tone of <u>Christian</u> morality to take offense at the stage.

It has been the practice of late to propose to the pupils on Sunday morning some prominent doctrine, requiring them to furnish in writing as many texts of Scripture as each one could collect, bearing upon it. From the sheets thus furnished Mr. Muhlenberg would read a selection at afternoon service and then give at length an exposition of the doctrine. This is an admirable exercise as it increases the general familiarity of the pupil with the Sacred volume and especially with those parts of it which have composed the regular Sunday lessons committed to memory during the Session. The proposition today was "What say the Scriptures of the future punishment of the wicked, and why do we believe that it will be everlasting?" Mr. Muhlenberg's remarks on the abundant proofs elicited were very fine and convincing, and he called attention to the fact that the happiness of the just was "prepared for them before the foundation of the world," while the torment of the wicked was "prepared for the devil and his angels," intimating strongly that "God willeth not the death of a sinner but rather that he turn from his wickedness and live."[118]

As next Sunday will be the last of the session, the communion will be administered and the term closed in a manner consistently with the character of the Institution. The calm retirement of this place is well calculated to keep alive a spirit of devotion. It is also a great aid to the formation of studious habits. Next session I propose by a proper course of mathematics to qualify myself to combine instruction in the "exact sciences" with my profession as a Painter, and nowhere could I enjoy greater advantages for such an object than at Flushing.

I had some conversation with Mr. Muhlenberg on the subject this evening. He seems highly satisfied with the arrangements about the drawing &c. for next session.

The weather continues very pleasant, and this evening the sunset was perfectly beautiful.

July 22
Close and vapoury in the morning, clear in the afternoon and so warm that the thermometer rose to nearly 100° in the shade. Everybody had on the lightest and loosest summer clothing and yet complained of the heat, but the ague must have made a great difference in me, for I felt quite comfortable in woollen with an under vest of Flannel.

July 23
Very beautiful with a fine cool breeze. Several instances of sudden illness occurred yesterday from exposure to the intense heat.

Wrote to Mr. Kemble and Mr. W. Young telling them of my plans for the next three months.

July 24
Morning warm and clear, but in the afternoon a drenching rain and frequent lightning made a grateful change in the summer air.

July 25
Shady sky and pleasant temperature.

In the evening, we attended the last "voluntary meeting" of the session. Mr. Muhlenberg suggested a plan to keep alive during the vacation the associations derived from our "Thursday evenings" of the session. He has selected the following chapters from St. John's Gospel—3, 5, 7, 10, 11, 13, 15, 17, being one for each Thursday, and proposes that at 8 o'clock on that evening each one should read his chapter and then spend awhile in such profitable reflections as may spring from the perusal, thus uniting us in spirit, while scattered over the country at our respective homes. This is an admirable Institution, and doubtless much genuine piety exists here. This, however, God alone can judge of, but it is apparent that more good order and diligence need not be desired. None of those improper expressions, so common among school boys, seem current here. At least I have never heard them once, and there is but little of those petty quarrels, bickerings and ill-will which disgrace all large assemblages of youth. The general sentiment here seems against them.

July 28
Sunday. The Last Sabbath of the session, and as the Sacrament is to be administered every thing conspires to promote calm and serious thought. Harmony and brotherly love were beautifully enforced by Mr. Muhlenberg at a meeting of the communicants before morning service, and Mr. Seabury's sermon on Christian Friendship served to strengthen this impression.

The evening service was postponed until after supper and the lovely sunset was just fading out when we assembled in the chapel to engage in the solemn offices of the Liturgy, for the last time. Mr. Muhlenberg's sermon was on the scriptural account of future happiness. What subject more appropriate! When his auditors were rejoicing in the prospect of the family circle, and the speedy enjoyment of home, what a ready transition to that final home in the heavens which we all hope one day or other to attain.

The devotional exercises in which we have been employed today will not, I am persuaded, soon be forgotten, nor will the truths which have been so faithfully presented to us readily be effaced from our minds. May they, on the contrary, sink deep and bring forth their fruit in due season.

July 29
I have today dismissed my classes. The pupils in drawing have given me every satisfaction, and in "Descriptive Geometry" James West has got thro' the graphic solution of spherical triangles.

Tomorrow I propose making my final arrangements in New York, and on Thursday I trust I shall be on the way home. Weather as lovely as usual of late.

July 30
Warm air, clouds and wind.

I have changed my plan and now intend passing the day I leave Flushing in New York and then proceeding to Baltimore the day following.

Everything at the Institute is to be conducted in the usual order to the last.

July 31
The last day of the session is one of uncommon beauty and everything looks cheerful and crowned with hope—good humour, good order and good feeling everywhere throughout the large household.

Received a parcel from Hull per the *Sir E. Hamilton*. Went to Mr. Seabury's to bid farewell. Took tea with Mr. Sherwood, and in the evening had everything in readiness for an early departure tomorrow morning "for Home."

I remained at Zanesville between two and three months. My father had taken a new house with more ground attached to it, and on the hill opposite the place which we first occupied. He and my brothers were constantly and busily occupied at the warehouse and store, but as it was to me a time of complete leisure I spent the greater part of it with my dear mother in reading to her, long conversations and taking her about that beautiful neighbourhood, whenever the skies and her health permitted. Sometimes I took long excursions alone either on foot or on horseback and this mode of life in the pure autumnal air completely obliterated all traces of the ague from which I had suffered so long at the East.

The time for my return to Flushing came at last, and I bid a long, lingering final adieu to my dear mother and my home. It was a dark, gloomy midnight. The thought of it and its sad associations, even at this distance of time produces an involuntary shudder.

The session of 1833–1834 glided away happily and usefully at the Flushing Institute. Alternate duties, studies and recreation, and pleasant visits at intervals to my friends in the city. I became very much attached to that kind of life, and to the friends I made at Flushing, and I had sufficient leisure and inducement to follow up my favorite employment of painting in connection with classical and other pursuits. The vacation commenced in the first of August and soon after I took an excursion up the Hudson, during which I made some hasty notes as follows.

August 12, 1834
The opposition [i.e., competition] on the river is running high. The little *Westchester* has lately been competing with the Old North River Line at $1 instead of $3 to Albany. The *Old Line* accordingly has reduced the fare to two dollars and put on the splendid *North America* pro. tem., at fifty cents to kill the opposition. I saw her leave the wharf this morning at 6. It was a curious spectacle. From stem to stern one dense mass of human beings, scarcely less than one thousand in all, of all people, nations and languages, joined together with a compactness which in anticipation of a fierce 12 o'clock sun was truly hideous. The *West Chester* left immediately after and I then walked quickly to the noble *Champlain* and at seven o'clock was again on my beloved Hudson. Its happy shores have become to me almost part of existence.

At 10½ I reached the Point, and crossed at once to Coldspring. I found Paulding and Miss Kemble on the lawn, and to my great delight we were joined in a few moments by Mr. Gov'r Kemble and Washington Irving. After an introduction and a little conversation, I found that my friends here had formed a large party, including Mr. Irving, for the Catskill mountains tomorrow, and thence to Stockbridge, Mass., where several of them will spend the rest of the summer. The Catskill mountain house[119] was my own destination, so that I was only too glad to join the party. Indeed it could not have fallen out more charmingly. I have calculated much upon my first visit to the Catskills, but I could not have hoped for such a pleasure as is now before me—the company of one whose name is not only identified with the choicest gems of American Literature, but with these very mountains too. Their most secret haunts have received a new interest from his graceful prose, and the genius of "Irving" is engraved on their rocks, and intwined with the spray wreaths of their water falls.

The incidents of the day connected me at once with those delightful "reunions" during my visit to Col. Thayer, so like in all but his absence. At 4 o'clock a boat appeared rounding the Point of Constitution Island, and then I had the pleasure of shaking hands with Lieut. Leslie, and [Thomas] Sully the Painter, with whom I had long been familiar thro' Mr. Leslie's frequent description. Robt. Weir, now professor of Painting at the Point, and two other gentlemen accompanied them. We all sat down to dinner about five—as choice a party as I ever had the pleasure of dining with, and not too large so that the "ice" was restricted entirely to our host's delicate wines, and an easy and spirited table-talk gave a double relish to the delicious "cuisine." Soon after the ladies

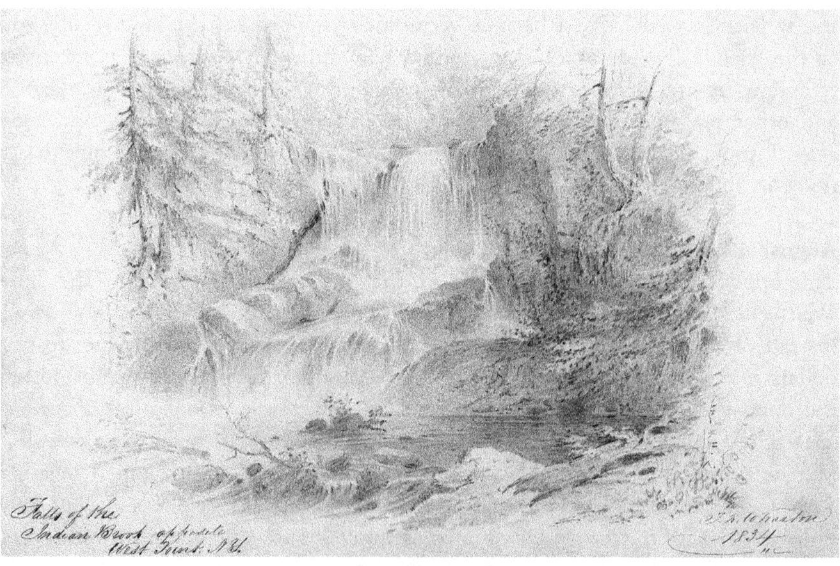

Figure 2.15 Falls of the Indian Brook opposite West Point, NY, 1834 (NYPL drawing 16). New York Public Library, Divisions of Prints and Drawings, New York.

withdrew Irving and Sully followed them, and set out on a moonlight excursion to the "Falls of the Indian Brook." I regretted much that I had declined joining them. Sully gave us a graphic description of the trip on their return. Irving's elegant and playful humour sparkled all the while as they wandered among the rocks of that beautiful and secluded dell, but he concluded that altho' it might do very well for the young people at the "witching noon of night" yet for himself he must conform his ambition to the retrospect of what he has already seen for the rest of his life.

There is a manly gentleness about him, and an unaffected simplicity that is perfectly charming; in conversation, affable and often sportive—no effort, no parade, and yet the most elaborate care could hardly produce more classic periods, and a silver thread of humor gleaming thro' the whole. He plays with the little ones on the grass-plots and enters into their amusements with the same ease and perfect adaptation that marks his intercourse with all around him. The scene of his exploit this evening is so like one of his own elegant pictures that I cannot forbear describing it—

> Our first essay was along a mountain brook among the Highlands of the Hudson "a most unfortunate place for the execution of those piscatory tactics which had been invented along the velvety margin of quiet English rivulets. It was one of those wild streams that lavish among our romantic solitudes unheeded beauties enough to fill the sketch book of a hunter of the picturesque—sometimes it would leap down rocky shelves, making small cascades, over which the trees threw their broad balancing sprays—and long nameless weeds hung in fringes from the impending banks, dripping with diamond drops—sometimes it would brawl and fret along a ravine in the matted shade of the forest, filling it with murmurs, and after this termagant career would steal forth into open day with the most placid demure face imaginable, as I have seen some pestilent shrew of a housewife, after filling her home with ill-humour, come dimpling out of doors, swimming and curtseying, and smiling upon all the world."

Sketch Book - The Angler[120]

Whilst our romantic friends were hunting moonshine among the ripples of the "Indian Brook," Mr. Kemble and his brother Richard, Mr. Paulding, Leslie, Father O'Reilly, an honorable senator from New England, and myself took the cool of the evening on the Lawn and Piazza until coffee was handed round, and after a "chasse" I walked leisurely down with Leslie to his Boat, and promised to be over at the Point the next day in time to make him a call before leaving for Catskill. The boat pushed off and I rejoined my friends on the garden chairs under a spreading chestnut, where we beguiled the time in animated conversation, in which the good Father played a conspicuous part, until the rest returned from their pilgrimage.

August 13

After breakfast Mr. Irving threw himself on the smooth green sward in front of the house and taking a book observed that the present style of imaginative works was far too hasty and negligent—dashed off with rapidity, and replete with crudities—arising, he thought, from a too ready compliance with the manner of [Sir Walter] Scott, which became necessary to him from the great demand for his works, but which, even in him, was attended with disadvantages that subsequent writers don't seem aware required the redeeming qualities of his commanding genius to make amends for.

Just at this moment Mr. Kemble's man Friday, Abram, emerged from the woodpath leading to the waterside, and I commissioned him to order me a boat at half past nine. The oarsman was punctual, and on landing at the Point I called upon Mr. Rogers, at the Hotel to inform him that Mr. & Mrs. Muhlenberg would be up in the morning's boat, according to their arrangement just before I left the city. I then repaired to Mr. Leslie's, stopping for a few moments with Col. Morris and Mr. Weir in crossing the Plain, and letting my eyes and thoughts rest intently for a while on my former delightful place of abode with the "Colonel," and the matchless scene up the River.

I spent a very pleasant half hour at Mr. Leslie's. Sully is a man of the first order—all the polish of cultivated society, and his taste refined to the utmost, and an amiable urbanity, which in union with his great abilities renders him an object equally of esteem and admiration. Naming a picture in which the artist had laboured to give the highest finish, "The execution" he observed,

> was faultless. The very radiations of the iris—even the indefinite little window reflected in the pupil of the eye—but at the true distance to embrace the <u>whole</u>. I was astonished to find how much, and yet how very little the painter had accomplished, with the utmost nicety of <u>detail</u>—the general <u>effect</u> was almost a nullity. In filling up a picture, he justly remarked, it is a beautiful thing to know where to stop—of this your brother"—to Mr. Leslie—and David Wilkie are fully conscious.

Here Mr. Leslie handed us a fine illustration of this principle, a little jewel of his brother's, "The Gypsey Girl," full of grace and delicacy, yet touched with the utmost freedom and spirit—nothing negligent—nothing redundant. This is one of Leslie's great excellencies, the happy mean between inattention on the one hand and superfluous effort on the other.

"I confess I was surprised"—continued Mr. Sully—"to hear a man of such acknowledged taste and discernment as Mr. John Q. Adams pass high encomiums on the picture in question." This now is an eye said he—"this is just as it should be, nothing wanting." "But there is a degree of poetry even in portrait painting" (the branch of Art in which Mr. Sully has attained his celebrity, and thus modestly referred to)—

> The impression made by a portrait ought to be exactly that left after a visit to some celebrated character in whose company we know beforehand that we could be but a few moments—to any inquiries as to the shape, colour and materials of his dress &c. our answers would be sufficiently vague and indefinite, but the expression of his countenance, the marked and leading traits of his features, in short the soul pictured in the face, here we should be at no loss, here we could expatiate, and the absence of these all essential points, or their feeble rendering can never be compensated for by the completest finish that the pencil can attain.

Mrs. Leslie was full of animation, and made me promise, should I bring my mother to the Point, to acquaint her with it immediately. I don't know anything that would do my mother so much good as the air of this delightful Plain. My once little friend Miss Emma is growing apace and bids fair to become a highly interesting and accomplished woman.

I next called on the Rev'd. Mr. Warner who begged me to establish my headquarters at his house as soon as I could arrange to come back again to the "Point."

> I may be absent—said he—when you arrive, as my health requires a visit to the "Springs," but my servant has orders that you shall be well attended to until my return, and I trust, he added warmly, that you will look upon this invitation as the expression of my sincere desire.

I lingered awhile with him at the door, and then hastened down to the wharf. Our party had arrived but Mr. Paulding having been taken unwell, Miss Kemble told me they had determined to wait another day. However, as my time was limited, and I was anxious to see as much as possible of the "mountains" I thought I had better go on before. The *Albany* soon came sweeping round the Point, and threw in her lines. The hitherto quiet dock was at once a scene of bustle and hurry, Porters loaded down with baggage, and a long line of passengers following. Messrs. Muhlenberg and Van Bokkelen were amongst them and wanted me much to stay another day at the Point, but I stuck to my plan and went on board. In a few seconds the rushing steam ceased at the signal of the engine bell, and we were ploughing a rapid furrow under the shadow of the Highlands, leaving a long wake of foam behind on the dark and silent River.

After dinner at 2 I went on the forward deck, and watched the changing curves of the Catskills as one peak after another came into view. The transparent blue colour of the chain deepened every moment and the slant afternoon sunbeams traced luminous lines of exquisite beauty on every salient angle. The river was perfectly still and bright sunbows glanced among the spray flung off from our cutwater.

At 5 we took our seats in the stage at Catskill landing—that is, I and half a dozen others—drove two miles to the village where we waited for the mail, paid our dollar and then hastened on at a round pace towards Pine Orchard—10 miles. Seven miles lay thro' a broken rugged country under very partial cultivation. We then commenced by starlight the ascent of the mountain, over a very good road with an inclination of one in five. Most of the passengers went up on foot, and the driver walked by the side of his horses, reining them up every five or ten minutes to rest and breathe. The air brushed past pure and keenly, flavoured with the spicy incense of the "Mountain Pine" and at 10 o'clock we all assembled at the tea table, in a capital house perched on the brink of the precipice—3,000 feet above the river,[121] which we left behind us.

The first thing, of course, on arriving at the top, was to take a peep over the ledge, which at this shadowy hour looked like a stupendous seacliff with a "spectral ocean surging at its foot."

The journey sharpened my appetite for a well-supplied table, and after an excellent supper I retired at once to my bedroom, anxious, in common with all visitors to the "Mountain House" to be on the Piazza at sunrise.

August 14
I slept well and was up and dressed at dawn—but what pen shall describe the scene when

> ____________________ Th' orient sun
> Shot parallel to th' earth his dewey ray
> Discovering in wide landscape all the East.[122]

Far beneath in that glorious valley gleamed the lovely Hudson threading its silver course with many a winding for upwards of 80 miles, until lost in the embrace of the distant Highlands. The mountains on the confines of Dutchess and Columbia counties lay bathed in a flood of golden sunlight, and swept in a vast curve around the checkered mass of country lying beneath, and on either hand rose two lofty peaks, some two or three hundred feet above the platform on which we stood, covered with thick forests, whole dark masses wrapt, the whole face of the mountain and sloped away in rapid curves to the plains far below. From this elevation, all inferior heights were sunk to flatness as all earthly distinctions to the superior glance of angels, and the country we had passed thro' though diversified with hills and deep romantic glens, seemed here reduced to an endless level, where not even the differences of colour produced by shadow convey the least idea of altitude or depression.

After enjoying this scene for some time, I went back to my room for my portfolio, and walked thro' the wood to the beautiful mountain lake about half a mile from the brink of the ledge. There are two such lakelets, hemmed in by forests and the tops of the higher Peaks and forming the reservoirs to the celebrated Falls of the Cauterskill. I made a sketch of the nearer sheet of water and then returned to breakfast, after which I went to the "Falls" and spent the morning in sketching and rambling among the rocky defiles until dinner at 3. At table a lady and gentleman who had seen me pencilling in the morning entered into conversation with me and requested permission to see my portfolio. The lady had been much in Italy and appeared well acquainted with pictures and painters. She herself had been a pupil of "Williams" of Edinburg; two of whose elegant "watercolours" I had seen at Mr. Wilke's in N. York. They were both pleasant and companionable people, and in the evening I showed them my sketches which they were kind enough to admire exceedingly.

Soon after sunset, a sudden sweep of clouds passed over the pure moonlight, a rushing storm of rain and lightning obscured half the mountains, while part of the wide expanse below lay still and quiet with the stars sparkling above it like crystals from the Eastern wave. I had always thought the gorgeous contrasts of "[John] Martin" extravagant till now. Here nature herself sets the seal of truth on his wildest creations.

At 9 o'clock the expected party gained the summit. The storm had passed by as suddenly as it came. After a short detour along the ledge by moonlight we retired to the well-lighted saloons and spent the rest of the evening in conversation and promenading among the numerous guests from below.

August 15

Soon after breakfast we all repaired to the "Falls of the Cauterskill," Governeur Kemble and I on foot, Mr. Irving and the rest with the ladies in a waggon that plies continually between the house and Falls, passing around the Lake and along the gurgling streamlet which conducts the water to the edge of the cataract. We regained our party at this point and placed ourselves under the direction of the guide. The rocks here form a stupendous semicircular chasm, thro' which the water, dashing along a natural spout, takes a bold leap of 180 feet into a broad granite basin then hurries along a platform of a few yards and takes a second bound of 80 feet more into the wild, chaotic ravine which forms the infant bed of the Catskill River. A deep cavity lies behind the principal Fall owing to the projection of the rocky ledge above. The pathway winds thro' it, and carries you over a dry gallery between the water and overhanging wall of granite. When visitors reach the edge of the second Fall, the water which was hitherto but a mere ooze is let off by the guide above in a fine graceful stream. Nature in one of her happiest moods has interposed a rocky point about half way down, which parts the water into a number of lesser gushes, and in an instant, the whole lower part resolves itself into a pure delicate veil of the finest gauze, waving to and fro in the breeze in fields of incomparable elegance. At the end of a long rod above is suspended a bucket in which refreshments are lowered when signalled for. Irving playfully insisted that it was intended to gather up the waters expended at each exhibition for a fresh display. The water becomes so scanty during the latter weeks of summer that the guides economise it by a rude dam above, at other seasons, however, it rushes down in a furious torrent, filling the channels beneath with foam and fragments torn from the rocks in its passage. The hollow that receives the falls is romantic in the highest degree. Bold heaps of rock manteled over with the richest mosses lie scattered about in profusion. Vegetation upsprings from every crevice. Large trees intertwine their roots over every foot of soil, and insinuate them with the utmost pertinacity into every fissure. Festoons of vines and ivys droop gracefully from the branches. In short nothing seems wanting to complete the beauty of this wild dingle but the destruction of those intolerable shanties which profane the verge of a precipice in every way worthy of the Sybilline Temple of Tivoli.[123]

The ladies entered into the spirit of the thing with the highest zest, and Mr. Irving made himself universally agreeable. Indeed, he entered into everything with as much glee as the most juvenile of the group and the points we explored tho' wild and rugged, and apparently quite shut out from the living, breathing world were so accessible that we revelled in their choicest beauties without paying the usual tax of over exertion, and we returned to the "Mountain House" in high spirits after a morning that will be to most of us a sunny spot for memory to rest upon.

The whole party having determined to go on to Stockbridge, descended to the River at noon in time for the Boat from below, but as I was going in the opposite direction, down the River, I lingered still on the mountain, and spent the evening in searching out some of its most poetical seclusions. In one place, I came suddenly upon a tall Pine grove, carpeted throughout with the deepest, loftiest lichens, white as snow, every sound excluded, not a breath stirred the pine tufts, not even a bird or an insect to disturb the intense stillness. It seemed as if "Nature" herself had formed and furnished it for her most secret retiring place where she might set at times and muse, uninterrupted even by the sweetest sounds of her own melodies.

August 16

At 6 I was on the road for the Village of Catskill. The air was piercing cold as the stage flashed along down the mountainside, but became mild and sunny when we reached the country below. The difference in temperature was very sudden; indeed, the guide at the Falls told us that he had known snow to fall among the upper defiles as early as the 15th of this month. The Stage stopped on the wharf at half past 9 and at 10 I was board the South boat *Ohio*. I took a Ticket for Tivoli intending to fulfil a promise I had made to Mr. W. Young in coming up the river that I would give him a call at Saugerties on my way back. On nearing the landing, I took my place in front of the Wheel house, the usual place for putting off passengers. I soon discovered my mistake, and that they were landing today astern. I hurried aft—but was too late—the thing is done so quickly that the passengers were all in the boat and ready to jump ashore, so that there was nothing left for it but to summon up my, stoicism, and purchase another Ticket for New York, as I had already determined to relinquish a second visit to West Point, being anxious to get back to the city where I expected there were letters awaiting me from home. It was late when

I reached Beekman Street, and after a short talk with Mr. and Mrs. Slocum I retired to my room.

August 17

Sunday. After a week of excitement and variety the fine breezes of the River last evening prepared me for the soundest sleep and I awoke this morning well-disposed to relish a cool and quiet Sabbath.

New York wears a quiet and sober look, no less novel than pleasing. The fashionable world are all away, crowding the Hotels at West Point, Lebanon Springs, Ballston, and Saratoga—in short to a thousand resorts for health and recreation from Portland to the mountains of the Susquehenna. Business, too, is in a measure suspended, and the presence of the old destroyer, cholera, gives an air of additional sedateness to the almost empty thoroughfares. New York exhibits the most striking contrasts. In a few short weeks, these silent streets will be filled with an ever-flowing tide of human life.

I attended Old Trinity. A stranger preached from the text, "For we walk by faith, not by Sight," shewing first the reasonableness of the walk of faith, and second, its entire adequacy to the wants of man in his greatest and last extremity, that it is the true alchemic touch which alone turns everything to gold. Under the latter head he sketched an illustrative example.

> I once thought, said he, that I had met an instance in which philosophy had justified the boast of her votaries, and inspired real peace in the last trying scene. A young man—full of promise—an intellect of the brightest order—with the most flattering hopes in the professional career that lay before him, but his glowing prospects all blasted, and in the very morning of life an incurable malady brought all the fond hopes of his family to an end, and devoted him to an early grave. In vain he sought new vigor in more genial climates. He returned to end his days in his father's home. From this time his days passed away in patient, intense suffering, but pain and weariness were alike incapable of extorting from him a complaint, and it was only in reply to the earnest inquiries of his friends that he could be brought even to allude to his sufferings. Meanwhile the subtle foe was undermining the tottering fabric. He declined from day to day, yet with the certain prospect of dissolution before him he appeared not in the least dismayed, and as on the subject of religion he maintained a steady silent reserve, we were induced to suppose that in common with but too many professional men, he had adopted some philosophic theory or other in which his mind was now wrapt up, and from which he derived his present calmness and support. But no—the stream of life had nearly ebbed away, when who shall describe the surprise and gratification of those around him when they heard from his own lips—I believe that I am going to heaven, I believe that for Jesus Christ's sake God

has heard my prayers, that thro' his merits my soul is safe. I only want to feel it with greater certainty. I only want to feel beyond a shade of doubt that my eternal salvation is secure. We now saw the source of his consolation. Speculative theories were far from his thoughts. The truest philosophy had thrown her halo around him. We now learned that for a long time past he had made the Bible his constant study, that he had lived by prayer and communion with heaven, that he had drunk deeply of the wellspring of life, and now that the cistern was giving way those purer streams gushed forth in all their freshness, and mingled their grateful flow with every expression. His pure and Simple faith now rested upon the Saviour crucified as alone worthy of a thought, and from him alone did he now derive support. Philosophy—cold—earth-born—poured not a drop into his cup of thanksgiving. To him to live was Christ to die was gain—here he walked by faith and now he ever lives to know the blessedness of the dead that die in the Lord."

Sept., 1834

I returned to the Institute at Flushing and altho' it was the vacation I passed two or three weeks very pleasantly with a few friends who still remained there, when one evening in the middle of September, as I was sitting with L. Van Bokkelen the mail brought me a letter from Dr. Hildreth of Zanesville with the paralyzing intelligence of my mother's death [on 10 Sept.].

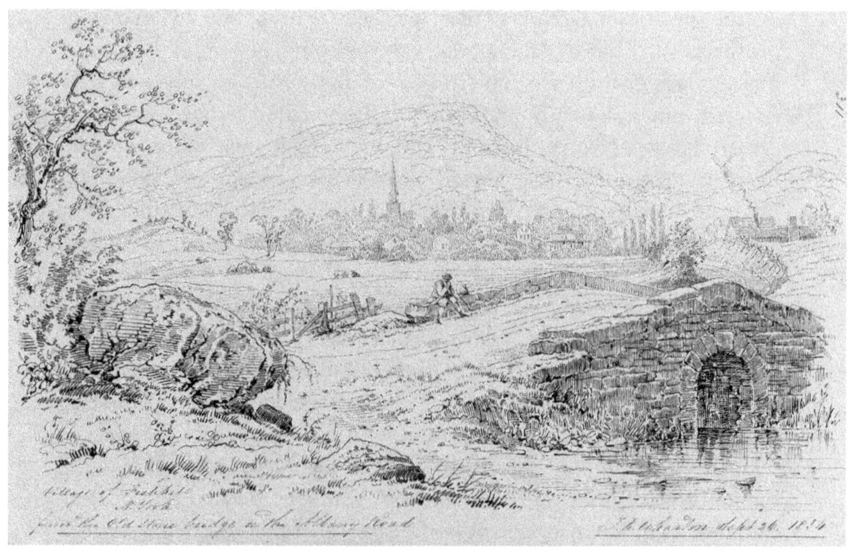

FIGURE 2.16 Village of Fishkill, NY from the Old Stone Bridge on Albany Road, 1834 (*Journal*, vol. 1, p. 311). New York Public Library, Archives and Special Collections, New York.

About the 20th of September, 1834, I went to the village of Fishkill, where I was an entire stranger, and took a room at the mansion house,[124] intending to spend some time in complete retirement.

I took my favorite books and painting materials with me. For the first week, I was quite alone, and soon familiarized myself with the many beautiful walks in this most beautiful neighbourhood. I spent part with my oil colours, sometimes taking my materials with me, and painting some of the most interesting features in the scenery on the spot in open daylight. I soon discovered, however, that this mode suited best for "studies" only, and not for "finished pictures." The effects of nature were more indelibly imprinted on the mind, but the tones on the canvass were too much modified by the surrounding glare. The high ridges on the North (or Albany road) commanding a superb view of the Catskills and River, were a favorite resort with me, and then the crossing of the "Old Stone bridge" with the picturesque village, buried in trees and relieved by the spire of its "ancient church" of historic fame[125]—its noble background of mountains, all furnished me with beautiful materials for my pencil, and often in the still evening I would take my copy of "Young" or "Collins" and wander off along the beautiful creek which winds throe the valley and chose a grassy bank for my seat shadowed over with fine trees, while broad beams of glorious sunshine still lit up the peaks of the Highlands. The lucent stream itself might have inspired those eloquent lines—

> While dashing soft from rocks around
> Bubbling runnels joined the sound.[126]

Where the tones and the sense go together as completely as in any example either ancient or modern. The course of this little stream for miles was a perfect "artist's studio" and the spot where it finally mingles with the Hudson, and which went by the name of "Fairy Island," was the most perfect little grotto for ideal and classic creations that Nature ever constructed.

After a while, quite a friendship sprung up between me and a gentleman and lady staying at the Mansion House—Lieut. [Abram?] and Mrs. Duryee. They were highly intelligent and agreeable, and their conversation elegant and full of interest. The Lieut. used to accompany me in my long rambles, he taking his angling apparatus and I my portfolio, and many a long and pleasant day we spent together. We harmonized well in most subjects of conversation, and agreed on objects of taste.

October 6th, 1834
Today commenced a new session and my friends at Flushing are reassembling to enter upon its duties.

The past vacation must ever be reverted to as the most momentous period of my existence. Part of it has been marked by peculiar and intense enjoyment, part of it by the deepest sorrow. My intellectual pleasures have been of a higher order than usual, my spiritual exercises more regular, and then that event!, which from my very childhood I have been accustomed to anticipate with terror, the loss of my most affectionate and most Christian mother—one to whom, under God, I am indebted for every blessing I enjoy—who has for years been my dearest, best and closest companion, whose tender and even excessive solicitude for my welfare has contributed to draw around me a host of invaluable privileges—in short, I possess nothing, whether of temporal good or the gifts of grace, that may not be traced to her maternal vigilance, her influence, and her constant, and fervent prayers. O! What joys and what trials we have shared together upon earth, but she has exchanged all for an "exceeding and eternal weight of glory in heaven." This event will render the past vacation for ever memorable. The ties that bind me to earth are weakened. The bonds that unite me with those above are indissoluble. May I henceforth so live that I may be ever ready to depart and to be with Christ and those dear ones who have gone before me.

October 11

Saturday night has arrived, and for some days past, owing to a variety of employments, I have had to suspend my daily record. They have, nevertheless been passed much to my satisfaction. Mr. and Mrs. Duryee and I have been a great deal together, and the interchange of pleasant conversation and continual kindnesses will not soon be forgotten.

I have finished three oil pictures and advanced considerably with the fourth, and shall treasure them as visible mementoes of my seclusion here, especially the "evening scene on Fishkill Creek."

I have written to Diller to say that I shall be at The Institute on Friday next, and commence with my classes on Monday following, the 20th. Tuesday the 14th I expect to spend with Mr. Kemble at Coldspring, and Wednesday & Thursday in N. York. I hope before long to have to go up the River again to meet the little girls and my brother Robert in Albany. I recd. a letter from him on the 9th last stating my Father's entire consent to my proposal of the 16th Ult. that Robert should bring my little sisters to me at Flushing and that he and I jointly should take the care of them. I have written to my Father to appoint a day for me to meet them in Albany and in the meantime shall have rooms provided for them in Flushing.

October 12

Sunday. At this very time last year, I parted for ever in this life with my dear mother [i.e., that was the last time Wharton had seen her]. All the particulars of our last intercourse rush like a flood upon me, and almost overwhelm me. My brother Robert's letter, dated Zanesville Sept. 29, 1834, is before me. He says—

> You will, I doubt not, be glad to learn that Mamma's remains were first carried to the church where, our burial service was read and

> an appropriate hymn sung—after which the procession moved on to the grave yard. The followers were numerous, which showed the respect for our departed mother. Dear Thomas, I feel as if I could not possibly realize the afflicting bereavement. Our loss—one of the best of mothers, and justly beloved by all who knew her—but while we mourn let it not be as those without hope—for we may with confidence rely that our loss is her gain, and as she is released from a world of sorrow and trouble she now rests with her Redeemer in everlasting glory. Let us try to attain unto this end—then we may hope to see her face in glory. R.J. Wharton.

Mr. Fisher at the Old Presbyterian Church preached with more than his wanted eloquence and fervour from the text, "And on a day the sons of God come to present themselves &c." It was deeply impressive. Towards the close he said,

> I have seen my Father die. You, too! have had your bereavements, and we all "ere long shall be numbered with the dead. Deploring friends will weep over our ashes, and the clods of the valley be heaped upon our remains. How then can we disregard the call of mercy? How can we close our ears to a Saviour's voice of compassion?"

After the services of the morning I took my accustomed walk on the Albany road.

Autumn now sparkles in every spray, and wraps the mountains in a garb of the richest brilliancy. Every breeze steals a golden tribute from the boughs. Those freshening gales which I had fondly hoped would bring back vigour to her dear but wasted frame, now sigh over our Mother's grave, but the sweet gales of divine love for ever play around her immortal spirit.

"Think," said Mr. Fisher in a powerful address in the evening, "Oh! Think of the instructions of those "who are now dead."

October 13

This morning Mrs. Duryee accompanied two agreeable girls (the Misses Hunters of Trenton, N. J. who arrived on Friday) to Tivoli, and as I leave almost immediately we had to say our farewells, with many wishes for the renewal of our intercourse. Duryee went with them to Fishkill Landing [now Beacon, NY], and there being no "Albany boat" today, the ladies took the *Dutchess* to Poughkeepsie, to proceed the next day.

After tea Duryee & I were pacing the room together, when after appearing a good deal dejected, he suddenly brightened up and proposed that we should surprise them before they took the boat tomorrow at Poughkeepsie. We accordingly laid our plans at once, and retired to rest.

October 14
We started off early and had a charming drive to Poughkeepsie. I need not detail the incidents of this most interesting day. Let it suffice that we both gave and received great pleasure from our little scheme, and indeed it turned out of important service to the ladies, and as we drove leisurely back we stopped occasionally in the romantic neighbourhood of Wappinger's Creek where I made some sketches to perpetuate the memory of the day, and its agreeable associations.

I bid adieu to Fishkill and my friend there on the 15th and in a few days resumed my duties and studies at the Flushing Institute.

Everyone seemed to sympathize deeply with me in my bereavement, and I soon felt more than ever that I was really among kindred spirits, whose society was congenial to me, and from whom, I felt also, that I should be unwilling, even with ever so strong inducements, to part.

[Vol. 1 ends here and there are no entries for the rest of 1834 through 1853.]

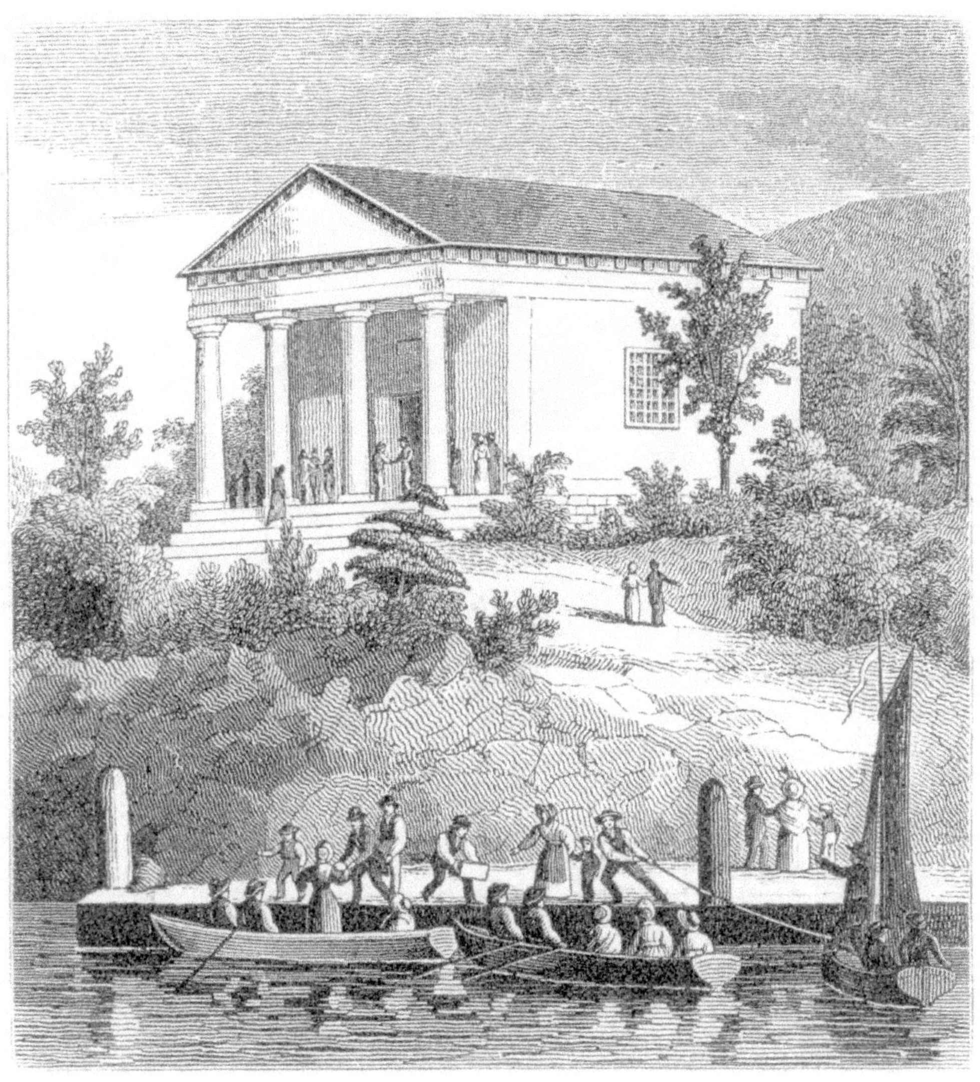

FIGURE 2.17 Chapel of Our Lady, Cold Spring, by Robert W. Weir, engraved by James D. Smillie, *New-York Mirror* 12, no. 19 (Nov. 8, 1834), 145.

Chapter 3

Return to the Northeast, 1853

[Wharton chronicles his family's trip from New Orleans to Boston and back. *Journal* 2, 1–256]

Notes of my Summer Tour of 1853

Journey from New Orleans to Boston and back,

&c. &c.

—

T.K. Wharton,

Camp Street,

New Orleans, La.

On the 13th June, 1853 I addressed the following letter to the Commissioners of the New Custom House, New Orleans, viz.

New Orleans, June 13, 1853

Gentlemen

I have struggled against my increasing debility until I can do so no longer and however reluctantly I feel compelled to avail myself of your kind offer of a "leave of absence," as my medical adviser says that it is indispensable to start for the north as early as possible, after making a few necessary arrangements—say next week—and that to become fully recruited will require an absence of 3 or 4 months in a high latitude. In asking this favor from you I would also respectfully state that I trust you will find it consistent with the interest of the Government to allow me my salary during my absence. I certainly should not ask it were it not that I cannot doubt that my present prostration arises from my constant and unremitting attention to the duties of the Office, ever since the commencement of the work, say for 5 years, summer and winter, in this enfeebling climate, without even so much as a week's change of air on the Lake Shore.

I would also respectfully add that during the period in which I acted as Superintendent, besides being indefatigable in my attention to the works, at a time, too, when a long space of previous inactivity called for unusual energy to bring up the works to a state of complete and efficient action, I also performed all the clerical details of the office, which had always before been paid for separately, thereby saving to the Government the sum of $875, during my Superintendency, by night work &c., and I trust you will not consider it immodest in me to refer to the state of the works, and that of the clerical Department in the Superintendent's Office at the time you entered on duty, as a proof of the faithfulness and success with which I filled both positions.

I trust you will excuse my intruding the above considerations upon you, and beg leave to assure you that whatever action you shall deem it proper to take will be fully satisfactory to me, as I know that you are activated by the purest desire to promote the interests of the Government, and the well-being, as far as in your power, of the employees in the works.

I remain, Gentlemen,

Respect' your obt. servt.

T.K. Wharton.

Commissioners of the

New Customs Ho., N. Orleans

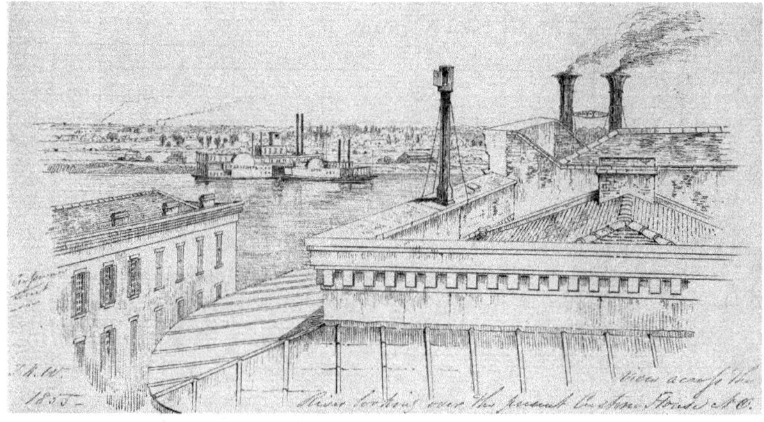

FIGURE 3.1 View across the river looking over the Custom House, New Orleans, 1855 (*Journal*, vol. 3, p. 77). New York Public Library, Archives and Special Collections, New York.

The following is the reply of Maj. [P.G.T.] Beauregard Superintendent and Commissioner—

Superintendent's Office,
June 13, 1853
New Custom House, New Orleans

Dear Sir

I have just received your note of this day accompanying your communication to the Board of Commissioners. I regret exceedingly to find that you are not much better. I hope, however, that you will soon commence to improve rapidly.

Your application for a leave of absence from next week for three or four months has just been considered by the Board and granted at once for three months, with leave to extend it further should it become necessary for the benefit of your health.

With regard to the application for your present pay to be continued during your leave of absence, altho' greatly disposed to grant it, considering it both just and proper, the Board does not think it has authority to act in the matter, but a copy of your communication, with a recommendation from the Board, that your application be granted, will be forwarded to the Honorable Secretary of the Treasury, and we feel confident that it will meet with his approval, which will be communicated to you as soon as received.

Before leaving here I shall want you to prepare me a synopsis of the contracts now existing, shewing their main features and conditions, also the Quantity of the principal materials which have been used on the Building up to the present moment, but this is in no great hurry.

Respectfully yours
G.T. Beauregard
Capt. & Brt. Majr. of Eng^{rs}.
Supt. &c.

Mr. T.K. Wharton

Immediately after the above correspondence I set about making the necessary preparations for a journey to New England, in which I was materially assisted by the kindness of Mr. Alexander Dunn and other friends, who volunteered to aid me in such matters as I was incapable of attending to personally from excessive weakness. My wife and mother in law soon dispatched those details which devolved upon them, and I engaged a trustworthy person and his wife to take charge of my house and furniture in my absence. I provided carefully for all such contingencies as were likely to arise whilst away, and made all my arrangements so as to leave behind me no cause whatever for solicitude or uncertainty.

On the 15th June I got my friend Mr. Dunn to secure for me good staterooms on board the Steamer "Aleck Scott" for her next trip to St. Louis and the interval soon sped away in the interest and excitement of preparation, which in a measure buoyed me up in spite of the tropical fierceness of the summer sun, so that we were all ready when the Steamer's day for departure arrived.

June 25, 1853
Francis[1] came for the baggage at half past 3 P.M. and at 4 the carriage was at the door. I felt so feeble that my heart misgave me. However, we all got in and bid adieu to our sweet, little cottage—Emily and myself, little Prescott and his nurse Catherine, and Mrs. Ladd & Ellen. In twenty minutes we were on board the "Aleck Scott" and were joined by Mr. Alex. Dunn and Dr. Wright who will be of our party. Looked at the staterooms selected by Mr. Dunn for me, and much pleased with them. Friends came on board to see us off. Saml Tracey and family, Mr. Wood and Miss Wallace, Messrs. A. Kearney, Irving &c., &c. Found Mr. W.P. Freret and family and others that I know, amongst our fellow passengers. Left the city all glowing and quivering with summer heat at 6 P.M. and watched the shores from the upper deck until day melted into starlight.

June 26
At Plaquemines (5 A.M.) not a cloud, pure and bracing on deck. Feel improved already, the river as smooth as glass, coast lovely, sugar fields bright in colour and very clean, fine trees and sweet looking homesteads, luxuriant background of Cypress, Oak &c. Uncle Tom and all his family fishing on the bank, or moving lazily along the river road and Levee. Every breath of this pure air seems to course thro' the system like a powerful elixir. After 5 years suffocation in the heat, dust, and stagnant atmosphere of New Orleans, the morning breeze at the bow seems laden with sovereign restoratives. I have not felt so buoyant for many months.

Hot and cloudless all day, fine air forward. No delay except for wood. Boat and passengers very pleasant. Officers obliging. One of them, Edward Tracey, was at Dr. Muhlenberg's at College Point, L.I. when I was there. He was then a boy of 11, now a stout, hearty, fine looking married man. We were very glad to meet after so long an interval.

My strength is increasing every hour. Prescott very restless all day. A little aperient [laxative] medicine restored him to his usual cheerfulness.

June 27
Day broke with a glow of the richest crimson mingling into the blue above like an Aurora Borealis. Rodney and Grand Gulf before breakfast. Sugar culture exchanged for cotton and corn. Country green and flourishing, and the

brightest sky above. Ladies reading, sewing, chatting and tending their babies. Gentlemen forward, in knots, talking, smoking, lounging. No noise, no bustle, comfort and decorum everywhere. Vicksburg at 1 P.M. Heat intense. Pleasant night and sound sleep.

June 28

Up at 5. Walked the deck till breakfast. Both banks low and sylvan. Dense forests with openings of corn and cotton lands. Islets shooting into the stream covered with bright green cotton wood, and separated from the main bank by "chutes" or bayous. Foliage of great beauty, every shade of green, mingled or contrasted with broad shadows from passing clouds, and brilliant clusters standing out in strong sunlight, all harmonized by the dreamy summer air.

Time glides along easily, and like our Steamer, rapidly. Pleasant men, good looking women and lively children. Conspicuous young lady with a poodle instead of a baby. My little boy promises to be an excellent traveller, quite sociable, and with the little girls especially.

Towards evening, on the front guards, a broad faced backwoodsman stepped up to us, and pointing to the shore, said very earnestly, "See that Bar." "See that Bar!" "Thar on the bank," and sure enough there he was, a huge black Bear, scooping and pawing the sand, and rolling about with enviable non-chalance, on a broad white beach between the stream and the forest.

Sun set with a superb glory, composed of strong yellow rays, shot with blue, and as well defined as the radiance with which painters encircle the head of "the Christ." Cool and pleasant night. Slept well.

June 29

Not a cloud. The sand Bars and impervious woods of Mississippi and Arkansas still stretching away on each side of us, but wilder than yesterday and fewer intervals of farm land, and even these set thick with girdled trees and other evidences of their being but recently brought under the plough.

Lay at the wharf Boat at Memphis from 3 P.M. to 7, discharging freight. Not a breath of air and such a concentration of heat I never experienced in my life—pouring down directly on the hurricane deck, reflected from the River, and bare lofty clay banks, and intensified by the furnaces below. Thermometer at 104 in the cabin and no escape. Add to which a large accession of passengers, about 50, came trooping on board, altho' the Captain assured them that we were already full, and the cabin floors spread over with mattresses at night, and in fact, that he was wholly unprovided for them, but they insisted on taking passage, and said they would put up with anything rather than wait longer for a Boat, some of them having been already a week on the lookout for a chance to get away, and utterly worn out with anxiety, and the heat and dust of Memphis.

June 30
Pleasant night for sleeping, and the vast human family on board seemed to get thro' it pretty well. Breezy day and light clouds to mitigate the heat. Shores low, woody and very monotonous, very few patches of cultivation, little signs of humanity, except an occasional woodyard with its primitive log cabin, and little corn patch. Men in linsey [light cotton or linen cloth], large framed women, and flaxen haired children. All else unbroken forest and long glistening sand bars.

We find Mr. & Mrs. Montgomery of New Orleans very agreeable and their little Lilly and Prescott are nice playmates. Messrs. Ansley, Cohen, Leeck, Stone and Hart, all of New Orleans, prove very pleasant travelling companions. We liked Mr. and Mrs. Simpson, too, very much. They left us at Memphis.

I am improving every day. Indeed we are all more or less benefitted, especially Prescott. Intensely hot in the afternoon. Sofas and chairs quite warm to the hand, and the woodwork of the Staterooms unmistakably hot. New Madrid at 5 P.M.

July 1, 1853
Cairo, mouth of the Ohio at 3½ A.M.

Sun rose without a cloud. Morning air fresh and elastic. Shores low and covered with the original forest—shelves and bars—with long level ranges of young cotton wood lying in front of the taller foliage.

Commerce at 8½, first high land above Cairo. Cape Girardeau at 10. Fine Catholic College of brick on the hill top,[2] and new Gothic brick church below on the river Bank. Large brick buildings everywhere, replacing the old town destroyed by the Tornado of 1850.

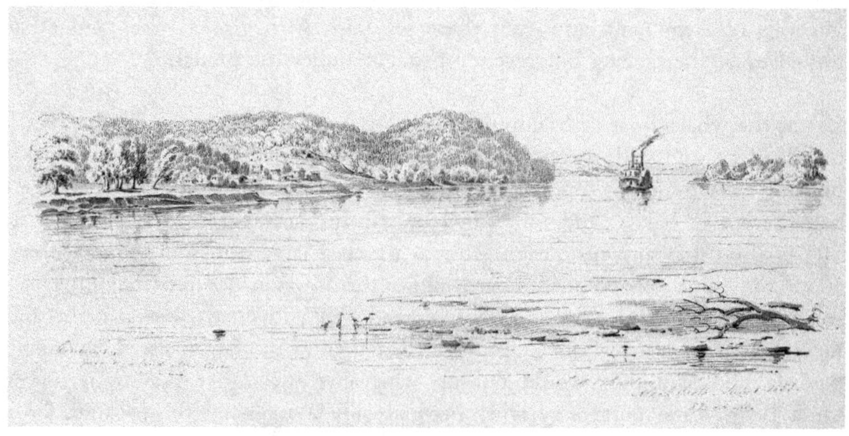

Figure 3.2 Commerce, first high land above Cairo, 1853 (*Sketchbook*, p. 1). New York Public Library, Archives and Special Collections, New York.

Telegraphed from here to St. Louis to secure staterooms in the LaSalle Packet tomorrow evening.

At Cape Girardeau the river assumes its finest and most impressive features. Every bend of its intricate course presents a new and charming combination of woody islands, rocky points, sloping hill sides clothed with wood, and far sweeping ranges of the richest forest growth—little towns straggling up the declivities, and fields of wheat just cut and shucked up, contrasting with the fresh tints of the young corn. The ladies spent the afternoon with us at the Bow, enjoying the pure breeze and enchanting scenery, and we lingered late on deck under the clear starlight. Slept well, and rose very early.

July 2

In time to see the most interesting points in the vicinity of St. Louis, where we arrived at 5½ A.M. (1,224 miles from New Orleans). Collected our baggage and drove up to the "Planter's" to breakfast, after seeing that our dispatch had secured the Staterooms for the Illinois Packet of the evening.

Met Mr. J.R. Shaw and his family of New Orleans at the Hotel. Found St. Louis much improved in 10 years, but the Planter's about the same, still kept by Stickney and his people, and the unfinished Court house opposite just as I left it in '43, same blocks of stone still lying about the open space around.[3] The city shews finely from the River, lofty brick buildings rising tier above tier from the long line of Steamboats at the Levee. Spires, domes and turrets, and beautiful greenwoods, and hill sides, spreading away from the suburbs to the utmost limit of vision.

Every comfort at the Hotel, cool quiet and inviting after the crowded Steamer. Still we were sorry to leave the *Scott*. She is a delightful Boat, perfectly safe, never exceeding 140 lbs. of Steam, and rapid at that, and a more attentive man to his passengers than Capt. Sellers I never met with.

At the Planter's the worst feature was the attendance at the ladies' ordinary. The dinner was good enough but the white servants slow, ill-trained and inefficient.

The improvements in St. Louis seem mainly confined to the central and South parts of town, the upper portion remaining as rude and delapidated as during my last visit.

After dinner the carriage was at the door, and we were soon on board the *Belle Gould*, having taken thro' tickets to Buffalo via LaSalle, Chicago, Toledo and Lake Erie. Distance to LaSalle 303 miles.

Very pretty Boat, nearly new, nice cabins, but crowded to its utmost capacity. We have two good Staterooms in the gentlemen's cabin, all in the Ladies' having been taken up before our dispatch came to hand. Mr. & Mrs. Montgomery on one side of us, and Messrs. Wright and Dunn on the other. Left the wharf at

5. Beautiful sylvan scenery on both banks, and Islands of fine trees interspersed. All on deck at the mouth of the Missouri. Great change in the water from turbid & muddy to dark and clear after passing that River. Superb sunset. Town of Alton rising behind a fine group of islands, and covering the sides and summit of an elevated rocky ridge. Lay to at the wharf boat for freight until 9½ P.M., 25 miles from St. Louis. A thunderstorm came up suddenly and cleared the air. Incessant flashes and heavy rain, passed off just as the Boat got under way.

Retired to our Staterooms early. No musquito Bars [netting]. None necessary, first time for years.

July 3

Sunday. Rose at 4½. Lovely morning, pure cool air. The Illinois shining like a mirror, narrow and clear, banks rising gently to the height of 200 feet, in ridges, with beautiful green trees to the summit, and bold glimpses of grey rock interspersed. Soil rich and loamy indicating great fertility, but the corn, which in Louisiana has attained its full growth, is here scarcely more than a foot high. The changes in vegetation, as we advance northward are strongly marked, both in kind and in the stage of growth.

Much complaint among passengers of accommodations &c., but I cannot see why. Surely they don't expect a crowded river steamer to be as well regulated as a private drawing room.

Quite warm in the middle of the day but not oppressive like the climates below St. Louis.

Frequent stoppings at little villages and landings. Slow progress. Shores low and belted with wood, Oak, Maple, Hornbeam, and gigantic Sycamores, festooned with the *Rhus radicans* [poison ivy] and other creepers. Glimpses of prairie and cornfields thro' the trees, and ponds glistening among the rank, Ivy-mantled woodlands. Mysterious little creeks emerging from the dark forest, and pure white cranes cooling themselves in the clear streamlets. Smooth river and large Pike leaping out of the water, and then darting off with the speed of lightening.

Meals abundant, strange dishes and all heaped on the table at once. Fine fish and fried frogs at breakfast.

Reached the turn of the river below Peoria at sunset (230 miles from St. Louis). Upper deck crowded. A nobler subject for an evening picture could scarcely be chosen. Such a glowing sky and such glorious reflections from the groups of trees and distant buildings, and a river of glassy smoothness gleaming like an opal towards the setting sun, and then withdrawing into recesses of the darkest shadow.

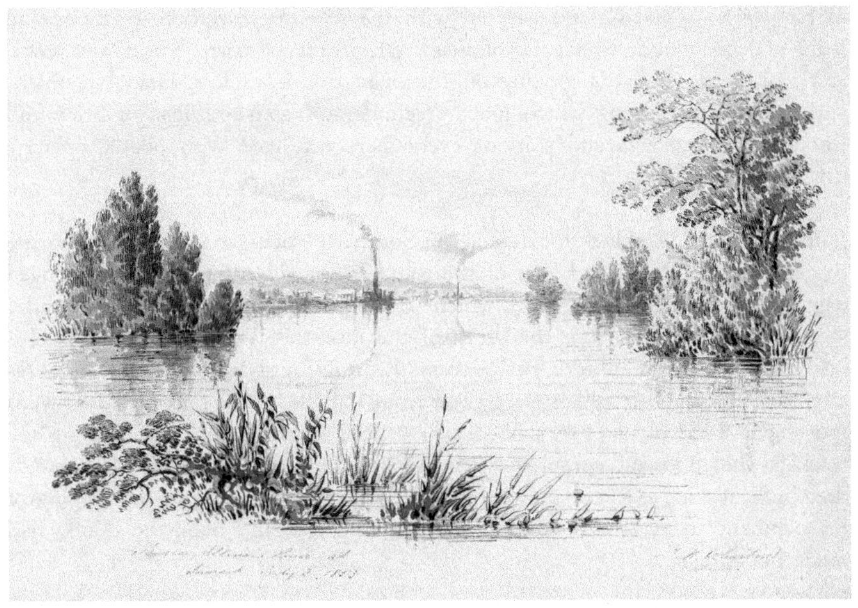

FIGURE 3.3 Peoria, Illinois River at sunset, 1853 (*Sketchbook*, p. 5). New York Public Library, Archives and Special Collections, New York.

Passed the long drawbridge at the entrance to Peoria Lake, and then made fast to put off passengers. A large number left us here amid a scene of confusion worse confounded, and suffocating heat. Among the incidents was the sudden illness of a lady who came on board at Memphis, and has been suffering a day or two from fever. She fainted on her way to shore, and was conveyed back to a Stateroom where she revived in time to leave the Boat. The picturesque meeting of a gentleman from shore with a young lady on board inspired the warmest interest. Such intense kisses were enough to fire the Boat. Fortunately for them our bachelor friends were in a remote part of the cabin.

We were much relieved by the loss of so much baggage, and so many people, and the Boat became all at once extremely comfortable and quiet. At a late hour Ice creams were handed round, and with the delicious temperature of the night allayed the feverish excitement of the afternoon.

July 4

Seventy-seventh anniversary of American Independence. Rose very early, roused up the whole party, had the baggage checked and breakfasted at LaSalle. Left in the cars for Chicago (90 miles) at 7 A.M. Had a slight chill immediately after breakfast, but battled with it until it passed off. Arrived at Chicago at 11½. Excellent road, good cars, interesting scenery, pure sunny air, fine broad prairies enamelled with flowers, and of the most resplendent green. Terraces as regular as a "glacis"[4] and covered with the smoothest verdure—groups and belts of Oak wood. Pretty farmhouses, enclosures of corn, wheat and Oats, and vast herds of cattle grazing on the open prairies. Clear, lucid streamlets, and neat towns, among which Joliet preeminent. Good buildings of brick and freestone. The streets and stations everywhere thronged with people opening the "festivities" of the day.

Left Chicago at 12 o'clock for Toledo, on Southern Michigan R. Road, preferring to get thro' the Rail Road part of the route as speedily as possible. Exchanged baggage checks here for Buffalo, which was attended with some trouble, and I still felt quite unwell from the "chill" of the morning. While attending to this business I observed quite a rush across the train, and learned a few minutes after that the cars on which we arrived from LaSalle, while making a backward movement from the Depot, passed over a poor woman who was crossing the track at the moment, completely severing her legs, and mutilating her hands dreadfully, leaving not a shadow of hope for her life. She was in the employ of the company to wash the paintwork of the cars &c., and habit, no doubt, had made her careless.

Montgomery, Cohen and Leech layover for a day or two at Chicago.

Good road and cars. 242 miles. Very rapid—as high as 36 to 40 miles per hour, but no less than 15 or 20 stoppings, giving us an opportunity of seeing & studying the population who were assembled in force at every little town to celebrate the 4th, tricked out in their best, the women all blazing with ruddy cheeks and red ribbons, and as the evening advanced, they would take passage with us for their homes in neighbouring villages, dotting the country every where along the line of the road. In fact, at Hillsdale [MI], where the day had been observed with unusual devotion, some 5 or 6 additional cars were attached to provide for the influx of people returning to the little towns of Ossio, Pittsford, Clayton, Adrian &c. One thing I could not but remark, the absence of everything to indicate a day of drunken frolic. All were in high spirits and full of fun, but I did not see more than two at all excited with liquor, and they but slightly.

The country very beautiful. We congratulated ourselves in choosing daylight for it. Noble farms, fine water courses, Lake Michigan of the deepest blue, breaking on a beach of smooth sand, large Ponds overspread with the broad leaves and snow-white Petals of the *Nymphaea Alba* [water lilies], and every few miles a neat thriving town, conveying an idea of comfort and competence, but no display or buildings of much pretension. I don't think I ever saw so large a spread of country where the mean is so well preserved between the extremes of indigence and wealth.

Arrived safely at Toledo at 1 o'clock at night, worn out with fatigue, and indeed some anxiety, for being somewhat behind time, and having to meet the night Express from Toledo at Adrian we tore along at a terrific rate for the last few miles, and I felt somewhat uncertain as to the effect of the "Fourth" upon the officers of the train after so many stoppings. Indeed we afterwards learned that a very bad accident occurred on the road at 7 this morning, about 4 miles from Toledo. An axletree of the baggage car broke, smashing the car in pieces and throwing the passenger car directly behind it off the Track, breaking it thro' the middle and seriously injuring 4 Persons. One had his abdomen torn open and leg fractured and could not survive. Another lost his reason from severe contusion on the head. The remaining four Passenger cars, crowded with people, were entirely uninjured.

I gave our baggage checks to the Porter of "Kingsbury's"[5] and drove at once to the Hotel to snatch a couple of hours of slumber before taking the Lake Steamer.

Comfortable house and good breakfast. Carriage from the cars and to the Steamer and handling baggage all promptly attended to without charge, and the Bill at the Hotel miraculously cheap. Indeed, I expressed a doubt of its correctness, but it was "all right."

July 5

Up again at 5. Breakfast at 6, and at 7 on board the *Northern Indiana,* a large, well built, and handsomely furnished Steamer for Buffalo. Left Toledo at 9 and took on the passengers by the morning train from Chicago at Monroe at 10½, then put out into the pale green waters of Lake Erie, under a beautiful sunny sky, and cold bracing north wind. The thermometer at Toledo at 6 A.M. this morning was only 64°.

Excellent staterooms, large airy cabins, scarce any vibration, and great speed. Took a refreshing sleep after dinner to repair the losses of the last week. On awaking about 4 P.M. we were coasting along a fine range of woody shore on the south side of the Lake, with the spires and buildings of Cleaveland in the far off distance. To the north nothing but the brilliant ripples of the Lake and the clear, blue sky above. On the land side, distant showers were passing over the country, and produced a fine variety of light and shade on the forest and details of the coast. The ladies collected in forward saloon for the benefit of the buoyant air and interesting Lake scenery. Three hours at Cleaveland and took on a vast concourse of people on the arrival of the train from Cincinnati. Retired at 10 leaving a dancing party in the forward saloon, and a pretty performer on the Piano in the ladies' cabin. Slept soundly—cold north wind streaming into my berth from the open window. Scarce any motion.

July 6

Rose at 5. Splendid morning but very cold. Shores closing in. New York mountains in the South East, Buffalo in sight. Steward collecting tickets. Waked up my party and had my baggage all laid together. Arrived at 7 A.M. What a scene of confusion ensued in selecting & landing baggage! I stood quietly by mine and surveyed the uproar at leisure, until the "fast people" had all gone ashore, then sent up my trunks &c. to the Mansion House, and followed with my party in the omnibus. Took a comfortable breakfast, purchased thro' tickets to Boston via the St. Lawrence River and then took the omnibus to the Cars for Niagara. Our fellow passengers from New Orleans, Mr. and Mrs. Stanley, accompanying us, while the rest, Messrs. Dunn, Wright, Stone &c. took the direct train to New York. Very pleasant men and quite sorry to part with them. Mr. Dunn would have continued with us but for an injury that he received on his foot in St. Louis.

Pleasant little rail Road of 22 miles to the Falls. Fine air, and pretty glimpses of the Niagara River. Ran down in an hour and ten minutes. Gave my checks to the Porter of the Cataract House, and got into the omnibus with my family, and in a very short time we were comfortably housed, with excellent bed rooms, and all our baggage and ourselves in the best order and high Travelling condition.

Here we take our first real rest since leaving New Orleans. Every thing looks so inviting, and those grand Falls just beneath our windows rolling their billows of silver dew high up into the bright blue sky, so that a rest of a day or two here before encountering another long section of Rail Road is a "fixed fact."

Found our friends Cohen and Leech in the cars. They laid over but half a day at Chicago, and then taking the South Shore Railroad thro', instead of the Lake at Toledo, reached Buffalo as soon as we. William Freret is here waiting to be joined by his father and family whom we left in St. Louis.

After a hasty toilet, I took little Prescott to the gallery of the House overhanging the rapids. He gazed at them with marked astonishment as they dashed by, foaming and glittering in the broad sunlight. Walked down to the Falls with Emily before dinner. Mrs. Ladd, Ellen and W. Freret went with us. Noble views of both Falls under a cloudless sky, and fine still atmosphere, giving the most glittering lucidity to the water sheets and exquisite delicacy to the spray wreaths, while the wood paths of the Island were flecked with bright gleams of sunshine, piercing the shadows of fine old Maples, Hemlocks, Oaks & Pine, and the silver sheets of the Cataract and Rapids glancing thro' the openings of the foliage.

Niagara is greatly improved since I was here last.[6] A noble Hotel (the International) has been added to its buildings, and the Cataract House, in consequence, greatly enlarged, new painted, fitted & furnished. The house is scrupulously clean, and the people civil and obliging. Excellent table and well-trained waters. The finest Salmon, and such vegetables! Young, fresh and tender. The Ices don't melt under your spoon as at the South. Perfect order, and numerous guests, tho' still many vacant seats. People rarely stay here more than a day or two, generally but a few hours, so that the Meals exhibit a constant succession of new faces. They have a good Band of Music at dinner, and a wide door at the end of the Dining Hall opening on the Rapids and letting in the mellow, dashing sound of waters between the strains of the performers.

In the afternoon, we made the entire circuit of Goat Island. Prescott gazed at the wondrous floods and held out his little hands as if to grasp them, laughing merrily for an instant, and then fixing a steadfast, thoughtful eye upon the waters as if he felt their deep inspiration and absorbing poetry. At the head of the Island is a beautiful calm spot where the rushing waters divide. I took him close to the brink, and sprinkled the crystal over him. We then pursued our way over the smooth turf, the wild rapids on the one hand and the quiet, green woodland on the other. We lingered some time near the beautiful Rapid between Goat and Moss Island. The pathway winds sweetly round it moistened by the light spray as it shoots along, and bathes the rich clusters of foliage and velvet moss which enchase this choicest "gem of the Falls."

Recrossing the bridge over the Rapids on the American side, I met my old friend Jacob Halsey, just from the Arkansas springs with his sister, and in very feeble health. Indeed, he was glad to take my arm in ascending the hill. As to myself this bracing air is reviving me rapidly. I slept last night with the cutting north wind across the Lake blowing on me without taking cold. After tea, we spent an hour in the Ball-room, a fine, large apartment, excellent Orchestra, Quadrilles & Waltzes every evening, retired at 10 & slept profoundly.

July 7
When I looked out in the morning the sun had anticipated me, and the spray twined its wreaths above the Falls tinged with a rich rosy light. I hastened to the woods below the town, and selected the best points of view. Then, after an excellent breakfast, Salmon, white fish &c. took my family over the same ground. W. Freret went with us. Brilliant atmosphere, every object glittering with Sunlight, the Falls, the woods, rocks, streamlets, rapids, islands, every thing fresh, lucid, impressive. Time plumed his swiftest wings. I secured a sketch of the Falls embracing the entire sweep in a fine foreshortened curve, while the rest looked over the Daguerrotype Establishment, and the apparatus for conveying visitors down the precipice to the Boat at the Base of the Falls, the lofty stairway contiguous to it &c. &c.

Returning to the Hotel we examined the curiosity shops, bought a pair of beautiful bead mocassins for Prescott, and other toys, and then came the unwelcome task of preparation for departure.[7] We would willingly linger out our summer here, but must hasten onwards.

Early dinner at 1 and then adieu to Niagara. Started at 2 P.M. in the omnibus for Lewiston (7 miles). Several ladies and gentlemen besides my party. Dust rolled round us in volumes. Fine distant views of the Falls, Suspension Bridge,[8] the lofty rocky banks of the Niagara River, and their abrupt termination, where they suddenly sink into a beautiful undulating country at Lewiston—at this

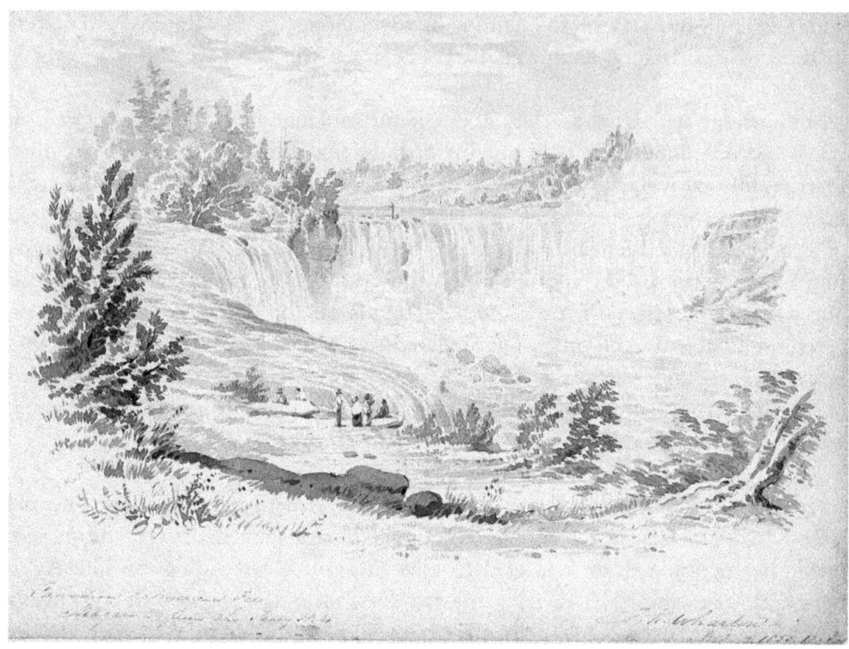

FIGURE 3.4 Canadian and American falls, Niagara from the Ferry Slips, 1853 (*Sketchbook*, p. 10). New York Public Library, Archives and Special Collections, New York.

point forming a superb gorge for the passage of the river. High on the headland rose the plain Tuscan shaft to the memory of General Brock,[9] and far away on the horizon gleamed the waters of Ontario, while the Niagara River, emerging from the precipices around us occupied the middle distance, and wound thro' a rich scene of fertility until it mingled with the distant Lake.

Long, steep and dangerous descent from the highlands at Lewiston. Locked the wheels but the drag chain gave way. However, we reached the Steamer New York in safety at 3½ P.M. A fine new boat, full of passengers. Baggage soon followed us. Left at 4 P.M., carrying off a poor, old lady who had come on board by mistake, while her husband had gone to the other boat, the *Niagara*. We landed her soon after at a point below where the *Niagara* had just come to and restored her to her anxious partner.

At 4½ we entered Lake Ontario—Fort Niagara on one side—Fort George and the pretty town of Newark[10] on the other. The "stars and stripes" and the "cross of St. George." The Lake as smooth as a mirror. Sunny sky. To the north nothing but the clear fresh waters of a mellow greenish blue tint. Southward a long line of woody shore, level clay banks, with a belt of farms, and neat farm houses, along the margin, and an occasional village with its spires. Schooners upon the Lake gliding quietly along and looking like "Painted ships upon a painted ocean."

The "Niagara" astern rapidly sinking in the distance.

On board every thing new, sweet and clean, in perfect order and so spacious that our large complement of passengers creates no confusion. The only annoyance was the tediousness of the clerk in distributing the Staterooms, and that appeared unavoidable, as every man asked questions enough to form a complete "hand book" of cross-examination. Distance from Lewiston to Ogdensburg 299 miles.

Towards evening the air became so calm that the Lake looked like polished steel, and differed but little in colour from the sky above. A more lovely afternoon on the water I never beheld. Its poetical, almost magical influence seemed to hold everyone of our large company as by a potent spell. A quiet, subdued manner and unwonted stillness prevailed in every part of our beautiful Steamer.

We retired early and slept well, the motion being very slight.

July 8

Rose at 4. Pure bracing air on deck. Crimson sunrise, and the sky overspread with mottled clouds. Just entering the "Thousand Islands" in the St. Lawrence River. Banks rising gently from the water, and well wooded, the Islands too, dotted and grouped with trees—the Pine shooting up at intervals, the river

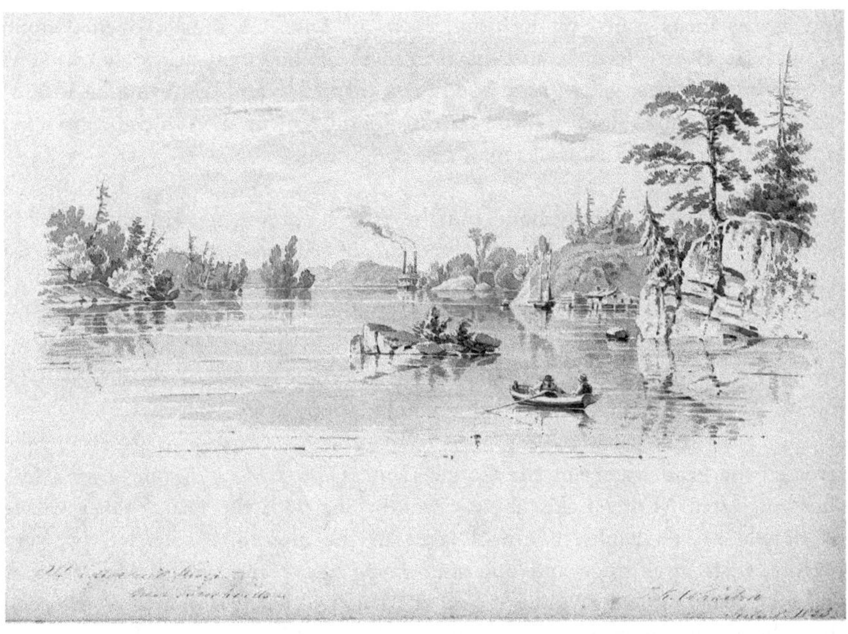

FIGURE 3.5 St. Lawrence River near Brockville, ON 1853 (*Sketchbook*, p. 12). New York Public Library, Archives and Special Collections, New York.

scenery very beautiful. Islands, Islets and rocks with a few clusters of bushes, all strewed over the water and "thick as leaves in Vallombrosa,"[11] but vegetation here looks stunted, thin and ragged. The air sharp and bleak, and the scanty soil encumbered with huge blocks of granite and yielding a precarious return in the few spots where man has been daring enough to attempt cultivation. Lumber seems the chief source of revenue, and many stations for sawing, deposit & shipment of timber occur on both sides of the [St. Lawrence] River.

Had the baggage checked for Boston via Vermont Central Railroad. Breakfasted on board and reached Ogdensburg at 7½ A.M. Took our seats in the cars, close to the Steamboat landing, and started for Boston at 8 A.M.—406 miles of rail road.

Changed cars at Rouse's Point (118 miles) at 11 A.M. Commenced raining. Crossed the two branches of the head of Lake Champlain over long modern viaducts on Piles. Pretty Champaign country, woods and streams, and enclosures under tolerable cultivation, covered with stumps, however, and looking very new and desolate. Road very good and cars comfortable. Very fast and no time to think or do anything but go ahead. Threw off the Burlington cars at Essex Junction—47 miles from Rouse's Point and 241 from Boston, and then darted along the Vermont Central R. Road to Northfield, 43 miles further, where we stopped at 2 P.M. and snatched a hasty dinner in 20 minutes, like the General's celebrated repast, and then off again—208 miles from Ogdensburg and 198 from Boston. Country improved rapidly after leaving St. Albans, in every particular—natural scenery, productions, dwellings, villages and farms, and as the mists rolled off beautiful views of Lake Champlain opened upon us, with its Points, Islands, and distant ranges of mountain delicately tinted as it were on the finest gauze, with the purest pigments, and conveying an idea of space almost illimitable to us who have so long been confined to the contracted landscape of the level alluvial regions at the South.

The rain ceased at an early hour and the broken surface of Vermont exhibited both far and near an endless succession of changes, exquisite groups of woodland, mountain, rocks, and craggy moss grown precipices, streams rippling over beds of clean gravel, and pastures of glossy green, dotted all over with simple wild flowers—while groups of healthy looking cattle roamed at large on the hillsides, or cooled themselves in the sparkling brooks at their base. The White River presenting new and fine combinations at every turn.

Crossed the head waters of the Connecticut at 3½ P.M. and soon after a fine sheet of water, Mosby Lake, about 5 miles long with the neat Shaker village of Enfield on its banks, beautiful lakes in the afternoon encircled by lofty heights, ridge after ridge and one spur rising above another in infinite series and ever changing forms, and I was glad I had selected this branch of the road thro' the mountain passes of Vermont and New Hampshire, rather than the comparatively tamer section thro' Burlington and Rutland.

Passed Salisbury, now Franklin, the birth place of Daniel Webster at 5½ P.M. The Farm is a beautiful one and very neat buildings, well kept enclosures & fine stock. The picturesque Merrimac winding gracefully thro' it—the bottom lands studded thick with stately Elms, from which it borrows its name of "The Elms" or "Elmwood."

Concord at 6 P.M. where we changed cars for the last time—76 miles from Boston. Passed like lightening thro' Manchester, Nashua and Lowell, and a sweet pretty country, every thing so neat, and pure, and substantial, and presenting the greatest possible contrast to the delapidated appearance of things in the lazy South. The winding Merrimac, now close beneath our wheels, now sweeping away into the far off distance, now crimsoned with sunset, and then gleaming in the quiet starlight. Beautiful home of the thrifty, painstaking, intelligent sons of Freedom. We shot into Boston a little before 9 P.M. Order and regularity every where. Took a coach which conveyed us all and our baggage to the Revere House in a few minutes. Found excellent rooms and an excellent supper awaiting us.

Mrs. Ladd and Ellen left us here for her Father's, and we were not long in seeking our chamber, after the fatigues and dangers of our long but delightful journey of over 2,800 miles. As to the dangers they are not few, for the speed on the Railroads is terrific, and the accidents frequent. I would willingly compromise for half the speed, with double the safety and a fairer chance to see the country we pass thro'. That around Boston, however, we hope now to examine in detail.

July 9

Rose late and felt much refreshed after a good quiet breakfast, tho' the whirl of the cars and the languor from loss of sleep and other contingencies of travelling still cling to us. Prescott, however, is extremely fresh and lively, and has grown rapidly during the journey. He has given very little trouble, and carried himself admirably thro' all the ups and downs of the way, making friends every where and winning golden opinions from all sorts of persons. Men, women and children all take to him.

After breakfast his great-grandmother, Mrs. Prescott, came with Mrs. Ladd to see us. She is a very fine old lady of 72—healthy and active—went up three flights of stairs like a girl.

Mr. George Prescott, Emily's uncle, called at 11 and will return after dinner to aid me in selecting a Boarding House. The morning passed quickly and pleasantly. It is now half past 1. Mr. and Mrs. Prescott and Mrs. Ladd have left, and Emily and the little boy are sleeping sweetly, and no wonder after such a sleepless journey. They suffered far more than I in this particular, but we have all been amply repaid for our deprivations by what we have seen and the past fortnight will be enrolled among the most interesting epochs in our lives.

After dinner Mr. Prescott called and walked with Emily and me to see some rooms at No. 21 Somerset Street—a square or two off. Nice large parlour, Bedroom and closet, well supplied with suitable furniture, and a bed room for Catherine close at hand. Fine, large substantial house on the hill side. Streets around scrupulously clean, elegant mansions rising on every side, and contiguous to the most frequented parts of the city and most objects of interest. I immediately engaged the rooms, and returned to the Revere House, ordered a carriage for ourselves and baggage, and we were fully settled in our new home in time for Tea. Every thing in the house seems so comfortable and home-ish, that we are quite delighted, and much obliged to Mr. Prescott for pointing out to us such excellent quarters. The charge for every thing, except washing and light, is Eighty dollars per month.

Rain set in about sunset, and continued all night. Very refreshing after the late drought.

The people here complain of the heat, but we find the temperature very pleasant, about February weather in New Orleans, and no musquito Bars required, which is a real privilege. I have not seen a "Bar" since we left St. Louis, but I notice the fabric for sale in Hanover Street here, labelled with the very original title of "Sketa netting."

July 10

Sunday. Beautiful after the rain, calm & quiet, scarce a sound but the mellow chimes of Old Christ Church,[12] but for the stately houses in every direction we should hardly feel that we were in the centre of a vast commercial city. Not the fronts only but the back offices and yards of the dwelling houses are as clean and tidy as a parlour. From our bed room window we look down into several, and see the Oleander, Fig, Spruce, Pine, Oak, Maple and luxuriant grape vines and Noisette Roses, all in fine order, and well pruned and watered. In fact—"water, water everywhere," and that of the purest kind. Every house has its "Gutta Percha" hose, and even on the lofty hills of the city, you see the jets rising still higher as the servants direct the streams over the pavements, and bathe the tall creepers that climb around the doorways and windows. I had no idea of the neatness and beauty of this city. We are indeed very pleasantly situated and little Prescott is as happy as a Marquis.

Mr. George Prescott and his wife called at 11 to invite us to dinner, but unfortunately I had a "chill" and could not go. I feel much mortified to be still so inefficient. I was apparently quite well just before they came. I do hope these tantalizing chills will soon leave me. They say the air of New England is a sufficient antidote. I observe, however, that the people here talk a great deal about the East wind, and seem more apprehensive of ill effects from it than I have ever noticed elsewhere, but why I cannot tell. I have always longed for a pure ocean breeze, and the East wind here blows directly from the Seaward.

Em. and I took a long and profound sleep after dinner, tho' I perspired freely after the "chill" and flush that followed it.

July 11

Pleasant morning after a night of showers. Took a short ramble to the "Common" and "Statehouse" before breakfast. What noble avenues of Elm, Limes & Maples &c. Fine hills and depressions, intersected with the neatest walks—wide and kept constantly swept and clean, new mown grass in between. Pretty pond and fountain, and beautiful distant glimpses of the country and Charles River, entwined with groups of children and adults, loitering under the splendid arches of foliage and enjoying the sweet morning air. Drinking founts at intervals, for the Public, of tasteful design in Iron. The entire enclosure 48½ acres, surrounded with handsome Iron Palisades on Granite, fine Granite steps, and Pillars, and Iron Gates. Stately mansions of the wealthier citizens the "Lawrences," "Emersons," "Appletons" &c. The old Hancock House[13] and solid public buildings all around, with streets as clean and sweet as a running brook.

Sent notes to Col. Thayer and A.B. Young and wrote to Major Beauregard & A.T. Wood.

In the evening took Emily and Prescott in the omnibus to her relatives [i.e., maternal grandparents], No. 7 Albion Street, and stayed to Tea.[14] Old Mr. [Jonathan] and Mrs. [Betsy] Prescott are a fine hearty couple of 72 and 74 years. Mr. P. looks after his business as briskly as the youngest man amongst us. Mrs. Ladd has taken a severe cold. All attribute it to the "East wind." George and his wife returned with us to Somerset Street and remained until bed time. Very pleasant visit. They are all very urgent for us to remove at once to their house. I propose accepting their invitation in a week or two. For the present, however, I find it necessary to be nearer the business part of the city, until I regain strength enough to make distance no object.

July 12

Raw East wind, light clouds. Emily's Father, Mr. D[arius]. Ladd, called and sat sometime. He is over 60 years of age, but would readily pass in New Orleans for 48 or 50. Rather slight, of a quick, restless habit.

July 13

Sunny, cool and pleasant. Therm. at noon 75°. Went round to the Athieneum, on Beacon Street (close at hand) with Emily & Mr. Ladd. Took season tickets. The building is exceedingly beautiful and spacious, fine brown stone, rusticated Basement, Corinthian Pilasters, tasteful Panels, openings, cornice and Blocking Course. But the window mouldings are scarcely strong enough, giving insufficient relief.[15] The Collections of Paintings and statuary fell far below my expectations. Still there are some pleasing works, sweet Landscape on the Wissahiccon, and a fine marble by [Edward A.] Brackett, *The Shipwrecked*

Mother, worth the whole collection.[16] Had a "chill" while in the rooms but soon walked it off when we returned to the open air.

Letter from my brother Robert and note from Gridley J.F. Bryant, Architect.

July 14

Beautiful day like autumn at the South. Long walk on the Common before breakfast. Pleasant ½ hour with Mr. Bryant during the morning. Visited the Custom House. Fine piece of construction, solid Granite, Grecian Doric, Stone to the top of the Dome, roof of Granite tiles, ribbed. Building small, but pleasing effect, and well placed. Rotunda adorned with Corinthian columns of white Marble, Choragic Monument of Lysicrates. Inner face of the dome panelled as usual. Skylight of stained glass, all prettily designed and offices convenient, but being so small, and so filled with desks and officials, have a crowded and close appearance, especially after being so long used to the gigantic proportions of the New Custom House at New Orleans.

Went over a large part of the business regions with Mr. Ladd, called at the Bank, and Post Office. Made purchases and returned to dinner.

In the evening walked with Emily to 7 Albion Street thro' the Common and Tremont Street. Took little Prescott and Catharine with us. How bright and beautiful everything looks in that noble Park. There is a cemetery on the South Side full of fine trees, with rows of Lilacs and Sumacs next to the iron railing, the bright red tufts of the latter in full blow. To my fancy it is much prettier than our China Tree at the South, tho' similar in foliation.

Returned in the omnibus to Tea. Visits from the ladies of the house after Tea.

July 15

Beautiful weather—much warmer. Usual walk before breakfast. Went to the Post Office at 10. Found a letter from Mr. Guesnon, N. Orleans, enclosing a copy of the letter from the Hon. Secretary of the Treasury, approving fully of my leave of absence and allowing my salary during the time I am away. Mr. G. also encloses letters from Robert John and my Mother, and one from Catharine's Father in England, acknowledging receipt of £3, which she asked me to send for her May 11.

Called at the Bank of Commerce and took Certificate of Deposit for $350, for travelling expenses back &c. &c. Sat sometime with Mr. Bryant. He showed me various documents, letters &c. and gave me a good many facts, throwing light upon our Granite troubles at the New Custom House some time ago, and his removal as Inspecting Agent, and Mr. Wood as Architect by Mr. Meredith (then Secretary of the Treasury). I never before understood it as fully, and the facts, as thus stated, certainly do little credit to the honorable Secretary.[17]

Emily and the little boy went down to dine and visit South Boston with the Prescotts. Mr. Ladd and I took the omnibus to Bunker Hill Monument and enjoyed a fine Panorama of the suburbs from the Esplanade around the now finished Obelisk. Beautiful Granite, chaste and simple, springing into the clear blue sky to the height of 220 feet. Worthy and elegant memento of "that eventful day."

After dinner went to Albion Street for Emily and returned at 7. Found a beautiful note from Col. Thayer, dated at Fort Warren, and saying that he would be with us tomorrow.

July 16
Cloudy with South East wind, symptoms of rain. Mild air, fresh and pure on the Common before breakfast.

Mr. G. Prescott called with a letter from Alex. Dunn. I replied to it at once and in full, enclosing the two last letters received from my brother Robert. Took a walk with Mr. Prescott to the Statehouse. Went thro' the Basement Floor, and saw the Marble Statue of Washington in its recess on the northern side.[18] It is a creditable piece of sculpture, but the head lacks dignity and force, and the posture is not sufficiently erect.

Set in rain after dinner. Answered Mr. Guesnon's letter of July 6, 1853.

Theodore and Miss Metcalf, and Miss Brodhead came in and spent the evening with us.

July 17
Sunday. Sallied out early to breathe the gentle west wind and enjoy the sunny atmosphere. Threaded the intricate, noiseless streets down to the Market opposite Faneuil Hall, expecting to find the usual bustle of a "Sunday marketing" and inspect the beautiful treasures of land and sea. But no—everything was locked up and silent—only a few figures loitering in the shadow of the long, mossy structure, and here and there a couple of Irish women returning from early prayers. I continued on towards the Harbour, and reached the end of the Long Wharf from which I had a noble view of the Bay, all gleaming and sparkling in mellow sunshine, dotted all over with vessels, and rich in Islands and jutting Points of land spread out in long perspective, while the buildings of East Boston and the Navy yard on the one hand, and South Boston on the other formed fine side scenes to the picture.

Returning I observed more carefully the architectural effect of the Custom House. The Porticos are very fine and the columns exquisitely wrought in solid block, but when they are continued round the body of the building and engaged ¼ into the wall, the effect is tame and unpleasing. The Dome, too, has so much unrelieved dead work about it that it looks lumpish and oppressive.

Indeed, it has no business there at all, except for the fine finish it gives to the Rotunda in the interior. A Dome on pure Grecian Doric Temples is just as incongruous as a glossy black beaver on the head of a well-dressed woman. Took a turn under the fresh green avenues of the Common, and then sat down with a keen relish to breakfast.

Noticed in the morning Paper that Gen. Brock's monument, which we saw standing on Queenston heights on the 7th Inst. was blown down with gunpowder on the 9th by order of the British Government, to make place for a new and more elegant structure to be created on the same site. The old monument had suffered much from a hurricane which tore away nearly all the work above the capital of the shaft.[19] Sir Isaac Brock fell on the field Oct. 13, 1812.

Emily and I wrote a joint letter to my mother in answer to hers received the other day.

After dinner, we walked down to Albion, Prescott with us. Spent the afternoon and took tea. The walk home was very beautiful, fine sunset lighting up the hills beyond [the] Charles River. The Common was crowded with promenaders, and we walked thro' it to take a look at the Fountain, then in full play from the middle of the Pond, rising about 60 feet, with fine horizontal jets near the Base.

Spent part of the evening at the rooms of the Brodheads and then received a visit from Miss Channing (niece of the celebrated Dr. [Walter] Channing) who, with her father, have rooms in the house. Her father is a physician of good repute.

July 18
Lovely weather, South East wind. Walked down to the Public garden on Charles River, which, when finished will be a charming spot, and a very appropriate appendage to the Common. Thence to the New Mill Dam across the River, then home to breakfast, thro' Mount Vernon Street and Louisburg Square, which, with Beacon and contiguous streets, form the most stately and magnificent portion of the city.

One thing strikes me very forcibly and that is the absence of weather stains and discolorations on the Facades, no matter what the material—granite, freestone and brick fronts that have been standing for years are just as fresh and sharp and clean as if executed yesterday.

Finished a pencil sketch of Niagara Rapids at the head of Goat Island.

At 10 I had the pleasure of welcoming my old friend, Col. Thayer. He had been prevented leaving the Fort on Saturday, and only arrived in town this morning. He sat talking with us for three hours, and it seemed to me but half the time. It is so long, so very long, since we last met, and he is now much

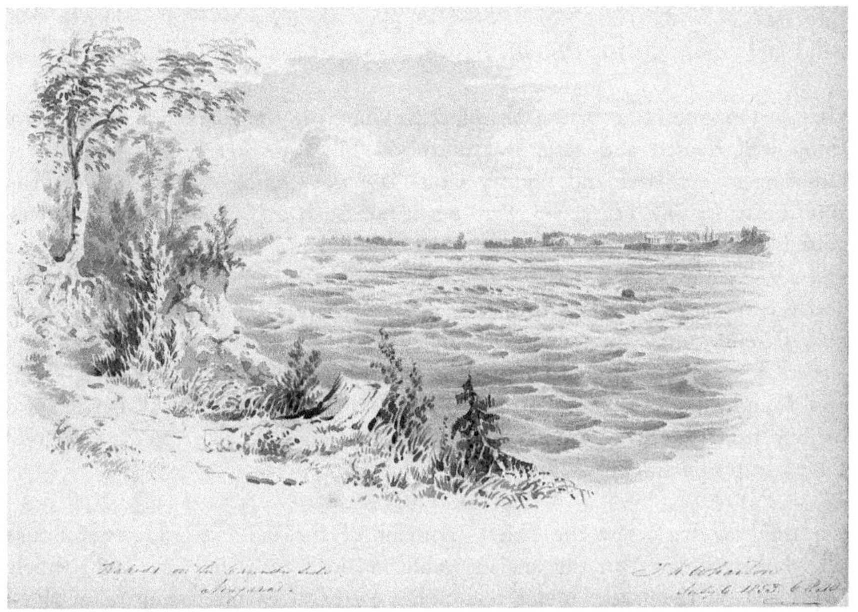

FIGURE 3.6 Rapids on the Canada side, Niagara, 1853 (*Sketchbook*, p. 8). New York Public Library, Archives and Special Collections, New York.

advanced in life, having been in constant and active service in the Engineer Corps for 47 years. He is thinner than when I last saw him, but looks fresh and well, and as interesting and delightful in conversation as ever. We shall see much of each other during the summer, altho' we fear that an order from the War Department, appointing him one of the Commissioners to investigate the Armory Question now at issue, may interfere with our intercourse by calling him away for a time from the works here. But there is a hope of his being released from the Commission. He feels that it is exacting too much from him, when his duties here are so onerous and responsible, and his health impaired, and he told me plainly that if the course adopted by the Department were insisted on he should without hesitation resign. He has been engaged since he resigned the Superintendency at West Point on the Fortifications in the Harbour, Fort Warren, Fort Independence &c. about 20 years.[20]

Soon after the Col. left Mr. Ladd called in with a superb bouquet of white Lilacs, Holly Hocks, Carnations and other fine specimens of northern Flora. It is surprising to see the splendour of the Flowers and Foliage of these chilly regions where climate has done so little and art achieved such wonders.

Emily and little Prescott went down to Albion Street after dinner, but feeling unwell I remained on the sofa. During their absence wrote a letter to Mrs. Huling.

July 19
Mild and sunny, air from South East.

George Prescott came before breakfast to shew me the market. I found every thing well classed and very neat and tidy, for a market house. Meats very tempting except Beef and Poultry which are not choice at this time of year. But the fruits and vegetables were beautiful. Such a profusion of raspberries, gooseberries, black, blue and whortle-berries,[21] white & red currants, cherries and a few early peaches, besides the usual tropical fruits, all in great perfection, and very cheap. And the Fish Department was a perfect treat, superb halibut, cod, salmon, and salmon Trout, brilliant fresh mackerel and huge blood red Lobsters, with a plentiful filling in of haddocks, striped bass, sea perch, eels and flounders, and at very reasonable prices, the finest salmon 25¢ per lb., and halibut from 8¢ to 12¢, according to supply, mackerel 8¢ & 12¢ each, and others in proportion.

On the way back saw the oldest remnant of the old city—a corner house on Market Square—in the ancient gable fashion, with the date 1680 rudely impressed on the stucco under one of the Peaks.[22] An interesting relic, which I should be glad to see stripped of Sundry modern trappings, such as Sign boards &c., and preserved in its pristine simplicity but its "business value" is too great now to admit of such considerations.

After breakfast took Emily and Prescott down to Albion Street, then walked over South Boston Bridge[23] and took the omnibus to the extreme point, where I spent an hour in rambling over the remains of ancient redoubts, and military works, and along the pebbly beach at their feet. The dark blue waters of the Bay came rippling in as clear as crystal, and the pleasant sea breeze swelled the sails of vessels of every class as they threaded the intricate channels, among the Islands and Fortifications that embellish the Harbour. Fort Independance rose just opposite and Deer Island buildings beyond, and formed so pretty a group that I could not resist the temptation to make a rough sketch on the back of my guide Map.

From the heights, too, I had fine Panoramic views of the city, its adjacent Peninsulas covered with buildings and backed by blue hills, woods and slopes dotted with villas, and pretty suburban towns at intervals. Then the crisp, dark looking waters of the harbour with its Forts, Islands, snowy sails, and the clear firm line of the Ocean on the far off horizon.

South Boston is interesting, too, from its large number of charitable Institutions, erected on fine commanding sites, with beautiful grounds around them, and wearing an air of substantial comfort and permanence, tho' the structures themselves are extremely plain and unpretending, but large and roomy. The streets are well laid out, without much regularity as to the style and class of buildings, but embracing many beautiful residences and gardens, and quite a number of tasty, well-placed Gothic cottages.

Leaving the omnibus at Harrison Avenue, I called at 7 Albion, but finding dinner over I walked back to my rooms, and left Emily with her friends until evening.

Spent the afternoon in writing, went for Emily at 5, got home between showers, which had set in lightly. Every omnibus was crowded, and Court and Washington Streets are full of them. Lines run to every quarter of the mazy suburbs, and all pass thro' these principal avenues and Tremont Street. All drive fast, whilst other vehicles of every description are flashing about in between, so that it is no very safe or easy matter to effect a crossing for ladies or children. Still I hear of no accidents.

Retired early after so much exercise.

July 20

Dark & murky, torrents of rain, cool East wind. I secured ½ an hour's walk before breakfast, while the rain fell more lightly.

Disappointed by the weather of a proposed trip to Mount Auburn [Cemetery], I sat down and finished a final drawing of the view from South Boston Point, and as it cleared up about 11 and turned out extremely fine, I set out with Mr. Ladd, and first called upon Mr. Bryant, then took a long walk thro' all the business streets, and principal avenues in the East side of the city—noting all the churches, and other public buildings—in fact everything of interest as we passed along, and returned to dinner at half past two much interested and gratified by the researches of the morning. The Unitarian Church in Bedford Street[24] is a pleasing specimen of modern Gothic, and well executed in mellow tinted sandstone with far more purity of detail than we usually find, decidedly the best I have yet met with in Boston.

July 21

Large fire at a short distance, corner of Court and Howard. No jangling, continuous bells, no noise. I might have passed it by unnoticed but for my servant. Dressed and walked down to the spot. Quite a number of people collected but no excitement, and even the Engines were worked with the coolest and most Oriental gravity. But they managed the fire with great skill, and subdued it in an incredibly short time. The "Alarm bell" simply tells the "number" of the Fire District, when the fire occurs, and would pass unobserved except for those who understood its meaning. It has a singularly wild & melancholy cadence when heard in the still night.

After breakfast Mrs. Ladd came and took Prescott to Albion Street and Emily and I walked down to the Worcester Depot and started on the 9 o'clock cars to Saxonville to pay a flying visit to Aunt Julia [Glazier, née Prescott] & bring Ellen to town. Distance 21 miles. Time 1 hr. 25 min.

Very pretty country. Cottages, villas and gardens every where. The taste for the old English gable & pointed style carried to the verge of insanity. Such a profusion of high peaked roofs, tall chimneys, barge boards, pinnacles, pendants & spandrils!—all new painted—chiefly stone colour, and dotting the hill sides, and springing up amongst the green trees in every direction. Running streams, too, gave great freshness, and the beautiful Cochituate Ponds, which supply the City of Boston added an interesting feature to the scenery.

When we got to Saxonville we took a long ramble with Aunt Julia and cousin Fanny [Frances Merrit] thro' the cool shady woods, and over meadows and wheatfields, skirted by the clear brook which winds thro' the bottom land, and sniffed with the delight of children the spicy air of the Pine groves.

Returned in the afternoon train. Took Albion Street on the way for Prescott, and got back to Somerset Street at 6 P.M. after a day of much pleasant incidents.

July 22

Bright and sunny, west wind changing to North East. The midday sun quite warm—warm to us, but not unpleasantly so even when walking briskly in the full radiance.

After breakfast Mrs. Ladd and Ellen came to say that George had planned an excursion to Mount Auburn Cemetery,[25] and would join us with his wife and old Mrs. Prescott at 9. They soon arrived at the rendezvous in Hanover Street, and we all set out, taking the little boy and Catherine, and forming a goodly party of 9 all told.

It is a pretty ride of 4½ miles, thro' the shady suburb of West Cambridge, and by the time-honored piles of old Harvard. The grounds comprise a surface of 110⅓ acres, thickly wooded and intersected with a perfect labyrinth of curving walks and avenues, broad and narrow both, and very neatly kept, winding over hill and dale, thro' alcoves of the deepest shadow, and open sunny glades decked with beautiful flowers, with ever and anon a sweet blue landscape peeping thro' the trees, especially from the highest point which is elevated above the neighbouring Charles River 125 feet. On this knoll a fine Granite shaft is now in progress, say about one third up, and when finished will be about 60 feet high, and command a superb coup d'oeil.

The monuments are very numerous and chiefly of white marble or warm coloured freestone, the latter harmonizing well with the bright foliage. Many of them are very tasteful, especially those of Magoun, Binney, Lawrence and Oxnard, the last both as to design, execution and exquisite beauty of position pleases me better than any other in the whole enclosure. The position of the Chapel is well chosen and the building would be very effective, but for the unsuitableness of Granite for Gothic details, all of which in this structure are painfully imperfect, tho' the architect must be as much to blame as the material, from the fact that the interior, which is of strong plaster over brick, is designed with equal disregard to purity. There is no excuse for this but ignorance. The Entrance Gates are also of Quincy Granite—Egyptian style—which is much better adapted to the severe character of the stone and has a pleasing effect.

We loitered in this charming Seclusion until 1 o'clock, when we returned to the city, dined and then set out again for North Chelsea Beach [now Revere Beach]—about 4 or 5 miles in the direction of Lynn. Here we spent a pleasant hour on the Sands, inhaling the pure sea air and in sight of the dark blue ocean, but as the wind was from the land there was no surf—nothing but diminutive ripples chasing each other to the shore. The Bay was dotted with white sails, and enclosed on the North by the town of Lynn with a range of well-wooded hills in its rear, and the Peninsula of Nahant stretching far to seaward. On the South by low promontories and tongues of land, swelling into rounded hills, or sinking into green salt-flats, until lost in the level line of the ocean.

We got back to our rooms at half past 7 after a day of rare enjoyment, and wholly unattended by that languor with which such lengthy excursions usually close. Indeed there is a buoyancy in this climate which seems to preclude fatigue.

After tea the "Brodhead" family and Mr. & Mrs. Andrews came in and we passed a very lively, social evening, ending with an excellent bottle of Champagne in Mr. Brodhead's rooms, and retired at half past 11. Slept very soundly and up again in time for a short walk on the Common before breakfast.

July 23
Cloudy, symptoms of rain, south wind. Sat for half an hour with Mr. Bryant. Made an engagement to go with him to Lawrence on Tuesday morning.

He tells me that the cornice of the Central Gateway at Mt. Auburn Cemetery is in one stone and weighs 55 Tons. Its extreme dimensions are 24' 6" x 11' 3" x 4' 6". The original block, when detached from the Quarry was upwards of 100 Tons, before it was cut and brought into shape. In setting, it was raised from the ground by screws, and then slid into its place on the top of the hoisted stone. The whole height of the Central portion of the structure is 27' 2", width of opening 10 feet with plain vertical Jambs of 4 feet each—wings on each side well proportioned, well cut inscription in alto relieve on the Facia over the principal opening:

—Then shall the dust return to the earth as it was,
and the spirit shall return unto God who gave it—[26]
Mount Auburn
Consecrated Sept. 24, 1831.

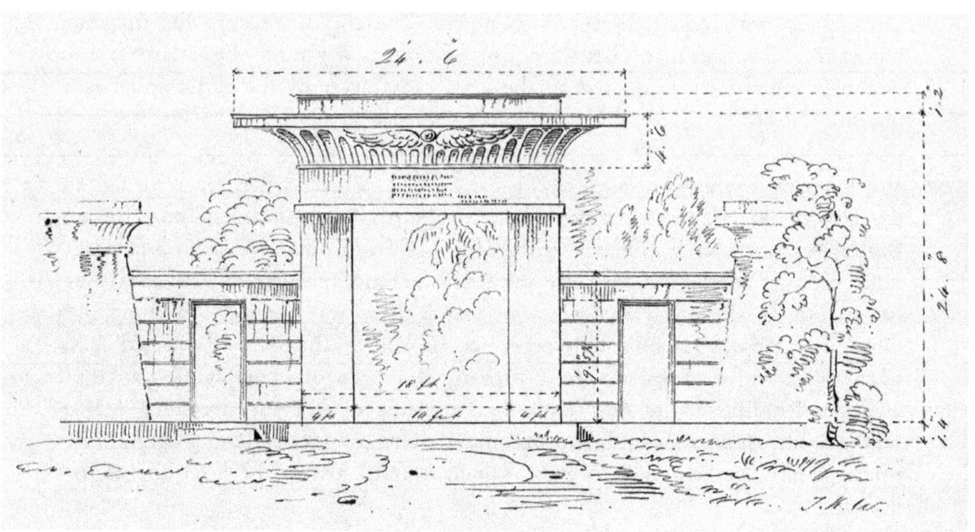

FIGURE 3.7 Central gateway at Mt. Auburn Cemetery, 1853 (*Journal*, vol. 2, p. 55). New York Public Library, Archives and Special Collections, New York.

The annexed rough sketch shews the central Portion of the gateway at Mount Auburn, and its principal dimensions, the cornice stone alluded to above &c. &c.

Mr. Bryant kindly furnished me with such drawing materials as I needed, and told me that anything he had of that kind was at my service, and if I wished to make a drawing at any time he would have a board prepared for me either at his office or sent up to my rooms, his library, also, he gave me access to. By the bye, thro' the politeness of a friend my name has been entered on the Books of the Librarian at the Athieneum, so that Emily and I can avail ourselves of that noble collection during our stay in Boston. They have a fine copy of "Audubon" and other rare and valuable works.

Rainy afternoon, chill wind from the South East.

July 24
Sunday. Charming day after the rain of the night, pleasant air from the South East.

In Boston, the Sabbath is literally a day of rest. Not even old Governor [John] Winthrop and his little colony, 223 years ago, could look out upon a more peaceful Sunday morning than now greets the strangers in this thriving metropolis. The stillness and seclusion of the ancient Shawmut hills are perpetuated in the weekly noiselessness of these city streets. Today they are radiant with sunshine, and the chimes of Christ Church steal pleasantly on the ear, swelling and falling with the breeze, and so they have done from Sunday to Sunday since they were first hung in the year 1774.

July 25
Showers in the night, clouds and sunshine today. Salt air from South West. Lovely afternoon.

Passed part of the morning in the Library and Reading Room of the Athenieum, familiarizing myself with the classification of the Books, so as readily to find any work I may have occasion to refer to.

The collection is a large one, some 55,000 volumes, and the rooms spacious, tasteful and very silent, the arrangements for reading &c. very commodious, and the librarian polite and attentive. The rooms appear to be much frequented by both sexes, and certainly a more delightful place of resort need not be desired, especially in connection with the galleries of Painting and Statuary which are in the same beautiful edifice.[27]

Finished a Pencil drawing made at Mt. Auburn the other day, including the family tombs of "Oxnard" and "Webster," forming to my fancy the most pleasing group in the cemetery. The latter has the following names and dates inscribed—

Webster					
John R.	died	1820	aged	18 months	
Harriet W.	"	1833	"	10 years	
Grant	"	1797	"	80 "	
John White	"	1805	"	80 "	
Sarah White	"	1807	"	77 "	
Elizabeth Davis	"	1812	"	76 "	
Redford	"	1833	"	72 "	Father to Prof. J. White Webster
Hannah	"	1833	"	67 "	

The remains of the notorious Professor John White Webster are interred within the same enclosure.

Note from Mr. Bryant proposing to defer our visit to Lawrence until Wednesday owing to unexpected and pressing business.

July 26
Went down to the Revere House and saw by the *Picayune* that on the 19th and 20th Inst. the deaths from Yellow Fever in N. Orleans were as high as 60.

From the Revere to the Reading Room to see the morning papers &c., and returned to breakfast thro' a brisk rain and raw South wind. The rain prevented a trip I had proposed to Nahant.

Letter from Robert John enclosing note of introduction to the Revd. P.H. Greenleaf. Answered at once.

Granite floor of the Interior of Post Office reeking with wet from condensation, shewing that this feature is not confined to a Southern climate. The sidewalks outside, at the time, were pretty dry, the rain having ceased towards noon, tho' the air continued dense and sultry, but the thermo. only indicates 76° at 12 N[oon].

Mr. Gilbert Brownell, a brother of the Bishop, kindly sent word that he had recorded my name at the Merchants' Exchange reading room, where I shall find all the papers in the country during my stay.

Made a sketch of the old house, corner of Ann Street and Dock Square, alluded to before. The face of the wall is rough cast, with broken junk bottles instead of pebbles in the mixture, making a very firm, enduring coat. The annexed sketch shews the date impressed into the plaster, and the simple ornaments which are introduced to relieve the plain surface. It is connected with the early history of Boston, and perpetuated in [James Fenimore] Cooper's novel of *Lionel Lincoln*.[28]

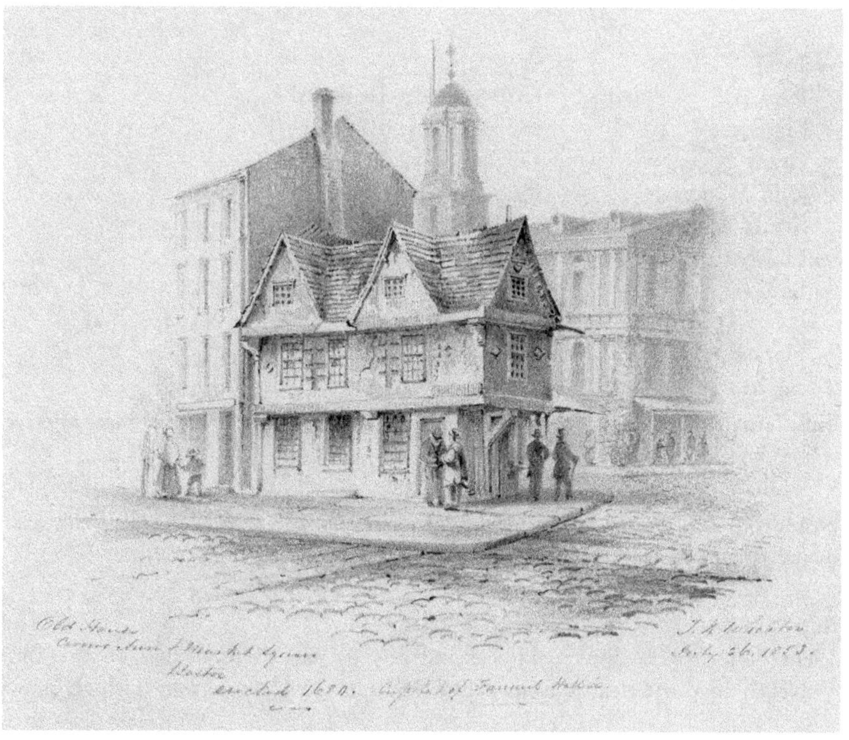

FIGURE 3.8 Old house, corner of Ann Street and Market Square, Boston, 1853 (*Sketchbook*, p. 68). New York Public Library, Archives and Special Collections, New York.

July 27
Gloomy rains and chill South East wind. Spent the morning chiefly at the Athieneum in the Picture Gallery and library, drawing &c.

Calling for a moment at the Revere I was so fortunate as to meet my old friend Major [Thomas] Leslie of New York, just arrived, and on his way to Eastport, Maine. He called upon Emily after dinner and spent an hour with us. The rain having ceased we passed the rest of the evening together until tea time, strolling round the Common and its vicinity, and as it is his first visit, I pointed out to him the various objects of interest, buildings &c., embraced in our walk. Took him thro' the rooms of the Athieneum &c. The last time I saw him was 1847 when he was stationed in New Orleans, during the [Mexican] war. We saw much of each other at that time, he being at the Florance House, and I with my family at Mr. Cornell's on the adjoining Square.

July 28
Pleasant west wind after the rain, fine & mild all day.

Mr. Ladd and I started at 9½ in a pretty little Steamer for Nahant. Threaded the intricate channel among the hundred Islands of the Harbour, and then across a fine Bay open to the broad Atlantic, but today as smooth as a sheet of plate glass.

We landed at 10½ and spent an hour in rambling over the more prominent points of the Peninsula which rise in rugged points of rock to heights varying from 20 to 60 feet, crowned with grassy mounds and slopes and washed by the Ocean. The connection with the mainland is by a flat, sandy Isthmus, which forms a beautiful beach, stretching away in a wide curve towards the town of Lynn.

I was not pleased, however, with Nahant. It has a bleak, comfortless look, without any of that seclusion and grandeur, which you would expect from its marine position. The rocks present a chaotic assemblage of sharp, jagged fragments, but no picturesque grouping, nothing artistic. Plenty of Hotels, however, and neat cottages. Good roads, carriages and people every where. I am rather disposed to suspect that my disappointment with Nahant is due more to an over wrought fancy, than a real deficiency in local interest. I have for years longed to stand once more on the ocean-cliff, and watch the surges tossing and chafing at my feet, and then again those strange little eloquent fairies called "early impressions" are ever at hand where fancy is busy. My earliest types of all that is grand and lovely in marine scenery were drawn from the noble headlands and beautiful bays which lie between Scarboro' and Flamboro' on the Yorkshire Coast and to this day I cannot feel fully satisfied with anything less redundant in all that is characteristic and engrossing in the poetry of the sea shore. Still the lover of nature will always feel that the simple ocean alone is a volume of sublimity and beauty—even apart from its varied and romantic surroundings.

Took the Stage to Lynn and thence by the Eastern Rail road to Boston, reaching there about 2 P.M. Emily had spent the morning in returning calls, and had just got back when I arrived. I had hoped to find Nahant sufficiently interesting to take her over for a whole day, but do not think she would be repaid for the trouble. Took a long sleep and a long walk after dinner.

Dr. & Miss Channing & young Brodhead passed the evening with us. Very pleasant.

July 29
Mild air from the South West, thin veil of clouds.

Walk as usual before breakfast.

Not feeling very well I spent the greater part of the morning in the house. However, I read the papers at the Mercantile Reading room, and at noon walked over to the Athineum with Emily to show her the geography of the place whenever she chooses to visit it. After dinner Mrs. Robbins brought her carriage to take Emily & Mrs. Ladd thro' the environs. I excused myself and took a long sleep on the sofa, which refreshed me exceedingly. Then a ramble with Ellen and little Prescott on the Common, the evening being delightful. Emily & Mrs. Ladd did not return until quite dark, after a charming drive thro' Cambridge, Brookline & Roxbury, visiting the Forest Hills Cemetery, Reservoir &c.

July 30
Cool and pleasant air from S. West, sunny sky. Therm. at noon 76°, which is seldom exceeded here. The morning Papers shew a gradual increase of "Fever" in New Orleans, 43 deaths last Saturday the 23rd.

Morning spent in making purchases, and at Bryants, Merchants' Exchange, & Athineum &c. Met Mr. Trufant of New Orleans at the Revere [House].

They have a way here of pronouncing the President's name [Franklin] "Perse." At first I thought it an individual peculiarity but thus far I have found it universal.

Answered a letter from Alex. Dunn, N. York, dated 26th Inst.

Emily spent the day in Albion Street and took the little boy. I went for them towards evening and returned in the ever ready omnibus. Let me note here that the omnibuses in Boston are not only numerous beyond belief, but the drivers are the civilest and most accommodating I ever met with. Great competition may partly account for it. The lines run thro' to the suburbs in every direction—South Boston, Dorchester, Roxbury, Brookline, Brighton, Jamaica Plain, Cambridge, Charlestown, Chelsea and East Boston Ferry—and even to Mt. Auburn 4½ miles off.

July 31
Sunday. Lovely day, pure blue sky, cool breeze South West to South East.

Rose very early and walked over the long Mill-dam Causeway, across the Charles River. It forms a principal avenue to the city in the direction of Brookline, entering thro' Beacon Street, one of the finest in the city. I passed thro' the Public Garden. The profusion of Mignionette [*Reseda odorata*] and other Scented Flora was perfectly delicious, but I was surprised to find myriads of musquitoes in the lowest part of the ground, evidently engendered in the neighbouring Salt Marsh.[29]

The chimes of the old Church were musical as ever, and among other tunes I recognized with pleasure the national air of England.[30] Heard the "Te Deum" at Temple Street church.

Sent notes to Edward Bogert of New York, and Horace W. Brown of Long Island.

A.M. walked down and took tea in Albion Street. A firm shower while there but the sun shone out again when we returned. The musquitoes were quite annoying on Tremont Street, where it lies contiguous to the low grounds. Latitude does not seem to determine the locale of this venimous little nuisance, and wherever there exist large tracts of wild marsh, there they most do congregate. Such tracts form quite a belt around Boston, and along its sedgy margin. There they buzz, buzz, and sometimes even venture forth on the waftings of the breeze a little way up the slopes as they did today. But I have never found them on the high grounds of New England.

August 1, 1853
Beautiful weather, South East wind.

There will be a continuous stream today on the Old Colony Railroad to Plymouth Rock, to celebrate the embarkation of the Pilgrims from Delft Harbour, August 1, 1620, in the immortal Mayflower. By the bye, two of the Pilgrims, W. Bradford and W. Brewster, were brother Yorkshiremen from Scrooby.

Col. Thayer called and sat awhile at 9 and we engaged to visit him at the Fort on Friday next.

Spent a social evening by invitation at Mr. Robbins, Chestnut Street. Some very pleasant young ladies there, music and a delightful little supper. I like the frank "abandon" and social warmth of the Boston people, and the more so as I was prepared to expect nothing but gelid [icy] reserve and austere verticality.

Carriage at the door at 11. Took Emily home first, then drove down to Albion Street with Mrs. Ladd and Ellen. It was near 12 when I got back. The weather had changed to a drizzling rain and raw East wind.

The Convention which has been in session for many weeks, proposing a "revised Constitution" adjourned "sine die" at 2 o'clock at night. The lights streamed cheerfully from the State house as we drove by. The closing scene was marked by the same good order and harmony which have characterized the whole session. The New Constitution will be presented to the people of the State at the November elections.[31]

August 2
Moist & cloudy, after the rains of the night, cold north wind.

Rose too late for my walk before breakfast.

Part of the morning at the Reading Room. Read a bold article in the July *Blackwood* on the "Fine Arts" and "Public Taste of 1853," criticizing severely and repudiating the leading features of the "Turner" School.[32] "Spernit et odit"[33]—deploring the caprice which lavishes patronage on tasteless works from the mere possession of a "name" and closing with remarks on the real standard of "Taste," the foundations of which it conceives to be laid in a grand all-pervading truth, which it designates as the "morals of life" and from which it supposes to spring everything that is truly excellent equally in manners as in art—tho' in language, to say the least, curious, and to me very vague and intangible.

The *New Orleans Bulletin* estimates the mortality of the week (July 23rd) by yellow fever, at 500, and states that it is raging to an extent wholly without precedent. The *Dispatch* gives 126 deaths by Fever on the 30th Ult.

August 3
Sunny day, South West wind.

Recd. a letter from C[harles]. Knap Pittsburg 30th Ult. Answered immediately.

Met Messrs. Moody, Chism & Marks of New Orleans.

Took the omnibus to Charlestown to deliver Robert's letter of introduction to the Revd. P.H. Greenleaf. After much fruitless inquiry had to return to town without finding him. Being so near the [Bunker Hill] Monument I should have gone to the top but the air was too misty for distant views.

Going to Albion Street with Emily & Prescott after dinner I found that had I taken the extreme South end instead of the extreme North. I should have found another Concord Street on the "Neck" and the gentleman I was in quest of in the morning. I was misled by the "Directory" and an imperfect map.

August 4
Heavy rains in the night, with brisk wind from the East. Set in rain thro' the morning.

Letter from E.C. Bogert, New York, and one from Col. Thayer postponing our visit to the Fort until next week as the rainy weather has made the island too wet and muddy for Emily to go over it with comfort.

We had engaged to dine out today but the rain prevented. It held long enough for me to step over to the Athieneum and read the papers. The dispatches from New Orleans are as gloomy as the day, the Fever raging with unabated virulence.

Spent the day in working up some of my sketches in Sepia, to preserve their character more distinctly than in rough Pencil outlines.

Several friends spent the evening with us.

August 5
Warm sunny sky. Light air from S. West to S. East.

Wrote to Col. Thayer engaging to visit him at The Fort on Tuesday next.

Morning at the Picture Gallery and Reading Room.

Pleasant evening with Judge [Theron] Metcalf and family. He presides at present at the Supreme Court and is a genial, well informed companion, and able jurist.

August 6
Dense sea fog during my walk before breakfast. East wind and cloudy threatening sky. Rain set in about 6 P.M.

I ordered a carriage at 11 A.M. and having packed up took leave of our friends in Somerset Street to redeem our promise of passing sometime with Emily's relatives in Albion Street, where we were pleasantly domiciliated by dinner time. We had scarcely arrived when Emily's cousin Aurelius Ladd drove up to invite us for a couple of weeks to his place 4 miles in the country. We engaged to go next Thursday.

No dispatches, no letters, no papers from New Orleans for the last 48 hours.

Calling at a Cigar Store a little amateur of 10 years old, neat and well dressed, stepped up to the counter with "What is your *smallest* cigar?" Shades of the Pilgrims!

August 7
Sunday. Heigho! The wind & the rain, and the rain, it raineth every day.[34]

Fog and dripping moisture from the Eastward, but so pleasant and comfortable indoors as to make the weather outside a matter of complete indifference.

Indeed, here, as everywhere else, there is more real enjoyment in a "home" in a couple of hours, than in the best conducted boarding house in a couple of weeks.

Cleared up in the afternoon to allow Mr. Prescott and me a walk over to Roxbury but spoiled the courtesy by wetting us on our return. I have so much to see, however, that I must keep on the move.

August 8
Moist and cloudy, but no rain, quite pleasant towards evening.

By appointment I joined Mr. Bryant at the Maine Railroad Depot at 10 A.M. and left in the cars for Lawrence, 27 miles. This is a very fine manufacturing town, containing now upwards of 10,000 people, where 8 years ago there were but a few cottages scattered over a sterile range of hill sides skirting the Merrimac. Its sudden importance is due to the enterprise of the Hon. Abbott Lawrence and others, and bids fair to rival the finest manufacturing plants in New England.[35] A dam of 22 feet high furnishes the power and the supply of water is unlimited.

We first visited the "Pacific Mills" now nearly finished and the largest in America—800 feet long when complete, 75 feet high, 5 Stories—and substantially built of brick on massive stone foundations, and intended for the manufacture of Mousseline de Laines [very fine woollen dress fabric]. Another Factory is in progress between it and the River, immediately on the Bank, this, tho' not near so high as the "Pacific," extends along the Merrimac to the vast length of 1,000 feet.

We next went to a large cotton Factory in full operation, the "Bay State," all the complicated machinery working with exquisite precision, and amazing rapidity, and the noise so deafening that we had to communicate with each other by signs, tho' the operators seemed in no way incommoded by it. They are chiefly Irish, the rate of wages now paid being too low to secure the services of those sprightly "Factory girls" whom we read of.[36]

From the Cotton Mill to the "Essex Machine shops," a noble structure and presenting fine samples of the more complex operations in Iron and Steel. The first story is assigned to "Locomotives" of which there were 8 or 10 nearly finished. The upper stories to spinning machinery &c. We also stepped into the offices and draughting room, at a short distance from the works. The drawings were finely executed and many of them of great size, say on sheets 10 or 12 feet long.

After a general survey of the town which is rapidly springing up on all sides, of large, substantial brick stores, dwellings, factories, churches, civil offices &c., we walked to the Franklin Hotel to dinner, and then proceeded to the other end of town, and inspected the works at the new county prison, now rapidly advancing under the Superintendence of Mr. Bryant. The three commissioners joined us and we spent at least two hours on the spot. The site is well chosen, building of split granite, with brick backing. Hammered Quoins, sills, Jambs and Lintels, and the arrangements for comfort, and cleanliness, light, ventilation, and the Security of the prisoners, truly admirable. A pretty little stream, the Spiggot River, flows by it, and by cutting away a contiguous hill and filling up the marshy margin, a striking range of terraces will be formed towards the stream and returned in a lofty embankment, faced with granite on the side fronting the high road. The Bridge which carries the road over the stream is so rural and combines so prettily with the quiet brook scenery that I stole off for a short time and retained a sketch of it.

We were in the cars again at 4¼ P.M. for Lowell, which we reached at 17 minutes to 5 (11 miles) and at 5 off again for Boston (26 miles), which we went over in exactly one hour.

This is the oldest [rail]road in America (except a short one at Quincy for the transportation of Granite), and no serious accident has ever happened on it, nor any passenger lost his life. It is certainly the easiest and pleasantest road I ever travelled on, and the country quite interesting.

I rejoined my family at tea, highly pleased with the excursion of the day, and feeling under great obligation to Mr. Bryant to whose politeness I was indebted for having seen so much of interest in so short a time.

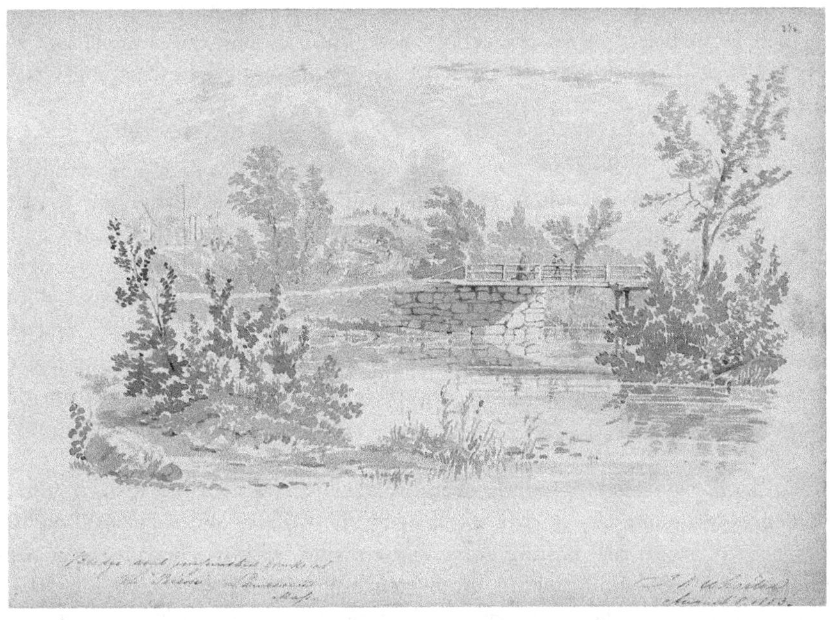

FIGURE 3.9 Bridge and unfinished works at the "'Prison," Lawrence, MA, 1853 (*Sketchbook*, p. 13 1/2). New York Public Library, Archives and Special Collections, New York.

I was delighted, too, to find my little boy a great deal better after being quite feverish and restless for the last day or two. The appearance today of his seventh tooth fully accounts for it.

August 9

Morning opened with a brilliant sky and not a cloud, while the light air from the South West blew fresh and elastic.

At 9 A.M. Emily and I and the little boy with his nurse left the wharf in the little steamer *Mayflower* for Hull, 21 miles down the Bay, where by appointment Col. Thayer was to meet us with a boat, and take us over to Fort Warren, on George's Island—separated by a channel of one mile from Hull—and protecting the entrance to the Harbour. Plenty of passengers and very pleasant trip of an hour among the Islands.

Arriving at the Hotel on the Beach we were disappointed not to meet the Col. and after waiting an hour without any signs of a Boat from the Fort opposite, we gave up all hope of crossing, and concluded that something very unexpected had interfered with the engagement. So we made up our minds to enjoy the fine pure air and pretty scenery of the Island we were on until time to leave for town.

We found the Hotel and one on the hillside quite well filled, and groups of ladies and gentlemen strolling about the beach or in the saloons and galleries, with quite an unusual proportion of children playing about the skiffs, and sail boats or dipping their feet in the clear crystal water as the tide came rippling in. Inch by inch it stole up the pebbly slope until its tiny waves moistened the very walls of the building, and flashed back the images of the laughing groups in many a radiant reflection.

Before dinner I walked to the summit of the Island, which commands an enchanting view of the whole Harbour, with the city of Boston far away to the West, and the magnificent works at Fort Warren occupying a conspicuous position in the near scenery, while Points, Islands and Headlands lay scattered in rich profusion with fine blue hills to the Southward, and Eastward the boundless ocean, all bathed in glowing sunshine. The grand, the wild and the beautiful, all in happy combination, and displaying a variety and richness of harbour scenery that will compare favourably with the most celebrated on this side the Atlantic.

The Island, or more properly Peninsula, is composed of two rounded eminences—the one on which I stood being the highest, say about 400 or 500 feet—covered with rich pasture grass, and crowned with the remains of ancient redoubts, and containing within the entrenchments a signal station for vessels entering from Sea. The high road winds between the hills, with neat cottages, and farm houses on each side, and fine orchards of apples and pears, loaded

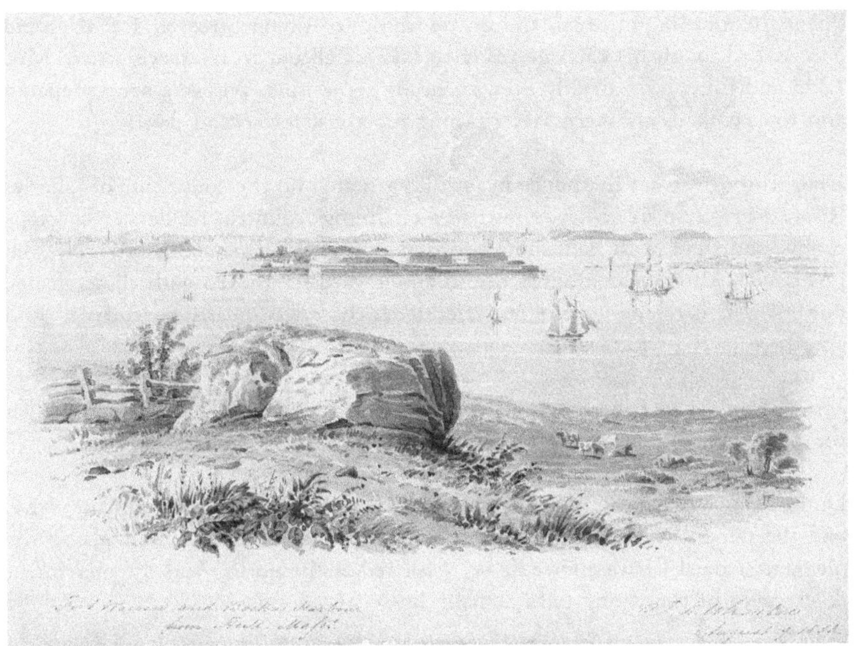

FIGURE 3.10 Fort Warren and Boston Harbor from Hull, MA, 1853 (*Sketchbook*, p. 15). New York Public Library, Archives and Special Collections, New York.

with fruit. A clear little Pond lies in the hollow, and is quite a picturesque object, when combined with the surrounding foliage and homesteads.

I was so pleased with my explorations that I insisted upon Emily's taking the same walk with me after dinner, and we climbed "The braes" together, a fine breeze mitigating the glare of the afternoon sun.

We got back to the Hotel just as the Boat appeared in sight, and at 4½ P.M. were again on board. Had a pleasant run to town and reached Albion Street by 6 P.M. Here I found a letter from Col. Thayer (which I ought to have got last night), stating that as the weather had continued so inclement, he should not expect us, and fixing our visit for Thursday in case it cleared off and promised a fine day. His letter was written during the Sea-fog of yesterday morning.

Letters also awaited me from Mr. Guesnon, N. Orleans, my brother Robert John, and sisters Marianne and Emily, and Mr. D. Ladd of Boston.

August 10
Charming weather, South West wind.

Answered the letters from Col. Thayer & Mr. Guesnon.

Spent the morning in town, and on returning to Albion Street at 1 P.M. found Mr. A. Ladd with his carriage ready to take us all out to his place, where Mrs. Ladd and Ellen have already been spending some time. We were soon prepared and took with us the necessary clothing for a visit of several days.

Delightful drive, and the house beautifully situated on the south side of Charles River, just opposite Mt. Auburn, a charming country residence, spacious rooms, and Hall, with handsome bedrooms upstairs to match. Thoroughly well furnished with every convenience, and ample garden, stocked with choice fruits, flowers, and vegetables—and our friends as cordial & hearty as you will find anywhere in the wide world.

Mr. & Mrs. Ladd have 5 young children, so that with my little boy and Ellen the rising generation is fully represented.

Dinner was awaiting us when we arrived, and the pure country air, the drive, and the tempting display fresh from the garden, all combined to make it the pleasantest meal I have enjoyed since I arrived at the north. And the merriment & garrulity of the young ones actually knew no bounds.

After a Bottle of Heidsieck [Champagne] and a cigar, Mr. Ladd & I drove to town for the "Doctor," the youngest child being quite unwell. Returned thro' Charlestown, East & West Cambridge, and by the lovely country seats and gardens around "Old Harvard."

Supped heartily and enjoyed a profound and refreshing night's rest, far from the hustle & disturbance of the crowded city.

August 11
Pure, sunny sky, and a breeze from the West so gentle that it scarce stirred the leaves. Therm. at 9 [A.M.]—85°—hot for this parallel, so we have concluded to spend the morning at home. I had a pleasant walk, however, before breakfast, returning met vast droves of sheep & cattle on their way to Brighton—the next town—today being market day for the surrounding villages and country in every direction for miles around. The Market is held at Brighton every Thursday.

Wrote to Dr. C. Hamilton of New Orleans, and passed the heat of the day in preserving the details of sketches made at Hull on Tuesday. 93° in the shade in the middle of the day, and felt most decidedly warm. Indeed, it is the first time I have perspired freely since I came to Boston.

A fine breeze sprung up in the afternoon, and at half past 6 Mr. Ladd, Emily & her mother and I got into the carriage for a drive. We took a circuit of 12 Miles; thro' charming lanes, over hill and dale, and such a richly diversified country as is rarely found in the environs of a vast city. At times the road wound thro' deep valleys overhung with dark masses of Elm and Pine, and moss grown piles of ancient granite, and then suddenly opened upon superb country seats, with fine gravelled avenues, lined with splendid foliage and close mown lawns, forming a succession of exquisite Parks, and exhibiting in perfection the beautiful art of "Landscape gardening" as applied to a country of unexampled variety and picturesqueness of surface and foliage. The villas, too, are on a large scale, and very tasteful—Gothic, Roman, and modern Italian, with every embellishment that opulence can bestow—fine ranges of greenhouse appearing thro' the trees, and choice borders of flowers, with hedges of Thorn or Privet neatly trimmed, delicious green slopes, dotted over with groups of shrubs and detached Elms of grand proportions, and great masses of dark forest in the background—and every now and then a fine glimpse of the city, or a Sheet of water, or a tapering village spire, while groups of gayly dressed females gave animation to the grounds and galleries [porches or piazzas]. And in several instances, a handsome horse & gig might be seen from the road, standing all ready at the principal entrance of a mansion, giving a stylish air to grounds and residences which were in themselves "beautiful exceedingly."

We drove thro' Brighton, Brookline, Jamaica Plain, and by the great reservoir that supplies the city with the pure Cochituate,[37] then round the head of Jamaica Pond, all glowing with the bright crimson sunset, and reflecting the rich woody hills that compose its margin. Then home again under the dewy, freshening influences of the young moon.

What an inestimable blessing to breathe this pure air, and revel in the enjoyment of this lovely country, instead of stifling in the deadly atmosphere of the city we have left far away behind us!—where death is daily more busy and counting his victims by hundreds.

August 12

We really have hot weather at last, glowing skies, dusty highroads, gentle West wind, and at 9 A.M. 85° in the shade. But the heat does not oppress, the air is still buoyant and elastic. At 12 N. it stood at 93°.

Spent the morning on writing and drawing.

Drive to the city in the cool of the afternoon, Mr. Ladd, Emily, Ellen & I. Called at G. Prescott's, Post Office, Reading Room &c., and returned to a late Tea.

During my morning walk, I passed a remarkably well kept place, owned by a "Canny Scott" and cultivated as a fruit garden. He has 10 acres in all, seven of which are planted with choice strawberries, with young orchard trees coming forward at suitable intervals. The strawberry vines are planted in rows wide apart, and treated with scrupulous care. 3 or 4 hands were busy weeding at the time & freeing the bold "runners" from entanglements. The net proceeds range from $2,000 to $3,000 per annum.

August 13
Weather unchanged at 9 A.M. 85° in the shade. At 12 N. still 85°, the wind having changed to east, but the same bright, fervid sky.

Finishing up sketches all the morning, with the drawing room windows all open to let in the pleasant sea breeze, and refresh my eye with the rich Dahlias of the garden in front. Thunder clouds came up at 1 P.M. and by 4 P.M. the thermometer had fallen to 76°.

Drove Emily & her mother in the carriage to East Cambridge in the evening & had to return at full speed to escape the rain which fell freely towards nightfall with thunder and vivid lightening.

August 14
Sunday. Sunny morning, westerly breeze, 83½°at 9 A.M., 91° at 12, and maximum in the afternoon 92°. A heavy rain & thunderstorm passed over towards evening & reduced the temperature 10 or 12 deg.

Geo. & Mrs. Prescott came over by invitation & spent the day, and as Mrs. Ladd's sister & family are staying here for a few days, we numbered 18 in all at dinner—9 adults & 9 children, all in high glee and in no way discomposed by the unusual sultriness of the day.

August 15
Pleasant change in the weather—North East wind—grey clouds—68° at 9—rose to 72° by 12 N., and turned out extremely pleasant, bright sky, cool air.

After drawing for 2 hours, walked to Winship's nursery, lying on each side the Worcester Railroad with Terraces of flowers & ornamental trees and shrubs bordering on the Track, and fine stock of Plants and Trees covering an area of 40 acres under excellent management.[38]

Mr. Ladd drove to town and brought back his mother, sister, and a young lady (from Bangor) to dine. Afternoon of fun and frolic in the garden amongst the new cut grass.

August 16
Cool & breezy, light clouds, East wind—70° at 9 A.M. 73° at 12.

Long walks before and after breakfast—up hill & down dale. Pretty country seats and farm houses every where, surrounded by well stocked orchards, gardens, and pastures, and the hill tops crowned with the original forest, with glimpses at intervals of the city spires, and the public buildings of Cambridge and Harvard.

Spent a good deal of the day in Tinting [pictures].

Emily's mother & Ellen left for Saxonville.

August 17
Fine sunny morning—south wind—72° at 9 A.M.

Mr. Ladd & I drove into town to the Post Office &c., and were caught in the rain on our return at noon. The change came suddenly & by 2 the therm. had fallen to 64°.

Answered a letter from Mrs. Ireland, New York, received on the 14th, and apprising me of the death of my old friend W. Horace Brown, and very recently of his son George by the accidental discharge of a gun.

Rain with little intermission throughout the afternoon and evening.

Dispatch from New Orleans of the 14th gives 200 deaths by fever in that day, and 1,530 for the week preceding, the disease still increasing both in virulence and the number of victims. It has already been in New Orleans about 3 months, the first cases having been reported from the middle to the end of May.

August 18
Thick, misty clouds, dripping rain, scarce any wind. 66° at 7 A.M. 69° at 9. 73° at 12 N, contrasting very strikingly with the end of last week, when the deaths from sunstroke & heat were very numerous even in Boston, and New England generally, and in the city of New York on the 13th Inst. amounted to 100. Spent the morning in sketching and taking outdoor exercise between showers.

The soil here is so light that even after a heavy rain the side paths and tracks across the meadow lands afford very respectable footing, so that in showery weather one need not be wholly confined to the house.

Heavy rain between 2 and 3 P.M. and thermometer fell from 75° to 70°.

August 19
Cold wind from North West—very fresh, 62° at 9 A.M., with dull grey clouds, and altogether quite wintry. Warmed myself by a brisk walk before breakfast. Fine wood fire blazing in the parlour. 68° at 12 N.

After breakfast Emily & I took a pleasant walk amongst the cottages, and pretty country houses which are here springing up on every side. Indeed Brighton will soon form a very considerable suburb to the neighbouring city.

Leaving Emily at the house I continued my walk alone to Brighton village. Attempted on the way to make a sketch of Winchester's elegant mansion & grounds, on the banks of Charles River, just under Mount Auburn.[39] But the highway was so thronged, and my employment excited such expansive gapes and stares, that I felt as if I was engrossing more than my share of the public interest, and abandoned the field.

Returning at 12, Mr. Ladd had the carriage ready so we took lunch and Emily & I got in with him and drove to "Fresh Pond" [in Cambridge]. We had a charming little jaunt of near four hours. The afternoon was brilliant. We found an excellent house there and plenty of good boats. Mr. Ladd chose a sail boat and shot over the Lake with a fine westerly breeze, Emily got into a good row boat and I took the "sculls," and skimmed along the pure crystal water, and enjoyed the exquisite scenery of its shores. It is years since I had a pair of oars in my hands, and it was Emily's first boating experiment. So that what with the beauty of the sky above, the scenes around, and the fine bracing exercise, it was a perfect luxury to us both. We had some pleasant walks, too, and noticed at intervals on the banks the ranges of wooden storehouses where the Ice is collected in winter that supplies the world. Fresh Pond Ice is everywhere considered the best. I secured a sketch of this pretty Pond, and we then ordered our carriage & drove rapidly home to a late dinner.

August 20
Sky as clear as a bell. 68° at 9. 74° at 12.

Being Saturday we announced our intention of returning to town. The carriage was ordered at 11 and Mr. Ladd drove us in by a different road from any we have tried yet, and, if anything, more beautiful. We have had a delightful visit, and promised to go again before the season is over.

Found our friends on Albion Street all well, and much pleased to see us after an absence of ten days.

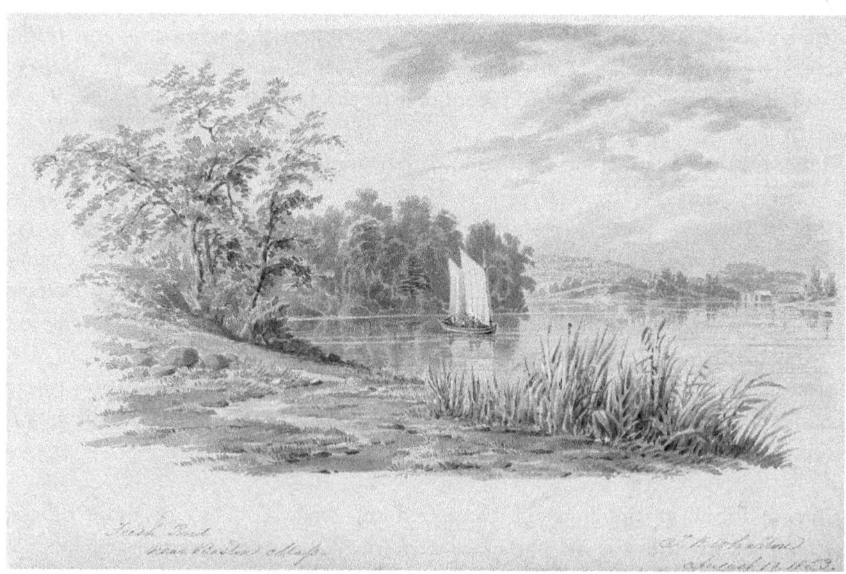

FIGURE 3.11 Fresh Pond near Boston, MA, 1853 (*Sketchbook*, p. 16). New York Public Library, Archives and Special Collections, New York.

A letter from Cousin Fanny awaited us, pressing us to go out and spend some time at Saxonville. Will go probably the latter part of next week.

After dinner replied to Robert John's letters of Augt. 4th and 9th.

August 21
Sunday. Sky of the deepest blue and a fine air from the South West.

Took a long walk with George thro' South Boston to Dorchester Heights and the Reservoir, and lingered there for some time enjoying the noble Panoramic views from the summit—the Harbour, the city and its suburbs, the far away ocean—and then, to the Southward, the fine broken outline of the Milton Hills—with beautiful bays and islands to seaward, and villages out of number brightening up the deep green of the woods and hill sides. There are truly but few cities which can boast of such beautiful and diversified environs as Boston.

In the afternoon wrote to sisters Emily and Marianne, and then took little Prescott and his nurse a good long walk on Shawmut Avenue and South Boston Bridge, leaving Emily at home with her books &c.

Met several New Orleans acquaintances on the Avenue.

August 22
Morning bright and sunny, South West wind. Heavy clouds passed over in the afternoon, with change of wind to North East.

Very unwell and feverish. Obliged to take medicine and stay at home in the afternoon.

The Postman brought me a long and welcome letter from Mr. A.T. Wood, architect of the New Custom House, New Orleans. He urges the terrible epidemic as the reason of his not writing before. He uses strong language—

> The faculties are stunned and awed, the senses are oppressed with the deepest gloom—never have I known such cause for sadness, and you know I am about the last man to cry out. In this epidemic neither age nor condition is exempt from the hands of the destroyer. The infant, the aged, the vigorous, the infirm. The Creole, and the stranger, all are subject to be prostrated, and many never to rise again. I congratulate you on your absence from the city, now the "City of Sorrow."

How little ought I to feel my occasional ill health when I think of the serious danger to which my dear family and I would have been exposed had we remained in New Orleans. I replied to Mr. Wood's letter at once.

Engaged to visit Quincy with Mr. Bryant on Thursday next.

August 23
Bright & sunny, cold bracing north wind.

Detained in the house from the effects of medicine, but feel better for it.

Our fellow traveller Alex. Dunn made us a good long sociable call. He has just arrived in Boston and will remain about 2 weeks. My little boy is just 11 months old today and looks remarkably hearty and forward—a lively intelligent countenance, and the prettiest smile in the world. His motions, too, are so rapid that he has to be watched very closely, especially as his penchant seems to be for climbing up stairs, indicating an aspiring turn of mind, but suggesting the possibility of his "Vaulting ambition o'erleaping itself."[40]

August 24
Charming weather with a light air from S.East, but I am still too bilious to enjoy it.

Wrote to Col. Thayer. I intended to visit him at the Fort today but do not feel well enough.

In the middle of the day Emily & I took a tour amongst our friends and made some half a dozen visits.

Change of wind in the afternoon to South West, with cloudy threatening sky.

August 25
Close and sultry, light veil of clouds, W. to N.W. wind.

Met Mr. Bryant by appointment at the State House at 9. Looked over his plans for the enlargement of the edifice, which is now rapidly advancing under his direction.[41] In spite of a violent nervous headache, I went up to the top of the Dome, and was fully repaid by the splendid coup d'oeil of the City and environs.

Arranged to meet Mr. Bryant at the "Old Colony Depot" at 1¼ P.M. and proceed together to Quincy. Then went to the Athieneum and spent an hour in the Library and Reading room.

Calling at the Winthrop House to see Mr. Moody of New Orleans, I looked over a file of the *Picayune* and was much shocked to see the death of Mrs. Sarah G. Hamilton, wife of Dr. C. Hamilton (my family physician) on the 7th Inst. of "fever." She was at my house the evening before we left New Orleans, looking extremely well, and kindly assisting Emily in her preparations for the journey. This is the first death that I have heard of amongst our friends since the commencement of the fatal "Fever," which still appears to be on the increase.

Met Dr. Channing who told me there was a letter for me at Mr. [T. Larkin] Turner's, Somerset Street. I found it to be a kind note from Col. Thayer, which I answered immediately.

Received, also, and answered a letter from Mr. D. Ladd.

At 1½ Mr. Bryant & I met at the Depot and took the cars for Quincy, where we found Mr. Rogers and 5 others of the Granite Contractors awaiting us, and a handsome dinner all ready in a large private dining hall at the Hotel.

After doing ample justice to the game and champagne we prepared to visit the Quarries.[42] Mr. Penniman took Bryant and myself behind a noble span of "Bays," and the rest got into their gigs, and we shot along at a rapid rate thro' a very interesting country, and by the old mansion of John Quincy Adams, the old Granite Church &c., and in twenty minutes were at the Quarries. There are some half dozen of them, scattered over the lofty ridges for several miles, with fine, romantic roads connecting them, and the most superb Panoramic views from the summits, where the giant masses have been detached from the primeval rock, forming deep chasms, hemmed in by stupendous walls of solid granite, except on one side in each Quarry, which has been graded to facilitate the passage of the huge blocks to the neighbouring sheds. Here the operatives are hard at work with their instruments and bush hammers, shaping and facing the rough material, and in every direction are lying vast piles of Obelisks, Cornices, Piers and Architraves in every stage of progress, from the rude split mass to the fine hammered, sharp angled ashlar or column stone. At all the Quarries, I found more or less of the stone for the New Custom House, all ready for shipment—all the anta-caps complete, and all the Capitals and Column stones, except two of each, which are in the hands of the cutters, and can easily be finished in two or three weeks, so that we may consider the entire requisition up to the bottom of the Entablature as ready for delivery. The contractors took me to one of the Quarries to see a stone which had been quarried under the order to get out the columns on the Canal Street Front, each in one entire block. It is a magnificent mass of 105 Tons weight and was taken from the bed and put in its present position outside the Quarry at a great expense, say not less than $800 or $1,000. The other three stones were got out at other quarries, but since the order for entire columns was countermanded, have been cut up for immediate use.

After mounting to the top of the ridge and taking a grand bird's eye view of the Harbour, city and country around, and then examining the operations of splitting, cutting, finishing &c., more in detail, and the powerful iron steam-cutter in use at Mr. Munn's Quarry, we drove back to the Hotel and bid adieu to our hospitable friends. Took the return cars at seven minutes past 6. The distance to town is only 8 miles. Sweet scenery, inlets of pure water, and a fine sweep of country round Dorchester Bay all studded with pretty cottages, while

"Savine Hill" covered with dark cedars, adds interest and variety to the bright glossy green of Elms and Orchard Trees.

Mr. Munn, the principal contractor for the New Custom House, is absent on a Western tour, but I expect to see him on his return, as I shall visit the Quarries again and take more leisure for examining them. Indeed, I had no idea of the extent of the granite interest here, and that its operations were conducted on a scale of such magnitude, and there is no placing a limit to their growing importance.

August 26
Lovely day with a keen north wind and a sky of unsullied purity.

Emily and I, little Prescott and Catherine took the Worcester Train at 9 o'clock and were with our friends in Saxonville at 10½. They were waiting for us at the Depot. Quite a family re-union at dinner, after which I drove Emily, cousin Fanny and Aunt Julia all around Cochituate Pond, and thro' the lovely lanes and winding roads of this beautiful country for two or three hours.

The "Pond" is a gem of a Lakelet, with high points of living green, and woody knolls jutting into it, and dark Pine woods contrasting with the livelier foliage of the Oak and Elm, and sprays of Silver-birch hanging gracefully over the water. The Conduit House is a small tasteful structure of solid split granite, with fine hammered Quoins, and architraves of openings, and window heads, well cut. Here we all got out and rambled awhile on the greensward by the edge of the water.

Took a long walk before ten and again after ten to familiarize myself with the features of the surrounding country and breathe the pure air of the hills, which has already had a sensible effect upon me, and removed the head-aches and bilious symptoms which have annoyed me so much of late.

Enjoyed a real sound country sleep and rose much refreshed, and greatly improved by the change from the city.

August 27
South S. East wind, cloudy & prospect of rain.

Wrote to Mr. Guesnon and Major Beauregard.

The delays at the New Custom House have been very hurtful to the interests of the granite contractors, as well as generally injurious to the Building. The granite has been got and at a great expense on the supposition that the progression would be pretty regular. But the work has been so much retarded by the discussions relative to the plan that the granite has not been required, and has consequently been left in the hands of the contractors, and not only encumbers their works, but keeps them out of the use of a very large amount of capital. I, therefore, have addressed the following language to Major Beauregard, the present Superintendent, as it is but just to diminish as much as possible, the inconveniences to the contractors from the delays that arose under the Superintendency of Col. Dakin, and Mr. L.E. Reynolds:

> I visited the several Quarries at Quincy this week, and found all the stone for the New Custom House complete up to the Entablature except two column stones, and two Capitals, which can easily be finished in two or three weeks. Thus the whole of the 2nd half of the Third Requisition will in that time be ready for shipment, and the greater part of it has been all boxed up for months, impeding the operations of the Quarry and occupying room in the sheds &c., which is much needed for constantly accumulating orders, so that the contractors are very anxious to receive instructions to ship. I named to them the several causes that had interfered with the resumption of stonework on the Building, and the fact that it was already greatly encumbered by stone lying all around it, and preventing the possibility of receiving more until the setting should recommence. I told them also of the solicitude which you and Mr. Penn had expressed on the subject, and that it was your wish to give them the order at the earliest practicable period, but I feared that the difficulty of procuring labor this "fatal" summer would materially interfere with the progress of the works and occasion unlooked for delay, so that they were satisfied that the inconvenience has been unavoidable. Still we cannot feel surprised at their desire to ship, when the delay not only interferes greatly with their business by the accumulation of bulky material, but also involves considerable loss by so large an amount of capital lying idle. I should be glad, therefore, if you would favor me with a line to say when there is a probability of your being able to give them an order to commence delivery—that I may state to them the prospects if you think proper that I should do so, &c., &c.

The country around Saxonville is broken up into hills of moderate elevation, well clothed with woods and groves, with intervals of bosky thicket and open pasture land. Pine and Oak are abundant and fine isolated Elms and Chestnut. The farms and orchards looking well, grain and fruit abundant. The narrow stream of the Sudbury winds among the uplands, and furnishes water power for the Factories of woollen and other goods in Saxonville, and adds a pleasing feature to a country abounding in picturesque groups, and fine touches of nature. The water is clear and fish plentiful. Trout, Pickerel, Perch, and Cat Fish for all the world like those at the South.

Spent the afternoon very pleasantly with Emily and Fanny in the thick Pine woods, gathering the large juicy whortleberries that grow there in profusion. The wild grapes, too, are ripening fast, the bunches heavy and well-flavoured.

After an early tea Fanny and I took a long ramble by the pleasant wood and meadow paths on the bank of the Sudbury, following its course for about a mile and then ascending to the high grounds and returning by the hill-road to avoid the damp air of the valley in the close of the evening.

Soon after dark the weather became stormy, rain fell freely and the flashes were frequent and vivid, but soon passed over.

August 28

Sunday. Lovely morning, the air purified by the storm, the sky as blue as a sapphire, and pleasant wind from the north west. The soil is so light that I found dry roads and grass-paths when I took my walk after breakfast, and the rains of the night had brightened the face of the whole country, and the green of the lighter foliage and the fields by the road side was perfectly dazzling, especially where contrasted with dark masses of Pine and Hemlock which diversify the Scenery, and give splendid contrasts both of tone and outline.

We all went to the Congregational Church on the hill top at 11. The building comfortable and well furnished, small organ, roomy, well cushioned pews, good carpet, and well arranged pulpit and platform for speakers, the congregation large and attentive. Minister very young but pleasant in manner, and gave us a very neatly written discourse from the text "Thy Kingdom come," shewing the various means used by divine providence for the establishment and extension of his kingdom upon earth, and the causes still operating to continue that extension until the "earth shall be filled with the knowledge of the Lord as the waters cover the sea." The other exercises consisted of short prayers, scripture reading and two hymns, the whole not occupying more than an hour and a half.

The afternoon service commenced at two o'clock, but my head ached so much that I just took the ladies to the door and then walked rapidly for miles over the green fields, and winding highroads, inhaling the fresh breeze of the hills, and the pure, spicy breath of the Pine groves, until I succeeded in walking away all pain and just got back in time to escort the church party home again.

August 29

Pure and cloudless sky, cool air from the West but so light that it scarcely stirred the delicate leafing of the Birch Tree.

After breakfast, I took Emily and Fanny to the Revd. Mr. Northrup's to ask permission to take his boat for a short row on the river. He kindly gave me the key of his boat house, and said it would give him pleasure for me to use it as often as I desired it. We proceeded at once down the hill where the Boat house has been built on the margin of a pretty lakelet formed by the Dam which arrests and spreads out the current of the River above the Mills. We found the Boat an excellent one, and furnished with oars, and a good pair of sculls. I chose the latter and took a long pull up the stream beneath the splendid foliage that hung over it and cast reflections of unparalleled brilliancy and beauty all around us. By and by we came to a place where a large tree had been blown down and spread itself entirely across the stream. A large crook in the main stem formed a natural bridge thro' which I could readily have forced a passage, but the direct rays of the midday sun admonished us that it was time to return, and we dipped gently down the current, locked up our Boat and returned the key to the worthy clergyman with many thanks for his kindness. Emily & Fanny seemed to enjoy it exceedingly, and to me it is always a luxury to glide along a bright, clear stream, with a good pair of oars in my hands, a bright sky above, and those I love in the boat with me.

Returning to dinner I called at the Post Office and found a letter from Mr. A. Ladd urging us to join him and his family on a trip to Belfast, Maine, next Thursday, but we shall be obliged to decline.

I also got the morning papers by the cars.

After dinner, I drove the ladies over to Framingham village (2½ miles) to do some shopping. It is a good example of the New England villages that we hear so much about. Its nearness to Boston (22 miles) and the railroad passing thro' it, secure for it quite a large and affluent population, attracted by the exceeding beauty and variety of the surrounding country, and fine mansions with their highly improved domains add a new embellishment to a place which has long been noted for the substantial and even elegant residences of its thrifty agriculturists.

The public common in the centre of the village are spacious and well planted, and the lofty spires of two Gothic churches rise gracefully from the masses of foliage, and give a fine masked character to the place. The roads in every direction are excellent, and the environs diversified by woody hills, and green grassy valleys, with streams of the purest water gliding thro' them. Altogether it is a lovely seclusion, and more to my taste for a country residence than anything I have yet seen around Boston.

August 30

Another lovely day after a cold dewy night. West wind. Bright blue sky.

Answered Mr. A. Ladd's letter, and then Fanny and I mounted our horses and rode over the country for two or three hours—by Cochituate Ponds and Village, thro' bright green meadows, and deep woody bridle paths, then emerging upon hill roads commanding vast sweeps of blue distance everywhere the same smiling picturesque country, the same well tilled farms, and comfortable homesteads, the same spacious orchards, bending with luscious, ruddy fruits, the same noble elms, and dark, shadowy groups of Pine, while clear Ponds sparkled like diamonds in the sunshine, and light clouds above flung mottled shadows over the fields and woodsides. It is a charming country, and the ride was exhilarating and delightful. I was only sorry that Emily could not join us, as she is unused to horseback.

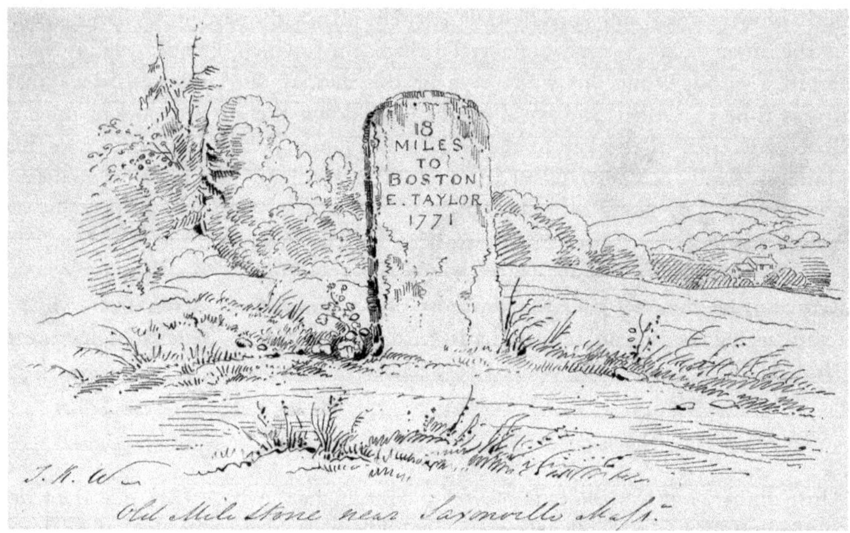

FIGURE 3.12 Old Mile Stone near Saxonville, MA, 1853 (*Journal*, vol. 2, p. 102). New York Public Library, Archives and Special Collections, New York.

At a turn of the road we were attracted by a mile-stone of the "olden time." Thus, executed in rough granite, the letters cut deep.

Got the morning paper on our return, and was pleased to see a considerable diminution in the mortality of New Orleans on the 27th—159 by Fever.

After an early tea Emily, Fanny & I took to the Boat and explored the river for a considerable distance above the "Sylvan bridge." The air had subsided to a dead calm, and nothing could surpass the beauty of this secluded forest stream, the lofty groves on each bank hung with vines and creepers depending into the water, and every leaf reflected with the nicest precision, and brightened by a liquid gloss even more beautiful than the original object above. I pulled easily and we glided along for nearly two hours, watching the changes as the sunlight gradually melted away, and awaking the echoes with glees and boat songs, so that the night dews had begun to fall when we regained the boat house, and hastened up the hill to reach home before the darkness fully closed in.

August 31

Pleasant morning with shady, mottled clouds and fine breeze from the South. The sun shone out bright towards noon, but did not deter Emily, Fanny and myself from taking a walk over to the head of Cochituate Pond (nearly 2 miles). Arrived there, we descended a steep, grassy slope, thro' an orchard, to the water's edge. A tuft of Pine trees formed a fine shade, and we found a chair by the gravelly margin all ready to our hands. Here the girls rested themselves until I took a sketch of the Pond from the hill side above which commands the best view of it, shewing to advantage all the Points projecting into the water, and richly wooded, while the clean smooth grass furnished me with a seat, and a spreading tree protected me from the sun's glare.

Returning we had a fine breeze in our faces, so that the girls enjoyed the exercise without suffering from the heat.

After dinner, I went out alone and made a careful sketch of the picturesque bridge at the entrance to the village. The whole group is so beautiful as it stands that I copied it with unusual care, leaving no detail to be supplied by memory. I then took the little boy and nurse thro' the meadows along the river bank, and over the hill by the church, and gave him a fine colour in his cheeks. He is growing fast and acquiring solid strength in this pure country air.

After tea Emily pleaded fatigue and remained at home while Fanny & I finished the day with a good long walk round the Pond, and by the Pine woods in the river valley.

This pleasant interchange of exercise—riding, and walking, rowing and drawing, together with the elastic atmosphere has had a very marked effect upon me, and I have almost forgotten that my health had ever declined so low as it did in New Orleans. The greatest amount of exercise I take only seems to whet my appetite for more, and then the absence of all business cares, the pleasant

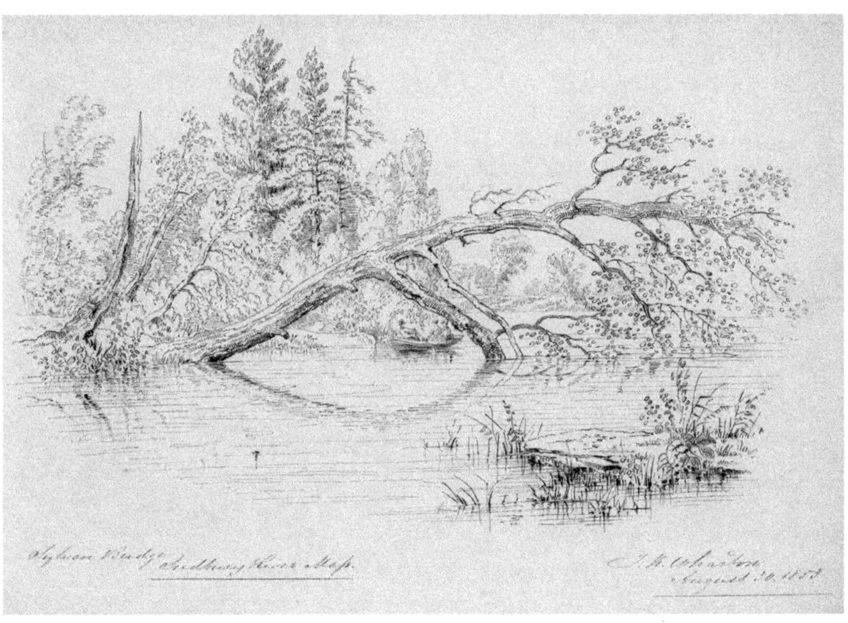

FIGURE 3.13 Sylvan Bridge, Sudbury River, MA, 1853 (*Sketchbook*, p. 21). New York Public Library, Archives and Special Collections, New York.

society, the constant companionship of my wife and little boy, and so much around me that is interesting and beautiful both in art and nature, all conspire to raise the tone both of health and spirits, and make this the most delightful summer I have passed for years. The only drawback is the sad daily dispatch from the suffering city we have left behind us.

September 1st, 1853
Cool, pleasant air from the north, thin veil of pearly clouds.

Spent the morning in long walks thro' the country around with my sketch Book—and in the cool of the afternoon took Emily and Fanny to see some beautiful points of view in the immediate neighbourhood. The path led us thro' a hay field where the hands were busy with their hay forks, and the air filled with fragrance. Then along a hill side covered with blooming clover, at the foot of which lay a fine sheet of water, still as glass, and reflecting with incomparable brilliancy, the tall Pines, Oak and Chestnut springing from its bank.

We took little Prescott and Catherine along with us.

September 2
After the river dews passed off the sky was left without a cloud, the sun blazed out with uncomfortable intensity, and the air from the West was so light that it did nothing towards mitigating the heat.

Spent an hour or two out with my Sketch Book, but had to take shelter from the sun towards the middle of the day. In the afternoon, however, I took a

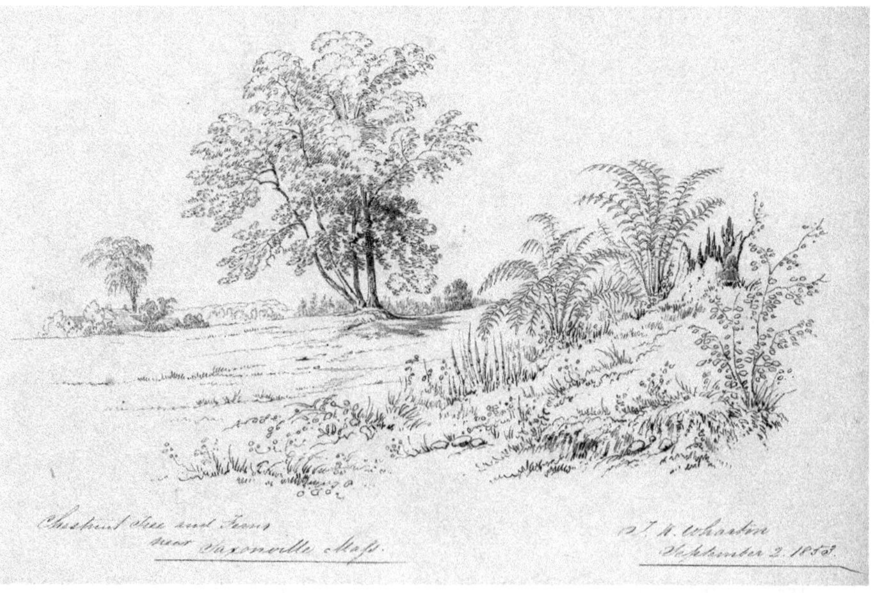

FIGURE 3.14 Chestnut tree and ferns near Saxonville, MA, 1853 (*Sketchbook*, p. 25). New York Public Library, Archives and Special Collections, New York.

long ramble by the woodpaths and meadows on the river side—every now and then ascending the uplands, which rise from the stream in successive ridges and afford fine general views.

The "Aurora Borealis" after nightfall was very beautiful at times, composing a vast, uniform, luminous arch, and then shooting upwards in clear, radial coruscations. It seems rather early for this phenomenon.

September 3
Pleasant breeze from the South West, clouds and sunshine.

Little Prescott suffers a good deal with his teeth. I have had to call in Dr. [John W.] Osgood who prescribes simple correctives.

Walked to the South end of Cochituate Pond, and took a sketch of it, introducing the Gate house, from an eminence rising abruptly from the carriage drive at the margin of the Pond, to the height of about 80 feet. The sun was well shaded while I took my sketch and I was favoured with a fine breeze during my noontide walk back again. Saw no less than three snakes on the way, about 2 feet long, sunning themselves near the streamlets by the roadside. They were of the harmless striped species of which I have seen several specimens in my rambles here.

Whilst at the Pond I looked in at the Gate-house. The Granite work is excellent, faced inside with good brick, over the entrance door is a white marble Tablet, thus, with the following Inscription, which may hereafter form the theme of many a learned "Paper" in the "Philosophical and antiquarian Transactions" of future centuries—

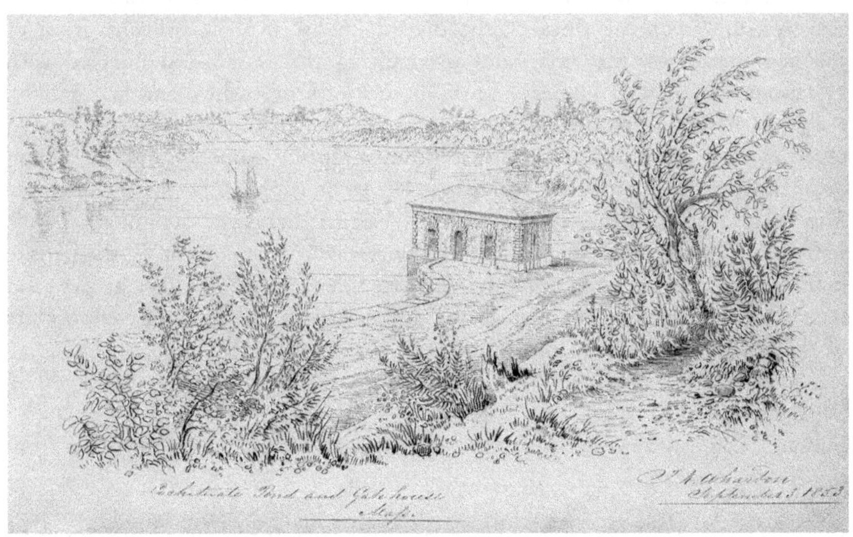

FIGURE 3.15 Cochituate Pond and gatehouse, MA, 1853 (*Sketchbook*, p. 26). New York Public Library, Archives and Special Collections, New York, NY.

Boston Water Works	
First Division	Length 30,085 Feet
Commenced Augt. 1846.	Completed Oct. 1848
Resident Engineer	Contractors
T.E. Sickles	Carmichael, Gonder & Co.
Assistants	McCullough and Clark
M. Conrad	Francis Blair
W.E. Ferguson	Geo. T. Wheeler
G.A. Hyde	

The Total Cost of the Waterworks	
including Interest to May 1, 1853	$6,071,351.14
Deduct Revenue	673,860.78
Net Cost	$5,397,490.36

A letter from Robert John at the Post Office on my way home. Answered it immediately after dinner.

The Papers today indicate a further diminution in the mortality at New Orleans. Dispatch of the 31st Ult., 103 deaths by Fever, 110 on the 30th.

In the afternoon Emily felt unwilling to leave the baby, so Fanny and I went out in the Boat and explored the river until it narrowed down to a few rods wide and the current became almost too strong to pull against. A rude bridge, too, thrown across the stream at a few inches above the surface, effectually stopped all further discoveries. We were delighted, however, with what we saw. Every turn of the banks disclosing new beauties. All the elements of the scenery—the trees, the thickets, the distant knolls, and the brilliant green of the near meadows, the rich vines overhanging the water, and purpled with heavy clusters of wild grapes—down to the tufts of rushes, and water lilies, and wild flowers that decked the margin of the stream, all seemed grouped together as if on purpose to furnish studies for the painter—and so rich in detail and composition that nothing was left to be supplied by the imagination. The more faithful the copy, the better. I carried away one combination in a rude, hasty sketch, while Fanny held the boat against the current by the pensile branches of a Silver birch. And we took in a few pounds of fine grapes, and then returned home to tea just as the dew began to fall, and the yellow tints of the sky to sober down into pearly grey.

September 4

Sunday. Beautiful morning with thin, light clouds, and just a breath of air from the South West.

Little Prescott slept soundly and is as lively as a lark this morning. Dr. Osgood called and thinks him almost entirely well.

Walked for over an hour before church time, but the sun was too hot for enjoyment, except where a massive old oak, or a group of Chestnuts and Pine trees flung a shadow over the road.

Mr. Northrup preached from the text "To you who believe he is precious"—1 Pet. 2 c. 7—shewing that those only who resemble Christ can fully understand and really delight in his purity, his excellence, and resplendent moral perfections. It was communion Sunday so I left Fanny and her mother after the sermon and hastened home to rejoin Emily who had remained with the little boy lest he should have any return of his bad symptoms, but the morning passed off without any.

In the afternoon Mr. Northrup preached from "Verily, verily, I say unto you, except ye be born again, ye cannot see the kingdom of God." He argued that the tastes and affections of the unrenewed soul are totally incompatible with the joys of heaven, and that this fact alone would present a sufficient obstacle to its admission there. Hence the necessity of an entire change, and that this change should take place in the "present state," he showed from the absence of any scripture proof that such a change is possible after the soul leaves the body. Time, he considered, as duration limited—eternity as duration infinite, and Death the Portal thro' which the soul passes from the one to the other—being nothing more than a change of condition and locality, and involving no alteration in the character, affection, and tendencies of the soul. Nor have we any hint in the sacred writings to shew that any remedial process whatever takes place after death, but everything to confirm the broad truth, that the general character of the soul, for good or for evil, and that, too, for ever, is formed during its union with the material body upon earth.

Took a good walk after tea with Prescott, who has been very lively all day, and is now almost quite well.

September 5
Clear, sultry day—scarcely a breath of air, tho' the vane indicates a northwest wind. This is too much like the weather we fled from to be wholly to our taste.

At 10 A.M. the therm. was nearly up to 80° in the shade, but the wind suddenly swung round to the East, blowing fresh and spreading broad masses of cloud over the blue sky, so that the temperature improved rapidly.

In the afternoon, I went with Emily and Fanny to visit the High School under the charge of a young man named "Pierce" [Henry Rueben Pierce]. The building stands alone, with a neat Doric Portico of wood. The school room large, well ventilated, clean and furnished with every convenience. Between 30 and 40 scholars, apparently from 12 to 16 years—boys and girls—about equally divided. Good intelligent faces, neatly dressed and their answers and references to grammatical rules &c. prompt and accurate. The recitations while we were there were in English Grammar, Parsing and Green's Analysis of Sentences.[43]

The questions were put by the teacher from his raised platform, and each pupil when addressed rose up and gave such answers as were required, remaining at their respective desks.

Mr. Pierce closed with a short prayer, and we left much gratified, and promising to repeat our visit before returning to Boston.

We then took a long walk over the high and open hills to the South and returned to a late Supper and soon after retired, as all felt more or less fatigued by the relaxing heat of the early part of the day, and the exercise of the afternoon.

September 6

Damp and close, with dull grey sky and cool air from the South. Cleared off at 11 and became very hot with but little breeze.

Made a circuit of several miles thro' the farms to the Southward, and climbed some eminences which are higher than any I have visited yet, overlooking the country for a great distance in every direction and presenting a beautiful interchange of hill and valley. Cultivated fields, and hill-sides planted with apple trees, and standing corn ready for the Bin. Intervals of wild forest extended in long wavy lines, while clusters of white specks and tall spires indicated the villages, scattered among the blue hills and woods along the horizon. Scenes, altogether, of great pastoral beauty. Nearby, an orchard of full 20 acres covered a range of sunny slopes and hung heavy with ruddy fruit, and at a turn of the road stood a neat country school house with groups of clean, healthy looking children taking their recess on the green grass plots around.

The general character of the soil is light and thin, and in many places encumbered with granite boulders and coarse gravel. The stones, however, are used for fencing, and the hand of industry and thrift have given an air of cheerfulness, comfort and abundance to the whole face of the country which you look for in vain where the soil is prolific, and the atmosphere enervating and luxurious. The orchard named above belongs to a Mr. Leland. His farm contains 100 acres all in good cultivation. The homestead and outbuildings are old but roomy and substantial. The whole valued, without the stock, at $9,900.

Little Prescott is quite hearty and active today and the Doctor's services will scarcely be needed again unless this unusually close, trying weather should affect him.

Dr. Osgood drove round this afternoon and invited me to accompany him on his visits to his patients in the neighbourhood. It took us about 3 hours, thro' a pretty country and the village of Natick, and by a large, picturesque sheet of water, forming a link in the chain of the Cochituate Lakes, which I had not seen before. The Doctor's conversation was sprightly and intelligent and I enjoyed the drive extremely. He, like nearly all the well-educated, thinking people I have met with thus far, is strongly opposed to the multiform phases of fanaticism which prevail here.

We passed a weatherworn, paintless, decrepid looking frame house which has stood the blasts of more than 150 winters. Its owner—an old woman whose appearance forcibly brought to mind the days of Salem witchcraft—was passing from the mansion to the barn as we went by and completed the picture of comfortlessness and desolation which marked the spot, tho' she rejoices in the possession of at least Fifteen thousand dollars. A little further on a nice, well-built brick school house presented a pretty contrast of red rosy cheeks and happy faces.

September 7
After a hot, stifling night, we have another blazing hot day, somewhat relieved, however, by a pleasant air from the South West. The thermometer rose at 12 N. to 82° in a very cool, shady position.

Spent the morning in the neighbouring woods with my sketch Book, the glare of light being altogether too dazzling to draw from nature in the open country.

Meeting Mr. Northrup he told me he had set the carpenter to work on his boat and supplied it with an additional pair of Thol-Pins [oar pivots], &c., &c., so as to make it more convenient for a single oarsman, and begged I would use it whenever I wished to do so. Accordingly, after dinner Emily, Fanny and I went down to the water, and had a delightful row of two hours, with a bright atmosphere, and strong refreshing breeze playing in gusts over the stream. The change in the oar-locks was well done and enabled me to pull with great rapidity and ease. We moored under several grape vines and gathered at least 8 Pounds of heavy purple clusters.

Suddenly the air fell calm and I noticed a huge pile of cumuli rising above the woods from the northward. The hint was sufficient, and I put the bow down stream, pulling briskly and aided by a steady current, so that we sped along with great velocity and reached home just as the sky was fully darkened over with every appearance of a rain storm. Its force, however, seemed expended before it reached us, but rain enough fell to lay the dust and give life and elasticity to the night air.

September 8
Sky mottled over with clouds, cool north wind and very pleasant after the late hot weather.

Wrote to Alfred Kearney, New Orleans.

Spent the day in rambles thro' the country round. In the afternoon Emily and Fanny accompanied me. We took the beautiful woodpath along the river bank below town, and then climbed the uplands till we reached a fine shady group of Pines, where the girls selected a smooth sitting place while I took a sketch of a very romantic bend in the river. We then crossed the hills and returned home to tea by the high road.

September 9
After a cool night, the sun rose without a cloud and the breeze from the north scarcely perceptible.

Drove with Emily and Fanny over to Framingham to make purchases, and enjoy the pleasant autumnal air. We took quite a long circuit thro' beautiful shady lanes on our return. In every direction, the country is interesting, but especially attractive in the immediate neighbourhood of Framingham.

The wind changed to the Eastward after dinner with strong symptoms of rain. Nevertheless, we all took a walk in the same direction as yesterday and my companions sat under the shade of a fine chestnut ("alta Castanea"), while I filled in some details in my sketch Book.

By the by, while at the store this morning, the girls were taken with a sudden desire to try the Scales. Emily's weight was 115 lbs., Fanny's 119, and mine 132½.

September 10
Cool and humid, thick clouds, East by South wind.

Good brisk walk before breakfast, and a drive over to Natick during the morning to buy shoes, having tried in vain all the stores in Framingham and Saxonville, and my incessant pedestrianism pleading strongly for fresh facilities. At the 5th and last store in Natick I succeeded in getting a "fit."

The Dispatch of the 7th lnst. from New Orleans is still encouraging, mortality being reduced to 53 of all diseases inclusive of "Fever," but increasing in Mobile and elsewhere.

Wind changed to North and clear sky.

After dinner Dr. Osgood called by appointment and drove me over to Nobscot hill, the highest point in the neighbourhood (about 4 miles off). The afternoon was charming, and the country more broken and rocky as we approached the highlands, but still well clothed with wood, and laid out in fine farms and orchards, narrow belts of morass in the hollows, filled with cranberries and aquatic plants.

We made several calls on the way (professional visits). Arrived at the foot of "Nobscot," we tied up at a fence corner, and ascended some high spurs of the hill commanding fine bird's eye views of the surrounding country and villages, to the North, East and South, while to the West the eminence hung immediately above us, rising to the height of some hundreds, and covered with a dense growth of trees of all kinds & sizes, peculiar to the country, with points of grey rock peeping out among the leaves, the hill shewing an almost vertical face immediately opposite us while the ascent on the other side is easily performed by a ridge road passing directly over the summit. This road, however, takes a circuit of several miles and our time was too limited to attempt it. On the way back, the Doctor made more visits and it was nearly sunset when I regained my family.

Judging from the extent of the Doctor's practice, this atmosphere, pure as it is, does not in any great degree ensure exemption from disease. The most malignant seem to be pthisis [pulmonary wasting disease], and the Typhoid forms of Fever. The most common diseases of the Liver and alimentary canal, while intermittents are rare, and are confined to very wet localities, and those who are greatly exposed to alternations of heat and cold in moist bottom lands.

My little boy was taken with "chicken pox" the day before yesterday, which prevents our return to Boston this week. We shall prolong our visit a few days until he is quite over it.

September 11

Sunday. Bracing air from N. West. A sky of unsullied purity, and the deepest autumnal blue, a lovely Sabbath morning. The foliage begins to indicate a change in the season. A dash of ochre mingles with the lively summer green, and the Rock-Maple is already dressed in lustrous scarlet. Fruits are maturing fast, Peaches, Plums, Pears, Grapes and Apples, while the Farm work of the Season is nearly done, Corn and Buckwheat almost ready to be housed.

Wrote to Mr. George Prescott. Revd. Mr. Northrup preached from 1 Peter. 2 c. 11 & 12. I beseech you, therefore, brethern as strangers & pilgrims abstain from fleshly lusts which war against the soul, having your conversation honest &c., &c., dwelling upon the baneful effect of a reduced moral standard on the higher nature of man, that as the flame on the moral altar diminishes in lustre, the intellectual ray burns more feebly until it is finally quenched, giving examples from the nations of antiquity and modern biography. And, further on, assuming the probability that each soul bears a relation to, and exercises an influence upon some other soul by which its ultimate destiny is fixed, he argued the paramount obligation to adopt that line of conduct, and that only, which is pointed out by holy scripture, and enlightened reason, as alone being productive of a happy influence.

In the afternoon he preached from the Text—"And to him gave all the prophets witness,"[44] recounting the several prophecies of the Hebrew scriptures, and shewing how they all centered in Jesus Christ, as the rays converge to a common focus.

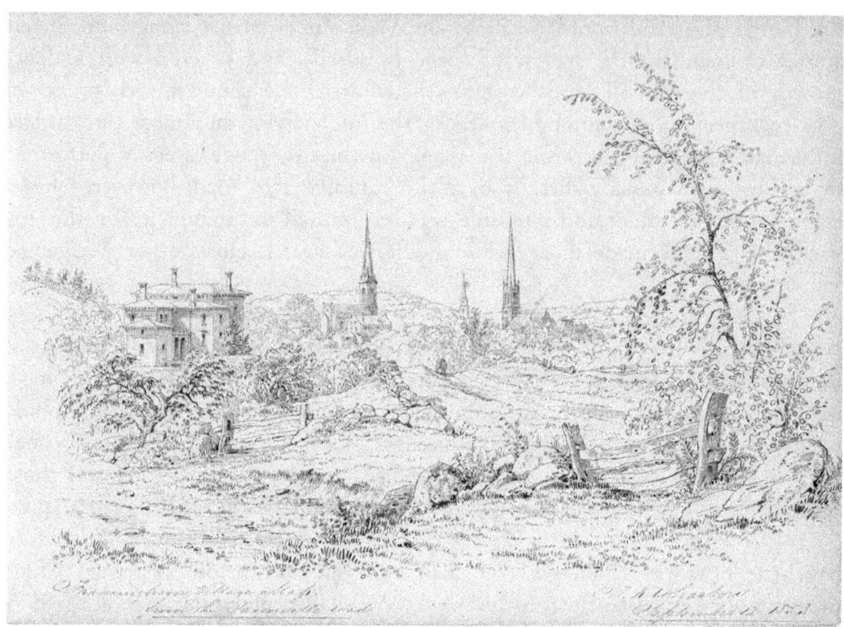

FIGURE 3.16 Framingham Village, MA from the Saxonville road, 1853 (*Sketchbook*, p. 30). New York Public Library, Archives and Special Collections, New York.

September 12

At day break the low grounds were all powdered over with a white frost. The sun rose without a cloud, and the keen nitrous air poured new life into the veins. Got up early and took a long walk by the Pine woods before breakfast, but had to move briskly to quicken the circulation and produce a healthy glow.

After breakfast, I had a delightful walk over to the village of Framingham to sketch it from the approach by the highroad which strikes me as very beautiful and most decidedly "English." Altho' the walk was a long one, some 5 miles, I preferred it to the chaise as I wished to be at liberty to wander about over the hill and fields to select a good position. I made a careful drawing, standing under the shade of a woodside, and cooled by a pleasant West wind.

Returning home the sun had acquired power enough to bring out a light perspiration, tho' when I got back at noon the thermometer indicated but 61 degrees.

In the afternoon "we three" took to the Boat again, and resolved unanimously that each River excursion is more charming than the preceding one. Before we started I first rowed little Prescott round the Pond, and then sent him home with his nurse. He is quite well again.

September 13
Delicious air from the West. Milder than yesterday, but still sharp and elastic, with a sparkling bright sky.

Rambling over the fields in the morning I found myself unexpectedly on the banks of Cochituate, at the bottom of a deep Bay, encircled by knolls overhanging the water, and draped with silver Birch and light copse wood, mossy paths permeating them in every direction. A clean sandy beach lay along the margin, dotted over with shining pebbles, and large pickerel were basking near the shore, as still as fossils embedded in opal.

In the afternoon, the ladies & little Prescott went out with me and seated themselves on the grass while I made a sketch of a pretty combination of foliage and water near the village.

September 14
Mild, balmy air from the south west. Very dry and dusty. Sky shaded with light clouds. Long rambles in the woods, and less frequented parts of the neighbourhood with my sketch book.

The Papers by the morning train are encouraging. Fever in New Orleans still decreasing. Deaths on the 8th Inst. 49. Whole number of deaths from the 22 May, by fever, between seven and eight thousand.

Wind changed to South after dinner, and the clouds gradually deepened. We all, however, started to walk over to Cochituate, but had not gone far before the drops began to steal down and warn us to return, much to our disappointment, tho' the rain will really be a blessing as the whole country begins to be parched and dried up with drought and dust.

Towards sunset the rain commenced in good earnest, continuing thro' the night.

September 15
Thick, murky clouds, driving rain, strong South East wind, gradually veering to the West.

Received a letter from Geo. Prescott in reply to mine. We had proposed returning to Boston today but the rain prevented us.

Went out very little, and spent the day in tinting with Sepia the outline of Niagara Falls, and that of the Rapids at Moss Island in my Sketch Book.

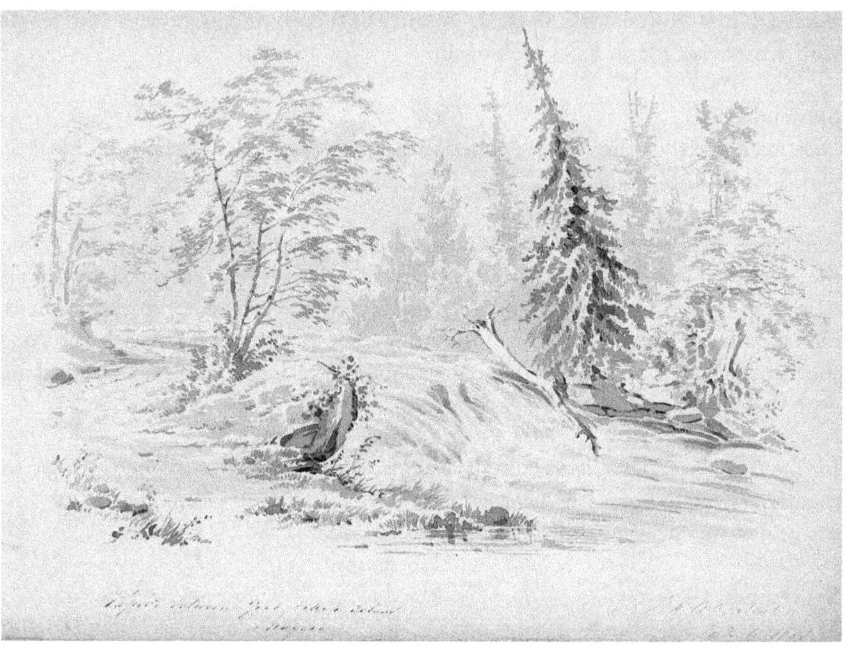

FIGURE 3.17 Rapids between Goat and Moss Islands, Niagara, 1853 (*Sketchbook*, p. 9). New York Public Library, Archives and Special Collections, New York.

September 16

Cool north west wind, ragged clouds and gleams of sunshine. At 9 the sun shone out and scattered every vestige of cloud, and the wind blew fresh and pure from the north.

I took a farewell walk over the hill by the Church, and thro' the beautiful woods which overhang the Sudbury.

Nature appeared in her brightest colours, as if to rivet the attachment which these scenes have inspired, and to deepen the regret at parting.

Mr. [Marshall] Glazier and I took a pleasant drive over to Sudbury village (4 miles), the road winding over high uplands, and overlooking a rich woody country, with the blue outline of Wachuset (2,018 feet high) on the horizon at a distance of about 20 miles west.

The hour for parting with our kind friends at length arrived, and an unwelcome one it was to all parties. We have been induced to prolong our visit considerably beyond the time we at first intended, and everything has been done that could be thought of to make it pleasant to us. Indeed, we have enjoyed it more than any part of our summer tour yet, and are sincerely sorry to have it draw to a close. Our friends, too, share our feeling.

Fanny and Mr. Glazier went with us to the cars. We were off at 1½ P.M., and in one hour were safely put down at Mr. Prescott's in Albion Street, where we found that Mrs. Ladd and Ellen had arrived two days before us, and all were expecting us.

Towards evening went to the Tremont and Winthrop House,[45] but found no one that I knew. Read the New Orleans papers. The Fever spreading in every direction thro' the State of Louisiana and up the River, tho' fast decreasing in the city.

Saw with deep regret many familiar names on the lists of mortality—none, however, of personal friends.

Returned thro' my favourite walk on the Common by the Fountain which rose like a column of moving snow-flakes against the deep blue sky, while the colours of the prism were enwreathed with the spray opposite the declining sun.

September 17
Change of wind to North East, and every appearance of rain.

While taking a walk, I met on Harrison Avenue the wreck of the locomotive "Bunkerhill" which exploded the other day and killed the Engineer. It was mounted on heavy wheels, drawn by seven powerful draught horses, and bore unmistakable evidences of age and decrepitude, fixing an indelible stigma on the company which continued to run it. The accident happened on a short branch of the Eastern Road near Newburyport, but a few minutes before a large Pic-nic party assembled on the very spot to return to their homes.

Drizzling rain in the afternoon. Spent the time in tinting sketch on the St. Lawrence &c., &c.

They build quick in Boston. Three weeks ago, they were setting the granite basement of a large four story house on Tremont Road and it is now roofed in. They are also at the Fourth Story of J[onas] Chickering's immense Piano Factory on the same road, quite close to the Marsh. The Stone Basement of this Building was not quite complete when we left for Saxonville. The work, too, seems well done.

September 18
Sunday. Dull rainy weather, light air from S. East. Went out very little during the day, having taken some cold from the damp, raw winds.

September 19
Damp and misty, south west wind. Cleared off warm and sunny towards noon with brisk breeze.

Spent the morning with Emily and Mrs. Ladd in making purchases. Drawing after dinner and then a long walk with Prescott thro' Washington Street to the Tremont and Winthrop and by the Common home again to tea.

By the *Picayune* I see the death of A. Toutant on his Plantation in St. Bernard. I saw him shortly before I left. Handsome, florid, and very robust. 27 years of age. He died of Fever.

September 20
Hot sunshine, floating clouds & brisk wind from the South.

Spent the morning in calling upon friends, and at the Picture Gallery, Library, Reading Rooms &c.

On my return from the Athieneum to dinner found a long letter from Major [P.G.T.] Beauregard, of 9th Inst. from Magnolia Plantation, in answer to mine of 27th Ult. Alludes to the death of his brother Alfred. Gives a very favourable account of the progress at the New Custom House, notwithstanding the epidemic, laying from 450 to 500,000 Bricks per month in interior walls, and expects to be ready to commence the Second Tier of Ground arches in about 6 weeks, but still uncertain as to the Granite work.

Took Emily, Mrs. Ladd, old Mrs. Prescott and Ellen to the Mechanics' Fair at Faneuil Hall after dinner. I drew but little pleasure from the visit as the air in the apartments was steamy and vitiated, and after walking so much in the forenoon sun I was very far from well, and suffered too much to take any interest in the perplexing variety of objects piled up on all sides.

I was struck, however, with the beauty of some slabs and mantels of Welsh Slate enamelled in imitation of rich marbles, and executed with wonderful delicacy and taste.

The Daguerreotype Department was unusually rich and some specimens of chased silver elegant in the extreme. Among the portraits were Mrs. H.B. Stowe[46] and her delectable husband, coarse featured and commonplace, especially the lady—interesting people, those!!

September 21
Dull and gloomy, cooler than yesterday, drizzling rain. East wind.

Spent the whole morning in drawing Rapids at Niagara in Sepia, the afternoon in answering letters from my sister Emily and Major Beauregard.

September 22
Cool air from the West, ragged grey clouds, fine burst of sunshine.

Received a letter from Robert John and answered it immediately. Wrote to cousin Fanny.

From New Orleans, we learn the death of two friends, Mr. Harry Hill and Dr. W.K. Stone,[47] besides other familiar names.

In the afternoon took Emily to the Horticultural Exhibition. It is held in a vast Tent on the Common, and Flora and Pomona[48] vie with each other in the richness and perfection of their treasures. The show of grapes and pears, dahlias and quilled asters, was superb. The vegetables, too, were generally fine, some gigantic. One mammoth gourd weighed 150 pounds. A leaf of the "Victoria Regia" attracted general notice. It measured nearly 5 feet in diameter, and its reticulated fibres resembled strong basket work. It was taken from the celebrated plant at Salem [by John Fiske Allen].[49] There were some beautiful varieties of "Erica" and "Fuchsia" among the growing plants. Indeed, everything was superior of its kind and we only regretted that the lateness of the hour did not permit us to examine more minutely. One large Basket was filled with an assortment of fruits and lined with mosses, and so full, florid and glossy were the contents, that they looked more like the exaggerated imitations in waxwork than real products of northern gardens. Eden itself could hardly boast of a more lustrous and seducing display.

I have at length seen a "strong minded" woman, tripping across the street at the corner of State and Court. Brown silk upper works, short in the skirt, and long white trousers drawn tight over the instep, full at the knee, a regular "Bloomer," coarse, strong features—tout ensemble ungraceful, inelegant to the last degree.

September 23
Pleasant, sunny day, with wind changing to East.

Mr. George Prescott suffered greatly during the night with violent nervous headache, so he determined to omit business for today and proposed to me to take a short trip into the suburbs. I suggested Brookline, where there is a beautiful Episcopal Church which I have long desired to add to my Sketch Book.[50] We took the omnibus in Tremont Street and were fortunate in having my friends Mrs. Judge Metcalf and daughter as fellow passengers. We had a very lively pleasant ride out, and a walk of half a mile to the church. It is a fine specimen of rural Gothic pointed style, spire in the angle, pure in detail and well executed in light freestone, of a warm brown tone, hammered carefully in the ornamental parts, tracery of windows, mouldings, buttress-caps and copings, angles &c. Charming situation well wooded rising grounds, and highly improved property around it—clean velvety turf between it and the winding road—and a gigantic Elm with long drooping tresses of glossy foliage standing in bold opposition to the finely broken outlines of the church.

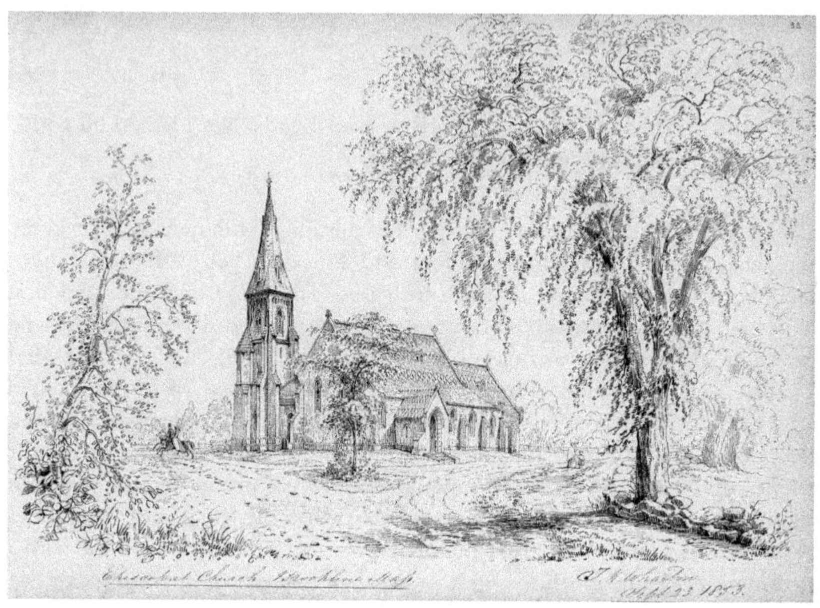

FIGURE 3.18 Episcopal Church, Brookline, MA, 1853 (*Sketchbook*, p. 33). New York Public Library, Archives and Special Collections, New York.

I selected a point of view embracing this noble tree, and made a careful drawing. We then walked briskly to the Depot and took the cars, arriving at home in time for a 3 o'clock dinner.

In the afternoon I took little Prescott to a Toy shop in Washington Street and let him exercise his infantile judgment in making a selection. Today is the first anniversary of his birthday, and he already prides himself on being able to stand and even walk a few steps by himself. He has received an elegant silver fork and spoon from his grandmother and great-grandmother, to accompany a beautiful silver goblet which was presented him by a friend a year ago, and he seemed as much delighted with his newly acquired treasures as if he understood their real value.

September 24
Charming weather, mild sunny atmosphere, west wind.

I left home at 9 with the intention of going down to Fort Warren to see Col. Thayer, taking Ellen with me, but learned at the Colonel's office that the Fort sloop had left early this morning, so we deferred the trip and went to the Museum.[51] The building is finer than the collections. That of Ornithology, however, is quite rich, and I saw with pleasure many common and beautiful species which are associated with my woodland excursions both on this and the other side of the Atlantic—such as the following—

Phasianus Colchicus—	English Pheasant
Perdix cinerea	" Partridge
Bonasa simbellus	Ruffed Grouse
Tetrao cupido	Pinnated do.
Meleagus Gallopavor	Wild Turkey
Pysanga Rubra	Scarlet Tanager
Yphantes Baltimore	Baltimore Oriole
Cardinalis Virginiensis	Cardinal Grosbeak
Campephilus principalis	Ivory Bill Woodpecker
Colaptes Auratus	Golden—do.
Sialia Wilsoni (Motacilla Sualis)	Blue Bird
Fringilla Tristis	Yellow—do.
Ceryle Alcyon	Belted Kingfisher
Cyano corax cristatus	Blue Jay

These and similar simple varieties were more suggestive and pleasing to me than the gorgeous plumage of India and Brazil.

While at the Museum I was taken with a sudden faintness and oppression tho' I felt perfectly well when I left home.

It gradually went off as we walked back to Albion Street, but left me weak and languid, so that I had to take some sleep before dinner. Tho' greatly improved, my health is far from re-established, and I fear will not be until the veritable cold weather sets in.

On reaching home I was much gratified to find cousin Fanny, who had come in by carriage with Mrs. Glazier to spend the day. She left again on the 6 P.M. train.

September 25

Sunday. Went to bed early, slept well, & rose late, feeling much better. A sharp air from the north west, and blue sky sparkling with sunlight.

Dressed warm and took a brisk walk before breakfast. Did not feel well enough to go to Church, which was a great disappointment as I have not been since I arrived in Boston to a city church and fully expected to go today.

Walked out to South Boston in the afternoon with the little boy and Ellen, and then, towards evening, with George Prescott to the new Gasometer building &c. The structure is circular, of brick on granite base, 118 feet diameter, 65 feet high to top of wall, conical Roof 35 feet high, capped by a cupola of 11 feet, 30 feet deep below level of ground, with walls 28 inches thick, laid in Cement, decreasing to 12 inches at the top, and containing in the aggregate nearly 2,000,000 of Brick. The walls are up and the framing of the roof ready to receive the metal plates.

September 26
Clear and bracing, pleasant sun, sharp air from the West.

Spent the day chiefly in tinting sketch of Boston Harbour. The day, however, was too tempting to remain altogether a captive within doors, so that I took a short ramble both in the morning and afternoon notwithstanding a slight bilious chill and unpleasant feelings that followed.

Received and answered a note from Mr. G. Penniman of Quincy.

September 27
Dull cloudy day, raw East wind.

Kept close in-doors until evening.

Spent the time in colouring my sketch of "Fresh Pond" which makes by far the prettiest contribution to my sketch-book.

Towards sunset I put on my cloak and took a brisk walk to the Winthrop House and back. Bought a few bunches of beautiful grapes for Em. The market shops, fruiterers and confectionaries are abundantly supplied with them—both the greenhouse and out-door varieties, and fully ripe and luscious Peaches, Pears, Apples and Quinces lay about in tempting heaps, and autumn is far advanced. The people tread more rapidly thro' the streets, the air blows fresh and keen, giving a rich, rosy glow to the young girls, and tipping the nose of mature age with mottled purple. Silks and woollens displace the lighter fabrics, and summer absentees again fill the city.

September 28
Another dark, gloomy day with drizzling rain from the north East, and heavy showers at intervals.

Dispatch of yesterday—14 deaths in New Orleans, and 13 in Mobile by yellow fever.

September 29
Cold, piercing north-wester, thin ragged clouds.

We were all prepared to go to Randolph at noon but I was taken with another bilious attack so that we had to postpone it, and Emily went in quest of Dr. Ayer. When he came, he made such enquiries and examination as convinced him that the Liver was the seat of disease—that the bile is not carried off promptly by the biliary ducts, and hence the Liver becomes clogged, and the whole system vitiated and weakened, especially the nerves & stomach. The chest, however, being perfectly sound and healthy. He advised the same course as Dr. Hamilton of New Orleans—substituting Extract of Taraxacum for Blue

Mass.[52] It is a satisfaction to find that two judicious physicians agree so exactly, and that there is no organic derangement or lesion, of a serious character. They both attribute the difficulty to my long residence of 5 years without change in the city of New Orleans, and think that it will require much time and patience and some medicine before I am thoroughly restored, even in a good atmosphere.

September 30
Sky without a cloud, after a frosty night. Piercing North West wind. Tho' far from well, it was too tempting to stay within doors, so I took the little boy out with his nurse to enjoy the sparkling sunlight and pure air.

Theodore Metcalf called upon us during the morning. He is a fine, intelligent young man, with excellent natural endowments improved by European travel.

The afternoon was mild and I felt much better, so I took the little boy thro' Washington Street and over the Common which today appeared in its gayest dress of shining green, and the foliage as rich and glossy as at midsummer. Laughing groups lingered around the Fountain and watched the glittering jets enwreathed with sunbows.

We stopped at a toy shop and I bought Prescott a pretty horse & waggon, when we got back Mamma tied a string to it, and the little fellow took hold of one end and walked round the room with it as firmly and knowingly as most boys at twice his months. Indeed his limbs are very strong, and he now begins to walk quite actively and seems to enjoy it. Articulation will soon follow and then adieu to babyhood. He still nurses and both mother and child seem the heartier for it. Whatever is natural is best.

October 1st, 1853
Charming weather, cool & bracing air from South West. Prescott and I sunned ourselves in Washington and Dover Streets.

Pleasant visit from New Orleans friends—Mr. & Mrs. Cook and Josey. They think of returning by the 1st November.

October 2
Sunday. Mild and cloudy, South West wind.

A polite note from Mr. Bryant inviting me to spend tomorrow with him at Nahant, but am not sufficiently recovered from my bilious attack to accept it.

Wrote to Col. Thayer at Fort Warren.

Walked out for a short time twice today but the medical treatment I am undergoing weakens me too much for my usual exercise.

October 3
Beautiful weather, piercing wind from South West.

It is very tantalizing to be an invalid under the paralysing spell of drugs when every thing is so gay and jocund around. I tried twice during the morning to walk out well wrapped in my cloak but was too faint to go far. I persevered, however, a third time, and succeeded in gaining a brisk walk of half an hour without any unpleasant feeling whatever.

After dinner, I spent an hour in painting, and then put on my cloak again and took another walk, much to my advantage, tho' in the very teeth of a cold, searching West wind, which had now almost risen to a gale.

October 4
Very beautiful day. Pleasant brisk breeze from the South West.

Tho' weak from the effects of medicine I am much better, and my physician thinks his services no longer needed, except just to look in and see that all goes on right in two or three days. He sat with me over an hour this morning and we had a very animated conversation on the leading topics of the day. He, in common with the prudent and thinking majority here, deplores the wild fanaticism which perpetuates bitter feeling between the north and south, and which in another phase is doing its mischief here by the advocacy of laws, which are incompetent to attain the end proposed. Legislation will never cure intemperance, nor will northern interference ever do anything to promote the real good of the slaves.

Towards evening took a pleasant walk with Emily and the rest up Washington Street and then continued it with the little boy for over an hour along the back Bay, while Emily went further into town shopping &c. She came back after I did, bringing with her our New Orleans friend Lawson Stone whom she met in the street. The last time we saw him he spent the evening at our house previous to sailing for Cuba to spend the winter in '52. He has been in Boston sometime and was frequently at Framingham during our visit to Saxonville, so that it is rather singular we never met.

October 5
Soft & mild, cloudy, light air from South West.

Wrote to Morgan of the Literary Depot, New Orleans, relative to my back numbers of *Harper*[*'s*] which I can easily obtain here.

Walked out with Emily thro' the neighbouring streets, and then again with the little boy and his nurse. Feeling generally much stronger tho' troubled with a distressing giddiness in the head which I still hope that good air and exercise will rid me of eventually.

We are just opposite the Back Bay of Charles River, on the low Isthmus connecting the city with Roxbury. The Bay forms a wide expanse of shallow water, ebbing and flowing with the tide, and mottled over with sedgy tufts, a wide margin of marsh skirting the opposite side along the confines of Brookline and Jamaica Plain. It is traversed by two long pile bridges, intersecting each other and carrying respectively the Tracks of the "Providence" and the "Worcester" Rail Roads, whose rushing trains sweep inward or outward at all hours of the day, and half the night long. The Stone Dam from Beacon Street towards Brighton forms its northern boundary. Westerly the fine hills of Brookline and contiguous villages give one a beautiful glimpse of woods and green fields, dotted with houses and churches. The compact streets and spires of Roxbury cover the Southern slopes, while the long low neck between is rapidly filling up with blocks of new buildings, lofty and elegant, along the wide avenues of Washington Street, Shawmut and Tremont Road. Public Squares are laid out at Suitable intervals, and the Marshy Bay' itself is being filled up and reclaimed, and will eventually furnish dwellings for a dense population.

Tremont Road seems entirely of new made ground forming a vast embankment of some 8 to 10 feet high, connecting with the middle of the neck by cross streets formed in the same way, the building-lots between being unfilled, and make the Basement stories of the dwelling houses which are going up in every direction.

Even on the west side of Tremont Road towards the Marsh, improvement is busy, and Jonas Chickering's Mammouth Factories are hastening towards completion, covering the greater part of a Square (say an area of 34,300 sq. ft.) and 6 stories high—in short the chief forces of the city in the way of improvement and speculation seem concentrated at this time on Boston Neck, and will very soon convert an unsightly range of flats into a noble suburb of wide streets, and lofty, tasteful, and well constructed edifices.

After dinner accompanied Emily and the rest to the Roxbury omnibus, then took a long walk, but found it hard work. The wind had changed to South East and blew very fresh, baffling the efforts of the Sprinkling Carts and filling the street with clouds of dust.

At midnight, we were awakened by the delicious strains of brass instruments in the street below, the Bugle, French Horn and Ophicleide [a deep-toned, brass instrument] played with exquisite taste and brilliancy. The air "Oft in the Stilly night" rose "like a steam of rich distilled perfume" and a set of short variations on "a popular air" were given as none but thorough musicians could give them.

October 6

Pleasant sunlight, heavy clouds along the horizon. Strong West wind, cold and piercing. Towards noon it blew very hard. This did not deter me from taking a very long walk over the Western part of the city and traversing the Common in different directions. The noble elms are changing fast and stained with dashes of rich ochre of every shade, but the glossy carpet still retains its living green.

I had one of those distressing faint turns on the Common but nerved myself against it and walked the more rapidly until it passed off.

Returning by Tremont Street I met a young lady who used to be an object of general remark in Camp Street, N.O. for the fleetness of her step and the wild, bizarre character of her dress and manner. I have often seen her sweeping along the banquette [sidewalk], with her pale, disturbed, but quite intelligent countenance directed straight forward, utterly regardless of the remarks which her appearance elicited. She appeared this morning with the same black velvet bonnet, thrown carelessly back, and enlivened by gay artificial roses and ostrich plumes—the same black dress. The same hurried or "inspired" manner—the only addition was a rich scarlet silk shawl—a recent acquisition—the reward, probably, of some literary effort of unusual merit, for she, too, fills her urn from the Castalian Fount.[53]

It is surprising what a number of familiar faces from the South one encounters, this summer, in the streets of Boston, and it is well that it should be so. Apart from the advantages of summer travel to the individual, there is nothing so well calculated to allay the ill-feelings and disarm the prejudices, that have too long disfigured the sentiments of the opposite extremes of our country. The New Englander begins to learn that the Southern gentleman is not the tyrant he supposed him, while the Southerner discovers that fanaticism is the badge of a "class" and not an all-pervading taint of the northern people and northern character.

The Postman brought me a letter from Col. Thayer advising me to take a trip to the "Island" instead of drugs, and says that the sloop shall be sent up for me whenever I appoint a day.

A letter, also, from Alfred Kearney in New Orleans giving me many details of the "Fever" &c., but stating that the city is fast becoming safe and healthy while the watering places and Plantations are still suffering severely.

They have a pretty habit here of planting grape vines in their back yards—no matter how small the spot of ground—and training them over their walls and trellises. I noticed one in Tremont Street this morning which not only covers the end of the house but trails along the Iron balcony of the second story towards the street, forming a graceful network of green leaves, and displaying a profusion of ripe clusters of the darkest purple, and set so thickly along the vine that it is hard to tell whether the green or purple tint predominates—leaves or grapes. The fruit attains great perfection in this climate, and does not seem to mildew, as in more Southern latitudes.

Lawson Stone called and sat an hour looking over my sketches around Saxonville and Framingham, and giving me details of their local history, with which he is familiar, having been born and brought up in that neighbourhood, and several members of his family still residing and holding property there.

October 7

Brilliant sky, lively sunlight, the wind which has been blowing hard all night from the westward still sweeps in piercing gusts thro' the streets, and gives a cold wintry look to the water and neighbouring hills.

I walked a great deal this morning and am recovering strength very fast, which speaks well for Dr. Ayer's treatment. He called before dinner, pronounced me well, and gave me some directions so as to anticipate those bilious attacks which are my bane, and master them without the use of "blue mass" keeping that as a "corps de réserve." He is a strong advocate for horseback exercise, fresh air, and good substantial food—medicines very sparingly.

In the afternoon, I took Ellen to Chickering's new Factory on the Neck. Its dimensions as near as I could step them were 262 feet on each of 3 sides of a hollow square, forming a front on Tremont Road and two wings towards the Marsh, each 50 feet in width and from 75 to 80 feet high. The Marsh at this point is crossed by a well-trodden embankment, and a wide road from the city to Roxbury. We continued our walk for some distance over the embankment, enjoying fine sunny views of the Brookline and Roxbury hills and Charles River on the one hand, and on the other the swelling outline of the city crowned with the Dome of the Capital. Spires at frequent intervals, tier above tier of red brick houses. The green trees of the common, the tall obelisk on Bunker Hill, Charlestown and Cambridge all embraced within the circle of vision. The pure, keen wind, too, was exhilarating.

Reading in the evening. Laughed over Peter Pindar's abuse of George the Third and Sir Joseph Banks.[54] The following passage is strong in its way—

> True fame is praise by men of wisdom given
> Whose souls display some workmanship of heaven
> Not by the wooden million—nature's chips—
> Whose twilight souls are ever in eclipse;
> Puppies! Who tho' on idiotism's dark brink,
> Because they've heads, dare fancy they can think."

This sneer at the "masses" is becoming more and more inapplicable under the elevating influence of successful Republicanism. The "people" in 1853 differ widely from the "people" at the close of the last century. The difference is great even where "Peter" lived and wrote. Greater still here!

October 8

The wind has died away and the air from the West just ripples the water. Keen, too, and health giving, with a sky of unstained purity.

Walked a good deal today, went into town, took the little boy with me. Called in at Chickering's new and elegantly furnished sale rooms at the Masonic Temple.

Some of his best Pianos were there—choice both in tone and finish. Saw a veritable broadcloth cloak in the street. They are rare here. The gentlemen have a deplorable fashion (even the best dressed) of wearing heavy grey "Bay State" shawls, perhaps to counterbalance the intrusions of the "strong minded" women upon the male costume, for there is nothing that I can see to recommend them except cheapness. They are unsightly, inconvenient, and ill adapted to the male wearer, tho' substantial and comfortable for a woman.

Cousin Fanny was here today from Saxonville for a few hours, and Mr. & Mrs. Ladd from Brighton.

The autumn is fleeting away, and we must soon begin to prepare for our return to the South.

October 9
Sunday. Mild, dry and sunny. South wind.

Walked with Geo. Prescott to the end of the Long Wharf and back before dinner. The Fort Sloop *Gen. Warren* happened to be in and I embraced the opportunity to send by the Skipper to Col. Thayer and fix Thursday next for a visit to him.

Much pain today and far from well.

Storm of rain, thunder and lightning in the night.

October 10
Calm and moist. Light air from North West. Clouds parted and the sun broke thro' warm and genial at 9.

Wrote to J.M. Reid and P. Guesnon, New Custom House, New Orleans.

Towards evening Emily and I went into town to make purchases, and were caught in a heavy storm of rain, thunder and lightning. The confusion in Washington Street was indescribable but we managed to secure seats in an omnibus and got home dry just after dark.

The weather cleared up in the night, and day broke with a sparkling sky, and strong severe North West wind.

October 11
Mr. Prescott and I were up at 5 for an excursion to the sea shore. Breakfast was soon dispatched, and we were in the omnibus for Dock Square by ½ past six. Started on the cars of the Eastern Railroad at 7 and got to Newburyport (34 miles) at ½ past 9. Took a carriage down to Plum Island—mouth of Merrimac—3 miles—ordered dinner at the Hotel and then walked down to the Ocean beach, and visited the Lighthouse on the wild open shore, the wind blowing quite a gale from the North West and bitter cold.

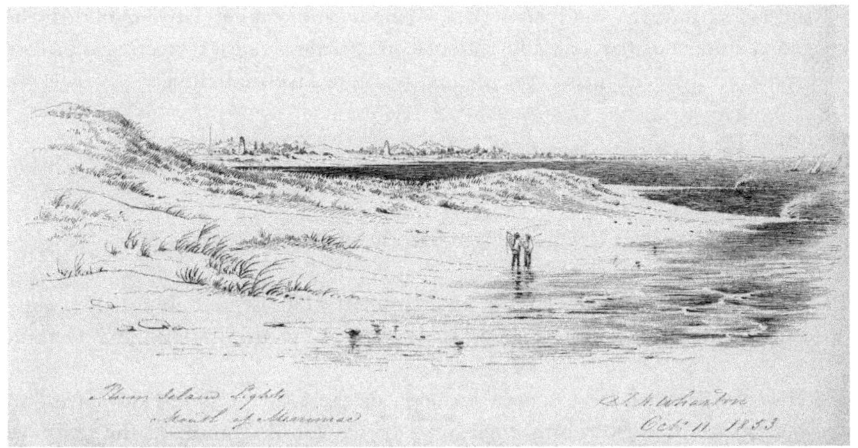

FIGURE 3.19 Plum Island lights, mouth of Merrimac River, 1853 (*Sketchbook*, p. 35). New York Public Library, Archives and Special Collections, New York.

Pursued the fine arts under difficulties and got two sketches of the weatherbeaten coast of New England. Savage and lonely to the last degree.

After dining upon game, killed on the Island, our carriage returned for us and we drove back to Newburyport, walked over the town and the bridge across the Merrimac. Met Mr. Bryant, the architect, hastening to the Boston cars, and fell in with a friend from New Orleans, while passing thro' High Street, where, by the by, I noticed particularly the residence of the present Attorney General—the Hon. Caleb Cushing—a large, square, 3 Story Frame house, plain but comfortable, set well back from the street on a high grassy slope graded into terraces with steps, and fruit and flower gardens in the rear. This part of town wears an air of opulence, and is adorned with spacious buildings, both public and private, fine trees and neat gardens. But the general appearance of the place is bleak and uninviting and the surrounding country sterile.

There is a small Custom House by the water side—of stone, with well executed Portico. Near it lay a large clipper ship, newly launched, of exquisite proportions and heavy tonnage, highly creditable to the naval architects of the place. Large Mills and Factories were conspicuous, and near the town an enclosure of several acres, covered with flakes and stacks of dried codfish—one great source of revenue to this industrious and painstaking people.

At ½ past 4 we took the cars to Haverhill, 15 miles, sweeping along thro' the interesting scenery of the Merrimac, the woods and hill-sides dressed in the gayest colours of autumn. At Haverhill we changed cars to the "Maine Road" and returned to Boston thro' Lawrence, reaching home at ½ past 8 P.M., after a day of great enjoyment—having made a circuit of nearly 90 miles, and passed thro' a country abounding in picturesque features, and exhibiting evidences of successful industry and enterprise—labour and capital have moulded the rugged character of the soil, and softened its sterner qualities, creating a picture of beauty and general prosperity denied to more favoured climes.

October 12
Beautiful day, fine breeze from South West.

Spent the morning in town amongst friends, making purchases &c.

Presented a letter of introduction to Hammatt Billings and found him quite an acquisition, with fine taste and execution both in drawing and architecture.

Met my old friend Isaac Osgood, formerly of the Coast La., but now living in New York. Learned from him intelligence of Dr. Hawks' family & the marriage of Olivia to Edward Bogert &c.

Called upon Lawson Stone. Introduced to his uncle, Mr. Knight, and found him a pleasant old gentleman, full of quiet humour.

Saw old Jacob Barker of New Orleans in State Street among the Brokers.

Received a letter from Col. Thayer to say that he had my card of Sunday and the Boat would be in waiting for me tomorrow.

In the afternoon Mr. Billings sent me Ruskin's *Modern Painters*[55] which he had alluded to in his conversation this morning.

October 13
The day opened charmingly with a bright sun and stiff breeze from the South West. Quite fair for my voyage to the Fort.

I was on board the Sloop *Gen[l] Warren* at 10 and we had a rapid run of an hour down the Bay. The wind blew hard, and the dark icy waters were crested with foam. The Islands rose sharp and clear against the blue sky, and the green slopes lay bathed in sunlight. The harbour was all alive with vessels darting along under reefed topsails. Our craft was 42 Tons so that there was plenty of room to move about, whenever the dip of the deck would let us, but altho' under shortened sail, she heeled a good deal, and the spray flew gaily over her bows.

Arrived at the Fort, the waves set too strong on the seawall to run alongside, so that we had to land with some risk and inconvenience in the jolly-boat, which danced like a cockle shell on the short sea, and was pretty moist from stem to stern. It took but a few minutes, however, and I soon had the pleasure of shaking hands with my excellent friend, the Colonel. He had almost given me up in such an obstinate South Wester.

After a little talk over the warm fireside we sallied forth to explore the fortifications, and first took the circuit of the outer parapet rising to the height of 69 Feet above tide water, enclosing an area of about 12 acres and faced with granite, beautifully cut, and jointed, and 8 feet in thickness, sodded on the top with clean turf, as are all the outworks, glacis, embankments &c., showing fine sharp angles and broad regular surfaces, apparently cut in green velvet and contrasting beautifully with the wild, broken outlines of the neighbouring reefs and islands, and the dark blue waves at their feet.

On this exposed elevation, the wind tried hard to rob us of our hats and cloaks, but it was so pure and healthy that I should have been sorry had there been less of it, and it did not prevent my enjoying every detail of the Scenery both near and remote. The smooth green escarpments below, the sharp, clean granite of the works, the ocean on one hand, and on the other the Harbour with its numberless variety of objects, and a long sweep of sea coast extending away from the city towards Chelsea, Lynn, Nahant, and Marblehead, and terminating in the high cliffs of Rockport and Cape Ann.

Several hands were at work on the top of the walls, setting granite, finishing up the Parapets, and bedding the Square blocks for the Pintels [pivots] within the gun circles. The works are intended to mount over 300 guns, and such is their admirable position that a sufficient number of them can be brought to bear upon any point of the winding and narrow ship channel to sink any force that an enemy might venture to introduce. When a vessel enters the channel, she comes bow on to the north wall of the Fort, and exposed to the fire of all the guns on that side, and passing on but a short distance further becomes entangled at most stages of the water in counter currents immediately under the guns of "the western" section of the works.

The fortifications are now hastening towards completion having been in progress upwards of 20 years under the able direction of Col. Thayer, who has finished within that time the noble works at Fort Independence, 3 miles below town, besides taking the oversight of other important military constructions at the north, and attending regularly to his duties as member of the Board of Engineers, so that his position has been one of unbroken labor and responsibility, requiring the constant exercise of abilities of the highest order. Nor has he since his connection with the corps had any material relief from duty, having been all the time under government orders except for a six weeks' tour to the West last year. He entered the Corps early in life and is now between 60 and 70.

We descended one of the exquisitely cut spiral staircases to the "Quarters" and took a delightful dinner together as in old times, and then went over all the intricate details of the interior—the ponderous masonry and beautiful brickwork of the casemates, their groined arches, vaults, bomb-proof magazines, Storehouses, quarters for officers and soldiery, guardrooms, posterns &c., with

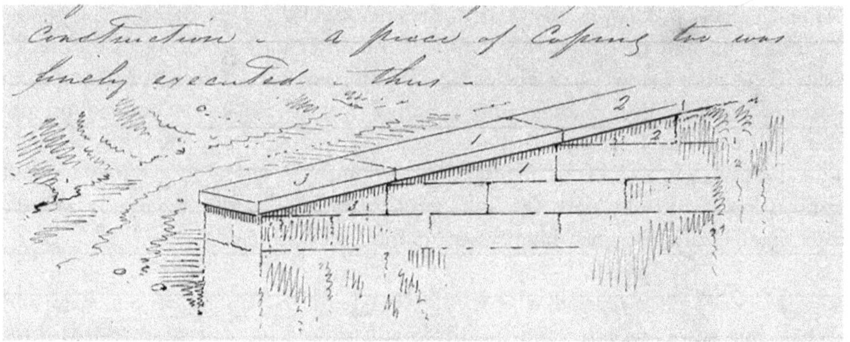

Figure 3.20 Capstones on stonework at Fort Warren, Boston Harbor, 1853 (*Journal*, vol. 2, p. 152). New York Public Library, Archives and Special Collections, New York.

the minuter arrangements for comfort and convenience—cisterns, air and fire flues, cellars and subterranean chambers—all exhibiting workmanship of the most complete and enduring character. One range of groined arches of brick some 25 feet span by 6 feet rise, and a "voûte de cloître" of solid granite over a chamber, the sides forming a trapezium, may be selected as examples of admirable construction.[56] A piece of coping too was finely executed, thus—each top stone 1,1—2,2—3,3—&c., forming a single block. The projection of the inclined coping being cut in the top of the stone and the whole forming one of the course—instead of levelling the course stone, and setting a separate coping stone over it.

The Colonel then showed me his mortar mill which is on the same principle as our own at the New Custom House, but much deeper in the bed, causing greater friction and requiring greater power to work the wheel. I examined the materials, too, brick, sand &c., in short my kind companion pointed out everything that he thought would interest me, and at half past 3 we walked down to the boat, which I had directed to be in readiness. As I stepped on the Colonel reminded me that it was just 20 years since we were first acquainted with each other, and playfully asked what I thought of the prospects for the next 20. My visit today carried me back to the happy months I spent with him at West Point. There is a Hejira in the lifetime of every one—a period to date from, and around which the brightest memories cluster. Such to me was my first long and intimate intercourse with Colonel Thayer. It has coloured more or less my subsequent existence and always for good, so that my renewal of it today was attended with the liveliest pleasure. And he, too, seemed to share my feelings. Indeed, a little remark he made served to shew me how genuine was the kindness he exhibited towards me in olden times. I happened to ask him how he came to visit such unusual places as Hull and vicinity when last in Europe. He said it was merely a whim that struck him at the time, a desire to visit my native place, which he had so often heard me speak of when a boy.

After assuring me that I should soon see him in town, the boat pushed off for the sloop which we soon boarded, set sail, and bounded merrily on our way homeward. The weather had become quite squally with sudden flaws, and the wind a little forward of the beam. We, gained, however, on every tack, having the benefit of flood tide. As we passed up the Harbour the sea abated, and presented less resistance. A splendid flood of golden light burst thro' the clouds, and lit up the city and the Islands with a shining glory, and just as the grey twilight closed in we hauled down our sail in the slip below the Custom House, after a well fought struggle with head wind of just two hours and five minutes.

I hastened up to the omnibus at the corner of Washington and Court Streets and in a short time rejoined my family in Albion Street and recounted the incidents of the day.

October 14
Cloudless sky, warm sun, west wind.

Spent the morning in town with Emily, little Prescott and the rest making purchases &c. Had a pleasant rencontre in Washington Street with Mrs. J. Osgood of the Coast below N. Orleans.

After spending the morning amongst the shops, and the bustle and noise of Washington Street, we were glad enough to remain quiet in the afternoon—Emily and the rest with their work, I writing to Col. Thayer &c.

Mr. Billings called and sat sometime, examined my sketch Book and conversed on art &c. Geo. Prescott and his wife left for New York to be absent a few days.

October 15
Clear sunny day, west wind.

Wrote to Mr. A. Dunn, N. York.

Spent the morning in town, and a good deal of time on the Common in conversation with a friend.

The colors of the foliage are perfectly dazzling, just enough green left for a contrast, with vast sheets of the brightest orange and yellow blazing in the sunlight.

Called at Mr. Bryant's office. Found Mr. Chapin of Quincy there. Sent word by him to Mr. Penniman that I would go to Quincy on Tuesday next.

The afternoon was beautiful tho' the wind had changed to the eastward. I took the little boy and Ellen to the Common and spent an hour amongst the lively groups which frequent it.

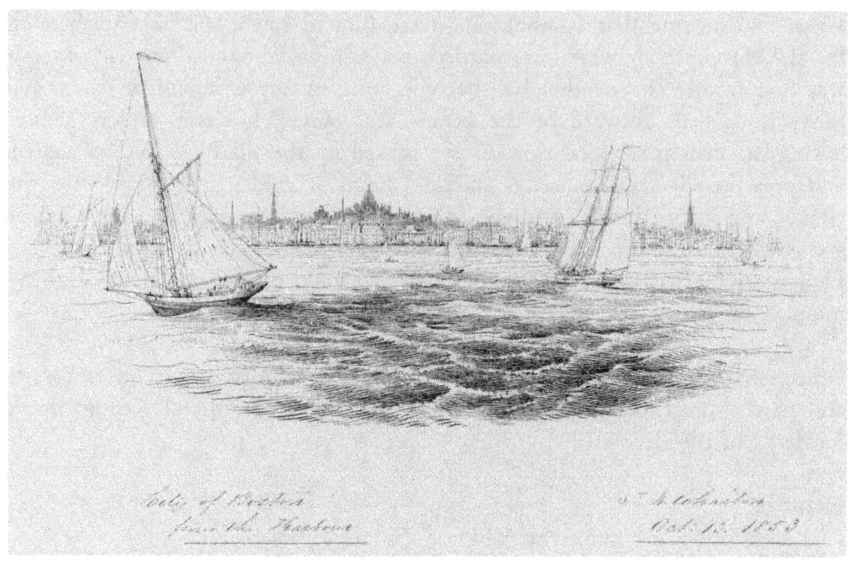

FIGURE 3.21 City of Boston from the harbor, 1853 (*Sketchbook*, p. 37). New York Public Library, Archives and Special Collections, New York.

On my return took the pencil and transferred to my sketch book an outline I made on the way to Fort Warren.

I have been surprised at the prevalence of Unitarianism, universalism, deism and atheism—infidelity, in short, in all its protean shapes, and changeful phases in a city which possesses such unusual advantages as this for the cultivation of intellect and the pursuit of truth. I can only account for it from the tendency of our nature to delight in opposites, and pass to violent extremes. The thirsty man drinks immoderately, surfeit succeeds to hunger. The annals of New England are disgraced by the rigors and severities of the puritanical and cognate persuasions, and hence the transition from the inflexibility of Calvinism, and such like sects, with their austerities and unlovely harshness (too often assumed as a mere cloke for impiety) to the free and dashing vagaries, and feeble restraints of so-called rationalism, and actual irreligion. The Bible I have heard spoken of in terms of irreverence that were absolutely shocking, and glancing over the columns of the *Investigator*[57] I find similar attacks upon all that we have been accustomed to hold sacred. I am still, however, willing to hope, that even here the poison is not so widely spread as to be ineradicable.[58]

October 16
Sunday. Lovely weather. Pleasant Northwest wind.

Emily and I went to Bishop [Manton] Eastburn's church in Summer Street.[59] The Bishop's assistant, young Mr. Smith, preached from Luke 11.42—"These

Things ought ye to have done and not left the others undone." His sermon was a choice example of good, useful preaching, with sufficient elegance in diction and imagery to please the most polished ear, tho' this was its lowest merit. He pointed out in plain, specific terms those duties, and that course of life which are imperative and indispensable under a profession of Christianity, and nothing short of which will satisfy the demands of that implanted principle called "conscience." He then showed how the sincere and hearty follower of Christ will aim at higher ground, and that where the simple dictates of conscience cease, his "sensibilities" and "affections" would carry him forward, and stimulate him to acts, which tho' not perhaps indispensable to his safety, are the strongest and most unmistakable evidence of generous devotion to his principles and real love to his God and Saviour. The question with every right-minded Christian will be not how little may be done consistent with the soul's safety but how much he can accomplish towards extending the principles he has espoused, promoting the cause of humanity, and exhibiting the beauty, purity, and solid worth of genuine piety. Those things which compose the very essence of all virtue and morality will be "done," while those things which are less obvious but prompted by the sensibilities and affections of the sincere heart will "not be left undone." He spoke admirably of self-denial—of the sense of power arising from every victory over our wayward inclinations. He spoke, too, of resigning our cherished enjoyments for the happiness of others—that it was sweeter far to feel that we had given up everything in a worthy cause, than to be put in possession of objects, no matter how much coveted, for the mere end of selfish gratification.

It was, in short, one of those sermons which could not be listened to without benefit, and certainly no congregation could be more attentive. I suppose there must have been some 600 or 700 present. The organ very fine and skilfully played, the voices, also, fine and the parts well balanced, producing rich and mellow harmony. The selection of Music simply bad—the "Te Deum" laboured, inelegant, inexpressive and tasteless. The "Benedictus," however, was an exception and exhibited some exquisite passages. The moment we entered the door the verger conducted us to a pew, and I noticed that he was on the alert whenever a stranger entered, thereby saving him much embarrassment.

What a contrast there is between the thronged thoroughfares of Boston during the week, and on Sunday. Omnibuses innumerable, vehicles of every imaginable size and fashion, huge broad-wheeled freight waggons, and fast walking foot passengers choke up the streets (narrow for the most part) on work-days. But on Sunday, only the people going to and from church, a few carriages, and a line or two of omnibus to accommodate distant church-goers.

In the afternoon, I took old Mrs. Prescott, Mrs. Ladd and Ellen to the Common, for the pure sunny air, tho' the wind had veered to the Eastward.

Every day tinges those beautiful trees with a brighter hue, tho' the clean sward retains its summer verdure. The walks were all alive with the humbler classes of Citizens, for whom this noble Park furnishes a charming and healthgiving retreat, where they can pass quickly from their dingy abodes to an atmosphere of untainted purity, and enjoy the face of beautiful nature, and take their quiet Sabbath walk by the sparkling Fountain, and thro' green alleys that princes might envy.

October 17
Calm, clear and sunny, bland air from the West.

Drawing, and a walk on the Common for exercise.

In the afternoon, we all went down to the North End to call upon Mr. A. Ladd's mother, quite a family gathering happened to be there including Aurelius and his wife. He had his carriage at the door, and politely drove us home after our visit.

October 18
Pleasant weather, cool air from North West. Changed to East in the afternoon.

At 10 A.M. Emily and I took the "Old Colony" cars for Quincy, which we reached in 20 minutes, then a carriage to Mr. Penniman's at the Quarries, two miles further. We met with a hearty reception from Mr. & Mrs. Penniman, and after a glass of Brandy & water to mollify the keen air Mr. P. and I left the ladies and walked up to the Quarry by the old Railroad Track, the first,

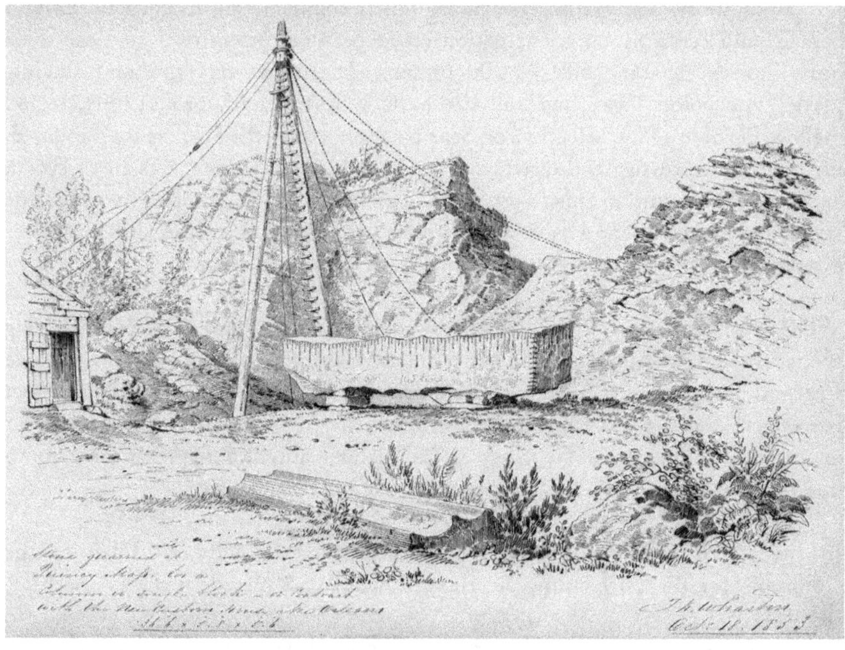

FIGURE 3.22 Stone quarries at Quincy, MA, 1853 (*Sketchbook*, p. 39). New York Public Library, Archives and Special Collections, New York.

in fact, that was laid in this country. It was constructed to run the granite from the Quarries to the Shipping point on Neponsett River, commenced May 8th, 1826, finished May 1, 1828. Gridley Bryant Engineer, T.H. Perkins, Wm. Sullivan, J. P. Davis and David Moody building committee. I made a hasty sketch of it, and at the Quarry, of the large block got out for one of the Columns of the New Custom House N.O. under the order requiring 4 Columns, each in single blocks. Its dimensions are 36'6" x 5'8" x 5'6" or 1137.7 cubic feet—say $87^{6}/_{13}$ Tons (or allowing for the irregularity of its faces 105 Tons, which is the computation given me by the Inspecting Agent).

I also got an outline of the fine view seaward from the summit of the Quarry, overlooking the Harbour as far as the outer Lights.

We then joined the ladies at the dinner table, and enjoyed the excellent fare with a keen country relish, after which Mr. Penniman had his fine span of horses at the door, and drove us over to Milton hill for the superb panorama which it commands, and a lovelier autumnal scene could hardly be conceived. The blue waters far away over the Harbour to the open ocean, the distant city, towns and villages, hills, and lowlands, filling up the middle distance with the Neponsett river winding thro' it. Then all around and below splendid groups of foliage, in gold and crimson, and sheltering beautiful country seats which nestle lovingly among the gay leafing.

We had but a rapid glimpse as it was now near time for the cars, so we rattled along at the highest speed back to Quincy, and got there just in time. Here we bid adieu to Mr. & Mrs. Penniman, who kindly urged us to come out and spend a week or two with them.

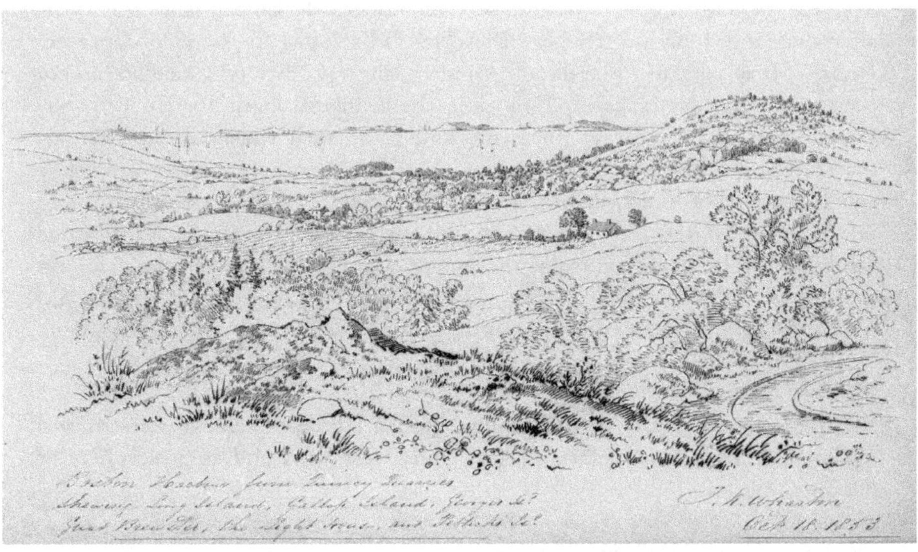

FIGURE 3.23 Boston Harbor from Quincy Quarries, 1853 (*Sketchbook*, p. 38). New York Public Library, Archives and Special Collections, New York.

At 3 we were on the road again, and a short easy trip closed our delightful day's excursion.

Little Prescott was beyond measure happy to see us back again. Only once before has Emily left him for so many hours at a time. He walks now very nicely, and takes a greater interest in little books than anything else. He holds them open and imitates in the most unique style the sound and gestures of a reader.

The Milton Hill, which we visited today, offers the most attractive sites for country residences to be found in the vicinity of the city, both as to beauty and variety of scenery, purity of atmosphere, fertility of soil, nearness to town (only 7 or 8 miles), and evidences of opulence in the fine mansions and pleasure grounds with which the sunny slopes are richly embellished. The range of Blue Hills lay off a few miles to the South and present fine bold curves against the sky, rising to the height of 636 feet above tide water. The rugged features of the Quarry region offer a succession of picturesque masses and contrasts to the cultivation of the level lands and lesser eminences.

October 19
Charming Indian Summer weather—blue sky, hazy distances, soft bland air from the west.

Drawing for an hour or two, then walked into town with Ellen to the Reading Room, Post O. &c. Made purchases and returned to dinner. The sun shone down the long narrow streets with the glare of midsummer, and lit up the foliage in the Common with hues that in a picture would be considered false, and to the last degree hyperbolical.

We all, the old people too, walked over to South Boston and spent the afternoon and took tea at Levi Prescott's. His house is some distance up Fourth Street, making a walk of a mile each way. His two daughters very pretty and agreeable especially Emmeline, the youngest, about 16. The little boy was so bent upon fingering the Piano and made such violent demonstrations that Emily concluded it better to send him home with his nurse. Emmeline and I went to see him safe thro' the crowded streets. We had a delightful walk just between sunset and twilight, and the water view from the long Bridge exhibited a delicate admixture of the purest evening tints. The tide was in and the surface without a ripple. Music with and without the Piano, lively talk &c. thro' the evening, and a moonlight walk home closed a very agreeable visit.

October 20
Still beautiful as ever with the genuine Indian summer stillness, warmth and mellow blue haze over remote objects. Quiet west wind and an atmosphere of untainted purity.

Drawing and long walk in the morning.

In the afternoon Mr. William Prescott came round with his gig and fast "Bay" and drove with me thro' the whole range of suburban villages, commencing with Roxbury, then by Jamaica Pond and Plain, Brookline, Brighton, Watertown, Mount Auburn, to Fresh Pond, and around Fresh Pond thro' Cambridge and Cambridge-port home, making a circuit of about 25 miles, thro' scenery unsurpassed for beauty and variety, possessing advantages by nature of the highest order, all moulded by the hand of taste and lavish outlay of wealth into combinations of exquisite grace. Groups of exotic and purely ornamental shrubs and trees intermingled with the noble natural growth, and lawns of living green brightened over with parterres, and intersected with long sweeping avenues, entered by massive granite gateways and leading up to mansions whose possessors ought to be happy, if wealth and comfort, with everything to delight the eye and please the fancy can make them so.

At Jamaica Pond the banks were bathed in a flood of autumnal lustre, so dreamy that the imagination took wing to summer climes and for the time forgot the stern and severe features of the north. Nothing broke the polished surface but a clean white pleasure boat, and a noble specimen of the Black Swan sailing calmly along the margin and arching his slender jetty neck with a bill of glowing vermillion.

At Fresh Pond we put up our horse for half an hour and went down to the Boat house, made our selection, and passed the time in rowing to the opposite woods and around the sedgy banks of the head of the Pond.

At Cambridge Mr. Prescott pointed out to me the house where Prof. [John White] Webster lived, and where he was taken by the officers—a quiet and comfortable retreat—surrounded by beautiful trees and in a neighbourhood rich in everything to polish and adorn life, but all thrown away on a nature debased by avarice, and sensual passions and vices.

The night was just closing in as we crossed Cambridge Bridge and it was quite dark by the time we reached Albion Street.

October 21

Bright and sunny. South west to South East wind.

Drawing until 11 then took little Prescott and Ellen a good long walk returning thro' the Common to breathe the genial summer like air. Stopped at Balch's rooms and saw a new picture of [Samuel Lancaster] Gerry's, New Hampshire scenery, lake and mountain with autumnal effects, very good. Also at Chickering's new sale room in the "Temple" and examined some superb specimens of his manufacture.

The provision shops, at intervals, now exhibit a bountiful supply of fine game, amongst which the ruffed grouse, woodcock, and various ducks stand preeminent, especially the first, of which you may see as many as eight or ten brace in a single window.

Walked into town again in the evening. I never saw Washington Street so crowded. I had almost to fight my way by inches. The extreme beauty of the weather tempts the people, and especially the ladies to do their purchases while the sun shines.

Met Mrs. Levi Prescott and Emmeline on Tremont Street and walked with them to the corner of Summer & Washington where we waited at least half an hour for a South Boston omnibus. Several passed but so jammed that it was not worth while stopping them. At last one came by with only every seat occupied, and as it was getting very late they got into it, trusting to the chance of settling down comfortably when fairly in. The Boston omnibuses are surprisingly elastic, everybody rides, and the people in nine cases out of ten, civil and accommodating.

I walked rapidly down the long winding narrow street but it was quite dark when I got home.

October 22

A change has come at last. East wind and light showers, forerunner of steady raw wet weather. I secured a walk, however, and some sketches of vessels in South Boston Bay before breakfast, and did the marketing for today and Sunday, George and his wife being still absent in Philadelphia, and the old gentleman having left yesterday for Ashburnham. I got such Lamb, striped Bass, cauliflowers &c. as would be a rare treat in our Southern markets. It is a great convenience, too, in addition to regular market-houses, to have so many provision shops, all over town, where you can purchase everything you need for the table, and have it sent home to you punctually at any time you name. No sales are made here on Sundays.

Received an answer from Mr. A. Dunn, New York.

While talking to a friend at the Merchants' Exchange we were joined by Mr. Greenleaf of New Orleans, son of Prof. S[imon]. Greenleaf who died at Cambridge not many days ago. The Father had long been at the head of the Law Department of Harvard University, and sustained a high reputation as a jurist and a man of private worth. He died at an advanced age, of apoplexy, on the 6th Inst. I have been slightly acquainted with his son for some time past. He is a successful merchant and much esteemed. His brother, the clergyman to whom I have a letter of introduction from my brother Robert John, has already left for his new charge at Madison, Ia [Indiana]. I regret to have missed seeing him.

The relentless east wind is strewing the soil everywhere with withered leaves, and many a noble Elm on the Common already appears in wintry nakedness.

I got home just in time to escape a driving rain, and the afternoon set in raw and cheerless. The showers were too frequent for out-door exercise so I spent the afternoon and evening in drawing and reading Ruskin's *Modern Painters*, with which I am more and more pleased both for the novelty and soundness of his views on art, and the purity of his style.

October 23

Sunday. Warm South west wind with drifts of massy, unsettled looking clouds spread over the sky, the sun blazed out quite hot at 11 and I took the little boy and Ellen some distance on the Neck towards Roxbury, returning by Tremont Road. The play of light and shade across the masses of the city, and the brown sedgy tufts scattered over the intermediate marshes produced effects of exceeding beauty. The only drawback was the recent geological formation of the foreground, consisting chiefly of broken pots, city rubbish and oyster shells.

In the afternoon Emily and I went to the Unitarian Church in Washington Street.[60] I had never been in a Unitarian Church before, and wished to know something of their views and mode of worship. The sermon differed widely from what I expected. It was based on the two texts "Without me ye can do nothing" and "I can do all things thro' Christ which strengtheneth me." Showing how Christ was the fountain head of all moral power in the life of man, and the source of everything that dignifies and ennobles his nature, and gives loveliness and moral beauty to the world in which we live. The preacher dwelt upon the transformation which that world has undergone since Christ stooped from his lofty habitation to tread on its soil, to stand by its ocean-tides, to kneel on its sod, to climb its mountain paths and write on its sand, scattering as he went blessings on its distressed tribes, healing their diseases, comforting their sorrows, and establishing a system of pure and heavenly teaching which has been referred to by all subsequent ages as the very essence and projection of all moral worth. He recognized Christ, not only as the highest authority in the Church of God, but the very centre, the indwelling principle of vitality, the very life blood of that church, and in the most unmistakeable language as he proceeded asserting his divinity, and pointing out the exalted and eternal attributes of that divinity. The discoveries of astronomy, said he, open one after another new worlds to the admiration of man, dropped as it were from some exhaustless stellar sea, within the reach of science—so the telescopic tube of simple faith is continually descrying new glories in the boundless heaven of Christ's divinity, and the humblest spot of earth may be our observatory from which to catch a glimpse of those perfections which angels desire to look into, and which it will be the happiness of eternity to contemplate and adore. The sermon was full of fine thoughts and I do but mar their beauty by attempting to retrace them. The services consisted of a chapter from the Bible—extemporaneous prayer, and three hymns beautifully given by four voices—bass, tenor, first & Second soprano. The style simple and well harmonized, and a well-played organ accompaniment. Altogether very unpretending but more touching and impressive far than the music of last Sunday at "Trinity." There they have the finest material but spoil all by an ambitious struggle after scientific effect and laboured intricacy. Solemnity, simplicity, and careful modulation should ever characterize the "Music of the Church."

October 24

Cold, raw morning, North west wind, changed to North East at 10 with drizzling rain.

Walked over to South Boston before breakfast, sketched marine details &c. Called at the provision shop and ordered dinner. They weigh here only the clean tender useful meat and the least possible amount of bone. Very different from the slovenly system pursued in our markets of lumping the inferior parts with the good and throwing all into the scales together at the same price per pound. In fact, housekeeping is a far more simple, cheap and satisfactory undertaking in Boston than New Orleans, and whatever is nominally higher in price is so much better selected, and so much choicer in quality, that less in bulk is required and that, too, well worth the difference. The admirable arrangements for warming every house, simplifying the operations of the kitchen and supplying a constant and beautiful stream of pure Cochituate, contrast very strongly with our imperfect provision for the same and such like purposes.

Walked down to the Merchants' Reading Room at 11. Called on the way at two Daguerreotype Saloons on Washington Street, elegantly furnished and containing some very superior specimens.

The *Picayune* of the 14th Inst. contains the announcement of the Board of Health that there exists no further danger from yellow fever in the city of New Orleans, tho' it still gathers in its victims among the interior towns and as far north as Jackson and Yazou City Miss.

The streets begin to look chill and wintry. Heavy overcoats, mantles, and fur linings are in the ascendant. The grand old Elm near the Fountain is shorn of his honours and nothing left but a gaunt megatherean[61] skeleton against the cold grey sky.

Thick, murky air and pitiless rains after dinner. The evening closed on a chord of wind and rain and driving mist. Everybody and everything in the streets looked wet, dripping and cheerless, and such a night of tempest as followed—a night of horror on so exposed and dangerous a coast. How many a cry of despair will be drowned forever by its ruthless blasts. How many a wreck will strew the lonely shore. In this northern zone with what force and energy nature performs her mysteries, bringing together the most violent opposites and startling with unlooked for contrarieties, but the other day bathing the whole country in a flood of softened radiance, lovelier far than the intense lustre of the South, and now springing out with one rude dash every fairer attribute, and deforming the earth & sky with driving storm, and uncouth, joyless deluge.

October 25

Wind changed in the night to the West and swept away all traces of the storm, except the deep pools in the unfilled building lots, and the general well washed appearance of the streets and fronts of the houses. It blows very hard today and bitter cold, but scarcely a cloud in the clear blue sky.

George and his wife arrived at day break, after a dreary night on the Long Island Sound and Stonington Railroad. They bring very discouraging accounts of the crowded condition of public accommodations in New York. Unless you engage rooms a week in advance it is next to impossible to get sleeping room for anything more than a "single gentleman" and he, of course, can be put away under a clothes press in an emergency. What with the Crystal Palace, the Springfield horse fair, and the Boston Mechanics' fair &c. &c., the stranger fares but sadly, and as the excitement and motley, tho' subsiding here, are likely to continue for some weeks longer in New York. I feel tempted to change my plan and make Philadelphia my first stopping place on the way home.

> These Palaces of Crystal, Cattle shows,
> Museums, Panoramas, Workmen's fairs—
> Have crazed the world—so every traveller vows—
> And made it "madder than the maddest" of March hares—[62]

Went into town with George. Called at Whipples and examined his beautiful gallery of Daguerreotypes which is richer than any I have yet seen in Landscape and Architectural subjects. George left me here and went to his office.

Called at the Revere House and Athenieum, met Dr. Channing and other friends and called at William Prescott's. Some heavy walls had just been blown down opposite his house, where extensive repairs and changes are in progress. I saw one poor fellow carried off in a litter and with both legs broken. He was alive but apparently insensible. 3 men were killed.

Received a letter from J.C. Morgan informing that he has had all my back numbers of "Harper" bound and ready for me, that the city is filling up fast, and very little fever—date 17th Inst.

[October 26]

Much pleasanter weather, light breeze from the West, and sharp biting air, thin dappled clouds, and streaks of feeble sunshine. Walked over to South Boston and made a sketch of the Harbour. Went into one of the extensive Foundries[63] and saw a fine piece of ornamental casting—a double faced cornice for a Stationary Engine, of great size and weight. Two hands were engaged in finishing it, drilling bolt holes &c.

Returned to Albion Street and took the little boy and his nurse over to the Common. This fine bracing air improves him every day. In fact, we all feel its

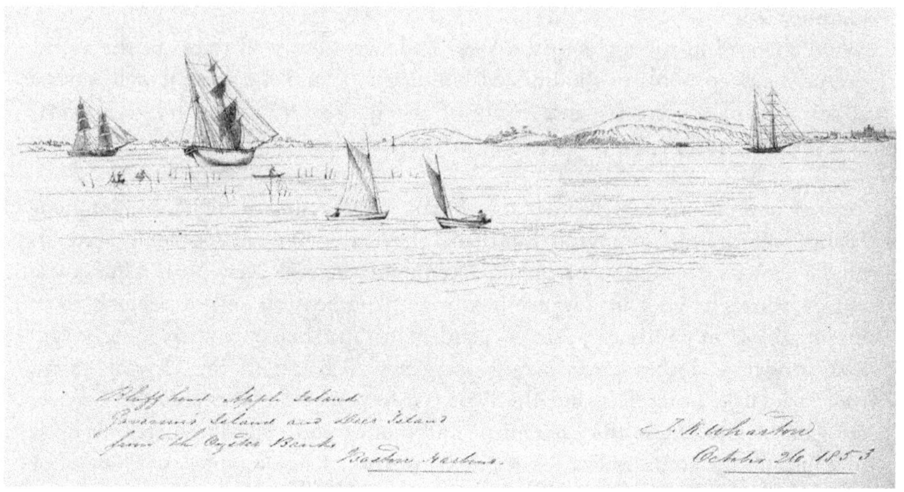

FIGURE 3.24 Bluff Head, Apple Island, Governors' Island, and Deer Island, Boston Harbor, 1853 (*Sketchbook*, p. 42). New York Public Library, Archives and Special Collections, New York.

invigorating effect, and Emily especially. She has gained so much in height and weight, and such red rosy cheeks since we left the South that she will hardly be recognized by our friends when we get back.[64] So that the main object of our summer tour will be amply secured—health. Indeed, a more interesting and delightful summer I never spent, nor could it ever be less desirable to remain at home. Every circumstance, in fact, has worked in our favour.

On my return home Theodore Metcalf called and sat with us until near dinner time. After dinner we all went out to Roxbury and spent the evening and took tea at Mr. Emme's. Whilst there Emily and I took a stroll upon the heights which command a noble coup d' oeil of the city and harbour, much marred, however, by a perfect huddle of tasteless suburban cottages, built by speculators to catch the eye of citizens who have a hankering after villas and "out of town" boxes. They cluster along the lofty terraces, and not only obscure the fine masses of the remote and middle distance, but mutilate and disfigure the bold features of the foreground which, in its primal condition, must have been very effective—large nodules and projections of pudding stone formation of a rich grey tone, filled in with smooth green turf, intersected with winding paths, and plentifully dotted over with groups of dark cedars and various species of copse wood peculiar to the soil, and the usual admixture of fine elms, oak, and hickory on the descending slopes. But all these particulars of "beautiful Nature" are fast being obliterated by a rapidly extending population. The site is not much over two miles from the State House, and the numerous lines of omnibuses and fine Avenues make it particularly attractive to gentlemen who do business in town. Indeed, the nucleus of a large city is already concentrated at the base of the hills, and the Neck which unites it to the city will soon be one unbroken range of streets of the best class.

Mr. Emmes returned from his office in town soon after we reached the house, and the evening hours passed very pleasantly. The old lady was with us and enjoyed the visit as much as any of us. Indeed, she walked a full half mile from where the omnibus stopped to the house. In going back, we took another line which started from the adjoining square, and got home in time for a good long night's rest.

October 27
Dull grey sky, high wind from the South west, mild air, light showers during the day.

Walked into town and called upon Bryant &c. Spent the rest of the day chiefly in drawing, reading &c.

The reclamation of the vast Marsh opposite is determined on.

> The Commissioners have fulfilled their duties, the questions of title have been settled, and this great public improvement, so important for the interests of the community, will now go on. A putrid and worthless bay will be changed to solid and wholesome dry land, not by filling it, as too often has been done in former instances by mud from the neighbouring flats but by clean gravel. And a wide extent of territory which has lain idle, will be converted into valuable property. 570,870 square feet of it will be added to the Public garden now in progress at the foot of the Common, and secured forever for the use of the citizens of Boston.[65]

So says the *Post* of Today.

October 28
Cold north wind, turbid atmosphere, soaking rain. The distant hills were enveloped in mist until just after sunset when a broad line of quiet yellow light established itself behind their wavy profile and with a change of wind to South west encouraged a hope of fine weather for the morrow.

I did not leave the house at all but spent the day in reading &c.

October 29
The sun rose without a cloud, and the air tepid and springlike from the South West.

Went down to the city wharf to make enquiries about the Provincetown Schooners for Emily's cousin Sarah.

Met Mr. Billings who told me that he called with his chaise last Monday week to drive out with me thro' the neighbourhood but not finding me at home left a message with the servant who, Irish-like, forgot to deliver it.

Received a note from Mr. Bryant inviting me to accompany him to Nahant next Tuesday.

Took Emily to see Whipples' and Hale's Daguerreotype Saloons, and Boddington's Landscape at Balch's. Called in at Chickering's and examined his superb Pianos, and had a delightful walk home by the Common, which, tho' destitute of foliage is still beautiful, and shews the distant hills to greater advantage than when closed in with a wilderness of leaves, while the green turf looked sparkling and gem-strewn in the pure sunlight.

Saw the death of old Mr. Evariste Blanc of New Orleans in the *Picayune* at the Merchants' Reading Room.

Towards sunset walked up to the highest point on Broadway, South Boston, to enjoy the effects of a fine evening sky on the intricate ranges of the city below and opposite, and the groups of Islands and distant hills stretching away seaward and southward. This lofty summit is melting away fast, and its whole contents will soon be removed to the Flats at its base, along the shallow borders of Dorchester Bay, where a large body of solid land laid out in valuable streets and building lots has already been created out of the soil taken from the heights. That part of the summit, however, which contains the Reservoir and adjoining Esplanade will be retained.

October 30

Sunday. When I took my walk before breakfast the Bridge and Wharves at South Boston, roofs of houses and every upturned surface, were profusely powdered with hoar frost, and the pools glassed over with thin ice. A dense mist hung over the harbour out of which spectral sails would emerge lazily into sunlight, while others retired into the downy obscurity. The tall buildings of the city showed dimly amongst its highest wreaths, and over all arched the pure blue interlaced with sunbeams and filmy cirri [clouds].

Emily and I attended morning service at St. Paul's.[66] The pastor, Mr. [Alexander H.] Vinton, preached from Romans 15: 29, "And I am sure that when I come unto you, I shall come in the fullness of the blessing of the Gospel of Christ." The sermon was addressed mainly to his own congregation, from whom he has been absent some months, travelling in Europe for health. They, in the meantime, having taken the opportunity to repair and embellish the church which was reopened this morning. It is a large and costly edifice, Ionic inside and out, and the congregation is one of the most numerous and opulent in Boston. This morning every pew was filled and nothing but rich costumes everywhere.

The walls and ceiling were overlaid with ornament, but altogether too much fresco, painted panels within real panels, painted rosettes alternating with real ones, painted projections multiplying the lines of the actual stucco, and the space between the columns of the elliptical apses covered with a painted glory corruscating [sparkling and glittering] from behind the Tables of the Law in the centre compartment and losing its rays in wreaths of painted clouds. Now all this is well done, but to my taste, quite out of place. No deception, no falsehood should have place in the Temple of God. Nothing should be introduced there which is not what it seems to be. Every ornament and every point of relief should be real and palpable, solemn, chaste, and apposite in design, solid and truthful in execution, emblematical of the simplicity, purity, dignity and truthfulness of the doctrines taught within it walls, and as far as the feebleness of art will admit, of the grandeur of that Divine Presence which sanctifies the shrine.

The pulpit and Reading Desk, however, were fine massy carvings in solid walnut, and the Font quite a tasteful design in white marble. The Organ is not yet restored to its place. The music was subdued and full of harmony. The thoughts of the preacher were conveyed in that faulty style too common in the sermonizing of the present day, clothing instruction and sacred themes in language so strictly technical and ecclesiastical as rather to confuse the general hearer than rivet the attention and affect the heart, language so widely different from that in common use, that it fails to create distinct impressions, and is robbed of all energy and precision, drawing a veil of vagueness and mist around the most substantial truths, while the glowing radiance of Revelation is shorn of its lustre, shrouded in opacity, or perceived only in fitful gleams thro' the dusky air. Not that I would appear a self-constituted judge of my teachers, not that I am unconscious of the many valuable lessons that I might have derived from the sermon of this morning, but I do regret that any minister of the church whose purity of doctrine and appropriate ceremonials I so much venerate, should fail to animate his discourses with that deep and searching and penetrating vitality, which arouse the conscience, convince the reason and warm the heart in the simple teachings of Christ and his apostles. And so much depends upon the choice of language. Clearness, precision, and force should be stamped upon every sentence, and as far as possible those mystical and figurative modes of expression should be avoided, which however suitable in a treatise designed for the eye of the theologian, are powerless and unimpressive as an element of general public teaching.

We got to church late and the pew-opener feared he could not find us both seats together. However, glancing up and down the sea of heads, he espied a pew near the altar-rail and marshalled us up the long aisle. The owner happened to turn, and politely stepped out and held open the door for us. He and his lady handed us their books with a manner indicating cordial welcome, instead of that askance look which strangers so often complain of among the pew holders of wealthy churches.

In coming out we exchanged recognitions with our friends the "Brodheads."

Reading in the afternoon and a walk with George just before tea.

October 31
Keen air from the North West and a sky of faultless blue. A very masterstroke of beautiful weather.

Wrote to C. Knap, Pittsburg.

Received a letter from J.M. Reid in answer to mine. He says my house has been well taken care of. The interior brickwork of the New Custom House finished up to the springing of second tier of arches on the 1st Inst. Says that Maj. Beauregard's Father died a few days before he wrote, and his own son in law at Thibodeaux of yellow fever.

I see, too, by the papers that my neighbour Mr. [D.W.?] Ashbridge has lost his infant daughter. I used to think that the loss of a child could hardly occasion poignant grief. I think differently now.

Walked to the Post Office, read the papers at the Reading Room. Called upon Theodore Metcalf. Went together to visit Billings. Looked in at the New Opera House near Washington Street below Winter, now in progress. The walls are up near to the roof. It will be an immense structure, and very commodious, but destitute of external ornament, like the Music Hall near Winter Street. Its situation, hemmed in on all sides by lofty buildings and approached by narrow alleys from Washington & Tremont, prevents any architectural display.

By the by, I have often had occasion to notice in this granite country the poor ambition of certain architects to execute delicate monuments in that material. You might as well attempt to model the Venus in coarse Pottery or imitate a Corregio [canvas] with the materials of a house painter. A notable example of this occurs in an otherwise beautiful granite front on Winter Street—the Central Church.[67] It consists simply of an Entablature supported by two full columns and two angular Pilasters. The order is the corinthian of the "Monument of Lysicrates" and the whole work as well done as granite will admit of. But the Capitals are painfully clumsy and destitute of all grace and proportion. The delicate lines of the foliation and volutes are entirely lost. Indeed, no trace of the beauty and spirit of the original is retained, and the most palpable idea suggested is that of the labour and skill required to shape out of such a heavy grained stone even these rude imitations of the elaborate orders. The coarseness and brittleness of the grain presents an insurmountable bar to all minute detail. Grand masses should alone be attempted with members, large, simple and in strong relief.

I was more than ever struck with this truth in passing the Central Church today. The sunlight fell upon it with intense purity, and in the very direction to show the capitals to the greatest advantage.

A row of English elms on Tremont Street, a few scattered here and there on the Common, a Weeping Willow or two, and the quivering Aspen are the only trees which retain their verdure. All others, including the American Elm are quite stripped.

Walked over to the reservoir at the summit of Dorchester Heights towards evening and took a sketch of the Blue Hills and Dorchester Bay.

November 1, 1853
Light frost in the night followed by a day of incomparable beauty. Pure bracing air from the south west and a sky of the clearest blue with a few filmy cirri resting in the highest vault of heaven.

Having engaged to spend the day at Nahant with Mr. Bryant I rose very early and breakfasted at 6. The carriage was at the door soon after and I joined Mr. B. at the Eastern Railroad Depot a few minutes before 7. But few figures were moving in the quiet streets except here and there a "family man" with his market basket on his arm, and the housemaids sweeping the sidewalk before the neat brick dwellings, and the frosty air was charged with smoke from the fresh kindled fires.

At Lynn, we took a carriage, and bowled rapidly over the fine neck road, and smooth hard sea beach of the Isthmus, and reached the Hotel at the point of the Peninsula at 8½.

All the gay groups that dotted with blue, yellow, and scarlet the grassy slopes around when I was here in the summer have taken their flight to warmer haunts, and the place has resumed its primitive seclusion. The public houses, except Whitney's,[68] are all closed. The numerous country-seats locked up for the winter, and but few dwellings retain their occupants. The fine avenues of trees planted along the road sides by Mr. Tudor, with the gardens around his villa, are all bare and lifeless. The house itself is always interesting, as it is one of the few examples of Gothic cottage architecture executed in solid stone.

In every direction around Boston—in villages, woods and fields, high peaked roofs, barge boards, pinnacles and pointed windows shew the prevailing taste for the old English cottage style. But all in wood, neatly painted with warm straw colour and in some cases of a dark tint in imitation of brown sandstone.

The great Hotel has been purchased by Col. Pason Stephens [*sic:* Paran Stevens] who is already principal proprietor of the "Revere" and "Tremont," a hotel in Mobile [the Battle House], and another at one of the southern watering places. He is about to expend $60,000 in additional buildings and improvements here, and reopen next season under the management of his son, a young man of about 25 who with his Father were on the ground today. Mr. Bryant is the architect for the work, and had his Portfolios of Plans &c. with him to settle preliminaries with the contractors and others for an immediate commencement.

After warming myself in the temporary office I left the gentlemen to their deliberations and sallied out to explore the Peninsula. I first made the entire circuit of the shores, marking the more striking features, and the finest points of view, then examined them more in detail and made sketches of several interesting points, but necessarily hasty as the air was sharp and piercing, tho' the therm'o. rose at noon to 54° in the shade.

The scenery was far more impressive to me than on my previous visit—partly from its loneliness which harmonized well with the rugged character of the rocks, and the grand expanse of ocean, and partly from the pure intensity of the sunshine, and the exquisite tones spread over the nearer surfaces and the long line of Coast and Islands on the horizon. The sea was of the deepest blue, graduated towards the sky line with unusual delicacy so as to convey a palpable idea of its convexity. A very slight sparkling agitation varied its general hue, but the might of the ocean betrayed itself where the masses swayed to and fro' against the broken bases of the rocks, in mantling creamy foam wreaths, of the purest unmitigated white, and jets of spray leaping over the smaller groups detached from the main rock, and then, as the wave withdrew, trickling down their rough sides in dazzling lines of light, like the silver threads of a cascade in the dry season. The formation is chiefly Trap, showing in places the dip of the strata with great precision in long parallel lines inclining downwards in the direction of the land at an angle of about 45°. The highest points are more or less rounded by the weather, but further down they are jagged and seamed and cleft into an endless variety of sharp, cuneiform laminae, and hold square shaped protrusions, and these again subdivided and reticulated by an intricate system of lines crossing each other in every direction, some of gossamer fineness, some bold, free and decided. The highest pitch of shadow was concentrated in oblique, gaping fissures, and every jutting prismoid exposed to the sunlight stained with a hue peculiar to itself, the sober greys and russets predominating, but rising in places to clear, ochry yellow, red and purple, and all fused, and blended, and mellowed down by the radiant atmosphere into the loveliest extension of rock-colouring ever met with. Then the rich olive greens of the marine Algae, clinging to the bases, all wet with the sea and specked with snow white flakes of foam, led the eye by easy gradations into the mysterious depths of colour which robed the ocean.

As I went from point to point, with new beauties developed at every step, I felt how such a mind as that of "Webster," ever alive to what is grand and beautiful in the works of God, should make choice of this as his favourite resort and frequent study.

Mr. Bryant's Father—a fine old gentleman of more than 60, came during the morning and we all dined together at "Whitney's." Drove back to Lynn at sunset, and then the cars for home, which I reached just as the family were sitting down to tea.

By the by, Mr. Bryant told me that he designed the church at Framingham in the early English style and Billings that with the crocketted spire, both which appear in my sketch of the village.

Letter today from Mr. P. Guesnon of New Orleans in answer to mine and enclosing a draft for $100.

November 2
Another day without a cloud and buoyant air from the West.

My unusual rambles over rock & hill yesterday have disinclined me for exercise today so I spent the morning in drawing and writing, and took but a short walk with the little boy over South Boston Bridge.

Wrote to Maj. Beauregard & Messrs. Guesnon & A. Dunn. Just as Emily was dressing to go with me to the rehearsal of the "Germania Society" at the new Music Hall, some friends called from Salem, and soon after Mr. & Mrs. Penniman who had driven in from Quincy. After they left Em. and I took a pleasant evening walk and made some purchases on Washington Street preparatory to starting for the South. I think we shall get away about the 15th.

Every paper brings instances of the severity of the gale on Monday night the 24th Ult., and swells the long catalogue of disasters. It is now beyond doubt that the Tow-Steamer *Ajax* foundered at sea off the New England Coast and that 13 persons went down in her.

November 3
Charming weather, warm sunshine, light air from the West.

Emily and I were in town nearly the whole morning, in the afternoon I stayed at home and transferred to my sketch book the rough notes made at Nahant.

November 4
The sky last evening threatened rain but the sun rose as cloudless as ever, with white frost and west wind.

Took the Roxbury omnibus at 9 and traversed the highlands, avenues, and surrounding fields in every direction. Passed many beautiful residences with gardens still shewing some lingering remains of vitality in the clear green of the arbor vitae, the tresses of the weeping willow, and the sunshine flashes from the red berries of the mountain ash, and the orange circlets of the marigold. I sought in vain, however, for a point to sketch from. There was detail enough—fine nodules of rich, dark cedars and distant views of the city, but in no place could they be assembled into a picture without falsifying the facts—either by restoring objects to what they once were, or suppressing those that now exist, in the shapes of unsightly wooden improvements which vitiate the picturesque everywhere—and I have no patience with the common vice of painters in sacrificing truth and fidelity to pictorial effect—a certain margin is always allowable to the pencil as well as the pen, especially in the play of light and shadow—atmospheric variety and other accidents, but the form and specific characteristics of all marked and leading features should be retained inviolate under any circumstances.

On return found a letter from Mr. Guesnon enclosing duplicate draft and saying that Mr. Wood had obtained leave of absence for six weeks and will leave for the north on the 10th November.

In the afternoon Emily and I went into town to get something for the old lady who is today 73 years. She is healthy and active, with a serene pleasant temper, and quite as full a relish for life and passing events, and as quick an enjoyment of them as she had 20 years ago.

November 5
Still beautiful weather, ice formed in the night, clear sky, west wind.

Spent the morning in town making purchases &c., and at the reading room.

After dinner George and I went to examine a beautiful little model of a machine for planing off "excelsior" filling for mattresses. It was mainly invented and lately much improved by the old gentleman, and he is now having the model and drawings made to file an application for a Patent.[69] He has one of the machines in operation at Ashburnham which yields him quite a nice little income, and gives him constant employment without overtasking him. He is extremely vigorous and constantly on the move—frequently goes out to Ashburnham to look after his manufacture, spending often a week or two at a time there. He is 75 years old.

Towards evening Emily and I took a walk over to South Boston, called at Levi Prescott's for the girls and all went together to the top of the Reservoir Hill. Enjoyed the fine sunset effects on the Panorama around and took a social cup of tea with the family before returning home.

The air is so buoyant and elastic that I almost begrudge the time necessarily spent within doors, especially as we must so soon exchange this health-giving breeze for the stagnant malaria of the South.

November 6
Sunday. Raw, cold and gloomy, west wind and sluggish rains, altogether too wet and disagreeable to go out except for very short distances.

Spent the day chiefly in reading and a short walk with George in the morning and little Prescott in the afternoon.

November 7
Keen west wind and every pool glassed over with fine ice.

When I walked out before breakfast the air was joyous in the extreme and the sun rose without a cloud. The frost stood ready by the housemaids as they "dashed off" the sidewalks and chained the water in glittering fetters. These early ablutions might be dispensed with on frosty mornings—slippery and dangerous.

Spent the morning in making perspective of "model" for the old gentleman. Went into town in the afternoon to see Mr. Bryant, read the papers &c.

After tea George and I went into town again to the Mercantile Library, and spent an hour in looking over the books &c., and enjoyed the walk thro' the clear frosty air and moonlight with infinite relish.

The last few weeks of cold weather have done more for me than all the summer beside. A few more such would put me back again exactly where I stood before I ever went to the South.

November 8
Hard frost in the night—north west wind and dull grey clouds threatening snow.

Wrote to Col. Thayer and J.M. Reid N. Orleans.

Called at "Billings" and returned the volume he lent me and looked over Turner's *Rivers of France*.[70] The engraver has evidently exerted himself to convey the peculiar effect of Turner's pictures in black and white, but it will not do. We lose both the brilliancy and fidelity of the originals and the delicacy and precision of the steel plate. I found a copy of Ruskin's book on Washington Street, and bought it among other purchases this morning preparatory to our journey.

A light snow fell all the time I was out, continuing thro' the afternoon and dissolving as it touched the ground, the wind shifting to South East.

In the afternoon Mr. Bryant's young man came with a drawing board and case of Instruments and I commenced a set of drawings of the old gentleman's machine to accompany his application for a Patent.

November 9
Rains and high wind during the night and this morning. Ragged, stormy looking clouds drifting across the sky. The whole day was so dismal out of doors that we confined ourselves to the house.

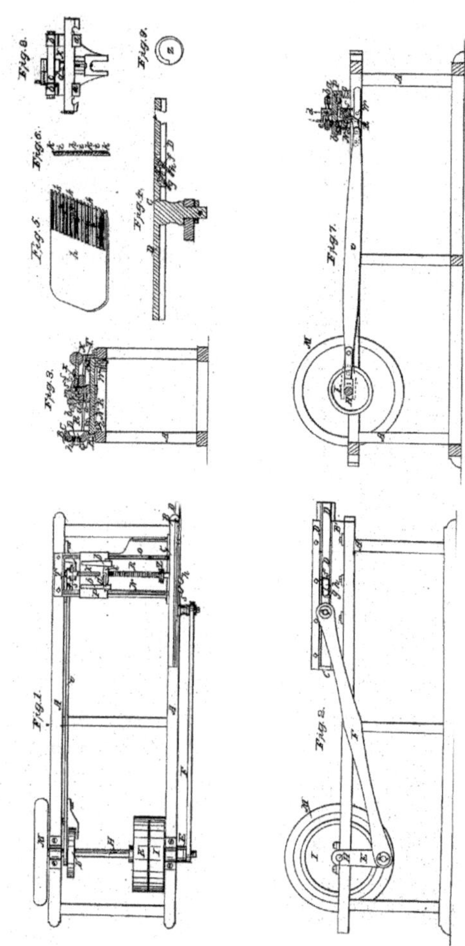

FIGURE 3.25 "Machine for Reducing Wood to Slivers" (US patent no. 10,893, May 9, 1854).

Close drawing, and lined in the Plan, Elevation and Perspective of the "Model."

Letter from A. Dunn in N. York, in answer to mine.

November 10
Gale of wind, and heavy rain all night. Cleared off very cold with high wind from North West and bright sun.

George presented me with an excellent box of instruments which is of great value to me as I find it difficult to get well-made instruments in New Orleans.

At the Reading Room saw the *Picayune* and *Bulletin* of the 1st Inst. Frosts had been general all over the State and the yellow fever was considered nearly extinct.

Drawing steadily until 5 in the evening, then took a rapid walk into town and back for exercise. Washington Street was as usual crowded with bright looking people, and as I threaded amongst them in walking back the moon flashed her silver shafts over the busy scene and the pure nitrous air quick[en]ed the step of the most active.

A letter from my sister Emily.

Wrote to Mr. A. Dunn.

Emily very busy preparing for our return home.

November 11
Thick ice formed in the night, bright blue sky, light air from the north.

Wrote to my sister Emily.

Went into town to King's to buy more instruments.

Called and sat awhile with Bryant. Read the New Orleans Papers of the 2nd & 3rd at the Reading room.

Spent the rest of the day in drawing and receiving callers.

After tea Mr. Bryant called and sat talking with us until 10. Mrs. B. was prevented coming by illness.

November 12
Rose quite early to finish the set of drawings. Warm and humid with a soft Indian summer mist and Southerly wind.

Met an appointment with Mr. Bryant at 11. He spent an hour with me introducing me to several friends—amongst whom we called upon Mr. [Arthur Delavan] Gilman, Architect, who has just returned from Europe and brought some fine works of art which appear to advantage in his well lighted and handsome rooms on Tremont Street. His office is quite a gem in its way, beautifully situated, spacious and furnished with every architectural convenience, and the walls exhibit abundant proof of the talent of its occupant. An article, too, in today's *Journal of Music* entitled "Pilgrimage to Salisbury" shews him to possess fine literary taste, and intense appreciation and love of English scenery. He designed and executed the elegant "Winchester" mansion at the foot of Mt. Auburn which we admired so much during our visit to Mrs. A. Ladd.[71]

On return found a letter from Charles Knap.

Went to town again towards nightfall on business.

Almost crushed to a jelly in the omnibus in going so preferred walking back. I do think there were no less than 20 persons inside and out—mostly ladies—seats filled first, then the laps of the sitters.

When George returned from his business in the evening he was very much delighted with the drawings, which I am glad of, as I have taken great pains with them, and been very careful to make them a fit accompaniment to so well executed a model.

November 13
Sunday. Another disagreeable day so that we were again prevented going to church. Air thick and foggy, drizzling rain and East wind. Heavy rains in the afternoon and dark murky atmosphere. Everything drenched and dreary out of doors. Everything pleasant and comfortable within.

November 14
Quite a gale from the north west with misty driving rains until 9 when It chased off with a strong wind from the north and very cold.

Took Emily to meet an engagement with the Dentist (Dr. Preston), then went to the Bank to get a supply of gold for the journey. Met a New Orleans friend while looking over the *Picayune* of the 5th at the Reading room. Made some purchases at Cotton's Artist Repository.

Called for Emily and returned home to dinner.

Towards evening Levi Prescott and his family came over from South Boston to pay us a farewell visit, but we did not get the full benefit of it as we were engaged to tea at Mr. Bryant's, and he would admit of no excuse when Em. told him that she needed every moment to prepare for our journey. Indeed, the day having been so severe, he politely sent his carriage for us at 6.

Mrs. Bryant is a lady of refined and cultivated taste and very engaging manners. The drawing rooms were brilliantly lighted and well stored with objects of "virtu," and the conversation very animated until we withdrew to the tea-room. Then Messrs. [George] Snell and [Merrill G.] Wheelock arrived. They had been invited to meet us but we looked in vain for Billings. The interchange of thought was spirited and well sustained, chiefly aesthetic, as the beautiful works of art around were eminently suggestive, and the ladies bore their past well with great animation. An elegant supper and excellent champagne kept up an even balance between the "spirituelle" and the "physique" and midnight approached but too soon. In short we had an evening of unmixed enjoyment and one to be remembered. The moon was at her zenith as we drove home, and the pure air had settled down to a calm elastic and delicious & untainted with the dank vapours of our Southern lowlands.

November 15
Charming weather with a gentle west wind.

Spent the morning among my architectural friends, looking over their designs &c. Snell showed me his pencil sketches in France and Italy and then took me over the new Music Hall, which does him great credit. The grand room is 130 x 80 or 85 ft., very lofty ceiling, simple and chaste in ornamentation, the sides relieved with Corinthian pilasters, and the ceiling reticulated with deep sunk panels, both tending to break the sound wave, and modify the reverberation. Ventilations of large size are inserted at frequent intervals in the vaulting over the semicircular windows, 17 in number, and a few feet below them the gas jets are placed in great numbers along the top of the cornice around the room, shedding a softened radiance from above, when lit, far superior to the glare of lights placed near the level of the eye. Indeed, the arrangements throughout for light, air, and the seating of an immense audience are admirable, and so are the acoustic properties of the room, as far as I could judge by stationing the architect at one end and myself at the other, and throwing out the voice with different degrees of force and pitch.

Immediately after dinner I took Emily to finish her engagement with the Dentist. While she was there I went to Chestnut Street to pay a farewell visit, lingered among my favourite alcoves on the Common, and by the Fountain which looks pleasant even at this season in so bright a sunshine. And as to the Common, what it loses in the absence of leafage, is in a degree made up by the charming outlines revealed of the distant country and many a spire in remote parts of the city, concealed during the warmer months.

Passing by the Tremont I heard my name called aloud from a carriage window, and turning round saw Monroe Poole of New Orleans who had just stepped out and was hurrying after me. He had returned but recently from Demerara [British Guiana] and the West India Islands, and was now starting for Salem when he will take a ship for the mouth of the Amazon. He spoke in raptures of the climate of South America, and his ruddy beaming countenance and full figure corroborated every word he uttered.

Rejoining Emily we took a turn among the shops for an hour and then walked home to tea.

By the by, I notice a good feature in the shops here, the employment of so many females as clerks, a position so suitable and lucrative for them in retail dry goods and fancy establishments that I should be very glad to see the example generally followed elsewhere. Most avenues open to women for securing a livelihood are so laborious and so ill paid, that the greatest industry will hardly keep them above starvation.

Received a letter from A. Dunn in answer to mine of the 10th, favourable as to getting rooms at the St. Nicholas, N. York. The crowd is dispersing.

November 16
Mild air from the North West, threatening sky.

Spent the morning in town. Called upon several friends, had a long and pleasant conversation with young Mr. [Merrill G.] Wheelock, and examined his Portfolio of designs for Store fronts, Suburban cottages &c., decorative details for the new opera house and other works.

At 3 o'clock I went to the concert of the "Germania" Society.[72] Had to go alone as Em. was too busy getting ready for the South. Every part of the new music Hall, galleries, and a good deal of the standing room, filled with attentive listeners. The music was beyond all praise. The full strength of the society—no vocalism all instrumentation—and so mellow, so full, so grand in forte and so tender in the more delicate harmonies, the very perfection of orchestral music.

The bird's eye view, too, of the vast assemblage, (perhaps 3,000) as seen from above, was singularly fine, under the subdued daylight let in from the openings near the ceiling. The general tone of colour was grave from contrast with the delicate tints and gilding of the walls. But close inspection showed a brilliant and kaleidoscopic distribution of the richest dyes, and in not a few instances the satins and velvets were thrown into shade by the splendid complexions and flashing eyes of the wearers. The entrances to the different parts of the hall and galleries from the surrounding lobbies are very numerous, so that I could easily try the effect of sound in a variety of positions. And in all I found it pure and clear, without deadness or confused vibration. Indeed I think it the finest room for Music I ever saw—tho' it has been a good deal complained of by lecturers. The fault, however, may lay with them and not the acoustic qualities of the room. Bad articulation is so common amongst them, and the nasal twang heard in conventicles, that half they utter would be only half intelligible in the best adjusted apartment under heaven. The outside entrances are insufficient judging from the length of time it took to discharge the auditory. Several of my Boston friends were there, and I could not help envying them the privilege of such a superb weekly entertainment.

In the evening Mr. and Mrs. Bryant and Mr. [Alpheus Carey] Morse called to pay us a farewell visit. Indeed, we have made quite a circle of friends here whom we find it very hard to leave behind. By the by, to Mr. Morse is due the chief credit of the ornamentation and artistic effect of the Music Hall.

November 17
Easterly wind and cloudy sky.

Wrote to Mr. Dunn to meet me at the St. Nicholas in New York tomorrow evening. We must get off in the cars in the morning unless the weather should be very severe indeed. Morning partly in town finishing up arrangements for going, partly receiving farewell visits at home.

Packing and other preparations for an early start consumed the evening until near midnight. In the meanwhile, an easterly storm set in, and the weather became wet and comfortless so I ordered the carriage conditionally as I am unwilling to expose my family to bad weather at the very outset.

November 18
Looked out at five—still raining—thick mist, and cold wind from the North, so I determined to wait another day and went to bed again.

Received and answered letters from sister Emily and Col. Thayer. Went to the Merchant's Exchange and looked over the papers for railroad information &c. Saw in the N.O. *Picayune* the marriage 8th Inst. of Mr. A.T. Wood to Miss Wallace, which accounts for his leave of absence and northern tour.

Examined the model of a newly invented brake for railroad cars. (By the way, models of new machines &c. are constantly on exhibition at the Merchant's Reading Room, where men of money "most do congregate.") The inventor was at hand to explain &c. The pressure is applied near the inner face of the wheel, and the friction distributed over a cluster of discs affixed to the axle and working against alternate stationary plates pressed together by a strong lever which can be readily relaxed or tightened by a single brakeman for every car in a train by connecting chains, and will stop the whole instantaneously if required. It appears to be a great improvement on the present mode of applying the friction to the periphery of the wheel, increasing the amount of frictional surface, according to the Inventor's figures, in the proportion of 1 to 30, and that, too, in small compass, and with very simple adjustments.

November 19
The whole house in motion before daylight. Pleasant tepid air outside, light breeze from S. West, and the moon struggling hard to shew her face.

Breakfast was on the table at 6 and the carriage at the door at 7¼. Bryant sent me an envelope covering the announcement of Mr. Woods' marriage. We bid adieu to our kind friends and drove to the Worcester Depot, in good time to secure pleasant seats in the cars and dispose of the baggage.

We form quite a party—Emily, self and Mrs. Ladd, Ellen, little Prescott and his nurse.

The trip to New York was short and rapid. The atmosphere balmy and full of radiant, luminous haze. Scenery coarse and uninteresting except in the beautiful valley of the Connecticut. The railroad, however, passes thro' the most uninviting parts of the country and the speed is so great and the volumes of steam and smoke so dense that one gets but an occasional glimpse of anything attractive. I may mention, however, Barnum's oriental mansion at Bridgeport, which appeared quite effective, tho' we could but steal a hasty glance at it thro' the column of vapour.[73] The conversation of a New York gentleman, who sat next me, beguiled the hours with racy sallies, good sense, and frequent allusions to persons I had known years ago. The motion was easy and gliding—the ladies rather somnolent, and would have been very hungry but for a parcel of crackers &c. slipped in at starting by Mrs. Prescott, and very fortunately as there was no stop for dinner. The little boy behaved well and soon made himself a general favourite.

On we sped—stopping for a while before we crossed the Norwalk draw, and then moving slowly over it, giving us ample time to scrutinize the scene of the late frightful tragedy.[74]

Nearing the great city everything was new to me. I looked and looked in vain for the familiar scenes of my boyhood. Nothing remained as it was, except a jutting point or two, and Mill Rock, at Hell-Gate. The Lunatic Asylum on Blackwell's Island, and the old Shot Tower, everything else was as strange to me as if I had never even read of it. The mason's trowel has effaced all the ancient landmarks.

At Stamford, the baggage expressman came round and took my baggage checks, name and Hotel, giving me his card on which the numbers of the checks were entered. I had nothing further to do with Trunks, Carpetbags &c., until I found them all safe at the Hotel.

In the upper part of the city the Locomotive was detached. To Canal Street by horse power. Here we stopped—in the middle of the street—and such a scene of confusion, dirt and uproar I never saw—disgraceful to the city—or the city "Fathers"—and indelibly disgraceful to the Railroad company for not providing at least a decent terminus.

Little Prescott entered into the spirit of the scene, and shouted at the top of his little lungs in mimickry of the ruffian hackmen &c. around us.

After a short struggle, we succeeded in extricating ourselves from the gripe of this "unterrified" and with the aid of a well-cushioned carriage reached the St. Nicholas [Hotel] all whole and sound. Here we were at once provided with elegant apartments, and were glad to be at rest.

This is the most sumptuous Hotel in this most sumptuous city, and nothing which modern ingenuity has devised for the comfort of the travelling public has been omitted.[75] While the decorative details, both without and within are surpassingly elegant, but after an absence of 10 years it is a deep disappointment to find nothing that reminds me of New York as it was—not even a familiar sign—not a vestige of what existed in my spring time of life—not an object that I had seen before, except the name on the corner of Prince Street, which still looks as formerly, tho' the building to which it is affixed is entirely new.[76] Still the changes are all for the better, and are only to be regretted as detaching one from the fond and endearing recollections of early life. Broadway at this point is superb compared with what it was.

Mr. A. Dunn joined us very soon after we arrived and took tea with us, and at 10 we retired and slept off the fatigues of the day.

November 20

Sunday. After a late breakfast, I took a walk up Broadway to look about me a little. The morning mist had rolled off and the sun shone down warm and radiant on the rich facades of this noble street. The effect of Grace Church[77] at the head of it is very fine, tho' defective in detail.

From Bond Street upward I began to feel at home again, tho' many new and very splendid edifices have sprung up since I was here last. Round St. Mark's, too, and in Tenth Street things looked familiar and I found H.K. Bogert's name on the same door as in old times. B.L. Levan's, too, in Lafayette Place,[78] but both families had gone to church, so I missed the pleasure of seeing them. I left cards and then returned to my family at the Hotel.

Wrote to George Prescott and spent the rest of the morning in writing &c.

Mr. A. Dunn dined with us and towards evening we all walked up to Union Place, returning by the Fifth Avenue.

The architectural improvements are much greater than I was prepared to expect, block after block, and street after street of really magnificent mansions—spacious and lofty—executed in solid material—chiefly dark freestone and in fine taste—elegant Italian combinations—and now and then blocks of Gothic—Grand entrances and massive balustrades—richly sculptured cornices, while glimpses thro' the ample openings showed the gorgeous character of the arrangements and furniture within.

The ecclesiastical structures too, and public' buildings, which break the splendid vistas by their superior mass, are finely designed, and exhibit much that is really good in Gothic and the classic orders. Grace church with its elegant early English Parsonage, all done in fine white freestone, and festooned with glossy ivy, and embellished with well kept gardens, presents as beautiful a group as the cultivated eye would desire to repose upon. And, to me, especially attractive from its rich assemblage of Gothic features which I have never seen attempted on this side of the Atlantic to the same extent and with as great success.

New York is indeed pre-eminent in city architecture, and profuse display of solid wealth. Boston is far behind it. Still there is nothing here to compare with that glorious Common. The fine slopes, and sweeping irregularity of surface, the scrupulous cleanliness, the home comfort, and above all the exquisite beauty of the suburbs. In all, these Boston stands unrivalled, and the time will come, and that soon, when her artistic improvements will be commensurate with the elegance of her site, and superior local advantages. The rivalry between these two leading cities is already great, and whenever it shall take the shape of municipal embellishment in the city of Boston, her wealth, and facilities for procuring the finest building material, will soon enable her to compete favorably with her proud commercial sister.

The fifth Avenue, Waverly Place, and upper part of Broadway were thronged with people returning from church, and every now and then I had the pleasure of exchanging recognitions with friends of former times.

The purlieus of the university[79] remain unchanged, but the names on the door plates are unfamiliar. The current of motion is all the time up-town for the best class of residences.

November 21
Today we pursued our investigations under appalling difficulties in the shape of drizzling rains, muddy streets, and the various disabilities springing from the fact of having much to see and do, and little time to do it in. However, we succeeded in spending some hours at the Crystal palace,[80] and having the aid of a friend who was perfectly familiar with every part of it. We saw everything that was best worth seeing, and far more than we possibly could have done in the same time had we taken the thing in routine—tho' days might be spent with pleasure in examining its treasures in detail—the designs in gold and silver—the porcelain and china, and the cabinet of minerals struck me as most attractive.

In statuary, the "Eve" of Pagani was worth all the rest put together not excepting the "Powers" group.[81] The paintings were but dimly lighted owing to the gloom without, and but few seemed to possess merit. However, I was not disappointed as I expected little in that Department. But the display in the various mechanical arts was highly creditable to American industry, and finely enriched by contributions from abroad.

We returned to the Hotel at 2 and I then went to the Erie Rail Road Office and purchased my tickets for Cincinnati tomorrow morning.

Called at my old friend's, M.E. Thompson, with whom I first began the study of architecture. I found him in his office, looking even better than I ever saw him before, tho' he was in years when I was in his office a mere boy. He showed me some of my first drawings made 21 years ago, which he has scrupulously preserved.[82]

Indeed it was a very pleasant meeting and only added to my regret that I must hasten thro' a city where I have so many friends of my boyhood still living, and where there is even yet so much left to remind me of the happy past.

I returned to the Hotel at 4, wet and very tired indeed, but an excellent dinner at 5 put all right again.

Mr. Dunn came and spent the evening with us.

We missed seeing the Bogerts when they called owing to a servant's blunder in delivering their cards.

Bed time soon came and after suitable preparations for an early start in the morning we indulged for a few hours in visions of steam-cars, steam whistles, and the well-balanced advantages and discomforts of steam travel in general.

November 22

We were up at 5 and drove off for the cars at 6½—foot of Duane Street. Here after a struggle I got my baggage all checked for Dunkirk (with the aid of the carriage driver) and then crossed the Ferry to Jersey City where the cars were in waiting. It was a raw, dreary, drizzling morning, so that the glimpses of New Jersey thro' the dripping glass were desolate enough—alternate rocks and marshes, moist and clammy. The cars were excellent—on the broad gauge all thro' to the Lake, and the speed at times so great as to make each particular hair stand erect. As we neared the Delaware the clouds rolled off from the mountain sides, and strong gleams of sunshine flashed across the wide valleys. For miles and miles, the dark, swollen river swept along by our side, chasing and fretting in its rocky bed, and huge cliffs hung over it, and rich mossy Hemlocks mingled their green with the seared leaves of the Oak and Chestnut. White, shining cascades threaded down the grey crags and mingled with the tide below, and the Delaware and Hudson Canal followed along the opposite bank at the base of the vertical ledges which in many places have been blasted away to create a channel for it.

The vast bends of the river and the impending mountains were so majestic that the loss of the foliage was scarcely felt, but rather enhanced their rude grandeur.

Then came the Susquehanna, sweeping in broad curves, thro' fertile valleys and grand pine-clad ridges, and the declining sun bathed the whole in a flood of most transparent golden light.

Night then set in, and hour after hour sped along in unvarying monotony. One after another fell fast asleep in spite of the throbbing and heaving of the train, the noise of the wheels, and resonance of the steam as it re-echoed from the rocky tunnels. We laid the little boy on a seat and he slept sweetly.

Towards midnight I was the only one awake, and that only at intervals for every now and then, tho' bolt upright in the seat, I fell into a short dose as profound as it was fleeting. This is one of the finest and best managed roads in America, but the time allowed for refreshment is necessarily very scanty—only one meal from New York to Dunkirk—469 miles. However, I had provided a large parcel of crackers, and made all hands take a good cup of hot tea &c. before leaving the St. Nicholas, so that we escaped starvation. We had 20 minutes for dinner and tea combined at Deposit, and everything plain and good. We arrived there at 2 P.M., say 187 miles from New York—making a very good division of the day.

At Hornelsville (342 miles) the passengers for Buffalo changed cars, but we were undisturbed and flew along at a fearful rate to Dunkirk which we reached at midnight.

The weather had changed again and as we were obliged to see our baggage rechecked at this point for Cincinnati I got quite a sprinkling while standing for full 20 minutes waiting for my checks to be called out and changed. The place for doing it is badly chosen, just at the extremity of the Depot exposed to the wind and rain from the Lake. However, I left my family under shelter, and soon dried myself at the Stove in the ladies' waiting room.

The Buffalo train came along and we were scarcely settled in our places before we got to the State Line (28 miles) when the gauge changes, and, of course, a change of cars. And such a struggle as ensued for places! The new cars were not sufficient for the mighty herd, and as the herd consisted chiefly of well-dressed savages, miscalled men, whose speed and muscle enabled them to take their seats in advance of the women and children, those who had families suffered in proportion—especially as the men aforesaid appeared utterly benighted as to the courtesies which usually prevail in civilized communities. I succeeded, after a while, in getting all my family in place, and scarcely had I done so when another change in the gauge and another change of cars, and another scene of confusion and selfish rudeness occurred at Erie—19 miles further.[83] For a little time, however, two additional cars were put on and with the assistance of a very pleasant, civil conductor I got my family comfortably seated and everything went smoothly until we got to Cleveland—611 miles from N. York, at 9½ A.M. on the 23rd.

November 23

Being several hours behind time we had to layover here until the afternoon express train for Cincinnati. Took a carriage and went at once to the American [Hotel][84] where we all took a good cleansing from the dust and cinders of the cars, and soon sat down to an excellent breakfast.

The day proved warm and sunny and we spent some time in walking thro' the wide streets of this busy thriving port. Its position is quite lofty, commanding a noble view of the Lake, but in every other direction it seems to be hemmed in by the dense primeval forest. Everything looks new and incomplete, and the greatness of the city is still in promise, not in fruition.

Soon after two we drove to the Depot and had the choice of seats in fine spacious cars. A balmy sunshiny afternoon, and cheerful pleasant looking fellow passengers. We started punctually at 2:50 and the whole trip to Columbus was as pleasant as could be. The lofty forests on each side tho' stripped of their leaves, and unbroken by rock or mountain were still grand and majestic, and vast cleared farms at intervals, opened a view into the distance all radiant with yellow sunlight.

The motion was rapid and easy, the stoppings frequent and managed without jarring or confusion. And at Columbus—135 miles—where we changed cars at 8 P.M. the arrangements were so good—the new cars so spacious and comfortable and all done under an ample Depot, that it made a pleasant contrast to the discomfort and disorder of the Lake shore road. But O! How tired and sleepy we all were by this time.

At 10 we took supper at Xenia, and soon after caught a glimpse of the Miami on whose banks I spent many a happy day in my boyhood. There it lay in a fine curve the light mist curling upward on the steep hill sides, and over all the clear moon in her last quarter looked lovingly down—bright and glistening, as burnished silver.

I looked at my wife and my little boy and felt how much happier I am now than in those free and joyous hours of which the scene before me was so suggestive.

At one o'clock we reached Cincinnati. No trouble with the baggage—the checks being collected on the cars by the Agent. The omnibus in waiting to take us to the Hotel, and in half an hour we were all safely lodged at the Burnett house,[85] in fine, spacious, well-furnished rooms—our trunks &c. in good order, and all quite thankful to have passed so safely and upon the whole pleasantly thro' the Railroad part of our journey.

November 24

After a 10 o'clock breakfast I went to the Banking House of Wood and Dunlap to enquire for my sister Emily. Mr. Wood had seen her but a few minutes before on her way to church (it being Thanksgiving Day) and kindly offered to bring her to me which he did in a few minutes. I was delighted to find her looking better than I had ever seen her, and she was much surprised to see me as she had not received my last letter. I took her immediately to the Hotel and we soon formed a cheerful and happy group around the fireside.

I left them all in high glee and went to make arrangements about a Boat. Mr. Wood went with me, and by the advice of Mr. Dunlap decided upon the *Susquehanna*, as every way the most eligible in port. She does not leave until Saturday—has pleasant accommodations and the captain & officers bear an excellent character.

I could be accommodated in a far more splendid and costly manner by going on the mail Boat to Louisville, and taking a large Boat there. But we have had so many changes already and have been so much in the crowd that we prefer going down in a more quiet and unostentatious manner, and above all I wish to avoid a cotton cargo, which I hope to do by taking a Boat from this place, as they generally load full here, or nearly so, while the Louisville Packets calculate largely on the Cotton region. I know by experience the danger and discomfort of a cotton cargo—especially with a family. I was on board the *Packet Memphis* when she took fire some years ago.

After dinner, I took Emily and Mrs. Ladd down to look at the Staterooms and as they were quite pleased with them I engaged them at once, so that our arrangements are now complete.

My sister rejoined us at the Burnett when we got back and the evening sped along merrily. We retired early, rose late [November 25], and after an excellent breakfast at 9 o'clock, found ourselves entirely recovered from the fatigues of travel, save and except the swimming in the head, and buzzing in the ear, which leave the impressions of the Railroad Train for days after the journey is over.

November 25
By the by I wrote to Mr. Reid immediately after I got here at 2 last night, requesting him to have the house ready for us on his arrival.

The close, humid air of the last few days has given place to a light frost and clear brilliant sky. We are much pleased with Cincinnati. There is an air of space and freedom about the city—wide streets—large solid buildings—fine freestone fronts—and a buoyant, healthy look of plain, simple, substantial prosperity. The thoroughfares are full of active movement and business like dispatch, but not choked, encumbered, distracting like the Eastern cities. Our time is so short that we can see but little of it, and I only regret that we cannot stay a month.

We were detained in the house during the morning by callers &c. amongst whom was Mrs. Huntington whom I knew years ago as a bright sparkling girl of 19. She is now the mother of two children but as handsome as ever.

Sister Emily spent the morning and dined with us, and in the afternoon we all took a walk thro' the best parts of the city, and all concluded that it would be the pleasantest place to live in of any we have seen this summer. Comfort and abundance are everywhere apparent—even the coal smoke which clouds the air is redolent of in-door comfort. The solid masonry—stone and brick—untouched by plaster—tells of opulence and comfort. The well clad people, and their wholesome ruddy looks, all tell of comfort. It is, in short, the most home-ish place of all, and next to New Orleans, the place of all others I have visited that I would choose to reside in. The recollections of my boyhood still cluster thick around it, while recent improvements have but added to its magnitude without crowding and oppressing it, and effacing those familiar features which connect it with the past. It is quite possible that there may be many drawbacks but do think it would take long to discover them.

Just before tea I got a dispatch from my brother Robert at Madison to know what boat I should proceed on. Replied at once.

The family with whom my sister Emily is now staying called upon us and invited us to spend the evening. We did so, and had a pleasant social visit—varied with Piano music—solos, duos, and trios. My sister has greatly improved both in voice and instrumentation, and the whole thing was so like old times.

I always enjoyed myself in Cincinnati. There is a heartiness and unostentation about the people that wins wonderfully upon a stranger, tho' I can scarcely consider myself a stranger where my brother and sisters so long had a home. And in the very next county to where we all had our home when we first came from England 23 years ago.

I have never been back to Piqua since we left it in 1832, and should have taken it on our route this time had I not discovered that the Columbus and Xenia road was every way more desirable for family travel.

November 26
Light frost in the night, lovely weather. Clear sunshiny and bracing.

Rose quite early and all appeared at breakfast at 8, with excellent appetites and feeling delightfully after a night of profound sleep.

Wrote to Geo. W. Prescott Boston and Charles Knap, Pittsburgh before breakfast. Sister Emily joined us just after.

Spent the morning in seeing friends and making arrangements to be off again. Then settled my account at the Burnett and went down early in the afternoon to the Steamer. My sister went with us and stayed sometime. I then took her to the Covington Ferry to pay a visit over the river and went back to the boat where we soon domesticated ourselves and had plenty of time to get settled before the hurry of departure.

The accommodations are limited compared with the Louisville and St. Louis Packets, but the best choice we have from this point, and we shall probably have more real comfort than on the favourite and in consequence, more crowded steamers. We shall, however, be fully able to satisfy ourselves on all points between Cincinnati and Louisville.

November 27

Sunday. The captain was disappointed in his pilots so that we did not get off last night. This is the first trip of the Boat for the season. Some of the arrangements are necessarily incomplete. But we all had a good night's rest, and consoled ourselves with the reflection that had we started we should have made but little progress as the fog settled down very dense all night. Indeed, it hangs over the hills and river in heavy vapours today, and seems little disposed to disperse. In the meantime, we are filling up with passengers and two boats have come in from New Orleans from which I have got papers and intelligence. One of them was at least three hours this morning in wedging into place between our boat and the next above. But with the aid of steam, guys and capstan they gradually forced her bow up to the Levee. The pressure of the current on the steamers, Barges &c. lying in consecutive tiers above, and bow on to the Levee makes it very difficult to open a berth for an incoming Steamer.

Our Staterooms do very well and the meals are plain and wholesome. The Beefsteak, however, does less than justice to the fame of the Ohio graziers. I could not help exclaiming in my efforts at mastication—"Oh! that this too too solid flesh would melt."

Emily is quite unwell today. The travelling, change of diet, loss of rest &c. have made her quite bilious, so she has been obliged to take blue mass and confine herself to her Stateroom.

At half past 2 P.M. we at last moved off, after taking on a full complement of passengers. Among them were the Bateman family—Kate, Ellen and the Baby—with their parents. As to babies, the cabin was a perfect Babel—at least half a dozen infants, besides children from 6 to 14. Kate Bateman is 11 and Ellen 8. They have large clear cut features, and Kate decidedly handsome. Their faces, manners, and conversation are alternately those of grown women, and buoyant high-spirited children, all life and sparkling intelligence. They say they have never been inside a school—their mother teaches them everything.

A thick mist broods over the river so that we proceed slowly and the fine hills on both sides look wan and spectral. I could but just discern the tomb of [President William Henry] "Harrison" 'thro' the fog and the old house at North Bend [Ohio]. I regret it the less as Emily cannot enjoy the landscape. She remained in her berth all day.

At Aurora, 26 miles below Cincinnati, we are obliged to lay up for the night, so that we may calculate upon another good sleep. And if it only clears off we shall still pass some of the richest scenery by day light and Emily will have the benefit of it, as she must be well again tomorrow and I would not on any account have her miss the "beauties of the Ohio."

November 28

It is now 8 A.M. We have had a fine night's rest, and have just breakfasted, but still lying by the wharf Boat at Aurora. Phoebus what a name! for such a place, and on such a morning too; impenetrable fog shrouds the opposite side of the river. Nothing visible but the small section of brown bank immediately at our side. It rises about 20 feet—grooved and channelled by rains and graded at the wharf Boat for the receipt & delivery of merchandise. A level road runs along the top and moving figures appear dimly thro' the mist. A little beyond are a few produce stores, a printing office and "Exchange." Some brick and some wood, and all enveloped in vapour so dense that they dissolve away from the eye at a few rods distance on either hand.

At 9¼ the air begins to clear up, and we are again under way.

This is one of the few boats that I have ever been able to write upon. The motion is so easy, that I find but little difficulty.

Oh for the art of easy writing—
That should be also easy reading.

Emily is up and dressed, and well today.

During the morning, the air remained charged with moisture, the sun shone thro' semi-opacity like the gleams in the opal, and the scenery looked as if the lights and shadows had been tinted in strongly and then toned down with a slight wash of the sponge. After dinner, however, everything came out sharp and clear, and as we approached the beautiful hills of Madison, Ia. [Indiana], I took Emily and Mrs. Ladd on deck to enjoy the rich and changing Panorama.

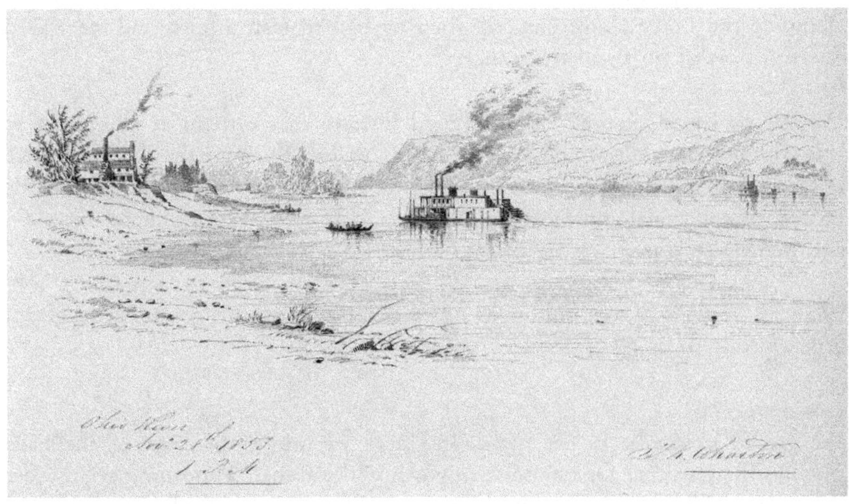

FIGURE 3.26 Ohio River, 1853 (*Sketchbook*, p. 49). New York Public Library, Archives and Special Collections, New York.

The captain brought seats and I stepped below to write a hasty line to my brother Robert, which turned out to be unnecessary as the first object I recognized when we neared the town was my brother himself on the lookout for us standing on the deck of a steamer at the wharf. He had been on the alert ever since he got my dispatch and we very fortunately had to make a stoppage here of more than an hour. It was a delightful meeting. I saw no change except for the better, tho' it is now nine years last July since I have seen him. He was then living in Cincinnati, and did not look near as healthy as at present.

After a short talk with my family in the cabin, he and I stepped into an omnibus and went in quest of his wife and family. We found them in their pleasant home, and I liked my sister in law very much indeed. It is the first time I have seen her. She is quite handsome, full of sprightliness and character and very pleasant manner. My little nephew [Robert H. Wharton] and niece [name unknown], and the baby [Charles H. Wharton] filled up the picture, and formed an interesting and pretty group.

Jane put on her mantle and we all got into the omnibus again to join my party at the Boat, going about a mile below town to a point where the Captain of the Steamer said he should take a barge in tow. We talked very fast as we had much to say in a very short time.

Arrived at the point indicated I found the landing so bad that I suggested we had better drive back to where we left the Boat, and just got there in time. But too late for Jane and the children to go on board, so that [they] stood on shore, and the two families had to content themselves with signalizing each other by waving hats and handkerchiefs and other pantomimic interchanges.

Robert came on board with me, and we improved every instant until we run alongside the Barge above named, when he had to leap ashore, and we waved our adieus with no small reluctance.

We felt very glad that we had the good fortune to see them at all—short as was the interview—it would have been the easiest thing in the world to have missed them, and had we been on a "fast favourite" we certainly should, so this proved an additional and most satisfactory incident to reconcile us to our plain and homely steamer.

Emily is fortunately too, quite well again, so that altogether it was a delightful little episode to us all.

November 29
We got to Louisville in the night, and here we are at the head of the Falls this morning waiting for our turn to go thro' the Canal, a consummation most devoutly to be wished for. But as to the when—all the ordinary modes of computation fail. Whoever casts his lot on a Cincinnati boat must be well

prepared to "bear all things, believe all things, hope all things, and endure all things."[86] Yet I do not see very well how we can change for the better. It is so rainy that it would be perfect nonsense to go on shore with so large a family, and a change of boat is but a conjectural advantage, so that we had better remain quiet. It may do very well after all. The Boat, at least, is strong, safe and easy. The principal objections are the limited space of cabin and Staterooms, and the large concourse of passengers without any chance for companionship. The great charm of travel on the Western boats of the best class is in the pleasant associations with which one becomes surrounded in so long and familiarizing a trip. We enjoyed it on the *Aleck Scott* but miss it here. Some of our passengers leave us this morning for the *Sultana* being in great haste to meet their engagements in New Orleans. I learn, however, that she is to take on cotton at Memphis or Vicksburg, and so of the Louisville Packets generally. Anything rather than a "Cotton Boat" for me.

The cabins, guards, and upper deck are so thronged that I find it difficult to secure a sketch without being disturbed. Yet I succeeded in getting 4 outlines as we passed along yesterday, and the "Falls of the Ohio" this morning. "Falls" on the principle of "lucus a non lucendo."[87] No cataract, hardly rapids, but simple eddies, and a little plashy [wet or splashing] chafing of the current over points of rock, chiefly submerged, and long shallow sand bars. The entire fall seems to be about 25 feet in 3 miles, along the curve of the river.

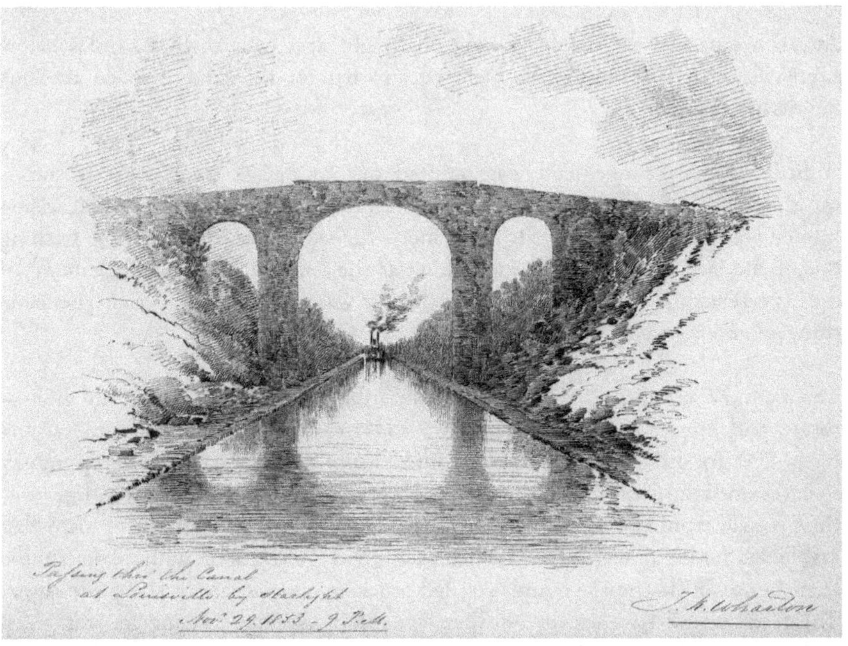

FIGURE 3.27 Passing through the canal at Louisville by starlight, 1853 (*Sketchbook*, p. 52). New York Public Library, Archives and Special Collections, New York.

Strong wind and driving rains all morning but cleared off cold in the afternoon. Evening is now approaching and we are still here waiting for an upward boat to work her tedious way thro' the canal and give us a chance. In the meantime, the staterooms vacated this morning have been filled up, and sundry sturdy, stalwart figures added to the swarm in the forward cabin.

Just at sunset a broad gleam of radiance shot thro' the clouds and lit up the opposite banks with flashing light like burnished or molu [faux gold]—while everywhere else on earth, sky and water, sober greys and simple purple tints were busily weaving the pall of night.

At 6 P.M. we got into the canal, working stern foremost to get the benefit of the wave from the wheels to increase the buoyancy forward where the greatest weight is concentrated.

We are 150 miles from Cincinnati.

November 30

At 7 when I went on deck our boat was lying at a wood yard about 30 miles below Louisville; the atmosphere bright and frosty and the wood piles, flatboat roofs, and rugged earthy banks all profusely powdered with white rime. It must have been a very long passage thro' the Canal to have made so little progress, but it is' partly due to the heavy Barge alongside which we still keep in tow to relieve the Steamer of part of her freight in the present low stage of water.

At 9¼ we passed the *Sultana* taking on freight at a little town 40 miles below Louisville. Our passengers who went over to her for the sake of speed are thus far disappointed.

A little above a Stone Mill was pointed out to me as a curiosity. It stands on the bank of the river, a limestone bluff of some 150 feet high rising immediately behind it and the machinery turned by a strong spring gushing out of the face of the rock. I was talking at the time to a "travelled German" of great pretensions. He simply thought that "it was nothing at all" that the same thing might be seen in "every little village in Ga-a-rmany."

The country around is composed of an infinite series of Limestone hills—round and lumpish—covered with thin soil and heavily timbered, and varying from 200 to 400 feet in height—some shewing a bare face of grey, mossy rock, seamed into horizontal strata, and dotted over with cedars. At intervals, they recede from the margin of the river, and leave a wide space of rich, flat, arable land—in almost every case under good cultivation, with plain simple farm houses near the river, and well fed stock moving leisurely along the shore. The trees are all bare except one lonely weeping Willow, waving its still green tresses over a humble river side cottage—while great sycamores as far as the eye can reach fling their snowy branches high above the turbid water.

At 5 P.M. we entered the coal region, and soon after made fast to the Cannelton wharf boat to take in a supply.

The little towns of Hawesville and Trabues' extensive coal mines are just opposite, say 125 miles from Louisville.

Higher up the river the coal veins lay on the top of the Limestone strata near the summit of the hills, about 200 feet higher than the bed of the river, but at Trabues the pits have been opened in the face of the bare rock close to the bank of the river, forming large black cavities, rudely arched, and cut out of the solid Limestone. Rail Tracks run from the mouths of the Pits to the river, and the coal is transported with rapidity in capacious Trucks to the Flat-boats in waiting.

At Cannelton where we are now lying, we notice a fine large cotton Factory of stone—relieved by well-proportioned turrets and quite imposing among the humbler structures which compose the village. The works are owned by a company in Boston.[88]

December 1, 1853
Light broke lazily thro' the dull grey threatening clouds. We have reached the wide part of the River, low woody banks, long shoals and sand bars and tame uniform scenery.

We have just risen from breakfast at 8 o'clock and are passing Mount Vernon—234 miles below Louisville.

Variable weather all day—broad gleams of sunshine at times, and then dark gloomy sky with passing rain.

The limestone formation still lingers with us, approaching the river and then retiring in long sweeps of ridgy upland—while vast blocks and fragments lie scattered along the shore, and the stupendous height of the forest trees on the first level bears witness to the richness of the alluvial deposit in the intervals along the margin of the river.

At half past one we moored to the bank to take in coal at a station some 270 miles below Louisville, and were soon joined by the *Sultana* with other boats and lay side by side for some time. We should have gained nothing on the score of time by a change of boats, and as to comfort I observe the lower deck of the *Sultana* covered over with sheep, horses, and stock in general, suggesting divers unsavoury recollections of a trip I made some years ago to the mouth of [the] Cumberland on a boat similarly freighted.

Towards evening we passed a bold range of cliffs, grouped in broad plain surfaces and semi-circular bastions, coursed with firmly marked horizontal belts, and surmounted by dense forests, with rich clusters of moss and evergreens traversing their upper lines. A large dark cavity in one of the projections shewed the entrance to the "Cave in the Rock" and a splendid radiance from the descending sun burst over the whole in a rich glow of amber light.

This point is 284 miles below Louisville, and the banks immediately relapse again into flat stretches of fertile alluvion covered with wild, unceasing forest. At long intervals, however, high conical ridges continued to throw their broad shadows over the stream while a single spark of daylight lasted.

December 2

We lay too all night just above the Sisters, two islands about 320 miles from Louisville, where the channel is narrow and circuitous, with but 7 feet of water and the Captain wisely preferred day light for it.

I was upon deck before sunrise. A lovelier morning for the season I never beheld, and such a clear elastic atmosphere.

We were working carefully thro' the passage stern foremost. Close by us lay the Steamer *Dick Keyes* hard aground. Further into the stream 3 coal boats also aground and two sunk on the reef. The scene forcibly reminding me of one of Hugh Evans' ditty—

> To shallow rivers to whose falls
> Melodious birds sing madrigals
> There will we make our beds of roses &c.[89]

We swung in close to shore and then floated thro' just touching on the shallowest part, as we draw seven feet one inch. The risk would have been great had we tried it at dark. Better to lose a night than to have to wait for a rise in the river like our unfortunate friend the *Keyes*. This is her first trip, and according to the superstition of the river she starts with a bad reputation for luck &c.

As to our boat it is pleasant to find so much care and good judgment in the Captain and his Pilots. However, the "heroic age" of Steamboating on the Western waters is fast passing away, and many have already learned the plain lesson that "discretion is the better part of valour."

At half past 8 we passed thro' the rapids formed by a "wing dam" thrown up at a narrow part of the river to increase the water on the shoals above. At the foot lay the *Cincinnatus* 9 days from New Orleans. She was lightening onto a barge at the Bank before attempting the reefs.

At 9 we are just going over another bad place in sight of Smithland. They are heaving the lead. "Mark under water twain," "Mark twain," "Mark above water twain," "Quarter less twain," "Nine feet"—"Nine feet Scant," "Eight feet," "Eight feet scant"—and so back again until we are safely over it.

N.B. "Mark twain" is 2 fathoms or 12 feet. "Quarter less twain" 10½ feet or 12 feet less a quarter of a fathom. The other two are 12 feet large—and 12 feet scant.[90]

Smithland at the mouth of [the] Cumberland, which we have just gone by is 328 miles from Louisville.

A little above the mouth of [the] Tennessee lay the *Tecumseh* fast in the sand. She left Louisville a day ahead of us.

Passed Paducah at 10¼ A.M., 340 miles and 50 from the mouth of Ohio. *Sultana* a little in advance.

Strong wind blowing, keen and cold, and waves running so high that my pen staggers every time it touches the paper.

At 3 P.M. we reached the ancient and dilapidated town of Cairo, at the mouth of the Ohio, looking even more decrepid and worm-eaten and forsaken, than ever. A few scattered buildings on the point, falling year by year into a more complete state of decay, and all around a perfect rendezvous of ruined flatboats—outlawed steamboat hulls—wharf boats in the last stage of senility, and other fragmentary relics of a former prosperous river marine.

The only appearance of activity seemed concentrated around the proposed terminus of the great Cairo and Chicago railroad, which is now in rapid progress, and will when complete form over 700 miles of as fine internal communication as is to be found in the West.

Unawed by the savage wildness of the spot I had the temerity to make a couple of sketches to preserve the uncouth features of its unambitious dwellings and locale.

We stayed but an hour, and casting off our Barge, at 4 P.M. were fairly embarked on the broad bosom of the Mississippi.

We are getting more and more pleased with our Boat, her Captain, and general management, and if the numerical force on board could just be diminished by one half—especially in the ladies' cabin, we should have little left to desire on the score of comfort.

I went on deck after tea. The wind had died away, and the new moon and evening star shone with singular brilliancy in the clear frosty air. A belt of rich orange still lingered over the dark solemn woods, and far spread river—while the intense depth of the vault above threw out the planets and constellations with a splendour peculiar to the dry atmosphere of the West.

Below the bright coal fires blazed cheerfully, and the ladies were distributed in cosy groups—some with their work, some with their books and some with their husbands. They all seem quite pleasant people, and when I wish their numbers diminished it is simply in view of the limited size of the cabins, and the swarm of little children which keep every thing in a state of perpetual agitation. We have 100 cabin passengers on board, of whom 15 are women, and the children number a full dozen.

At 7 we were at Mills' Point, 38 miles below the mouth, and stopped an hour putting off freight &c.

The steward brought on board three brace of beautiful wild-ducks, just killed, which he purchased at the ridiculous price of 15 cents apiece. These with a noble wild Turkey which he got at Cairo, will be a pretty addition to our larder tomorrow.

December 3

We had a fine run all night. I was up and on deck at day break—not a breath of wind but a piercing nitrous air, and ice of half an inch in thickness formed on the water buckets where exposed.

After breakfast, I was walking on the upper deck, breathing the fresh, frosty atmosphere, when our showy little, moustached German joined me. He had already told me that he was a consul of Hanover, Brunswick and Luneburg. He now gave me an account of the manufacturing operations in Prussia and especially in woollen fabrics, in which he says his brothers are largely engaged at Frankfort upon Oder—having a branch house in New York under the style of Ludwig and Emile Sanson [*sic*: Samson]. Says his own profession is that of physician but he often feels tempted to engage in mercantile pursuits for which the position of his brothers would offer peculiar advantages. But he has been unused to commercial operations, and, moreover, in Germany would lose somewhat by it in social estimation. I told him that was a European prejudice, which must sooner or later be totally obliterated. He thought, however, that it was a "very respectable prejudice," for he conceived it next to impossible for a man engaged in traffic and pecuniary accumulation to possess what he called "large feelings."

Just at this moment, I happened to glance my eye along the majestic ranges of forest which line the level, earthy banks on either side, and noticed the indications of a change of climate as we approached the "South." Clusters of young Cotton Trees with the leaves still clinging to them—Willows here and there quite green, and herbs and creepers along the brink of the river showing a long line of tangled verdure.

I directed his attention to it, and he placed his eye glass in the cavity of his imperial brow, and remarked that he had never lived in the country and had not paid any attention to such matters, indeed did not know the difference between a Plum and a Pear tree. As he professed to write Latin I suggested that he must be one of those whom Virgil has immortalized in the line "*Non omnes arbusta juvant, humilesque myricae*."[91] "Ah yes!" said he, "but, of course, I know the officinal plants, those composing the materia medica; and as to flowers I do know the difference between a rose and a forget-me-not, a myrtle and a jessiminy."

At this point I found the air so sharp and cutting that I proposed to go down into the cabin.

We were then passing the earthy bluffs near Randolph, 181 miles below Cairo. They seem to be about 80 feet high, seamed and furrowed by the rains, and stained with variegated patches of red and yellow ochres. After skirting the left or eastern bank for a couple of miles They suddenly sink again into the level lowland. The stage of water is much lower than when we went up in the summer, and interminable ranges of tawny sand bars heave their huge length high out of the stream like the fabled "Kraken" of Norwegian seas.

The day continued without a cloud and as afternoon came on the difference in climate became more and more apparent. Large trees with a full suit of leaves clinging to them dotting the otherwise naked forest.

We arrived at Memphis at 3½ P.M. and much to my disappointment the Captain concluded to take a lot of cotton which immediately offered, amounting to some 380 Bales, this, together with the necessary detention and large influx of fresh passengers put me entirely out of conceit with my choice of a Boat.

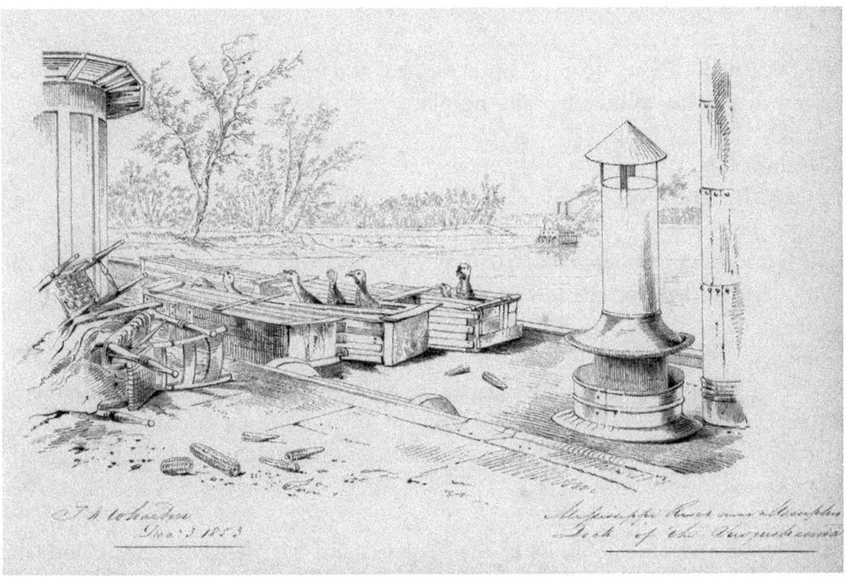

FIGURE 3.28 Mississippi River near Memphis, TN, 1853 (*Sketchbook*, p. 57). New York Public Library, Archives and Special Collections, New York.

Tho' I should not be surprised if even the largest and best have disadvantages equally objectionable especially as there are no exclusively "Passenger boats" on the river. All make what may be termed "trading" voyages, and take any and every thing that offers, except perhaps the strictly cotton boats, such as the monster *H.W. Hill* which left while we lay at the wharf well filled with passengers and buried in Bales.

Our own Boat with her crowded cabins, her horde of deck passengers below—and freight of every kind and description, choking up every avenue from hold to hurricane deck—presents a scene of most admired confusion and discomfort which is the more annoying to me as I supposed that at this late season there would be but little travel southward, and had looked forward with so much pleasure to the trip down the river at this bracing time of the year and in a fine "Western Boat," so proverbial for "appliances and appointments."

I have made a serious mistake in trying a Cincinnati boat. I did it under the impression that I should avoid the danger of a cotton cargo with my family. On the contrary I have the inferior accommodations and some <u>cotton</u> to boot.

We all walked up the bluff and thro' the main street, taking a hasty view of this busy and fast increasing place, but were not very favorably impressed with what we saw. Everything seems in a transition state—raw, crude, untidy, unfinished, but promising a future of greatness. Yet it never can be a pleasant place. It is decidedly sickly both in summer and winter, and its exposed position on the bluff renders it obnoxious to the intensest heat of the one, and the blustering rigor of the other. But for business it offers greater inducements than any point between New Orleans and St. Louis.

We returned to the Boat in time for tea and then waited patiently for our release from this uninviting landing place.

December 4
Sunday. Beautiful sunny day, cloudless sky, mild air.

We were under way again at 10 last night and this morning at 8 passed the *H.W. Hill* taking cotton at Helena, 59 miles below Memphis and 307 from Cairo.

Some of the passengers who engaged at Memphis changed their minds owing to reports of cholera and yellow fever in New Orleans brought by upward bound boats within the last few hours. They are as usual, doubtless, greatly exaggerated.

We are now within the limits of the "Cypress and Myrtle." The air is bland, the shores rich and level cotton farms at intervals with the deadened Timber still standing in gaunt and savage ranks amid the tillage, some kinds of forest trees with their leaves yet unshed, and in the remote swamps back from the river a dense growth of tall cypress trees with their flat spreading tops all covered with brown leaves, sere and lifeless but still clinging to the twigs.

We passed at 11 A.M. our old friend the *Aleck Scott* bound up.

Southward and still southward we pressed along, aided by the powerful current, the air becoming constantly warmer, and a soft blue haze settling gradually down upon the river until by evening we were entirely enveloped in the smoky atmosphere of the Southern "Indian Summer," which wholly concealed the distant woods as the river swept round long sandy flats, and far reaching islands.

The Mississippi side was in many places covered with the tall green tufts of the Cane-brake, thick and impervious like a miniature forest, over which towered the lofty sycamores, cypress, Tulip and Cotton Trees, still mostly nude and lifeless, but more and more intermingled with single trees and even whole groups dressed in living green. And the weather today is so beautiful that it invites one to study this transition region and mark the rapid changes to a summer climate as we pass along.

At 4½ we reached Napoleon at the mouth of Arkansas—450 miles below the Ohio—rounding to for a few moments at the Wharf Boat to land a passenger.

The whole cabin has been quiet and pleasant today. There are Bibles on board and some have read them.

December 5
Warm sunny sky without a cloud. We have had a fine run all night and are now, at 8 A.M., about 60 miles above Vicksburg.

The green now predominates and the banks look less and less naked. Short tresses of moss depend from the cypress trees. The cotton farms shew extensive and careful culture, and the plantation houses and outbuildings are spacious and comfortable. Everything indicates an approach to a sunny and opulent region. Indeed, by noon the temperature was uncomfortably warm, and the fires in the cabins are wholly dispensed with. The deciduous Trees on the banks are at about the same stage of foliage as in New England on the First of October.

At 1½ P.M. we made fast to the Wharf Boat at Vicksburg and landed quite a number of passengers and light freight. Here I got a *New Orleans Picayune* of the 3rd Inst., which announced the sudden death of my old friend Dr. [Abner] Hester. He has been subject to haemorrhage of the lungs for over 15 years, and has frequently told me that he thought his life very precarious.

We moved off again at 3 P.M.

Vicksburg has a sluggish, unbusiness like, unprogressive air about it. Scattered over rugged hills of crumbling brown earth, washed in places with deep ravines, and the steep streets and roads suggesting uncomfortable ideas of tenacious, ochry mud in wet weather, and intolerable dust in dry.

The yellow fever is considered quite extinct here, at least so says the *Sentinel*. Vicksburg is 650 miles below Cairo and 400 miles from New Orleans.

At 7½ we stopped for a few moments at Grand Gulf 53 miles below Vicksburg. A lovely moonlight night, and such a mild summer air—altogether too pleasant to remain in the cabin so Emily and I sat out on the guards, and sang duos &c. Mrs. Ladd sat with us and we stayed out until the night air began to cool down.

Our numbers are greatly reduced by the weeding out at Vicksburg and other points, and the cabins are now lively and cheerful without being crowded and encumbered. So that with the charming weather, and the obliging good humour of the Captain and officers, a well-furnished table and plenty of room to move about freely, the latter part of our trip is becoming as pleasant as we could desire. Our spruce, dapper little German, and others among the men formed quite a fund of amusement & entertainment which would be no mean accession to the "Comic Muse." As an example of jolly, rotund, and inflated self-importance the German is a perfect study in his reiterated "my dear Saare" is inimitable.

December 6

Fine sunrise, simple river scenery, long level clouds of mist on the horizon and wreathed among the forests. A single flatboat casting dark Shadows on the Stream, and above the most exquisite passage of glowing yellow rays, thro' the rose and violet into the purest blue. The mist suddenly lifted itself and spread over the whole sky. It settled down about 8 A.M. into thick fog forbidding further progress. Fortunately, it happened at a wooding station, so making a virtue of necessity we fastened to the shore and went to work on a pile of Fuel.

We passed Natchez—114 miles from Vicksburg at 1½ last night and Fort Adams 56 miles further down at 7 A.M. this morning. The wooding point where we now lie is a little above the mouth of Red River.

The trees on the lofty bluffs at Fort Adams show a good deal of rich autumnal colouring, tho' some are still quite green and summer-like, while others, especially along the summit lines, are already quite bare. On the level banks opposite lies the large cotton plantation (formerly owned by Col. Coffee), but now reduced to little more than half its original extent, the capricious river, year by year, stealing away its fertile acres, and washing away the point for the formation of new bars and an altered channel.

About 11 the sun blazed out, and with the aid of a light breeze scattered the mist, and the rest of the day was like midsummer in New England.

When the fog dispersed, we were at the mouth of Red River 221 miles from New Orleans, and at 1½ P.M. were passing along the Sugar Plantations of Pointe Coupée, the cane looking quite green shewing that there has been no black frost yet, and the Sugar Houses in full operation.

Here, too, are the first live Oaks, with their vast round masses of dark foliage scattered here and there among the lighter species which embosom the Plantation houses—lustrous orange and citron trees within the garden enclosures, and far away in the background beyond the cane fields, the interminable line of rank, mossy cypress.

Some vestiges of cotton culture still appear at intervals, and on the opposite side of the river the sand bars are covered with a luxuriant growth of young Cotton Trees, one of the last lingering characteristics of the river above. But here all green and shining with summer leafage, and floating summer clouds sail along overhead, casting broad shadows across their long curved ranks of verdure, and summer birds carol among the branches.

At Bayou Sara we put off a passenger and got a New Orleans paper at 20 minutes past 2. From the paper we learn that our magnificent little German has been recognized by the President as Consul of Brunswick and Luneburg for the State of Alabama. His name is given "Julius Sanson" [*sic*: Samson].[92]

At 5:20 we got to Baton Rouge, 36 miles from Bayou Sara, and about 150 from New Orleans. Here I was pleased to see Mr. Andrews and his wife come on board. Mr. A. is a clerk of Major Beauregard's in his military office for the transaction of business of the Forts and Engineer Corps. From him I got quite a fund of late information as he only left New Orleans on Saturday last.

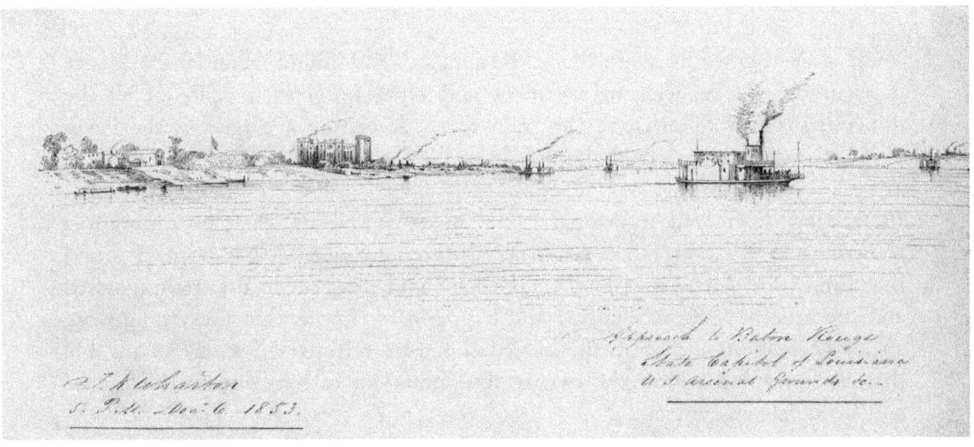

FIGURE 3.29 Approach to Baton Rouge and State Capitol of Louisiana, 1853 (*Sketchbook*, p. 59). New York Public Library, Archives and Special Collections, New York.

Much, too, in regard to the New Custom House, and with few exceptions everything favourable. I regret, deeply, however, to hear of the death of our faithful "Brady" by yellow fever. We have a beautiful moonlight, and no indications of fog, so may hope to reach the city in good time tomorrow.

December 7

Towards midnight the vapours gathered but we continued running slowly all night until about 5 this morning when the mist became too thick to proceed and we are now at 7 fast to the bank, about 25 miles above the city waiting for clear weather. The sun is making a strong effort to beam thro' and we shall probably not have to wait long.

At half past 9 we were fairly under way again and about noon arrived at New Orleans, bid adieu to our worthy Captain and fellow voyagers and a short drive brought us all safely to our home again. With what feelings of joy and gratitude I entered it I need not tell.

I left it with but a precarious hope of ever seeing it again, and here I am in excellent health, with my family around me all well and hearty, and everything looking so pleasant, and cheerful, and joyous and home-like—and then the house and furniture have been so well taken care of—everything clean, dry and well-aired—and the shrubbery around all green and thriving roses in bloom. Every object outside and in as pleasant as could be wished, and after such a fearful summer here, far pleasanter than could be hoped for. Arthur and his wife have kept the whole thing in excellent order, and they have been exempt from the fever so that I was very happy in selecting them to take charge in my absence.

In the afternoon, I went down to the Custom House and had a cordial and hearty meeting with all my friends there.

Went over the works with Major Beauregard and found abundant evidence of vigorous and superior management and rapid progress in spite of all the difficulties which followed in the train of so desolating a plague as the Fever of '53, the darkest epoch in the annals of New Orleans.[93]

In walking down and returning, I met hosts of friends, each of whom had something to tell that I had not heard before, and when I got home I found that Emily and Mrs. Ladd had made such rapid progress in domestic matters, and the little boy seemed so free and happy in his home, that everything wore an air of modest enchantment. Indeed, I have rarely passed a day in my life that has encircled within the twenty four hours so many elements of intense and heart felt enjoyment.

The appearance of the streets, too, so orderly and roomy, and even cleanly, after the confusion, oppressive hurry and unmitigated filth of New York, is striking enough—and so quiet and spacious all around my dwelling, with China Trees and shrubs and the grassy square still green and summerish, attractions enough of every description to make me in love with home.

Our summer travel has opened to us infinite sources of new enjoyment. Nature and art have combined to gratify and delight us, and social intercourse with remote parts of the country to remove prejudices and correct hasty impressions. It has had the effect, too, of enabling us to judge more impartially of our home, and has given prominence to advantages which consuetude and daily contact had well-nigh concealed from us so that a healthy judgment (as well as healthy constitutions) is likely to result from our long, and most delightful and gratifying summer tour.

The wealth, refinement, and intellectual culture of the Eastern States, the teeming plenty and boundless resources of the West, have passed in review before us and successively challenged our admiration while they have ministered to our pleasure. But still there is something about the genial "South" which after all chains and rivets our love. And with all its faults of climate, and exposure to physical danger still makes one cling to it and prefer to dwell here than amid all the opulence, and magestic "nature" of the more rugged and inflexible North.

The following is a recapitulation of Distances taken from Tables in use on the different routes. They may vary a little from those entered The Journal.

New Orleans	to	St. Louis	1,224 miles
St. Louis	"	LaSalle	310
LaSalle	"	Chicago	100
Chicago	"	Toledo	247
Toledo	"	Buffalo (by Lake)	238
Buffalo	"	Niagara	22
Niagara	"	Lewiston	7
Lewiston	"	Ogdensburg (Lake and St. Lawrence)	299
Ogdensburg	"	Boston	406
			2,853
Boston	"	New York	236
New York	"	Dunkirk	469
Dunkirk	"	Cleveland	142
Cleveland	"	Columbus	135
Columbus	"	Cincinnati	120
Cincinnati	"	Mouth of Ohio	541
Mouth of Ohio	"	New Orleans	1,050
			2,693
Total distance in miles			5,546 miles

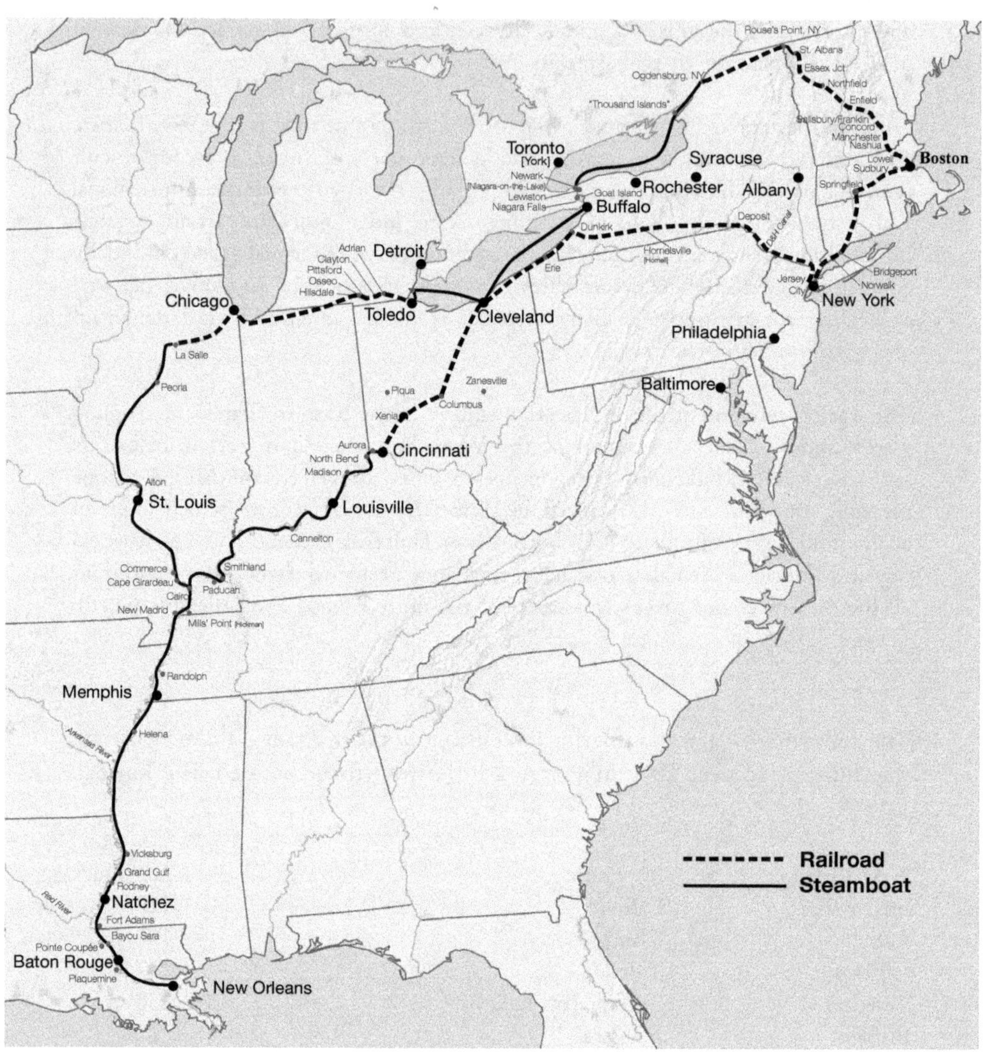

FIGURE 3.30 Map of Thomas Kelah Wharton's travels, 1853. Map by S.A. Walton.

Wharton

The family traces its roots back to a Norman lord, Humphrey Wharton of Wharton (early 12th C), Thomas Wharton, First Baron Wharton (1495 - 1568), and to various Lords Wharton in the 16-17thC. This line derives from a second son's line in the 17thC. The ancient family seat is Wharton Hall (castle) near Kirkby Stephen, Cumberland.
2
1
Capt. Robert KELAH (? - <1839)
? BARKIN (? - 1839)
John BARKIN (? - ?1811)
Thomas¹ WHARTON (1757 - 1812)
?
1
2
3/2
1
Elizabeth GOODYEAR (? - 1810)
Anne BARKIN (1780 - 1835)
Thomas² WHARTON (1789 - <1845)
Anna Marie REDDIE (1787 - 1864)
née Ralph
See Prescott/Ladd genealogy
2
1
Emily Julia LADD (1835/6 - 1932)
Thomas Kelah WHARTON (1814 - 1862)
Maria HULLING (1827 - 1848)
1
2
Penemiah McCOY (1822 - 1849)
Robert John WHARTON (1818 - 1854)
Jane F. BROOKS (1825 - 1912)
Thomas Prescott WHARTON (1852 - 1910)
Louise/a P. CAMEROW (? - before 1910)
Robert H. WHARTON (1847 - 1898)
? WHARTON (<1852 - ?)
Charles Henry WHARTON (1852 - 1863)
Moved in with aunt after father dies
Adopted by aunt by 1865

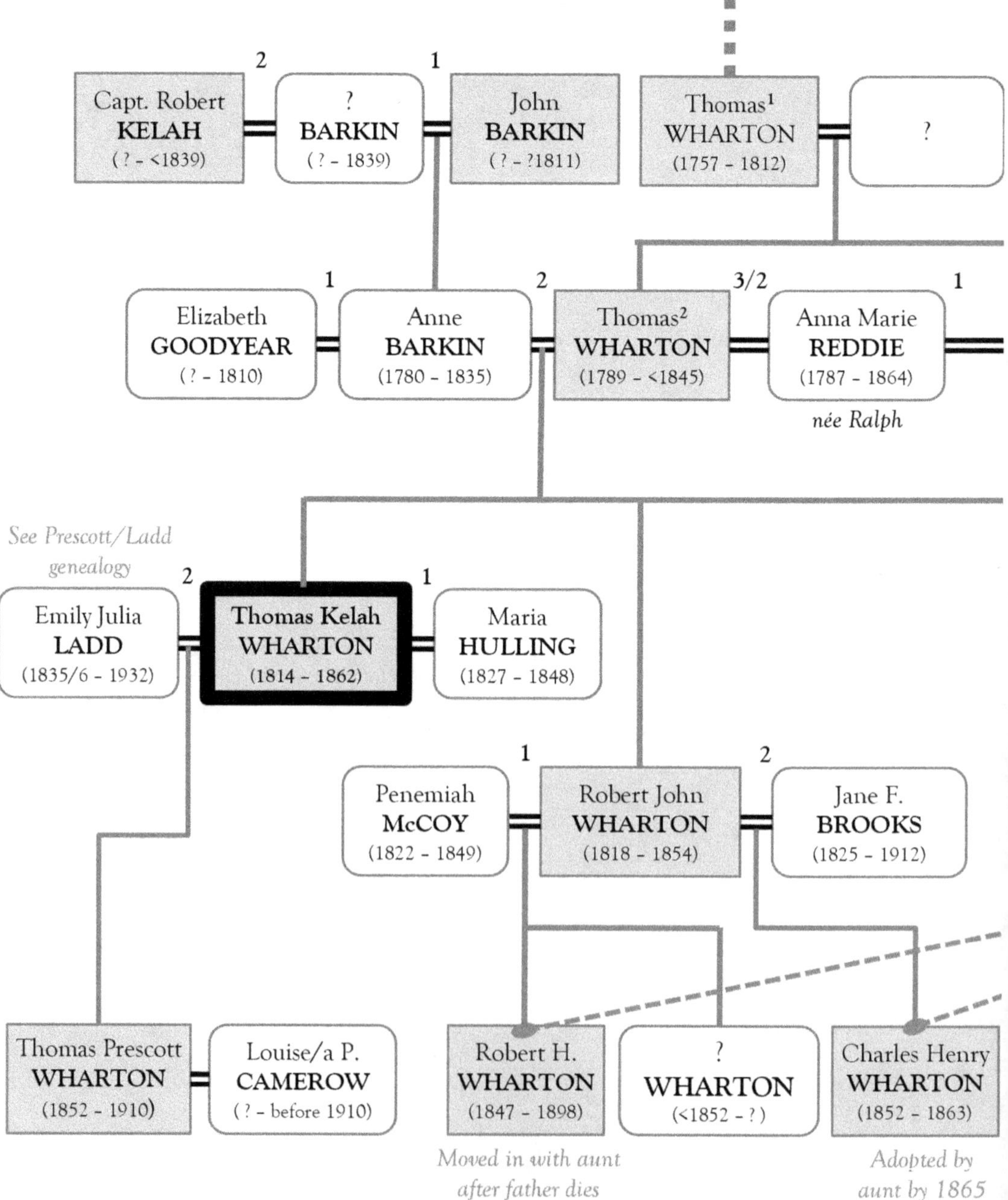

Family Genealogy

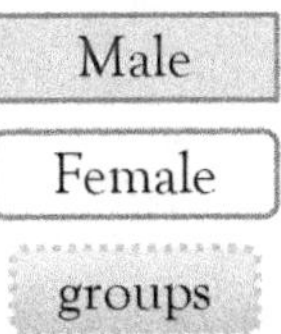

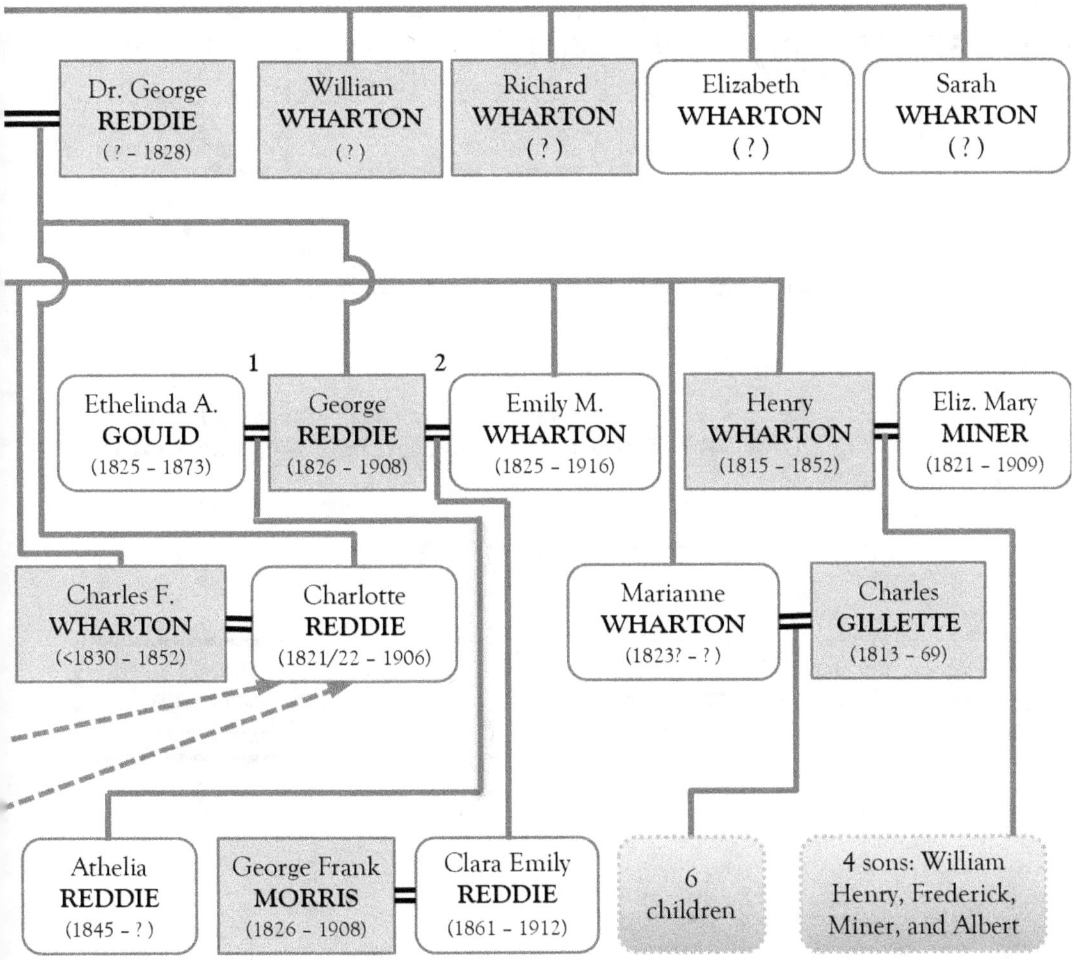

Dr. George **REDDIE** (? - 1828)

William **WHARTON** (?)

Richard **WHARTON** (?)

Elizabeth **WHARTON** (?)

Sarah **WHARTON** (?)

Ethelinda A. **GOULD** (1825 - 1873)

1

George **REDDIE** (1826 - 1908)

2

Emily M. **WHARTON** (1825 - 1916)

Henry **WHARTON** (1815 - 1852)

Eliz. Mary **MINER** (1821 - 1909)

Charles F. **WHARTON** (<1830 - 1852)

Charlotte **REDDIE** (1821/22 - 1906)

Marianne **WHARTON** (1823? - ?)

Charles **GILLETTE** (1813 - 69)

Athelia **REDDIE** (1845 - ?)

George Frank **MORRIS** (1826 - 1908)

Clara Emily **REDDIE** (1861 - 1912)

6 children

4 sons: William Henry, Frederick, Miner, and Albert

Prescott/Ladd Family Genealogy

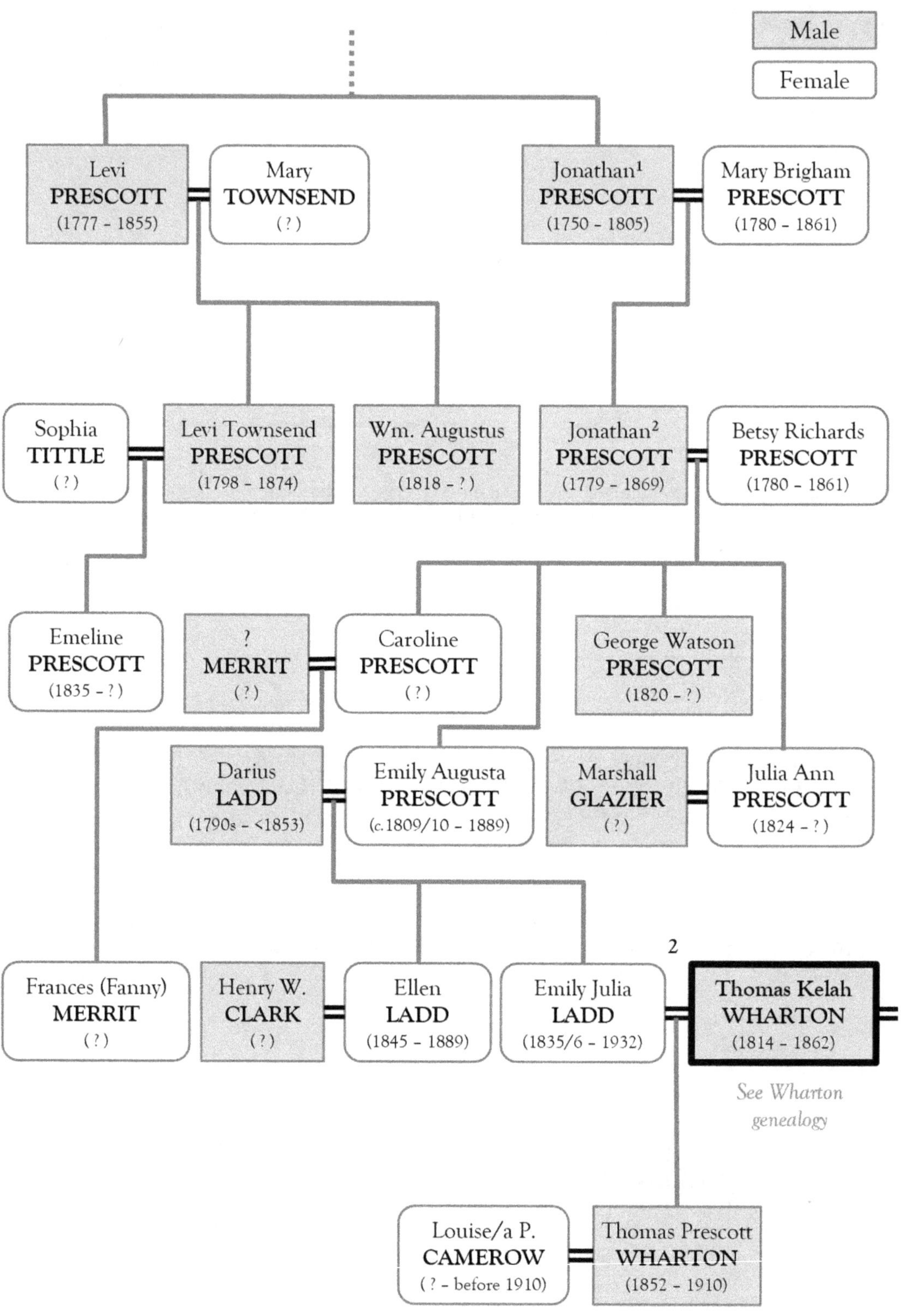

Chapter 4

Biographical Register

The following people appear in Thomas Kelah Wharton's diary for 1830–1834 and 1853. Most of these biographies are based upon the *Appleton's Cyclopedia of American Biography* (New York: D. Appleton, 1888–91), and for the artists, George C. Groce and David H. Wallace, *The New York Historical Society's Dictionary of Artists in America 1564–1860* (New Haven: Yale University Press, 1975). Many of the New Orleans residents have been identified by Samuel Wilson, Patricia Brady, and Lynn D. Adams (eds.), *Queen of the South: New Orleans, 1853–1862: The Journal of Thomas K. Wharton* (New Orleans: Historic New Orleans Collection, 1999), and residents of New York and Boston for the relevant city directories for those years.

For genealogical information on the Prescott and Ladd families, see William Prescott, *The Prescott Memorial, or, a Genealogical Memoir of the Prescott Families in America* (Boston: Henry W. Dutton & Son, 1870), 62, 84, 115–16, and 156; and Warren Ladd, *A Genealogical and Biographical Memoir of the Descendants of Daniel Ladd, etc.* (New Bedford, MA: E. Anthony & Sons, 1890), 98 and 124. Additional familial details have also been deduced from FindAGrave.com, Ancestry.com, FamilySearch.com, FindMyPast.co.uk, and marriage and death notices in the *New York Times* and other period newspapers. Further sources are cited in the notes.

Names in Small Caps refer to cross-referenced entries in this register.

Abilene, ___ (?): A preacher at the Middle Dutch Church, the original of which was at West 20th Street and Sixth Avenue in the Bowery (Thomas Kelah Wharton is not referring to the "other" Middle Dutch Church, the Middle Collegiate Church on Lafayette Place, because it was only begun in 1836).

Allen, John Fiske (1785–1865): A bookkeeper in Salem, MA, who rose to run a large import-export business, made a fortune, and then devoted his time to horticultural pursuits. By 1852 he had obtained a specimen of the Amazonian *Victoria regis* (today named *Victoria amazonica,* first reported in 1837 by Sir R.H. Schomburgk) from Caleb Cope of Philadelphia and cultivated it in a special greenhouse behind his home on Chestnut Street in Salem. In August 1851,

Allen was successful in obtaining the first hothouse flower and then also enlisted the country's foremost chromolithographer, William Sharp, to illustrate and popularize this natural wonder.[1]

Ansley, ___ (?): The Ansley family was a well-known and extended family in New Orleans.[2]

Ashbridge, D.W. (?): A New Orleans resident living near Camp and Robin in 1854, and then on Fulton at the corner of Common in 1866.

Ayer, James Cook (1818–1878): Graduated from the medical department of the University of Pennsylvania but never practiced, instead devoting his attention to pharmaceutical chemistry and the compounding of medicines. His success led him to establish a factory in Lowell, MA, for the manufacture of his medicinal preparations, which became one of the largest of its kind in the world.

Balch, ___ [William Y.?] (?): Owner of a gallery in Boston in 1853, though the 1852 city directory shows no such *gallery*. There was a William Y. Balch, gilder and picture frame manufacturer (shops at 10 and 92 Tremont Street, respectively), who is likely the person to whom Thomas Kelah Wharton refers.[3]

Banks, Sir Joseph (1743–1820): Naturalist and traveler. He accompanied Captain Cook to the South Pacific, circumnavigated New Zealand, and surveyed the east coast of Australia.

Barclay, Henry (1778–1851): New York financier and industrialist responsible for building large parts of the industrial infrastructure in Saugerties, NY, including a paper mill and the Ulster Iron Works.

Barker, Jacob (1779–1871): A keen financier, who started as a businessman in New York, though he later repeatedly lost a vast fortune but each time always managed to recover. He worked in trade and credit, stock speculation and insurance, supplying oil to the government, acting as a state senator, and helping establish the Exchange Bank on Wall Street. He moved to New Orleans in 1834 and spent his last years with his son, Wharton Barker, in Philadelphia.

Barton, John G. (1803–?): One of the resident instructors at the Flushing Institute in 1835 and a candidate for Episcopal orders in 1837.[4]

Bateman, (H)Ellen (1845–?): American child actress billed variously as Ellen or Hellen, who performed with her sister Kate in *The Babes in the Wood*. She retired from acting in 1856 and married Claude Greppo in 1860.

Bateman, Hezekiah Linthicum (1812–1875): American actor and stage manager. His and Sydney Frances Bateman's two daughters, Kate and Ellen (known across the country on stage as "The Bateman Children"), were still touring in 1853, but in 1855 he took a position as a theatre manager in St. Louis, later moving to similar positions in New York and eventually London.

Bateman, Kate Josephine (1842–1917): American child actress and daughter of an acting family, she was educated for the stage since childhood and performed with her sister Ellen in *The Babes in the Wood*. She retired in 1856 but returned to the stage in 1860; in 1866, she married George Crowe (1841–1889), formerly editor of the *London News*. They settled in England and in 1868 she returned to the stage under her maiden name for several decades.

Bateman, Sidney Frances (1823–1881): Playwright and matriarch of the Bateman acting family, and daughter of Joseph Cowell, an English actor who had settled in America. Later she returned to England and managed the Sadler's Wells Theatre in London until her death.

Beauregard, Pierre-Alfred Toutant (1825–1853): Brother of Maj. P.G.T. Beauregard, who owned a plantation in St. Bernard parish, LA. This the same man Thomas Kelah Wharton refers to as "A. Toutant" (see *Journal* September 19, 1853), who died on September 4.

Beauregard, Pierre Gustav Toutant (1818–1893): Appointed superintendent for the construction of the New Orleans Custom House in 1852. During the Civil War he was a Confederate general notable for firing the first shot of the war at Fort Sumter in 1861.

Bedell, Gregory Townsend (1793–1834): An 1811 graduate of Columbia College in New York, Bedell ministered in Hudson, NY and Fayetteville, NC before establishing the Episcopalian St. Andrews church in Philadelphia in 1822 and later the *Philadelphia Recorder* newspaper, which broadcast distinctly Low Church Episcopalian evangelism. His son, Gregory Thurston Bedel (1817–1892) was also a noted Episcopalian minister, and from 1859 to 1889 assistant bishop and bishop of Ohio. Between them they published more than a dozen important Episcopalian theological tracts and catechisms.

Bennett, William James (1784–1844): London-born painter, aquatint engraver and etcher in the topographical landscape tradition who immigrated to America about 1826 and was elected a full member of the National Academy of Design in 1828.[5]

Billings, Hammatt (1818–1874): Architect who designed numerous churches and public buildings and monuments throughout the United States and executed decorative designs and drew illustrations for numerous books. The National Monument to the Forefathers, formerly known as the Pilgrim Monument, at Plymouth, MA is after his design.

Blanc, Evariste (?–1853): Originally from Bayou St. John, LA, Blanc began his career as a hardware merchant and ship chandler and by 1830 he had become a lime merchant. He parlayed that line of work into becoming a noted brick maker in New Orleans, and the owner of the Blanc Brick Co. at Julia and St. John streets. His ca. 1834 house at 1342 Moss Street on Bayou St. John, later the Our Lady of the Holy Rosary Rectory, has been recorded by the Historic American Building Survey (HABS LA–168).[6]

Bogert, Edward C. (?): Son of Henry K. Bogert, merchant and broker, and in 1860 the partner in Bogert & Kneland, with an office at 49 William Street, New York, in 1860.[7]

Bogert, Henry K. (?): Insurance executive (e.g., director of the Neptune Insurance Co. and Merchant's Insurance Co. in 1833), secretary for the New York Institute for the Blind in 1832, and vice president of the New York City Chamber of Commerce in 1845. He had his office on 10th Street in New York City from the 1830s to the 1850s.[8]

Bogert, Olivia Hawks (?–1899): Daughter of the Rev. Dr. Francis L. Hawks and married to Edward Bogert on October 1, 1853, at Calvary Church in New York.

Bonaparte, Joseph-Napoleon (1768–1844): The elder brother of Emperor Napoleon Bonaparte, King of Naples and Sicily (1806–08), and later King of Spain (1808–13, as José I). After 1815, he lost these positions and styled himself Comte de Survilliers and moved to the United States from 1817 to 1832. Although numerous localities in America offered him a home, he settled in Bordentown, NJ.

Both, Jan (ca. 1615–1652): Baroque painter and etcher, master of Italianate Dutch landscape painting.

Boyd, Alexander (?): A Presbyterian minister of Newtown, Bucks County, near Philadelphia, PA.

Brackett, Edward Augustus (1818–1908): American sculptor trained in Cincinnati in the 1830s and noted for busts in Washington and New York in the late 1830s. He moved to Boston in 1841, was introduced to the circle of Dana, Longfellow, and Allston, and had a prolific career in sculpture until about 1873.[9]

Breneman, John S. (?–1837): He had come to the Flushing Institute from W.A. Muhlenberg's earlier Sunday Church School in his native Lancaster, PA. He was ordained an Episcopal minister in 1836 and died shortly thereafter.[10]

Brock, Sir **Isaac Brock** (1769–1812): Major-general, served extensively in the British army since age fifteen, with service in Jamaica, Barbados, and Canada. He was made knight of Bath for achieving the surrender of the entire army and artillery when facing General Hull in Detroit during the War of 1812, and was killed in the Battle of Queenstown on Oct. 13.

Brodhead, ___ (?): Perhaps either Daniel D. Brodhead, a broker at 29 State Street, or Josiah A. Brodhead, a merchant on Cornhill, both in Boston.[11]

Brown, George (?): Son of W. Horace Brown, he died when a gun accidentally discharged.

Brown, W[illiam?] Horace (?): Thomas Kelah Wharton gives this Long Island resident's forenames in both orders. There is a William Horace Brown, Esquire, to whom a serenade by a Mr. Knight was dedicated in 1840.[12]

Brown, John Walker (1814–?): A native of Syracuse, NY, he took a degree at Union College in 1832, and was ordained a deacon in 1836 and a priest in 1838 by the General Theological Seminary. He opened the Astoria Female Institute under the auspices of St. George's Church, Astoria, NY in 1838.[13]

Brownell, Gilbert (?): Brother of Bishop T.C. Brownell.

Brownell, Thomas Church (1779–1865): Founder of Trinity College in Hartford, CT and bishop of the US Episcopal Church from 1852 to 1865.

Bryant, Gridley (1789–1867): Engineer, father of G.J.F. Bryant, notable for inventing the portable derrick in 1823. He obtained the contract for building the US Bank in Boston, and other public buildings, and was master builder and contractor to supply stone for Bunker Hill monument. In order to bring the stone from his quarry in Quincy he developed the plan for the Granite Railway Co., fashioning cars, tracks, turntables, switches, turnouts, and other machinery.

Bryant, Gridley J.F. (1816–1899): A leading Boston architect and engineer of the mid-century. His major works include the Massachusetts State House extension and the Boston jail (now a hotel).

Buckingham, Ebenezer, Jr. (1778–1832): A pioneer in and deputy surveyor of Ohio, leading citizen of Zanesville, OH, he was killed while supervising the reconstruction of the Y-Bridge when he tried to save a pier from being washed away during a freshet.[14]

Camidge, Charles Joseph (1801–1878): BA (1824) and MA from St. Catherine's Hall, Cambridge with an extensive career, including vicar of All Saints, Pavement (York) and Nether Poppleton (York), curate of St. Sampson's (York), chaplain to the York Workhouse, honorary canon to the Cathedral Church of Ripon, governor of Wakefield Grammar School (1856–76), and vicar of Wakefield (1855–75). Married to Charlotte Hustwick in Hull in 1828.

Car(e)y, Henry (ca. 1799–1857): A minor essayist on the fringes of the Knickerbocker group in New York, he was described as a "gentleman of elegant leisure" as result of his being longtime president of the Phœnix Bank of New-York.

Catherine (?): The Whartons' servant and nursemaid to young Thomas Prescott Wharton. Her surname is not known but she was English and her father was still in England in 1853.

Channing, Walter (1786–1876): Physician "of good repute" who was listed in the Boston City Directory of 1853 as living at 21 Somerset Street. Brother to William Ellery Channing.

Channing, ___ (?): Daughter of Dr. Walter Channing and niece of Rev. Dr. William Ellery Channing.

Channing, William Ellery (1780–1842): Celebrated preacher with fervent religious eloquence, brother of Dr. Walter Channing. His views defended the doctrine of Christ's divinity. He published diverse essays in journals like the *North American Review* and the *Christian Examiner*, and was associated with the "Anthology Club." He became known as the founding thinker of the Unitarian Church (founded in 1825), strengthening the group's identity and position throughout the 1830s and 1840s.

Chickering, Jonas (1797–1853): Noted piano manufacturer in Boston who improved the cast-iron frame for the square piano (from the Alpheus Babcock patent) and patented a number of improvements to the pianoforte (US Patent nos. 1,389, 1,802, 3,122, and 3,238). At the London Exhibition in 1851 he exhibited a complete single-piece cast frame for grand pianos. His factories, and especially his new one in 1853 after the previous one burned, reached a production of two thousand pianos a year by midcentury.[15]

Coffee, Col. ___ (?): Possibly John Coffee (1772–1833), an American planter and state militia general in Tennessee, or his son, both of whom as landowners may have received the southern honorific of "Colonel."

Coggeshall, Russell (1788–1864): Whaling magnate from Newport, RI.

Cole, Thomas (1801–1848): American artist who was the principal founder of the Hudson River School. Like Thomas Kelah Wharton, he was born in England and, on coming to this country, spent some of his early years in Ohio. "Cole's landscapes, particularly following his first trip from America to England, France and Italy in 1829–32, have a freely developed, painterly quality, and rich coloring that go well with the extremely dramatic arrangements of billowing clouds, massive gnarled trees, deep chasms, towering peaks, and golden light that are common in his pictures."[16]

Courtenay, Edward Henry (1803–1853): Graduated first in his class from the USMA in 1821, and was assigned to the engineer corps. He served as assistant professor of natural and experimental philosophy and of engineering at West Point from 1821–24; professor of mathematics at the University of Pennsylvania (1834–36); division engineer of the Erie Railway (1836–37); and then again entered the government service as a civil engineer. He finished his career as professor of mathematics at the University of Virginia (1842–53). He was employed in the construction of Fort Adams in Newport, RI and Fort Independence in Boston Harbor.

Cozzens, William B. (1787–1864): Hotel keeper. For ten years he was proprietor of the American Hotel in New York City, and then opened Cozzen's Hotel at West Point on the Hudson River.

Crowe, Kate Bateman: See Bateman, Kate Josephine.

Cushing, Caleb (1800–1879): Statesman, served as a US congressman from Massachusetts for several years and as attorney general under President Franklin Pierce (1853–57).

Dakin, James Harrison (1806–1852): Noted architect who designed the Old Louisiana State Capitol, the State Arsenal, and St. Patrick's Church in New Orleans. He was the sometime architectural partner with James Gallier, Sr, though they were more often rivals. His design for the Customs House was passed over in favor of that of A.T. Wood, though he later held the superintendence of its construction for a time, proposing major changes that would have created a central atrium for ventilation, but which were scuppered by fighting between the Anglo and creole New Orleanians. After resigning from the project in September 1851, he returned to Baton Rouge to finish superintending his design for the State House. Thomas Kelah Wharton refers to him as Colonel, as he served briefly at this rank during the Mexican-American War.

Davies, Charles (1798–1876): After graduating from the USMA he served at West Point, where he became a professor of mathematics. He served as treasurer of the USMA (1841–46) and became a professor of mathematics and philosophy at the University of New York (now NYU) in 1848. He wrote important works on mathematics and geometry.

Davis, J.P. (?): One of the building committee for the Granite Railway Co. railroad, which was laid from Boston to Quincy in 1826–28 and was built in order to transport granite for the Bunker Hill Monument.

Diller, Jacob W. (1800–1880): Born in England, he became a mathematics instructor at the Flushing Institute, was later ordained and became deacon at St. George's, Flushing (1834), and was for nearly forty years the rector of St. Luke's Episcopal Church in Brooklyn.

Dunn, Alexander (?–1863): A retired steamboat captain who accompanied Thomas Kelah Wharton on the trip north in June 1853, and helped organize their travel arrangements that fall.

Durand, Asher Brown (1796–1886): An artist who began his career as engraver (the trade of his artist father, Cyrus Durand) but who became a very prominent painter of the Hudson River School.

Duryée, Abram (1815–1890): Mahogany importer in New York who later became a noted general of Zouave regiments during the Civil War. He had just joined the New York Militia in 1833 when Thomas Kelah Wharton called him a lieutenant, possibly referring to his position as police commissioner in New York since 1823.

Dwight, Timothy (1752–1817): An academic, educator, and a Congregationalist minister, theologian, and author known for his poems and songs. He served as the eighth president of Yale College (1795–1817) and was a pioneer in higher education for women.

Dykes, Thomas (1761–1847): Vicar of St John's Church in Drypool, Hull.[17]

Earl, ___ (?): An elusive but important figure in Thomas Kelah Wharton's story as he was the intermediary who brought the offer of employment for young Wharton from Martin E. Thompson, "which my Father is now considering" (*Journal*, March 3, 1832 [Rodabaugh (note 6), 136]). The *Journal* does not indicate how Wharton's father came to know Mr. Earl, though we learn that he was somehow related to Thomas Slocum (*Journal*, May 28, 1832).

Eastburn, Manton (1801–1872): Born in England, he studied theology in New York and became assistant bishop of the Diocese of Massachusetts in 1842 and bishop from 1843–72 at Trinity Church, Boston, which was destroyed in the Boston Fire of 1872.

Edwards, Jonathan (1703–1758): Calvinist preacher and mystic who graduated from Yale in 1720 and became president of Princeton. He was an important early American theologian and philosopher associated with Reformed Theology and theological determinism.

Farrington, ___ (?): The Farringtons, an old colonial family of Long Island,[18] owned a farm adjacent to the Flushing Institute.

Fellenberg, Philipp Emanuel von (1771–1844): A Swiss philanthropist, educational reformer, and a follower of the Swiss pedagogue Johann Heinrich Pestalozzi (1746–1827), Fellenberg purchased an estate in Hofwyl, Switzerland, in 1799, where he founded a self-supporting agricultural school for poor children. His method combined manual training and agricultural and academic instruction, and the school grew to add a classical institute for middle-class students, a girls' school, and a teaching institute, all of which sought to narrow the gap between the classes through education.

Fetter, Emmanuel (1809–1889): Born in Lancaster, PA and a student at Flushing Institute and then Columbia College (BA and MA). After teaching briefly back at Flushing, he became a professor of Greek language and literature at the University of North Carolina from 1837–68. He was known as Manuel Fetter as an adult.[19]

Finley, Robert (1772–1817): After graduating from Princeton in 1793, he became a tutor, studied theology (receiving a Doctor of Divinity degree), and was a trustee of the university (1806–17). His work led to the formation of the American Colonization Society, the society for the return of free African-Americans to Africa.

Fracker, J.T. (?): A "colonel" from Zanesville, OH, and head of the Zanesville Artillery for the state militia, though not a graduate of the USMA.

Franklin, Walter E. (?): From Lancaster, PA, where he had come to the attention of W.A. Muhlenberg in his Sunday Church School there. Franklin followed Muhlenberg to his Flushing Institute for further studies.

Freret, William Alfred (1833–1911): Son of New Orleans mayor and engineer William Freret (1804–1864), and founder of the Freret Cotton Press Company, the first industrial firm in New Orleans. W.A. Freret trained in engineering and architecture in England and designed several major buildings in New Orleans in the late 1850s. After serving in the Confederate artillery and engineers during the Civil War, he became head of the federal government's Office of the Supervising Architect in the 1880s.

Gallier, James, Jr. (1827–1868): Born in England, he immigrated to America in 1832, where he attended both the Flushing Institute and St. Thomas's Hall in Flushing (both under Rev. F.L. Hawks and Thomas Kelah Wharton) and the University of North Carolina (1848–49). In 1849 he took over his father's architecture practice in New Orleans and superintended the erection of the building of Christ Church, among other notable buildings. He first worked in New York for James H. Dakin, though in his New Orleans phase they became professional rivals despite occasionally partnering on projects. His design for the US Customs House in New Orleans was passed over in favor of that of A.T. Wood.

Gallier, James, Sr. (1798–1866): Born in Ireland, he immigrated to America in 1832, and published *American Builder's General Price Book and Estimator* (1833). He set up as an architect in New Orleans in 1835 and designed the Merchants Exchange, the old and new Christ Church, St. Patrick's Church, the Commercial Exchange (later the Masonic Temple), and the Municipal Hall (the old New Orleans City Hall, now Gallier Hall).

Gerry, Samuel Lancaster (1813–1891): American landscape painter who was mainly active in New England. He was an original member of the Boston Art Club and its president in 1858.

Gilman, Arthur Delavan (1821–1882): An architect who became an important architectural critic and theorist. As early as 1844, in an attack on both the Greek and Gothic revivals, he praised by contrast the simplicity and appropriateness of American Colonial architecture. He designed and built Boston's old City Hall, which is regarded as his best work.

Gimbrede, Thomas (1781–1832): French engineer who emigrated to the US in 1802 and was the instructor of drawing at the USMA from 1819 until his death.[20]

Glazier, Marshall (?): Husband of Julia (Prescott) Glazier and uncle (in-law) to Emily Julia Ladd Wharton, he ran a hack, livery, and boarding stable in the center of Saxonville, MA.

Glazier, Julia Ann Prescott (1824–?): The youngest sister of Emily A.P. Ladd, who lived in Saxonville, MA. She married Marshall Glazier in 1851.

Gouverneur, Samuel Laurence (1799–1865): New York lawyer (Columbia College, 1817) and civil servant and private secretary to President James Monroe, to whom he was related by blood and by marriage. He had married the president's daughter, Maria Hester Monroe, in the first wedding at the White House in 1820, and was at that time the postmaster of the city of New York.

Greenleaf, ___ (?): Son of Simon Greenleaf and a successful merchant. Brother of P.H. Greenleaf.

Greenleaf, P.H. (?): Son of Simon Greenleaf and an Episcopal minister in Charlestown, MA.[21]

Greenleaf, Simon (1783–1853): Lawyer, jurist, and reporter of the Supreme Court of Maine. He was appointed Royall Professor of Law at Harvard in 1833, then transferred to the Dane professorship and became professor emeritus after his resignation in 1848. He had two brothers, Jonathan and Moses, a clergyman and an author, respectively.

Greppo, (H)ellen Bateman: See Bateman, (H)Ellen.

Guesnon, P. (?): Administrator for the Treasury Department in the construction of the New Customs House in New Orleans. This is likely the same person as Philip Guesnon, collection clerk for the Bank of New Orleans.

Gurney, Thomas (?): Columbus, OH merchant and active abolitionist originally from Bristol, England. The Gurney and Wharton families both emigrated about the same time and then moved together to Zanesville. Thomas Kelah Wharton implies that Mr. Gurney and his father's mercantile businesses were somehow connected, and the families were clearly close in Ohio.[22]

Hale, Luther Holman (?): Proprietor of a daguerreotype gallery in Boston noted for advancing that city to the forefront of photography before the Civil War.[23]

Hamilton, Charles (?): Noted physician in New Orleans in the 1850s. His first wife, Sarah, died of yellow fever in 1853; he married his second wife, Margaret Bender, in 1856.

Hardcastle, ___ (?): A merchant of Dayton, OH, where he had a warehousing business with a Mr. Machir in the 1820s and 1830s. A business friend of Thomas[2] Wharton, he was a noted early supporter of railroads in Ohio.[24]

Harvey, Jacob (?): The son-in-law of Dr. David Hosack, who was one of the founding partners, with Abraham Bell and Robert H. Bowne, of the shipping firm Abraham Bell & Co., with offices on Pine Street in New York. He was later president of the Washington Marine Insurance Co.[25]

Hassler, Ferdinand Rudolph (1770–1843): Swiss-born and trained surveyor who became acting professor of mathematics at West Point from 1807–10 and then first superintendent of the United States Coast Survey from 1816–43. He also was head of the nascent Bureau of Weights and Measures.

Hawks, Francis Lister (1798–1866): A native of North Carolina and graduate of that state's university (1815), he initially practiced law and politics. He later entered the Episcopal Church as a lay preacher and then ascended to deacon, pastor, and was eventually offered numerous bishoprics by the 1830s, largely due to his strong, charismatic preaching style. He was connected to Trinity College, New Haven, CT, and the General Theological Seminary in New York, as well as churches in New York and Philadelphia. After a stint of less than a year at W.A. Muhlenberg's St. Paul's College at College Point, on Long Island, and then a mismanaged attempt to run his own boys' school in Flushing (St. Thomas's Grammar School, 1839–43), he moved west and south. He became rector of Christ Church in New Orleans (1845–49) and the first president of the University of Louisiana (later Tulane). Besides theology, he was an important writer on church history, a contributor to popular intellectual religious periodicals, and coauthor of Commodore Matthew Perry's memoirs of his opening of Japan (1855–56).

Herring, James F. (1794–1867): Initially a tinter of prints and maps in New York and Philadelphia, Herring settled in New York as a portrait painter. He and his partner, James B. Longacre, collected information and portraits of famous Americans under the superintendence of the American Academy of the Fine Arts for a *National Portrait Gallery of Distinguished Americans*, 4 vols. (New York, 1834–39).

Hervieu, Auguste (fl. 1819–1858): French painter and illustrator best known for traveling to America as a tutor to Frances Trollope's children, including the future author Anthony Trollope. His illustrations appeared in many of her most popular books, including *Domestic Manners of the Americans* (1832). Although his relationship with her and her family generated much gossip—Hervieu was considered a struggling young artist while traveling with Trollope—it was his earnings from engravings that kept the Trollopes solvent during their American travels.[26]

Hester, Abner (1813–1853): A Virginia native who grew up in Tennessee and received an MD from the University of Pennsylvania (1837), he became a noted New Orleans doctor and editor of the *New Orleans Medical and Surgical Journal*. He died, ironically, of cholera after penning an important paper on yellow fever.[27]

Hildreth, Charles (?): Founder of the Muskingum Medical Society in Ohio in 1842, who had been practicing in Zanesville for a number of years before that.

Hill, Harry (?–1853): Head of the New Orleans cotton exporting firm of Hill, McLean & Co., he was reputed to be "at least as eccentric as he was supposed to be rich."[28]

Hitchcock, Ethan A. (1798–1870): An 1817 graduate of the USMA (and grandson of Gen. Ethan Allen of Revolutionary fame), he served at many posts in the South before becoming commandant of cadets and instructor of infantry tactics at West Point (1829–33) and later serving with distinction in the Seminole Wars, the Mexican-American War, and, reactivated, during the Civil War.[29]

Hosack, Alexander Eddy (1805–1871): A physician and the eldest son of Dr. David Hosack. He settled in New York, devoting himself especially to the practice of surgery and was the first practitioner in the city to administer ether as an anesthetic. He was also noted for his study of methods of inflicting capital punishment for the purpose of discovering the most humane method.

Hosack, David (1769–1835): A physician, botanist, educator, and a founder of the New-York Historical Society, he was internationally recognized in several scientific fields. After attending the College of New Jersey (now Princeton University), he studied medicine under Benjamin Rush in Philadelphia, and later became professor of botany at Columbia. He was one of the first physicians in America to use the stethoscope and to advocate vaccination. He established the Elgin Botanical

Gardens, whose main group of greenhouses stood between 50th and 51st streets toward what is now Sixth Avenue in Manhattan. The land was later granted to Columbia College by the state of New York and is now the part of Rockefeller Center opposite Saint Patrick's Cathedral. Hosack married three times: first to Catherine Warner of Princeton; second to Mary Eddy, who died in 1824; and third to Magdalena Coster, widow of Henry A. Coster, whose money allowed the building of Hosack's Hyde Park estate that Thomas Kelah Wharton visited.

Hosack, Eliza Bard (1808–1888): The second daughter and the fourth of six children of Dr. David Hosack. She never married and is buried in the family plot at Trinity Church in Manhattan.

Hosack, Emily (1810–1893): The youngest daughter and the fifth of six children of Dr. David Hosack by his first wife, Catherine Warner. She married ophthalmologist Dr. John Kearney Rodgers (1793–1851) in 1846, and is buried in the family plot at Trinity Church in Manhattan.

Hosack, Magdalena (?): Widow of Henry A. Coster and the third wife of Dr. David Hosack.

Huling, Frederick Watts (ca. 1792–1861): Father of Thomas Kelah Wharton's first wife, Maria Huling. He was a native of Perry County, PA (though often mistakenly said to be from Tennessee), a lawyer, and a cotton planter of Holy Springs, MS who enslaved forty-one persons in 1840. He served as a mounted infantry private in Cheatham's Detachment of the Tennessee militia in the War of 1812 and in 1832 fought in the Black Hawk War under Andrew Jackson. Living in Clarksville, TN in 1831, he was elected justice of the peace for Montgomery County and simultaneously became Democratic speaker of the Tennessee House of Representatives for two terms (1831–35). He was a circuit judge for the Eighth District of the state of Mississippi from 1836 to at least 1840 and seems to have been by then a Whig. He had the first two-story house in Marshall County—built in Holly Springs in 1838 and later known as the Strickland Place—and he was the principal of sixteen trustees for the University at Holly Springs (chartered February 9, 1839). That same year he served as a member of the convention to charter Centenary College in Jackson, MS. He later moved to Plaquemines Parish, LA and finally to Amite City, LA where he was struck by a train and killed on June 22, 1861.[30]

Huling, Maria Hulling, Maria: See Wharton, Maria H.

Huling, Sara Brown (ca. 1796–1859): Married Judge F.W. Huling in 1818.

Huntington, Frederick Dan (1819–?): Originally from Hull, England, he withdrew from the Unitarian denomination and took Protestant Episcopal orders in 1860, eventually rising to bishop of central New York in 1869. He published many sermons and addresses and contributed to various reviews and periodicals.

Hustwick, Robert (1759–1835): A coach builder and heraldic painter in Hull, England.

Ingham, Charles Cromwell (1797–1863): Born in Dublin, Ireland, he settled in New York in 1817 as a portrait and miniature painter. He was also a founder and vice president (1845–50) of the National Academy of Design.

Irving, Washington (1783–1859): American author, essayist, historian, and ambassador best known for his stories "The Legend of Sleepy Hollow" and "Rip Van Winkle." He was close friends with Gouverneur Kemble, James Kirke Paulding, Henry Car(e)y, and James Renwick.

Johnson, Samuel Roosevelt (1802–1873): A graduate of Columbia University (1820) and the General Theological Seminary (1823), he was an Episcopal clergyman and disciple of Rev. W.A. Muhlenberg. He was the pastor of St. James in Hyde Park, NY, when Thomas Kelah Wharton was staying there with Dr. David Hosack in 1832. Johnson also built a Muhlenberg-inspired church school, later the Bard Infant School, in Hyde Park and was later a professor at the General Theological Seminary in New York.

Johnston, Abraham R. (1815–1846): Son of Col. J. Johnston of Piqua, OH, he graduated the USMA in 1835, saw service in the 1st Dragoons in the Indian Territories, and was killed in the battle of San Pasquale, CA during the Mexican-American War.[31]

Kearney, Alfred (1813–1877): A ship broker from New Rochelle, NY, he was a member of the firm of A. Delagrave & Co., commercial merchants and dealers in paints, plaster, and other building materials, which supplied materials for the construction of the new Custom House in New Orleans.

Kemble, Gouverneur (1786–1875): From a mercantile family in New York, he and his brother William Kemble, along with Gen. Joseph Gardiner Swift, founded the West Point Foundry in 1817. This institution stood in Cold Spring, across from West Point, and manufactured ordnance, locomotives, and steamboat engines, as well as cast-iron machine parts to order. Kemble was a sociable and versatile man, a lifelong friend of Washington Irving and James Kirke Paulding, a patron of painters like Asher Durand and John Gadsby Chapman, and his Saturday dinners to which Thomas Kelah Wharton was invited were famous in the region. He served two terms as a US representative under President Van Buren.

Kemble, Mary (ca. 1794–1880): Sister of Gouverneur Kemble and wife of Robert P. Parrott (of Parrott Gun fame).

Kemble, Richard F. (1800–88): A merchant and the youngest brother of Gouverneur Kemble, Richard had inherited the family home in New Brunswick, NJ, where he lived until the death of his wife Charlotte Morris in 1838, at which time he moved to Cold Spring to live with his sister, Mary, and her husband, Robert Parrott (of Parrott Gun fame).

Kemble, William (1795–1881): Brother of Gouverneur Kemble and a merchant in New York City. William was the business face of the West Point Foundry in the city and was, at the time that Thomas Kelah Wharton was visiting Cold Spring, building his own country home just to the west of his brother's.

Kerfoot, John Barrett (1816–1881): Educated at Dr. Mulenberg's Flushing Institute from its opening in 1828 (he had been previously noticed as a promising child at age six in Mulenberg's Sunday Church School in Lancaster, PA), he became the rector of St. James College in Maryland, first bishop of the Episcopal Diocese of Pittsburgh, and a president of Trinity College in Hartford, CT. He was also instrumental in reunification deliberations between the Northern and Southern Episcopal Church after the Civil War.[32]

King, James Gore (1791–1853): A businessman and Whig politician in New Jersey who was a banker in New York and president of the Erie Railroad. His country estate known as Highwood stood on a wooded crest of the Palisades, but was only partly finished in 1832 when Martin E. Thompson tried to get Thomas Kelah Wharton the commission for its completion. The plain, square, two-story house with cupola, surrounding loggias, and an attached greenhouse, stood on 180 acres and was, like the David Hosack estate, noted for its grounds and vistas.[33]

Knap, Charles (?): A partner in the Fort Pitt iron foundry in Pittsburg, which supplied the iron plates that surmounted the brick column capitals at the new Custom House in New Orleans. Knap was generally the financial and office manager for this foundry and for its predecessors, Wade & Totten (with William J. Totten) and McClurg, Wade, & Co. (with Joseph McClurg and William Wade).[34]

Ladd, Aurelius [Towne?](1813–97): Thomas Kelah Wharton refers to him as a cousin of Emily Ladd Wharton with five children. However, no Aurelius Ladd is recorded in the *Genealogical and Biographical Memoir* of the Ladd family, nor do any of her first cousins, at least, have a middle name of Aurelius (though classical Latin given names run in the family). We may here be seeing a more distant cousin, Aurelius Towne Ladd (b. Waldo, ME), who married Lydia Washburn and whose son, Aurelius B. Ladd (1848–1912), was a noted mining engineer and head of the Engineering Corps during the invasion of Cuba in the Spanish-American War. An "Aurelius I. [T.?] Ladd" owned a plot in Mt. Auburn Cemetery, though he is apparently not interred there.[35] This would comport with Thomas Kelah Wharton's noting he had an estate on the south side of the Charles opposite Mt. Auburn with a fine house and orchard.

Ladd, Darius (1788–after 1853): Father of Emily Ladd Wharton who had married Emily Augusta Prescott in Boston on April 13 (or March 31), 1831. They initially lived in New Hampshire but relocated to New Orleans in the early 1830s. After 1838, Darius removed permanently to Boston and he and his wife lived apart, though Thomas Kelah Wharton's *Journal* does not explain why. They had three children, Harrison (who died young), Emily, and Ellen.

Ladd, Ellen J. (1843–?): Emily Ladd Wharton's sister, who lived with her mother in Massachusetts and then the Whartons in New Orleans. She later married Henry W. Clark.

Ladd, Emily Augusta Prescott (ca. 1809/10–1889): Emily Ladd Wharton's mother, daughter of Jonathan and Betsy Prescott,[36] and elder sister to George Watson Prescott. She married Darius Ladd in 1830 and then after his death moved with Thomas Kelah Wharton and Emily Wharton to New Orleans until the end of her life.

Ladd, Emily Julia: See Wharton, Emily Julia Ladd.

Lawrence, Abbot (1792–1855): Merchant and half of the firm of A.&A. Lawrence, prosperous in the sale of foreign cotton and woolen goods on commission.

Lely, Sir **Peter** (1618–1680): Dutch painter, born Pieter van der Faes, whose career was mainly spent as a court painter for Charles I and the English nobility from 1641 until his death.

Leslie, Charles Robert (1794–1859): English artist and a member of the Royal Academy in London. Noted as a genre, historical, and portrait painter as well as for his writings on painters and paintings. He was briefly the instructor of drawing at West Point in 1831–32, and then on the death of Thomas Gimbrede, in 1833 he was appointed professor of drawing at West Point but resigned after only a few months because his English wife would not stay there. This led to his young brother Thomas J. Leslie taking the post.

Leslie, Thomas Jefferson (1796–1874): Soldier and brother of Charles J. Leslie, he graduated from the USMA in 1815. In 1829, he was brevetted captain for ten years of faithful service.

Livingston, Robert L. (1774/5–1843): One of a long line of Robert Livingstons to have held the estate of Clermont in Red Hook, NY on the Hudson. He was a manager of the first US steamboat company—his father, Robert R. Livingston (1746–1813), had worked with Robert Fulton to perfect that craft—but then lost a fortune in trying to run it.

Mahan, Dennis Hart (1802–1871): A professor of military engineering at West Point, he was a member of many scientific societies in the United States and one of the corporate members of the National Academy of Sciences in 1863. He was also the father of the naval historian Alfred Thayer Mahan.

Martin, John (1789–1854): English painter known for his large Romantic paintings with subject matter drawn from the Old Testament and Milton.

Mason, James Murray (1798–1871): Grandson of George Mason of Revolutionary War fame and Democratic senator from Virginia (1847–61), he was appointed Confederate diplomatic commissioner to France and England (1861–65).

McIlvaine, Charles Pettit (1799–1873): Chaplain and professor of ethics at the USMA (1825–28), during which time he worked hard to reform the skepticism that was rife among officers and cadets. He was rector of St. Ann's Church in Brooklyn from 1827–32, a position for which he declined the presidency of the College of William and Mary. In 1832 he became both the second president of Kenyon College in Gambier, OH, and Bishop of Ohio; he later served twice as chaplain of the United States Senate.

McVickar, John (1787–1868): An economist, churchman, and moralist, as well as a professor at Columbia College.

Meredith, William M. (1799–1873): Having studied law, he served in the legislature and was president of the select council of Philadelphia and a member of the state constitutional convention of 1837. He became secretary of the US Treasury in 1849, though he resigned when Taylor lost to Fillmore.

Merrit, Frances (Fanny) (?): Unmarried daughter of Caroline Prescott Merrit, the oldest sister of Emily A.P. Ladd (i.e., Emily Wharton's cousin). In the 1860 census, she and her mother were living with Marshall and Julia Glazier in Saxonville, MA.

Metcalf, Julia (?): The only daughter of Judge Theron Metcalf, she remained unmarried as of 1879.

Metcalf, Julia Tracy (?): A native of Litchfield, CT and the wife of Judge Theron Metcalf.

Metcalf, Theodore (1812–1894): A noted pharmacist in Boston in the mid-nineteenth century and a friend of Oliver Wendell Holmes. At the time of Wharton's visit, he was still a bachelor.[37]

Metcalf, Theron (1784–1875): Took a degree at Brown University (1805) and then a law degree from Litchfield College (1807). He practiced law in Dedham, MA for thirty years and intermittently served in state government. He was an associate justice of the Massachusetts State Supreme Court from 1841–65.[38]

Milnor, James (1773–1844): A Philadelphia lawyer, he entered political life in 1805 and was a Pennsylvania representative to Congress (Federalist, 1811–13). After returning home, he became a candidate for orders in the Protestant Episcopal Church, was ordained and received a doctorate as well as being a catechist and lay reader, and accepted the rectorship of St. George's Church in New York city, where he remained until his death.

Moody, David (?): An "ingenious mechanic" and superintendent of the Boston Iron Works on the Boston & Roxbury Mill Dam, and, having been hired by Francis Cabot Lowell to build the machinery for the Boston Machinery Co. in Waltham, he became a founder of the textile industries in Lowell, MA. He was also instrumental in the Bunker Hill Monument Association and was on the building committee for the Granite Railway Co. railroad, which was laid from Boston to Quincy in 1826–28, built in order to get granite for the monument.

Morgan, J.C. (?): Owner, with a Mr. Bravo, of the Literary Depot next to the post office on Exchange Place in New Orleans, one of the largest bookstores in the South before the Civil War. Morgan and Bravo were also publishers, bookbinders, and stationers.[39]

Morris, George Pope (1802–1864): Journalist who established the *New-York Mirror* (1823), *New Mirror* (1843), *Evening Mirror* (1844), and founded the *National Press* (1846). Nathaniel P. Willis was with him in all these ventures.

Morris. William Hopkins (1827–1900): Son of G.P. Morris and an 1851 graduate of West Point. He served in the military from 1846–54 and then again for the Union during the Civil War. He was the assistant editor of the *New York Home Journal* (1854–61), invented a repeating carbine and revolver (1869 and 1877), and authored several books on tactics.[40]

Morse, Alpheus Carey (1818–1893): Boston architect from Haverhill, MA, noted for his interior of classical pilasters and the coffered ceiling of Boston's Music Hall (designed by George Snell in 1852) and later many notable elite homes in Providence, RI.

Morse, Samuel Finley Breeze (1791–1872): American painter and telegraph inventor. He was active in the formation of the National Academy of Design and then spent some years in London. After his return to New York in 1833, he devoted less time to painting and more to the perfection of the electric telegraph.

Mount, William Sydney (1807–1868): A Long Island painter tangentially part of the Hudson River School and known especially for his genre paintings.

Muhlenberg, Frederick Augustus (1802?–1837): Medical doctor and brother of Rev. William Augustus Muhlengerg. He worked at the Flushing Institute as its physician and professor of physiology, hygiene, and the natural sciences. His death was eulogized by the Rev. Dr. Samuel Seabury and reworked for the Institute's "Eunomian Society" as *Tribute to the memory of Frederick Augustus Muhlenberg, M.D.* (Boston: Marden & Kimball, 1837).

Muhlenberg, Peter (1746–1807): Brother of Rev. William Augustus Muhlengerg, who lived at the Flushing Institute.

Muhlenberg, William Augustus (1796–1877): Episcopal clergyman, founder of the Church School movement, and leading exponent of the idea of the "social gospel." He founded the Flushing Institute (1828) and Saint Paul's College (1838) and became rector of the Church of the Holy Communion in New York in 1846. His greatest and most lasting achievement was the founding of Saint Luke's Hospital (where Wharton's widow, Emily, spent her remaining years).[41]

Munn, Luther (?): Partner of Joseph and Lysander Richards as Richards & Munn Co., granite quarriers, in Quincy, MA since 1829, who were often on the cutting edge of machine working of granite. Luther also acted as the agent for several Quincy-area quarries with the US government in contracting for the granite for the New Orleans Custom House from 1849–56.

Northrup, Birdsey Grant (1817–1898): Connecticut native with degrees from Yale (1841) and Yale Divinity School (1845), he spent a decade as a Congregational minister in Saxonville, MA. He was a longtime member of the American Missionary Society, the Boards of Education in Connecticut and Massachusetts, and a diplomat for the United States when Japan was first opened to the West. He was instrumental in founding Arbor Day in Connecticut in 1886 and then nationally the next year.

Nott, Eliphalet (1773–1866): For many years president of Union College in Schenectady, NY, he invented the first stove suitable for anthracite coal and held ten patents on such devices.[42]

O'Reilly, Philip (?–1854): A Catholic (Dominican) priest born at Scabia, County Cavan, Ireland, he received his education in Bologna, Italy. He made missions and built churches on the banks of the Hudson wherever the number of Catholics made it possible. He ministered to congregations at Rondout, Cold Spring (where he was the first priest of St. Mary's in the Highlands, the chapel Thomas Kelah Wharton designed with Gouverneur Kemble), Saugerties, Newburgh, and Poughkeepsie until 1837, when he was appointed pastor of St. John's Church in Paterson, NJ.[43]

Onderdonk, Henry Ustick (1789–1858): Conservative Episcopalian churchman educated at Columbia College (1805). He studied medicine in London and Edinburgh, and practiced in New York City, where he also edited the *New York Medical Journal*. Later he studied theology and became the bishop of Pennsylvania in 1836.

Osgood, John W. (?–1867): A medical doctor established in Saxonville and later Centre, MA, who was a vice-president of the Middlesex Medical Association.[44] When Thomas Kelah Wharton called upon him for young Prescott and joined him on his rounds in the Saxonville area, he lived in a house on the south side of Saxonville.

Parsons, Samuel Bowne (1771–1841): Quaker horticulturist in Flushing who founded the well-known Parsons Nursery in 1838. Parsons introduced the pink-flowering dogwood, hardy rhododendrons, azaleas, the European weeping beech, the Valencia orange and the first frost-resistant honeybee to the United States.

Paulding, Gertrude Kemble (ca. 1780–1841): Wife of James Kirke Paulding and sister of Gouverneur Kemble and William Kemble.

Paulding, James Kirke (1778–1860): Noted American author and part of the *Salmagundi* group (with Washington Irving) and political appointee as assistant to the Bureau of Naval Commissioners (1815–23) and Secretary of the Navy under Van Buren (1838–41). He was also Gouverneur and William Kemble's brother-in-law by their younger sister, Gertrude Kemble Paulding.

Penniman, George (?): One of the proprietors of the Granite Railway Company granite quarry at Quincy, MA. Penniman, Octavius G. Rogers, and Joshua Emerson had purchased the railroad (incorporated 1826) and quarry in 1847 and hired Gridley Bryant as their agent.

Perkins, Thomas Handasyd (1764–1854): A philanthropist and Massachusetts state senator (1805–23). In 1827 he was the early promoter of the Quincy Railway, the first railroad in the United States, and was lieutenant colonel of a military corps in Boston.

Pierce, Henry Ruben (1828–1862): Born in Covington, VT, he graduated Amherst College in 1853 and served as principle of Saxonville, MA High School for the next school year and then at a series of New England high schools until the Civil War. He died in the Battle of New Burn, NC on March 14, 1862.

Poinsett, Joel Roberts (1779–1851): After experience in foreign delegations (and some military service/advising) to Chile and Mexico in the 1820s, Poinsett became a congressman for South Carolina (1821–25). He served as the controversial American minister to Mexico (1825–29, where he first encountered the red-leafed plant that he later cultivated and introduced to the US under his name), and then secretary of war under Martin Van Buren (1837–41). In retirement, he devoted much of his time to naturalism and cultural institutions such as the National Institute (which later formed the core of the Smithsonian). He was a good friend of Gouverneur Kemble.

Prescott, Betsy Richards (1780–1861): Wife of Jonathan[2] Prescott (i.e., Thomas Prescott Wharton's grandmother).

Prescott, Emeline (1835–?): Born in New York, she was daughter of Levi and Sophia Prescott.

Prescott, Emily: See Ladd, Emily A.P.

Prescott, George Watson (1820–?): Eighth child of Jonathan and Betsy Prescott and brother of Emily Prescott Ladd (i.e., Emily Wharton's uncle). With his father, Jonathan[2] Prescott, he obtained US Patent 10,893 in 1854 for a machine to make wood shavings (excelsior) for mattresses.

Prescott, Jonathan[1] (1750–1805): Brother of Levi Prescott and father of Jonathan[2] Prescott (thus, maternal great-grandfather of Thomas Prescott Wharton), he married Mary Brigham in ca. 1776.

Prescott, Jonathan[2] (1779–1869): Father of George W. Prescott, grandfather of Emily Wharton, and therefore maternal great-grandfather of Thomas Prescott Wharton. Described as an "active, energetic man, possessing a strong and active mind and firm decision of character," he was originally a tanner in Maine and after the War of 1812 went into the fur trade with his sons, quite successfully. He held patents on coloring and tanning leather (March 6, 1818), and the excelsior machine mentioned in Thomas Kelah Wharton's journal on November 5, 1853.

Prescott, Julia Ann: See Glazier, Julia.

Prescott, Levi (1777–1855): Cabinet maker in Bolton, MA and brother of Jonathan[1] Prescott. He married Mary Townsend, and they are the parents of Levi T. Prescott.

Prescott, Levi Townsend (1798–1874): first cousin of Emily Ladd and veteran under Gen. Scott and Col. Aspinwall of the Niagara campaigns (including the battles of Lundy's Lane and Chippewa) during the War of 1812. He was an insurance agent in South Boston and married Sophia Tittle (Prescott) of Beverly, MA.

Prescott, Mary Brigham (1780–1861): Wife of Jonathan[1] Prescott and maternal great-grandmother to Thomas Prescott Wharton.

Prescott, Sophia Tittle (1795–1861): The daughter of a shipmaster in Beverly, MA, she married Levi T. Prescott in 1823.

Prescott, William Augustus (1818–?): First cousin of Emily Ladd and brother of Levi T. Prescott.

Preston, Nathaniel Ogden (?–1866): First rector of the Episcopal Church of the Annunciation in New Orleans.

Preston, Alonzo F. (?): Dentist in Boston residing at 18 Bedford Street.

Reddie, Anna Maria (1787–1864): Born in London (*née* Ralph) and wife of,

- *first*, Dr. George Reddie, married April 6, 1811 in Calcutta. Their connection may likely have come through James Ralph (1782–1857), presumably her bother, who witnessed both their marriage and George's will, who was an officer in the East India Company army and paymaster in Hyderabad. After Dr. Reddie's death in India in 1827 she inherited his estate worth over £72,000 [nearly £6 million in 2018 when adjusted by purchasing power; over 50 times that much by relative share of GDP] and moved back to Scotland (presumably to the home of her brother-in-law, James Reddie, an advocate in Glasgow) about 1833 with her two surviving children, George[2] and Charlotte. By 1836 she moved with them both to Connecticut, where she built Bhurtpore Cottage in the Hindustani style in New Haven.

• *second,* the third wife of Thomas[2] Wharton, married June 1, 1836 in New York. After Wharton's death, in 1845 she petitioned the state of Connecticut for her surname to be legally reverted to Reddie.

As a double widower, by the 1860s she lived in Fond du Lac, WI with her widowed daughter, Charlotte Reddie Wharton, and Charlotte's son, Charles Henry Wharton.[45]

Reddie, Charlotte: See Wharton, Charlotte Reddie.

Reddie, Emily Margaretta (or **Margaret**) **Wharton** (1825–1916): The youngest sister of Thomas Kelah Wharton, christened on January 16, 1826 in Sculcoates near Hull. She became the second wife of George[2] Reddie Jr. (son of Dr. George and Anna Maria Reddie) after the death of his first wife in 1873 (and thereby also becoming her own stepsister; see Charlotte Reddie).

Reddie, George[1] (?–1827): English doctor educated at the Royal College of Surgeons in Edinburgh (studied 1785–90) who entered the Indian Medical Service in 1792. As a surgeon in the medical branch of the East India Company, he served as a lieutenant with the Regiment of Native Cavalry at Fort William in Calcutta, Bengal in 1811; with the British 6th Infantry in India in 1818; with the commissaries general the 29th Native Infantry in Jamaulpore in 1825, where he was promoted to captain; was head of the medical department during the siege of Bhurtpore in 1825–26; and rose to be superintending surgeon of the province of Bengal in the later 1820s. While stationed in India, he and Anna Maria Reddie had at least five children, of which only two survived. He died of fever in October 22, 1827 while stationed at Kanpur (then Cawnpore), Uttar Pradesh, India.[46]

Reddie, George,[2] **Jr.** (1826–1908): Son of Dr. George[1] Reddie and Anna Maria Reddie; born in India, lived briefly in Scotland, and then grew up in Connecticut. In the 1840s he migrated to Wisconsin and purchased seventy acres of farmland near Fond du Lac. He married,

• *first,* Ethelinda (1825/6?–1873), with whom he had a daughter, Athelia, in 1845, and then,

• *second,* Emily M. Wharton, his cousin-in-law through the Thomas[1] Wharton–Anna Maria Reddie marriage, with whom he had one daughter, Clara Morris Reddie.

While in Fond du Lac, he seems to have entered the lumber business while also farming. In 1866 the family began a migration to California but stopped short in Hamilton, Caldwell Township, MO, where he became a "pioneer lumberman" (i.e., the first lumber dealer) and first warden of the Episcopalian mission. He ran a lumberyard there until 1898.[47]

Reid, James M. (?): Architect at the US Custom House in New Orleans. He was a partner in a private architectural practice with, separately, Thomas Kelah Wharton and Benjamin Morgan Harrod.

Reynolds, Sir **Joshua** (1723–1792): English painter famous for his portraiture, knighted in 1769. He was one of the founders and the first president of the Royal Academy in London.

Reynolds, Lewis E. (1816–1879): Architect from Norwich, NY, he trained in New York and Louisville, KY. He set up practice in New Orleans in 1845 and became one of the city's most prominent architects of the 1850s.

Robinson, James (?): Presbyterian minister in Ohio in the 1820s and 1830s who preached at the Pleasant Hill Church south of New Concord, OH, starting about 1820.[48] Thomas Kelah Wharton recorded that Robinson preached his farewell sermon in Zanesville on April 8, 1832.

Samson, Julius (?): Consul of the Duchy of Brunswick and Lüneburg (now in Lower Saxony, northwestern Germany) to the state of Alabama in Mobile. He was instrumental in concluding a number of commerce treaties between the US and Brunswick in the 1850s.

Scott, Winfield (1786–1866): Initially educated as a lawyer, Scott entered military service just before the War of 1812. He commanded troops to some success on the Niagara frontier during the war, notably winning at the Battle of Chippewa though not at Lundy's Lane, where he had two horses shot from under him and was severely wounded in his arm. In 1832, he negotiated peace treaties with several Native American tribes at the end of the Black Hawk War. He fought during the Seminole and Creek Wars, became commander-in-chief of the US Army in 1841, and was instrumental as commander during the Mexican-American War of 1846–48. Although a Virginian, he retained command of the Union Army at the outbreak of the Civil War until his retirement in November 1861.

Scott, Sir **Walter** (1771–1832): Scottish historical novelist and playwright whose works enjoyed great popularity in the British Isles and America in the first half of the nineteenth century. His portrayal of Scotland gave a nucleus to Scots' identity and nationalism.

Seabury, Samuel (1801–1872): Fourth in a line of famous Seabury Episcopal ministers, he was educated at Columbia University and until 1834 was the professor of languages at the Flushing Institute and St. Paul's College. He then took up the editorship of *The Churchman*, a New York weekly Episcopal magazine, until 1849. From the 1830s to the 1860s he was a rector in New York City, and for the last decade of his life he was a professor at the General Theological Seminary.

Simmons, John (1799–after 1860): An émigré ironmaster from Staffordshire who became superintendent of the Ulster Iron Works in Saugerties, NY, under William Young. He later briefly followed Young to the Mt. Savage Iron Works in western Maryland before returning to Saugerties.[49]

Slocum, Thomas Stillé (1774–1849): He began life as a saddler in New York City, but after a brief stint on a farm in Illinois, he returned to New York in the early 1820s and ran a relatively high-end boardinghouse, "liberally patronized by Newport people," at 53 Cliff Street and later at 65 Beekman Street.[50]

Smillie, James David (1807–1885): Scottish engraver, noted for his steel engravings of landscapes and figure pieces by well-known artists, who immigrated to New York in 1829. He was elected to the National Academy of Design in 1851, and did much to develop the engraving of banknotes in the US.

Smith, Henry (1798–1847): An 1815 graduate of the USMA who then served in the quartermaster corps for seventeen years. He fought in the Black Hawk War of 1832 before spending his last three years in the army on engineering duty (1833–36). He then worked as a civil engineer in Michigan until he was reactivated for the Mexican-American War, where he was killed at Veracruz.[51]

Snell, George (1820–1893): An architect born in London, educated at the Institution of Civil Engineers, and who immigrated to Boston in 1849. He is known for the Boston Music Hall, the Hotel Oxford, the South Boston Church Home for Destitute Children, the Concord Public Library, and the granite bank building on State Street.[52]

Spalding, Asa (?): A physician in Flushing, Long Island, originally from Connecticut, and who had served as a surgeon during the Revolution. He was also Flushing's fourth postmaster.

Stevens, Paran (1802–1872): "The father of the American hotel system," Stevens was a hotelier who began by managing his father's hotel, the Tremont House in Claremont, NH. By 1843 he was managing the New England Coffee House in Boston and shortly moved up to run the finest hotels in the city: the Revere House on Bowdoin Square in 1847 and then by 1853 the Tremont House at 73 Tremont Street. A real estate tycoon, he later owned some of the finest hotels in New York, Philadelphia, and Mobile, and was said to have collected hotels "as assiduously as Commodore Vanderbilt collected railways." His widow continued to be active in the New York and Newport social set into the end of the century.[53]

Stickney, Benjamin (?): A hotelier originally from Massachusetts who moved to St. Louis in 1837 and opened Planter's Hotel, a four-story, three-hundred-room hotel at Fourth and Pine streets. By 1858, it was run by Stickney in association with a Mr. McKnight and later a Mr. Kelsey, and was *the* hotel to stay in when visiting St. Louis. A room cost $4.25 per person per day, including four grand meals. When Stickney retired in 1860, he was considered one of St. Louis's most prominent men, and served on the board of directors of the St. Louis Gas-Light Company, the Missouri Pacific Railroad, and the St. Louis National Bank. Noted Army engineer Gen. Amos Stickley was Benjamin's son.[54]

Stowe, Harriet Beecher (1811–1896): Noted American abolitionist and author of *Uncle Tom's Cabin* (1852), Stowe was outspoken on a wide range of social issues of the day and worked on numerous causes with her husband, Calvin Ellis Stowe, a biblical scholar and public education reformer.

Sullivan, William (1774–1839): Son of the Massachusetts governor James Sullivan (in office 1807–08), William was a member of the building committee for the Granite Railway Co. railroad, which was laid from Boston to Quincy in 1826–28 and that was built in order to transport granite for the Bunker Hill Monument.

Sully, Thomas (1783–1872): American painter and émigré from England in 1792 with his parents. Sully initially trained in Virginia with his older brother, the noted miniaturist Laurence Sully, and later in Boston with Gilbert Stuart, as well as in London. He became most famous for his life-sized historical paintings of American politicians and military heroes.

Taylor, James H. (1807?–1835): Graduated West Point class of 1830, stationed at West Point as a brevet second lieutenant from 1831 to 1834, and then served in the Indian Territory (Oklahoma), where he drowned in 1835.

Thayer, Sylvanus (1785–1872): A graduate of Dartmouth College, he spent one year at West Point. After serving in the War of 1812, he was sent to Europe from 1815 to 1817 to study military schools, fortifications, and armies. On his return, he was appointed superintendent of the USMA at the age of thirty-two and undertook its reorganization in the light of what he had learned abroad. He was a good friend of Gouverneur Kemble. Thayer is traditionally considered the "Father of the Military Academy." His resignation—in disgust—from West Point is referred to in the *Journal* entry of March 25, 1833.

Thibault, Aimée (1780–1868): Noted French miniature painter who worked in New York and Baltimore in the mid-1830s.

Thompson, Aaron Kitchel (1817–1873): A merchant in New York and son of Martin E. Thompson, the architect.

Thompson, Martin Euclid (1787–1877): Trained as a carpenter, he became a self-taught architect (much like A.J. Downing in landscape architecture) in New York City and a cofounder of the National Academy of Design. He designed numerous important Greek revival private residences and commercial buildings, including the Second Branch Bank of the United States on Wall Street (1824; its facade is now preserved in the Metropolitan Museum of Art in New York), the Merchants Exchange Building (destroyed 1835), and the Central Park Arsenal (1847–51). He has been described as an "artistically advanced and a magnificent designer but professionally conservative—a man who, although . . . he used the term architect, never entirely released himself from the earlier system of the architect-contractor."[55] It is in Thompson's office that Wharton received his only formal architectural training in America, though he would have had some exposure to it in his summer at West Point and may have had some rudiments before emigrating.

Tillotson, Robert Livingston (1786–1878): Lawyer, secretary of state of New York (1816–17), and US attorney for the Southern District of New York (1819–28).

Toutant, A. (d. 1853): See Pierre-Alfred Toutant Beauregard.

Tracey, Edward (ca. 1823–?): Officer on board the *Aleck Scott*, a Mississippi riverboat, and also a student at Dr. W.A. Muhlenberg's at College Point, Long Island, in the 1830s.

Travers, Helen (?): Daughter of John Travers.

Travers, John (?): Mechanic and ironmaster, specializing in rolling mills, who worked for William Young at the Ulster Iron Works in Saugerties, NY.

Trollope, Frances Milton (ca. 1780–1863): English author who fled a poor marriage by immigrating to Cincinnati in 1829 to start a business, but when that adventure was a failure, she returned to England in 1831 and published the "rude yet witty" caricature *Domestic Manners of the Americans* (1832). She subsequently became an acclaimed novelist and essayist, as did her son, Anthony.

Turner, T. Larkin (?): Druggist who lived at 21 Somerset Street and had a shop at 95 Cambridge Street, Boston. He was a member of the Massachusetts College of Pharmacy from 1851 and was instrumental in the establishment of the American Pharmaceutical Association.[56] He was also married to Elizabeth D. Whiton, so perhaps the post office thought she and Thomas Kelah Wharton were related (see *Journal*, August 25, 1853).

Van Antwerp, John [Jacobus] (?–after 1785): A tailor and property owner in New York City who, with his (probably second) wife Margaret, had eleven children, of which six survived: Simon, John, James, Nicholas, Damile, and Mary.[57]

Van Antwerp, Margaret (1722–?): Born Margaret Peeck Bogert[58] (see Bogert family entries, above), she married Jacobus (John) Van Antwerp on April 18, 1745.

Van Bokkelen, Libertus (1815–1889): He helped establish St. Paul's School (later College) on Long Island in 1837, and in 1842 became an Episcopal minister. In 1845 he founded the first church military school in the US, St. Timothy's Hall in Catonsville, MD. In the early 1860s, as school commissioner of Baltimore County, he reorganized education in Maryland and was director of the National Teachers' Association.[59] He would have been about eighteen when he was Thomas Kelah Wharton's promising pupil at Flushing (*Journal*, February 21, 1833).

Varley, John (1778–1842): British watercolorist. He had many pupils, including Peter deWint and David Cox.

Vinton, Alexander Hamilton (1807–81): Low Church Episcopalian clergyman who was a graduate of Brown and then Yale (in medicine, which he practiced for three years) before entering the Episcopal seminary, from which he graduated in 1835. He received doctorates in sacred theology from the University of the City of New York in 1843 and from Harvard University in 1853. He was in charge of St. Paul's Church in Boston from 1842 to 1858.

Wallace, Elizabeth J. (?): Second wife of Alexander Thompson Wood.

Ward, James (1769–1859): English painter known for his animal paintings, and an engraver. Many of his early works are considered examples of the English Romantic sublime, and thus could be considered forerunners of the Hudson River School.

Warder, Jeremiah (1780–1849): The son of a noted Philadelphia merchant, he worked for his father's shipping firm of John Warder & Sons (later Warder Brothers) and inherited $10,000 worth of land in Springfield, OH in about 1829 or 1830. There he ran a thriving milling business and operated other industries and became the wealthiest man in the community. In 1832 he organized the Springfield Lyceum, from which the first library developed.[60] Thomas Kelah Wharton made a drawing of Springfield for his "excellent friend Mr. Warder" (*Journal*, March 2, 1832), which was later engraved.

Warner, Thomas (1784–1848): A graduate of Union College in Schenectady in 1808, he became the chaplain and professor of rhetoric and moral philosophy at the USMA in 1828. He was also brother of Henry Warner.

Warner, Henry (1787–1875): A graduate of Union College in Schenectady in 1809 and noted New York City lawyer. The younger brother of the Rev. Thomas Warner, he purchased

Constitution Island, with adjacent marsh and farmland, across the Hudson River from West Point in 1836. He planned to build a grand resort hotel there, as well as a summer retreat for his family, but when his fortunes collapsed in the Crisis of 1837, he moved permanently to a modest house on the island. His attempt to reclaim marshland in the adjacent marsh resulted in conflict with GOUVERNEUR KEMBLE and the West Point Foundry, as it was thought the impounded water fostered miasma and malaria in the neighboring town of Cold Spring. Henry was the father of two famous daughters, the best-selling authors Susan (1819–1885) and Anna (1824–1915) Warner.

WEBSTER, DANIEL (1782–1852): Conservative constitutional lawyer, orator, Whig congressman and senator from New Hampshire, and secretary of state under Harrison and Tyler. He was a strong nationalist and argued forcefully for federalism from what is often considered an elitist (as compared to the Jacksonian Democrats) position and was then most remembered for the Compromise of 1850 on slavery issues in order to (temporarily) preserve the Union.

WEBSTER, JOHN WHITE (1793–1850): A socially well-connected professor of the Harvard Medical School who murdered Dr. George Parkman on November 23, 1849. Webster was found guilty and hanged on August 30, 1850. Dr. Parkman's remains are in Mount Auburn, though THOMAS KELAH WHARTON erroneously believed Webster to be in the Webster family plot there (see *Journal*, July 25, 1853); in fact, Webster is buried at Copps Hill Burying Ground in Boston's North End.[61]

WEIR, ROBERT WALTER (1803–1889): American painter and National Academician most well known for his large Italian and historical canvases. In the context of this diary, the large paintings depicting the interior of the West Point Foundry by his son, John Ferguson Weir (1841–1926), should be noted. R.W. Weir succeeded T.J. LESLIE as drawing instructor at West Point in 1834.

WHARTON, ANNA MARIA: See REDDIE, ANNA MARIA.

WHARTON, CHARLES FREDERICK (1820–before 1854): Younger brother of THOMAS KELAH WHARTON, christened on November 13, 1820 in Cottingham, just northwest of Kingston-Upon-Hull. In November 1840, he married CHARLOTTE REDDIE WHARTON.[62]

WHARTON, CHARLES HENRY (1852–1863): Son of THOMAS KELAH WHARTON's older brother, ROBERT JOHN WHARTON.

WHARTON, CHARLOTTE REDDIE (1821–1906): Born in India to Dr. GEORGE[1] REDDIE and ANNA MARIA REDDIE, she married CHARLES F. WHARTON in 1840. After his death in the early 1850s, she moved with her also-widowed mother to a fine house at 30 E. Arndt Street, Fond du Lac, WI, where brother, GEORGE[2] REDDIE Jr., had settled. By the 1860s she had adopted her two nephews, ROBERT H. WHARTON and CHARLES H. WHARTON, after their father (and her brother-in-law), ROBERT JOHN WHARTON, had died and their mother had remarried. She died on December 29, 1906. See also notes to ANNA MARIA REDDIE.

WHARTON, EMILY M.: See REDDIE, EMILY MARGARETTA.

WHARTON, EMILY JULIA LADD (1835/36–1932): Born in New Orleans, she was the second wife of THOMAS KELAH WHARTON. They were married in New Orleans on December 18, 1851, when she was only sixteen. Her obituary called her Evelyn. (See 307n4, below)

WHARTON, HENRY (1815–1852): Younger brother of THOMAS KELAH WHARTON, baptized November 20, 1815 in Sculcoates, just outside Kingston-Upon-Hull. In 1839 in Columbus, OH, he married "the belle of Franklin County" and daughter of Isaac and Hannah Storret Miner, Elizabeth Mary Miner (1821–1909), with whom he had four children, Willian Henry (12/8/1841–3/16/1841), Fredrick (8/6/1842–7/23/1843), Miner (?–?), and Albert (1852?–?). He was a "sickly man" and died of consumption.[63]

WHARTON, MARIA HULING (1827–1848): Eldest daughter of Judge F.W. HULING (1792–?) of Holly Springs, MS and THOMAS KELAH WHARTON's first wife. Their marriage on October 18, 1845 was officiated by REV. FRANCIS HAWKS. She died April 11, 1848, aged twenty-one.

Wharton, Marianne (Mary Ann) (1823?–?): Sister of Thomas Kelah Wharton, christened on September 3, 1823 in Sculcoates, just outside Kingston-Upon-Hull. In 1852 she married Rev. Charles Gillette (1813–1869), an episcopal minister, rector of Christ Church, Houston, and church school principle of St. Paul's College at Anderson, TX and later St. David's in Austin. In 1858 in Austin he founded Wharton College (chartered 1860), named after his wife, which operated until 1861, and then informally until 1865. They had six children and moved back to Brooklyn in 1865, where Gillette became secretary to the Commission of Home Missions for the Colored People.[64]

Wharton, Robert H. (1847–1898): Son of Robert John Wharton born of his first wife in southern Ohio. Adopted by Charlotte Reddie Wharton (his aunt) in Fond du Lac, WI by 1865 (very probably in 1854 when his father, Robert John, died or when his stepmother, Jane (*née* Brooks) Wharton, remarried in Indiana in 1856; Jane's son, Charles H., went to live with the Reddie widows in 1854, so it would be logical that her stepchild would have as well).

Wharton, Robert John (1818–1854): Younger brother of Thomas Kelah Wharton christened 19 Aug 1818 in Cottingham, just northwest of Kingston-Upon-Hull, and immigrated to Ohio with his father, Thomas[2] Wharton, in 1829. He lived in Cincinnati as an unmarried boarder and worked as a bookkeeper. He married twice:

• *first*, by about 1846 to Penemiah McCoy (1822–1849; other sources suggest she went by a common name starting with "N") and with her had a son, Robert H. Wharton, and a daughter whose name is unknown. She died of consumption on October 25, 1851, and Robert John soon moved to Madison, IN, where he was cashier for Firemen & Mechanics Insurance Co., the local agent for a mission of the Protestant Episcopal Church of the United States, and superintendent of the Christ Church Sunday school building (1852–54).

• *second*, about 1851 to Jane F. Brooks (1825–1912), with whom he had a second son, Charles Henry Wharton. Robert John died of cholera on July 3, 1854, and both his sons were adopted by his widowed sister-in-law, Charlotte Reddie, in Fond du Lac, WI. In 1856, Jane remarried O. Alexander Houston of Columbus, IN; she died February 25, 1912.[65]

Wharton, Thomas[1] (1755–1812): Father of Thomas[2] Wharton and four other children (William, Richard, Elizabeth, and Sarah) and grandfather of Thomas Kelah Wharton.

Wharton, Thomas[2] (1789–before 1841?; certainly before 1845): Father of Thomas Kelah Wharton, born in Hull and baptized February 16, 1789. He married three times:

• *first*, on March 31, 1809 in Rowley (ten miles west of Hull) to Elizabeth Goodyear, daughter of Richard Goodyear of Pocklington (fifteen miles east of York), who died March 24, 1810;

• *second*, on May 13, 1811 in Sculcoates (Hull) to Anne Barkin (mother of Thomas Kelah Wharton; baptized September 25, 1780; died September 10, 1835). Anne was the daughter of John Barkin of Bishop Harmouth, County Durham, and later stepdaughter of Captain Robert Kelah of Hull, who had married Anne's presumably widowed mother); and

• *third*, on June 1, 1836, to Anna Marie Reddie, in New York City.

Wharton, Thomas Kelah (1814–1862): born April 17, 1814 to Thomas[2] Wharton and Anne Barkin Wharton; baptized on April 19, 1817 at All Saints' Church in Sculcoates, a northern suburb of Kingston-Upon-Hull, England. Died May 24, 1862 in New Orleans, age 48.

Wharton, Thomas Prescott (1852–1910): Son of Thomas Kelah Wharton. On December 10, 1905, he married Louise P. Camerow, daughter of John Camerow. They had no children.

Wheaton, Walter V. (?): Post surgeon at the USMA during the cholera epidemic of 1832.

Wheelock, Merrill Greene (1822–1866): Boston artist who was active in starting the Boston Art Club and an architect who was responsible for the design of the Masonic Temple at Boyleston and Tremont (built 1867).

Whipple, John A. (?): Proprietor of a daguerreotype gallery in Boston noted for advancing that city to the forefront of photography before the Civil War.[66]

White, John Chambers (1770–1845): British naval commander born to a New York merchant family. His father, Henry White, and mother, Eve Van Cortlandt, remained loyal during the American Revolution and the family fled to London in 1783, where John joined the Royal Navy. He is noted for his command of the HMS *Slyph* during the French Revolutionary Wars and then of numerous ships of the line during the Napoleonic Wars. He rose to the rank of rear admiral by 1830, then vice admiral within a decade, and was made a Knight Commander of the Order of the Bath (KCB) in 1841.

Wilkes, Horatio (?–1840): Third son of Charles Wilkes (d. 1833) and a commercial merchant in New York with his offices at 35 Wall Street and his home at 28 Laight on Hudson Square. He had two daughters, Cornelia and Louisa.[67]

Wilkie, Sir David (1785–1841): Scottish painter and member of the Royal Academy, known for his historical paintings and group scenes.

Williams, Hugh William (1773–1829): Scottish watercolorist known as Williams of Edinburgh and Grecian Williams, he was known for landscapes and dramatic skies, as well as for the published accounts of his travels.

Winthrop, John (1587/8–1649): The governor of the Massachusetts Bay Colony for twelve years in the period 1629–49, known for his authoritarian rule but also for (relative) religious tolerance.

Witherspoon, John (1723–1794): Scottish-born Presbyterian minister and signer of the Declaration of Independence. He was president of the College of New Jersey (now Princeton University) from 1768 to 1776.

Wood, Alexander Thompson (1799–1854): Architect who practiced in London before opening an architectural academy in New York in 1831, although by 1833 he was working in New Orleans. In July 1835, he killed architect George Clarkson, a former employee, in a fight and spent five years in state prison. He was appointed architect for the Custom House in 1848 but was dismissed two years later. However, he returned in 1851 to ensure his original plans were followed.

Wright, John (?): New Orleans pharmacist and co-owner of John Wright & Co., pharmaceutical agents.

Young, Adam (?): An engineer working at iron foundries, rolling mills, and furnaces and the younger brother of William Young. He seems at one time in the early 1830s to have been briefly the manager of the West Point Foundry and often followed his brother to iron concerns, though he also worked independently of him.

Young, Ammi Burnham (1799–1874): Bostonian and architect for the first New Orleans Custom House (1837 and 1847). He was later first supervising architect of the Office of Construction of the Treasury Department (1852–60) and designed numerous federal buildings.

Young, William (?–ca. 1855): Irish engineer from the Belfast area who was recruited to America in 1817 to build the West Point Foundry in Cold Spring, NY. He was president of the Ulster Iron Works in Saugerties, NY, from 1830–40 and then was recruited by Samuel Swartwout to become president of the Mount Savage Iron Works near Cumberland, MD, for the Maryland & New York Iron & Coal Co. from 1840–ca. 1844. He retired to and died in New York City and is buried in Cold Spring, NY.

Appendix

Known Works by Thomas Kelah Wharton

Building Designs

Thomas Kelah Wharton trained as an architect, but other than the Chapel of our Lady in Cold Spring, NY, all his known designs date from the later 1840s and 1850s when he returned to the practice after the death of his first wife, when he left his earlier career of drawing and language instructor at various Episcopal church schools. Unless otherwise noted, he furnished the designs and presumably had a hand in overseeing the construction of the buildings listed. Although the following list is as complete as we have been able to muster, further searches in the garden plan books at The New Orleans Collection (THNOC) and the New Orleans archives may provide more information on residential projects by Wharton from 1848–1862.

*Those designs marked with an asterisk indicate uncertainty as to Wharton's involvement.
†Those designs marked with a dagger are destroyed or were never built.

Cold Spring, New York

1833–1834: **Chapel of Our Lady.** The design by Wharton was based upon sketches by Gouverneur Kemble and influenced heavily by Grecian temple designs by Martin E. Thompson for clients like David Hosack. Built in 1834, augmented in 1890s, and renovated back to original plan in the 1970s and 2000s. Listed on the National Register of Historic Places.

New Orleans, Louisiana

1845/6: **Second Episcopal Christ Church,** riverside corner of Canal and Bourbon streets. While still teaching at Rev. Francis L. Hawks' Episcopal school in Holly Springs, MS, Wharton furnished large-scale preliminary designs and perspective drawings (and perhaps floor plans) for a central-spired, Gothic church to Hawks, who then delivered them to architects James Gallier Sr. and James H. Dakin for construction. Gallier wrote that Wharton's was only a "sketch design [to which] I had to make so many alterations in the plan before it could be made practically fit to build from, as to make it amount to a new design."[1] THNOC, however, considers Wharton the designer, as did a local paper in December 1852 when they printed a letter by Wharton about establishing a drawing department at the local Mechanics' Institute.[2]

1845–1862: **St. Paul's Episcopal Church**, Camp and Gaiennie streets. Wharton provided drawings for renovations of the second church on this location, and it was entirely rebuilt in about 1855.

Late 1840s: **Second Municipality City Hall**, St. Charles Avenue at Lafayette Square. Wharton is known to have done the perspective drawings for the principal architect, James Gallier Sr. The hall was completed 1851 and is now known as Gallier Hall.[3]

1847–1853: †**Magazine Market**, lot bounded by Sophie Wright Place, St. Mary Street, and Magazine Street. Destroyed by fire in 1858.

1850: †**Steele Methodist Chapel** (aka, the Street Chapel), 1200 block of Felicity Street at Chestnut.[4]

1852–1862: **US Custom House**, Canal Street. From January 1848 Wharton was a draftsman and later superintendent of construction for the building originally designed by A.T. Wood in 1845.

Early 1850s: **John Thornhill house**, 1420 Euterpe Street between Prytania and Coliseum. Planation-style colonnaded two-story house with galleries on three sides.[5]

Early 1850s: **Seaman's Home**, 1735 Erato Street. A hotel or boardinghouse for merchant marine men, this commission with which Wharton was involved seems to have been designed in connection with James Gallier Sr. The construction contract went to William K. Day of New Orleans (*Journal*, March 3 and 16, 1857, etc.).

1853: ***St. Anna's Asylum**, 1823 Prytania Street at St. Mary. Wharton provided designs to "The Society for the Relief of Destitute Females and Their Helpless Children," for a three-story Renaissance revival building with a central two-story classical (Doric) section and triangular pediment set on a rusticated ground story, a central Italianate cupola, and crenelated wings.

1855: **Coliseum Square Baptist Church**, western tower redesign, 1376 Camp Street at Terpsichore. The church's tower, originally designed by John Barnett, failed during construction and Wharton, along with Richard Easterbrook and L.E. Reynolds, were brought in to redesign a new square-topped and corner-buttressed tower for this red-brick Gothic church.[6]

1855: †**Touro Synagogue**, St. Charles Street. Wharton submitted a "general design . . . with buildings accessory thereto," for the new synagogue at the request of William Florence and was prepared to furnish a full set of plans should his design be accepted. He may also have collaborated with his good friend W.A. Freret Jr., the architect who ultimately received the commission for the classical Ionic design, which may have reused elements from the first Episcopal Christ Church, which was being rebuilt at the same time.[7]

1857–1858: **Alexander Harris house**, Prytania Street and Jackson Avenue.

1858: **Southwestern Bible Society House**, 727 Camp Street. Wharton reworked the facade that had been designed by John Barnett into a three-bay, three-story pilastered front with foliated capitals and denticulated lintel below the cornice.[8]

1859: **Bosworth-Hammond house**, 1126 Washington Avenue. Two-story, five-bay colonnaded front with the center three bays slightly bow-fronted and a slightly taller square pediment over the central bay.[9]

1859: **Marine Hospital**. Wharton may have assisted the main architect, A.B. Young, in designing it; he was assistant to the superintended of construction in 1859 and "Engineer in Charge" in 1861, once the construction passed to the Confederate government.[10]

1861: †**Paul Cook house**, St. Charles Avenue between Arabella and Joseph streets, with back to Danneel. Brick mansion and spacious gardens of unknown style, but which included gas and running water, this was Wharton's last known and largest work.[11]

n.d.: †**Methodist Chapel**, Dryades Street.

n.d.: †**Kemp Hall & Co. building**, Canal Street.

n.d.: **Richard Terrell cotton press**, St. Thomas Street.[12]

Columbia, Tennessee

1847: *†**Ashwood School for Girls**. A carpenter Gothic, three-range hall school on the southwest side of the town, near the turnpike to Mt. Pleasant (now Route 243). Though it burned in 1850, a small (watercolor?) painting of the building survives, possibly by Wharton, raising the possibility that he was the architect.[13] This church was built by the Episcopal Diocese of Tennessee, and Wharton knew Rev. James Hervey Otey (1800–1863), its first master, as well as Rev. E.H. Cressy, the principal and rector of the nearby St. John's Church, but no evidence has yet come to light to definitively mark this commission or the painting as by Wharton.

Natchez, Mississippi

1850s: *†(?) Planation of Thomas Thornhill.[14]

Holly Springs, Mississippi

Mistakenly Attributed/No Evidence: 1857: **Cedarhurst.** A brick Gothic residence built for Dr. Charles Bonner. The attribution is hypothetical but quite unlikely, as such a commission ought to have appeared in Wharton's copious diary for that year.[15] *Mistakenly Attributed*: 1858, **Airliewood.** A stuccoed Gothic residence built for William Henry Coxe. The house was in fact designed by the Philadelphia firm of Sloan and Stewart. John Stewart was the construction architect and Fletcher Sloan, Samuel Sloan's younger brother, was the building superintendent.[16]

Austin, Texas

1858: †(?)[**Marianne**] **Wharton College.** Wharton designed a building or buildings for his brother-in-law, Charles Gillette (1813–1869), an Episcopal priest who had married Wharton's sister, Marianne. Gillette was in 1858 developing plans for a college that was chartered in 1860 but closed 1865.[17] It is unclear whether any of Wharton's designs were ever put into effect, and the plans are not known to have survived.

Sewanee, Tennessee

1860: †**The University of the South's main building.** Wharton furnished a full proposal as one of twenty-four entries in the design competition for the main building of the Episcopal university and seminary planned by Bishop Leonidas Polk, bishop of Louisiana. His 17,500-square-foot design features a three-story (that is, two stories above with a fully fitted-out half-sunken basement), neoclassical building with a grand central entrance staircase to the elevated main floor. The central auditorium block of 40 by 70 feet was flanked by T-shaped wings consisting of 20-by-60-foot "corridor extensions" and perpendicular 41-by-81-foot "wings" featuring a library and art gallery, respectively. The basement held the administrative offices and further rooms for drawing, sculpture, mineral collections (the school being on the western piedmont of the Appalachians), and a museum. Offices and classrooms would have been on the underspecified second floor, and the prospectus repeatedly refers to other specialty schools being planned for the university that would have had separate buildings. Six two-story Corinthian columns front the central block with full-width pediment carved in bas-relief with Pallas Athaene (personifying intellectual arts) at the center, surrounded by Demeter (agriculture), Hephaestos (useful arts), Hestia ("presiding deity of the social hearth"), and Apollo (poetry and music), with a background of "suitably intermingled such emblems of Commerce, the fine and useful Arts, and polite Learning, as naturally belong to the subject, and exhibit the legitimate fruits of mental polish and social union."

The proposal also includes a watercolor elevation of the front of the building, floor plans for the basement and main floor, and a detail plan and elevation of the main auditorium. The only known publication by Wharton is an accompanying twenty-one-page brochure, *General and Mechanical Description of a Design for the "University of the South,"* dated September 15, 1860.[18]

New York Public Library Drawings

The New York Public Library's Manuscripts and Archives Division, mss. col. 3306 comprises Wharton's eight-volume journal and one-volume sketchbook. Wharton redrew earlier sketches from his previous 1830s journeys in the New York section of the journal when he recopied volume 1 in 1854. The sketches are titled by Wharton himself and reproduced verbatim in the lists below. They are mostly signed either "T.K.W." or "T.K. Wharton" (omitted here to reduce repetitiveness) and are dated. If a sketch is dated by Wharton, that is part of the caption; a date in [square brackets] is the date where the sketch appears in the journal if it is not the same as the date in the caption. If the sketch is untitled, we have supplied a descriptive title in [square brackets]. Sketches in the sketchbook are standalone, without text, and in many cases dated as noted.

Journal, volume 1 (1830–1835)

p. 1 Clee-Thorpes opposite Spurn Head, Mouth of the Humber. 1830 [April 3, 1830].
2 Flamboro' Head and Tiley Bay, Yorks. 1830 [May 4, 1830].
3 Scarboro' and Castle. Yorkshire. 1830 [May 4, 1830].
4 Marmond Hills and Kennard's Head. Scotland. 1830 [May 6, 1830].
6 The Hebrides. (Lewis). 1830 [May 6, 1830].
9 The Diana at St. Mary's Bay, Newfoundland. 1830 [May 20, 1830].
12 The Diana and New York Bay from the Battery. 1830 [June 3, 1830].
20 Palisadoes. Hudson River. 1830 [July 1, 1830].
21 West Point from the North. 1832 [July 1, 1830].
23 Gap in the Highlands from the Old Fort, Constitution Island. 1832 [July 1, 1830].
51 Sciota Crossing, 1830 [July 14, 1830].
56 Our Home in the Woods. Piqua, Ohio. 1830 [July 16, 1830].
67 Court House. Dayton, Oh. 26 Jan. 1832 [May 31, 1831].
71 Springfield, O. from the N. East. Feby 10, 1832.
73 Icicles at Mill Creek Falls, Springfield, Ohio. February 24, 1832.
75 Falls of Mill Creek, Springfield, Ohio. February 11, 1832.
77 Mound Hill, Springfield, O. February 9, 1832.
79 Court House. Springfield, Ohio from Werden's Hotel. Feby 9, 1832.
83 Limestone Rocks on Brick Creek near Springfield, Ohio. Feby 14, 1832.

87 Lock of the Lateral Canal at Columbus, Ohio. March 2, 1832.
107 Freestone Culvert on the National Road, 21 Miles East of Zanesville O. April 4, 1832.
115 Iron Works on the Licking River near Zanesville Ohio. April 1832.
136 Poughkeepsie Landing, Hudson River. 1833 [July 6, 1832].
203 Works of the West Point Foundry at Coldspring N.Y. Nov. 16, 1832.
205 Works of the West Point Foundry from the head of the "Ravine." Nov. 1832.
207 Crow's Nest and The Point of Constitution Island opposite West Point. Nov. 1832.
209 Village of Coldspring and the Chapel of our Lady.[19]
213 Residence of Gov. Kemble Esq. Coldspring N.Y. 1833.
215 Euterpe Knoll. Hyde Park N. York. Sept. 11, 1839.[20]
217 Crystal Cove. Hyde Park. New York. Sept. 11, 1839.
219 Flushing Bay, Long Island with "Palisadoes" in the distance. July 27, 1833.
311 Village of Fishkill N. York from the Old Stone bridge on the Albany Road. Sept. 26, 1834.

Journal, volume 2 (1853–1854)

p. 55 [Central Gateway at Mt. Auburn Cemetery]. [July 23, 1853].
59 [Gable of house built in 1680]. [July 26, 1860].
65 Marsh near Boston. [July 31, 1853].
102 Old Mile Stone near Saxonville Mass. [August 30, 1853].
105 The Meadow Path. Sudbury River, Saxonville. [August 31, 1853].
108 [Sketch of Inscription Stone at Boston Waterworks]. [September 3, 1853].
152 [Capstones on stonework at Fort Warren, Georges Island, Boston Harbor]. [October 13, 1853].
185 Circular Reservoir. Dorchester Heights. [October 31, 1853].
234 Bank of the Misissippi [*sic*] near Bayou Tunica. 1853 [November 30, 1853].
255 Sudbury River, Saxonville. 1853 [December 7, 1853].
280 Steel Chapel, Felicity Road New Orleans. May 28, 1854.[21]
282 [Cast iron caps for N.O. Customs House piers]. [May 28, 1854].[22]
284 Arches of Central portion of [N.O. Customs House] Building. June 1, 1854.[23]
302 Mill Falls at Saxonville, Mass. 1854 [January 31, 1854].[24]
371 College Point in 1839. [May 21, 1854].
377 Trinity Church, Lafayette from "our Cottage." [May 31, 1854].[25]
396 Marble Tablet. North Side. N. Orleans Waterworks. 1854 [June 24, 1854].
406 New Orleans Waterworks. Corner Richard and Religious Streets. 1854 [July 9, 1854].[26]
430 [Column capitals]. [September 2, 1854].[27]
476 Riggers fitting the mast for Derrick New Custom House. Top 160 feet from the ground. Nov. 15, 1854.[28]

Journal, volume 3 (1855–1856)

p. [iii] Section thro' the Collector's Room New Custom House New Orleans. Dec. 18, 1854.[29]

[v] Plan of Collector's Room. New Custom House. New Orleans. Scale 1/16 Inch to the foot. Dec. 18, 1854.

14 Plan and section of Cast Iron Cap (reversed) for the Brick Columns of Vestibule and U.S. Court Room. N. Custom House. New Orleans. Scale 1 inch 6 ft. [January 31, 1855].[30]

27 Lever for testing Cast Iron Beams &c. New Custom House. New Orleans. 19 Feb. 1855.[31]

33 Cast Iron Caps &c. New Custom House, New Orleans. Feb. 28, 1855.[32]

41 [Perspective of octagonal column] Scale ¼ Inch to foot. March 1855. [March 20, 1855].[33]

43 Elevation of Angular face of Octagonal Capital. Scale 1 Inch to foot. [March 20, 1855].

48 Marble Cutting at the New Customs House New Orleans. 1855 [March 31, 1855].[34]

59 Sketches of Beams & Girders suggested for Floors of N. Custom House, N. Orleans. [April 30, 1855].[35]

62 Mississippi River, 4 Miles Above New Orleans. May 3, 1855.[36]

65 Lauillebaurre's Old Plantation House on the River 4 Miles above N. Orleans. May 3, 1855.

67 St. Patrick's Cathedral New Orleans from the River Bank 4 miles above. May 11, 1855.

71 Coliseum Place, New Orleans. May 24, 1855.[37]

77 View across the River looking over the present Custom House N.O. 1855 [May 31, 1855].

87 The Marine Hospital from the upper walls of the New Custom House, New Orleans. June 30, 1855.[38]

91 Lighthouse on Lake Pontchartrain entrance of the New Canal. July 3, 1855.[39]

101 Window opening on new levee front. N. Custom Ho. New Orleans showing the Granite work, Brick backing and Iron anchors, Scaffolding &c. July 25, 1855.[40]

111 Lake Terminus of the Shell Road from the Pier of the Jefferson and Pontchartrain Railroad. Augt. 7, 1855.[41]

112 Residence of Jas. Robb Esqr. Washington Avenue, New Orleans. Augt. 9, 1855.[42]

Journal, volumes 4–6 (1855–1861)

These volumes contain no sketches.

Journal, volume 7 (1861–1862)

95 Cretica Flowers, Synjenesia &c. &c. drawn hastily, but from nature. [March 23, 1861].[43]

Sketchbook (1853)

This 12-by-8¾-inch leather-bound book, its cover embossed in gold reading, "Sketch-Book 1853 – T.K. Wharton N.O.," is the sketchbook that Wharton took with him on his travels from New Orleans to Boston and back in 1853, although pages 62–72 include scenes from after his return. After each entry, a key in [square brackets] indicates the medium of drawing: **I**: ink, **P**: pencil, **W**: watercolors, or **S**: sepia-tone watercolor.

p. 1 Commerce, first high land above Cairo. Aleck Scott. July 1, 1853. 8½ a.m. [**I**]

2 Mississippi River below Cairo. June 30, 1853. [**I**]

3 Turn of the River Mississippi 50 miles above Cape Girardeau. July 1, 1853, 5½ P.M. [**S**]

4 Illinois River at Kingston 211 miles above St. Louis. July 3, 1853, 6 P.M. [**I** with **S**]

5 Peoria, Illinois River at sunset. July 3, 1853. [**I** with **S**]

6 Mouth of Maumee River below Toledo. Lake Erie, July 5, [1853] 9½ a.m. [**S**]

7 Lighthouse, Maumee Bay, Lake Erie. July 5, 1853, 9¾ A.M. [**S**]

8 Rapids on the Canada side, Niagara July 6, 1853, 6 P.M. [**S**]

9 Rapids between Goat and Moss Island, Niagara. July 6, 1853. [**S**]

10 Canadian and American Fall, Niagara from the Ferry Slips, July 7, 1853, 10 A.M. [**S**]

11 French Creek, Thousand Islands, St. Lawrence River. Sunrise, July 8, 1853. [**S**]

12 St. Lawrence River near Brockville. July 8, 1853. [**S**]

13 Fountain and Masonic Hall, Boston Common. 1853. [**S**]

13½ Bridge and unfinished works at the "Prison." Lawrence, Mass. Aug. 8, 1853. [**W**]

14 Point Alderton. Entrance to Boston Harbour. Aug. 9, 1853. [**W**]

15 Fort Warren and Boston Harbour from Hull, Mass., Aug. 9, 1853.[44] [**W**]

16 Fresh Pond near Boston, Mass. August 19, 1853. [**W**]

17 Observatory and Catholic Church, Charles River &c. Cambridge Mass. from Brighton. Aug. 20, 1853. [**I**]

18 Nobscot Hill. Framingham, Mass. August 28, 1853. [**I**]

19 Distant view of Village of Framingham Mass. August 28, 1853. [**W**]

20 Sudbury River at Saxonville Mass. August 29, 1853. [**I**]

21 Sylvan Bridge, Sudbury River Mass. Aug. 30, 1853. [**I**]

22 Cochituate Pond, Mass. Aug. 31, 1853. [**I**]

23 Railroad Bridge, Saxonville Mass. Aug. 31, 1853. [**I**]

23^{V} Purple Gentian, Saxonville Mass. Sept. 8, 1853. [**I**]

24 Saxonville Mass. from the South East. Sept. 1, 1853 [**I**]

25 Chestnut Tree and Ferns near Saxonville Mass. Sept. 2, 1853. [**I**]

26 Cochituate Pond and Gatehouse, Mass. Sept. 3 1853. [**I**]

26^{V} Pond at Saxonville, Mass. Sept. 1853. [**I**]

27 Sudbury River, above Saxonville Mass. Sept. 3, 1853. [**I**]

28 From the Grave Yard, Saxonville Mass. Sept. 7, 1853. [**I**]

29 Sudbury River below Saxonville, Sept. 9, 1853. [**I**]

29^{V} Bracket and Chimney of Building opposite. N.d. [architectural sketch] [**I**]

30 Framingham Village Mass. from the Saxonville road. September 12, 1853. [**I**]

31 Near Saxonville, Mass. Sept. 14, 1853. [two horses in meadow] [**I**]

32 Near Saxonville, Mass. Sept. 13, 1853. [reedy pond with two small bridges] [**I**]

33 Episcopal Church, Brookline, Mass. Sept. 23, 1853. [**I**]

34 Long Island, Gallop Is^{d}, and Fort Warren, Boston Harbour. Octr. 13, 1853. [**I**]

35 Plum Island Lights Mouth of Merrimac [River]. Octr. 11, 1853. [**I**]

36 Plum Island Beach, near Newburyport, Mass. Octr. 11, 1853. [**I**]

37 City of Boston from the Harbour. Octr. 13, 1853[45] [**I**]

38 Boston Harbour from Quincy Quarries, shewing Long Island, Gallop Island, Georges Is^{d}, Great Brewster, the Light House and Pettick's Is^{d}. Octr. 18, 1853. [**I**]

39 Stone quarried at Quincy Mass. for a Column in single block—on Contract with the New Custom House New Orleans. 36'6" x 5'8" x 5'6". Octr. 18, 1853. [**I**]

40 Approach to the Quarries at Quincy, Mass. by Bryant's Old Rail Road. October 18, 1853. [**I**]

41 Customs House, Boston Mass. Octr. 13, 1853.[46] [**I**]

41^{V} [Sketch of a small sloop]. [**I**]

42 Bluff head, Apple Island, Governors' Island and Deer Island from The Oyster Banks, Boston Harbour. October 26, 1853. [**I**]

42^{V} Barberry. [**I**]

43 Savin Hill and Blue Hills from South Boston. Octr. 31, 1853. [**I**]

44 Egg Rock from N.E. Point of Nahant, Mass. Novr. 1, 1853. [**I**]

45 Trap Rocks at Nahant, North Side. Novr. 1, 1853. [**I**]

46 Cove on South Shore at Nahant, shewing Deer Is^{d}, Bluff Head, and Blue Hills. Novr. 1, 1853. [**I**]

47 Horse Ferry, Ohio River, Thick Mist. Novr. 27, 1853, 4 P.M. [**I**]

48 Ohio River, Novr. 28, 1853, 11 A.M. [showing lone house on left shore, side-wheel steamboat in distance, and horse riders on right bank] [**I**]

49 Ohio River, Novr. 28, 1853, 1 P.M. [showing houses on left bank and stern-wheel steamboat in middle of river] [**I**]

50 Ohio River, 7 miles above Madison, I[ndian]a., November 28, 1853, 2 P.M. [showing flatboats being polled] [**I**]

51 Corn Island, Falls of the Ohio at Louisville, Ky. Novr. 29, 1853. 9 A.M. Misty rain. [**I**]

52 Passing thro' the Canal at Louisville by starlight. Nov. 29, 1853. 9 P.M. [**I**]

53 Limestone Rocks, Ohio River, Novr. 30, 1853, 4 P.M. [showing houseboats] [**I**]

54 Cairo, Junction of the Ohio and Mississippi Rivers. November [Dec.][47] 2, 1853, 3 P.M. [**I**]

55 Tavern at Cairo, Mouth of the Ohio. Decr. 2, 1853, 4 P.M. [**I**]

56 Bluff banks near Randolph. Mississippi River 65 miles above Memphis. Dec. 3, 1853, 11½ A.M. [showing houseboat] [**I**]

57 Mississippi River near Memphis. Deck of the Susquehanna. Dec. 3, 1853. [showing turkeys being shipped in crates] [**I**]

58 Diving Bell at Bayou Tunica, Mississippi River. Decr. 6. 1853, 12 M [meridian=noon].[48] [**I**]

59 Approach to Baton Rouge, State Capitol of Louisiana, U.S. Arsenal grounds &c. 5 P.M. Dec. 6, 1853. [**I**]

60 Mississippi River, 52 miles below New Orleans. 1853. [**I**]

61 Fort Livingston on the Gulf of Mexico. Barataria, Louisiana, 1853. [**I**]

62 River and Levee at New Orleans from the North East Angle of New Custom House, 4th story. Oct. 1855. [shows many ships in the harbor] [**I**]

63 Oblique Section thro' one of the Ground arches, New Custom House New Orleans. Curious arrangement of joints as exhibited when the work was cut thro'. Novr. 10th, 1855. [**I**]

64 Bhurtpore Cottage, near New Haven in 1839, West Rock &c. our last home at the North. T.K. Wharton. Nov. 27, 1855.[49] [**I**]

65 Wyton Bar near Hull, Yorks. Wyton House in the distance. Our last home in England 1829. From nature. [**I**]

66 Town of Lynn from Nahant. July 28, 1853. [with fishermen on rocks] [**P**]

67 Chelsea Beach. July 22, 1853. [**P**]

68 Old House, Corner Ann and Market Square, Boston, erected 1680. Cupola of Faneuil Hall. July 26, 1853. [**P**]

69 Tombs of Webster and Oxnard, Mt. Auburn near Boston, Mass. July 22, 1853. [**P**]

70 Wreck of the "Princess," 20 miles below Baton Rouge, La. Augt. 25, 1859 9½ A.M. [**P**]

71 [Unidentified. Stone building with tile roof and Romanesque lancet windows in square tower]. [**P**]

72 [Unidentified. Same stone building as on p. 71 from opposite side. Gatehouse?].[50] [**P**]

73 [Unidentified. Two buildings, one a mill, beside the sea or lake. Also, two boats tied up to a tree stump]. [**P**]

74 [Unidentified. Timber buildings with thatched roofs]. [**P**]

75 Roger's Slide, Lake George [NY]. [**P**]

76 [Unidentified. Stone house with a thatched roof by a stream]. April 1856. [**P**][51]

Other Drawings and Paintings

The New York Public Library Prints and Photographs Division has many dozens of Wharton's images, including many original drawings. These include the twelve "Views of Ohio" series pen-and-ink drawings, many Hudson Valley pen-and-ink drawings and pencil sketches, and several watercolors of sites in Greece, Portugal, the Middle East, and India. These latter are in all likelihood drawn from intermediate images, as it is not known that Wharton ever left the United States after he arrived from England. There must also have been a good number of other paintings and drawings that have been lost to the ages or are no longer identified with his name—for example, the various paintings and drawings that Wharton notes as having been given to friends and supporters during his New York period—and one can hope that more will come to light.

Wharton's further work, which may include unsigned drawings that may be candidates for attribution to his hand, may reside in the federal records of the construction of the New Custom House in New Orleans[52] as well as the numerous newspaper and periodical articles he is known to have written later in his New Orleans phase.[53] Some of his earlier work may be in the James Harrison Dakin Collection of architectural drawings and lithographs,[54] as Dakin worked with James Gallier Sr., and it is possible that Wharton did work for them when he first arrived in New Orleans. Some of Wharton's drawings from the New York Public Library were shown there in an exhibition entitled *Wild New York: The Printmaker and the Natural Landscape from the Age of Exploration Through the Twentieth Century*, March 15–June 28, 1997. The Metropolitan Museum of Art also holds a small number of his works.

The two standard reference works, cited below, are Gloria-Gilda Deák, *Picturing America, 1497–1899: Prints, Maps, and Drawings Bearing on the New World Discoveries and on the Development of the Territory That is Now the United States* (Princeton, NJ: Princeton University Press, 1988), and I.N. Phelps Stokes and Daniel Carl Haskell, *American Historical Prints, Early Views of American Cities, Etc., from the Phelps Stokes and Other Collections* (New York: The New York Public Library, 1932).

Drawings in the New York Public Library (1829-1859)

The NYPL drawings in the Miriam and Ira D. Wallach Division of Arts, Prints and Photographs: Print Collection are all unbound (acc. MEKY). In this section, the manner of Wharton's signature, or lack thereof, is noted. After each entry, a key in [square brackets] indicates the medium of drawing: **I**: ink, **P**: pencil, **W**: watercolors, or **S**: sepia-tone watercolor, with further details as necessary.

No. 1 Twelve Views Miami and Montgomery Counties Ohio. T.K. Wharton. 1831. [This is a title sheet for nos. 2–13. These are considered a set and referred to as his "Twelve Views of Ohio," ink drawings in a wrapper, 14 x 23.1 cm.] [Deák 398][55] [**I**]

2 Crane of the Miami River Ohio. T.K. Wharton. 1831. [**I** with **W**]

3 South East View of Pequa, Ohio. T.K. Wharton. 1831. [**I**]

4 French's Mill Pequa Ohio. T.K. Wharton. 1831. [**I**]

5 Davis Clearing 1½ Miles South West of Pequa, Ohio. T.K. Wharton. 1831. [**I**]

6 Islet in the Miami between Pequa and Troy Ohio. T.K. Wharton. 1831. [**I**]

7 Mill on the Miami Near Pequa, Ohio. Indian Summer. T.K. Wharton. 1831. [**I**]

8 Dalzell's Clearing 1 Mile South West of Pequa, Ohio. T.K. Wharton. 1831. [**I**]

9 Bofson's Factory Near Troy, Ohio. T.K. Wharton. 1831 [**I**]

10 Troy, Ohio. T.K. Wharton. 1831. [**I**]

11 Head of the Miami Canal Dayton, Ohio. T.K. Wharton. 1831. [**I**]

12 Dayton from the South East. T.K. Wharton. 1832. [**I**]

13 Bridge Over the Miami at Dayton, Ohio. T.K. Wharton. 1832. [**I**]

14 Columbus, Ohio from the South West. T.K. Wharton. 1832. [**I**]

15 Washington's Memorial Baltimore. James D. Smillie, engraver. T.K.W. 1833. [Deák 413] [**I** with **W**][56]

16 Falls of the Indian Brook opposite West Point, N.Y. T.K. Wharton. 1834.[57] [**P** signed in **I**]

17 Caatskill Falls. T.K. Wharton. August 1834. [**P** signed in **I**]

18 Silver Lake Near Caatskill Mountain-House. T.K. Wharton. August 1834. [**P** signed in **I**]

19 Kirkstall Abbey Near Leeds, Yorkshire. Built AD 1200. From an original sketch by T.K.W in 1829. T.K. Wharton. 1836. [**P**]

20 Rough Sketch of Rapids near the Source of the Hudson River. T.K. Wharton. August 1839. [**P** signed in **I**]

21 Lake George from the Ruins of Fort George, N.Y. T.K. Wharton. August 1839. [**P** signed in **I**]

22 Catskill Mountains from W. Youngs. Saugerties, N.Y. T.K. Wharton. 1840. [**P**]
23 Bloodhound [head]. T.K. Wharton. February 1840. [**P**]
24 Setter. T.K. Wharton. Feby 25, 1840. [**P** and **I**, signed in **I**]
25 Athens. T.K.W. N.d. [**S**]
26 Interior of the Cave at Elephanta. T.K.W. 1840. [**S**]
27 Temple of the Sybil, Tivoli. T.K. Wharton. 1840. [**S**]
28 [Interior of a ruined church with triple Romanesque lancet windows and Tudor crypt vault arch.] T.K. Wharton. 1841. [**S**]
29 [Mirror-engraved lettering, park by manor house, and detail of a ruined Romanesque (Norman) arch-stone and zigzag molding bearing date 1841.] Unsigned. N.d. [Presumably 1841] [**I**]
30 Distant View of the Acropolis, Athens. T.K. Wharton. 1841. [**W**]
31 View on the Tagus, Portugal. T.K. Wharton. 1841. [**P**]
32 Washington Irving's House at Hell Gate N.Y. T.K.W. Dec. 4th 1841. [Deák 513] [**P** signed in **I**][58]
33 Islip Church, Long Island 1842. T.K.W. [Deák 518] [**P**]
34 Source of the Arve [River], Pennine Alps. T.K. Wharton 1842. [**W**]
35 Sketch of ruined Arch. T.K. Wharton 1842. [**W**]
36 M^t. Hermon and Sea of Gallilee. T.K. Wharton. 1842. [**S**]
37 Entrance to Indra Subba, Hindoostan. T.K. Wharton. 1842. [**W**]
38 North Gate, Old Delhi, Hindoostan. T.K. Wharton. 1842. [**P**]
39 Capta Castle, Bootan [Bhutan], East Indies. T.K. Wharton. 1842. [**P**]
40 Sketch of an ancient Country Church, Eng^d. T.K. Wharton. 1842. [**S**]
41 Phoenix Tower, Chester, from which Charles I beheld the defeat of his army on Rowton Moor A.D. 1642. From an original sketch by T.K.W. in 1829. T.K. Wharton. 1842. [**W**]
42 Ancient House in Smithy Door, an old street in Manchester, from an original sketch by T.K.W. 1829. T.K. Wharton. 1842.[59] [**W**]
43 Roman Remains Found in Lombard Street, London in 1785.[60] Unsigned. N.d. [**P**]
44 [Night scene: Moonlight on an overgrown river]. T.K.W. N.d. [**P** with conté crayon]
45 [Night scene: Moonlight over River with Bridge and Tower on Bluff]. T.K.W. N.d. [**P** with conté crayon]
46 View from Pine Mountain, Mass.[61] T.K.W. Jany 15, 1845. [**P**]
47 Cathedral Catholique Place d'armes, New Orleans. T.K.W. June 1845.[62] [**P**]
48 First rough sketch of a Design for Christ Church N. Orleans. T.K. Wharton. Holy Springs, Miss. 1845.[63] [**W** with **I**]
49 Glimpse of the American Fall[s] Niagara. T.K.W. Sept. 1847. [**W** with white crayon]
50 Interior of Vestibule Canal Street Front, New Custom House New Orleans. T.K. Wharton. March 1, 1853 [or 1855?]. [Deák 691][64] [**I**]

51 [Two women in brightly colored dresses at a gate between fields]. T.K.W. Feby 26, 1859. [**P** with **W**]

Sketches of the David Hosack Estate, Hyde Park, New York (1832)

Seven items in the Hosack Album, a collection of twenty-five drawings of the David Hosack Estate in Hyde Park, NY, entered the Metropolitan Museum in 1994 (acc. 1994.187.1–25). See *Journal*, July 9, 1832, and Kevin J. Avery, *A Catalogue of Works by Artists Born before 1835, American Drawings and Watercolors in the Metropolitan Museum of Art* (New York: Metropolitan Museum of Art, 2002), 1: 363 and 391.

1. Bridge over Crumelbow Creek (1994.187.11): Watercolor on off-white wove paper. View across the creek with a prominent young tree in left of frame of the three-span bridge on tapering piers. Through the central span a waterwheel is seen in the distance.

2. Greenhouse (1994.187.12): A view of the tropical glass house in which Hosack grew citrus and other fruits.

3. View of David Hosack Estate from Western Bank of the Hudson River (1994.187.13): Looking at the estate nestled within the tree line from across the Hudson from West Park, NY, with rocks in the foreground and sailboats on the river.

4. View of David Hosack Estate with a Sundial (1994.187.14): A view of the rolling landscape of the estate principally filled with four young trees. The small sundial is at left in the foreground.

5. View of the David Hosack Estate from the South (1994.187.15): A view of the two main buildings of the estate, the mansion at left and the Doric greenhouse on the right, with trees on near left, framing the long view of the buildings. A path runs diagonally across the foreground.

6. View of David Hosack Estate from the East (1994.187.16): A view of the mansion in the center of the drawing, extensive greenhouses to the left and the Doric gatehouse (?) on the right. A small farmhouse with smoking chimney lies in a notched vale in the foreground.

7. Grove of Poplars with a Memorial Bust (1994.187.17): View of a small hillock with three benches surrounding a small memorial bust on a plinth, with mountains in the distance.

Paintings and Other Drawings

Painting of New York City from Brooklyn Heights (1834)
Owned by Mr. & Mrs. Robert Lee Gill, New York, NY.[65] There is also an anonymous copy after the engraving, a black-and-white sandpaper drawing, 18¾ x 27 in., shown at Kennedy Galleries, New York.[66]

Christ Church, 901 Canal Street, New Orleans (1846)
Watercolor of the facade of the church, 17⅝ x 22 in. The Historic New Orleans Collection, 1945.1.2.

Interior of Christ Church, 901 Canal Street, New Orleans (1846)
Watercolor perspective of the nave of the church, 17¾ x 22 in. The Historic New Orleans Collection, 1945.1.2.

Ashwood School for Girls, Columbia, Tennessee (1847?)
Small watercolor of the carpenter Gothic buildings seen from a moderate distance in a Romantic landscape attributed to Wharton by style and association to the school's principal and master, but see above under Buildings.[67]

Views of Natchez, Mississippi (ca. 1850)
An exquisitely detailed pencil drawing finished in gouache, showing both the upper and lower town of Natchez, 10.6 x 7.0 cm. New York Public Library, Stokes Collection. Ref. Stokes and Haskell, ca. 1850–D-5 and –D-10.

US Patent 10,893 (1853)
Wharton did the drawings for George W. Prescott and Jonathan Prescott of Boston, MA, "Machine for reducing wood to slivers," patented May 9, 1854. See *Journal,* November 9, 1853. The location of the original patent drawings is unknown.

The Elms, Natchez, Mississippi (1859)
Pencil sketch dated August 23, 1859, of the "suburban villa" known as the Elms just outside Natchez, built beginning in 1801. Wharton was a visitor there in 1849 and likely later. This seems to be part of the journal (see August 1859) and may be the drawings in the sketchbook, 72–73 (see note 48, above). Privately owned by the owners of the Elms.

University of the South, Sewanee, Tennessee (1860)
Pen and watercolor, front elevation and floor plans with specifications. University of the South Archives, Sewanee, TN, acc. no. 1600010258. See above under Buildings.[68]

Prints from Wharton's Illustrations

All engravings of Wharton's drawings are executed by others from his originals, for as far as is known, he never learned the art of engraving, though it is clear that he did try his hand at lithography.

Springfield, Ohio (1832)
This engraving, dated February 23, 1832, derives from the sketch in the journal from February 10 (volume 1, page 71) made for Jeremiah Warder in Springfield (see Biographical Register). Engraving reproduced in Benjamin F. Prince (ed.), *The Centennial Celebration of Springfield, Ohio* (Springfield, OH: Springfield Publishing Co., 1901), frontispiece.

New York from Brooklyn Heights (1834)
Steel-plate engraving by A.W. Graham (active 1830s) and printed by Robert Miller (active New York, ca. 1830–1843) in the *New-York Mirror* April 19, 1834 (see *Journal,* March 23, April 6, and May 11, 1834 and figure 3.13 above). The *New York Evening Post* (April 18, 1834) said, "The foreground is beautiful and the buildings and spires of the city, with their reflection in the water of the East River, are given with a good effect." MMA acc. 24.90.1259: Image size 6 x 8¾ in. (15.3 x 22.2 cm); plate size 9¹/₁₆ x 11⁵/₁₆ in. (23.0 x 28.8 cm). Copies in collection of Thomas Addis Emmet, EM12734, NYPL, ID 256195; 26.5 x 34.5 cm; NYPL, ID 1090702; [Amos F.] Eno Collection of New York City views (Eno 153); and copy, 20 x 24 cm (7¾ x 9¼ in.), in Mid-Manhattan Picture Collection, NYPL, ID 716102.

Washington's Monument, Baltimore (1835)
The image was engraved by James David Smillie and appeared in the *New-York Mirror* in 1835. The *New York Evening Post* said, "The Mirror of the present week . . . is embellished with one of those beautiful engravings which have added so much to the value of that weekly miscellany. The present engraving . . . by T.K. Wharton, a young artist of fine taste and great promise, and engraved by Smillie, the production, of whose burin are of known excellence." The original drawing was owned by Smillie (ex-John H. Levine Collection), 26.7 x 40.3 cm. NYPL Print Collection, ID 118492 [Deák 413]. Other versions exist: 20 x 15 cm exists at NYPL Prints and Photographs Division, ref. Smillie [13], ID 1926969; and 24 x 19.5 cm, Massachusetts Historical Society, Guild Library-Lg.

Institute at Flushing, New York (1833–1844)
Published in New York by Endicott & Sweet, 1834. Image size 6 x 9 in. (23.0 x 15.5 cm); sheet size 12½ x 19¾ in. (315 x 500 mm). Bloomsbury Auctions, Americana, 2007, lot 20. "Lithograph by Endicott, after I. K. [*sic*] Wharton," 11⅝ x 16 in. (29.5 x 40.7 cm), Yale University Art Gallery, Mabel Brady Garvan Collection, 1946.9.207. See figure 2.3 above.

The Flushing Oaks, Long Island, New York (1833–1844)
Lithograph published by T. Moore of Boston. Image size 10⅝ x 13⁵⁄₁₆ in. (27.0 x 33.8 cm); sheet size 13⅜ x 16¼ in. (33.9 x 41.2 cm). The Edward W. C. Arnold Collection of New York Prints, Maps and Pictures, 54.90.1148.

Reading, Penn. from the south (ca. 1838)
"Drawn from nature, and on stone by T.K. Wharton. Thos. Moore's lithography, Boston." Lithograph, 9¾ x 12¼ in. (24.8 x 31.2 cm). Thomas Moore operated his lithography studio in Boston from July 1836, when he bought out his employer, John Pendleton, until 1840 when he himself sold out to Benjamin Thayer. Described in its title as "Printed by Peter S. Duval": Duval (1804/5–1886) was a French-born and trained lithographer working in Philadelphia.[69]

Hand-colored lithographs of two reported sizes: 21.9 x 32.7 cm [Deák 489] and 13.3 x 10.3 in. [Stokes and Haskell C.1838-F-42].[70] NYPL, I.N. Phelps Stokes Collection of American Historical Prints, ID 118633; Library of Congress cph.3c07307.

New Haven from the S.E. (1836–1840)
"Drawn from nature, and on stone by T.K. Wharton. Thos. Moore's lithography, Boston." Lithograph, 14 x 20½ in. (35.5 x 52.0 cm). This recently discovered print, coupled with that of Reading, PA, above, hints at a larger collaboration between Moore and Wharton with other city views yet to be found. Library of Congress Prints and Photographs Division, call no. "PGA - Wharton (T.)—New Haven . . . (B size) [P&P]" (digital file: LC-DIG-pga-08537).

Views of New York City (1840s?)
Wharton supposedly made a number of sketches of New York City that were intended for publication in Booth's illustrated history of the city, but they were either not included in the final product or have lost explicit attachment to his name in favor of the engravers who rendered them for the press.[71] NYPL lists them as from "vol. 8," but it was only ever issued in one- or two-volume editions.

Municipal Hall, Lafayette Square, New Orleans, 1847 (1848)
Lithograph by F. Bedford of the new Greek Revival City Hall designed by James Gallier Sr. (London: Standidge & Co. 1848). Lithograph with watercolor, 20½ x 28 in. The Historic New Orleans Collection, 1935.1.[72]

Hatch Silver Service Set (1861)
A seven-piece silver service set given to Francis H. Hatch, collector of the Port of New Orleans in May 1861, with engravings based upon Wharton's sketches.[73] Made in New Orleans by Terfloth and Küchler, coin silver (THNOC, acc. 2008.0329.2.1–7).

Notes

Preface

1. "Public Improvements. Church of Our Lady at Cold Spring," *New-York Mirror*, Nov. 8, 1834, 145. See also figure 3.17.

2. See also chapter 3, note 70, below, for Kemble's contribution to the design.

3. Thomas Kelah Wharton's journal is located at the New York Public Library, Manuscripts and Archives Division, mss. col. 3306, and is available on microfilm (call no. *ZL-441). The editors of *Queen of the South* [note 5, below], iv, confusingly say that they survive in "hundreds of loose manuscript pages, six bound manuscript volumes, and a sketchbook." The eight journal volumes are purchased, pre-bound blank books of the day. There are seventy-seven drawings in his (bound) sketchbook in the NYPL Manuscripts and Archives Division and fifty-one loose drawings in a separate collection in the NYPL Prints and Drawings Division. Cataloging is apparently contradictory as to whether the sketchbook is part of the same manuscript collection. The notice of the acquisition of two quarto volumes and one "oblong" quarto (the sketchbook) covering 1853–1854 is in E.H. Anderson, "Report of the Director for the Year Ending December 31, 1920," *Bulletin of the New York Public Library Astor, Lenox, and Tilden Foundations* 25, no. 4 (1921): 200–242 at 214–215.

4. There is a sadness in the details here, as the *New York Times*, June 6, 1932, 15, got Emily's name wrong in her own obituary:

> Mrs. T.K. Wharton.
>
> Widow of Prominent New Orleans Architect Succumbs at 97 here.
>
> Mrs. Evelyn [sic] Ladd Wharton died Saturday at St. Luke's Home for Aged Women . . . at the age of 97. She was the daughter of Mr. and Mrs. Darius Ladd of New Hampshire, and was born in New Orleans, where her parents moved soon after their marriage.
>
> She married Thomas K. Wharton, a prominent New Orleans architect, and moved to New York soon after his death. In 1908 financial disaster overtook Mrs. Wharton, and through the efforts of Mrs. Ichabod T. Williams she became the beneficiary of an endowment in St. Luke's Home, where she had since lived.
>
> A diary kept by her husband was considered of such literary and historical value that it was purchased by the New York Public Library.

Emily's funeral was held at St. Luke's Home and she is interred in Woodlawn Cemetery. It is unknown what the financial disaster was, but it does suggest that Wharton left her financially well off; it is also possible that William Augustus Muhlenberg, who founded St. Luke's Home, could have, out of compassion, arranged a place for her in her old age after Thomas Kelah's own death in 1862. Thomas and Emily's son, Thomas Prescott Wharton, pre-deceased her in 1910.

5. James H. Rodabaugh, "From England to Ohio, 1830–1832: The Journal of Thomas K. Wharton," *The Ohio Historical Quarterly* 65, no. 1 (1956): 1–27, and 65, no. 2 (1956): 111–151. Thomas Kelah Wharton, Samuel Wilson, Patricia Brady, and Lynn D. Adams, *Queen of the South: New Orleans, 1853–1862: The Journal of Thomas K. Wharton* (New Orleans and New York: Historic New Orleans Collection and The New York Public Library, 1999). The only other sustained works on Wharton other than brief biographical mentions known to us are Norris F. Schneider, "English-Born Artist Recorded Early History of Zanesville," *The Times-Recorder*, January 13, 1957 [copy in CRA, folder "Ohio 1830–32"], and sections on Wharton in Daniel Wilson Randle, *A Question of Style: the Architectural Competition for the Central Building of the University of the South (1860)* (master's thesis, University of Texas at Austin, 1979).

6. As we were putting the final touches on our draft in late 2016, we learned that Kenneth John Myers, then a curator at the Freer Gallery in Washington, DC, and now at the Detroit Institute of Arts, had been planning a book, *A Young Artist in a New Nation: The 1830–34 Journals of Thomas Kelah Wharton*, that was supposedly forthcoming from Syracuse University Press in 2000. It, too, never appeared.

Introduction

1. *Journal*, December 7, 1853.

2. This section is transcribed and published as James H. Rodabaugh, "From England to Ohio, 1830–1832: The Journal of Thomas K. Wharton," *The Ohio Historical Quarterly* 65, no. 1 (1956): 1–27, and 65, no. 2 (1956): 111–151.

3. These volumes have been extensively mined and copiously illustrated, though not fully transcribed, in Samuel Wilson, Patricia Brady, and Lynn D. Adams (eds.), *Queen of the South: New Orleans, 1853–1862: The Journal of Thomas K. Wharton* (New Orleans: Historic New Orleans Collection, 1999).

4. *Journal*, April 30, 1832 [Rodabaugh, 147–148]. Arthur P. Ponsonby, *English Diaries: A Review of English Diaries from the Sixteenth to the Twentieth Century with an Introduction on Diary Writing* (London: Methuen & Co., 1923), 2: The consciousness of the writer of an immediate recipient exercises a restraint on the author and produces a certain sort of self-consciousness which may be entirely absent in the pages of a diary.

See also Lynn Z. Bloom, "'I Write for Myself and Strangers': Private Diaries as Public Documents," in Suzanne L. Bunkers and Cynthia A. Huff (eds.), *Inscribing the Daily: Critical Essays on Women's Diaries* (Amherst: University of Massachusetts Press, 1996), 23–37.

5. Marilyn Ferris Motz, "Folk Expression of Time and Place: 19th-Century Midwestern Rural Diaries," *Journal of American Folklore* 100, no. 396 (1987): 131–147.

6. *Journal*, August 13, 1832. Sok Chul Hong, "The Burden of Early Exposure to Malaria in the United States, 1850–1860: Malnutrition and Immune Disorders," *Journal of Economic History* 67, no. 4 (2007): 1001–1035.

7. The average height and weight for forty-year-old British males for this period was 5 ft. 8 in. and 155 lbs. (1.72 m and 70 kg). Roderick Floud, "Height, Weight and Body Mass of the British Population since 1820," *Historical Paper 108* (Cambridge, MA: National Bureau of Economic Research, 1998), tables 3 and 4.

8. Christine Stansell, *City of Women: Sex and Class in New York 1789–1860* (Urbana: University of Illinois Press, 1987), 76–83. E. Anthony Rotundo, *American Manhood: Transformations in Masculinity from the Revolution to the Modern Era* (New York: Basic Books, 2001), offers far more insight into the ways in which men negotiated nineteenth-century friendship, gender relations, and marriage than Wharton offers in terms of glimpses into his own experiences in that regard.

9. Karen Halttunen, *Confidence Men and Painted Women: A Study of Middle-Class Culture in America, 1830–1870* (New Haven, CT: Yale University Press, 1982), 34–36.

10. Stansell, *City of Women*, 93.

11. Here I am playing on the title of John Higham, *From Boundlessness to Consolidation: The Transformation of American Culture, 1848–1860* (Ann Arbor, MI: William L. Clements Library, 1969), which neatly summarizes the transformation Wharton seems to have experienced in the period not covered in his journal.

12. "Deaths," *The Hull Packet and Original Weekly Commercial, Literary and General Advertiser*, March 27, 1810, 3.

13. "Marriages," *Hull Advertiser and Exchange Gazette*, May 18, 1811, 3.

14. "For Quebec (with passengers)," *Hull Advertiser and Exchange Gazette*, March 1, 1822, 2.

15. "Deaths," *The Hull Packet*, November 7, 1834, 3.

16. Though now in ruins, John F. Curwen, *The Castles and Fortified Towers of Cumberland, Westmorland and Lancashire North-of-the-Sands* (Kendal: CWAAS, 1913), 401–404 provides a compelling reconstruction plan and details.

17. *History, Directory & Gazetteer, of the County of York* (Leeds: Edward Baines, 1823): 2: 314. The home would today be about one thousand feet due north of the main rail station and just inside the A165, though the area is entirely redeveloped after severe World War II bombing damage. He was born on Mason Street, where the Hull History Center now stands. Wharton also mentions that before emigrating, his father lived on Albion Street, parallel but three streets south of Pryme (*Journal*, March 29, 1832). On Wyton, see *A History of the County of York East Riding*, Victoria History of the Countries of England (Oxford: Oxford University Press, 2002), 7: 169–172. Rent for Wyton Bar cost £245 in 1841, and the residents then charged tolls to make up that rent and a profit; Martin T. Craven, *A New and Complete History of the Borough of Hedon* (Driffield: Ridings Publishing Co., 1972), 100.

18. *Journal*, May 4, 1830 (Rodabaugh [note 2, above]), 7.

19. *Hull City Directory*, 1826 [copy in CRA with letter of Michael Bordman, Humberside City Council, to WKS, January 24, 1984]. "To be Sold by Private Contract," *Hull Advertiser and Exchange Gazette*, June 1, 1821, 2; "Exports," *Hull Packet*, March 10, 1829, 1.

20. "For Palermo, & Mesisna," *Hull Packet*, July 11, 1815, 2; "Hull – For New York," *The Hull Packet and Original Weekly Commercial, Literary and General Advertiser*, April 30, 1816, 2; "Sales by Private Contract," *Hull Advertiser and Exchange Gazette*, November 25, 1825, 2; "Advertisements & Notices," *The Hull Packet and Humber Mercury*, November 11, 1828.

21. "Thomas Wharton's Bankruptcy," *Hull Advertiser and Exchange Gazette*, April 10, 1829, 2; "In Wharton's Bankruptcy," *Hull Advertiser and Exchange Gazette*, May 29, 1829,

2; "Thomas Wharton's Bankruptcy. Audit and Dividend," *The Hull Packet and Humber Mercury*, March 27, 1832, 1; "Bankruptcies," *Worcester Herald*, April 11, 1829, 4; "Court of Exchequer, Westminster," *The Hull Packet and Humber Mercury*, May 31, 1831, 2; "Wharton's Bankruptcy," *Hull Advertiser and Exchange Gazette*, April 13, 1832, 2; "Final Dividend. In Thomas Wharton's Bankruptcy," *The Hull Packet*, February 26, 1841, 4.

22. Rodabaugh (note 2, above). Additionally, see Norris Franz Schneider, *Y Bridge City: The Story of Zanesville and Muskingum County, Ohio* (Cleveland, OH: World Pub. Co., 1950). Wharton's warehouse, formerly known as Northrup's Warehouse, was advertised for sale in the *Ohio Republican* on March 24, 1832 and was removed by eminent domain in 1836 when navigational improvements to the Muskingum River were undertaken by the state. Thomas Sr.'s third son, Henry, was still seeking recompense from the state in 1840, his father having moved to New Haven, CT after remarrying. *Journal of the Senate of Ohio, at the First Session of the Thirty-Eighth General Assembly* (Columbus, OH: Samuel Medary, 1839), 618.

23. *Journal*, March 3 and April 2, 1832 (Rodabaugh [note 2, above]), 136 and 140.

24. *Journal*, March 19 and 23, 1833. A sampled search of New York City directories from 1828–45 turned up no Earl or Earle on Beekman Street.

25. *Journal*, April 17, 1832 (Rodabaugh, 146).

26. *Journal*, June 1830 (Rodabaugh, 13). For the slightly later growth of the tourist culture in America, see John F. Sears, *Sacred Places: American Tourist Attractions in the Nineteenth Century* (Amherst: University of Massachusetts Press, 1989).

27. Brian P. Luskey, *On the Make: Clerks and the Quest for Capital in Nineteenth-Century America* (New York: New York University Press, 2010).

28. Charles E. Rosenberg, *The Cholera Years: The United States in 1832, 1849, and 1866*, 2nd ed. (Chicago: University of Chicago Press, [1987] 2009).

29. Christine Chapman Robbins, *David Hosack: Citizen of New York* (Philadelphia: American Philosophical Society, 1964), 3–4 and 181–183. And see Victoria Johnson, *American Eden: David Hosack, Botany, and Medicine in the Garden of the Early Republic* (New York: Liveright Publishing Corporation, 2018), esp. 311, 316.

30. In general, see James McLachlan, *American Boarding Schools: A Historical Study* (New York: Scribner, 1970), chapter 4; David Hein, "The High Church Origins of the American Boarding School," *Journal of Ecclesiastical History* 42, no. 4 (1991): 577–595; and William J. Reese, "Soldiers for Christ in the Army of God: The Christian School Movement in America," *Educational Theory* 35, no. 2 (1985): 175–194. For a full modern appreciation of Muhlenberg's movement, see Walter Lawrence Prehn, *Social Vision, Character, and Academic Excellence to Nineteenth-Century America: William Augustus Muhlenberg and the Church School Movement, 1828–1877* (doctoral thesis, University of Virginia, 2005). Muhlenberg's two vision statements by the time of his hiring Wharton were his *The Application of Christianity to Education: Being the Principles and Plan of Education to be Adopted in the Institute at Flushing, L.I.* (Jamaica, L.I. [NY]: Sleight & George, 1828), and Muhlenberg and Samuel Seabury *Christian Education: . . . the Studies and Discipline of the Institute and an Essay on the Study of the Classics on Christian Principles* (New York: Protestant Episcopal Press, 1831).

31. The three-story, 108-by-45-foot building had a four-column classical portico and symmetrical wings with some twenty-five to thirty-six rooms (depending on partitioning), two large parlors with marble mantles and folding doors, and sat on six acres with formal gardens, ornamental trees, and outbuildings, including coach, wood, and ice houses; "Flushing

Institute–For Sale or Let," *The Atlas* [London], March 9, 1838, 4. It sold the following February for $8,200; *New-York Spectator*, February 21, 1839, 3. The best general description of the Flushing Institute is Alvin W. Skardon, *Church Leader in the Cities: William Augustus Muhlenberg* (Philadelphia: University of Pennsylvania Press, 1971), chapter 3. See engraving in chapter 3, above and an early photo of the building in the Eugene L. Armbruster photograph collection at the New-York Historical Society, http://nyheritage.nnyln.net/cdm/singleitem/collection/p16124coll2/id/15613/rec/16.

32. John Fowler, *Journal of a Tour in the State of New York, in the Year 1830* (New York: Augustus M. Kelley, 1831; rpt. 1970), 32 and 34–35.

33. S.D. McConnell, *History of the American Episcopal Church; From the Planting of the Colonies to the End of the Civil War* (New York: Thomas Whittaker, 1890), 326–327. "Institute at Flushing, L.I. New York," *Church Register*, February 23, 1828, 62–63.

34. "Institute at Flushing, L.I. New York," *Church Register*, Feb. 23, 1828, 62.

35. These appear to be quotations from Muhlenberg's prospectus for the Flushing Institute, *Application of Christianity to Education* (note 30, above), quoted in the *Church Register*.

36. J. Edwin Orr, *America's Great Revival* (Elizabeth, PA: McBeth Press, 1957), and Terry D. Bilhartz, *Urban Religion and the Second Great Awakening: Church and Society in Early National Baltimore* (Rutherford, NJ: Fairleigh Dickinson University Press, 1986). By the 1850s, Muhlenberg would moderate his position and put for the "Muhlenberg Memorial" that proposed a way—never ratified by the Episcopal Church's bureaucracy—for reincorporation of the various flavored of American Anglican Protestantism under the Episcopal leadership.

37. Skardon, *Church Leader in the Cities* (note 31, above), 91.

38. "Classified Advertising: The Institute at Flushing, L.I.," *New-York Spectator*, September 1, 1836, 3.

39. "St. Paul's College," *New-York Spectator*, May 21, 1838, 1 (reprinted in *Daily National Intelligencer*, May 22, 1838, 2). *The Churchman's Almanac for the Year of our Lord 1839* (New York: Sherman and Trevett, 1838), 22. The introductory core consisted of grammar, Latin, Greek, geometry, rhetoric, and there were both junior- and senior-level philosophy courses. A full set of topics and books for the curriculum is printed at "The Institute at Flushing, L.I.," *New-York Spectator*, October 1, 1832, 1. John Frederick Woolverton, "William Augustus Muhlenberg and the Founding of St. Paul's College," *Historical Magazine of the Protestant Episcopal Church* 29, no. 3 (1960): 192–218.

40. Anne Ayres, *The Life and Work of William Augustus Muhlenberg, Doctor in Divinity* (New York: T. Whittaker, 1889), chapter 8. Henry D. Waller, *History of the Town of Flushing, Long Island, New York* (Harrison, NY: Harbor Hill Books, 1975), 181–183. "The Institute at Flushing, L.I.," *New-York Spectator*, September 2, 1833, 3.

41. "Deferred Articles: St. Paul's College," *Vermont Chronicle*, October 8, 1835, 164. Prehn, *Social Vision* (note 30, above), chapter 4. And, in general, see Diana Butler Bass, *Standing Against the Whirlwind: Evangelical Episcopalians in Nineteenth-Century America* (New York: Oxford University Press, 1995), chapter 3, on the shift of the mainline Protestant Episcopal Church toward fighting radical evangelicalism in the 1830s. See also Wharton's comments during his 1853 Boston sojourn (chapter 3 above) and Mary Kupiec Cayton, "Who Were the Evangelicals? Conservative and Liberal Identity in the Unitarian Controversy in Boston, 1804–1833," *Journal of Social History* 31, no. 1 (1997): 85–107.

42. John G. Cawelti, *Apostles of the Self-Made Man* (Chicago: University of Chicago Press, 1965).

43. Elijah A. Smith, *Map of the Town of Flushing and Environs* (New York: G. Hayward, 1841).

44. Allan Nevins and Milton Halsey Thomas (eds.), *Journal of George Templeton Strong* (New York: Macmillan, 1952): 115 and 200; Waller, *History of the Town of Flushing*, 187. Hawks had also been embroiled in 1838–39 in a scandal over alleged sexual affairs. He countersued the accuser for libel, which he won, though the impression is that he paid off the defendant to plead guilty to make the scandal go away.

45. Hawks's various educational ventures were Episcopal boarding schools but are not considered to have been in the Muhlenbergian mold (Prehn, *Social Vision*, 314n4).

46. *Journal*, Aug. 31, 1854. That he says "8 years" is confusing as he was hired originally by Muhlenberg in 1832 and left with Hawks for Mississippi in 1843/1844, which is nearly a dozen years. Wharton is here referring to an eighteenth-century poem by Mark Akenside (1721–1770), "The Pleasure of Imagination," II.738–742:

> With hallow'd ruins; when the Muses' haunt,
> The marble Porch where Wisdom wont to talk
> With Socrates or Tully, hears no more
> Save the hoarse jargon of contentious monks,
> Or female Superstition's midnight pray'r;

The Poetical Works of Mark Akenside (Edinburg[h]: Apollo Press, 1781): 81.

47. *Circular of St. Thomas' Hall, Holly Springs, Miss.* ([Holly Springs, MS?]: Kilpatrick and Morrill, Printers, 1844). No copy of this prospectus is known to survive. The move was noticed in numerous religious weeklies of the day. A review of the circular in the *Guardian: Devoted to the Cause of Female Education on Christian Principles* (March 15, 1844) notes that the school's organization seems to have been the same as St. Thomas's in Flushing, and quotes from the conclusion of the prospectus thus:

> The proprietors are aware that some of the institutions of the country offer their advantages for a smaller sum than that named above. With this they of course find no fault, but for themselves frankly say that they cannot perform what they undertake this prospectus for a less sum than $250.

Citing the cost to find competent teachers and noting that "Economical Education (as it is sadly miscalled)" is "*necessarily* superficial education," Hawks and Wharton appealed to the parents of potential students, asking them to reflect how much it would cost to educate their sons in modern languages through tutors alone, and proposed that they would "make for the South an institution equal to any of similar rank in the United States" (41).

48. *Journal of the Proceedings of the Annual Convention of the Protestant Episcopal Church in the State of Mississippi* (Jackson, MS: The Southern Office, 1844), 8–9, 16, 28. Ruth Watkins, "Reconstruction in Marshall County," *Publications of the Mississippi Historical Society* 12 (1912): 155–213 at 197 and 202. See also *Journal of the Proceedings of the Twenty-Second Annual Convention, of the Protestant Episcopal Church, of the Diocese of Mississippi* (New York: Stanford and Swords, 1848), 17–24.

49. William Baskerville Hamilton, *Holly Springs, Mississippi, to the Year 1878* (Holly Springs, MS: Marshall County Historical Society, 1984), 78. *St. Thomas Hall Catalogue*

(1895–1896), 1 [photocopy in CRA, folder, "South 1843–1862"]. "St. Thomas' Hall, *The Guard* [Holly Springs, MS], June 5, 1844, 3; this advertisement ran repeatedly in 1843 and '44 in *The Guard*.

50. Hawks addressed the convention and they resolved that the failure of the school was not his fault and a number of years later he was enticed to move back to New York when Calvary Church offered a gift of $30,000 for the discharge of the debts at Flushing. *The Tulane News Bulletin* 11, no. 7 (April 1931): 112 [copy in CRA].

51. *Biographical and Historical Memoirs of Mississippi* (Chicago: Goodspeed Publishing Co., 1891): 325–326. *A Tribute to the Memory of the Rev. Francis L. Hawks, D.D., LL.D.* (New York: Bible House, 1867), 29–31.

52. Sir Charles Lyell, *A Second Visit to the United States of North America* (New York, 1849), cited in Allan Nevins, *American Social History as Recorded by British Travelers* (New York: H. Holt, 1923), 342.

53. Pers. comm., Rev. Bruce McMillin, Christ Episcopal Church, Holly Springs, MS, June 28, 2017.

54. Hamilton, *Holly Springs*, 78 and 117. Sears returned to St. Thomas's as its president from 1859 until the Civil War, served notably and lost a leg at the Battle of Nashville in 1864. After the war he served as professor of mathematics at the University of Mississippi until 1889.

55. James Gallier and Samuel Wilson, *Autobiography of James Gallier, Architect* (New York: Da Capo Press, 1973), 40. Not mentioning Wharton is all the stranger since Gallier's son, James Jr., had been Wharton's student at both Flushing and Holly Springs for about six or seven years (32–32, 38) and must have learned much of his own architectural skills there. Then again, never one to keep his opinion to himself, Gallier Sr. thought little of any other architect's abilities: "During the practice of my profession at New Orleans, I could find no person capable of giving me much assistance in making drawings; I was therefore obliged to do nearly all the drawings myself" (which of course affected his eyesight and health, 42), and in describing the New York architectural scene just as he and Wharton arrived there almost simultaneously in the spring of 1832 he says, "The majority of people could with difficulty be made to understand what was meant by a professional architect," and "There was at that time, properly speaking, only one architect's office in New York" (18), by which he meant the office of Towne & Davis, not Martin E. Thompson.

56. He also apparently left some of his belongings with the Hulings, for he notes in his journal years later that Judge Huling had returned his Ohio sketches that had been found in a trunk that had lain unopened for a number of years at the plantation.

57. Mary N. Woods, *From Craft to Profession: The Practice of Architecture in Nineteenth-Century America* (Berkeley: University of California Press, 1999), James F. O'Gorman, *Some Architects' Portraits in Nineteenth-Century America: Personifying the Evolving Profession*, Transactions of the American Philosophical Society 103, no. 4 (Philadelphia: APS, 2013), and see the list of known houses by Wharton in chapter 6, below.

58. Stanley C. Arthur, *A History of the U.S. Custom House, New Orleans* (New Orleans: WPA Administration of Louisiana, 1940). "Cornerstone Laying at Custom House," *Daily Picayune* [New Orleans], Feb. 10, 1849, 2. Within the cornerstone of the building is apparently a piece of parchment dated February 22, 1849 bearing the name of "T.K. Wharton, draftsman."

59. Mark Twain, *Life on the Mississippi* (Boston: James R. Osgood and Co., 1883), 424.

60. See Molly Iker, "Hard Times in the Big Easy: The Medical, Social, and Political Effects of the Yellow Fever Epidemic of 1853 in New Orleans," *Voces Novæ: Chapman University Historical Review* 4, no. 1 (2012): 117–144.

61. For general statistics, see Josiah Curtis, *Report of the Joint Special Committee on the Census of Boston, May, 1855* (Boston: Moore & Crosby, 1856).

62. Thomas Mallon, *A Book of One's Own: People and Their Diaries* (St. Paul, MN: Hungry Mind Press, 1995), xi–xii.

63. Arthur P. Ponsonby, *More English Diaries; Further Reviews of Diaries from the Sixteenth to the Nineteenth Century with an Introduction on Diary Reading* (London: Methuen & Co., 1927), 4.

64. Kimberly Katz and Salim Tamari, *A Young Palestinian's Diary, 1941–1945* (Austin: University of Texas Press, 2009), xi.

65. See Sally Wolff, *Ledgers of History. William Faulkner, an Almost Forgotten Friendship, and an Antebellum Plantation Diary: Memories of Dr. Edgar Wiggin Francisco III* (Baton Rouge: Louisiana State University, 2010). See also Read Bain, "The Validity of Life Histories and Diaries," *Journal of Educational Sociology* 3, no. 3 (1929): 150–164, and Molly McCarthy, "A Pocketful of Days: Pocket Diaries and Daily Record Keeping among Nineteenth-Century New England Women," *The New England Quarterly* 73, no. 2 (2000): 274–296.

66. Rachael Langford and Russell West, "Introduction: Diaries and Margins," in Langford and West (eds.), *Marginal Voices, Marginal Forms: Diaries in European Literature and History* (Amsterdam: Rodopi, 1999), 8, cited in Irina Paperno, "What Can Be Done with Diaries?" *The Russian Review* 63, no. 4 (2004): 561–573 on 561.

67. See Wilson, et al., *Queen of the South* (note 3, above).

68. See Matthew Goodman, *The Sun and the Moon: The Remarkable True Account of Hoaxers, Showmen, Dueling Journalists, and Lunar Man-Bats in Nineteenth-Century New York* (New York: Basic Books, 2008).

69. *Journal*, July 25, 1853.

70. *Journal*, August 22, 1832.

71. *Journal*, December 21, 1860 (Wilson, et al., *Queen of the South*, 238), simply notes,

> Human nature is a sad complication of inconsistencies. The news of the dissolution of the Union reached us today and as much jubilation and gun firing was expended on that "event" as on the original consolidation of said Union less than a Century ago.

72. Rosenberg, *The Cholera Years* (note 28, above); Asa Briggs, "Cholera and Society in the Nineteenth Century," *Past and Present* 19 (1961): 76–96; and although it is about Leeds in the UK, R.J. Morris, *Cholera 1832: The Social Response to an Epidemic* (London: Croom Helm, 1976) provides useful analysis of the cultural context of these kinds of outbreaks.

73. *Journal*, September 22, 1853.

74. *Journal*, June 25, 1853.

75. *Journal*, July 13 and 24, 1833. These must have been Hosack's servants, slavery having ended in New York state in 1827.

76. Craig D. Townsend, "Episcopalians and Race in New York City's Anti-Abolitionist Riots of 1834: The Case of Peter Williams and Benjamin Onderdonk," *Anglican and Episcopal History* 72, no. 4 (2003): 488–505, and John R. McKivigan, *The War Against Proslavery*

Religion: Abolitionism and the Northern Churches, 1830–1865 (Ithaca, NY: Cornell University Press, 1984).

77. Thomas Hart Benton, *Thirty Years' View, Or, A History of the Working of the American Government for Thirty Years, from 1820 to 1850* (New York: D. Appleton and Company, 1880), 153.

78. *Journal*, December 12, 1860 (Wilson, et al., *Queen of the South*, 238), emphasis in original.

79. "The Fine Arts. Exhibition of the National Academy of Design. Fifth Notice," *New-York Mirror*, June 13, 1835, 395. For the general story of the art world in this period, see Russell Lynes, *The Art-Makers: An Informal History of Painting, Sculpture, and Architecture in Nineteenth-Century America* (New York: Dover Publications, 1982).

80. Woods, *From Craft to Profession* (note 57, above); Andrew Saint, *Architect and Engineer: A Study in Sibling Rivalry* (New Haven, CT: Yale University Press, 2007); and see Mary Ann Stankiewicz, Patricia M. Amburgy, and Paul E. Bolin, "Questioning the Past: Contexts, Functions, and Stakeholders in 19th-Century Art Education," in Elliot W. Eisner and Michael D. Day (eds.), *Handbook of Research and Policy in Art Education* (New York: Routledge, 2004), 33–54.

81. *Journal*, January 30 and December 25, 1861 (Wilson, et al., *Queen of the South* [note 3, above]), 244, and NYPL Prints Collection for Wharton, no. 19. By contacting various grammar schools in Manchester, we have only succeeded in confirming that Wharton was not a student at the Manchester Grammar School. There are no student records surviving from the early nineteenth century for the Hull Grammar School, the obvious site for his education, but see Thomas Laughlin, "The School Curriculum from the Fifteenth to the Nineteenth Century," in *The City and the School: Hull Grammar School 500th Anniversary of Endowment, 1479–1979* (Hull: Hull Grammar School, 1979); John Lawson, *A Town Grammar School through Six Centuries* (Oxford: Oxford University Press, 1963), 185–197; and "Education," in *A History of the County of York East Riding: Volume 1, the City of Kingston Upon Hull* (London: Victoria County History, 1969), 348–370. One possible influence on Wharton's training is from John Scott (1777–1834), Hull Grammar School headmaster from 1801–1810, as his father, Thomas, was a noted architect *and* an early evangelical; see Arthur Pollard, "Scott, Thomas (1747–1821)," *Oxford Dictionary of National Biography* (Oxford: Oxford University Press, 2004).

82. As he was described by the famed naturalist John James Audubon, who happened to travel from New York to Philadelphia with him when Wharton Sr. had arrived in America in 1829; Robert Williams Buchanan and Lucy Green Bakewell Audubon, *The Life and Adventures of John James Audubon, the Naturalist* (London: S. Low, Son, & Marston, 1869), 159.

83. John Roach, *A History of Secondary Education in England, 1800–1870* (London: Longman, 1986), chapters 1, 2, 13. See also Sophia Woodley, "'Oh Miserable and Most Ruinous Measure': The Debate between Private and Public Education in Britain, 1760–1800," in Mary Hilton and Jill Shefrin (eds.), *Educating the Child in Enlightenment Britain: Beliefs, Cultures, Practices* (Farnham, UK: Ashgate, 2009), 21–40. Charles Frost, *Notices Relative to the Early History of the Town and Port of Hull* (London: J.B. Nichols, 1827), xiv, though note that there he is not styled "Esq.," but the fact that Thomas Sr. was a subscriber (i.e., financial backer) to an 1827 book on the history of Hull puts him toward the striving gentlemanly middle class. Private art tutors were certainly available: Branwell Brontë (brother

of Charlotte, Emily, and Anne and only three years Wharton's junior) was home-educated by his father, but then in the early 1830s studied under the artists John Bradley of Keighley and William Robinson of Leeds in his failed attempt to become an artist.

84. Printed letter of Wharton to John Ray, newspaper clipping, December 16, 1852 [photocopy in CRA, folder, "N.O. Society"].

85. James T. Callow, *Kindred Spirits: Knickerbocker Writers and American Artists, 1807–1855* (Chapel Hill: University of North Carolina Press, 1967), 94.

86. "International Copyright Law," *Register of the Debates in Congress* 13 (Washington, DC: Gales and Seaton, 1837), appendix, 248.

87. Roger Hale Newton, *Town & Davis, Architects, Pioneers in American Revivalist Architecture, 1812–1870* (New York: Columbia University Press, 1942), 53.

88. *Journal*, November 4, 1853, emphasis in original.

89. In reconstructing Gouverneur Kemble's art collection from his and other family members' probate records, loans to galleries and exhibitions, and travelers' notice of paintings on display at his home, there is no evidence of any known works by Wharton, though he mentions getting paintings ready to send to Kemble (*Journal*, July 13, 1833).

90. *Journal*, May 30, 1832.

91. *Journal*, May 4 and July 1, 1830 (Rodabaugh [note 2, above]), 6 and 16.

92. *Journal*, November 1, 1853.

93. Thomas Kelah Wharton, "Kirkstall Abbey, near Leeds, Yorkshire" (signed "1836, from original sketch in 1829"), pencil on paper, New York Public Library, call no. MEKY.

94. *Journal*, July 28, 1853.

95. *Journal*, July 17, 1853.

96. *Journal*, July 22, 1853.

97. *Journal*, October 26, 1853. See David Schuyler, *Apostle of Taste: Andrew Jackson Downing, 1815–1852* (Amherst: University of Massachusetts Press, 2015).

98. *Journal*, August 9, 1853. Ronald Dale Karr, "Suburban Land Development in Antebellum Boston," *Journal of Urban History* 41, no. 5 (2015): 862–880.

99. Arthur Ponsonby, *English Diaries* (note 4, above), 27–28. At times the phrasing of the journals is quite similar, as when Darwin writes, "It is not possible to give an adequate idea of the higher feelings of wonder, astonishment and devotion which fill and elevate the mind."

100. Thayer owned a copy of Francesco Milizia's *The Lives of Celebrated Architects, Ancient and Modern*, Mrs. Edward Cresy (trans.) (London: J. Taylor, 1826), which is now in the USMA library. Sadly, no correspondence between Wharton and Thayer has been found among Thayer's papers; pers. comm. Keith Huffaker, US Army Heritage and Education Center, December 1, 2014. Cindy Adams (ed.), *The West Point Thayer Papers, 1808–1872* (West Point, NY: Association of Graduates, 1965) misidentifies a passing secondhand mention of Wharton.

101. Ibid., 57.

102. Paul E. Johnson, *Sam Patch, the Famous Jumper* (New York: Hill and Wang, 2003), 53–57.

103. Robert C. Reinders, *End of an Era: New Orleans 1850–60* (New Orleans: Pelican Publishing Co., 1964), 16.

104. The standard work on this transition of labor, capital, and industry is Sean Wilentz, *Chants Democratic: New York City & the Rise of the American Working Class, 1788–1850* (New York: Oxford University Press, 1984), but little of that work speaks to Wharton's experience. As an educator and artist as well as being apparently insulated in his

life in Long Island and later Mississippi, he seems to have stood outside and alongside these massive changes to American society. On craft workers and "the trades," where Wharton might have sympathized with "artisan republican" values, see 140–142.

105. After the 1850s, Boston's South End became an area known for parvenus and was mocked as the part of town where "the mistaken movement of society in that direction [had] ceased." Betty G. Farrell, *Elite Families: Class and Power in Nineteenth-Century Boston* (Albany: SUNY Press, 1993), 25.

106. Carroll Smith-Rosenberg, *Religion and the Rise of the American City: The New York City Mission Movement, 1812–1870* (Ithaca, NY: Cornell University Press, 1971), 30–43 and chapter 2 on revivals. Richard Lee Rogers, "The Urban Threshold and the Second Great Awakening: Revivalism in New York State, 1825–1835," *Journal for the Scientific Study of Religion* 49, no. 4 (2010): 694–709.

107. Butler, *Standing against the Whirlwind* (note 41, above), 11.

108. Ibid., 39–42. Michael Graziano, "America's "Peculiar Children": Authority and Christian Nationalism at Antebellum West Point," *Religions* 8, no. 1 (2017). In fact, when Muhlenberg was developing St. Paul's at College Point, he envisioned a "Cadets Hall" that "would be to the church what West Point and Annapolis were to the Army and Navy," which Alvin Skardon (*Church Leader in the Cities* [note 31, above], 81) tied to Muhlenberg's close friendship with Sylvanus Thayer at the US Military Academy.

109. James D. Davidson, "Religion among America's Elite: Persistence and Change in the Protestant Establishment," *Sociology of Religion* 55, no. 4 (1994): 419–440. For a comparison, see Edward Digby Baltzell, *Philadelphia Gentlemen: The Making of a National Upper Class* (New York: Transaction Publishers, 1989).

110. Alexander Eddy Hosack, "David Hosack, 1769–1835," in Samuel Gross (ed.), *Lives of Eminent American Physicians and Surgeons of the Nineteenth Century* (Philadelphia: Lindsay and Blakiston, 1861), 289–337 at 335–336.

111. He was, for example, one of the "subscribers" to (i.e., helped pay for the printing of) Muhlenberg, *The Rebuke of the Lord: A Sermon Preached in the Chapel of the Institute at Flushing, L.I., on the Sunday after the Great Fire in New-York on the 16th and 17th Dec., 1835* (Jamaica, L.I. [NY]: I.F. Jones & Co., 1835).

112. *Journal*, October 23 and September 4, 1853.

113. *Journal*, February 12, 1855. Wharton may have read this ditty in *The Church of England Quarterly Review* 11 (1842): 115.

114. Carl Lamson Carmer, *The Hudson* (New York: Rinehart, 1939), 202, 207, 235.

115. Robert L. Root, *"Time by Moments Steals Away": The 1848 Journal of Ruth Douglass* (Detroit: Wayne State University Press, 1998), 32.

116. Ibid., 28–31.

117. From Sir Charles Lyell, *A Second Visit to the United States* (1849), cited in Howard Mumford Jones and Bessie Zaban Jones (eds.), *The Many Voices of Boston: A Historical Anthology, 1630–1975* (Boston: Little, Brown & Co., 1975), 219.

118. Anthony Bergen, "John Quincy Adams and the World's First Deadly Railroad Accident," *Dead Presidents* (blog), May 22, 2014, http://deadpresidents.tumblr.com/post/86537072057.

119. See Richard H. Gassan, *The Birth of American Tourism: New York, the Hudson Valley, and American Culture, 1790–1830* (Amherst: University of Massachusetts Press, 2008), esp. chapter 5; Sears, *Sacred Places* (note 26, above), chapter 1; and for the Niagara Falls collection, J. Teather, "The Niagara Falls Museum and the Exhibitionary Complex of

Early Canada," *Museum History Journal* 1, no. 2 (2008): 253–284. For a comparison of what the Wharton's would have seen had they stopped on the way to Ohio, see E.T. Coke, *A Subaltern's Furlough: Descriptive of Scenes in Various Parts of the United States* (London: Saunders & Otley, 1833), chapter 3.

120. See Halttunen, *Confidence Men and Painted Women* (note 9, above).

121. *Journal*, December 7, 1853.

Chapter 1: Thomas Kelah Wharton's Autobiography

1. Wharton consistently misspells Kemble's given name of "Gouverneur," which was his mother's family name.

2. Here Wharton compressed the actual timeline: Muhlenberg had purchased a one-hundred-acre farm on College Point, Long Island, and started building the foundations of St. Paul's in 1836. The Panic of 1837, however, interrupted his plans and in particular his receiving various financial promises from wealthy supporters. Thus, the temporary wooden buildings he had erected were all that were ever built. The college was in operation by 1837. Alvin W. Skardon, *Church Leader in the Cities: William Augustus Muhlenberg* (Philadelphia: University of Pennsylvania Press, 1971), 78–83.

3. The Astoria Female Institute was opened under the auspices of the Protestant Episcopal Church of the United States as a daughter house of St. George's Church, Astoria, NY in 1838. In 1843 it was described as follows:

> Its location is excellent, and combining the most beautiful scenery with an animated water prospect. The institute enjoys, moreover, the advantage of retired rural walks and pleasant groves, in its vicinity; and in order to encourage a taste for floral horticulture, a portion of the flower garden is laid out to each pupil. The rector with his family, the resident teachers and pupils, who are limited in number to thirty, form one household, and the government of the whole is paternal. Here are taught all the useful and ornamental branches of education, common in the best arranged female seminaries. In the immediate neighborhood are several superb private residences, surrounded by all the luxury of the most splendid scenery. There is also an extensive carpet factory, one for hats, and others for chairs, candles, wool-cards, &c. besides gardens and nurseries filled with fruit and ornamental trees, plants, &c.

Benjamin Franklin Thompson, *The History of Long Island: From Its Discovery and Settlement, to the Present Time* (New York: Gould, Banks & Company, 1843), 2: 151, and Williams's *New York Annual Register* (New York: J. Leavitt, 1840), 28.

4. See Wharton's drawing of the facade, now preserved in the prints room of the New York Public Library (acc. MEKY no. 48).

Chapter 2: New York and the Hudson Valley, 1832-1834

1. James H. Rodabaugh, "From England to Ohio, 1830–1832: The Journal of Thomas K. Wharton," *The Ohio Historical Quarterly* 65, no. 1 (1956): 1–27, and 65, no. 2 (1956): 111–151.

2. Footnote in the journal: "Fringilla tristis and Motacilla sialis."

3. Probably Jesse Tomlinson's Western Hotel at 288 High Street above 8th (*McElroy's Philadelphia City Directory* for 1837); the same address later became 828 Market Street after the 1854 renumbering and renaming of the city streets.

4. The "Oratorio" by Franz Josef Haydn. The Chatham Garden Theatre had been built in 1824 but struggled through ten sets of managers in eight years before being rented to Lewis Tappan and William Green. In early 1832, they let it to the Presbyterian minister Charles Grandison Finney, who turned it into the Free Presbyterian Chatham Street Chapel. In November 1835, the diarist Philip Hone was "astonished at the magnificence of the scene" of a performance of the Sacred Music Society. He described an audience of between two and three thousand, of which a large number were women, and nearly one hundred choir members: "The ground floor, which is very capacious, and two large galleries were so crowded that I could scarcely find standing room behind the benches." Quoted in V.B. Lawrence, *Strong on Music: The New York Music Scene in the Days of George Templeton Strong* (Chicago: University of Chicago Press, 1988), 64.

5. James Stuart and Nicholas Revett, *The Antiquities of Athens*, 3 vols. (London, 1762–1816) had great influence in popularizing the architecture of ancient Greece in the United States. Greek Revival style did not become universal in America until the late 1820s when the Greek independence movement against Great Britain once again firmly bound ideals of the new American republic and the democratic ideas of Greece.

6. A fourth-century BCE monument near the Acropolis of Athens.

7. "Mr. Preston is a plain, good man with an amiable countenance . . ." (*Journal*, March 4, 1832 [Rodabaugh {note 1}], 137).

8. Commonly called the *Erechtheum*. This Ionic temple stands on the Acropolis and is celebrated for its Porch of the Maidens, with the pediment supported by six caryatids.

9. These are likely Wharton's "Twelve Views of Ohio," now in the New York Public Library Prints and Drawings Division (acc. MEKY no. 2–13).

10. *Athena Guardian*, commonly known as the Parthenon. This is possibly now the undated drawing title "Athens" in the New York Public Library (acc. MEKY no. 25).

11. It is claimed that the *Courier & Enquirer*, a New York weekly, printed an extra ten thousand copies of its Sunday cholera issue. Charles E. Rosenberg, *The Cholera Years: The United States in 1832, 1849, and 1866* (Chicago: University of Chicago Press, 2009), 22.

12. On this cholera outbreak, see David Meredith Reese, *A Plain and Practical Treatise on the Epidemic Cholera: as it prevailed in the city of New York, in the summer of 1832; including its nature, causes, treatment and prevention* (New York: Conner & Cooke, 1833). Chloride of lime, a bleaching powder of calcium chloride and calcium hypochlorite—$CaCl_2$ + $Ca(ClO)_2$, first used in 1826—was a strong disinfectant that was spread liberally everywhere to try to suppress the contagion, though Reese thought it relatively ineffective (61).

13.

> Then Samuel said to all the house of Israel, "If you are returning to the Lord with all your heart, then put away the foreign gods and the Astartes from among you. Direct your heart to the Lord, and serve him only, and he will deliver you out of the hand of the Philistines." 1 Samuel 7: 3 [NRSV].

14.

> I am not worthy of the least of all the steadfast love and all the faithfulness that you have shown to your servant, for with only my staff I crossed this Jordan;

> and now I have become two companies. Deliver me, please, from the hand of my brother, from the hand of Esau, for I am afraid of him; he may come and kill us all, the mothers with the children. Genesis 23: 10–11 [NRSV].

15. "He humbled himself and became obedient to the point of death—even death on a cross," Philippians 2: 8 [NRSV].

16. The Tower of the Winds, Athens.

17. Grace Church stood at the corner of Broadway and Rector Street from 1808 to 1846, immediately to the south of Trinity Church.

18. "But they all alike began to make excuses. The first said to him, 'I have bought a piece of land, and I must go out and see it; please accept my apologies,'" Luke 14: 18 [NSRV].

19. Psalm 91: 6.

20. Wharton's entry is of interest because it indicates that this distinguished miniaturist was in the United States at least two years earlier than has been supposed. See entry for Thibault in George C. Groce and David H. Wallace, *The New York Historical Society's Dictionary of Artists in America 1564–1860* (New Haven, CT: Yale University Press, 1975).

21. Here there are two page spreads, 135–136 and 136–137, left blank for drawings, but only one was used. Instead he added an annotation, "T.K. Wharton's private journal continued."

22. Wharton's visit to the Hosack estate is only very briefly noted in Christine Chapman Robbins, *David Hosack, Citizen of New York* (Philadelphia: American Philosophical Society, 1964), 183, and she mistakenly gives "Kenneth" as Wharton's middle name.

23. Parterre: ornamental garden with paths between the beds.

24. Dr. Hosack acquired his property in 1827 and had it laid out by the Belgian André Parmentier, the first professional landscape gardener in America. The house that Wharton tells us about, after being enlarged by a subsequent owner, was taken down in 1895 to make way for the present mansion for Frederick W. Vanderbilt designed by Stanford White. For the estate's history, see Patricia M. O'Donnell, et al., *Cultural Landscape Report for Vanderbilt Mansion National Historic Site* (Boston: NPS Cultural Landscape Program, 1992).

25. It appears that Hosack's premature death in 1835 prevented this volume from ever appearing, but this must be the volume now known as the *Hosack Album* that came into the Metropolitan Museum of Art in 1994 (acc. 1994.187).

26. See his sketch of this bridge, now MMA, acc. 1994.187.11.

27. Possibly the one preserved today as MMA, acc. 1994.187.12.

28. A horse-powered ferryboat, where the horses trod on a circular horizontal treadwheel that turned the paddlewheels.

29. Charles Lucian Bonaparte, *American Ornithology or, The Natural History of Birds Inhabiting the United States, not Given by Wilson*, 3 vols. (Philadelphia: Carey, Lea & Carey, 1825–33). This was an augmentation of Alexander Wilson's, *American Ornithology; or, The Natural History of the Birds of the U.S.* (Philadelphia: Porter & Coates, 1815–22+), which was the pre-Audubon "Audubon." See also Laura Rigal, *The American Manufactory: Art, Labor, and the World of Things in the Early Republic* (Princeton, NJ: Princeton University Press, 1998), chapter 5, "Feathered Federalism."

30. Sereno Edwards Dwight, *The Life of President Edwards* (New York: G. & C. & H. Carvill, 1830)—president of Princeton though a graduate of Yale—and John Witherspoon, *A Practical Treatise on Regeneration* (London: for Edward and Charles Dilly, in the Poultry, near the Mansion House, 1764).

31. See the sale catalogue of only his medical books: *Catalogue of the Entire Medical Library of the late Doctor David Hosac [sic]* (New York: Charles C. Shelley, 1867).

32. David Hosack, *Memoir of De Witt Clinton* (New York: J. Seymour, 1829).

33. To this point, these included: *An Inaugural Dissertation, on Cholera Morbus* (New York: Samuel Campbell, 1791), *An Inquiry into the Causes of Suspended Animation from Drowning* (New York: Thomas and James Swords, 1792), possibly a bound copy of "Observations on Vision," *Philosophical Transactions of the Royal Society of London* 84 (1794): 196–216, *An Introductory Lecture on Medical Education [at Columbia College]* (New York: T. & J. Swords, 1801), *Observations on the Surgery of the Ancients* ([New York]: n.p., 1807), *Case of Aneurism of the Femoral Artery* (New York: n.p., 1808) also appearing in French (Paris: Migneret, 1809), *Observations on Croup or Hives* (New York: C.S. Van Winkle, 1811), *Sketch of the Origin and Progress of the Medical Schools of New York and Philadelphia* ([New York?]: n.p., 1812), *Observations on the* Peripneumonia Typhodes, *now Prevailing in Several Districts of the United States* (New York: C.S. Van Winkle, 1813), *An Introduction Discourse, to a Course of Lectures on the Theory and Practice of Physic* (New York: C.S. Van Winkle, 1813), *Observations on Febrile Contagion, and on the Means of Improving the Medical Police of the City of New-York* (New York: Elam Bliss and J. Seymour, 1820), *Observations on Ergot* (New York: C.S. Van Winkle, 1822), and *Essays on Various Subjects of Medical Science*, 3 vols. (New York: J. Seymour, 1824 and 1830).

34. If Wharton's statement is correct, it took at most eight days for his mother's letter from Zanesville, OH to reach him at Hyde Park, NY, possibly forwarded through his city lodging or Thompson's office in New York City.

35. Probably Adeline Emily Coster, daughter of Hosack's third wife, Magdalena, who was the widow of Henry A. Coster.

36. Joseph-Napoleon Bonaparte, the elder brother of Napoleon Bonaparte.

37. James Thatcher, "An Excursion on the Hudson," *The New England Farmer and Horticultural Journal* 9, no. 19 (November 26, 1831): 148–149 and 156–157 at 149. The two-part article describes Hosack's estate in great detail.

38. Probably William Roscoe, *A Discourse on the Origin and Vicissitudes of Literature, Science and Art, and Their Influence on the Present State of Society* (Liverpool: Harris & Co., 1817).

39. *Hibiscus syriacus*, also known in England and America as Syrian ketmia. See Ann Leighton, *American Gardens in the Eighteenth Century: "For Use or Delight"* (Amherst: University of Massachusetts Press, 1976), 429.

40. John Witherspoon, "On Regeneration," in *The Works of John Witherspoon, D.D.* (Edinburgh: Ogle & Aikman, 1804), 175; and see note 29, above.

41. Here one and a half pages have been left blank for sketches of Hyde Park, probably copies of those that went to Hosack and now the MMA *Hosack Album*. Although those would have long before left Wharton's possession, both they and the sketches in the *Journal* seem to all come from a now-lost master sketchbook.

42. Properly, *Hoc opus, hic labor est*: "This is the task, this is the toil." Virgil, *Aeneid*, VI.126 (or VI.129, Loeb ed.).

43. Wharton had commented at length on this area when he first passed it on the way to Ohio:

> The Highlands are conspicuous more for the simple grandeur of their grouping and their majesty of outline than from their height, the highest not exceeding

> 1,600 or 1,700 feet. Ragged peaks, and barren rocky pyramids there are none, but grand swelling curves of the richest foliage, half hiding and half revealing the vast masses of sienite beneath, tho' in some places the leafy screen is drawn aside, and lofty mural precipices of bare granite spring aloft high above the river, and cast broad shadows over its bright waters. I insert opposite a sketch of the gorge as it appears from West Point, with the old ruins on Constitution Island in the foreground, Newburg,—Polipell's Island & the Shonga mountains in the distance, Bull Hill, Breakneck, Coldspring Landing & Stony Point on the right, Butter Hill [i.e., Storm King] on the left—euphonious names!!!

Journal, July 1, 1830 (Rodabaugh [note 1], 16).

44. *The Nahant March* was composed by J.H. Walch in 1831. The folk tale of Cinderella had been numerously adopted as an opera by Jean-Louis Laruette (1749), Nicolas Isouard (1810), Stefano Pavesi (1814), and most famously, Gioachino Rossini (1817).

45. Charles Davies, *Elements of Descriptive Geometry, with their Application to Spherical Trigonometry, Spherical Projections, and Warped Surfaces* (Philadelphia: H.C. Carey & I. Lea, 1826).

46. The Sandy Hook Lightship, established in 1823, was one of the noted floating lighthouses that served until permanent shore lighthouses could be built.

47. It is unclear to whom Wharton is referring: there were no members of the US Congress before 1832 named Wood who were military men, nor were there any US generals named Wood who served in politics in this period.

48. "But whenever you pray, go into your room and shut the door and pray to your Father who is in secret; and your Father who sees in secret will reward you," Matthew 6: 1 [NRSV].

49. Wharton probably means Saugerties, NY (also known as Ulster) and the Ulster Iron Works (see note 114, below), as John Travers, an ironmaster, had connections with William Young and John Simmons there, and we learn that O'Reilly later took the ministry in Saugerties.

50. At this point in the journal, Wharton left the lower half of the page blank, presumably for a copy of his "River view." This may be the one he inserted earlier in the journal for July 1, 1830, since that drawing is actually dated 1832. Recall that his "book of early sketches in Ohio" had been packed away with Judge Huling after the death of his first wife in 1848 until it was found again and sent back to Wharton in the later 1850s (photocopy from the journal, page 413, under the date July 25 [no year or volume indicated] in CRA).

51. This is the bridge "through whose framework we glanced with delight at the sparkling eddies of the river." *Journal,* April 5, 1832 (Rodabuagh [note 1], 144).

52. Probably William Young's wife, Kiera, and her sister.

53. Unfortunately, we do not know for certain where Wharton attended school in England.

54. Coal from the Lehigh Valley in Pennsylvania was brought to New York by way of the Delaware & Hudson Canal, built between 1825 and 1828, and entered the Hudson at Kingston.

55. The Highland School for Boys in Garrison, NY, across from West Point, opened in 1830; William Cullen Bryant, *Highlands Sketches: the Hudson River in the Eye of the Beholder* (Nelsonville, NY: Mount Taurus Press, 1993), 80.

56. This view of *New York, from Brooklyn Heights* (after a work by John William Hill, and thought to date from 1836, but clearly here demonstrated as being known in 1832) is in Bennet's series of American city views. See Groce and Wallace, *Dictionary of Artists in America* (note 19).

57. Fort Putnam, an old redoubt built in 1778 and partially restored between 1907 and 1910.

58. 1 Thessalonians 5: 21.

59. Sully painted a series of presidential portraits for West Point, including full-length versions of Thomas Jefferson and James Monroe, now on display in the Haig Room in Jefferson Hall of the USMA. Charles Henry Hart, *A Register of Portraits Painted by Thomas Sully, 1801–1871* (Philadelphia: n.p., 1909), 121, no. 1210. See also "Dawson Tells Some of the Secrets of Restoring Old Masters," *New York Times*, March 27, 1910.

60. The only graduate of the USMA named Smith who was a captain in 1832 was Henry Smith, and Cullum's *Register* has him fighting in the Black Hawk War at the Battle of Bad Axe River on August 2, and then shifting to engineer duty in January 1833. It is likely therefore that he was back at West Point after the war for reassignment.

61. To support President Monroe (his father-in-law), S.L. Gouverneur defended the propriety of the First Seminole War (1814–19), in which Monroe had dispatched Gen. Andrew Jackson to recapture runaway slaves in Seminole lands. In the process, Jackson demonstrated his ruthlessness and also exceeded his initial mandate by also seizing the Spanish towns of Pensacola and St. Marks. See biographies of both Jackson and Monroe, but also David S. Heidler, "The Politics of National Aggression: Congress and the First Seminole War," *Journal of the Early Republic* 13, no. 4 (1993): 501–530, and Milton Meltzer, *Hunted Like a Wolf: The Story of the Seminole War* (1972; rpt. Sarasota, FL: Pineapple Press, 2004).

62. This drawing, or likely a painting made from it, was exhibited at the NAD in 1834, where one reviewer said of it, "This little picture is hung so high that it is hardly possible to judge correctly of its value; it struck us however, as being rather lumpy, and wanting in the rich varieties of both shade and color which are so conspicuous in our Highland color." Meanwhile, in the same show, his "Landscape" was noted as a "very clever little picture." See "Miscellaneous Notices of the Fine Arts, Literature, Science, Drama &c.," *The American Monthly Magazine* 3, no. 4 (June 1, 1834): 281–286 at 284, nos. 106 and 116. The rock formation known Saint Anthony's Face (not to be confused with Anthony's Nose, the mountain to the south) existed on Breakneck Ridge until its destruction by quarrying in the later nineteenth century.

63. "For just as by the one man's disobedience the many were made sinners, so by the one man's obedience the many will be made righteous," Romans 5: 19 [NRSV].

64. The letter survives in the Thayer Papers; see November 8, 1832 in Cindy Adams (ed.), *The West Point Thayer Papers, 1808–1872* (West Point, NY: USMA Association of Graduates, 1965). The editors of those papers misidentified "Wharton" in the letter as "Possibly reference to Walter V. Wheaton, USMA post surgeon during cholera epidemic of 1832."

65. The Good Clerk of Copmanhurst is a character from *Ivanhoe* by Sir Walter Scott.

66. "And these will go away into eternal punishment, but the righteous into eternal life," Matthew 25: 46 [NRSV].

67. This may be Encke's Comet, which appeared in 1832.

68. Charles Davies, *A Treatise on Shades and Shadows and Linear Perspective* (New York: J. & J. Harper, 1832). The "Treatise on Optics" could be any number of works, but

likely either Henry Coddington, *An Elementary Treatise on Optics* (Cambridge, UK: J. Smith for J. Deighton & Sons, 1825) or Sir David Brewster, *A Treatise on Optics* (London: Longman, Rees, Orme, Brown & Green and John Taylor, 1831).

69. A letter survives from Kemble to Wharton at West Point dated November 18, 1832 that clearly shows Kemble as the driving influence in the design. Kemble says, "I send a draft of the church, and a pretty dirty one it is. But it may answer your purpose to run over the lines and the paper can be cleaned afterwards," (Alice Campbell, a great-grandniece of Gouv. Kemble, to WKS, photocopy in CRA). Wharton, then, presumably put Kemble's sketch into formal orders and gave sufficient information for builders to construct the chapel.

70. Originally known as St. John's Square, it was a park on the west side bounded by Laight Street on the north and Beach Street on the south (the later now known as Ericsson Place, as the inventor John Ericsson of USS *Monitor* fame lived here right next to the Kembles, and the West Point Foundry had its steam engine shops at the foot of Beach Street at the Hudson), and Hudson and Varick on the west and east, respectively. It is now the point where the Holland Tunnel disgorges onto Manhattan streets.

71. Characters in Lawrence Sterne's *Tristram Shandy*. The original oil on canvas is properly titled "A Scene from Tristram Shandy ('Uncle Toby and the Widow Wadman')" (1829–30; original now at the Tate Gallery, London, acc. N00403). This must be a copy, as the Tate copy was back in the UK by 1847 and probably returned with Leslie when he resigned the post of drawing master at West Point in 1834. Gouverneur Kemble's copy remained in the family after his death in 1875, and it was exhibited at the 1893 Columbian Exhibition in Chicago.

72. Robert Walter Weir, "Bay of Naples" (ca. 1830; Boston Museum of Fine Arts, acc. 1993.71).

73. Probably Robert Walter Weir, "The Fountain of Cicero" (1829; private collection).

74. William Sidney Mount, "Long Island Farmer Husking Corn" (1834; Long Island Museum, Stony Brook, NY, acc. 1975.016.0008). Wharton must be misremembering how early he saw this painting at Kemble's, as it had not been painted yet where this entry falls in the journal.

75. This must be Cole's "Aqueduct Near Rome" (1832; Washington University, St. Louis, MO, acc. WU1987.4), not to be confused with his later "Roman Campagna" (1843; Wadsworth Athenaeum, Hartford, CT, acc. 1948.189).

76. A hotel built in the 1750s; see "Another Landmark Going. The Old Walton House on Pearl-Street to be Demolished," *New York Times*, March 22, 1871, 8, and Robert H. Gibbons, "The Walton House," *New York Times*, December 2, 1904, 8.

77. This was a sort of after-hours reading and discussion club at the Flushing Institute. From "eunomia," the Greek word for "good order." Eunomian societies were common social clubs in nineteenth-century colleges.

78. Latin for "Behold the oak," playing on ideas of "from little acorns grow mighty oaks."

79. "As he spoke through the mouth of his holy prophets from of old," Luke 1: 70 [NRSV]. The quotation is Psalms 90: 9.

80.

> Come now, you who say, 'Today or tomorrow we will go to such and such a town and spend a year there, doing business and making money.' Yet you do

not even know what tomorrow will bring. What is your life? For you are a mist that appears for a little while and then vanishes. Instead you ought to say, 'If the Lord wishes, we will live and do this or that.' As it is, you boast in your arrogance; all such boasting is evil. Anyone, then, who knows the right thing to do and fails to do it, commits sin. James 4: 13–17 [NRSV].

81. This is the historic Bowne house. Thomas Bowne was a Quaker who defied Peter Stuyvesant and by so doing gained religious freedom for the Quakers in the colony of New York. It was the founder of the Society of Friends George (not Thomas) Fox, who preached under the oaks in June of 1672: "The Fox Oaks were two in number and stood near each other. One of them fell on the twenty-fifth of October 1841, and the other in the year 1863. A stone, near the sidewalk, on the west side of Bowne Avenue, opposite the Bowne house, marks their site." Henry D. Waller, *History of the Town of Flushing* (Flushing, NY: J.H. Ridenour, 1899; rpt. Harrison, NY: Harbor Hill Books, 1975), 70.

82. Parker and Clover was a frame shop that served as a "prominent . . . outlet" for art in New York; see Malcolm Goldstein, *Landscape with Figures: A History of Art Dealing in the United States* (Oxford: Oxford University Press, 2000), 18.

83. Wharton seems to have meant the firm of Anthony and Gabriel A. Arnoux at 145 Fulton Street. (*The New York City Directory, for 1842 and 1843* [New York: John Dogget, Jr., 1842], 17).

84. Samuel Hicks, merchant, 80 South Street (ibid.).

85. Possibly Thomas Shaw Bancroft Reade, *Christian Experience as Displayed in the Life and Writings of Saint Paul* (London: Hamilton, Adams & Co, 1832) or an earlier edition of Robert Philip, *Christian Experience; or a Guide to the Perplexed* (London: Book Society for Promoting Religious Knowledge, 1833).

86. "I passed by the field of one who was lazy, by the vineyard of a stupid person; and see, it was all overgrown with thorns; the ground was covered with nettles, and its stone wall was broken down. Then I saw and considered it; I looked and received instruction. A little sleep, a little slumber, a little folding of the hands to rest, and poverty will come upon you like a robber, and want, like an armed warrior," Proverbs 24: 30–34 [NRSV]. Ecclesiastes 11: 1 is on the value of diligence: "Send out your bread upon the waters, for after many days you will get it back."

87. Many of these men are identified in Hall Harrison, *The Life of the Right Reverend John Barrett Kerfoot, D.D., LL.D., first Bishop of Pittsburgh* (New York: J. Pott, 1886), 11–12, 57. Kerfoot in his diary makes no mention of Wharton, probably because Wharton was not headed for ordination and must have been "merely" the drawing and geometry instructor.

88. A reference to the "Spring" section of James Thomson's "The Seasons" (1726); see *The Poetical Works of James Thomson* (Boston: Little, Brown and Co., 1854), 2: 10–11.

89. The "infidel" David Hume was the celebrated skeptical philosopher and historian, author of *Dialogues on Natural Religion* (London, Geneva, and Edinburgh, 1779).

90. Rev. Samuel Charles Wilkes, *Christian Essays* 2nd ed. (London: J. Hatchard & Son, 1828), 1–57, originally published in the *Christian Observer* and also in *The Religious Magazine, or Spirit of the Foreign Theological Journals and Reviews* 1, no. 3 (March 1828): 201–212.

91. From the Greek "eumathes," meaning "quick at learning." This seems to have been a society for the instructors at the Institute. See note 76, above, and see Anne Ayres, *The Life and Work of William Augustus Muhlenberg* (New York: Harper & Brothers 1880), 106.

92. Timothy Dwight, *Sermons* (New Haven, CT: Hezekiah Howe and Durrie & Peck, 1828), 1: 515–534, sermon 28. Dwight, grandson of Jonathan Edwards and president of Yale from 1795 to 1817, delivered a series of 173 sermons printed as *Theology Explained and Defended* (Middletown, CT: Clark and Lyman, 1818–19).

93. Acts 27: 13.

94. Rev. Samuel Seabury, *The Efficacy of a Mother's Prayers; Illustrated in the conversion and labors of Augustine, bishop of Hippo. A narrative delivered in the chapel of the Institute at Flushing, L.I.* (New York: Protestant Episcopal Press, 1833).

95. This probably refers to Thomas Dick, a Scottish astronomer known for fusing science and Christian philosophy. It is unclear which work Wharton is referring to here, as Dick's *Practical Astronomer* did not appear until 1845 (London: Seeley, Burnside, & Seeley; New York: Harper & Brothers, 1846), but it may likely be the first or second edition of Elijah H. Burritt, *The Geography of the Heavens, and Class Book of Astronomy*, which Dick had edited for the third edition (Hartford, CT: F.J. Huntington, 1836).

96. Psalms 51: 4.

97. David Hume, *The History of England* (London: A. Millar, 1754–61) and subsequent editions.

98. "Moreover by them is your servant warned; in keeping them there is great reward," Psalms 19: 11 [NRSV].

99. Thomas C. Doremus went into partnership with James Snydam in the 1820s and they built a large dry goods business on Pearl Street.

100. Wharton is probably referring to "Expulsion from the Garden of Eden" (1828; Boston Museum of Fine Arts, acc. 47.1188) and "The Subsiding Waters of the Deluge" (1829; Smithsonian Museum of American Art, acc. 1983.40), both of which were purchased by Hosack and inspired by the tortured landscapes of the mid-Hudson, though they would hardly be considered Catskill mountain scenes.

101. Thayer was to leave West Point on June 9, 1833, his birthday, famously setting a routine of visiting the steamboats in the evening for several weeks and then, one evening, unexpectedly and without notice or baggage, simply boarding a boat and disappearing down the river. For the full story, see James W. Kershner, *Sylvanus Thayer: A Biography* (New York: Arno Press, 1982).

102. *The New York Evening Mirror*, founded in 1831 by George Pope Morris and Nathaniel Parker Willis.

103. Wharton's view of New York from Brooklyn Heights was published in the *New-York Mirror*, April 19, 1834. A view of the Washington Monument in Baltimore appeared in the *New-York Mirror*, July 4, 1835. The twelve Ohio views, which were never printed in Wharton's lifetime, are preserved in the NYPL Prints and Drawings Division (see chapter 6).

104. Wharton subsequently did exhibit a painting of "The Falls of Indian Brook, opposite West Point," at the NAD show in 1835, of which only a sketch survives (see *Journal*, August 12, 1834).

105. "Go therefore and make disciples of all nations, baptizing them in the name of the Father and of the Son and of the Holy Spirit, and teaching them to obey everything that I have commanded you. And remember, I am with you always, to the end of the age," Matthew 28: 19–20 [NRSV].

106. Richard Baxter, *A Call to the Unconverted*, introduction by Thomas Chalmers (Philadelphia: Presbyterian Board of Publication, 1825), and subsequent editions. Baxter was a prominent and controversial English Puritan divine and originally wrote *A Call* in 1657.

107. Claude-Marie-Paul Dubufe (French, 1790–1864) *Adam and Eve* (1927). This show was at the American Academy of Fine Arts, in Barclay Street, established in 1808. See Kendal B. Taft, "*Adam and Eve* in America," *Art Quarterly* 22 (1960): 171–179 and Carrie Rehora Barratt, "Mapping the Venues: New York City Art Exhibitions," in Catherine Hoover Voorsanger and John K. Howat (eds.), *Art and the Empire City: New York, 1825–1861* (New Haven, CT: Yale University Press, 2000), 47–82 at 55–56.

108. Perhaps Edward Young (1683–1765), *Night Thoughts on Life, Death, and Immortality* (New York: Richard Scott, 1816).

109. William Sidney Mount, "Bishop Benjamin T. Onderdonk (1791–1861)" (ca. 1830–1833; formerly in the chapel of Columbia College [University], now New-York Historical Society, acc. 1953.71).

110. The General Society of Mechanics and Tradesmen of the City of New York, founded in 1785, which, from 1820, had a lending library on Chatham Street.

111. 1 Corinthians 1: 18.

112. Frances Trollope's tour and her book, *Domestic Manners of the Americans,* which had reached the public in March 1832, caused a great stir.

113. Now Clermont Manor State Historic Site. The estate was known as Miramont, and is now the central third of the Bard College campus. These islands are part of what is now called Tivoli Bays, the river to the east of the rail line having partially silted in since its construction.

114. This is the Ulster Iron Works, incorporated in 1831, with Young as president and manager, and William Kemble as the New York agent. In 1834, it consumed 3,100 tons of pig iron and 100,000 bushels of bituminous coal from Virginia. The next year, it employed 150 men and was said to have "embrace[d] all the recent improvements in the manufacture of iron and is believed to be the most complete in the United States." It had a large refinery with the "powerful blast cylinder" and four-and-a-half-ton forge hammer that Wharton notes, ten puddling furnaces and the rolling mill powdered by two water wheels. It could produce weekly one hundred tons of first-quality merchant iron in "all shapes and sizes of iron, viz. flat, round, half round, oval, square, hoops, bands, boiler plate, &c." Edwin Williams, *The New York Annual Register* (New York: J. Leavitt, 1830), 146.

115. Trap rock is an intrusive igneous rock, like that of the Palisades.

116. Wharton uses this term three times to refer to the camshaft. Otherwise an unattested term, his hand is quite clear here.

117. This and the extract that follows are paraphrases from Plato, *The Republic,* bk. 10.

118. Paraphrase of Ezekiel 18: 21, perhaps from a popular sermon of the day.

119. The Catskill Mountain House (above Palenville, NY; closed 1941; burned 1963) was the jewel of the mountain hotels in this period, and Wharton had previously mentioned seeing it at a distance through Dr. Hosack's telescope. At first it possessed a continuous high porch typical of the early spa hotels. For more information, see Roland Van Zandt, *The Catskill Mountain House* (New Brunswick, NJ: Rutgers University Press, 1966).

120. Washington Irving, *The Complete Works of Washington Irving* (Paris: Baudry's European Library, 1843), 329.

121. This number, championed by the Mountain House's second owner, Charles Beach, has long passed into lore as the hotel's elevation, though it is actually only 2,250 feet above sea level.

122. Paraphrase of Milton, *Paradise Lost,* 5.140–142. Lines 136–143 read, "But first from under shadie arborous roof, / Soon as they forth were come to open sight / Of day-

spring, and the Sun, who scarce up risen / With wheels yet hov'ring o're the Ocean brim, / Shot parallel to the earth his dewie ray, / Discovering in wide Lantskip all the East / Of Paradise and Edens happie Plains."

123. The circular temple of Vesta, more often known as the Temple of the Sybil, overlooks the Falls of Tivoli.

124. James Stuart called it a "capital hotel . . . [with] one of the best breakfasts I ever saw. . . . [T]he house being large and well kept, affords great temptation to strangers to pass some time here in a quiet cool situation." James Stuart, *Three Years in North America* (1833; Carlisle, MA: Applewood Books, 2007), 1: 467–468.

125. The First Reformed Dutch Church, which Wharton saw, was built about 1784. The New York Provincial Convention met in the first church (built 1736) from September 5, 1776 to February 11, 1777, before moving to Kingston.

126. William Collins, "The Passions, an Ode to Music," in Collins, *Odes on Several Descriptive and Allegoric Subjects* (London: A. Millar, 1747), ll. 62–63.

Chapter 3: Return to the Northeast, 1853

1. A servant? It is unknown whether the Whartons had any enslaved people, though certainly Wharton's father-in-law did at his plantation downriver in Plaquemines Parish.

2. St. Vincent's Seminary and College (1843–1902) was established as one of the first colleges west of the Mississippi. Robert Sidney Douglass, *History of Southeast Missouri* (Chicago: Lewis Publishing Company, 1912), 1: 413–418.

3. Planter's House was the first luxury hotel in St. Louis, opened in 1841 with 150 lavish rooms. The courthouse, designed and built by Col. Joseph C. Laveille, was begun in 1826 but grew to five times its original intended size by the time it was completed in 1861. Wharton passed by it during its second reconstruction and remodeling, when the entire east wing was torn down and rebuilt.

4. A gentle slope. The term derives from fortification where the land outside the walls was cleared of trees and gently sloped away so that the defenders had a clear field of fire against attackers. Wharton probably learned this concept at West Point.

5. The Kingsbury Hotel, on Summit near Walnut Street, opened as the Ohio House in 1847 and changed names in 1852.

6. Wharton must have visited sometime between 1835 and 1843, as he mentions when he was on his way to Ohio when he first arrived in the US that "we must pass them by this time, and trust to a propitious future," *Journal*, July 8, 1830 (James H. Rodabaugh, "From England to Ohio, 1830–1832: The Journal of Thomas K. Wharton," *The Ohio Historical Quarterly* 65, no. 1 [1956]: 1–27 at 25 and continues in 65, no. 2 [1956]: 111–151). For a contemporary relation of visiting the falls area at that time, see "A Visit to Niagara," *The Living Age* 25, no. 2 (November 1844): 37–40, wherein the anonymous writer relates the town, then mostly owned by one development company, was still "meager" and under development, though the hotels "crowded with visitors . . . making the *grand tour*" (37).

7. The 1844 anonymous traveler reported that, indeed, at Goat Island, "a pontage [bridge-fee] is levied of 2*s*., and your name registered, while refreshments, guide-books, Indian articles, &c. all court your acquaintance at the expense of your purse" (ibid., 39).

8. John A. Roebling of Brooklyn Bridge fame built the world's first rail suspension bridge over the Niagara gorge just downstream (north) of the falls, but this famous one

was not opened to traffic until 1855. Wharton must have seen Roebling's temporary bridge (built 1848) and the construction work on the permanent bridge. William R. Irwin, *The New Niagara: Tourism, Technology, and the Landscape of Niagara Falls, 1776–1917* (University Park: Pennsylvania State University Press, 1996).

9. Wharton is describing the first monument to British general Isaac Brock, which was built on Queenston Heights in 1823–24. Its capital was partially demolished by an explosion in 1840, apparently set by anti-British domestic rebels. Construction on a second monument took place from 1853–56. Brock and his aide-de-camp were interred in both monuments' bases.

10. Now Niagara-on-the-Lake, Ontario.

11. A reference to Milton, *Paradise Lost*, I. 299–304: "he so endur'd, till on the Beach / Of that inflamed Sea, he stood and call'd / His Legions, Angel Forms, who lay intrans't / Thick as Autumnal Leaves that strow the Brooks / In Vallombrosa, where th' Etrurian shades / High overarch't imbowr."

12. That is, the Old North Church of Paul Revere fame.

13. The Hancock House, which stood to the west of the State House, was built in 1737 and demolished in 1863. See also Rebecca J. Bertrand, *Myth and Memory: The Legacy of the John Hancock House*, master's thesis, University of Delaware, 2010.

14. Albion Street ran between Dover and Castle streets (now E. Berkeley and Herald streets, just south of Interstate 90) one block east of Tremont in Boston's South End. In the early nineteenth century, the area, "although laid out into streets," was apparently slow to develop. But "beginning with the fifties it rapidly grew into a region of symmetrical blocks of high-shouldered, comfortable red brick or brownstone houses, bow-fronted and high-stooped, with mansard roofs, ranged along spacious avenues, intersected by cross parks, whose central gardens were enclosed by neat cast iron fences." Walter Muir Whitehill, *Boston: A Topographical History* (Cambridge, MA: Belknap Press, 1968), 122.

15. The Boston Athenaeum at 10½ Beacon Street was designed by Edward C. Cabot and built between 1847 and 1849. Enlarged and rebuilt in 1913, it still retains its original appearance from Beacon Street.

16. This great marble statue was begun in 1848 and sold to the Athenaeum in 1851, displayed early on in Philadelphia and New York, and was very rapidly recognized as one of the most important American sculptures of the day. "Brackett's Wreck," *The New American Whig Review* ns 9 (May 1852): 470; M.W.B., "The Shipwrecked Mother and Child," *The Ladies' Repository* 30 (September 1861): 118–119.

17. The only focused history of building is Stanley Clisby Arthur, *A History of the U.S. Custom House, New Orleans* ([New Orleans]: US Custom Service, Region V, [1984]), originally written for the Louisiana WPA in 1940.

18. By the British sculptor Sir Francis Chantrey.

19. See Robert Malcomson, *Burying General Brock: A History of Brock's Monuments* (Niagara-on-the-Lake, ON: Friends of Fort George, 1996).

20. For the general history of these Third System forts, including Thayer's work on Fort Warren on Georges Island and Fort Independence on Castle Island, see Jay Schmidt, *Fort Warren: New England's Most Historic Civil War Site* (Amherst, NH: Unified Business Technologies Press, 2003); Gerald Butler, *The Military History of Boston's Harbour Islands* (Charleston, SC: Arcadia Publishing, 2000); and "Fort Warren, Boston," *Harper's Weekly* 5, no. 258 (December 7, 1861): cover and 770. More generally, see Harry L. Hawthorne, "History of the Sea-Coast Fortifications of the United States. II. Boston Harbor," *Journal of*

the United States Artillery 6 (1896): 359–375 and Joseph E. Kaufmann, *Fortress America: The Forts That Defended America 1600 to the Present* (Cambridge, MA: Da Capo Press, 2004). See also Sylvanus Thayer, *A Special Report on the Sea Wall, Built in the Year 1843, for the Preservation of Ram Head at the Northwest End of Lovell's Island, in the Harbor of Boston, Massachusetts,* U.S. Engineer Dept. Papers on Practical Engineering no. 2 (Washington: W.Q. Force, 1844).

21. Various berries of the genus *Vaccinium,* which includes bilberries; much like blueberries.

22. This was the Old Feather Store (also known as the Old Cocked Hat) located at Dock Square and North (Ann) Street, stood in what is now the plaza to the west of Faneuil Hall. It was demolished in 1860.

23. The South Boston Bridge was close to Albion Street and in the 1850s still an attractive promenade. It is now the line of Berkeley Street through Back Bay.

24. The New South Church at the corner of Summer and Bedford streets was designed for the Unitarian Congregationalists by Charles Bulfinch in 1814. It is odd that Wharton would call it a Gothic building, as it was an octagonal first story, surmounted with a stacked steeple of square and octagonal section, and the windows are decidedly Romanesque.

25. Mount Auburn Cemetery was a popular place of pilgrimage for many years, combining, as it still does, beauty of landscaping and a place of burial for Boston's famous dead. Its 135 acres are "the oldest garden cemetery in the United States, . . . established in 1831 by the Massachusetts Horticultural Society in connection with an experimental garden." *King's Handbook of Boston,* 5th ed. (Cambridge, MA: Moses King Publisher, 1883), 232.

26. Ecclesiastes 12: 7.

27. Katherine Wolff, *Culture Club: The Curious History of the Boston Athenaeum* (Amherst: University of Massachusetts Press, 2009).

28. James Fenimore Cooper, *Lionel Lincoln; or, the Leaguer of Boston* (New York: Charles Wiley, 1825) is a historical novel.

29. The Salt Marsh, or Back Bay, would eventually be entirely filled in and become a fine residential district. Except for the railroad lines crossing it at different angles, at high tide it was, at the time of Wharton's visit, a sheet of water extending from the public garden all the way to Roxbury and Brookline.

30. "America" (also known as "My Country 'tis of Thee"), first sung in 1831, is set to the tune of "God Save the King."

31. This was the third of four Massachusetts Constitutional Conventions. See Lawrence B. Evans, "The Constitutional Convention of Massachusetts," *The American Political Science Review* 15, no. 2 (1921): 214–232.

32. "The Fine Arts and Public Taste in 1853," *Blackwood's Edinburgh Magazine* 74, no. 453 (July 1853): 89–104, takes issue with a great deal of John Ruskin's aesthetics.

33. "He scorns and hates it," which seems to be from one of Horace's *Epistles* VII.20.

34. This was the refrain from a popular song of the day, "The Wind and the Rain," by Charles Mackay.

35. Lawrence was second only to Lowell as an important and model industrial town in Massachusetts, but is unfortunately now most remembered for the great Bread and Roses strike of 1912. See Lawrence A. Peskin, *Manufacturing Revolution: The Intellectual Origins of Early American Industry* (Baltimore: John Hopkins University Press, 2007); Donald Cole, *Immigrant City: Lawrence, Massachusetts 1845–1921* (Chapel Hill: University of North

Carolina Press, 1963); and Ardis Cameron, *Radicals of the Worst Sort: Laboring Women in Lawrence, Massachusetts, 1860–1912* (Urbana: University of Illinois Press, 1995).

36. The reference here is to the successful social engineering experiment of Lowell, MA, where William Cabot Lowell built a series of factories that specifically employed women aged eighteen to twenty-two; provided them with housing, education, moral instruction, and reasonable pay; and then limited their length of employment in order to send well-educated and dexterous women out into society with a modest savings. These mill girls were eventually pushed out by new (male) immigrants, who demanded longer-term employment and, incidentally, would initially work for less. See Laurence F. Gross, *The Course of Industrial Decline: the Boott Cotton Mills of Lowell, Massachusetts, 1835–1955* (Baltimore: Johns Hopkins University Press, 1993) and Jeff Levinson, *Mill Girls of Lowell* (Boston: History Compass, 2007).

37. The great reservoir built to contain the pure water flowing through the Cochituate aqueduct from Long Pond (which Wharton would visit as well) had only opened five years before and was one of the most notable civil engineering works in the country at the time. See Michael Rawson, *Eden on the Charles: The Making of Boston* (Cambridge, MA: Harvard University Press, 2010), chapter 2. Although he is not explicit about it, many of Wharton's visits to Jamaica Pond (the city's previous aqueduct source) and Fresh Pond (which fed the Cochituate) around greater Boston seem to be out of interest in the waterworks for the city.

38. See "Winship Nursery," *The Country Gentleman* 1, no. 25 (June 23, 1853): 391.

39. "Fernhill," the Watertown, MA estate of Col. William P. Winchester, was a Palladian-inspired five-bay classical revival mansion built in 1849–50 by Arthur Gilman, noted Boston architect and proponent of filling and developing Back Bay. Roger G. Reed, *Building Victorian Boston: The Architecture of Gridley F. Bryant* (Amherst: University of Massachusetts Press, 2006), 120–121.

40. A reference to Macbeth's soliloquy in *Macbeth*, act 1, scene 8.

41. Bryant's addition to the State House was on the northern side. It had to be removed when the Brigham addition in yellow brick was made in about 1893. Walter H. Kilham, *Boston after Bulfinch: An Account of its Architecture 1800–1900* (Cambridge, MA: Harvard University Press, 1946), 66.

42. In 1854, the granite quarries in Quincy employed about 1,000 people and did a trade of about $500,000. Dr. Dugan, "Commercial and Industrial Cities of the U. States. Number Xl: The Town of Quincy in Massachusetts," *Hunt's Merchant Magazine and Commercial Review* 33 (1850): 303–313 at 313.

43. Presumably Samuel Stillman Greene, *First Lessons in Grammar, Based upon the Construction and Analysis of Sentences* (Philadelphia: Cowperthwait, Desilver, and Butler, 1848).

44. Acts 10: 43.

45. The Winthrop House was a hotel on the lower three levels, and the Scottish Rite Masonic Temple was on the upper three. It was located at the corner of Tremont and Boylston at the corner of the Common, and was destroyed by fire in 1864.

46. Harriet Beecher Stowe's most celebrated book, *Uncle Tom's Cabin*, had appeared in 1852. Its immediate success thrust her into national and, indeed, international prominence. Her husband, Calvin Ellis Stowe, a prominent educator and scholar, was in 1853 professor of sacred literature at the Andover Theological Seminary. "Mrs. Stowe had not foreseen the storm of wrath which *Uncle Tom* was to evoke. In the South, her name was hated. . . . The

Southern Literary Messenger declared the book a 'criminal prostitution of the high functions of the imagination,' saying that the author had 'placed herself without the pale of kindly treatment at the hands of Southern criticism.'" (DAB)

47. This must have been a false rumor reaching Wharton: Dr. Warren Stone of New Orleans was one of Louisiana's greatest antebellum surgeons and had founded the New Orleans charity hospital in 1839. He was also one of the first to use ether as an anesthetic, but he did not die until 1872 (*Queen of the South*, 14 n. 18).

48. The goddesses of flowers and fruit trees, respectively. They were a popular motif deriving from the story of the nymphs Pomona and Vertumnus by Orpheus (see Padraic Colum, *Orpheus: Myths of the World* [New York: Macmillan, 1930], 119–122). A generation later they would become standard bearers for the Aesthetic Movement under William Morris.

49. A giant water lily whose floating, two-meter-wide leaves can support 30 kilograms, or 70 pounds; its flower opened and closed daily and was the wonder of Boston and other cities.

50. The church was chartered in 1849, and William Aspinwall and Harrison Fay obtained plans for the gothic church from Richard Upjohn, the architect of Trinity Church in New York and later of Rev. Muhlenberg's St. Paul's College at College Point, NY. The cornerstone was laid in July 1851 and the church completed by the end of 1852. Robert Payne Bigelow, *A Sketch of the History of St. Paul's Church in Brookline* (Brookline, MA: n.p., 1949), 1–3.

51. The Boston Museum on Tremont Street was designed by Hammatt Billings in 1846 and became a Barnum-esque collection of what it claimed was the largest collection of wax figures in the United States in 1850, though it also contained serious zoological and botanical exhibitions. Mssrs. Bowen and Doyle had opened a similar museum on Tremont forty years before (*Boston Democrat*, November 22, 1806).

52. Extract of taraxacum is made from dandelions (*Taraxacum officinale*) and is a mild laxative. "Blue Mass" was a generic term for preparations prepared variably by each pharmacist, but all contained either mercury or mercury chloride (calomel).

53. A spring on Mount Parnassus, hence source of poetic inspiration. We never do find out the identity of the mysterious and colorful lady poet.

54. The poem comes from Peter Pindar, "Peter's Prophesy; or the President and Poet," in *The Works of Peter Pindar* (Philadelphia: M. Walis Woodward & Co., 1835), 284.

55. John Ruskin, *Modern Painters: Their superiority in the art of landscape painting to all the ancient masters, proved by examples of the true, the beautiful, and the intellectual from the works of modern artists, especially from those of J.M.W. Turner*, 5 vol. (London: Smith, Elder, and Co., 1843).

56. A cloister vault (*voute de clótre*) of ovoid section and rising equally from all four sides of the space enclosed. It is in effect a squared oval dome.

57. The Boston *Investigator* newspaper (1831–1904) was "devoted to the development and promotion of universal mental liberty." At this time, it was edited by Horace Seaver, a known freethinker, champion of the working classes, and a secular reformer in the rather staunch Protestantism of Boston. See Mary Kupiec Cayton, "Toward a Democratic Politics of Meaning-Making: The Transcendentalist Controversy and the Rise of Pluralist Discourse in Jacksonian Boston," *Prospects* 25 (2000): 35–68.

58. Mary Kupiec Cayton, "Who Were the Evangelicals? Conservative and Liberal Identity in the Unitarian Controversy in Boston, 1804–1833," *Journal of Social History* 31, no.

1 (1997): 85–107 and Conrad Edick Wright, *American Unitarianism, 1805–1865* (Boston: Massachusetts Historical Society, 1989).

59. Trinity Church, destroyed in the Boston Fire of 1872.

60. Probably the South Congregationalist Church (Congregationalist Unitarian) at Washington and Castle streets, founded in 1827, whose minister was Frederic D. Huntington (1819–1904).

61. Strictly speaking the *megatherium* was an elephant-sized ground sloth of Central and South America, but it was the then generic term for mastodon/mammoth fossils that were all the rage among scientific circles. The classic example of the mania was the unearthing of a full mastodon skeleton near Newburgh, NY in 1799, immortalized by a painting of the event by Charles Wilson Peale, who was present and directed the excavation.

62. This seems to be a poem of Wharton's own composition.

63. Probably the South Boston Foundry, founded by Cyrus Alger in 1809, which was where the South Station rail switching yards west of Foundry Street and north of W. 4th Street are today.

64. Though it sounds like he is describing a youth, it is worth remembering that Emily Ladd Wharton is only eighteen years old at this point. Wharton himself was thirty-nine.

65. The street plan for the Back Bay was not adopted until 1856, and contracts for the commencement of this vast undertaking were not signed until the summer of 1858.

66. Saint Paul's Church, conspicuous for its portico of Greek Ionic columns, stands on Tremont Street facing the Boston Common. Since 1908 it has been the Cathedral of the Episcopal Diocese of Massachusetts. Walter Muir Whitehill, *Boston: A Topographical History* (Cambridge, MA: Belknap Press, 1968), 244.

67. A Congregationalist Trinitarian church, founded 1835, and the minister was Rev. George Richards.

68. A public house at 71 Lincoln Street, C. Whitney, proprietor.

69. George W[atson] Prescott and Jonathan Prescott, Boston, MA, "Machine for reducing wood to slivers," US Patent no. 10,893, May 9, 1854, which shaved wood so that it "shall possess the greatest degree of elasticity possible. The wood, being reduced by cutters set obliquely in their stocks, all the material removed is consequently curled in long helices." The 1870 Prescott genealogy says that the excelsior machine, "abundantly supplied . . . the country . . . of late with this neat and useful article." The "old Gentleman" to whom Wharton refers is his grandfather-in-law, Jonathan Prescott. William Prescott, *The Prescott Memorial: or, a genealogical memoir of the Prescott families in America* (Boston: H.W. Dutton & Son, 1870), 84, no. 417.

70. J.M.W. Turner and Leitch Ritchie, *The Rivers of France*, introduction by John Ruskin (London: Longman, Rees, Orme, Brown, Green & Longman, 1837).

71. This passage was noted by Roger Reed, *Building Victorian Boston: The Architecture of Gridley J.F. Bryant* (Amherst: University of Massachusetts Press, 2007), 123–124.

72. The Germania Musical Society was a short-lived (1848–1854) but important classical musical group whose musicians emigrated from Germany after a successful tour of England. During their years of touring, which ended abruptly as the musicians decided to settle in one place, the society gave more than nine hundred concerts to over a million audience members.

73. P.T. Barnum commissioned the Austrian-American architect Leopold Eidlitz to build a Moorish Revival mansion, known as "Iranistan," in Bridgeport, CT in 1848.

74. On May 6, 1853, the engine, tender, two baggage cars, and two passenger cars of a northbound New York express train plunged off the open span of the swing bridge at

Norwalk, CT, killing forty-four people. Ships had right-of-way to open the bridge and trains had to pause, but the bridge superintendent apparently failed to hoist the warning signal (a red ball), indicating the draw was open. "The Norwalk Catastrophe," *New York Times*, May 9, 1853, May 1 and 11, 1853, 1.

75. The St. Nicholas had only opened in January 1853 and displaced the Astor as the most opulent hotel in New York City. It took up most of the block on the west side of Broadway between Broome and Spring streets (across from where Bloomingdale's is today). "The Lost 1853 St. Nicholas Hotel," *Daytonian in Manhattan*, February 31, 2012, http://daytoninmanhattan.blogspot.com/2012/02/lost-1853-st-nicholas-hotel-broadway.html; accessed May 10, 2014.

76. This probably refers to Niblo's Theatre and Concert Room and the new Metropolitan Hotel on the northeast corner of Broadway and Prince Street. William Niblo had built Niblo's Gardens and Theatre on that block in 1828, but the theatre burned in 1846, was rebuilt in 1849, and the hotel erected on the site of the gardens (the western half of the block) in 1852. Gerald Bordman and Thomas S. Hischak, *The Oxford Companion to American Theatre*, 3rd ed. (Oxford: Oxford University Press, 2004), 461.

77. Grace Church, at the head of lower Broadway near 10th Street, replaced the earlier Grace Church, which stood on Broadway just south of Trinity Street. Completed in 1848, it made the reputation of its young architect, James Renwick, Jr.

78. Families such as the Astors and Delanos lived on Lafayette Place in the 1840s and '50s.

79. New York University in Washington Square. That Wharton could judge the names on the name plates suggests that he was friendly with the university professors back in the 1830s.

80. The Crystal Palace, a glass and iron exhibition building consisting of four "naves" dominated by a central dome and flanked by numerous "courts," stood in the block that is now Bryant Park and the New York Public Library between 40th and 42nd streets and 5th and 6th avenues. Opened in 1853, it was destroyed in a fire five years later.

81. "Eve after her Transgression," by "Pagani of Milan" (probably Pelagio Pagani, 1775–1860) was in the Austrian exhibition. The group of sculptures at the focal center of the exhibition under the central dome by the American sculptor, Hiram Powers (1805–1873), consisted of four works brought together from a number of owners: another "Eve," the "Fisher Boy," the "Greek Slave," and a bust of Proserpine. Their tranquil and delicate effect were like "that of a mountain-girded lake, sleeping in the serene beauty of sunset" compared to the bold "Amazon" group next to it by the Berlin sculptor, August Kiss (1802–1865), which affected the viewer like "that which is experienced in . . . the contemplation of an ocean tempest." William C. Richards, *A Day in the New York Crystal Palace Exhibition and How to Make the Most of It* (New York: G.P. Putnam & Sons, 1853), 12–13, 21.

82. These have not been identified in the few Thompson papers that survive at Columbia University (Pers. comm, Jason Escalante, Avery Drawings & Archives, Columbia University, August 14, 2013).

83. North American rail gauge was not standardized at 4 ft. by 8½ in. until the Civil War, and each rail line was free to set its rails at whatever width it chose. This also prevented companies' rolling stock, whether passenger or freight, from running on another company's rails.

84. There is no "American" restaurant or hotel listed in *Williams' Cincinnati Directory, City Guide, and Business Mirror* (Cincinnati: C.S. Williams, 1853); Wharton may mean the United States Hotel at 6th and Walnut.

85. The Burnet House hotel, Abraham Coleman, proprietor, was built in Cincinnati, OH on the land owned by one of the pioneers of the Ohio Valley, Judge Jacob Burnet (one "t"). When this 340-room, $250,000 hotel designed by Isaiah Rogers opened in 1850, it was considered one of the finest hotels in the world and compared to the Tremont House in Boston and the Astor Hotel in New York. Molly W. Berger, *Hotel Dreams: Luxury, Technology, and Urban Ambition in America, 1829–1929* (Baltimore: Johns Hopkins University Press, 2011), 247–248; Blanche Lindow and Zane L. Miller, "Queen City History: The Burnet House and the Central Business District," *Cincinnati Magazine* 9, no. 8 (July 1976): 16–17.

86. 1 Corinthians 13: 7.

87. Literally, "A grove (is so called) for not giving light." It might here be applied to the falls as "a falls in name only." To the *lucus e non* principle . . . are referred all such paradoxical derivations and descriptions which involve a contradiction in the mere stating of them. See W.F.H. King, *Classical and Foreign Quotations* (New York: Frederick Ungar, 1958).

88. Cannelton cotton mill was designed by Thomas Alexander Tefft and built between 1849–1851. Wharton was mistaken about the Boston ownership as the mill was developed and financed mostly through money from Louisville, though it was to try to rival the textile mills in Lowell and Lawrence, MA.

89. The snippet is from the song "The Passionate Shepherd to his Love," sung by Sir Henry Evans in Shakespeare's *The Merry Wives of Windsor*, act 3, scene 1.

90. It is from this practice the Samuel Clemens—who began his career as a Mississippi River boatman—took the pen name of "Mark Twain" a decade later.

91. "Not all do the orchards please and the lowly tamarisks," Virgil, *Eclogue* 4, no. 2.

92. Dr. Julius Samson was apparently rather full of himself, as the following story from the *Weekly Alta California* [San Francisco], July 22, 1854, 1, the following year illustrates:

> The very best joke of the fortnight has been told of Dr. Julius Samson, Consul for Brunswick and Lünenberg, at Mobile, who, upon being on a visit to the military encampment at Camp Walton, was rudely set upon by some riotous boys, who affixed crackers to his coat-tails and set them on fire. Hugely indignant at such an outrage, he demanded personal and national satisfaction, which, not being forthcoming, he appealed to the Prussian Minister at Washington for redress. According to a telegraphic dispatch . . . very serious, results have followed. The Minister, having expressed to Mr. [William L.] Marcy [the U.S. Secretary of State at the time] the strongest indignation, especially at the grossness of the insult implied, in pinning Chinese crackers to the Consul's breeches, our Secretary construed the reference to "breeches" into a personal reflection on himself, whereupon he kicked Mr. Prussia out of doors. This event has greatly complicated the difficulty, and how or when the affair will terminate, none can say—being endless from the start.

93. See Jo Ann Carrigan, "Yellow Fever in New Orleans, 1853: Abstractions and Realities," *Journal of Southern History* 25, no. 3 (1959): 339–355.

Chapter 4: Biographical Register

1. John Fisk Allen, *Victoria Regia; or the Great Water Lily of America* (Boston: Dutton & Wentworth, 1854); Tatiana Holway, *The Flower of Empire: An Amazonian Water Lily,*

the Quest to Make It Bloom, and the World It Created (New York: Oxford University Press, 2013).

2. John Smith Kendall, *History of New Orleans* (Chicago: Lewis Publishing Company, 1922), 988–989.

3. *The Boston Directory for the Year 1853* (Boston: George Adams, 1853), 27.

4. *Journal of the Proceedings of the Fifty-Second Convention of the Protestant Episcopal Church in the State of New-York* (New York: Protestant Episcopal Press, 1837), 52.

5. Gloria-Gilda Deák, *William James Bennett: Master of the Aquatint View* (New York: New York Public Library, 1988).

6. "Julia Street with Poydras the Parrot," *New Orleans Magazine*, http://www.mynew orleans.com/New-Orleans-Magazine/February-2010/Julia-Street-with-Poydras-the-Parrot/; accessed October 23, 2014.

7. S.F. Kneeland, *Seven Centuries in the Kneeland Family* (New York: n.p., 1897), 449–450. "James L. Bogert's Will," *New-York Tribune*, August 26, 1881, 8.

8. Williams's *New York Annual Register* (New York: J. Leavitt, 1845), 12 and 220; Edwin Williams, *New York as It Is* (New York: T.R. Tanner, 1833), 106 and 112; Edwin Williams, *The New York Annual Register* (New York: J. Leavitt, 1832), 213.

9. Albert Ten Eyck Gardner, *American Sculpture: A Catalogue of the Collection of the Metropolitan Museum of Art* (New York: Metropolitan Museum of Art, 1965), 18.

10. *Catalogue of the Officers and Students of the General Theological Seminary of the Protestant Episcopal Church . . . 1888–1889* (New York: Trows, 1888), 38.

11. *The Boston Directory for the Year 1852* (Boston: George Adams, 1852), 36.

12. "Musical," *New-York Mirror*, February 15, 1840, 270.

13. John McClintock and James Strong, *Cyclopaedia of Biblical, Theological and Ecclesiastical Literature* (New York: Harper & Bros., 1891), 650.

14. James Buckingham and Mary J. Tilton, *The Ancestors of Ebenezer Buckingham* (Chicago: R.R. Donnelley & Sons, 1892), 23–29.

15. Gary J. Kornblith, "The Craftsman as Industrialist: Jonas Chickering and the Transformation of American Piano Making," *The Business History Review* 59, no. 3 (1985): 349–368.

16. John K. Howat, *The Hudson River and Its Painters* (New York: Viking, 1972), 36.

17. Thomas Dykes, John King, and William Knight, *Memoir of the Rev. Thomas Dykes with Copious Extracts from His Correspondence* (London: Seeleys, 1849).

18. Dorothy Farrington Parker, *The Farringtons, Colonists and Patriots: Descendants of John of Dedham, Massachusetts, Edmund of Lynn, Massachusetts, Edward of Flushing, New York* (Upper Montclair, NJ: D.F. Parker, 1976).

19. William Stevens Powell, *Dictionary of North Carolina Biography* (Chapel Hill: University of North Carolina Press, 1986), 193.

20. "West Point," *The New-York Mirror*, August 21, 1830, 51.

21. P.H. Greenleaf, *The Christmas Festival. A Sermon, Delivered on the Evening of Christmas Day, in Saint John's Church, Charlestown* (Boston: James D. Dow, 1843).

22. J.F. Everhart, *1794: History of Muskingum County, Ohio* (Columbus, OH: F.J. Everhart & Co., 1882), 146–147.

23. R.W. Keyes, "Luther Holman Hale and the Daguerrean Art," *Photographic Art-Journal* [New York] 1, no. 6 (June 1851): 357–359. D.T. Davis, "The Daguerreotype in America," *McClure's Magazine* 8 (November 1896): 4–16.

24. C.R. Conover, *The Story of Dayton* (Dayton, OH: Greater Dayton Association, 1917), 133.

25. Abraham Bell and Co. records at the Winterthur Library (Col. 194) and the University of Albany (Special Collections MSS-035). "Storage of Imported Goods," U.S. House of Representatives, 30th Congress, 2nd Session, report no. 141 (March 3, 1849), 31.

26. Linda Simon, "A Vulgar Pushing Woman. That was Robert Browning's description of the Fearless Fanny Trollope," *New York Times*, December 13, 1998, a book review of Pamela Neville-Sington, *Fanny Trollope: The Life and Adventures of a Clever Woman* (New York: Viking, 1998), online at http://www.nytimes.com/1998/12/13/books/a-vulgar-pushing-woman.html.

27. Obituaries in the *New York Journal of Medicine* 12, no. 2 (1854): 308–309, and the *Medical News and Library* 11, no. 129 (September 1853): 35. Abner Hester, "Medical History of Two Epidemic Yellow Fevers," *New Orleans Medical and Surgical Journal* 7 (July 1850): 82.

28. "Harry R.W. Hill," in Freeman Hunt, *Lives of American Merchants* (New York: Derby & Jackson, 1858), 2: 501–514. Quote from E.J. Donnell, *Chronological and Statistical History of Cotton* (New York: J. Sutton, 1872), 397.

29. George W. Cullum, *Register of Officers and Graduates of the United States Military Academy*, 3rd ed. (New York: Houghton, Mifflin and Co., 1891–) no. 177 (1: 167–179) [Hereafter, Cullum's *Register*].

30. William Baskerville Hamilton, *Holly Springs, MS, to the Year 1878* (Holly Springs, MS: Marshall County Historical Society, 1984), 8–13, 68, 75–6. Ruth W. Atkins, "Reconstruction in Marshall County," *Publications of the Mississippi Historical Society* 12 (1912): 155–213 at 155. Mary Carol Mille, *Marshall County: From the Collection of Chesley Thorne Smith* (Dover, NH: Arcadia Publishing, 1998), 33. William Henington Weathersby, *A History of Educational Legislation in Mississippi from 1798 to 1860* (Chicago: University of Chicago Press, 1921), 156 and Edward Mayes, *History of Education in Mississippi* (Washington, DC: US GPO, 1899), 106. Volney E. Howard, *Reports of Cases Argued and Decided in the High Court of Errors and Appeals, of the State of Mississippi* (Cincinnati: E. Morgan & Company, 1843), 6: 582. Pers. comm., Bobby Mitchell, Marshall County, MS Historical Society, July 28, 2014.

31. Cullum's Register (note 29, above), no. 813 (1: 611–612).

32. Hall Harrison, *The Life of the Right Reverend John Barrett Kerfoot, D.D., LL.D., first Bishop of Pittsburgh* (New York: J. Pott, 1886).

33. W. Jay Mills, *Historic Houses of New Jersey* (Philadelphia: J.B. Lippincott, 1902), 52–60.

34. Robert C. Totten, "History of the Fort Pitt Cannon Foundry," *Western Pennsylvania Historical Magazine* 3 (1920): 90–92.

35. Austin Jacobs Coolidge (ed.), *Catalogue of the Lots in the Cemetery of Mount Auburn* (Boston: A. Mudge & Son, 1867), 142, lot 2031.

36. Warren Ladd, *The Ladd Family: A Genealogical and Biographical Memoir* (New Bedford, MA: E. Anthony & Sons, 1890), 124 erroneously reports that Darius Ladd married "Emily Brewster, dau. of Jonathan and Betsey (Richards) Brewster" and that she married "Thomas R. Wharton." Of this, only the first names of Emily and her parents, Jonathan and Betsey, are correct, as verified by the journal and the Prescott Memorial.

37. "Death of Theodore Metcalf," *American Druggist and Pharmaceutical Record* 24, no. 18 (May 3, 1894): 240.

38. Mortimer Blake, *A History of the Town of Franklin, Mass.* (Franklin, MA: Committee of the Town, 1879), 172–173.

39. "The New-Orleans Literary Depot," *The New World* [New York] 7, no. 13 (October 1, 1843), following 400.

40. Cullum's *Register* (note 29, above), no. 1520 (2: 460–461 and 4: 82).

41. Anne Ayres, *The Life and Work of William Augustus Muhlenberg, Doctor in Divinity* (New York: T. Whittaker, 1889), esp. chapter 8.

42. Frederick M. Binder, "Anthracite Enters the American Home," *The Pennsylvania Magazine of History and Biography* 82, no. 1 (1958): 82–99.

43. *The Catholic Church in the United States of America* (New York: Catholic Editing Company, 1914), 3: 432; Alphonso T. Clearwater, ed., *The History of Ulster County, New York* (Kingston, NY: W.J. Van Deusen, 1907), 412–422.

44. Samuel Adams Drake, *History of Middlesex County, Massachusetts* (Boston: Estes & Lauriat, 1880), 1: 452.

45. In November 1840, Anna Maria's daughter, Charlotte Reddie (1821/22–1906) married Charles F. Wharton, Thomas Kelah Wharton's younger brother. In 1841/2 Charles and Charlotte were living with Anna Marie at Bhurtpore Cottage on West Street in New Haven, CT. By 1845 Anna Marie had moved to Hamden, CT, just north of New Haven, presumably leaving the cottage in the care of Charles F. and Charlotte. At this time, Thomas[2] Wharton having died, by a special act of the Connecticut State Assembly she successfully petitioned to have her surname reverted to Reddie. She was again a resident of New Haven in the 1850 census, but in 1851 she purchased a lot on the corner of what is now Arndt and Amory streets in the frontier town of Fond du Lac, WI, where the autumn before her son, George[2] Reddie (Jr.), had purchased farmland.

Charles F. Wharton had died by 1854, and his widow, Charlotte Reddie Wharton, then joined her mother in Wisconsin. By 1860 and the two Reddie/Wharton widows, mother and daughter, were living in Fond du Lac with their domestic, Philomena Dennillis (age twenty, from Belgium), and the two sons by separate mothers of Thomas Kelah Wharton's brother Robert John Wharton: young Charles Henry Wharton and (very likely) Robert H. Wharton (he does not appear in the 1860 federal census with the three women and Charles at that household, but Charlotte had adopted him by 1865). It was likely the near simultaneous death of both of Thomas Kelah Wharton's brothers in 1854 that triggered the consolidation of these branches of the family in Wisconsin. Anna Marie, Charlotte, Charles H., and Robert H. are all buried in Rienzi Cemetery in Fond du Lac.

Sources: British India Office Marriages, record no. N-1-8, fol. 414 and British India Office Wills & Probate no. L-AG-34-29-41 and Inventory L-AG-34-27-90, both on FindMyPast.co.uk; *New York Spectator*, June 3, 1836; *Morning Register* [Dublin, Ireland], March 28, 1828, 4; Connecticut marriage records on FamilySearch.org; *Patten's New Haven Directory, for the Years 1841–42* (New Haven, CT: James M. Patten, 1840), 100; *Resolutions and Private Acts: Passed by the General Assembly of the State of Connecticut, May Session, 1845* (Hartford, CT: John L. Boswell, 1845), 66 and "Connecticut Legislature May Session 1845," *Hartford Courant*, May 23, 1845, 2; Find-A-Grave.com memorials #72987110, #72987719, #72987721, #21045049, #21045056, and #21045041; pers. corr. with the Fond du Lac Co. [WI] Historical Society and Jefferson Co. [IN] Historical Society.

46. *Morning Chronicle* [London], April 8, 1818, 2. *Dublin Morning Register*, March 28, 1828, 4. *Aberdeen Journal* [Scotland], March 19, 1828, 4. *The East-India Register and Army List* (London: W.H. Allen, 1845), 47, 120.

47. Eva Glasener and Helen Booth, "George Reddie, Pioneer Lumberman of Hamilton," 1934, US GenWeb, 2008 http://files.usgwarchives.net/mo/caldwell/history/other/georgere301gms.txt; accessed June 26, 2014.

48. J. Hope Sutor, *Past and Present of the City of Zanesville and Muskingham County, Ohio* (Chicago: S.J. Clarke Pub. Co., 1905), 230.

49. Cuyler Reynolds, *Genealogical and Family History of Southern New York and the Hudson River Valley* (New York: Lewis Historical Pub. Co., 1914), 2: 694–696.

50. Both addresses are southeast of city hall and just south of where the Brooklyn Bridge lands in Manhattan today. Charles Elihu Slocum, *A Short History of the Slocums, Slocumbs and Slocombs of America* (Syracuse, NY: the author, 1882), 92–93; *Longworth's American Almanac, New York Register, and City Directory* (New York: Thomas Longworth, 1827), 144.

51. Cullum's *Register* (note 29, above), no. 139 (1: 139).

52. Obituaries in the *New York Times*, February 24, 1893, and *American Architect & Building News* 39 (March 4, 1893): 129–130; H. Withey, *Biographical Dictionary of American Architects* (Los Angeles: Hennessey & Ingalls, 1956), 563.

53. John S. Walker, *Memorial Services and Address in Honor of the Late Paran Stevens* (Claremont, NH: National Eagle Office, 1872); Amanda Mackenzie Stuart, *Consuelo and Alva Vanderbilt: The Story of a Mother and a Daughter in the 'Gilded Age'* (London: HarperCollins, 2012); *New Hampshire: A Guide to the Granite State* (Washington, DC: Federal Writers' Project, 1938), 131.

54. J. Thomas Scharf, *A History of St. Louis City and County, from the Earliest Periods to the Present Day* (Philadelphia: L.H. Everts & Co., 1883), 2: 1442. Mary Bartley, *St. Louis Lost. Uncovering the City's Lost Architectural Treasures* (St. Louis: Virginia Publishing, 1994). *Association of Graduates of the United States Military Academy, Annual Report* (1922), 177. See http://genealogyinstlouis.accessgenealogy.com/hotels.htm.

55. Talbot Hamlin, et al., *Greek Revival Architecture in America* (Oxford: Oxford University Press, 1944), 135, 136.

56. *The Boston Directory for the Year 1852* (Boston: George Adams, 1852).

57. Last will and testament of Jacobus Van Antwerp, March 11, 1785 (*Collections of the New-York Historical Society for the Year 1905*, 7–8).

58. "The Bogert Family," p. 3, no. 29, online at http://www.whittaker.org/Genealogy/Bogert.pdf; accessed August 9, 2015.

59. *National Cyclopædia of American Biography* (New York: James T. White Co., 1893) 3: 213.

60. James H. Rodabaugh, "From England to Ohio, 1830–1832: The Journal of Thomas K. Wharton," *The Ohio Historical Quarterly* 65.1 (1956) and 65.2 (1956): 1–27 and 111–151 at 126n39 and 138. Benjamin F. Prince (ed.), *The Centennial Celebration of Springfield, Ohio* (Springfield, OH: Springfield Publishing Co., 1901), frontispiece, says, "The engraving . . . was made from a drawing by an English gentleman who visited Mr. Jeremiah Warder, February 23, 1832."

61. Officially, see *Report of the Trial of Prof. John W. Webster: Indicted for the Murder of Dr. George Parkman, Before the Supreme Judicial Court of Massachusetts, Holden at Boston, on Tuesday, March 19, 1850* (Boston: Phillips, Sampson & Company, 1850), but more interestingly, see the statement of the murderer: John White Webster, *The Extraordinary Confession of Dr. John White Webster, of the Murder of Dr. George Parkman* (Boston: Hotchkiss, 1850); as well as the modern novelization by Helen Thomson, *Murder at Harvard*

(Boston: Houghton Mifflin, 1971), and exploration by Simon Schama, *Dead Certainties: (Unwarranted Speculations)* (London: Penguin Books/Granta, 1991), which was also made into a PBS documentary, *Murder at Harvard* (Alexandria, VA: PBS Home Video, 2003).

62. See also note 44, above.

63. *Centennial Biographical History of the City of Columbus and Franklin County, Ohio* (Chicago: Lewis Publ. Co., 1901), 296–297. Leslie Blankenship, "History of Green Lawn Cemetery [Columbus, Ind.], Founding & Incorporation," online at http://www.greenlawn cemetery.org/History_of_Green_Lawn.php. Find-A-Grave.com memorials #73702419 and #10123344.

64. "Gillette, Charles," *Handbook of Texas Online*, online at http://www.tshaonline.org/ handbook/online/articles/fgi28.

65. "Died," *The Weekly Herald* [New York], November 3, 1849, 352; Find-a-Grave.com memorial #79069665. *William's Cincinnati Directory and Business Advertiser, for 1850–51* (Cincinnati: C.S. Williams, 1850), 287. Women's Club of Madison, "History of Madison," *Indiana Magazine of History* 16, no. 4 (2920): 317–351 at 344, and see mastheads in Episcopal Church Board of Missions, *The Spirit of Missions* 17 (1852) or 18 (1853); Find-A-Grave.com memorials #76927758 (Robert John Wharton) and #25825841 (Jane F. Brooks Houston); Obituary, *Madison* [IN] *Daily Courier*, July 7, 1854, 2 and July 8, 1854, 2.

66. M. Grant, "John A. Whipple and the Daguerrean Art," *Photographic Art-Journal* [New York] 2, no. 2 (August 1851): 94–95. Davis, "The Daguerreotype in America" (note 23, above), 4–16.

67. See Wilkes v. Harper, 1 N.Y. 586, in Oliver L. Barbour, *Reports of Cases Adjudged in the Court of Chancery of New York*, 2nd ed. (New York: Banks & Brothers, 1887), 2: 338–359.

Appendix

1. Samuel Wilson, et al. (eds.), *New Orleans Architecture*, 8 vols. (Gretna, LA: Pelican Publishing Co., 1971–2000), 2: 23 and fig. 2; citing James Gallier and Samuel Wilson, *Autobiography of James Gallier, Architect* (New York: Da Capo Press, 1973), 40 and fig 23.

2. Newspaper clipping from unknown New Orleans newspaper, shortly after December 16, 1852 [CRA, folder "N.O. Society"].

3. Robert Cangelosi, "Thomas Kelah Wharton," in *KnowLA Encyclopedia of Louisiana*, edited by David Johnson (New Orleans: Louisiana Endowment for the Humanities, 2010–), January 25, 2011; online at http://www.knowla.org/entry.php?rec=522; accessed November 6, 2016.

4. Wilson, *New Orleans Architecture*, 1: 127; Danile Wilson Randle, *A Question of Style: The Architectural Competition for the Central Building of the University of the South (1860)*, master's thesis, University of Texas at Austin, 1979, 277; and see *Journal* 2: 280 for sketch.

5. Wilson, *New Orleans Architecture*, 1: 126.

6. Ibid., 1: 117.

7. Ibid., 2: 30 and see *Journal*, March 14, 1855, April 1, 1857, and May 1, 1858.

8. Wilson, *New Orleans Architecture*, 2: 127. See *Journal* 3: 71 for a sketch.

9. See *Journal*, May 2, 1859 and Wilson, et al., *Queen of the South*, 202–203 and 202n18. Historic American Building Survey HABS LA-1143 (=LA,36-NEWOR,73-1);

Jessie J. Poesch and Barbara SoRelle Bacot, *Louisiana Buildings, 1720–1940: The Historic American Buildings Survey* (Baton Rouge: Louisiana State University Press, 1997), 365.

10. Ascription to Wharton had rested on his widow's comment with the diaries, but had been called into doubt by Steven R. Ruttenbaum (National Archives and Records Administration) to Mrs. Joseph J. Domas, October 23, 1970 [CRA, folder "Washington"] that claimed the only record of Wharton in the Marine Hospital construction records was his 1859 assistantship. However, Wharton included a summary description of its characteristics, contracts, superintendents, and costs in *Journal*, January 17, 1861 and signed off as "Engineer in Charge." See also *Journal*, January 28, 1861.

11. Wilson, *New Orleans Architecture* (note 1), 8: 15.

12. Randal, *A Question of Style*, 277 refers to this a merely a "brick warehouse." See general note on cotton presses being constructed by architects such as Wharton in Wilson, *New Orleans Architecture*, 1: 145.

13. Posited by Daniel Wilson Randle, *A Question of Style* (note 4), 276:

> When Wharton saw his old friend of James Harvey Otey in New Orleans in 1859, the diarist noted that he had known the bishop a number of years earlier in Columbia, Tennessee [*Journal*, February 11 and 13, 1860]. Wharton's relationship with Hawks, the Episcopal Church, Muhlenberg, and architecture all would suggest he had a natural base of friendship with the educationally-minded Bishop [and] it seems more than remotely possible that Wharton may have been the architect for the building of the Ashwood School near Columbia that Otey was erecting . . . as early as 1847. If not the architect, Wharton was almost certainly the artist who painted the school.

Elsewhere, Randle suggests Bishop Leonidas Polk also had a hand in the design. See also William Bruce Turner, *History of Maury County, Tennessee* (Nashville: Parthenon Press, 1955), 131 and painting reproduced after 212.

14. Randle, *A Question of Style*, 277, hypothesized.

15. Mills Lane, Van Jones Martin, Marshall Bullock, and Gene Carpenter, *Architecture of the Old South: Mississippi & Alabama* (New York: Abbeville Press, 1989), 160, 162.

16. Ibid., 160, 163, 165. However, Lane mistakenly attributed the project to Wharton without any evidence or further investigation when Hubert H. McAlexander merely suggested Lane look into Wharton as a possible candidate architect. McAlexander soundly demolishes that hypothesis in "Rust-at-Airliewood"; online at http://www.rustcollege.edu/rust-at-airliewood/building.html and /notes.html, n. 12. Thanks to Professor McAlexander, to whom I owe this information.

17. "Wharton College," *Handbook of Texas Online*, Texas State Historical Association; online at http://www.tshaonline.org/handbook/online/articles/kbw15.

18. University of the South Archives, Sewanee, TN, acc. no. 1600010258 and the *General Description* is bound in "University of the South *Miscellaneous*, Glass III *Swaneeana* 1859–81." See Randle, *A Question of Style* (note 4), *passim*, but esp. 122–130 and 275–283. Wharton mentions seeking this commission on March 6, 1860 (Wilson, et al., *Queen of the South*, 222). See also Daniel W. Randle to Mr. Joseph J. Domas, July 30, 1876 [CRA, folder, "University of the South"], which mentions a number of letters on this project between Wharton and his wife, Maria, that Randle had found for the "Architecture of the University of the South Research Project." These letters have not been (re)located.

19. Wharton only delivered the designs for the chapel to Gouverneur Kemble in the summer of 1833 and it was not finished until 1834, so this image is either his imagination of what it would eventually look like in the landscape of 1832 or it is a sketch made in 1834 or 1835. Wharton may have been at the dedication of the Chapel on Sept. 21, 1834, for although he does not mention attending, he coincidently went to Fishkill, NY "about the 20th of Sept., 1834" to mourn the death of his mother (p. 124–25, above).

20. This was sketched four years after Dr. Hosack died, perhaps with fond memories of his early acquaintance.

21. Reproduced in Wilson, et al., *Queen of the South*, 30.

22. Ibid., 31.

23. Ibid., 32.

24. Wharton must have sketched this in later summer of 1853 when they spent some time at his wife's cousins' home in Saxonville.

25. Reproduced in Wilson, et al., *Queen of the South*, 30.

26. Ibid., 39.

27. Ibid., 44.

28. Ibid., 53.

29. This and the next sketch reproduced in ibid., 57 and 56.

30. Ibid., 63.

31. Ibid., 69.

32. Ibid., 70.

33. This and the next sketch reproduced in ibid., 73.

34. Ibid., 76.

35. Ibid., 81.

36. This and the next two sketches reproduced in ibid., 82, 83, 85.

37. This and the next sketch reproduced in ibid., 86, 87, and the former also in Lake Douglas, *Public Spaces, Private Gardens: A History of Designed Landscapes in New Orleans* (Baton Rouge: Louisiana State University Press, 2011), 42 with relevant diary extracts on the preceding pages.

38. Reproduced in Wilson, et al., *Queen of the South*, 89.

39. Ibid., 91.

40. Ibid., 94.

41. Ibid., 96.

42. Ibid., 98.

43. Ibid., 268.

44. Reproduced in James Truslow Adams, *The History of New England* (Boston: Little, Brown, and Co., 1927), 184.

45. Ibid., 356.

46. Ibid., 312.

47. Note in pencil on drawing: "[December] see Diary."

48. Curiously, he does not mention this "diving bell," which is likely salvaging goods from a sunken ship, in his journal.

49. Reproduced in Wilson, et al., *Queen of the South*, 106.

50. It is unclear if this is his sketch of "The Elms" in Natchez, MS. In the National Register Nomination, §8, 3 for this ca. 1801 mansion, they report that,

> In 1859, New Orleans architect T.K. Wharton, a guest at The Elms, described the house and grounds during the Stanton ownership as: beautiful exceedingly—

the air gushes thro' the noble trees, and the choice shrubbery with a purity and freshness unknown in the airiest parts of the city below—a bold well graveled carriage drive leads from the entrance gates to the mansion, and a fine ample billiard room stands off to the right amid the rich foliage of the garden while on the left a double terass [*sic*] rises above the level of a sloping lawn and backs a richly clothed ruin covered with English ivy and consisting of three arches—the remains of a conservatory that was destroyed by the Tornado of May 7, 1840. Fine galleries round the house 9 to 14 feet wide—Everywhere, exquisite order and tasteful arrangement.

To supplement his verbal description, Wharton drew a "fine outline of the house and grounds, taken from the South Entrance-Gate" on August 23, 1859; online at http://www.apps.mdah.ms.gov/nom/prop/470.pdf and Ann Beha Associates, *Natchez National Historical Park, Natchez, Mississippi. Historic Resource Study* (Boston, 1997), illustration 26.

51. Wharton's signature is uncharacteristically hidden in the grass in this sketch, and it the date is written ambiguously, possibly reading 1836 of 1856.

52. See National Archives and Records Administration, Fort Worth, Texas, Record Group 36, Entry 1679A: Records of the United States Customs Service, "Records Relating to the Construction of the New Customs House, 1848–1861" (1 linear ft.; 4 boxes), though these seem to contain only the textual records.

53. See "TKW, writings of" in the index of Wilson, et al., *Queen of the South*.

54. New Orleans Public Library, Louisiana Division, James Harrison Dakin Collection Architectural Drawings and Lithographs, ca.1832–1851, 184 drawings and 35 lithographs.

55. Six of the following Ohio sketches were reproduced in Eugene H. Roseboom and Francis P. Weisenburger, *A History of Ohio* (Columbus: Ohio Historical Society, 1953). All twelve are also available as digital files on the NYPL online with Digital IDs of, respectively, 54040, 54411, 54074, 54044, 54101, 54128, 54041, 54015, 54445, 54091, 54045, 54017, 54035.

56. NYPL online, Digital ID 54616. This sheet is also stamped in ink, "James D. Smillie Collection"; see the entry for the engraving of this image, below.

57. This is likely the preparatory sketch for the (now unlocated) painting exhibited at the NAD in 1835.

58. This is the house owned by John Jacob Astor in which Irving lived while writing *Astoria, or Anecdotes of an enterprise beyond the Rocky Mountains* (Philadelphia: Carey, Lea, & Blanchard, 1836) and just across the bay when Wharton was an instructor in Flushing.

59. Wharton was in Manchester and Leeds in 1829 (See NYPL Sketchbook, no. 42), though he also may have been copying from H.G. James, *Views of Old Halls, Buildings, etc. in Manchester and the Neighbourhood* (Manchester: Lithographic Press, 1825). See also his comments about being in Manchester as a youth in the *Journal*, January 30 and December 25, 1861 [Wilson, et al., *Queen of the South*, 244].

60. This drawing seems to relate to Thomas Allen, *The History and Antiquities of London, Westminster, Southwark, and Other Parts Adjacent* (London: G. Virtue, 1839), 1: 28–29 and figs. 1–6.

61. Pine Mountain is ten miles southeast of Springfield, MA. This must have been one of the last sketches Wharton made before leaving for Mississippi.

62. Reproduced in Wilson, et al., *Queen of the South*, iv and cited with an accession number of 1974.25.14.169 implying it is a copy (?) in THNOC. Also noted in James H.

Grady, et al., *Index of American Architectural Drawings before 1900* (Charlottesville, VA: American Association of Architectural Bibliographers, 1957), 16, no. 44.

63. Reproduced in Wilson, et al., *Queen of the South*, 35.

64. Ibid., 100. This is likely the drawing that was submitted with an article on the Custom House to *Harper's Magazine* on September 7, 1855. Also noted in Grady, *Index of American Architectural Drawings*, 4, no. 60 and cataloged as NYPL, John H. Levine Collection, ID 118831.

65. Inventories of American Painting and Sculpture, Smithsonian American Art Museum, IAP 80044372. See *Antiques*, May 1977, 997 and Bruce Weber, *Paintings of New York, 1800–1950* (San Francisco: Pomegranate, 2005), 7.

66. Reproduced in J.K. Howat, *The Hudson River and its Painters* (New York: Viking Press, 1972), 133–134, no. 6 and in James T. Callow, *Kindred Spirits; Knickerbocker Writers and American Artists, 1807–1855* (Chapel Hill: University of North Carolina Press, 1967), 101.

67. William Bruce Turner, *History of Maury County, Tennessee* (Nashville: Parthenon Press, 1955), following 212, and Randle, *A Question of Style* (note 4), 276.

68. See Randle, *A Question of Style*, fig. VI-8–10.

69. David Tatham, "The Pendleton-Moore Shop. Lithographic Artists in Boston, 1825–1840," *Old-Time New England* 62, no. 2 (1971): 29–46. John Bewley, "Philadelphia Lithographers: Peter S. Duval (1804 or 5–1886)," Keffer Collection of Sheet Music, ca.1790–1895, University of Pennsylvania Rare Books and Manuscript Library; online at https://www.library.upenn.edu/collections/rbm/keffer/duval.html; accessed August 1, 2017.

70. See John William Reps, *Views and View-makers of Urban America . . . 1825–1925* (Columbia: University of Missouri Press, 1984), no. 589 (q.v. no. 3636).

71. Mary Louise Booth, *The History of New York* (New York: W.R.C. Clark & Meeker, 1859; rpt. New York: W.R.C. Clark, 1866, 1867; also New York: E.F. Dutton, 1880).

72. Wilson, *New Orleans Architecture* (note 1), 2: 204 and Randle, *A Question of Style* (note 4), fig. VIII-34.

73. H. Parrott Bacot and Carey Turner Mackie, "Reflections in Silver: The Hatch Presentation Coffee and Tea Service," *Historic New Orleans Collection Quarterly* 18, no. 4 (2000): 8–10 and Mackie and Bacot, "From the Golden Age of New Orleans Silver: The Hatch Service," *Historic New Orleans Collection Quarterly* 26, no. 2 (2009): 1–3.

Index

Page numbers in *italics* are illustrations.
Those with a question mark are conjectural identifications.
See also the biographical register, pp. 267–87.

Abraham Bell & Co., 39, 273
Alger, Cyrus, 333n63
Allen, John Fiske, 267
American Academy of Fine Arts, 8
American regionalism, 2, 30
Arnold, Dr. (dentist), 73, 74
Ashbridge, D.W., 268
Astor, John Jacob, 343n58
Astoria Female Institute, New York, 34, 270, 318n3
Athenaeum, Boston, MA, 149, 158–59, 329n15
Athens, views of, 301
Austin, TX, building designs, 292
Ayer, Dr. James C., 200, 205, 268

Back Bay, Boston, MA, 203, 223, 330n29, 333n65
Balch, William, Y. 217, 224, 268
Baltimore, MD, views of, 300, 304
Banks, Sir Joseph, 55, 205, 268
Barataria, LA, views of, 298
Barclay, Henry, 110, 268
Barker, Jacob, 208, 268
Barkin, Anne, 5, 286
Barnett, John, 290, 291
Barnum, P.T., 16, 238
Barton, John G., 91, 96, 268
Bateman, acting family, 246, 268, 273
Baton Rouge, LA, views of, *259*, 298
Baxter, Richard, 104, 326n106
Beauregard, Pierre-Alfred T., 196, 268
Beauregard, P.G.T., 15, 25, 133, 149, 178, 196, 226, 229, 259, 260, 268
Bedel, Gregory T., 38, 269
Bedford, F. (engraver), 305
Bennett, William J., 71, 89, 269
Bhutan, views of, 301
Billings, Hammatt, 208, 211, 223, 226, 229, 231, 235, 269, 332n51
Blanc, Evariste, 223, 269
Bogert, Edward C., 163, 164, 207, 208, 241, 269
Bogert, Henry K., 239, 269
Bogert, Olivia Hawks, 207, 241, 269
Bonaparte, Joseph-Napoleon, 39, 53, 269
Boston, MA, 141–77, 195–237; city, views of, *212*, 294, 297, 298; Common 152, 240; Common, views of, 296; harbor, 154; Boston Museum, 198–99, 332n51; harbor, views of, *215*, *222*, 296, 297
Both, Jan, 92, 269
Boyd, Alexander, 6?, 102, 269
Brackett, Edward A., 149, 269, 329
Bradford, John Q., 13
Bradley, I., 65, 66
Breneman, John S., 88, 91, 94, 96, 269
Brighton-Allston, MA, 170–74
Brock, Sir Isaac, 144, 152, 269
Brockville, Ontario, views of, 296

Brodhead family, 151, 152, 157, 162, 225, 269
Brookline, MA, *198*; views of, 297
Brooks, Jane F., 286
Brown, George, 173, 270
Brown, Rev. John Walker, 34, 270
Brown, Thomas, house, 325n81
Brown, W. Horace, 163, 173, 270
Brownell, Gilbert, 160, 270
Bryant, Gridley J.F., 150, 158, 166, 176–77, 227–29, 233–34, 270
Bryant, William Cullen, 28
Buckingham, Ebenezer, Jr., 63, 270
Bullfinch, Charles, 330n24
Bunker Hill Monument, Boston, MA, 151, 164, 205, 271, 278

Cairo, IL, views of, 298
Caldwell, Matthew, 7
Cambridge, MA, 156, 162, 170, 172, 217; views of, 296
Camidge, C. Joseph, 41, 270
Canals, 7, 27, 54, 110, 111, 241, 248, 249–50, 300; views of, *249*, 294, 295, 298, *300*
Carey, Henry, 72, 91, 92, 94, 98, 99, 100, 107, 107, 111, 270
Catherine, 134, 148, 156, 178, 184, 285
Catskill ("Cauterskill") Falls, NY, 121, 122; views of, 300
Catskill Mountains, 47, 76; views of, *109*
Catskill Mountain House, Palenville, NY, 24, 46, 327n119–21; views of, 300
Central Church, Boston, MA, 226
Channing, Dr. Walter, 152, 177, 221, 270
Chapel of Our Lady, Cold Spring, NY, xiii, 79, 80, 98, 99, 289, 324n69, 342n19; views of, *80*, 99, *129*, 294
Chatham Garden Theater, NY, 319n4
Chelsea Beach (Revere), MA, 157; views of, 298
Chickering's Piano Factory, Boston, MA, 195, 203, 205, 217, 224, 270
Christ Church, New Orleans, LA, 13, 14, 274, 289–90; building designs, 301, 303
Churches, drawings and paintings of, 294, 296, 297, 301, 303
Cincinnati, OH, 243–45
Cleveland, OH, 141, 242–43
Cochituate Pond, Natick, MA, 156, 171, 178, 181–86, *185*, 193, 220, 331n37; views of, 297
Coffee, Col. John, 258, 270
Coggeshall, Russell, 8, 271
Cold Spring, NY, 9, 78, 79, 116; building designs, 289; views of, *80*, 294. *See also* Kemble, Gouverneur; West Point Foundry
Cole, Thomas, 9, 18, 22, 86, 92, 98, 106, 107, 271, 324n75
Coliseum Place Gardens, New Orleans, LA, 1, 26; views of, 295
College Point, Long Island, NY, 4, 10, 12, 33, 294, 318n2; views of, *87*
Columbia, TN, building designs, 291; views of, 303
Columbus, OH, views of, 294, 300
Commerce, MO, views of, *136*, 296
Constitution Island, NY, 57, 64, 73, 77, 78, 116, 285, 321n43; views of, *79*, 293, 294
Coster, Adeline Emily, 47
Coster, Henry A., 48, 275
Coster, Laura, 47, 48, 53
Courtenay, Edward H., 70, 271
Cozzens, William B., 57, 66, 73, 74, 75, 271
Crow's Nest, Hudson Highlands, NY, 57, 71, 77, 78, 81; views of, *79*, 294
Crystal Palace Exhibition, New York, NY, 24, 221, 240
Cushing, Caleb, 207, 271
Customs House, Boston, MA, 23, 150, 151–52

Daguerreotypes, 143, 196, 220, 221, 224
Dakin, James H., 171, 271, 272, 290, 299
Darwin, Charles, 23–24, 316n99
Davies, Charles, 48?, 59, 75, 271
Davies, Rev. George J., 20
Davis, J.P., 215, 271
Dayton, OH, views of, 293, 300
Diaries, 2–3, 15–18
Dick, Thomas, 95, 326n95

Diller, Jacob W., 86–88, 91, 95–96, 103, 126, 271
Diving bell, views of, 298
Dogs, sketches of, 301
Dorchester Heights, MA, views of, 294
Dubois, Bishop John, xiii
Dunn, Alexander, 133, 134, 137, 142, 151, 162, 176, 211, 218, 229, 232, 233, 236, 237, 239, 241, 271
Durand, Asher B., 9, 18, 21, 22, 107, 271
Duryée, Lt. Abram, 125, 126, 127, 271
Duval, Peter S. (engraver), 305
Dwight, Rev. Timothy, 94, 271
Dykes, Rev. Thomas, 90, 272

Earl, Mr., 7, 41, 98, 99, 272
Eastburn, Rev. Manton, 44, 107, 212, 272
Edwards, Jonathan, 51, 272
Elephanta, IN, views of, 301
Elgin Botanic Garden, New York, NY, 54
England: Cottingham (Yorkshire), 5; Hull grammar schools, 19–20; Kingston-upon-Hull (Yorkshire), 5–6, 19–20; Wharton Hall (Cumberland) 5; Wyton, Hull (Yorkshire), 6; views of Chester 301; views of Clee-Thorpes (Yorkshire), 293; views of Flamborough Head (Yorkshire), 293; Isle of Lewis (Hebrides), 293; views of Kirkstall Abbey, Leeds, 300; views of London, 301; views of Manchester, 301; views of Scarbororough Castle, 293; views of Wyton, Hull (Yorkshire), 298
Enlightenment ideals, 23–24
Epdemics (cholera, yellow fever, etc.), 8, 17, 43, 44, 45, 49, 50, 55, 60, 90, 92, 123
Episcopalianism, 9–12, 26; Church Schooling Movement, 9, 12
Erie Canal, 27, 32, 54
Eunomium Society, Flushing Institute, 87

Faneuil Hall, Boston, MA, 151, 196; views of, 298
Fellenberg, Philip E. von, 84, 272
Fetter, Emmanuel (Manuel), 89, 103, 272
Finley, Robert, 93, 272
Fishkill, NY, 33, 79, 125–28; views of, *124*, 294
Flushing, NY, 9, 93; Bay, 83; Bay, views of, *85*; views of, 294, 304, 305
Flushing Institute, Flushing, NY, 2, 8, 9–10, 33, 84, 85, 90, 310n31, 318n2, 324n77; views of, 35, 304
Fort Montgomery, NY, 75
Fort Putnam, NY, 66
Fort Warren, Boston Harbor, MA, 169, 208–10, *210*; views of, 294, 296, 297
Fracker, J.T., 90, 272
Framingham, MA, 181, 190, 192, 202, 204, 229; views of, *192*, 296, 297
Franklin, Walter E., 89, 91, 98, 103, 272
Freret, William A., 134, 142, 143, 272, 291
Fresh Pond, Cambridge, MA, 174, 200, 217, 331n37; views of, *174*, 296

Gallier, James, Jr., 272, 313n55
Gallier, James, Sr., 14, 36, 271, 273, 290, 299, 305, 313n55
Germania Society, 236
Gerry, Samuel L., 217, 273
Gillette, Charles, 286, 292
Gilman, Arthur Delavan, 233–34, 273
Gimbrede, Thomas, 60, 62, 64, 273, 277
Glazier, Julia Ann Prescott, 155, 156, 178, 199, 273
Glazier, Marshall, 194, 273
Gouverneur, Samuel L., 66, 68, 70, 71, 273, 323n61
Granite Railway Co., Quincy, MA, 270, 271, 278, 279, 283
Greenleaf, Rev. P.H., 160, 164, 218?, 273
Greenleaf, Simon, 218, 273
Guesnon, P., 150, 151, 169, 178, 206, 229, 230, 273
Gurney, Thomas, 37, 40, 273

Hale, Luther H., 224, 273
Halsey, Jacob, 143
Hamilton, Charles, 170, 176, 200, 273
Harrod, Benjamin Morgan, 281
Harvey, Jacob, 39, 41, 42, 45, 46, 47, 90, 92, 98, 104, 273
Hassler, Ferdinand R., 68, 273–74
Hawks, Rev. Francis L., 11–14, 20, 33, 34–36, 208, 272, 274, 312n44–45

Hell Gate, NY, views of, 301
Herring, James F., 70, 274
Herschel, Sir John, 16
Hervieu, Auguste, 107, 274
Hester, Abner, 257, 274
Highland School, Garrison, NY, 67, 68
Hildreth, Charles, 124, 274
Hill, Harry, 197, 274
Hindustan, views of, 301
Hitchcock, Capt. Ethan A., 61, 70, 80, 274
Holly Springs, MS, 12–13, 18, 34–36; building designs, 292
Horticultural Exhibition, Boston, MA, 197
Hosack, Alexander E., 47, 274
Hosack, David, Jr., 50
Hosack, Dr. David, 8, 18, 32, 42, 46–48, 50, 52–56, 90, 98, 100, 107, 273–75, 289, 320n24, 321n32–33; library, 51, 52; estate, Hyde Park, NY, 25, 46, 47, 49, 51, 55, 56, 82–83; views of, *47*, *51*, 294, 302
Hosack, Eliza, 47, 52, 92, 275
Hosack, Emily, 17, 47, 48, 50, 52, 92, 100, 275
Hosack, Magdalena, 47, 275
Hudson Highlands, 46, 56, 321n43; views of, 75, *79*. *See also* Crow's Nest
Hudson River, 27–28, 83; views of, 300
Hudson River School of Art, xiii, 9, 18, 21–22
Huling, Frederick W., 35, 275
Huling, Maria G. *See* Wharton, Maria H.
Huling, Sara B., 153, 275
Hull, MA, 168–69
Hull, UK. *See* England: Kingston-upon-Hull
Huntington, Rev. Frederic D., 41, 244?, 275, 333n60
Hustwick, Robert, 90, 275
Hyde Park, NY, 8, 9, 18, 25, 32, 41, 43, 45, 46, 54–56, 107; views of, *47*, *51*, *82*, *83*, 294, 302

Illinois River, 138; views of, *139*, 296
Indian Brook Falls, Garrison, NY, 19, 67, 117; views of, *116*, 300
Ingham, Charles C., 41, 42, 275
Iron works, views of, *67*, *78*, 294
Irving, Washington, 8, 9, 32, 81, 117–22, 134, 275, 301, 343n58
Islip, NY, views of, 301
Italy, Tivoli, 122; views of, 301

Jackson, Gen. Andrew, 99, 275, 323n61
Johnson, Rev. Samuel Roosevelt, 9, 51, 275
Johnston, Abraham R., 60, 71, 275

Kearney, Alfred, 134, 189, 204, 276
Kelah, Robert, 5, 286
Kemble, Fanny, 4
Kemble, Gouverneur, xiii, 9, 17, 18, 21, 22, 32, 53, 54, 57, 63, 64, 68, 69, 73, 75, 86, 98, 100, 110, 113, 116, 117, 121, 125, 276, 289, 294, 316n89, 324n69, 324n71, 342n19; dinners, 57, 61–63, 66, 68, 70, 73–75; estate, Cold Spring, NY, 80–81; estate, views of, *81*
Kemble, Mary, 63, 65, 66, 98, 116, 119, 276
Kemble, Richard F., 117, 276
Kemble, William, 80, 100, 276, 327n114
Kerfoot, John Barrett, 11, 91, 96, 102, 276
King, James G., 90, 276
Kingston, IL, views of, 296
Kiss, August, 334n81
Knap, Charles, 164, 226, 234, 245, 276
Knickerbocker Group, 9. *See also* Irving, Washington; Bryant, William Cullen

La Salle, IL, 139
Ladd, Aurelius, 23, 165, 170, 181, 217, 276
Ladd, Darius, 149, 277, 307n4, 337n36
Ladd, Emily A., 134, 142, 147, 149, 155, 156, 162, 163, 170, 172, 195, 196, 206, 236, 238, 244, 247, 258, 260, 277
Ladd, Emily J. *See* Wharton, Emily Julia Ladd
Lake Champlain, 146
Lake Erie, 141–42; views of, 296
Lake George, NY, views of, 299, 300
Lake Pontchartrain, LA, views of, 295
Lawrence, Abbot, 277
Lawrence, MA, 166, 330n35; views of, *167*, 296

Lely, Sir Peter (Pieter van der Faes), 277
Leslie, Charles R., 81, 116, 117, 118, 277, 324n71
Leslie, Lt. Thomas J., 32, 61, 63–66, 69–72, 74, 76, 161, 277
Livingston, Robert L., 109, 277
Louisville, KY, 248; views of, *249*, 298
Lowell, MA, 330n35, 331n36
Lyell, Sir Charles, 13
Lynn, MA, views of, 298

Madison, IN, 26, 217, 247; views of, 298
Mahan, Prof. Dennis H., 70, 73, 75, 103, 277
Martin, John, 121, 277
Mason, Capt./Maj. James M., 63, 65, 277
McCoy, Penemiah, 286
McIlvaine, Rev. Charles P., 26, 73, 277; sermons by, 40
McVickar, John, 92, 277
Memphis, TN, 135, 256; views of, 298
Meredith, William M., 150, 277
Merrimac River, views of, *207*, 297
Merrit, Frances [Fanny], 156, 178, 278
Metcalf, Julia T., 151, 165, 278
Metcalf, Theodore, 165, 201, 222, 226, 278
Metcalf, Theron, 165, 278
Miami and Montgomery Co., OH, "12 views" of, 300
Miami River, OH, views of, 300
Miller, Robert (engraver), 304
Milnor, Rev. Dr. James, 39, 42, 43, 278
Milton Hill, MA, 175, 215–216
Mississippi River, 133–37, 253–60; views of, *255*, 294, 295, 296, 298
Monroe, President James, 70, 273, 323n61
Moody, David, 164, 176, 215, 278
Moore, T. (engraver), 304, 305
Morgan, J.C., 202, 221, 278
Morris, George P., 16, 20–21, 70, 100, 106–8, 111, 278. *See also New-York Mirror* (periodical)
Morris, William Hopkins, 118, 278
Morse, Alpheus Carey, 236–37, 278
Morse, Samuel F.B., 21, 106, 278
Mount, William Sydney, 9, 21, 41, 81, 92, 106, 278, 324n74
Mt. Auburn Cemetery, Cambridge, MA, 23, 24, 156–58, 330n25; views of, *158*, 294, 298
Muhlenberg, Dr. Frederick A., 84, 105, 278
Muhlenberg, Peter, 84, 278
Muhlenberg, Rev. William Augustus, 4, 9–10, 26, 33, 61, 66, 69, 73, 84, 87, 88, 99, 102, 103, 105, 108, 113, 114, 119, 279; education philosophy, 96, 112, 113; sermons by, 62, 87, 88, 89, 93–95, 97, 100, 104, 112, 114
Munn, Luther, 178, 279
Music Hall Boston, MA, 226, 229, 235–37

Nahant, MA, 161, 227–28; views of, 297
Natchez, MS, 258; building designs, 291–92; views of, 303
National Academy of Design, 17, 19, 21, 22, 41, 100, 106, 323n62
New Customs House, New Orleans, LA, 1, 14, 25, 36, 51–52, 132, 133, 150, 177, 179, 196, 226, 260; views of, 294–95, 297, 298, 301
New Haven, CT, 33; views of, *34*, 298, 305
New Opera House, Boston, MA, 226, 236
New Orleans Academy of Sciences, 27
New Orleans Mechanics Society, 20
New Orleans, LA, 1, 2, 13, 175; building designs, 289–91; views of, 294, 295, 298, 301, 303, 305
New York, NY, 6, 7–8, 16, 25–26, 39–45, 86, 91–94, 98–101, 107–8, 111, 238–41; views of, *102*, 303, 304, 305; harbor, views of, *31*, 293
New York Review (periodical), 20
New-York Mirror (periodical), xiii, 19, 98, 106
Newburyport, MA, views of, *207*, 297
Niagara Falls, NY, 29, 142–44, 328n6–7; views of, *153*, *194*, 296, 301
Northrup, Rev. Birdsey G., 180, 187, 189, 191, 279
Nott, Eliphalet, 66, 279

O'Reilly, Rev. Philip, 63, 65, 74, 79, 117, 279

Oakley, Mrs., 42, 92
Ohio River, 246–53; views of, *247*, 298
Omnibuses, 155, 162, 218, 229, 234
Onderdonk, Bishop Henry, 9, 44, 279
Osgood, Isaac, 208
Osgood, Dr. John., W. 188–89, 185, 190, 279
Otey, Rev. James H., 291, 341n13

Palisades, NY, views of, 293
Parker and Clover's (framing shop), 89, 98, 100
Parkman-Webster murder, 17, 285
Parsons, Samuel Bowne, 89, 279
Paulding, Gertrude, 61, 63, 65, 66, 99, 279
Paulding, James Kirke, 9, 17, 32, 61, 63, 65, 86, 92, 98, 99, 111, 116, 117, 279
Peale, Charles Wilson, 333n61
Pendelton, John (engraver), 305
Penniman, George, 177, 200, 211, 214–15, 229, 279
Peoria, IL, views of, *139*, 296
Perkins, Thomas H., 215, 279
Philadelphia, PA, 38
Pierce, Henry Ruben, 187–88, 280
Pine Mountain, MA, views of, 301
Piqua, OH, 7, 32; views of, 293, 300
Poinsett, Joel Roberts, 32, 280
Polk, Leonidas, 292, 341n13
Ponsonby, Arthur, 15
Poole, Monroe, 235
Portugal, Tagus River, views of, 301
Poughkeepsie, NY, views of, 294
Powers, Hiram, 240, 334n81
Prescott, Betsy Richards, 280
Prescott, Emeline, 216, 218, 280
Prescott, Emily A. *See* Ladd, Emily A.P.
Prescott, Emily J. *See* Wharton, Emily Ladd
Prescott, George, 147, 148, 154, 197, 233, 280, 303
Prescott, Jonathan,[1] 280, 303
Prescott, Jonathan,[2] 280
Prescott, Julia Ann. *See* Glazier, Julia
Prescott, Levi T., 216, 218, 230, 234, 280
Prescott, William A., 217, 280
Preston, Alonzo F., 234, 280
Preston, Rev. Nathaniel O., 41, 280

Quincy, MA, 177, 179, 214–15, 331n42; views of, *214*, 297

Railroad Travel, 139–41, 28–29, 145–47, 142, 167, 195, 207, 237–38, 241–43, 244
Reading, PA, views of, 305
Reddie, Anna Maria, 33, 280–81, 286, 338n45
Reddie, Athelia, 281
Reddie, Charlotte, 281, 338n45
Reddie, Clara Morris, 281
Reddie, Emily M. *See* Wharton, Emily M.
Reddie, Ethelinda, 281
Reddie, George,[1] 281
Reddie, George[2] (Jr.), 281, 338n45
Reid, James M., 206, 226, 231, 244, 281
Reynolds, Lewis E., 179, 281, 290
Reynolds, Sir Joshua, 107, 281
Robinson, James, 42, 281
Roebling, John A., 328n8
Romantic ideals, 22–23
Ruskin, John, 208, 219, 231; and Turner School, 164

Samson, Dr. Julius, 250, 254–55, 258, 259, 281, 335n92
Saugerties, NY, 110, 322n49; views of, 301. *See also* Ulster Iron Works
Saxonville, MA, 178–94; views of, *182*, *184*, 294, 297
Sciota Crossing, OH, views of, 293
Scotland, Marmond Hills, views of, 293
Scott, Gen. Winfield, 32, 65, 70, 282
Scott, Rev. John, 19–20
Scott, Sir Walter, 282
Sea of Gallilee, views of, 301
Seabury, Rev, Samuel, 87, 88, 93, 96, 115, 282; sermons by, 86, 89, 91, 94, 95, 97, 100, 105, 114
Sears, Lt. Claudius W., 13–14, 311n54
Second Great Awakening, 10, 25
Sewanee, TN, building designs, 303, 292–93
Shaw, J.R., 137

Silver Lake, NY, views of, 300
Simmons, John, 109?, 282
Slocum, Thomas, 8, 32, 41, 86, 90, 92, 98, 104, 111, 272, 282; boarding house, 39, 40, 92, 98, 123
Smillie, James D. (engraver), 100, 282, 300, 304
Smith, Capt. Henry, 70, 282, 323n60
Snell, George, 234, 235, 282
Sollitt, J.D., 20
South Boston Foundry, Boston, MA, 333n63
Southern Michigan Rail Road, 140
Spalding, Dr. Asa, 103, 108, 282
Spence, Mrs. Edward, 90
Springfield, OH, views of, 293, 304
St. Lawrence River, views of, *145*, 296. *See also* Thousand Islands
St. Louis, MO, 137
St. Mary's Bay, Newfoundland, views of, 293
St. Paul's Church, Boston, MA, 224
St. Paul's College, Flushing, NY, 4, 10–12, 26, 33; views of, *35*
St. Paul's College, Holly Springs, MS, 12–13
St. Thomas's Hall, Flushing, NY, 11–12, 33
St. Thomas's Hall, Holly Springs, MS, 312n47
St. Vincent's College, Cape Girardeau, MO, 328n2
Steamboats, 115; travel on, 28, 134–39, 141–42, 144–46, 244, 245–60; views of, *136*, *139*, *247*, *249*, *259*, 296, 298
Stevens, Paran, 227, 282
Stewart, John, 292
Stickney, Benjamin, 137, 283
Stone, Dr. Warren, 47?, 197, 332n42
Stone, Lawson, 202, 204–5, 208
Stowe, Harriet Beecher, 283, 331n46
Strong, George Templeton, 4, 12
Sturges, Walter Knight, xiv–xv
Sudbury River, MA, views of, *183*, 297
Sugden, Capt. John, 6
Sullivan, Mr., 97, 98, 99
Sullivan, William, 215, 283
Sully, Thomas, 70, 116–18, 283; portrait theory, 118, 119
Switzerland, Pennine Alps, views of, 301

Taylor, James H., 75?, 283
Thayer, Benjamin (engraver), 305
Thayer, Col. Sylvanus, 8, 24, 26, 32, 53, 57, 61–65, 69, 70–76, 99, 116, 152–53, 283, 326n101; dinner with, 65, 70; education, advice on, 60, 62, 66, 74, 77; excursions with, 60, 65, 68, 70, 72, 80; generosity of, 72, 76
Thibault, Aimée, 45, 283
Thompson, Aaron K., 43, 56, 283
Thompson, E. and I., 6
Thompson, Martin E., 7, 8, 12, 19, 21, 22, 32, 40, 41, 44, 45, 56, 89, 90, 91, 92, 99, 100, 107, 110, 111, 240–41, 283, 289, 312n55; architectural studies under, 39, 99, 100, 107; works of, 44, 46, 90
Thousand Islands, St. Lawrence River, 145–46; views of, 296
Tillotson, Robert L., 109, 283
Toledo, OH, 140; views of, 296
Tourism, 29, 142–43
Toutant, A. *See* Beauregard, Pierre-Alfred T.
Tracey, Edward, 134, 284
Travers, Helen, 65, 284
Travers, John, 63, 109?, 284, 322n49
Tremont House (hotel), Boston, MA, 195, 196, 227, 235
Trollope, Francis Anne, 4, 8, 107, 274, 284
Troy, OH, views of, 300
Turner, J.W.M., 164, 231
Twain, Mark (Samuel Clemens), 14

Ulster Iron Works, Saugerties, NY, 65, 110, 322n49, 327n114
Unitarianism, 26, 212, 219–20
United States Military Academy, West Point, NY, 8, 24, 57, 59, 71, 77, 317n108; T.K. Wharton in residence at, 57–77
University of Louisiana (Tulane), 13
University of the South, Sewanee, TN, building designs, 303, 292–29
Upjohn, Richard, 332n50

Van Antwerpe, John, 40–42, 45, 99, 107, 111, 284
Van Bokkelen, Libertus, 11, 87, 119, 124, 284
Varley, John, 92, 284
Vermont Central Railroad, 146
Vicksburg, MS, 257–58
Victoria regis (*Victoria amazonica*) flower, 197, 267
Vinton, Alexander H., 224, 284

Wallace, Elizabeth J., 134, 237, 284
Ward, James, 98, 284
Warder, Jeremiah, 38, 41, 92, 284
Warner, Henry, 86, 284–85
Warner, Rev. Thomas, 70, 73, 76, 86, 119, 284; sermons by, 65, 69, 74
Webster, Daniel, 147, 285
Webster, John White, 159, 217, 285. *See also* Parkman-Webster murder
Weir, Robert W., xiii, 19, 21, 22, 81, 98, 100, 106, 107, 116, 118, 129, 285, 324n72–73
West Point, NY, 3; views of, *64*, 293, 300. *See also* U.S. Military Academy
West Point Foundry, Cold Spring, NY, xiii, 9, 21, 57, 71, 73, 110, 324n70; views of, *67*, *77*, *78*, 294
Wharton College, Austin, TX, building designs, 292
Wharton, Anna Maria. *See* Reddie, Anna Maria
Wharton, Anne, B. 2, 5, 33, 41, 52, 59, 60, 63, 66, 69, 119, 150, 152, 286; death of, 124
Wharton, Charles F., 5, 33, 285, 338n45
Wharton, Charles H., 285, 338n45
Wharton, Charlotte Reddie, 285
Wharton, Emily Julia Ladd, 14, 36, 133–260 *passim*, 277, 285, 307n4, 333n64
Wharton, Emily M., 5, 34, 169, 175, 196, 233, 243–45, 281
Wharton, Henry, 33, 285
Wharton, Humphrey, 5
Wharton, Maria H., 13, 14, 26, 35, 36, 285
Wharton, Marianne (Mary Anne), 5, 34, 169, 175, 286, 292
Wharton, Robert H., 286, 338n45
Wharton, Robert John, 5, 6, 26, 27, 34, 126, 150, 160, 169, 186, 197, 218, 245, 248, 286, 338n45
Wharton, Sir Thomas, First Baron Wharton, 5
Wharton, Thomas Kelah, 7–15; on architecture, 7, 8, 13–14, 20, 23, 44, 152, 155–56, 160, 171, 195, 199, 222, 224–25, 226, 239–40; as artist, 18–24; on art, 18, 21, 65, 67, 75, 104, 164, 217, 229–30, 240; on commerce, 154, 213, 218, 220, 236, 254; drawings, 299, 293–302; on education, 10–11, 19, 114, 115, 315n81; excursions, 49, 57, 61–62, 66–69, 89, 111, 115, 117, 119, 120, 124; on fashion, 197, 204; genealogy, *264*; health, 3, 57, 58, 103, 105, 108, 109, 111, 113, 133, 148–49, 200–1, 202; on industry, 38, 166, 196, 237; journal, 1, 2–3, 307n3–4; mother's death, 125–26; paintings, 299; patent drawings, 333n69, 230, 231, *232*, 234; poetry, 3; portrait, xx; prints and engravings, 304–5; on religion, 11, 25–26, 40, 180, 187, 191, 212–213, 224–5; on women and race 17–18, 23, 197; works of, mentioned, 50, 54, 55, 60, 63–77 *passim*, 86–89, 95, 98, 100–6 *passim*, 109, 111, 120, 125, 326n103–4
Wharton, Thomas Prescott, 1, 14, 36, 133–260 *passim*, 286
Wharton, Thomas,[1] 286
Wharton, Thomas,[2] 5, 6, 24, 32, 286
Wheaton, Dr. Walter V., 66, 71, 73–75, 286
Wheelock, Merrill G., 234, 236, 286
Whipple, John A., 221, 224, 287
White, John C., 66, 287
Wilkes, Horatio, 107, 287
Wilkie, Sir David, 118, 287
Williams, Hugh W., 107, 121, 287
Williams, Ichabod T., 307n4
Winchester, Col. William P., 234, 331n39

Winthrop, John, 158, 287
Winthrop House (hotel), Boston, MA, 176, 195, 196, 200
Witherspoon, John, 51, 56, 287
Wood, A.T., 134, 149, 150, 175, 237, 243, 244, 271, 272, 287, 290
Wright, John, 134, 137, 142, 287

Young, Adam, 287
Young, Ammi B., 287
Young, William, 75, 109–11, 113, 122, 287, 322n49, 327n114

Zanesville, OH, 7, 26, 32, 33; views of, 294

www.ingramcontent.com/pod-product-compliance
Lightning Source LLC
LaVergne TN
LVHW082157080826
844660LV00046B/1263